"Most academic books fit into a genre, but this one defies easy categorization. Part introduction, part commentary, and part theology, this book is most of all a guidebook. It moves toward repairing the fateful move of biblical scholarship two centuries ago to separate the Old from the New Testament in misleading and harmful ways—with Beale and Gladd we return to one whole Bible! A welcome touch is illustrations—graphic depictions that engage the imagination and remind us that Scripture is not just concepts and controversies but a window on our world in light of the Word of God who made it. Overall, a fresh and compelling exposition of how thirty-nine Old Testament writings intertwine with twenty-seven New Testament writings to yield the single most important narrative ever."

Robert W. Yarbrough, professor of New Testament, Covenant Theological Seminary, St. Louis

"This volume represents a remarkable achievement, equally suited for classroom adoption and personal use. While not entirely ignoring historical-critical issues, Beale and Gladd have given us a refreshing alternative that returns to the text and context of the New Testament itself, working their way through every major passage, always with a view toward the crucial ways in which the Old Testament serves as an indispensable background for rightly interpreting the teachings of Jesus and his apostles. The result is a creative, clear, and compelling work undergirded by a lifetime of faithful scholarship in service of the church."

Justin Taylor, managing editor, ESV Study Bible

"Beale and Gladd have written a book that is refreshingly different. They do not ignore historical questions but examine them briefly and concisely. The heart and soul of the book investigates the content of each writing in the New Testament in light of the Old Testament witness, considering the use of the Old Testament that informs the New Testament. Students, professors, pastors, and all those who study the Scriptures will often turn to this invaluable resource."

Thomas Schreiner, associate dean and James Buchanan Harrison Professor of New Testament Interpretation at The Southern Baptist Theological Seminary

"In addition to covering the basic territory of authorship, date, recipients, and more, Beale and Gladd use their expertise in the field to show students how deeply rooted the New Testament is in the Old Testament. The numerous pictures and images help bring the text to life. If you want students to understand each New Testament book in light of its place in redemptive history, this is the textbook for you."

Matthew S. Harmon, professor of New Testament studies, Grace College and Theological Seminary

"Biblical illiteracy is perhaps one of the greatest weaknesses of the global church today. Those of us with the vocation of teaching the biblical text to bright and eager university students are given a great responsibility—one rife with eternal consequences. The triumph of this new textbook is its capacity to teach *biblical* literature, to explain the New Testament in light of its place within the biblical narrative at-large, without neglecting the first-century historical and cultural backgrounds. This is a textbook we should all be teaching from, especially if we want our students to be biblically and theologically minded, recognizing Jesus Christ as the New Testament authors did—as the fulfillment of God's long-awaited promise to restore his good creation. In short, it's a brilliant New Testament introduction and one I look forward to using in my classroom."

Haley L. Jacob, assistant professor of theology, Whitworth University

"Beale and Gladd concisely survey each book of the New Testament through a biblical-theological lens. I plan to require this book for my seminary course that focuses on the theological message of each New Testament book."

Andy Naselli, associate professor of New Testament and theology, Bethlehem College and Seminary, Minneapolis, elder of Bethlehem Baptist Church

"With its special focus on biblical theology, this innovative and attractively presented new work by Benjamin Gladd and G. K. Beale should work well in the classroom. While not a conventional New Testament introduction, *The Story Retold* promises to be a helpful resource by introducing each New Testament book in light of the Old Testament against a redemptive-historical backdrop. Well done!"

Andreas J. Köstenberger, research professor of New Testament and biblical theology, Midwestern Baptist Theological Seminary

"*The Story Retold* is an outstanding resource for introducing students to the New Testament. It brings them straight to the fountainhead of New Testament doctrine—the Old Testament Scriptures. It combines profound biblical insight with lucid, readable prose and presents the best of contemporary biblical scholarship in a readily accessible way. I highly recommend this book."

Sean McDonough, professor of New Testament at Gordon-Conwell Theological Seminary

"This accessible introduction to the New Testament shines in highlighting biblical-theological connections between the New Testament and the Old Testament, and in so doing provides an unassumingly thorough orientation to New Testament theology. The book-by-book approach that highlights each book's redemptive-historical contributions will be particularly useful for students and pastors, and the running interaction with the biblical text ensures that everyone will come away better informed about the rich topographies of the final twenty-seven books of Scripture."

Brandon Crowe, associate professor of New Testament at Westminster Theological Seminary

"Greg Beale and Ben Gladd have written an unusual—and unusually good—introduction to the New Testament. They introduce the New Testament writings on the basis of the Old Testament writings that preceded them, grounding all (both Old and New) in the substratum of the narrative of creation-fall-judgment-redemption in Genesis 1–3, through which all subsequent biblical narratives (both Old and New) find their meaning. Despite this overarching unified purpose, the introduction is remarkably sensitive to particular issues of genre, cultural background, and kerygmatic emphasis of each particular part of the New Testament. I can only wish such an introduction had been available when I began my own academic study of the Bible over forty years ago."

T. David Gordon, professor of religion and Greek, Grove City College, Grove City, Pennsylvania

"Introductions to the New Testament tend to suffer from two consequences. First, they have a tendency to focus on what is behind the text rather than what is in the text. Second, very few of them incorporate the Old Testament explicitly in their analysis and thereby surrender the storyline that started in Genesis. *The Story Retold* stems these oversights. New Testament authors wrote their works as a continuation of the story of Israel—to understand them we need to keep the big picture in mind and see how they appropriate the Old Testament. Pastors, church members, and students will all benefit from this introduction."

Patrick Schreiner, assistant professor of New Testament language and literature, Western Seminary

"Beale and Gladd have produced a unique resource that moves far beyond what we have come to expect in a New Testament introduction. Students will enjoy studying the literature and theology of the New Testament on its own terms—as the unfolding of the literature and theology of the Old Testament. Perhaps the greatest value of this book will be in the patterns of thought and interpretive methods it cultivates in readers. Students will grow in their ability to discern the meaningful meshwork of connections between the Testaments while orienting the contents of the New Testament to the grand narrative of Scripture. We needed a resource like this, and two of the best have delivered!"

John Markley, associate professor of New Testament, Liberty University

"Greg Beale and Ben Gladd have written a singular and insightful New Testament introduction that situates each book within a biblical-theological storyline. They concisely cover the usual introductory issues, and then largely treat the books in light of the Old Testament. This volume offers a fresh and savvy approach and is well worth your read."

Terry L. Wilder, professor and Wesley Harrison Chair of New Testament, Southwestern Baptist Theological Seminary, Fort Worth, Texas

"The New Testament writers received their theology from the Old Testament and from the revelation of the person and work of Jesus Christ in history. *The Story Retold* brings together the Old Testament and the person of Christ, providing fresh insight for how the New Testament fulfills the Old Testament. This New Testament introduction will no doubt be a valuable resource for students, professors, and laypeople."

M. Jeff Brannon, associate professor and chair of biblical studies, Belhaven University

"Students of the Bible will greatly benefit from this fine volume. While briefly accounting for such issues as authorship and date of composition, the unique strengths of this New Testament introduction are found in its discussion of biblical-theological themes and in its extended summaries (really minicommentaries!) on each biblical book. The result is an introduction to the New Testament that assists us to grasp the message of the Bible as a whole."

David W. Chapman, professor of New Testament and archaeology, Covenant Theological Seminary

"Biblical revelation no longer needs to be viewed as a fractured collection of independent and unconnected ideas. With this work, the New Testament is seen in its glorious dependence on the Old Testament. And most importantly, the New Testament is now seen as building on and extending the Old Testament. Beale and Gladd are to be congratulated for this stellar job of unpacking and integrating the text. Simply terrific."

Jay E. Smith, department chair and professor of New Testament studies, Dallas Theological Seminary

"*The Story Retold* inaugurates an innovation in New Testament introductions where students are introduced to the books of the New Testament in the context of the Old. Beale and Gladd keep each book of the New Testament firmly tethered to the Old Testament narrative, which its authors presume. This new textbook is readable, reliable, and underscores the redemptive-historical threads of the whole Bible, with Christ as the focus."

Daniel M. Gurtner, Ernest and Mildred Hogan Professor of New Testament Interpretation, The Southern Baptist Theological Seminary

"Many of us are accustomed to reading the New Testament two dimensionally: we simply ask what a text means and how it applies to our lives. This introduction encourages us to read three dimensionally. We discover that reading the New Testament is not only about the text and us; true understanding of the New Testament requires a third dialogue partner—the Old Testament. Focusing on the way the New Testament authors incorporated the Old Testament allows the message of the New Testament to come into sharper focus than probably anything else could. I am happy to recommend this new resource."
Kenneth Berding, professor of New Testament at Biola University

"*The Story Retold* is aptly titled since it is the story of God's grand plan for humanity that began in Eden and culminated in the new Jerusalem told through the eyes of the New Testament writers. Following in the footsteps of Geerhardus Vos, Beale and Gladd have produced a unique work with its combination of biblical theology and Old Testament background. With superb graphics and wonderful readability, *The Story Retold* fills a significant void in the field of New Testament introduction and should be welcomed by those who teach in seminaries as well as by those who teach upper-level college courses."
James Bibza, professor of biblical and religious studies, Grove City College, Grove City, Pennsylvania

"Jonathan Edwards counseled that biblical theology is best understood through the historical lens of God's work of redemption. Here is an introduction to the New Testament that takes that counsel seriously. Beale and Gladd's book brings a lifetime of observation to bear on a project of illumining the narrative plan that unites the apostolic witness to Christ in the New Testament with God's preparatory work in Israel recorded in the Old Testament and related Jewish literature. Jesus' apostles wrote with a conviction that creation, kingdom, covenant, temple, exile, promise, and the conquest of sin all reprise their roles in the drama of the Christ event. Jonathan Edwards would take delight in how reliably this book's retelling of the story will rekindle that biblical conviction anew for readers in the church and the academy alike."
Don Westblade, department of philosophy and religion, Hillsdale College

G. K. BEALE AND BENJAMIN L. GLADD

THE STORY RETOLD

A BIBLICAL-THEOLOGICAL INTRODUCTION TO THE NEW TESTAMENT

IVP Academic
An imprint of InterVarsity Press
Downers Grove, Illinois

InterVarsity Press
P.O. Box 1400, Downers Grove, IL 60515-1426
ivpress.com
email@ivpress.com

InterVarsity Press® is the book-publishing division of InterVarsity Christian Fellowship/USA®, a movement of students and faculty active on campus at hundreds of universities, colleges, and schools of nursing in the United States of America, and a member movement of the International Fellowship of Evangelical Students. For information about local and regional activities, visit intervarsity.org.

Cover design and image composite: David Fassett
Interior design and layout: Jeanna Wiggins, Daniel van Loon, and Maureen Tobey
Cover image: recycled card stock texture: © Zakharova_Natalia / iStock / Getty Images Plus

ISBN 978-0-8308-5266-6 (print)
ISBN 978-0-8308-5603-9 (digital)

Printed in the United States of America ♾

InterVarsity Press is committed to ecological stewardship and to the conservation of natural resources in all our operations. This book was printed using sustainably sourced paper.

Library of Congress Cataloging-in-Publication Data
Names: Beale, G. K. (Gregory K.), 1949- author. | Gladd, Benjamin L., author.
Title: The story retold : a biblical-theological introduction to the New Testament | G.K. Beale and Benjamin L. Gladd.
Description: Downers Grove, Illinois: IVP Academic, [2019] | Includes bibliographical references and index.
Identifiers: LCCN 2019052325 (print) | LCCN 2019052326 (ebook) | ISBN 9780830852666 (hardcover) | ISBN 9780830856039 (ebook)
Subjects: LCSH: Bible. New Testament—Introductions. | Bible. New Testament—Relation to the Old Testament. | Bible. New Testament—Theology.
Classification: LCC BS2330.3 .B43 2019 (print) | LCC BS2330.3 (ebook) | DDC 225.6/1—dc23
LC record available at https://lccn.loc.gov/2019052325
LC ebook record available at https://lccn.loc.gov/2019052326

P 23 22 21 20 19 18 17 16 15 14 13 12 11 10 9 8 7 6 5 4
Y 42 41 40 39 38 37 36 35 34 33 32 31 30 29 28 27 26 25 24

FOR OUR STUDENTS

Past, present, and future

CONTENTS

PREFACE

Of the writing of New Testament introductions there is no end. A quick search for introductions to the New Testament on Amazon yields pages of choices. With a myriad of New Testament introductions, why write another? Our desire to write this book springs from teaching New Testament courses against the backdrop of the Old Testament. We are convinced that the New Testament stands in continuity with the Old Testament. The books of the New Testament were not written within a vacuum. Israel's story is the church's story.

New Testament introductions typically fall into two categories: those that go beyond the content of the writings and investigate the historical side (authorship, dating, audience, etc.) and those that explore the content of each book. The latter category tends to summarize each book and perhaps add some theological reflection. Recently, the trend has been for these introductions to explore the cultural background of the New Testament. While this is admirable, few introductions have sufficiently integrated the Old Testament in their survey. Fewer still are those that incorporate the story line of the Old Testament.

This introduction explores each New Testament book in light of the broad history of redemption—a story that began with Adam and Eve in Genesis 1–3 and ends with the creation of the new heavens and earth in Revelation 21–22. Every passage of the Bible, every paragraph, in some way contributes to this narrative. We do not attempt to explain all components of the New Testament—the cultural and historical background, sociological issues, and so on. Plenty of New Testament introductions do just that. Our central concern is to couch every major passage within the broad history of redemption. We endeavor to make sense of the New Testament in light of the Old.

The intended audience of this project is, first and foremost, college students who have some familiarity with the Bible. This textbook is primarily designed for use in a Christian college setting. Since both of us teach in a seminary context, we also wrote this introduction with an eye on seminary students. We exert most of our energy explaining how the major contours of each New Testament book are traced throughout the history of redemption. For historical issues such as authorship, dating, and provenance, we are broadly indebted to D. A. Carson and Douglas J. Moo's *An Introduction to the New Testament* (2nd ed.; Grand Rapids: Zondervan, 2005). Since we do not deal at length with these historical matters, it may be helpful to read this volume in conjunction with Carson and Moo's excellent work. For those wishing to delve more deeply into the biblical-theological connections we explore in this project, consult G. K. Beale's *A New Testament Biblical Theology: The Unfolding of the Old Testament in the New* (Grand Rapids: Baker, 2011).

A word about the layout of the volume. We attempt to explain each New Testament book in light of the Bible's story line through four avenues. Immediately following the introductory portion of each chapter, we include a section called "Biblical-Theological Themes," wherein we zero in on one or two prominent themes or passages within the book and briefly discuss its connection to the history of redemption. At the beginning of each major section, we also attempt to isolate one particular thread that runs from the Old Testament into the New Testament passage under discussion. Often we bring Genesis 1–3 or some aspect of Israel's career to bear on the New Testament passage. We also include a number of images that broadly correspond to the topic at hand. On occasion, we include specific images that directly relate to our discussion. Lastly, as we work through each major section of each New Testament book, we are on the lookout for some textual or conceptual relationship to the Old Testament. We are unable to examine all the Old Testament quotations and allusions in the New, but we do draw attention to a good number of them.

In this vein, the early church made considerable use of the Greek translation of the Old Testament, known as the Septuagint or the LXX. The majority of the Old Testament quotations in the New Testament are derived from the Septuagint. Its translation began approximately in the mid-third century BC and extended to the early first century AD. The LXX is the earliest translation and interpretation of the Hebrew Old Testament. As we study some of the contours of the Old Testament's use in each New Testament book, we sometimes consult the LXX. Unless otherwise noted, the default English translation of the LXX is *A New English Translation of the Septuagint* (NETS).

For us to explore how each New Testament book fits into the grand story line of the Bible, we must first construct that story line. The introductory chapter paints the story with broad strokes, and central to the plan of redemption is what will transpire at the very end of history. As we introduce each New Testament book, we often return to the story line of chapter 1. If the material in this chapter is unfamiliar, we recommend reading over it a few times to grasp the content and language, as it is foundational for our entire project.

In chapter two we introduce the readers to the general manner in which New Testament writers use the Old Testament. This promising field of study has blossomed in the last few decades, and much of our project is attuned to the way in which New Testament authors interact with the Old Testament.

The four Gospels stand apart from the remainder of the New Testament in their literary form and in their configuration. Most of the New Testament comprises letters, whereas the Gospels largely fall into the category of a genre known as Greco-Roman biography. Three of the Gospels, Matthew, Mark, and Luke, also display remarkable similarity. Because of these issues and a few others, chapter three briefly introduces the Gospels and touches on these matters.

This project would not be possible without the help of our institutions, Reformed Theological Seminary and Westminster Theological Seminary. We are especially grateful for the invaluable input from Michael Daling, Karen Jobes, Mark Strauss, and Guy Waters. We would also like to thank Tyler Milliken for his diligent and careful edits of this manuscript. Lastly, we are indebted to our editors at InterVarsity Press, Dan Reid (now retired) and Anna Gissing, who expertly guided the project along the way. We are also thankful to the host of IVP editors for their tireless efforts in producing this complex project. Above all, we are grateful to God, who gave us the desire to write this project and the energy to complete it. Our prayer is that this book would give glory to him alone.

To keep the project accessible, our default translation and chapter outlines rely on the New International Version (2011). We often use italics within the English translation to demonstrate emphasis or mark parallel wording with the Old Testament. Most of the time these parallels indicate that a New Testament passage is alluding to or quoting the Old Testament.

ABBREVIATIONS

GENERAL

AD	*anno Domini* ("in the year of our Lord")
ad loc.	ad locum (at the place discussed)
b.	Babylonian Talmud
BC	before Christ
ca.	circa
chs.	chapter(s)
frg(s.)	fragment(s)
Gk.	Greek
Heb.	Hebrew
m.	Mishnah
NT	New Testament
OT	Old Testament
par(s).	parallel(s)

BIBLE VERSIONS

Brenton	Brenton Greek Translation of the Septuagint
ESV	English Standard Version
HCSB	Holman Christian Standard Bible
KJV	King James Version
LXX	Septuagint
MT	Masoretic Text
NASB	New American Standard Bible
NET	New English Translation
NETS	New English Translation of the Septuagint
NIV	New International Version
NJB	New Jerusalem Bible
NKJV	New King James Version
NLT	New Living Translation

NRSV	New Revised Standard Version
OG	Old Greek translation of the Septuagint
REB	Revised English Bible
RSV	Revised Standard Version
Theod	Theodotion translation of the Septuagint
TNIV	Today's New International Version

ANCIENT WORKS

1-3 En.	1-3 Enoch
1-4 Macc.	1-4 Maccabees
1QM	Milḥamah or War Scroll
1QS	Serek Hayaḥad or Rule of the Community
Ag. Ap.	Josephus, *Against Apion*
Ant.	Josephus, *Jewish Antiquities*
Callim.	Isocrates, *Against Callimachus*
CD	Damascus Document
Cher.	Philo, *De Cherubim*
Dial.	Justin, *Dialogue with Trypho*
Geogr.	Strabo, *Geography*
Haer.	Irenaeus, *Against Heresies*
Hist. eccl.	Eusebius, *Ecclesiastical History*
Jdt	Judith
Jub.	Jubilees
J.W.	Josephus, *Jewish War*
Mos.	Philo, *De vita Mosis*
Paed.	Clement of Alexandria, *Paedagogus*
Phil.	Polycarp, *To the Philippians*
Pud.	Tertullian, *Modesty*
Pss. Sol.	Psalms of Solomon
Quaest. Exod.	Philo, *Quaestiones et solutiones in Exodum*
Res.	Tertullian, *On the Resurrection*
Strom.	Clement of Alexandria, *Stromateis*
T. 12 Patr.	Testaments of the Twelve Patriarchs
T. Job	Testament of Job
T. Mos.	Testament of Moses
T. Sol.	Testament of Solomon

MODERN WORKS

ABD	Anchor Bible Dictionary. Edited by D. N. Freedman. 6 vols. New York: Doubleday, 1992
BBR	*Bulletin for Biblical Research*
BECNT	Baker Exegetical Commentary on the New Testament
BTNT	Biblical Theology of the New Testament
BZNW	Beihefte zur Zeitschrift für die neutestamentliche Wissenschaft
CBQ	*Catholic Biblical Quarterly*
HUT	Hermeneutische Untersuchungen zur Theologie
Int	*Interpretation*
IVPNTC	InterVarsity Press New Testament Commentaries
JETS	*Journal of the Evangelical Theological Society*
JSNT	*Journal for the Study of the New Testament*
LNTS	Library of New Testament Studies
NIBC	New International Biblical Commentary
NICNT	New International Commentary on the New Testament
NICOT	New International Commentary on the Old Testament
NIGTC	New International Greek Testament Commentary
NIVAC	New International Version Application Commentary
NovT	*Novum Testamentum*
NovTSup	Novum Testamentum Supplement Series
NSBT	New Studies in Biblical Theology
NTS	*New Testament Studies*
PNTC	Pillar New Testament Commentaries
RB	*Revue biblique*
SNTSMS	Society for New Testament Studies Monograph Series
TJ	*Trinity Journal*
TNTC	Tyndale New Testament Commentaries
TynB	*Tyndale Bulletin*
WBC	Word Biblical Commentary
WTJ	*Westminster Theological Journal*
WUNT	Wissenschaftliche Untersuchungen zum Neuen Testament
ZECNT	Zondervan Exegetical Commentary on the New Testament

1

THE STORY LINE OF THE BIBLE

From Genesis to Revelation, the Bible presents a single, grand narrative that reveals who we are, who God is, and his goal for all creation. It is a rich story that puts God on display for all to see and marvel. This is a story that narrates God's gracious and merciful dealings with humanity, including remarkable suspense, intrigue, and twists and turns.[1]

Genesis 1–3 forms the core of the story and contains the basic elements of the script. Here we discover God's ultimate intention for all creation and how he plans on achieving that aim. As we make our way through Genesis 1–3, we will glean three interrelated points: (1) God creates the heavens and the earth to be his cosmic sanctuary, where he sovereignly rules and dwells. All creation is designed to house the glory of God. (2) God creates Adam and Eve as kings to rule on his behalf and as priests to serve and mediate his glory. Humanity is created to remain wholly dependent on God and represent him faithfully on the earth. (3) In an attempt to be independent of God, the original couple succumbs to the serpent's temptation. But, despite the fall, God promises to overcome evil and establish a perfect dwelling place for his glory and kingdom.

The grand story line of the Bible entails the general pattern of creation, fall, and redemption. Delving deeper into this cycle, the pattern begins with creation and the divine commission for humanity to rule over the earth and worship the Lord. Humanity then sins and disobeys. As a result, God's people are exiled from his presence in Eden. Beginning with Adam and Eve, the pattern repeats itself throughout the Old Testament. Each pattern picks up steam, and more characters emerge into the spotlight. What began in Eden with the first couple is repeated with an entire nation in the Promised Land. With more characters come more subplots, intrigue, suspense, and redemption. Although the story becomes more complex, the general pattern remains the same. The expectation is that one day, at the very end of history, the cycle will end and humanity will enjoy God's full presence in the new creation.

[1]This discussion is also found in G. K. Beale, "The Eschatological Conception of New Testament Theology," in *"The Reader Must Understand": Eschatology in the Bible and Theology*, ed. K. E. Brower and M. W. Elliott (Leicester, UK: Apollos, 1997), 11-52; and G. K. Beale and Mitchell Kim, *God Dwells Among Us: Expanding Eden to the Ends of the Earth* (Downers Grove, IL: InterVarsity Press, 2014).

THE CREATED WORLD AS GOD'S COSMIC TEMPLE

Genesis 1–2 portrays God creating an all-encompassing cosmic temple wherein he sovereignly rules. Genesis 1:14 contains an early hint of the creation of a cosmic temple: "And God said, 'Let there be *lights* in the vault of the sky to separate the day from the night.'" The word *lights* in the creation narrative is peculiar, as the same term is applied to the lampstand in Israel's tabernacle: "the lampstand that is for *light* with its accessories, lamps and oil for *the light*" (Ex 35:14; cf. 39:37; Num 4:9). The lights within the cosmos, therefore, function as cultic luminaries that shine throughout God's cosmic temple, just as the lights on the lampstand illuminate the Holy Place of Israel's temple. Even the seven lights on the lampstand in the temple symbolize the seven lights of the visible sky (sun, moon, and five planets).[2] Several scholars have even compared the construction of Israel's mobile tabernacle to the creation of the cosmos, concluding that God is indeed fashioning a cosmic temple in Genesis 1–2 (Gen 1:31; cf. Ex 39:43; Gen 2:1; cf. Ex 39:32; Gen 2:2-3; cf. Ex 40:33; Gen 2:3; cf. Ex 39:43).[3] Elsewhere in the Old Testament, the cosmos is compared to Israel's temple: "*He built his sanctuary like the heights, like the earth* that he established forever" (Ps 78:69; cf. Is 66:1-2; 1 Chron 28:2).

When God finished creating the cosmos, he "rested" from the creative process, but this resting is unlike our modern conception of rest. God's resting after six days entails his climactic enthronement as King over the cosmos (Gen 2:2; cf. 2 Chron 6:41; Is 66:1) since "it is connected to taking control in his role as sovereign ruler over the cosmos."[4]

Why does God graciously construct a cosmic temple? He desires to rule and reign over the created order, but he also wants to dwell intimately with it. The world is designed to house the veritable glory of God. Despite God's intimate communion with the first couple in Eden, his full presence dwells in the invisible heavens with the angels. Even before the fall, God and humanity remained separated—God in heaven and Adam and Eve on the earth. By creating a cosmic temple, God reveals that he intends on dwelling with humanity in all his fullness. Heaven and earth are to be joined together at the very end of history. Though perfectly created, the cosmic temple remains incomplete in Genesis 1–2. Sin can infest the original creation. The cosmos, then, must be altered to house the glory of God.

Eden as a temple. Another insightful detail we glean from Genesis 1–2 is the depiction of Eden as a sanctuary resting on a mountain. Although God dwells in his fullness in the invisible heavens, he dwells partially with Adam and Eve in the garden. The casual mention of God "walking" in the Garden of Eden (Gen 3:8) highlights his presence in the temple. In Leviticus, the Lord promises that he will "walk" among the Israelites and be their God (Lev 26:12). In Deuteronomy, the Lord commands the Israelites to keep their camp holy because he "walks" in the midst of their camp (Deut 23:14 NASB). In a similar manner, the Lord is "walking" in Eden because Eden itself is a sanctuary.

The book of Ezekiel even calls Eden a temple, referring to it as "the garden of God . . .

[2]Vern Poythress, *The Shadow of Christ in the Law of Moses* (Brentwood, TN: Wolgemuth & Hyatt, 1991), 18-19.
[3]J. Richard Middleton, *The Liberating Image: The* Imago Dei *in Genesis 1* (Grand Rapids: Brazos, 2005), 81-82.
[4]John H. Walton, *Genesis*, NIVAC (Grand Rapids: Zondervan, 2001), 165.

the holy mount of God" containing "sanctuaries" (Ezek 28:13-14, 16, 18). Ezekiel also describes a person resembling Adam in Eden wearing bejeweled clothing like a priest: "You were in Eden, the garden of God. . . . Your settings and mountings were made of gold" (Ezek 28:13). This individual's sin profanes the sanctuaries and causes him to be cast out: "Your heart became proud on account of your beauty, and you corrupted your wisdom because of your splendor. So *I threw you to the earth*" (Ezek 28:17).

Genesis 2:10-14 provides the reader with several seemingly incidental details about bodies of water: "*A river watering the garden flowed from Eden*; from there it was separated into four headwaters. The name of the first is the Pishon. . . . The name of the second river is the Gihon. . . . The name of the third river is the Tigris. . . . And the fourth river is the Euphrates." The river flowing out of Eden indicates the abundant life flowing from the presence of God. It gives life to the many trees growing on its banks, including the tree of the knowledge of good and evil and the tree of life (Gen 2:10, 17; 3:24). This water flows out of Eden to water the garden before flowing outward to give life to the rest of the earth (Gen 2:10-14). Similarly in later depictions of the temple, a river flows with trees of life on its banks. In Ezekiel 47, a river flows from below the threshold of the temple with trees on the bank of both sides. The waters of this river make seawater fresh (Ezek 47:8), give life to creatures (Ezek 47:9), and cause leaves of healing to blossom on the trees of its banks (Ezek 47:12). In Revelation, a river flows in the new Jerusalem, with "the tree of life, bearing twelve crops of fruit, yielding its fruit every month. And the leaves of the tree are for the healing of the nations" (Rev 22:2). This river of life abounding with God's presence flows from the inmost place of God's presence ("from the throne of God and of the Lamb") outward into the nations. In the Israelite temple, God's holiness is graciously manifest in the holy of holies and spreads outward to the Holy Place and then

FIGURE 1.1. GARDEN OF EDEN

the outer court, where all Israel assembles for worship symbolizing the whole world. In Eden, the river flows from God's presence into the garden and then the rest of the earth (Gen 2:10-14).

We can discern gradations of holiness as the presence of God increases from the innermost place of Eden / holy of holies outward to the earth and the lands. Just as the Holy Place contained the lampstand shaped like the tree of life and held the bread of the presence to sustain the priests, so the Garden of Eden was the place of the tree of life (Gen 2:8-9) and sustains Adam's existence (Gen 2:16). Just as the outer court of Israel's second temple provided a place for the nations to come, so the land and seas are outside the garden, where the nations of Cush and Assyria dwell (Gen 2:13-14). Of course, these lands were not yet populated. Notice in the illustration how Eden is the Holies of Holies, the garden is the Holy Place, and the outer world is the outer court.

Why is it important that we understand Eden as a sanctuary created for God's glory? This insight reveals two important points: God ultimately wants to dwell with the created order in all his fullness, and Adam and Eve play a critical role in accomplishing that goal.

FIGURE 1.2. EDEN AS THE INNERMOST SANCTUARY

ADAM AND EVE: THE CREATION AND FALL OF THE DIVINE IMAGE

After God created his cosmic temple, he began to enter into the cosmos, rule over it, and dwell with humanity. On day six, he created Adam and Eve at the pinnacle of creation to rule on his behalf. God's full presence remains in the invisible heaven, yet he comes down to Eden to dwell with Adam and Eve. This is similar to God dwelling in heaven yet residing in the holy of holies of the temple. God's aim is for the first couple to spread this glorious presence over the entire earth so that it may be transformed into the new heavens and earth. Once the earth is permanently transformed, God's presence will descend and fully dwell with mankind.

When God creates Adam and Eve in his image, they become his official representatives on earth. Genesis 1:26-27 says that God made Adam in his image or likeness, and Genesis 2 says that God placed him in a garden-like sanctuary. In Eden, Adam and Eve reflect and represent God as his divine image. In the ancient Near East, gods frequently established kings as their images to express their authority (even though these kings were images of false gods). Images of the gods were also placed in the innermost part of the temples. Adam is created in the image of God and placed in the Eden temple so that the divine presence would shine through him and God's rule would extend to the earth. As kings, the first couple are charged with mediating God's sovereign rule on the earth. As priests, Adam and Eve are to serve in God's garden sanctuary in Eden and expand his glory to the ends of the earth. As prophets, they were to learn, obey, and promote the divine law. We will now examine the offices of king and priest in more detail and connect them to the story line of the Bible.

Adam and Eve as kings. According to Genesis, God fashions Adam in his image to function as a vice regent (one who rules on behalf of another) over creation:

> Then God said, "Let Us make man *in Our image*, according to *Our likeness*; and *let them rule* over the fish of the sea and over the birds of the sky and over the cattle and over all the earth, and over every creeping thing that creeps on the earth." God created man *in His own image, in the image of God* He created him; male and female He created them. (Gen 1:26-27 NASB)

Just as God reigns over the cosmos in his cosmic temple, so Adam and Eve represent him and rule over the created order. God's heavenly reign extends through the first couple. Psalm 115:16 states, "The highest heavens belong to the Lord, *but the earth he has given to mankind*." The entire creation account of Genesis 1–2 highlights God creating the cosmos and bringing order to creation. In the same way, Adam and Eve are to gain control over the earth and subdue it. Adam, for example, rules over creation by speaking and naming the animals (Gen 2:19), just as God spoke and named parts of creation (e.g., Gen 1:5, 8, 10).[5]

Genesis 1:28 reveals the core of God's plan for Adam and Eve and humanity in general: "God blessed them and said to them, 'Be fruitful and increase in number; fill the earth and subdue it. Rule over the fish in the sea and the birds in the sky and over every living creature that moves on the ground.'" Just as God, after his initial work of creation, subdued the chaos, ruled over it, and created and filled the earth with all kinds of animate life, so Adam and Eve, in their garden abode, are to reflect God's activities in Genesis 1 by fulfilling the commission to "subdue" and "rule" over all the earth and to "be fruitful" and multiply (cf. Ps 8). Stephen Dempster notes that "the male and female as king and queen of creation are to exercise rule over their dominion, the extent of which is the entire earth."[6] As time would unfold, the

FIGURE 1.3. KARNAK TEMPLE, EGYPT

[5]W. Austin Gage, *The Gospel of Genesis* (Winona Lake, IN: Eisenbrauns, 1984), 31.

[6]Stephen G. Dempster, *Dominion and Dynasty: A Theology of the Hebrew Bible*, NSBT 3 (Downers Grove, IL: InterVarsity Press, 2003), 59.

couple and their progeny would continue to fulfill the commission of Genesis 1:28 by extending God's rule beyond Eden until the entire earth is subdued.

Adam and Eve as priests. Adam and Eve's priestly role also comes into focus: "The LORD God took the man and placed him in the garden of Eden *to work it* and *watch over it*" (Gen 2:15 HCSB). A priest is a servant of God—one who ministers before his presence and mediates it to others. As priests in the garden sanctuary, God charges the first couple with taking care of the garden by maintaining it and keeping out all unclean things. The two key terms in 2:15, *work* and *watch over*, often occur together and pertain either to Israelites "serving" God and "guarding" (or "keeping") God's word, while the combined wording refers to the role of a priest in his service to the tabernacle/temple (e.g., Num 3:7-8; 8:26; 18:7). Adam is to cultivate the garden and guard against theological corruption by keeping God's law and rooting out all forms of falsehood (Gen 2:16).

John Walton states that Adam and Eve "were gradually supposed to extend the Garden as they went about subduing and ruling" in order to "extend the food supply as well as extend sacred space (since that is what the Garden represented)."[7] God wanted to expand that sacred space and dwelling place from the limited confines of the garden temple of Eden to the entire earth.

The command to "fill the earth" in Genesis 1:28 implies that the earth is not yet filled with images that reflect God's glory. While the boundaries of the garden are clearly delineated (Gen 2:10-14), the command to multiply images of God would expand its boundaries until it filled the whole earth. The entire earth was to be one gigantic garden of Eden so that all of humanity would worship God by reflecting his attributes in all of life. As Adam multiplied children in his image,

FIGURE 1.4. IN THE GARDEN

[7]Walton, *Genesis*, 186.

they would expand God's dwelling place of his presence into the wilderness outside of Eden until the whole earth reflected his order and glory.

> *If* Adam and Eve obey God's commission by producing godly descendants, expanding the boundaries of Eden and filling the earth with God's glory, keeping his commands, and subduing evil, *then* the earth would be transformed into an incorruptible creation, evil would be abolished, and humanity would inherit incorruptible bodies. God would descend to earth to rule and dwell with humanity for all of eternity.[8]

THE FALL AND THE PROMISE OF REDEMPTION

In Genesis 3:1-7, we learn that Adam and Eve fail to keep God's law, fail to "rule over" the serpent, and fail to "watch over" the sanctuary of Eden (Gen 1:28; 2:15). What about the commission of Genesis 1:28? Has God's plan to fill the earth with his glory changed? No. The divine mandate remains intact after the fall, but there is a shift in how it will be accomplished. God will now go "with" humanity in accomplishing that original goal. Sin corrupted the divine image and infected the created order, but it did not abolish the image of God. The Lord promised to restore his image in humanity and accomplish the original aim of Genesis 1:28 through a covenant. Genesis 3:15 states that God "will put enmity" between the serpent and his ungodly offspring and the descendants of Adam and Eve. The two lines will wage war with one another, culminating in the decisive defeat of evil: "He [a righteous descendant of Eve] will crush your [the serpent's] head." Redemption is guaranteed.

From Adam to the patriarchs. Adam's commission to fill the earth with images of God is passed to Noah even though sin runs rampant. In Genesis 3, Adam and Eve disobey God's command to subdue the beasts and are

FIGURE 1.5. NOAH'S ARK ON MOUNT ARARAT

instead subdued by a serpent. In Genesis 4, Cain murders Abel. In Genesis 6–9, the earth is filled not with faithful images of God but with wickedness of humanity (Gen 6:5, 11). As a result, God brings a flood, paving the way for God to repeat Adam's commission to Noah. Just as God originally created the heavens and earth through waters (Gen 1:1-2) and blessed and commissioned Adam to be "fruitful and increase in number; fill the earth" (Gen 1:28), so God recreates the world through the waters of the flood and blesses and commissions Noah to "be fruitful and increase in number and fill the earth" (Gen 9:1, 7).

The comparison between Adam and Noah doesn't stop there: Adam and Eve sinned in

[8]See G. K. Beale, *The Temple and the Church's Mission: A Biblical Theology of the Dwelling Place of God* (Downers Grove, IL: InterVarsity Press, 2004), 81-121, for more in-depth demonstration of Adam as a priest and of Eden as a sanctuary that was to be expanded to encompass the entire earth.

a garden, and Noah sins in a vineyard (Gen 9:20-21). Instead of the sanctuary of God's presence expanding and filling the earth with images of God, the earth is filled with a people so rebellious that they are dispersed "over the face of the whole earth" (Gen 11:9). The unabated spread of sin after the flood raises a critical question: How will the commission of Adam ever be fulfilled in light of the prevalence and power of sin?

God passes down the commission of Adam to the patriarchs, while promising and guaranteeing its fulfillment through a number of covenants. In Genesis 12, the focus shifts from "all the earth" to one man—Abraham. From this one man comes offspring in whom "all peoples on earth will be blessed" (Gen 12:3). While the wide-angle lens of Genesis 11 pictures rebellious, scattered humanity, Genesis 12 zooms in on a promise that the offspring of Abraham will become a blessing to all the families of the earth. The cosmic scope of God's purposes through Abraham and his children is seen in the repeated promises to bless and multiply their offspring to fill the earth. These promises to the patriarchs grow out of God's original commission given to Adam in Genesis 1:28, which he passes down to Abram in Genesis 12:1-3:

> The LORD had said to Abram, "Go from your country, your people and your father's household to the land I will show you. I will make you into a great nation, and *I will bless you*; I will make your name great, and *you will be a blessing*. I will *bless those who bless you*, and whoever curses you I will curse; and all peoples on earth will be blessed through you."

God accompanied the original commission with a blessing (Gen 1:28), and he does so once more with Abram. God blessed Adam to fill the earth (Gen 1:28), so he blesses Abram to make him a "great nation" and bless "all . . . [the] earth." In Genesis 17, the connections to Adam's commission are more explicit: God promises to "multiply [Abram] exceedingly . . . [and] make [him] exceedingly fruitful" (Gen 17:2, 6 NASB; see 22:17-18), just as God blesses Adam and commands him to "be fruitful and increase in number" (Gen 1:28). His purpose for Abram grows out of the original commission to Adam. Through the Abrahamic covenant, God ensures that the Genesis 1:28 commission will be fulfilled *through* Abram's descendants and that he will be the "father of many nations" (17:4). Abram's immediate offspring, Isaac and Jacob, likewise receive the identical commission given to Adam (Gen 26:3-4, 24; 28:3-4, 14; 35:11-12; 48:3, 15-16).

ISRAEL: THE CREATION AND FALL OF THE CORPORATE ADAM

The second pattern of creation, fall, and redemption begins with the nation of Israel and their descendants. God redeems his people from Egyptian bondage by overthrowing the Egyptian deities in the ten plagues of judgment. He leads his people through the waters and, like Adam and Eve, creates Israel at Sinai.

Mount Sinai is reminiscent of Eden in that both are the dwelling place of God. Like Eden, Sinai comprises a tripartite structure—the outer courts (Ex 19:12, 23), the holy place (Ex 19:22), and the holy of holies (Ex 24:2). The goal of God's delivering his people from Egypt is to lead them to this holy mountain so that they might worship and experience him there: "When you [Moses] have brought the people out of Egypt, *you will worship God on this mountain*" (Ex 3:12; cf. 3:18; 4:31; 5:3; 7:16; 8:1, 20, 27, 28).

Once he creates his chosen people, God commissions them to be "a kingdom of priests" (Ex 19:6). Like the first couple, Israel must form a godly community that obeys God's law, rule over the entire created realm, and mediate God's presence. God covenants with them by obligating himself to grant life to those who perfectly obey (Lev 26:1-13; cf. Deut 28:1-14) and death to those who do not (Lev 26:14-46; cf. Deut 28:15-68). Resembling their parents in the garden, the Israelites immediately break God's law by committing idolatry through worshiping the golden calf (Ex 32). As William Dumbrell notes, "Like Adam, Israel is put into a sacred space to exercise a kingly/priestly role (cf. Ex 19:4-6) . . . like Adam, Israel is given laws by which the divine space is to be retained. Finally, Israel, like Adam, transgresses the law and so too is expelled from the divine space."[9]

The tabernacle and temple as a model of the cosmos. The mobile tabernacle in the wilderness wanderings and the permanent temple in Jerusalem are composed of three main parts, each of which represent a major part of the cosmos: (1) the holy of holies symbolize the presence of God with his heavenly host in the invisible dimension of the cosmos (Ex 25:18-22; Is 6:1-7; Ezek 1), (2) the Holy Place in the temple is emblematic of the visible heavens and its light sources (Ex 25:8-9; Ps 19:1), and (3) the outer court represents the habitable world where humanity dwelt (Ex 20:24-25; 1 Kings 7:23-26; Ezek 43:14). Daniel Block agrees, "Although the temple was an earthly replica of YHWH's true heavenly residence, it also functioned as a microcosm of the cosmos, perfectly proportioned and designed with cosmic and Edenic features."[10] Why are the three parts of the tabernacle and temple symbolic of the cosmos? The structure of the temple is a symbolic story of God's ultimate intention to dwell intimately with his people and creation. The general idea is that God's revelatory presence in the invisible heavenly dimension (the holy of holies) will break out and fill the heavenly (Holy Place) and earthly (outer court) regions.

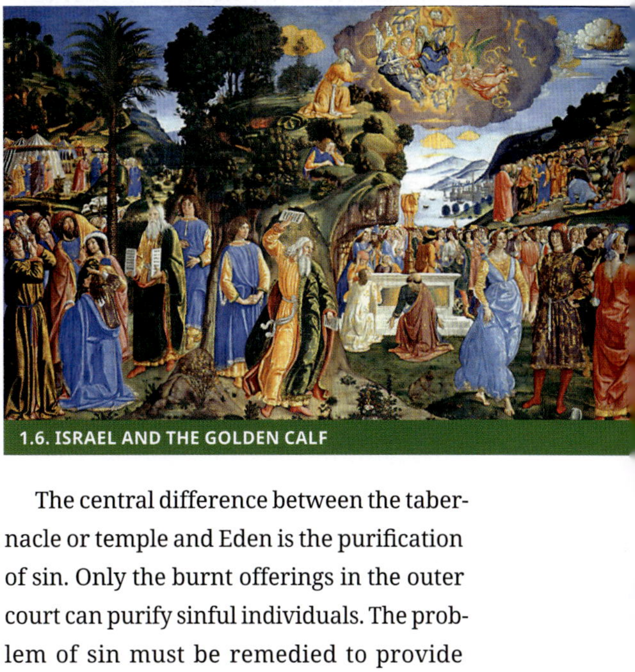

1.6. ISRAEL AND THE GOLDEN CALF

The central difference between the tabernacle or temple and Eden is the purification of sin. Only the burnt offerings in the outer court can purify sinful individuals. The problem of sin must be remedied to provide access to a holy God in the tabernacle, and the outer courtyard in Israel's temple is where provision was made.

Even though the tabernacle and temple are localized manifestations of God's presence, his presence was never ultimately to

[9]William J. Dumbrell, "Genesis 2:1-17: A Foreshadowing of the New Creation," in *Biblical Theology: Retrospect & Prospect*, ed. Scott J. Hafemann (Downers Grove, IL: InterVarsity Press, 2002), 62.

[10]Daniel Block, *For the Glory of God: Recovering a Biblical Theology of Worship* (Grand Rapids: Baker, 2014), 312.

be limited to one place; heaven and earth are designed to house the Lord's glory. Isaiah 66:1 reads, "This is what the LORD says: '*Heaven is my throne, and the earth is my footstool.* Where is the house you will build for me? Where will my resting place be?'" (see Is 6:1; Jer 23:24; Ps 78:69).

God's special, revelatory, glorious presence remains sequestered in the back room of the temple in the Old Testament epoch. The cosmic design of the temple indicates that this sequestered presence will break out from the heavenly holy of holies and fill every nook and cranny of the new cosmos. God's consistent purpose for his tabernacle was to expand and fill the earth so that his presence would fill it and sinful humanity might be forgiven and cleansed in the new heavens and earth.

Journey to and entrance into the Promised Land. We will now briefly trace the story of Israel and how that story never loses sight of God's original goal for creation and humanity. As Israel remains at the base of Sinai, Moses outlines in the book of Leviticus a series of regulations for Israel to obey if God is to dwell in their midst. The nation of Israel, a "kingdom of priests" (Ex 19:6), must ensure that they are ritually clean and qualified to approach the tabernacle and be near to God's presence. Numbers describes the various obstacles that Israel had to overcome in order to reach the Promised Land, where God's people would function as a corporate Adam in a new garden of Eden. Deuteronomy addresses this second generation with the same obligations of the first, yet these Israelites will enter this land of promise. The book of Joshua depicts Israel experiencing a mini-exodus (Josh 3) and the overthrow of the hostile nations living in the land. The book concludes on a positive note by affirming that "the LORD gave them rest [from their enemies] on every side" (Josh 21:44; cf. 3:1) and that "not one of all the LORD's good promises to Israel failed; every one was fulfilled"

FIGURE 1.7. JOSHUA CROSSING THE JORDAN RIVER

(Josh 21:45; cf. 23:14-15). But these comforting statements come with a warning: if Israel does not faithfully obey the covenant, they will incur the covenant curses and "will quickly perish from the good land he has given you" (Josh 23:16). The book of Judges highlights the incipient sin, though only briefly noted in Joshua, running rampant. Judges narrates a repeated pattern of Israel sinning, coming under bondage to a surrounding enemy, and then God raising up a judge to deliver them from their plight.

Israel in the Promised Land. First Samuel recounts the transition from the rule of the judges to that of kingship in Israel. Kingship itself was not evil (Deut 17:14-20), for God himself installed Adam as a king over creation. Israel's first king, Saul, was disobedient much like Adam. Saul's kingship was taken away and given to David, whom he persecuted. David initially displayed the marks of a faithful king. Yet his promising start toward successful kingship did not come to fruition, as 2 Samuel (and 1 Chronicles) sadly recounts. His adultery with Bathsheba and murder of Uriah signal the beginning of his demise. His own son, Absalom, even conspires against him (2 Sam 15). Although David regains his kingdom, 1 Kings 1–2 relates how his chosen heir, Solomon, begins his reign after an attempted coup.

The kingdom of Israel reaches its zenith under Solomon, who successfully builds the temple and establishes the kingdom more widely than his predecessors (1 Kings 3–10 / 2 Chron 1–9). Solomon represents the height of Israelite kingship and the epitome of Israel fulfilling the promises and hopes of Genesis 1:28. His sinful demise commences in 1 Kings 11, and further deterioration occurs with the division of the monarchy into southern and northern Israel. Instead of obeying God's laws, keeping the covenant, and ruling on behalf of God as Adam should have done in the garden, Israel's kings in the north and the south brazenly commit idolatry and rule selfishly (1 Kings 12–2 Kings 25). Righteous kings during the period of the divided monarchy are few and far between.

Israel in exile from the Promised Land. The fall of the nation of Israel was a long time coming. Despite the protestations of the prophets throughout the centuries (Elijah, Elisha, etc.), the northern tribes of Israel and her kings continue to sin and worship foreign deities. Second Kings 17 describes the Assyrian assault on the northern tribes and

FIGURE 1.8. JUDGMENT OF SOLOMON

their eventual destruction. For three years, the Assyrians fought the Israelites in Samaria and eventually succeed (2 Kings 17:5-6). Deporting thousands of the culturally elite and notable individuals, Sargon II exiles Israel to Assyria in 722 BC.

Approximately one hundred years later, the two tribes in the south, Benjamin and Judah, follow suit. Despite Josiah's reforms, God's decision to exile Judah remains firm: "The Lord did not turn away from the heat of his fierce anger, which burned against Judah because of all that Manasseh had done to arouse his anger. So the LORD said, *'I will remove Judah also from my presence as I removed Israel, and I will reject Jerusalem'*" (2 Kings 23:26-27; cf. 24:3). After a series of attacks, Jerusalem eventually falls to the Babylonians in 587/86 BC, and Nebuchadnezzar, the king of Babylon, exiles the two southern tribes in a series of deportations.

At the end of 2 Kings, God discloses *why* he sent Israel into exile: "I am going to bring disaster on this place and its people . . . *because they have forsaken me and burned incense to other gods* and aroused my anger *by all the idols their hands have made*" (2 Kings 22:16-17). Centuries before, Moses predicted this very thing in Deuteronomy 29:26-28: "They went off and *worshiped other gods and bowed down to them*. . . . In furious anger and in great wrath the LORD uprooted them from their land and *thrust them into another land*" (cf. Deut 28:64-68). Like Adam and Eve, the nation of Israel commit heinous idolatry, so God drives Israel from his presence into Babylonian exile, just like he drove the first couple out of the garden.

FIGURE 1.9. EZRA THE SCRIBE

Israel's return to the Promised Land. Israel spends approximately seventy years in captivity, but a glimmer of hope remains: Babylon fell to the Medes and the Persians, and Cyrus, the Persian king, decrees that Israel could return to its land and rebuild the temple (2 Chron 36:21-23; Ezra 1:1-4). If the temple could be rebuilt, then God would once again dwell among his people. The Israelites return to the land and begin reconstructing Jerusalem's walls and the temple (Ezra–Nehemiah). The temple is eventually completed, although it pales in comparison to its former glory (Ezra 6:13-18; Hag 1:12-14; 2:3). Despite physically living in the Promised Land and rebuilding the temple, Israel remains in *spiritual* exile because the postexilic community, like their ancestors, continue to disobey God's law. For example, Israel's priests present unclean sacrifices to the Lord (Mal 1:6-14), and the Israelite men break their marriage covenant with their wives (Mal 2:14-17). Zechariah 10–11 also condemns Israel's leadership for their selfish ways. According to Zechariah 10:2, the Israelites are even consulting idols because of the "lack of a [righteous] shepherd." Although living in the Promised Land, Israel is still physically in slavery to foreign powers,[11] continuing through the Roman occupation in the first century AD. Spiritually, the majority of the nation remains in unbelief, in fulfillment of the prophecy in Isaiah 6:9-13.[12] The second pattern of creation, fall, and redemption is recapitulated but without ultimate redemption. Israel still stands in need of complete physical and spiritual salvation.

RESTORED ISRAEL: THE SUCCESS OF GOD'S MESSIAH

Stretching back all the way to Genesis 1–3, the Old Testament writers and prophets foresaw a time when the third and final pattern of redemption would emerge. This epoch in Israel's career takes place at the very end of history. This pattern entails God's greatest act of creation, but instead of repeating the fall of Adam and Israel, a future figure will arrive on the scene and succeed in obeying the divine commission and resisting sin and temptation. The success of this figure will secure God's decisive act of redeeming creation and humanity in the new heavens and earth. At that point, God will descend from heaven and dwell with redeemed humanity in the new creation for all eternity.

The timing of Israel's restoration. Our English term *eschatology* comes from two Greek words—*eschatos* (last) and *logos* (word)—and means the study of the "last things." The final pattern or cycle of redemption should be considered eschatological, as it takes place at the very end of history. The Old Testament uses the phrase "latter days" or the "last days" to refer to this final phase of Israel's history (e.g., Gen 49:1; Num 24:14; Deut 4:30; 31:29; Hos 3:5; Is 2:2; Ezek 38:14-16; Dan 2:28-29, 45). All the events that take place within this period, whether acts of judgment or restoration, are eschatological. Like a seed germinating, sprouting, and eventually growing into a tree, the Old Testament writings begin with an eschatological seed in Genesis 1–3 and then develop into a vast tree

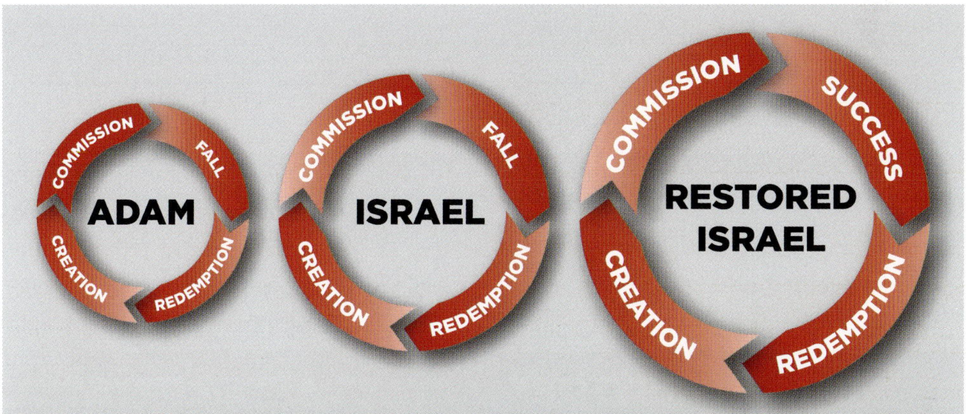

FIGURE 1.10. ADAM, ISRAEL, AND RESTORED ISRAEL

[11]Ezra, for example, confesses that "we [Israelites] are slaves," even though Israel had physically returned to the promised land (Ezra 9:9). Likewise in Nehemiah 9:36 the Levitical leaders confess that "we are slaves today, slaves in the land you gave our ancestors so they could eat its fruit and the other good things it produces."

[12]Isaiah prophesies that the spiritually hardened condition of Israel before the Babylonian exile (Is 6:9-10) would continue even when Israel returned from exile to the Promised Land (Is 6:11-13). See G. K. Beale, *We Become What We Worship: A Biblical Theology of Idolatry* (Downers Grove, IL: InterVarsity Press, 2008), 35-69.

by the close of the canon. That is, the remainder of the Old Testament writings expand in various ways on the ideas in Genesis 1–3. The period of the latter days is neither unrelated nor disconnected to the remainder of the Old Testament; it is the climax of Israel's story.

Determining the precise order of end-time events is difficult since they are tightly bound together. Nevertheless, the following is a general chronological overview of the Old Testament material of what will occur during the latter days:

1. Israel will endure a period of intense suffering and affliction instigated by an end-time opponent. This antagonist will deceive many within Israel, and those who do not succumb to false teaching will be persecuted (Dan 11:31-35).
2. God will vanquish Israel's enemies through a descendant of David, the Messiah (Gen 3:15; 2 Sam 7:13; Ps 2:8-9).
3. Those persecuted and martyred because of their faithfulness to God's law will be resurrected with incorruptible bodies and will rule with the Messiah in his eternal kingdom (Is 25:8; Ezek 37:12-13; Dan 12:1-3) and in his new temple (Ezek 40–48).
4. God will transform the present cosmos into an incorruptible one, the new heavens and earth, that will house God and redeemed humanity (Is 65:17; 66:22). The commission of Genesis 1:28 will be finally fulfilled.
5. God will cut a new covenant with restored Israel and the nations and pour out his Spirit on them (Jer 31:33-34; Ezek 36:26-27; Joel 2:28-29).

Thus, the latter days entail positive and negative elements with the negative elements generally preceding the positive. God first judges then restores.

THE LATTER DAYS AND THE NEW TESTAMENT

With the basic story line of the Old Testament now sketched, we turn to the New Testament's continuation of that same story. The period known as the latter days in which Israel's enemies are judged and the covenant community is restored at the end of history has now begun in the person of Christ. All

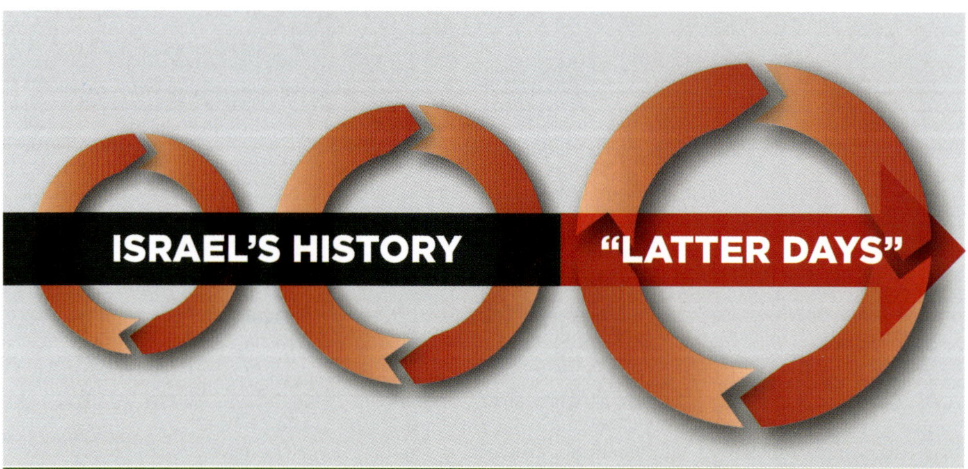

FIGURE 1.11. ISRAEL'S HISTORY, AND THE LATTER DAYS

that the Old Testament foresaw would occur in the end times has begun to be fulfilled in the first coming of Christ and continues until his second coming. The final pattern of creation, fall, and redemption has been initiated. But this time around, we witness genuine success. The divine commission to Adam and Eve in Genesis 1:28 is fulfilled, and God's glory begins to invade the earth. As the glory of God filled Israel's tabernacle, so too his glory dwells in Jesus. The presence of God, formerly contained in the holy of holies of the temple, has begun to burst forth into the world in the form of Jesus incarnate.

FIGURE 1.12. TWO WITNESSES OF REVELATION 11

The Old Testament end-time expectations of the great tribulation, God's subjugation of the Gentiles, deliverance of Israel from oppressors, Israel's restoration and resurrection, the new covenant, the promised Spirit, the new creation, the new temple, a messianic king, and the establishment of God's kingdom have all been set in motion through Christ's death and resurrection.

The expression "already but not yet" refers to two stages of the fulfillment of the latter days.[13] It is "already" because the latter days have dawned in Christ, but it is "not yet" since the latter days have not consummately arrived. Scholars often use the phrase "inaugurated eschatology" to describe the beginning stage of the latter days.

We can illustrate this critical phenomenon with a military metaphor. Christians live between D-day and V-day. D-day is the first coming of Christ, when the opponent is defeated decisively; V-day is the final coming of Christ, when the adversary will finally and completely surrender.[14] As Oscar Cullmann notes, "The hope of the final victory is so much the more vivid because of the unshakably firm conviction that the battle that decides the victory has already taken place."[15] Anthony Hoekema concludes,

> The nature of New Testament eschatology may be summed up under three observations: (1) the great eschatological event predicted in the Old Testament has happened; (2) what the Old Testament writers seemed to depict as one movement is now seen to involve two stages: the present age and the age of the future; and (3) the relation between these two eschatological stages is that the blessings of the present [eschatological] age are the pledge and guarantee of greater blessings to come.[16]

[13]The discussion of the "already but not yet" is adapted from Benjamin L. Gladd and Matthew S. Harmon, *Making All Things New: Inaugurated Eschatology for the Life of the Church* (Grand Rapids: Baker, 2016), 9-10.

[14]Anthony A. Hoekema, *The Bible and the Future* (Grand Rapids: Eerdmans, 1979), 21.

[15]Oscar Cullmann, *Christ and Time* (Philadelphia: Westminster, 1950), 87.

[16]Hoekema, *Bible and the Future*, 21-22.

Christ's life, trials, and especially his death and resurrection initiated the latter days (Acts 2:17; 1 Cor 10:11; Gal 4:4; Eph 1:7-10; 1 Tim 4:1-3; 2 Tim 3:1-5; Heb 1:1-2; 1 Pet 1:19-21; 2 Pet 3:3; Jude 18; 1 Jn 2:17-18). These pivotal events of his life inaugurated the new creation and the eternal kingdom. The Old Testament prophesied that the destruction of the first creation and the re-creation of a new heavens and earth were to happen at the very end of time, but Christ's ministry demonstrates that the end of the world and the coming new creation have begun in his death and resurrection. For example, 2 Corinthians 5:15 and 17 says Christ "died and rose again . . . [so that] if anyone is in Christ, he is *a new creature*; the old things passed away; behold, *new things have come*" (NASB). Revelation 1:5 refers to Christ as "the firstborn from the dead," and then Revelation 3:14 defines *firstborn* as "the Beginning of the [new] creation of God" (NASB). Likewise, Colossians 1:18 says that Christ is "the firstborn from among the dead" and "the beginning," so that "in everything he might have the supremacy." In Galatians 6:14-15 Paul says that his identification with Christ's death means that he is a "new creation."

The Old Testament predicted that the resurrection was to occur at the end of the world as part of the new creation (cf. Dan. 12:1-2). The resurrected Christ is the beginning of the long-awaited new cosmos since he was resurrected with a physical, newly created body. Recall the effects of Jesus' death in Matthew 27:51-52, "*The earth shook*, the rocks split and the tombs broke open. The *bodies* of many holy people who had died *were raised to life*." These strange phenomena are recorded by Matthew to signal to his readers that Christ's death was the beginning of the end of the old creation and the inauguration of a new creation. The death of Jesus is not just any death but the beginning of the destruction of the entire cosmos. The new cosmos that was promised to Adam and Israel upon perfect obedience has now been initially fulfilled in Christ's death and resurrection.

The New Testament writers, without hesitation, claim that the church is the restored Israel of God (Rom 2:25-29; 9:6, 24-26; Gal 3:29; 6:15-16; Eph 2:16-18; 3:6; 1 Pet 2:9; Rev 1:6; 3:9; 5:9-10). The covenant community in this new age stands in solidarity with the covenant community in the Old Testament. Through Christ's earthly ministry, death, and resurrection, all the Old Testament prophecies that concern latter-day Israel are initially fulfilled in the church (2 Cor 1:20).

The nature of the latter days in the New Testament. Now that we have outlined the basic eschatological underpinnings of the New Testament, we will probe the nature of its fulfillment. The "already but not yet" nature of eschatology in the New Testament is a bit unexpected from the vantage point of the Old. The Old Testament authors anticipated that end-time events would occur in all their fullness. The advent of the Messiah would signal the death knell of evil empires. He will destroy or "crush" pagan kings and their kingdoms (Dan 2:44). Such a defeat and judgment would be decisive and happen all at once at the end of history. But Jesus claims that the advent of the Messiah and the latter-day kingdom does not happen all at once (Mt 13). Paradoxically, two realms coexist—those who belong to the kingdom and those who belong to the devil. The kingdom has been inaugurated but remains to be consummately fulfilled. What the Old Testament foresaw as one fulfillment at the very end of history happens unexpectedly in two stages or in a staggered manner: an inaugurated and a consummated fulfillment.

Believers are caught in the "overlap of the ages." Christ has inaugurated the new age, yet the old age and its effects persist. The Old Testament writers generally did not foresee such an overlap of the ages since to them the old age was to give way decisively to the new age. We can graphically depict the Old Testament's expectation of the end of history (see figure 1.13).

The New Testament, however, outlines a different schema of fulfillment (see figure 1.14).

Though all facets of the latter days have begun to be fulfilled in Christ and the church, they have not reached their consummate state of fulfillment. The New Testament looks forward to the future when God will fully establish the kingdom (1 Cor 15:24), physically resurrect believers and unbelievers (James 4:5), and create the physical new heavens and earth (Rev 21:1).

Therefore, as we survey the New Testament, we will situate each book and examine every major passage in light of the overlap of the ages. We will consider how each New Testament author explored the depths of the Old Testament and latter days and exhorted his audience to live soberly in light of the coming climax of the history of redemption.

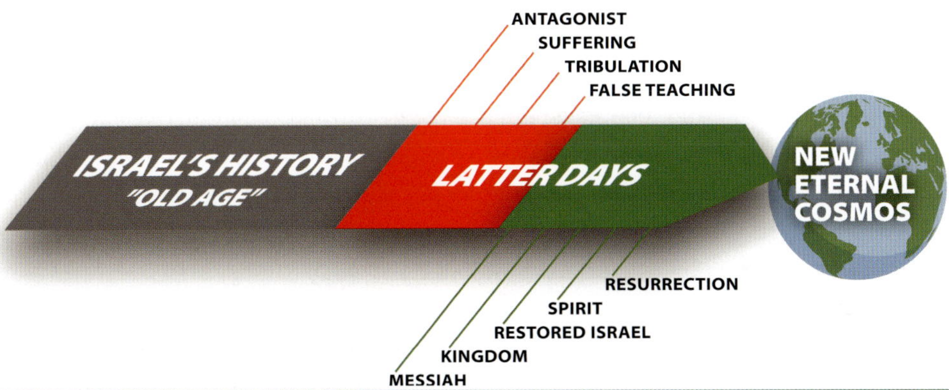

FIGURE 1.13. THE LATTER DAYS IN THE OLD TESTAMENT

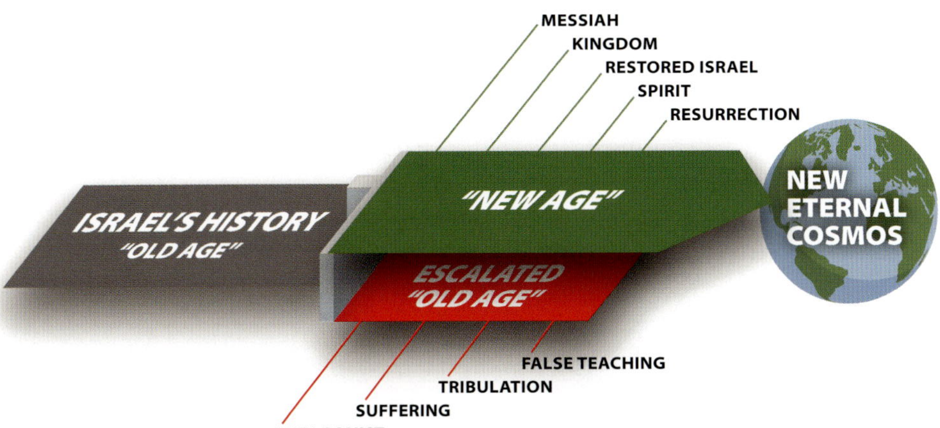

FIGURE 1.14. THE LATTER DAYS IN THE NEW TESTAMENT

2

THE USE OF THE OLD TESTAMENT IN THE NEW

With the foundation laid for understanding the broad redemptive-historical context of the New Testament, we now turn to a related field of interest—the New Testament's use of the Old Testament. Here we discover how the two Testaments are fused together in the person of Christ.[1] This chapter is incredibly important to our project in that it explains how we as authors understand how the Old Testament shapes the New. As we survey each New Testament book, we are quick to point out where its authors draw from the Old Testament and the manner in which they do so. We are also including this chapter as a basic introduction to this promising field.

The last several decades have witnessed a remarkable interest in the use of the Old Testament in the New. Scholars are growing more aware of how New Testament authors are indebted to the Old Testament. At key points in their argument, the apostles often lean on Old Testament passages, events, and concepts. One scholar has counted 295 separate quotations of the Old Testament in the New Testament. These make up about 4.5 percent of the entire New Testament, or about 352 verses.[2] Thus, 1 out of 22.5 verses in the New Testament incorporates a quotation. In Paul, for example, there are about 100 quotations. A few others suggest that the New Testament contains well over a thousand allusions. By way of comparison, the New Testament includes a handful of pagan and Jewish quotations. Although there are more allusions to this extrabiblical literature, they are nowhere near the same amount of allusions to the Old Testament. The difference is staggering.

THE CONTEXTUAL NATURE OF THE NEW TESTAMENT'S USE OF THE OLD TESTAMENT

For a variety of reasons, many scholars argue that Jesus and the New Testament authors did not cite the Old Testament in accordance with its original meaning. These scholars contend that, on occasion, the New Testament writers do not respect the original

[1]This chapter is a distillation of G. K. Beale, *Handbook on the New Testament Use of the Old Testament: Exegesis and Interpretation* (Grand Rapids: Baker, 2012).

[2]R. Nicole, "The New Testament Use of the Old Testament," in *The Right Doctrine from the Wrong Text? Essays on the Use of the Old Testament in the New Testament*, ed. G. K. Beale (Grand Rapids: Baker, 1994), 13.

meaning of Old Testament quotations or allusions. However, we are convinced that the New Testament authors, without exception, use the Old Testament contextually. That is, these authors respect, to one degree or another, the Old Testament's meaning in its original context.

FIGURE 2.1. PORTRAIT OF A SCRIBE

One of the strongest arguments for a contextual use of the Old Testament lies in C. H. Dodd's classic work, *According to the Scriptures*. He reasons that the New Testament authors are aware of the broad contexts of their Old Testament quotations and do not focus merely on single verses.[3] When we come across an Old Testament quotation or allusion, it is tempting to think that only the immediate or narrow context is in the mind of the New Testament writer. But the majority of Old Testament quotations and allusions in the New Testament are tethered to the immediate and broad context of the Hebrew Scriptures.

As an illustration, consider how we can see only the tip of an iceberg with the naked eye. But if we examine the iceberg under water, we would discover that it is much bigger than we first thought. The same could be said of Old Testament quotations and allusions in the New Testament. One concrete example of how this works is the citation of Isaiah 40:3 in Mark 1:3: "a voice of one calling in the wilderness, 'Prepare the way for the Lord, make straight paths for him.'" On the surface, it appears that Mark only has Isaiah 40:1 in mind and that Isaiah's original meaning appears a bit strained. How does Jesus of Nazareth fit into Isaiah's prediction of Israel's release from spiritual captivity? With further investigation, we discover that Mark wants his audience to consider all of Isaiah 40–66.

Mark's use of Isaiah 40:1 is a signpost that beckons the reader to recall Isaiah's broad message of return from exile, the new creation, and the victory of the messianic servant figure. John the Baptist's role in heralding Isaiah's second exodus in Mark 1 makes good sense in light of the broad context of Isaiah 40–66.

FIGURE 2.2. QUOTATION OF ISAIAH 40:1

[3]C. H. Dodd, *According to the Scriptures: The Sub-Structure of New Testament Theology* (London: Nisbet, 1952), 126-27.

How did the New Testament writers become familiar with the Old Testament? The apostles probably had varying degrees of education in studying the Old Testament. We do not know with great precision what their childhood education entailed, but we can be confident that they learned a great deal about Israel's Scriptures at home and through attending the synagogue. With the exception of Luke and possibly the author of Hebrews, all the New Testament writers are Jewish, so they knew the story of Israel quite well. Even though Luke is a Gentile, he obviously is well acquainted with the Old Testament.

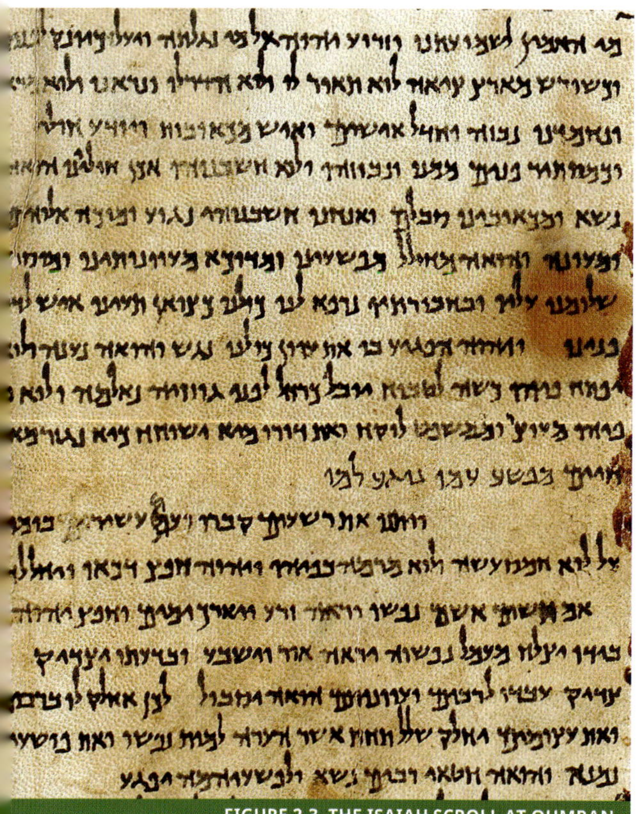

FIGURE 2.3. THE ISAIAH SCROLL AT QUMRAN

The New Testament writers also learned how to interpret significant portions of the Old Testament through their interaction with Jesus. The four Gospels are filled with Jesus interpreting the Old Testament and applying it to their current situation. According to Luke 24:27, Jesus even interprets vast portions of the Old Testament in light of his life, death, and resurrection. Jesus probably expected the disciples to imitate his exposition of the Old Testament. The person of Christ unlocks the ultimate meaning of the Old Testament, so the apostles returned again and again to the Hebrew Scriptures to refine their understanding. Second, as the New Testament authors reflected on the Old Testament, they began to imitate how the prophets interpreted earlier portions of Scripture. The more they read the Old Testament, the more they imitated it. Quite often Israel's prophets interpreted and applied the Pentateuch in their writings (Isaiah, Jeremiah, Ezekiel, etc.), and the apostles began to interpret the Old Testament in much the same way as Israel's prophets did so hundreds of years earlier.

What principles or presuppositions govern the New Testament's use of the Old? First and foremost, Jesus and the apostles believed that the Old Testament Scriptures were the sacred Word of God. For Jesus and his followers, what the Old Testament said, God said; and what God said, the Old Testament said. Second, the apostles were convinced that, like kings representing the nation of Israel in the Old Testament, Christ represents true Israel. He represents the Israel of the Old Testament and the Israel of the New Testament—that is, the church. Third, the apostles firmly believed they were living in the latter days. Everything the Old Testament expected to occur in the end times was beginning to take place in the person of Christ. Fourth, all of history is unified by a wise and sovereign plan so that earlier parts of redemption are designed to correspond to later parts. History is not random. All the events in the New Testament prophetically correspond to the events of the Old Testament. Fifth, as a consequence of the preceding point, the latter parts of biblical history function as the broader context to interpret earlier parts. We can have a better understanding of what the Old Testament authors mean by reading the New Testament. The entire sweep of the history of redemption, from beginning to end, has the same divine author who inspires each biblical author. Therefore, the Old Testament ultimately points to Christ, the center of the Bible's story line and the key to interpreting and bringing clarity to the entire Old Testament.

Much of the New Testament's use of the Old makes good sense if we keep these principles in mind. As we come across Old Testament quotations or allusions that originally referred to Israel but are now attached to Christ or the church, we should not be surprised. Christ is true Israel and so are all those who identify with him.

DEFINITIONS

In our survey of every New Testament book, we will use three tiers of correspondence between the two Testaments—quotation, allusion, and concept.

Quotation. A quotation is an intentional, high degree of verbal correspondence. It is a direct citation of an Old Testament passage that is recognizable by its clear and unique verbal parallelism. Many of these quotations are introduced by a formula, such as "And so was fulfilled what the Lord had said through the prophet" (Mt 2:15), "as it is written" (Rom 3:4), or other similar expressions.

Allusion. Allusions are a bit trickier. Depending on one's criteria, commentators differ about how many allusions exist in the entire New Testament. The count goes anywhere from about 600 allusions to 1,650 and even up to about 4,100.[4] We define allusion as a unique set of words that thematically correspond to a previous text and its context. Allusions do not reproduce the Old Testament passage verbatim. The telltale key to discerning an allusion is to recognize a unique parallel in wording, syntax, concept, or cluster of motifs in the same order or structure. For example, Matthew 13:42, 50 probably alludes to Daniel 3:6, 11. As we juxtapose these two passages, we can trace Matthew's allusion to Daniel (see figure 2.4).

The wording, syntax, and thematic correspondence between these two passages line up nicely. If we take a look at the immediate context, we can even recognize Matthew's careful attention to detail. Daniel 3 concerns the judgment that awaits the righteous Israelites—Shadrach, Meshach, and Abednego. King Nebuchadnezzar punishes them for not bowing down to the colossus that embodies the Babylonian empire (Dan 3:1-6). Since the three righteous Israelites hold fast to the law by not committing idolatry, they are sentenced to death in the fiery furnace. But, miraculously, they are delivered (Dan 3:25).

Matthew is very much aware of Daniel's narrative when he invokes the allusion in Matthew 13:42 and 50. A stark difference remains, though: in Daniel 3 the righteous are delivered from the fiery furnace, whereas

[4]See Nicole, "New Testament Use," 14, who cites this statistic from counting the allusions found in E. Hühn, *Die alttestamentlichen Citate und Reminiscenzen im Neuen Testament* (Tübingen: Mohr Siebeck, 1900).

Daniel 3:6, 11 (NASB)	Matthew 13:42, 50 (NASB)
3:6 "But whoever does not fall down and worship shall immediately *be cast into the midst of a furnace of blazing fire.*" 3:11 "But whoever does not fall down and worship *shall be cast into the midst of a furnace of blazing fire.*"	13:42 "and [they] *will throw them into the furnace of fire*; in that place there will be weeping and gnashing of teeth." 13:50 "and [*they*] *will throw them into the furnace of fire*; in that place there will be weeping and gnashing of teeth."

FIGURE 2.4. DANIEL/MATTHEW TEXTS

in Matthew 13 the unrighteous are ironically punished in the fiery furnace. The unrighteous in Matthew 13 have succumbed to idolatry and persecute the righteous saints, so God promises to punish them by means of their own devious invention! The allusion to Daniel 3:6 and 11 is even reinforced with a number of other allusions to Daniel scattered throughout Matthew 13 (e.g., Mt 4:11/Dan 2:47; Mt 13:32/Dan 4:12; Mt 13:43/Dan 12:3).

This is a wonderful example of how a New Testament author alludes to an Old Testament passage and then adapts it to make his point. Yet the meaning of the Old Testament passage is maintained throughout, though in this case it is ironically understood.

FIGURE 2.5. SHADRACH, MESHACH, AND ABEDNEGO IN THE FIERY FURNACE

Concept. The third and final dimension of the Old Testament's influence in the New operates on a conceptual or thematic level. Quotations and allusions refer to specific passages, while the concept is tied to a large swath of texts or a synthesis of those texts. Even if we are hard pressed to find a precise Old Testament passage in a particular New Testament passage, the basic term *God* is deeply wedded to the story of Israel in the Old Testament.

With a conceptual use of the Old Testament, it is difficult to put our finger on a specific text(s). Prominent themes run throughout a good portion of the Old Testament, such as creation, the exodus, exile, Israel, covenant, and law. We can only do our best to find a point of origin for those themes and trace them throughout the Old Testament writings, especially how they relate to the latter days.

In the stilling of the storm, for example (Mt 8:23-27; Mk 4:36-41; Lk 8:22-25), we can isolate the divine warrior motif, a theme found in the major epochs of Israel's career. It is possible that this theme originated in Israel's exodus, where God utterly defeats the false gods of Egypt (Ex 12:12). Later, in the period of the conquest, if Israel obeys God's decrees, God fights on behalf of the nation and wages war against the pagan nations that occupy the land (Josh 11:6-9). But if Israel disobeys, God fights against Israel (1 Sam 4:1-11; Lam 2:4-5). Likewise, at the very end of history, God will wage war one last time against the hostile forces allied against Israel (e.g., Zech 14:3). The stilling of the storm symbolizes Jesus' overthrow of Israel's enemies since the sea in the Old Testament represented the forces of cosmic evil (e.g., Job 39:15–41:34; Ps 74:13-14; Is 27:1; Dan 7:3-8; Rev 13:1-2). While a few Old Testament passages feature prominently in the background (see Ps. 65:5-7; 89:6-10; 107:23-32), there is a strong conceptual idea running throughout the event. Just as God fought on behalf of his people against their enemies throughout Israel's career, so now Jesus, identifying with Israel's God, fights for the disciples and all those who follow him.

In narrating the stilling of the storm, the three Evangelists most likely do not have a single Old Testament passage in mind as they connect Jesus with the divine warrior theme of the Old Testament. The audience must consider Jesus' actions in the stilling of the storm against the larger story of Israel. Thus, the New Testament often draws from broad Old Testament themes, motifs, and events. Despite not being able to pinpoint a precise Old Testament passage(s) concerning Jesus as the divine warrior, as readers of the New Testament we are still compelled to explore the wonderful array of relevant Old Testament concepts (though it is possible that, at least, Psalm 107:23-32 is in mind, but this does not appear to pertain to the divine warrior theme).

THE INTERPRETATIVE USES OF THE OLD TESTAMENT IN THE NEW TESTAMENT

A common misunderstanding is that the New Testament authors employ Old Testament quotations and allusions the same way in all their writings. Although the latter days have broken into history, and Old Testament predictions and anticipations are initially coming to fruition in the New Testament, not every quotation or allusion signals prophetic fulfillment. At times, New Testament writers are merely making a comparison with the Old Testament. On other occasions, the New Testament brings forward an Old Testament teaching whose authority remains relevant to the new covenant community.

FIGURE 2.6. JOSHUA ORDERING THE SUN TO STAND STILL

Our goal in this section is to outline the major ways the New Testament writers use the Old Testament. We will provide a handful of examples of each, but keep in mind that many of these uses are not mutually exclusive. Often a few of these hermeneutical uses are combined in the author's mind as he recalls the Old Testament with a quotation or allusion.

Direct fulfillment. Here a New Testament author wants to demonstrate *how* *something that has happened in Jesus' life or in the church is a fulfillment of a direct verbal prophecy from an Old Testament passage.* Some of these uses may have introductory fulfillment formulas of various types (e.g., "And so was fulfilled what the Lord had said through the prophet" or "it is written"). Frequently there is no introductory formula at all. This category of usage is the most straightforward and, usually, the easiest to understand: an Old Testament passage makes a specific prediction, and an event in the New Testament is seen as the fulfillment of the prediction.

Matthew 2:5-6. When Herod inquired from the priests and scribes where it was prophesied that the Messiah would be born, they replied, "'In Bethlehem in Judea, . . . *for this is what the prophet has written*: "But you, Bethlehem, in the land of Judah, are by no means least among the rulers of Judah; for out of you will come a ruler who will shepherd my people Israel."'" Here is a quotation of Micah 5:2, one of the Minor Prophets, and in the context of Matthew 2 this quotation indicates the fulfillment of direct prophecy as the following verses reveal that Jesus indeed was born in Bethlehem.

Matthew 3:3. Matthew introduces John the Baptist as the forerunner of Jesus: "*This is he who was spoken of through the prophet Isaiah*: 'A voice of one calling in the wilderness, "Prepare the way for the Lord, make straight paths for him."'" The first Evangelist portrays John the Baptist as fulfilling the prophecy in Isaiah 40:3 of the one who would prepare the way for the end-time coming of the Lord to restore his people from exile. This presents a high view of Jesus since it identifies him with the "Lord" in the Isaiah prophecy.

FIGURE 2.7. GREEK FRAGMENT OF THE MINOR PROPHETS

Luke 4:17-21. Jesus goes to Nazareth, attends a synagogue service, and is handed the scroll of Isaiah the prophet. He turns to Isaiah 61:1-2 and says, "'The Spirit of the Lord is on me, because he has anointed me to proclaim good news to the poor. He has sent me to proclaim freedom for the prisoners and recovery of sight for the blind, to set the oppressed free, to proclaim the year of the Lord's favor.' Then he rolled up the scroll, gave it back to the attendant and sat down. The eyes of everyone in the synagogue were fastened on him. He began by saying to them, '*Today this scripture is fulfilled* in your hearing.'" Jesus sees himself as beginning to fulfill this explicit verbal prophecy from Isaiah.

Indirect or "typological" fulfillment. This category is probably the most complex of all the various uses. The difficulty is largely bound up with one's understanding of the Bible—the divine and human levels of authorship, the broad story line of the Bible, and especially the manner in which the two Testaments correspond to the person of Christ. Our understanding of these critical issues drastically affects how we understand the nature of typology. We will first define indirect or typological fulfillment before exploring how it works in general.

Although some define typology in different ways, our view is that, like direct verbal fulfillment, it retains a fulfillment idea.[5] Whereas direct fulfillment is verbally explicit in the Old Testament passage, typology is less so. Both uses predict the future but do so in a different manner: one by words and the other by events, persons, and institutions. Our working definition of typology is *the study of analogical correspondences among persons, events, institutions, and other things within the historical framework of God's special revelation that are prophetic in nature*. At its core, typology retains a comparative element and a prophetic element.

The comparative aspect of typology applies to notable persons, events, and institutions in the Old Testament that correspond to later persons, events, and institutions. Typology thus pays close attention to prominent Old Testament historical narratives and critical events that relate to the story of Israel. Significant Old Testament patterns foreshadow or point forward to later New Testament patterns. As we wade through the New Testament in this volume, we will often point out cases of typology. When we do so, a few things need to be kept in mind:

1. Historicity: typology is anchored in the veracity of the historical events in Israel's career (exodus, conquest, etc.).
2. Prophecy: historical events, persons, and institutions prophetically anticipate or point forward to later events, persons, and institutions.
3. Escalation: the fulfillment of an event, person, or institution tends to be heightened (Christ as a Passover lamb is greater than the Passover lamb sacrificed in Egypt at Israel's Passover).
4. Retrospection: In the light of Christ's death and resurrection, New Testament writers have a deeper understanding of the prophetic nature of past events, persons, and institutions.

John 19:33, 36. According to John 19:33 and 36, the Roman soldiers did not break Jesus' legs, fulfilling Exodus 12:46 and Numbers 9:12: "When they came to Jesus and found that he was already dead, they did not break his legs . . . These things happened so that the scripture would be fulfilled: 'Not one of his bones will be broken.'" The historical description of the requirement that the bones of the Passover lamb not be broken anticipates the ultimate Passover lamb, Jesus Christ.

FIGURE 2.8. THE DEATH OF PHARAOH'S FIRSTBORN

John 19:36 also recalls Psalm 34:20: "He protects all his bones; not one of them will be broken." David, the psalmist, refers to God's deliverance of the righteous from their afflictions, especially his own. Psalm 34:20 applies Exodus 12:46 and Numbers 9:12 to King David, the righteous sufferer. John may take Psalm 34 as a cue for reading Exodus 12 and Numbers 9 as a type. Since Psalm 34 already applies

[5]For a broader notion of typology than our own, see B. J. Ribbens, "Typology of Types: Typology in Dialogue," *Journal of Theological Interpretation* 51 (2011): 81-96.

Exodus 12 and Numbers 9 to David, it makes sense that John would apply Exodus 12 and Numbers 9 to Jesus, the heir of David and the ultimate Passover lamb.

John 13:18. Jesus tells the disciples in John 13:18 that Judas's betrayal was a fulfillment of Old Testament prophecy from Psalm 41:9: "I am not referring to all of you; I know those I have chosen. But this is to fulfill this passage of Scripture: 'He who shared my bread has turned against me.'" Psalm 41:9 is a historical reflection of David about his trusted counselor, Ahithophel, who betrays him. Though Psalm 41:9 is clearly not a direct verbal prophecy of the coming Messiah, Jesus sees Ahithophel's betrayal of David as a pattern foreshadowing Judas's betrayal of himself. Accordingly, Judas "fulfills" the prophetic expectation of Psalm 41:9.

1 Corinthians 15:44-45. Paul's conception of Jesus' resurrection is largely dependent on his typological reading of Genesis 2:7: "If there is a natural body, there is also a spiritual body. So it is written, '*The first man Adam became a living being*'; the last Adam, a life-giving spirit" (1 Cor 15:44-46 HCSB). From Paul's perspective, the pre-fall Adam of Genesis 2:7 is still considered a natural or earthly being, though he had not yet sinned (1 Cor 15:46). Christ, however, has a different body of glory. Before the resurrection, Christ identified with the earthly body of the pre-fall Adam. At the resurrection, the Spirit transformed Christ's body into a heavenly one. Christ's glorified body was what the first Adam's body would have been transformed into had he not sinned. The first Adam prophetically corresponds to the last Adam. The first Adam's failure to obey God anticipates the success of the last Adam. The latter is greater than the former.

Analogy. New Testament writers use the Old Testament analogically when they *draw something from the Old Testament and compare it to something in the new covenant age in order to illustrate or draw an analogy (or perhaps a contrast) between the two.* The purpose is to emphasize a gnomic, broad, or universal principle. Sometimes it is difficult to distinguish between analogy and typology since typology also contains points of comparison. The main difference between the two is that analogy lacks the element of prophetic anticipation. According to the analogical use, the New Testament author is simply comparing two things.

1 Corinthians 9:9-10. First Corinthians 9:9-10 cites Deuteronomy 25:4 to support Paul's argument that servants of the gospel who "sow spiritual things" among people should benefit materially from those same people: "For it is written in the Law of Moses: '*Do not muzzle an ox while it is treading out the grain.*' Is it about oxen that God is concerned? Surely he says this for us, doesn't he? Yes, this was written for us, because whoever plows and threshes should be able to do so in the hope of sharing in the harvest." Paul sees that the statement from Deuteronomy 25:4 in its context had reference to the moral principle of justice or equity, which he applies to laborers in the gospel. Paul alludes to the general moral principle of justice that even animals should enjoy the benefits of their labor and thus analogically applies this to human laborers. Paul reasons analogically from the lesser (a law about animals) to the greater (applying the principle of this law to humans).

Revelation 2:20. In Revelation 2:20 Jesus confronts a problem of sin in the church of Thyatira: "I have this against you: You tolerate that woman *Jezebel*, who calls herself a prophet. By her teaching she misleads my servants into sexual immorality and the eating of food sacrificed to idols." The church of Thyatira is accused of permitting a group of false teachers to have free rein in influencing God's servants to compromise with idolatrous aspects of pagan society. Jezebel incites King Ahab and Israel to compromise and "fornicate" by worshiping Baal (1 Kings 16:31; 21:25). Similarly, false teachers in the church contend that participation in idolatrous aspects of Thyatiran culture is permissible. Just as Jezebel was from the pagan Caananite culture and came to have a prominent place in the covenant community as the wife of King Ahab, so one may presume that these false teachers in Thyatira were apparently recently converted pagans who professed Christian faith and had come to have some prominence in the church but had not shed all of their pagan allegiances. And just as Jezebel was merging worship of Israel's God with that of Baal, so it appears that the false teachers in Thyatira were combining the worship of Jesus and pagan idols.

Symbol. Symbols, like analogy, compares two things. But symbols function a bit differently in that the comparison is figurative. For example, a dove symbolizes peace. There is a peaceful quality to a dove, yet the dove is not literally peace. The same could be said about a red rose that symbolizes love and adoration. A rose is not literally love but rather a figurative expression of love. The Old Testament is filled with such symbols, and oftentimes they are reapplied in the New Testament. Something that was already symbolic for a historical reality in the Old Testament is used again as a symbol for some reality in the New Testament. Herein lies the difference between the analogical use and the symbolic use: one thing (e.g., an image, such as an animal or some aspect of the natural world) has already been figuratively compared to a person or institution in the context of the Old Testament itself. If the Old Testament has already employed a symbol and that symbol is picked up again in the New Testament, then the New Testament authors are probably employing the Old Testament image symbolically.

Matthew 24:29. According to Matthew 24:29, the Son of Man's coming to judge the temple in AD 70 is associated with the disruption of the cosmos: "Immediately after the distress of those days '*the sun will be darkened, and the moon will not give its light; the stars will fall from the sky, and the heavenly bodies will be shaken.*'" Matthew probably has in mind Isaiah 13:10 and 34:4, both of which concern judgment on foreign nations. Isaiah 13 refers to the nation of Babylon, whereas Isaiah 34 has many nations in view. Throughout the Old Testament, this cosmic language symbolizes the historical end of a sinful nation's existence through divine judgment and the emerging dominance of a victorious kingdom (e.g., Ezek 32:6-8; Hab 3:6-11). God executes the judgment by employing one nation to defeat another in war. Such figurative language is used because Old Testament prophets had a literal conception of the end of history, and they applied this language metaphorically to the ends of various epochs or kingdoms during the Old Testament era. The significance of these allusions to Isaiah here in Matthew 24 is that the destruction of the temple in AD 70 is symbolic of divine judgment falling on the nation of Israel. Ironically, God is judging not the pagan nations that are in mind in Isaiah but the nation of Israel!

Revelation 13:2. Another good example of the symbolic use is found in Revelation 13:2: "The beast I saw resembled a leopard, but had feet like those of a bear and a mouth like that of a lion. The dragon gave the beast his power and his throne and great authority." In Daniel 7:3-8 the images of the lion, bear, leopard, and "terrifying" beast, respectively, represent four successive world empires that persecute the saints of the covenant community. For Daniel, each beast symbolizes a political entity that is antagonistic to the people of God. The beast in Revelation 13 therefore symbolizes political power that persecutes in a similar way. Yet there is a difference. John combines the different animals from Daniel that represent different kingdoms and merges them into one antagonistic animal. Why does he combine all the animals into one? Piling up Daniel's multiple beasts into one may highlight the extreme fierceness of this beast, especially in persecuting God's people. Furthermore, merging Daniel's four beasts may also suggest the transtemporal nature of Revelation's beast since the ones in Daniel's vision represent kingdoms that span hundreds of years. Revelation 13 may suggest that there is one beast that symbolizes Rome, spanning the overlap of the ages between the two comings of Christ.

Abiding authority. Here again there may be some overlap with the analogical use since there is a comparison of an Old Testament passage with something in the New Testament. *This use underscores the reaffirmation of the authority of an Old Testament statement.* The teaching is just as true and authoritative today as when it was first spoken in the Old Testament passage. To grasp the significance of the abiding authority, it is imperative to examine the broad and immediate context of the Old Testament. Sometimes the introductory formula "as it is written" prefixes a quotation that indicates the abiding authority that continues into the present situation of the New Testament writer.

FIGURE 2.9. THE FALL OF BABYLON, AN EVENT PREDICTED IN DANIEL 7

Romans 3:2-4. A typical example of this kind of abiding authority occurs in Romans 3:2-4, in which Paul argues that the benefit of being a Jew is "great in every respect. First of all, that they were entrusted with the oracles of God. What then? If some [Jews] did not believe, their unbelief will not nullify the faithfulness of God, will it? May it never be! Rather, let God be found true, though every man be found a liar, as it is written, '*That You may be justified in Your words, and prevail when You are judged*'" (NASB). Part of "the oracles of God" refers to Old Testament promises about Israel's end-time salvation. Paul asks, Will "their unbelief . . . nullify the faithfulness of God" in fulfilling those promises? Romans 9:6–11:32 answers this question in the negative. God will remain faithful to his promise to Israel. In Romans 3:2-4, Paul anticipates his expanded discussion in Romans 9:6–11:32 by affirming that although the majority of Israel has not believed, this does not mean that God is or will be unfaithful to his Old Testament promise to save Israel in the latter days. Paul emphatically says in this respect, "May it never be!"

The Old Testament quotation in Romans 3:4 comes from Psalm 51:4, in which David confesses that he has sinned with Bathsheba. David contrasts his undependable sinfulness with God's unswerving truthfulness. God is justified in his words and prevails when he is judged by anyone trying to doubt his absolute faithfulness. David states this was true of God in his day, and Paul argues that the same is still just as true. The majority of the Jews are "unbelieving" and "liars," but God stands as unswervingly true and faithful to his promises to Israel (Rom 3:3-4). Paul also uses the formula "as it is written" in Romans 3:10 to introduce a number of Old Testament quotations (3:10-18) from the Psalms and Isaiah about humanity's sin and depravity and thereby demonstrate that what was true about humanity's fallen condition in the Old Testament is still true in his own day.

Prototype or blueprint use. As we mentioned above, New Testament authors often have the immediate and broad context of an Old Testament quotation or allusion in mind. The prototype or blueprint use is a development of this idea in that *sometimes a New Testament author takes an Old Testament segment and uses it as a model for a segment of text in his own writing.* The broad context of the Old Testament (perhaps a chapter or a portion of a chapter) serves as a blueprint for the New Testament passage. We can discern this particular use by observing a thematic outline that is traceable to a specific Old Testament passage and/or by discerning a cluster of quotations or clear allusions from the same Old Testament text.

Revelation 4–5. Daniel 7 provides the blueprint for the vision of Revelation 4–5. An overview of the two chapters together reveals that they exhibit a unified structure that more closely resembles Daniel 7 more than any other Old Testament passage. The point of Revelation's use of the Daniel 7 blueprint indicates that Daniel's prophecy of the kingdom of the Son of Man and of the saints has been inaugurated in Christ's death and resurrection. The judgment mentioned in Daniel 7 has also begun its fulfillment in Christ, especially in the climactic defeat of the kingdom of evil forces.

Irony. Irony is expressing one thing and meaning its opposite. *New Testament authors may use the Old Testament in such a way that stands in direct opposition to the meaning of the Old Testament.* This does not mean that the New Testament authors are unconcerned about the original context of the Old Testament. Indeed, the ironic use affirms it. Biblical irony can ridicule or mock to highlight ironic judgment, or it may encourage the faithful who, while suffering persecution and defeat, ironically overcome the world as they persevere faithfully. This literary use of irony may also be called antithetical or inverted employment of the Old Testament.

Galatians 3:13-14. The ironic use of the Old Testament is well illustrated in Galatians: "Christ redeemed us from the curse of the Law, having become a curse for us—for it is written, 'CURSED IS EVERYONE WHO HANGS ON A TREE'—in order that in Christ Jesus the blessing of Abraham might come to the Gentiles" (3:13-14 NASB). The quoted passage is from Deuteronomy 21:23, in which the curse of capital punishment is said to be executed on an evil Israelite criminal. Now, at the turn of the ages, this horrific punishment for the worst and most despicable of criminals was executed on the most honored Israelite: Jesus. The Deuteronomy text is turned on its head and reversed to indicate a curse on the most innocent of Israelites. Christ endured his Father's curse, so that sinners may receive God's blessing. The Deuteronomy passage is intentionally used in an inverted manner to indicate how the Messiah ironically was cursed to bring about a blessing on humanity.

Revelation 5:6. The depiction of the Lamb with "seven horns" in Revelation 5:6 appears to be taken from Daniel 7:7-8, 20-21, the only place in all of the Old Testament where an animal is portrayed with seven horns. Just as the evil beast in Daniel 7:7-8, 11, 19-27 is portrayed with the power of horns as conquering God's people, now Christ is portrayed with the same imagery to indicate that in the way evil conquers, so must the defeat of evil be portrayed. On the one hand, this imagery metaphorically indicates a divine retributive irony—the manner in which one sins becomes the way one is punished (e.g., see Ps 7:15-16; 9:15-16). On the other, the beast with two horns like a lamb in Revelation 13:11 is likely meant as ironic mockery that this figure is trying to assume a messianic role. The two-horned beast is doomed to failure from the start, though, because he is the antithesis of the true Messiah.

CONCLUSION

The purpose of this chapter is to help students gain some familiarity with the use of the Old Testament in the New. This is very important for our project and for our general understanding of Christ and the nature of the church. In the chapters that follow we will rely on some of this chapter's nomenclature. For the sake of brevity, we will not tag each Old Testament quotation or allusion with a specific hermeneutical use, but we will do so with the more prominent ones. Our hope is that students would recognize the brilliance of the New Testament's use of the Old and have a deeper appreciation of Christ's work as the climax of Israel's story.

INTRODUCTION TO THE GOSPELS

What are the four Gospels? Where did they come from? How do we read them? Are they trustworthy accounts? Without a firm understanding of the nature of the Gospels, questions such as these will plague readers. Reading the four gospel accounts is a little like watching a movie. It is easy to get so caught up in the plot that one fails to realize the cost, time, and energy devoted to developing the project. A movie is the result of thousands of hours of time, countless meetings, and large budgets. We can assume that the Gospels are also the result of much planning, time, energy, and great financial sacrifice. This chapter is a brief attempt to pull back the curtains and remove some of the mystery behind the production of the four Gospels.

DEFINITION OF GOSPEL

The word *gospel* in the New Testament comes from the Greek word *euangelion* "good news" and probably originates in the book of Isaiah (e.g., Is 40:9; 52:7; 61:1). But what does the term mean? The New Testament tethers the gospel to Christ's death and resurrection. Paul says that the gospel he communicated to the Corinthians was of "first importance." He then goes on to state that "Christ died for our sins . . . was buried . . . was raised . . . according to the Scriptures" (1 Cor 15:3-4; cf. Rom 1:1-4). Thus, as D. A. Carson points out, "The heart of the gospel is what God has done in Jesus, supremely in his death and resurrection."[1]

The four Gospels inform the reader of the same gospel, yet through a narrative. Whereas Paul uses the term *gospel* propositionally, the Gospels define the term by retelling the story of Jesus. For example, Mark 1:1 says, "The beginning of the *good news* about Jesus the Messiah." We should distinguish between the gospel proper (Christ's death and resurrection) and the effects or implications of the gospel (the kingdom, the new creation, etc.). Jesus' earthly ministry of casting out demons, healing the sick, proclaiming the kingdom, turning water in to wine, and so on contributes to our understanding of the gospel since his acts anticipate the cross and resurrection.

What makes the term *gospel* even more fascinating is that each account of Jesus' life bears the title "the *gospel* according to . . ." The gospel in the New Testament is also a

[1]D. A. Carson, "What Is the Gospel?—Revisited," in *For the Fame of God's Name: Essays in Honor of John Piper*, ed. Sam Storms and Justin Taylor (Wheaton, IL: Crossway, 2010), 162.

literary classification, and the titles of four Gospels demonstrate a conscious awareness of this reality within the early church. According to Martin Hengel, "The unusual titles of the Gospels already indicate that the evangelists . . . bear witness in their works to the one saving message of Jesus Christ."[2] We have *four* Gospels about the *one* gospel of Jesus! Roughly half of the New Testament falls into the category of narrative. Evidently, early Christianity had quite a penchant for using narratives to unpack the significance of the gospel.

THE GENRE OF THE GOSPELS

Imagine reading Harry Potter like *USA Today*. We would attempt to enroll immediately at Hogwarts and begin training for quidditch tryouts. We scoff at such a prospect, but why is that? How do we know Harry Potter and similar books are fiction? It does not claim to be fiction on the front or back cover. But we instinctively and unconsciously discern that it is fiction. By picking up the book and flipping through the pages, our brains gather data and signals that tell us the book is purely fictional so that by the time we begin reading the book, we understand its nature and how to read it.

The same could be said of the four Gospels. If we do not place them into the right literary category, we will fail to catch some of the nuances of their narratives. Before any interpretation can take place, the book's genre must be determined. As Richard Burridge notes,

FIGURE 3.1. PORTRAIT OF ST. MARK

FIGURE 3.2. MATTHEW 1:1 FROM THE LINDISFARNE GOSPELS

[2]Martin Hengel, *The Four Gospels and the One Gospel of Jesus Christ: An Investigation of the Collection and Origin of the Canonical Gospels*, trans. John Bowden (Harrisburg, PA: Trinity Press, 2000), 49.

> Genre forms a kind of "contract" or agreement, often unspoken or unwritten, or even unconscious, between an author and a reader, by which the author sets out to write according to a whole set of expectations and conventions and we agree to read or to interpret the work using the same conventions, giving us an initial idea of what we might expect to find.[3]

In the last few decades, many New Testament scholars have begun categorizing the four Gospels as Greco-Roman biography. In the ancient world, there existed a genre known as "Lives," a flexible genre that incorporates a variety of literary characteristics (history, praise, moral philosophy, story, etc.). The point of this type of literature is to *inform the readers of a leader and invite the readers to believe that message.*[4] The Gospels, like Greco-Roman biography, primarily narrate the story of a protagonist. In short, each chapter and literary unit in the Gospels somehow informs us of Jesus and his message.

If the Gospels are deemed to be Greco-Roman biographies, then we must keep something uppermost in mind when reading them: the four narratives are primarily about Jesus, the leader or hero of the narrative. We must continue to ask ourselves the question, What do we learn about Jesus in light of the present passage? In this vein, we must also examine each Gospel in light of the grand story line of redemption as set out in the Old Testament. Although it is tempting to interpret each Gospel in isolation, we ought to study the four narratives against the backdrop of the Old Testament. Jesus is the climax of God's dealings with humanity and creation, so we are compelled to place him at the center of that story.

As an example of reading each passage in light of Jesus and how he fits into the larger sweep of God's story, let us briefly consider Matthew's account of the stilling of the storm (8:23-27 NASB). This event details Jesus' sovereign power over the chaotic waters and the failure of the disciples to believe. Once the storm arises on the sea, the disciples cry out in fear, "Save us, Lord; We are perishing!" Jesus' reply to them appears rather surprising: "Why are you afraid, you men of little faith?" Scholars tend to focus on the disciples' lack of faith in Jesus' power. Although the disciples' response is an important piece, it is not central. The disciples' lack of faith is secondary to Jesus' identity. The narrative connects Jesus to Israel's Lord in the Old Testament who sovereignly reigns over chaotic waters, wherein his (and Israel's) enemies dwell. This explains why the disciples ask the question, "What kind of a man is this, that even the winds and the sea obey Him?" The disciples are conceptually aware of Old Testament passages that demonstrate God's absolute power over chaotic waters (Ps 65:5-7; 89:6-10; 107:23-32). They also know that the Old Testament anticipates the day when God will judge his water-dwelling enemies (see Dan 7:1-14). Therefore, as we progress through the Gospels, we must focus on how each passage pertains to Jesus and how the story of redemption climaxes in him.

EYEWITNESS TESTIMONY

Exactly how the Gospels came about has been the focus of much scholarship for the past two

[3]Richard A. Burridge, "Gospel Genre and Audiences," in *The Gospels for All Christians: Rethinking the Gospel Audiences*, ed. Richard Bauckham (Grand Rapids: Eerdmans, 1998), 114.

[4]Richard A. Burridge, *What Are the Gospels? A Comparison with Graeco-Roman Biography*, 2nd ed. (Grand Rapids: Eerdmans, 2004), 76.

centuries. Every conceivable hypothesis has been offered to explain their creation and publication, particularly the relationship between the Gospels and the historical figure of Jesus. The quest for the historical Jesus has, unfortunately, concerned itself with critically investigating the Jesus *behind* the Gospels. In this reappraisal the Gospels are not taken at face value but viewed as the product of early Christian beliefs and ideologies. In order to apprehend the Jesus of history, scholars have been preoccupied with stripping away the layers of the later church's theology and ideology. The net result is a reconstructed Jesus who looks nothing like the Jesus of Matthew, Mark, Luke, and John.

A far better way of establishing the "historical Jesus" is to allow the Gospels to present him on their own terms. For nearly two thousand years, Christians have taken the Gospels at face value and believed that the Jesus of the Gospels is one and the same with the Jesus of history. Bridging the gap between the historical Jesus and the gospel narratives is the category of eyewitness testimony. In recent years, this understanding of early Christianity has undergone considerable refinement, strengthening the long-held view.

Richard Bauckham's book *Jesus and the Eyewitnesses* is most insightful in this regard.[5] The crux of his argument is that in the ancient world, living testimony is to be preferred to secondhand tradition. In other words, the authors of the Gospels are primarily concerned with gathering content about Jesus *from those who had personally listened, seen, and experienced him*. Bauckham builds on Samuel Byrskog's work, *Story as History—History as Story*.[6] Byrskog argues that Greco-Roman historiography makes extensive use

FIGURE 3.3. THE TWELVE APOSTLES

[5]Richard Bauckham, *Jesus and the Eyewitnesses: The Gospels as Eyewitness Testimony* (Grand Rapids: Eerdmans, 2006).
[6]Samuel Byrskog, *Story as History—History as Story: The Gospel Tradition in the Context of Ancient Oral History* (Leiden: Brill, 2002).

of a category known as eyewitness testimony, which preferred a witness who participates in the actual events. In our modern world, we prefer "objective" testimony in an attempt to get at the bare facts. We typically prefer a neutral observer to a prejudicial one. In disputations involving car accidents or criminal activity, the neutral observer is held in high regard. But in the ancient world, historiographers prefer to interview those who are active participants.

The Gospels, some critics claim, come into existence through several stages: Jesus' actual words, the apostolic proclamation, and the written Gospels. The Gospel writers, they argued, should be understood primarily as collectors of "forms" or literary units that are created by a specific community to meet a specific need within that community. The Christian church later in the first century supposedly created Jesus' sayings (perhaps through purported prophetic utterances by those in the church who claimed Jesus was speaking through them). This same church also ostensibly created some of the narratives about what Jesus did. The task, therefore, for many scholars is to get back to the original words of Jesus by stripping away all the ideological layers produced by the later church. But eyewitness testimony questions much of what form criticism seeks to accomplish. Instead of determining how a particular form evolved and developed within a community over decades, the category of eyewitness testimony cuts through the presupposition of a long oral development of the Gospels without the control of the eyewitnesses.

One of the clearest examples of eyewitness testimony comes at the beginning of Luke's account: "Many have undertaken to draw up an account of the things that have been fulfilled among us, just as they were handed down to us *by those who from the first were eyewitnesses and servants of the word*. With this in mind, since I myself have carefully investigated everything from the beginning, I too decided to write an orderly account for you, most excellent Theophilus" (Lk 1:1-3). Here Luke explicitly states that he and others used "eyewitnesses" and "servants of the word" in their composition of Gospel accounts (cf. 2 Pet 1:16; Eusebius, *Hist. eccl.* 3.39.1-4). So, as we read the Gospel accounts of Jesus' ministry, we can be confident that we are getting firsthand testimony of the life of Christ.

AUDIENCE OF THE GOSPELS

When we turn to the epistles of the New Testament, the author typically mentions the audience at the beginning of the letter. For example, Paul says in 1 Corinthians 1:2 (NASB), "to the church of God which is at Corinth," and Peter in 1 Peter 1:1 (NASB), "to those who reside as aliens, scattered throughout Pontus, Galatia, Cappadocia, Asia, and Bithynia." But when we examine the four Gospels, the audience is never mentioned. We are left to determine the audience through a different avenue of inquiry.

For the past several decades, it has been (and still is) quite popular to view each Gospel as being written *in* and *for* particular communities. Until recently a better proposal was not offered. For instance, several prominent scholars claim that the book of John is most likely written to the community in Ephesus. The high Christology and other particular emphases in John's Gospel are included to address specific problems *within* the community. Not only was each Gospel written for a specific community in mind but

FIGURE 3.4. THE CHURCH OF ST. PETER IN ANTIOCH

each Evangelist writes his Gospel in that same community. In other words, the author exclusively writes a Gospel to suit the needs of his own community.

Some of this line of argumentation has considerable problems and lacks historical evidence. Much of the problem rests on how we read the Gospels. They are oftentimes read as epistles—a letter written to a specific church or churches with a particular set of problems. But the Gospels are not the same type of genre that Paul employs. The Gospels fall, as we argued above, into the category of Greco-Roman biography, whereas Paul's letters are part of the epistolary genre. With epistles, we do our best to recreate the occasion of the letter. We study the geographic location of its recipients, the history, the culture, the reason(s) why the letter is sent, and so on. But Gospels are noticeably different from letters, and we need to treat them as such.

Bauckham proposes that each of the four Gospels has an "open" audience; that is, they are not intended for one specific community or communities. They were written for *all* Christians.[7] For example, Mark may very well have been written in Rome (and his Roman congregation would certainly have obtained a copy of his Gospel), but once the Gospel had been copied, it spreads quickly throughout the eastern Mediterranean, moving from one congregation to another. In a few short years, the majority of Christians enjoy access to Mark's Gospel. If Bauckham is right, then the audience of each Gospel spans the entire Christian spectrum, from Jewish Christians, to Christian Jewish proselytes, to converted pagan Gentiles. What begins with twelve people in Palestine catches fire, rapidly expanding to many of the major cities throughout the eastern Mediterranean. For nearly three decades, the

[7]Richard Bauckham, "For Whom Were Gospels Written?," in *The Gospels for All Christians*, ed. Richard Bauckham (Grand Rapids: Eerdmans, 1998), 9-48.

apostles and Jesus' family testify to Christ's life, death, and resurrection and his fulfillment of the Old Testament expectations. The Gospels were written to reinforce and supplement this apostolic teaching within the early church.

While Bauckham's view is headed in the right direction in that the Gospels are intended to circulate widely and not intended solely for one isolated community, each Gospel probably has in mind the struggles of its local network of churches. Each Evangelist is certainly part of a local congregation, so it seems likely that the four Gospels are intended, at some level, to address some of the concerns of their local body of believers. The Gospel of Matthew, for example, is rich with Old Testament and Jewish imagery and language, leading many scholars to suggest that the First Gospel is written primarily, though not exclusively, for Jewish Christians in Matthew's community.[8]

Lastly, the four Gospels also contain evangelistic elements. To some degree, the four Evangelists also wrote with an eye to reach *unbelieving* Jews and Gentiles. The Gospel of John, for example, claims to have been written "*that you may believe* that Jesus is the Messiah, the Son of God, and that by believing *you may have life in his name*" (Jn 20:31). Thus, one of John's central aims is to reach unbelieving Jews.[9] As the Gospels circulated throughout the early church and Jewish and Gentile Christians learned more about Jesus, Christians would inevitably share what they had learned with their unbelieving family members, friends, employers, and so on. Therefore, the four Gospels are published to enrich the faith of all believers, address some of the needs of the local church, and proclaim the truth of the gospel to unbelievers throughout the entire known world.

SYNOPTIC PROBLEM

The term *synoptic*, coined by J. J. Griesbach, comes from the Greek word *synopsis*, which means "seeing together." Virtually all scholars today argue that interdependence exists within the Synoptics. Although a few argue that the Synoptics closely resemble one another because they depend on an earlier oral tradition, most scholars are convinced that Matthew, Mark, and Luke are interdependent. That is, the Gospels borrow textually from one another. There are simply too many textual similarities (vocabulary, syntactical arrangement of words, order of events, etc.)

FIGURE 3.5. THE FOUR EVANGELISTS

[8]See, e.g., Craig S. Keener, *The Gospel of Matthew: A Socio-Rhetorical Commentary* (Grand Rapids: Eerdmans, 2009), 45; Mark L. Strauss, *Four Portraits, One Jesus: A Survey of Jesus and the Gospels* (Grand Rapids: Zondervan, 2007), 31.

[9]D. A. Carson, *The Gospel According to John*, PNTC (Grand Rapids: Eerdmans, 1991), 662-63.

between the texts. If there is borrowing, then who borrowed from whom? Perhaps one Gospel is the source? Can one Gospel account for all the material? Why is Mark so brief in comparison? The Synoptics demonstrate great differences and divergences, but, as Carson and Moo so aptly put it, "What hypothesis best accounts for the combination of exact agreement and wide-divergence that characterizes the first three gospels?"[10]

The history of source criticism of the Synoptics can be roughly broken down into three stages. The first stage begins with the Augustinian hypothesis, which lasted over a thousand years. Augustine proposed that Mark used Matthew, and Luke used both of them. This hypothesis is named after Augustine (ca. 354–430) since he crystallized and promulgated it. The Roman Catholic Church eventually adopted this position.

The second stage is the Griesbach hypothesis or the "Two-Gospel" hypothesis. J. J. Griesbach (1745–1812) critiqued the Augustinian hypothesis by proposing that Matthew was the earliest, Luke borrowed from Matthew, and Mark borrowed from both of them. The difference between Augustine's view and this one is that Griesbach proposed that Mark drew from Matthew and Luke instead of Luke drawing from Matthew and Mark.

The next stage, known as the "Two-Source" hypothesis, maintains that Mark is the earliest

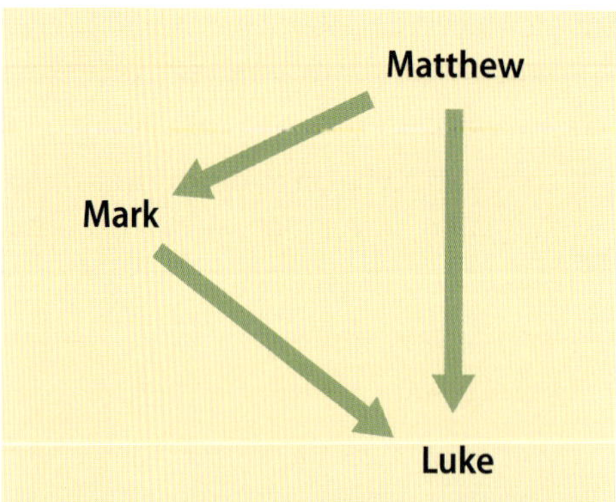

AUGUSTINIAN HYPOTHESIS

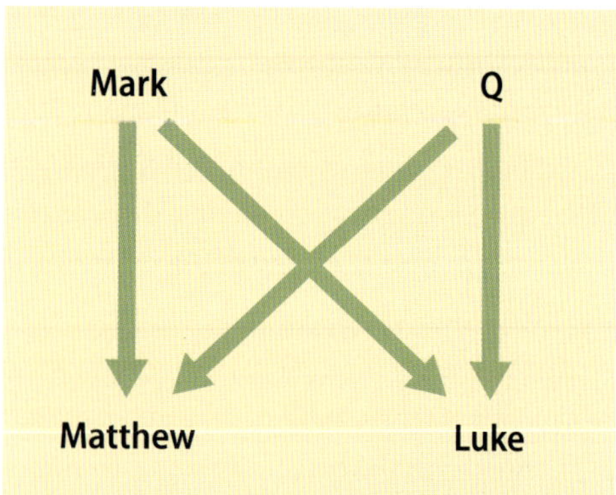

TWO-SOURCE HYPOTHESIS

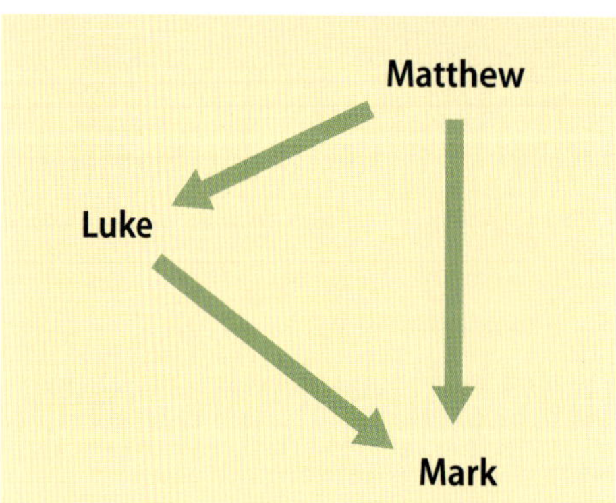

GRIESBACH HYPOTHESIS

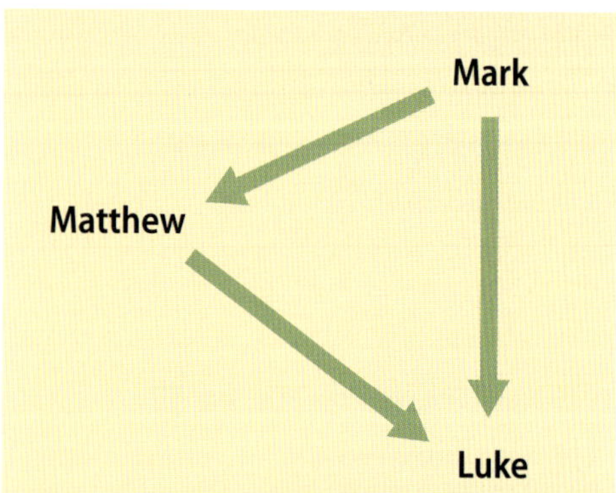

FARRER'S HYPOTHESIS

[10]D. A. Carson, and Douglas J. Moo, *An Introduction to the New Testament*, 2nd ed. (Grand Rapids: Zondervan, 2005), 88.

and that Matthew and Luke did not borrow from one another but from a second source called "Q." This theory was first postulated by C. H. Weisse (1801–1866) but was popularized by H. J. Holtzmann (1832–1910).

Scholars have attempted to piece together this second source and have labeled it "Q," standing for the German word *die Quelle* "source." The Q source is material that is common only to Matthew and Luke, and it is probably best to view this Q source as a combination of an *oral* and *written* tradition. Although the "Two-Source" theory is most persuasive, we remain cautious in our preference.

In recent years, many scholars are taking a hard look at Austin Farrer's hypothesis. This is perhaps one of the most viable alternatives to the two-source hypothesis in that it dispenses with the Q source and maintains a welcome simplicity.[11] This configuration is also attractive because it deems Mark as the earliest Synoptic, the view of the majority of New Testament scholars.

In the end, we prefer Markan priority because of (1) the length of Mark is considerably shorter than Matthew and Luke (Why would Mark abridge the other two Gospels?), (2) the order of events (Matthew and Luke never agree against Mark), and (3) Mark's awkward and rather primitive grammar.[12]

As a final remark, we need to recognize that, according to tradition, two major apostolic eyewitnesses stand behind the four Gospels. Mark was not an apostle but he did receive Peter's testimony. If Matthew and Luke depend on Mark, then Peter's testimony composes the bulk of the Synoptics' portrayal of Jesus. Furthermore, John the apostle (the son of Zebedee) wrote the Gospel of John. If this is correct, then the voices of Peter and John, two of the "inner three" disciples, stand behind much of what we have in all four Gospel accounts.

CANONICAL ORDER OF THE GOSPELS

When we open our Bibles to the beginning portion of the New Testament, we are presented with the order Matthew, Mark, Luke, and John. Why are they listed in this order? Paul's books are roughly organized according to length, but what about the Gospels? Two main options exist:

1. Matthew-John-Luke-Mark. This order is known as the Western tradition. We find it in Latin manuscripts and among writers and churches in the western Mediterranean. In this order, the *two apostolic voices are given priority* in order of length. (Luke and Mark were not part of the original Twelve.)
2. Matthew-Mark-Luke-John. This order appears in the Muratorian Canon (AD 200) and often appears in the eastern Mediterranean tradition. It is not until Jerome's Vulgate (fourth century) that this order becomes the standard. The order of the Gospels in this configuration represents a *chronological distinction.* According to the early church, Matthew was written first, then Mark, then Luke, and finally John.

[11]See Francis Watson, *Gospel Writing: A Canonical Perspective* (Grand Rapids: Eerdmans, 2013).
[12]Carson, and Moo, *Introduction to the New Testament*, 96-98.

THE GOSPEL OF MATTHEW

AUTHORSHIP

Although many modern scholars deny that the apostle Matthew (also called Levi [Mk 2:14; Lk 5:27-28]) authored this Gospel, the evidence tends to run in the opposite direction. Within the First Gospel, we can detect a unique emphasis on taxation (Mt 9:9; 10:3; 17:24-27), suggesting that its author was familiar with the tax trade. Not coincidentally, Matthew himself was a tax collector (9:9). The early church even attested to Matthew's authorship, and it was simply assumed that he penned the Gospel (e.g., Eusebius, *Hist. eccl.* 1.7.10; 3.24.5). Matthew was a Jew, and the First Gospel is trenchantly Jewish. Admittedly, although evidence for Matthean authorship is not particularly strong when we examine the Gospel internally or externally, there remains no better alternative. In the end, we ought to trust the early church's conviction that Matthew did indeed author the Gospel bearing his name.

DATE

The dating of the book depends on its relationship to Mark and Luke. If Matthew depends on Mark, which we believe to be the case, it must have been written after Mark. Determining when Matthew's Gospel must have been completed is difficult to say. We are convinced that Jesus' prediction of the judgment on the temple is forward-looking and prophetic in that it concerns the *future* destruction of the temple in AD 70. Therefore, if this prophecy by Jesus is true, which we believe it is, a date around the mid to late 60s is likely.

PURPOSE

Matthew places Jesus of Nazareth at the center of the story of the Old Testament. Israel's institutions, events, and individuals prophetically anticipate Jesus and his ministry. He is the climax of the history of redemption and the long-awaited ruler of Israel, the son of David and true Israel. Yet Jesus is more than a King; he is Immanuel—Israel's God in the flesh (Mt 1:23). Matthew desires that his largely Jewish readers affirm their belief in Jesus as the crucified Lord and follow him in all their ways.

OUTLINE

On a general level, the three Synoptics arrange their material geographically, progressing from Jesus' baptism in the Jordan to his ministry in Galilee and then on to Jerusalem. Each locale has its own story and its own place in the history of redemption. In Galilee, the populace, both Jews and Gentiles, welcomes Jesus. Jerusalem, however, is ironically the place of his suffering and death. Instead of the City of David embracing her Messiah, she scorns him, eventually nailing him to a cross. While broadly arranging the material geographically, Matthew also weaves five prominent teaching blocks into his narrative (chaps. 5–7; 10; 13; 18; 23–25), perhaps symbolizing the five books of the Pentateuch.

- I. Introduction to Jesus and His Mission (1:1–4:11)
  - A. Prologue and Genealogy (1:1–2:23)
  - B. John the Baptist and Jesus' Testing in the Wilderness (3:1–4:11)
- II. Jesus' Ministry in Galilee (4:12–18:35)
  - A. Kingdom Proclamation (4:12–7:28)
  - B. Kingdom Demonstration (8:1–11:1)
  - C. Rejection and Restoration (11:2–18:35)
- III. Jesus' Ministry in Judea and Jerusalem (19:1–28:20)
  - A. Triumphal Entry, Judgment on the Temple, and the Olivet Discourse (19:1–25:46)
  - B. Last Supper and Betrayal (26:1–27:31)
  - C. Crucifixion and Empty Tomb (27:32–28:20)

BIBLICAL-THEOLOGICAL THEMES

Jesus and the already but not yet of the kingdom. Much of what Jesus says and does in the Synoptics centers on the establishment of the end-time kingdom, an event that, according to the Old Testament, would take place at the very end of history. Jesus argues that the kingdom has indeed arrived, but his followers and the crowds struggle to believe his staggering claims. The arrival of God's eternal kingdom was to entail the outpouring of covenantal blessings and the creation of the new heavens and earth. So where is the fulfillment of these promises? Why is Rome still governing Israel? How can God's kingdom arrive yet Rome still wield authority over the Jews? The three Evangelists tackle these pressing questions in Matthew 13, Mark 4, and Luke 8, but Matthew's presentation of the parables of the kingdom is extensive and perhaps the best place to look for answers.

FIGURE 4.1. INSPIRATION OF ST. MATTHEW

Following Matthew's parable of the sower (Mt 13:1-10), Jesus claims that the disciples have received from him the "mysteries of the kingdom" (our translation). The expression "mysteries of the kingdom" is especially important in Matthew's Gospel and the Synoptics at large (Mt 13:11; Mk 4:11; Lk 8:10). The term *mystery* originates in the book of Daniel, especially chapters 2 and 4, where it concerns judgment on pagan nations and the establishment of God's end-time kingdom. Nebuchadnezzar dreamed about a colossus with four parts, each representing four pagan kingdoms (Babylon, Medo-Persia, Greece, and Rome). A "stone" then smashes the statue and eventually fills the entire earth, symbolizing the kingdom filling the whole earth (Dan 2:29-35). The prophet Daniel finally interprets the meaning of Nebuchadnezzar's symbolic dream (Dan 2:36-45). Nebuchadnezzar's dream and Daniel's interpretation of it constitute the mystery. The divine revelation is thus "hidden" (Nebuchadnezzar) but later "revealed" (Daniel). Mystery then becomes a framework for understanding revelation in Judaism and early Christianity that generally refers to a teaching or doctrine entailing new or surprising elements.

FIGURE 4.2. WORSHIP OF NEBUCHADNEZZAR'S STATUE

What does Jesus mean by the "mystery of the kingdom of God"? In the immediate context, the mystery is related to the parable of the sower and the following parables concerning the kingdom. The Old Testament expects the establishment of the end-time kingdom to be a decisive overthrow of God's enemies at one consummate point at the very end of world history (e.g., Gen 49:9-10; Num 24:14-19; Dan 2:35, 44-45).

What makes Jesus' teaching about the kingdom a mystery is the contrast with the Old Testament expectation of the kingdom. One of the main tenets of the prophesied latter-day kingdom is the consummate establishment of God's kingdom directly preceded by the ultimate destruction of unrighteousness and foreign oppression. The advent of the Messiah would signal the death knell of evil empires. Pagan kings and their kingdoms are to be destroyed or "crushed" (Dan 2:44), and the Messiah would "shatter all their substance with an iron rod" (Pss. Sol. 17:24). Such a defeat and judgment would be decisive and happen all at once at the end of history (see fig. 4.3).

But Jesus claims that the advent of the Messiah and the latter-day kingdom does not happen all at once. Paradoxically, two realms coexist simultaneously—some belong to the kingdom and others to the "evil one." The

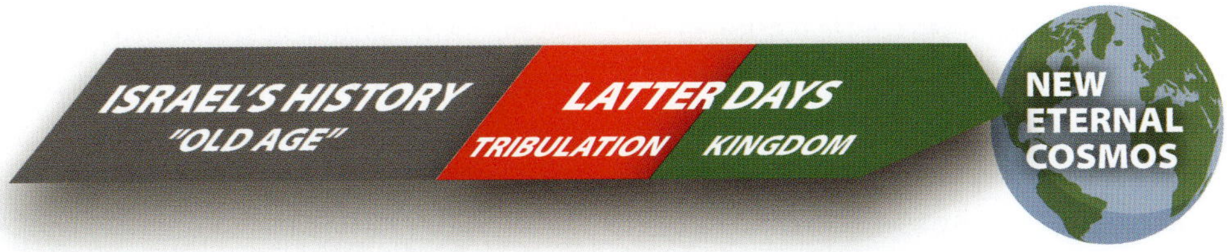

FIGURE 4.3. OLD TESTAMENT EXPECTATION OF THE ETERNAL KINGDOM

kingdom has been inaugurated but remains to be consummately fulfilled.

In a very real sense, the latter-day kingdom has begun through Jesus. His defeat of the devil during his wilderness temptation is nothing short of the fulfillment of Old Testament promises that portray God annihilating Israel's enemy through the Messiah. But the true enemy of Israel is not ultimately Rome—it is Satan.[1] Jesus, the "rock" that is "cut out, but not by human hands" (Dan 2:34), has "crushed" the devil and his demonic forces (Mt 21:44). Exorcisms of demons are a result of Jesus' victory over the devil and further advancement of the kingdom. At the very end of the age, the physical enemies of God (behind whom stand Satan and the forces of evil) will be completely and finally defeated. We thus have an "already but not yet" defeat of evil: first the unseen powers of evil in the first century and then the physical opponents of God and his people at the very end of the age.

The parable of the weeds (Mt 13:24-30) describes a field owner who sowed "good seed," but while he was sleeping "his enemy" came and "sowed weeds" (13:24-25). As a result, the weeds and the wheat grew *together*, making it difficult to separate them (13:26-28). The owner thought it wise to allow the wheat and the weeds to flourish concurrently (13:29). Only at the harvest will the wheat and weeds be ultimately separated. Fortunately, Jesus interprets the parable a few verses later (13:36-43) because of the disciples' apparent lack of understanding (13:36). According to the interpretation, the field constitutes the world, the good seed are the sons of the kingdom, and the weeds are the sons of the evil one (13:38). The point of the parable could not be clearer: kingdom citizens and unrighteous individuals dwell together (see fig. 4.4).

FIGURE 4.4. ETERNAL KINGDOM IN THE OVERLAP OF THE AGES

[1] N. T. Wright, *Jesus and the Victory of God* (Minneapolis: Fortress, 1996), 451-61.

The inclusion of two more parables—of the hidden treasure and the costly pearl (Mt 13:44-46)—demonstrate the immense worth or inauguration of the latter-day kingdom. This is again illustrated in the enigmatic saying found in Matthew 13:52: "Therefore every teacher of the law who has become a disciple in the kingdom of heaven is like the owner of a house who brings out of his storeroom *new treasures as well as old.*" Here the kingdom is likened unto a scribe or writer that furnishes "things new and old." Jesus' teaching concerning the kingdom involves both new and old insights. His teaching stands in both continuity and discontinuity with the Old Testament. The continuity of Jesus' teaching is that the unexpected "already but not yet" kingdom still truly fulfills Old Testament prophecies concerning the kingdom (Gen 49, Num 24, Dan 2, Mt 5:17). The kingdom has arrived! Yet, the kingdom remains a future reality. Mysteriously, its arrival does not signal the *complete* destruction of Israel's enemies and the devil as the Old Testament anticipates.

FIGURE 4.5. PARABLE OF THE WHEAT AND THE WEEDS

FIGURE 4.6. PARABLE OF THE HIDDEN TREASURE

Jesus as the divine warrior. One of the ways in which the three Synoptics paint their portrait of Jesus is by identifying him with Israel's God. What is true of God is true of Jesus. In that vein, Jesus is often identified with the divine warrior motif found throughout the Old Testament (e.g., Ps 18:7-15; 24:7-10; 68:4; 104:1-3).[2] God as a warrior can probably be traced back to Israel's exodus from Egypt and in the period of the conquest. If Israel obeys God's decrees, he fights on their behalf and wages war against the pagan nations (Josh 11:6-9). But if Israel disobeys, God fights against Israel (1 Sam 4:1-11; Lam 2:4-5). The divine warrior is also applied to the Old Testament's understanding of the latter days. At the very end of history, God will wage war one last time against the hostile forces allied against Israel (e.g., Zech 14:3).

[2]Tremper Longman III and Daniel G. Reid, *God Is a Warrior* (Grand Rapids: Zondervan, 1995).

Perhaps the clearest account of Jesus as the divine warrior is the stilling of the storm (Mt 8:23-27; Mk 4:36-41; Lk 8:22-25). This extraordinary event, one of the most memorable miracles in the Synoptics, is thick with Old Testament influence, particularly in Matthew's retelling of the event. In the Old Testament, the sea symbolizes rebellion and hostility toward God's creation. For example, Psalm 74:13-14 says, "It was you [the Lord] who split open the sea by your power; you broke the heads of the monster in the waters. It was you who crushed the heads of Leviathan and gave it as food to the creatures of the desert" (cf. Ezek 32:2; Dan 7:2). Yet only the Lord has the ability to judge sea monsters and calm the chaotic waters. Psalm 107:23-32, a key text behind the stilling of the storm (cf. Ps 65:5-7; 89:6-10), states,

> Some went out on the sea in ships;
> they were merchants on the mighty waters.
> They saw the works of the LORD,
> his wonderful deeds in the deep.
> For he spoke and stirred up a tempest
> that lifted high the waves.
> They mounted up to the heavens and went down to the depths;
> in their peril their courage melted away.
> They reeled and staggered like drunkards;
> they were at their wits' end.
> Then they cried out to the LORD in their trouble,
> and he brought them out of their distress.
> He stilled the storm to a whisper;
> the waves of the sea were hushed.
> They were glad when it grew calm,
> and he guided them to their desired haven.
> Let them give thanks to the LORD for his unfailing love
> and his wonderful deeds for mankind.
> Let them exalt him in the assembly of the people
> and praise him in the council of the elders.

Most if not all of these features take place within the Synoptics' account of the stilling of the storm, with one distinct difference: *Jesus* stills the storm. Throughout his career, events such as the stilling of the storm force the reader to recall God's interaction with Israel in the Old Testament. In identifying himself as Israel's Lord, Jesus possesses sovereign authority to silence the onslaught of "demonic forces," symbolized by the chaotic waters of the Sea of Galilee. Jesus, as Israel's God incarnate, symbolically judges evil.

FIGURE 4.7. ISRAELITES CROSSING THE SEA

In one of the most riveting displays of Jesus' divine identity, Matthew also displays his humanity. In contrast to the chaotic environment of the sea, Jesus soundly sleeps in the stern of the boat. Several Old Testament texts set the background for such strange behavior. Psalm 3:4-6 says, for example, "I [David] call out to the Lord, and he answers me from his holy mountain. *I lie down and sleep*; I wake again, because the Lord sustains me. I will not fear though tens of thousands assail me on every side" (cf. Ps 4:6-8). Sleep in the midst of trouble can be found only by trusting perfectly in God since he is wholly in control and governs all things, including enemies. Jesus, as a perfect human and a descendant of David, trusts in the sovereign hand of his Father, knowing that his life remains safe despite being in the throes of chaos.

INTRODUCTION TO JESUS AND HIS MISSION (1:1–4:11)

According to 2 Samuel 7, King David longs to build a permanent structure where the Lord could dwell with his people. God is at that time dwelling in the tabernacle, a temporary, mobile structure. God denies David's request since he was a "warrior and . . . shed blood" (1 Chron 28:3). Instead, the Lord promises David that one of his descendants will build the temple and that his descendants will rule over the kingdom "forever" (2 Sam 7:13, 16). Although Solomon initially fulfills these promises (1 Kings 8:22-66), he and David's descendants fails to rule faithfully by committing idolatry and pursuing personal gain. The Old Testament prophets foretell the advent of a righteous descendant of David who will defeat Israel's enemies in the latter days and establish the eternal kingdom (e.g., Is 9:6-7; 11:1-16; Dan 2:35, 44-45). Without hesitation, Matthew connects the person of Jesus to these expectations and announces their fulfillment.

Prologue and Genealogy (1:1–2:23). Many scholars rightly argue that Matthew's gospel resonates within a Jewish setting. Although the other two Synoptics, Mark and Luke, certainly configure their Gospels in accordance with the Old Testament, Matthew does so all the more. His Gospel contains about fifty-five Old Testament quotations whereas the other three combined cite a total sixty-five quotations.[3]

The first Evangelist, himself a Jew who no doubt had some form of training in the Hebrew Scriptures, draws heavily from the Old Testament to narrate Jesus' life, death, and resurrection. Using ten "fulfillment formula" quotations, Matthew explicitly connects the person of Jesus to swaths of the Old Testament (Mt 1:22; 2:15, 17, 23; 4:14; 8:17; 12:17; 13:35; 21:4; 27:9). All that Jesus says and does is seen through the lens of the Old Testament. The entirety of the First Gospel is studded with Old Testament quotations, imagery, and language.

Matthew is the only Gospel that opens with a formal genealogy, leaving little doubt to Jesus' identity (Mt 1:1-17). Whereas Mark lacks a genealogy and Luke places his between John's imprisonment and the wilderness temptation (Lk 3:21-37), Matthew immediately sets the tone of his Gospel with the genealogy. The prologue begins with "*the genealogy* [*biblos geneseōs*] of Jesus the Messiah." This critical phrase recalls Genesis 2:4 and 5:1: "*This is the account* [*biblos geneseōs*] of the heavens and the earth. . . . *This is the written account* [*biblos geneseōs*] of Adam's family line." In echoing the first few chapters of Genesis, Matthew typologically reveals

[3]"In addition to explicit quotations, numerous allusions and echoes of Scripture may be discerned in every part of this Gospel, roughly twice as often as in Mark, Luke, or John." Craig Blomberg, "Matthew," in *Commentary on the New Testament Use of the Old Testament*, ed. G. K. Beale and D. A. Carson (Grand Rapids: Baker Academic, 2007), 1.

that Jesus has come to establish the new creation as the last Adam. The whole of Matthew's Gospel could be considered as an account of Jesus inaugurating the new age in his earthly ministry, death, and resurrection.

Jesus is formally introduced as "the Messiah the son of David, the son of Abraham" (Mt 1:1). By not following the chronological sequence of Israel's history (Abraham lived before David), Jesus' Davidic pedigree remains primary throughout the genealogy. Although some of Matthew's genealogy remains elusive to us, the overall point cannot be missed: Jesus is the long-awaited king! Israel and her prophets waited expectantly for hundreds of years for the Messiah's coming, and he has now arrived in the person of Jesus of Nazareth. Even the genealogy's structure expresses this messianic theme. The structure breaks down into three chronological sections: pre-monarchical period (1:2-6a), monarchical period up until the exile (1:6b-11), and the deportation to the long-awaited Messiah (1:12-16). The arrangement of the genealogy displays a wonderful focus on Jesus as the ruler of Israel.

Why also mention the great patriarch Abraham? Matthew does so for at least one salient reason: God promises Abraham that he will be the father of a great nation that will occupy the Promised Land (e.g., Gen 12:1-9; 15:4-20). Jesus is the continuation and ultimate fulfillment of God's promise to Abraham in that he is a legitimate offspring of Abraham. He is *the* embodiment of what it means to be a descendant of Abraham, the true Israelite. To state the matter succinctly, Matthew presents the story of Jesus primarily (but not exhaustively) through the lens of the end-time king and true Israel. Perhaps Abraham is also mentioned because of God's promise that "all peoples on earth will be blessed through" him (Gen 12:3). Jesus is the means by which God will restore Gentiles.

FIGURE 4.8. KING DAVID PLAYING THE HARP

By including Abraham at the beginning of the genealogy, Matthew expects his readers to consider how this eminent figure fits into the grand story line of the Old Testament. God promised Abraham that he would be the "father of many nations" (Gen 17:5). This promise explains the presence of four Gentile women: Tamar, Rahab, Ruth, and Bathsheba (although it is unclear if Bathsheba is a Gentile according to 2 Sam 11:3). The inclusion of these women suggests that Jesus' mission stretches beyond the boundaries of Israel.

After establishing Jesus' role as king and true Israel in the genealogy (Mt 1:1-17), Matthew moves on to the birth narrative (1:18–2:23). Before Jesus is born, an angel tells Joseph to name the child "Jesus, because he will save his people from their sins" (1:21). This verse is particularly revealing in that the angel unveils the ultimate reason why Jesus, the end-time king and true Israel, has come—to save people from sin. The establishment of God's eternal kingdom is the result of Jesus' saving work.

The name Joshua, Jesus' Hebrew name, also recalls the great Israelite leader Joshua, who led the Israelites into the Promised Land (Josh 1:1–5:12) and won a series of military conquests (Josh 5:13–12:24). Jesus is a greater Joshua who will usher Israel into the Promised Land of the new creation upon defeating the devil.

The name Jesus (literally, Joshua) means "the Lord saves." It is a title that aptly summarizes God's character and plan of redemption in the Old Testament. He is known as the God who saved his people from Egyptian bondage (Ex 14:30; 18:8; Ps 106:21; Hos 13:4; see fig. 4.10) and plans to redeem them fully in the latter days. By assuming the name "the Lord saves," Jesus is the Lord incarnate who will accomplish an even greater redemption and deliverance—the salvation of individuals from the slavery of sin. As Craig Blomberg notes, "He will be a savior of his people, not from the physical oppression of the Roman occupying forces but from the spiritual enslavement of their sins."[4]

Following the naming of Jesus, Matthew sees a direct fulfillment of Isaiah 7:14 taking place in Jesus: "All this took place *to fulfill* what the Lord had said through the prophet: 'The virgin will conceive and give birth to a son, and they will call him Immanuel' (which means 'God with us')'" (Mt 1:22-23; see fig. 4.9). Isaiah 7:13-14 prophesies a young woman (or virgin) giving birth to a child named "Immanuel." The prophecy is initially fulfilled in the birth of Isaiah's son (Is 8:3-4; cf. 8:8, 10, 18). Yet Isaiah 9:1-7 predicts that a future Davidic king will be called "Mighty God, Everlasting Father, Prince of Peace," and Matthew confirms that Isaiah's prophecies are fulfilled climactically in the person of Jesus. The first Evangelist even translates the Hebrew word *Immanuel* for the readers, rendering the name as "God with us." The placement of Isaiah 7:14 here in Matthew 1:22-23 suggests that God's glorious presence is no longer found in the backroom of the physical temple in Jerusalem but in Jesus. The Old Testament awaited the day when God would dwell intimately with his people (e.g., Is 66:1-2), and Matthew signals its arrival. Heaven has come down in Jesus of Nazareth. As the First Gospel continues to unfold, Jesus advocates the destruction of the old idolatrous temple (e.g., Mt 21:12-17; 24:1-35) and the establishment of the end-time temple in himself and all those who follow him (e.g., 12:6; 21:43-44). "God with us" is found at the beginning, middle, and end of Matthew's Gospel, suggesting that the phrase is a unifying theme throughout the narrative (1:23; 18:20;

[4]Blomberg, "Matthew," 2.

28:20).[5] It may not be a stretch to claim that "these [three] references frame and support everything in between."[6]

Once Jesus, the sign child (Mt 1:22-23), is born, Magi come to worship him. Herod catches wind of this and orders the killing of children under the age of two (2:1-12). Chapter 2 fleshes out Jesus' role as king and true Israel on many levels. Herod the Great, the Roman-appointed ruler of Israel at this time, discovered that a rival "king" (Jesus) had been born, so he attempts to kill this rival ruler (2:1-12). Like the wicked Pharaoh in Exodus 1:15–2:10, who unsuccessfully attempted to murder all the male Israelite newborns, Herod is unsuccessful in attempting to kill Jesus, a greater Moses. The typological parallel between Moses and Jesus in the birth narrative should not be forgotten as we journey through Matthew's Gospel. The book of Exodus begins with a birth narrative in which God displays his sovereign hand of provision to his servant who will later mediate God's covenant to the Israelites (Ex 2:1-10). By juxtaposing the birth of Jesus and the birth of Moses, Matthew sets the stage for the bulk of Jesus' ministry. Like Moses, Jesus will bring his people out of slavery (sin), lead them to a new mountain (Jesus himself), mediate to them a new covenant (Jesus' teachings), so that they may dwell with God in a new Promised Land (new creation).

As Matthew will unpack in the next few chapters, we learn that Jesus is a threat to the devil's territory, not Herod's. The Son of David will rule and reign not over a plot of land in the Middle East but over the spiritual realm and the far reaches of the cosmos. Being warned in a dream that Herod will try to kill Jesus, Joseph and his family flee to Egypt. In fleeing to Egypt, Jesus retraces Israel's flight to Egypt hundreds of years earlier. There is little doubt that Matthew presents Jesus as true Israel (Mt 2:13-15).

According to Matthew 2:15, it is precisely at this point when Hosea 11:1 is fulfilled: "So he got up, took the child and his mother during the night and left for Egypt, where he stayed until the death of Herod. And so was

FIGURE 4.9. THE PROPHET ISAIAH

[5]Richard B. Hays, *Reading Backwards: Figural Christology and the Fourfold Gospel Witness* (Waco, TX: Baylor University Press, 2014), 38.
[6]Hays, *Reading Backwards*, 38.

FIGURE 4.10. KILLING OF EGYPTIAN FIRSTBORN

fulfilled what the Lord had said through the prophet: '*Out of Egypt I called my son*.'" Matthew claims that Hosea 11:1 is fulfilled in Jesus' journey to Egypt, even as a baby. Hosea 11:1-4 recounts God's devotion to Israel by redeeming her out of Egypt (11:1), but Israel did not remain faithful to him: "The more they were called, the more they went away from me" (Hos 11:2). Verses 1-4 highlight the Lord's faithfulness to his covenant and Israel's unfaithfulness to that same covenant.

The book of Hosea, not unlike other prophetic books, oscillates between the one and the many, or "corporate solidarity." Often in the Old Testament, an individual corporately represents a community or even a nation. The actions of a single person affect the entire community. For example, Saul's sin of killing the Gibeonites results in a famine in Israel (2 Sam 21:1), and David's sin of numbering the people engenders punishment on Israel (1 Chron 21:1-17).

The same concept operates in Hosea. The prophet Hosea is commanded to "take a wife of harlotry," so that Israel may see a graphic representation of their behavior. The symbolism between Hosea and Gomer is clear enough—Gomer represents unfaithful Israel and Hosea represents faithful Yahweh (Hos 1:2), and Hosea's children even represent Israel (1:6; cf. 12:2-5). Upon coming to Hosea 11:1 ("When Israel was a child, I loved him, and *out of Egypt I called my son*"), astute readers are keenly aware of the corporate solidarity that the prophet Hosea has already established. The book of Hosea also predicts a time when a leader representing the community will lead them out of exile: "The people of Judah and the people of Israel will come together; *they will appoint one leader and will come up out of the land* [of Egypt]" (Hos 1:11; cf. 7:11, 16; 8:13; 9:3; 11:5).

Using a blend of direct and indirect fulfillment, Matthew contrasts Israel as God's "son" in Hosea 11:1 with Jesus as the true "son" of God (Mt 2:15). The nation of Israel came out of Egypt, disobeyed, and incurred judgment. Jesus repeats the cycle by traveling out of Egypt, even as a child (2:14-23), and perfectly obeying his Father throughout his ministry (3:15). Where Israel grumbled, complained, and lacked faith in the Lord, Jesus faithfully obeyed the Father's will (4:1-11).

John the Baptist and Jesus' testing in the wilderness (3:1–4:11). Matthew transitions out of the birth narrative and into Jesus' adulthood in chapter 3, which begins with the character of John the Baptist. Readers are immediately confronted with a bizarrely dressed Israelite prophet demanding that the nation repent of her sins. Since the kingdom is at hand, John's message carries a sense of urgency. Israel must be prepared for the Lord's coming in the latter days. If they are not, they will be on the receiving end of God's wrath. Despite John's warnings, the majority of Israel refuses to repent (Mt 3:7-12).

By offering baptism for "repentance" (Mt 3:11), John the Baptist indirectly challenges Israel's institutional structures. He lays the foundation for Israel to be reconstituted according to different terms, especially regarding Israel's temple and the entire sacrificial institution. The prophet John announces God's restoration of Israel (Is 40:3), yet in order for this to happen, Israel must repent and surrender to John's baptism (Mt 3:2). Like the prophet Elijah, John's

FIGURE 4.11. MOSES DISPLAYS THE SAME UNBELIEF AS ISRAEL AND STRIKES THE ROCK

appearance reflects Israel's wretched and ungodly condition and their need for urgent repentance (2 Kings 1:8). Despite some Judeans responding to John's message (Mt 3:6), the Jewish leaders resist John. As a result, he recognizes that Jesus will "baptize" them with a destroying "fire" (3:11-12).

Matthew presents a razor-sharp contrast between Jesus' ministry and the Jewish leaders. All three Synoptics highlight the hostility of the religious leaders toward Jesus, but Matthew's presentation of this conflict is exceptional. At every pivotal turn in Jesus' career, he is met with unflinching animosity from the Jewish leadership (e.g., Mt 7:15-23; 12:22-45; 23:1-39; 24:4-5, 10-12, 23-24). It is not surprising, then, to find the Pharisees and the Sadducees, two groups that traditionally did not get along, presenting a united front against John's message. Upon seeing the Jewish leaders, John pulls no punches: "You brood of vipers! Who warned you to flee from *the coming wrath*?" (Mt 3:7; cf. 12:34). With the coming of the kingdom, God's end-time judgment is now at hand. As Leon Morris asserts, "John is linking this wrath with the coming of God's kingdom and accusing the Pharisees and Sadducees of simply looking for a way of escaping the punishment that their deeds had deserved."[7]

The presence of a dove at Jesus' baptism symbolizes the end-time Spirit who ushers in a new stage of God's plan of redemption, the dawn of the new creation (Gen 8:8-12; Is 32:15-16; Ezek 36:26-30).

FIGURE 4.12. THE PROPHET ELIJAH

The Jewish leaders are banking on their Jewish ancestry for God's acceptance, but John argues that "Out of these stones God can raise up children for Abraham" (Mt 3:9). God's people have always been and will continue to be defined by their faith in his promises, not their religious heritage. Here John the Baptist plants the seeds of the restored people of God, true Israel, who will grow into a mighty tree by the end of the First Gospel. Only those who align themselves by faith to Jesus and follow him are qualified to participate (8:19, 22-23; 9:9; 16:24; 19:21, 27-28).

In contrast to the Jewish leaders' rejection of John's baptism, Jesus embraces John's ministry of renewal (Mt 3:13-17). Jesus' baptism in the Jordan will "fulfill all righteousness" (3:15), an event that typologically recalls Israel's passing through the sea at the

[7]Leon Morris, *The Gospel According to Matthew*, PNTC (Grand Rapids: Eerdmans, 1992), 58.

exodus and the second generation passing through the Jordan to enter the Promised Land. Craig Keener notes that "Jesus' baptism, like his impending death . . . would be vicarious, embraced on behalf of others with whom the Father had called him to identify."[8] Israel's restoration is now at hand through the person of Jesus.

Immediately after being baptized by John in the Jordan River, Jesus enters the Judean wilderness (Mt 4:1-11). While all three Synoptics include the temptation narrative, only Luke and Matthew develop the event in some detail. In Mark and Matthew, the wilderness temptation immediately follows the baptism, whereas Luke includes this event after the genealogy. Jesus' forty-day wilderness temptation typologically recalls Adam and Eve's testing in the garden and Israel's forty years of wandering in the desert. While originally addressed to the nation of Israel, Jesus quotes three passages from the book of Deuteronomy during his temptation (Deut 6:13, 16; 8:3). In the original context of Deuteronomy, God instructs Israel about how they should have responded to him in the wilderness. They failed. Jesus, though, fully obeys the Lord. In contrast to Israel's failure to drive out the sinful nations from the Promised Land, Jesus drives out Satan from the world. His resistance to these satanic allurements was the beginning of his decisive defeat of the devil.

Likewise, Jesus' temptation in the wilderness recapitulates Adam and Eve's testing in the garden. Whereas Adam and Eve failed, Jesus succeeds. As the perfect last Adam and true Israel, Jesus obtains the blessings and glory for his success, the same blessings that Adam and Eve, the patriarchs, and Israel were to inherit upon a successful completion of their testing.

JESUS' MINISTRY IN GALILEE (4:12–18:35)

Often in the Old Testament, God's presence is associated with mountains. The Garden of Eden, for example, is the first mountain where God dwelt and manifested his glorious presence to Adam and Eve (Gen 2:8-14; Ezek 28:13-14). Sinai itself, the standard by which all encounters with God are measured,[9] is also portrayed as a grand temple (Ex 3:5; 19–24). Mount Sinai even "becomes the symbol for approaching God in

FIGURE 4.13. JORDAN RIVER

[8]Craig S. Keener, *The Gospel of Matthew: A Socio-Rhetorical Commentary* (Grand Rapids: Eerdmans, 2009), 132.
[9]Jeffrey J. Niehaus, *God at Sinai: Covenant and Theophany in the Bible and the Ancient Near East* (Grand Rapids: Zondervan, 1995).

worship."[10] Mountains also feature prominently in the latter days, as Isaiah prophesies that Israel and the nations will stream to the "mountain of the LORD's temple" in the last days (Is 2:2; cf. Mic 4:7). Throughout his Gospel, Matthew picks up on this important theme of God dwelling on mountains by placing several key events within Jesus'

FIGURE 4.14. JUDEAN DESERT WHERE JESUS IS TESTED

ministry on mountains (Mt 4:8; 5:1; 8:1; 14:23; 15:29; 17:1, 9, 20; 21:1, 21; 24:3; 26:30; 28:16). In fulfillment of these Old Testament expectations, the first Evangelist claims that Jesus is the true temple and Israel's God incarnate who once again meets with his people on a mountain. As God fashioned and commissioned the nation of Israel at Sinai, so too Jesus fashions and commissions true Israel on a mountain (Mt 28:16-20). God gave Israel the old covenant stipulations on Sinai, and Jesus gives the new covenant stipulations on a mountain. Scholars have long recognized that Matthew highlights Jesus' wisdom and teaching ministry more than the other Synoptics. By ascending a mountain and teaching Israel (the disciples and the crowds), his actions recall Moses teaching Israel at Sinai in Exodus 19–23. The Sermon on the Mount (Mt 5:1–7:29) is the first of five teaching blocks in the Gospel of Matthew (see 10:1–11:1; 13:1-53; 18:1–19:1; 23:1–26:1).

Kingdom proclamation (4:12–7:28). With Satan initially defeated (4:1-11), Jesus is empowered to begin the process of renewing creation, humanity, and Israel. The long-awaited Messiah appoints twelve disciples to reconstitute the twelve tribes of Israel (4:18-22) and expel demons from the land (4:23-25). As R. T. France observed, "The disciples of Jesus both correspond to the Old Testament people of God in that in their experience the history of Israel is repeated, and they also assume and carry to completion the destiny which in the Old Testament was to be Israel's."[11] The appointment of the disciples establishes a faithful people group to live in the new creation.

Matthew insists that Jesus typologically corresponds to Moses on multiple levels. But the first Evangelist is also quick to point out that Jesus is a *greater* Moses. Dale Allison argues, "[Matthew] composed a book in which Moses, while remaining normative, becomes a symbol of someone greater, a promise awaiting fulfillment, a book in

[10] L. Michael Morales, *Who Shall Ascend the Mountain of the Lord? A Biblical Theology of the Book of Leviticus*, NSBT 37 (Downers Grove, IL: InterVarsity Press, 2015), 89.

[11] R. T. France, *Jesus and the Old Testament* (London: Tyndale, 1971), 65.

which the exodus becomes history anticipating eschatology."[12] In Exodus 19–23 Moses instructs the Israelites at Sinai how they are to remain holy in the midst of a pagan environment. If the nation responds to the covenant with complete obedience, God promises to vanquish their enemies and give them life, an existence that is fit for the new heavens and earth (Deut 6:2; 30:15). But, like Adam and Eve, the Israelites failed to obey and succumbed to pride and idolatry. In the Sermon on the Mount (Mt 5–7), Jesus rehearses the well-known story but with a twist: instead of failure, Israel is marked by obedience to the covenant. Participants of true Israel will obey these commands because their representative, Jesus, obeyed in the wilderness.

The "law" that Jesus prescribes on the Sermon on the Mount is not antithetical to the law that Moses issued; rather, it is the fulfillment of Moses' instruction (Mt 5:1–7:29). Jesus even says in 5:17 that he did not "come to abolish" the Mosaic commandments but to "fulfill them." Jesus is essentially claiming that he and his teaching, particularly the Sermon on the Mount, fulfill Old Testament patterns and expectations. The Mosaic covenant anticipated Jesus' person, his acts, and teaching on the kingdom.

With the arrival of the new age, members of true Israel are called and empowered to live as citizens of Christ's kingdom. These ethics are not antithetical to those in the old covenant or Mosaic administration (see Deut 6:4!), but they are internalized, reaching

FIGURE 4.15. VIEW FROM MOUNT SINAI WHERE MOSES GIVES ISRAEL GOD'S LAW

[12]Dale C. Allison, *The New Moses: A Matthean Typology* (Minneapolis: Fortress, 1993), 273.

their intended state of fulfillment (Jer 31:31-34; Ezek 36:25-27). This is not to say that the Mosaic covenant lacked an internal dimension (Ex 20:17; Ps 119), but it was largely external in nature by physically separating Israel from her neighbors. These end-time kingdom ethics are not deeply intertwined with Israel's status as a theocratic nation living in the "old age." Instead, they are intended for a community of saints, a people group that has been reconstituted around King Jesus in the eschatological "new age."

Kingdom demonstration (8:1–10:42). Chapters 5-7 disclose what is required of those living within the kingdom, whereas the following chapters reveal who is admitted to the kingdom. When Jesus descends from the mountain, he continues to demonstrate the inbreaking of the kingdom and, astonishingly, his role as Israel's God incarnate (Mt 8:1-9:38; cf. 14:13-36; 15:29-39; 17:13). Jesus immediately heals a leper (8:1-4) and welcomes a Roman centurion who was a Jewish proselyte or a "God-fearer" into the end-time community of Israel (8:5-13; see Lk 7:3-5).

The placement of the stilling of the storm in Matthew's narrative is remarkable. All three Synoptics graphically narrate the fierceness of the storm on the Sea of Galilee. But Matthew strangely refers to the storm as a "quaking" or "shaking": "And behold, there arose a great *shaking* on the sea, so that the boat was being covered with the waves; but Jesus himself was asleep" (Mt 8:24, our translation). The term *shaking* is used fourteen times in the New Testament. It is connected to the crucifixion (27:54), resurrection (28:2), Paul and Silas's imprisonment (Acts 16:26), and several times in Revelation. The occurrences in Revelation are illuminating since they all have overtones of *judgment* associated with them (Rev 6:12; 11:13; 16:18). This may explain why Matthew decides to use the unique word—judgment is at hand.

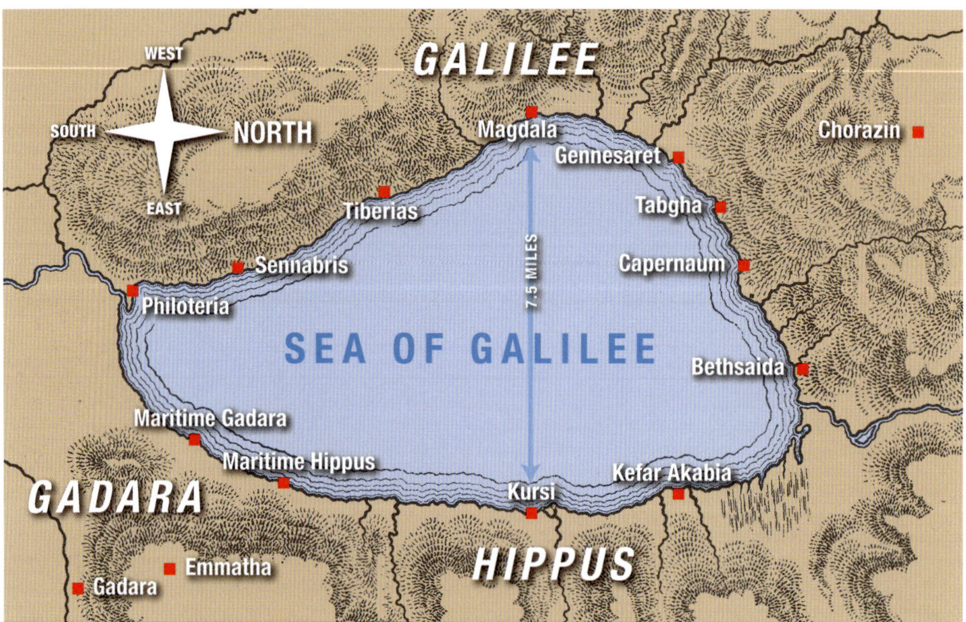

SEA OF GALILEE WITH PROMINENT CITIES

FIGURE 4.16. SEA OF GALILEE

Since only God possesses the ability to calm chaotic waters (e.g., Ps 89:8-10; 107:25-30), Matthew's audience must identify Jesus with Israel's Lord in stilling the storm. When we add this insight into Matthew's enigmatic use of "quaking," we conclude that Jesus, as Yahweh, has judged the devil and his demonic allies. His judgment on Satan and his minions fulfills the prophetic expectation that the Lord would one day redeem Israel and vanquish her enemies in the latter days (e.g., Is 11:13; 29:5). Genesis 3:15 expects an end-time ruler would crush the head of the serpent, and that prophecy is remarkably coming to fruition. The word here used for "rebuking" the wind is the same word used when Jesus "rebukes" the demons later in the narrative (Mt 8:26; 17:18). Matthew drives this point home in the following passage when Jesus expels the demons from the two demoniacs (8:28-34). Notice how Jesus judges the onslaught of evil: "[he] rebuked the winds and the waves" (8:26). This is precisely how he exorcised the demons in the previous context—"he drove out the spirits *with a word*" (8:16).

In forgiving and restoring a paralyzed man, Jesus demonstrates his divine identity once more (Mt 9:1-8). His identity as Israel's God surfaces again in 9:18-25, in which he miraculously raises a girl from the dead. The new creation has certainly broken in and through the person of Jesus. The narrative then focuses on the call of Matthew or Levi (Mk 2:14-17) and the extended commissioning of the Twelve, composing the second major speaking discourse (Mt 10:1–11:1; see 5:1–7:28; 13:1-53; 18:1–19:1; 23:1–26:1). Armed with Jesus' authority, the disciples continue the expansion of the end-time kingdom (10:1-42).

Jesus' various healings throughout Matthew (and the other Gospels) illustrate that he is the last Adam reversing the effects of the fall. We should understand these historical, miraculous healings as acted-out parables in that physical healing symbolizes genuine spiritual healing. At Christ's second coming, then, the bodies of believers will be thoroughly and finally healed at the resurrection. The physical and the spiritual will be fully restored in the new heavens and earth.

Rejection and restoration (11:1–18:35). As Jesus' ministry progresses in Galilee, so does his rejection. The closer Jesus approaches Jerusalem, the more resistance he encounters. This portion of Matthew's narrative turns on recalcitrant Israel and her rejection of Jesus as the Son of Man. Since Israel rejected John the Baptist, she will certainly reject the object of John's proclamation—Jesus (Mt 11:1-30). Chapter 12 of Matthew focuses on Jesus' messianic identity. He claims that he is the fulfillment of Isaiah's predictions and the means by which the Lord will restore captive Israel (Mt 12:15-21; Is 42:1-4). Jesus is not only the king of Israel but also the "Lord of the Sabbath" (Mt 12:1-14) and the one who, as Israel's God, can plunder the strongman (i.e., Satan; Mt 12:22-37). He is Israel's king and her Lord.

Jesus' exposition of the nature of the kingdom in Matthew 13:1-52, the third teaching discourse, is one of the most succinct descriptions of the kingdom in the Gospels. The kingdom stands in direct and indirect fulfillment of the Old Testament expectations yet contains some new, even surprising elements. Chapter 13 is filled with parables relating to the nature of the kingdom, but the purpose of parables in general can be most difficult to ascertain. Are they merely heavenly stories with an earthly meaning? Can they be categorized as simply proverbial sayings undergirded with moralism? The Old Testament offers some help in this regard. The prophets originally ministered to Israel by speaking plainly to them in the form of didactic speech or sermons (e.g., Moses, Elijah). Yet Israel refused to listen, so later prophets were instructed to use a different manner of communication, such as parables and symbolic actions. For example, in Ezekiel 24:3 the Lord commands the prophet to relay a "parable" to the wicked Israelites: "Tell this rebellious people a *parable* and say to them: 'This is what the Sovereign Lord says: 'Put on the cooking pot; put it on and pour water into it.'" The passage goes on to describe a boiled lamb in detail (Ezek 24:4-5), symbolizing God's thorough judgment on Israel in taking her to Babylon (Ezek 24:6-13).

Symbolic actions affect the audience in two ways: those already hardened toward God will be further hardened and ultimately judged; the righteous yet complacent individuals will respond appropriately by obeying the prophet's message. For example, Nathan's parabolic confrontation of David in 2 Samuel 12:1-14 illustrates the latter. The prophet Isaiah's interaction with Israel highlights the former. The Lord commands Isaiah to further *harden* Israel in Isaiah 6:9-10: "He [the Lord] said, 'Go and tell this people: "Be ever hearing, *but never understanding*; be ever seeing, *but never perceiving*." *Make the heart of this people calloused; make their ears dull and close their eyes*. Otherwise they might see with their eyes, hear with their ears, understand with their hearts, and turn and be healed.'" A few verses later, Isaiah performs several symbolic acts that further harden Israel (Is 7:3-9; 8:1-4).

Isaiah 7:3 says that one of Isaiah's children is named "a remnant shall return," so that whenever little "remnant will return" is late for dinner, his mother would call out

"Come home 'remnant will return.'"[13] The child and his name become a symbolic reminder to Israel. Whenever Israelites see the child go anyplace, they are reminded that if they do not change their sinful ways, God would punish them by making them leave their land and go into the captivity of another country from which only a small remnant would return. The parabolic aspect of the prophet's message is then closely linked to the hardening commission of Isaiah 6:9-10 and therefore may be considered one of the means by which God blinds and deafens the people.

Parables in the Gospels fall very much in line with the Old Testament's conception of parables. Jesus stands on the shoulders of Old Testament prophets, both in word and deed. His parables often remain an enigma to individuals hardened toward the message of the kingdom. If the listener remains impassive or apathetic, the parable is meaningless. But if the listener tirelessly pursues understanding the parable, then its meaning is eventually unlocked. Here in chapter 13 the parables of the kingdom describe the unusual fulfillment of the end-time kingdom. The "secrets of the kingdom" (Mt 13:11) concern the unexpected arrival of the kingdom. The parables explain that although the end-time kingdom has broken into history, the complete and final destruction of Israel's enemies and the devil will occur at the very end of history (cf. 24:36–25:46).

In chapter 13, Matthew prefers the phrase "kingdom of heaven" (Mt 13:11, 24, 31, 33, 44-45, 47, 52) over Mark and Luke's phrase "kingdom of God" (Mk 4:11, 26, 30; Lk 8:1, 10). Matthew's preference stems not from a desire to avoid the title *God* but to draw a distinction between heaven and earth.[14] Matthew's heaven terminology also signals the arrival of the heavenly kingdom on earth. The heavenly dimension of God's kingdom irrupts into the earthly ministry of Jesus. By referring to the phrase "kingdom of heaven," Matthew argues that the end-time kingdom has begun its descent and has initially broken into the earthly sphere.

The horrific death of John the Baptist (Mt 14:1-12) prompts Jesus to seek solitude to mourn the loss (14:13). John's death ominously foreshadows Jesus' own fate (17: 11-13). The narrative transitions into the feeding of the five thousand, the only miracle recorded in all four Gospels (Mt 14:14-21; Mk 6:32-44; Lk 9:10-17; Jn 6:1-13). The public meal recalls the Israelite Passover celebration (Ex 12), symbolizing God's redemption of Israel from Egypt. Rehearsing the meal annually looked forward to God delivering his people out of exile once more in a second exodus (Ex 12:14). Jesus, as Israel's Lord, feeds this group of five thousand and their families, signifying God's care of Israel and their deliverance from bondage. The end-time people of God continue to come out from spiritual exile through accepting the words and deeds of Jesus.

The feeding of the five thousand gives way to Matthew's account of Jesus walking on the water (Mt 14:22-36). Similar to the stilling of the storm in 8:23-27, the disciples are alone in the boat being "buffeted by the waves" (14:24). Unexpectedly, Jesus walks on the lake from the shore and identifies himself: "It is

[13]This section on Isaiah 6–7 is taken from Gregory K. Beale, "The Purpose of Symbolism in the Book of Revelation," *Calvin Theological Journal* 41 (2006): 57-58. Reprinted by permission of *Calvin Theological Journal*.

[14]Jonathan T. Pennington, *Heaven and Earth in the Gospel of Matthew*, NovTSup 126 (Leiden: Brill, 2007; repr., Grand Rapids: Baker Academic, 2009).

I. Don't be afraid" (14:25-27). The language here recalls Exodus 3:13-14, when God reveals himself to Moses as "I AM WHO I AM." As the Lord revealed himself by delivering his people from Egyptian captivity and leading them through the chaotic waters of the Red Sea, so too Jesus reveals his identity as Israel's Lord incarnate by delivering the disciples on the Sea of Galilee. The event once again demonstrates Jesus' intention to spearhead a second exodus.

Chapter 15 intensifies the brewing hostility between Jesus and the Jewish leaders (see Mt 12:1-14, 22-45). Since Jesus and his teaching fulfill the entire Mosaic law, its dietary restrictions are no longer in force in the new age (e.g., Lev 11:1-47). Jesus claims that "what goes into someone's mouth does not defile them, but what comes out of their mouth, that is what defiles them" (Mt 15:11; cf. 15: 18-20; Acts 10:14-15). The Jewish leaders argue for ritual uncleanness based upon the external, whereas Jesus states that true uncleanness originates from within. The same could be said of the old covenant. Mosaic legislation teaches that one can become ritually impure because of external contaminants, but Jesus drills down to a deeper level of uncleanness—the human heart. True and complete ritual cleansing is now found in Jesus. After he heals a Canaanite woman's daughter (Mt 15:21-28), a sign that Gentiles are now joining true Israel, he feeds four thousand men plus women and children (15:29-39). The narrative reaches a high point in Matthew 16:16 when Peter finally acknowledges Jesus as "the Messiah, the Son of the living God."

FIGURE 4.17. STATUE OF ST. PETER

Matthew's Gospel underscores the title *Son of God* more than Mark and Luke, attaching it to key events in Jesus' ministry. Jesus is declared to be God's Son when he, even as an infant, went to Egypt and retraced the nation of Israel's steps (Mt 2:15; Hos 11:1). As a recapitulation of the second generation of Israel going through the Jordan, at the baptism in the Jordan River, God declares Jesus to be his Son (Mt 3:17). And just as Israel was called God's "son" as she wandered in the wilderness (Deut 1:31), so during the wilderness temptation Jesus is called the "Son of God" twice (Mt 4:3, 6; cf. 8:29). Certainly, the title is wedded to Jesus as true Israel. According to Exodus 4:22, Israel is even called a "firstborn son," so Matthew typologically presents Jesus as *the* Son who repeats Israel's career and succeeds where the nation faltered. As the narrative unfolds, the title *Son of God* thickens and begins to incorporate a "vertical dimension of Jesus' personhood" that is "virtually tantamount to an affirmation of deity."[15] Jesus claims to possess intimate knowledge of his Father in Matthew 11:27. Toward the end of Matthew's narrative, Jesus affirms that he is the "Son of God" to the Jewish leaders and then goes on to cite Daniel 7:13, an act that is taken as blasphemy (Mt 26:63-66).

When God announces to the disciples that Jesus is his Son, he is affirming Jesus' identity as the divine Son and true Israel. After all Jesus has said and done up to this point in his career, the disciples are beginning to perceive Jesus' true identity. But such excitement is short lived, as Jesus sternly rebukes Peter for his unbelief in Jesus' prediction of his suffering and death in Jerusalem (Mt 16:21-28).

The Transfiguration, one of the climactic events of Jesus' ministry, discloses his divine identity to Peter, James, and John (Mt 17:1-8). As God's Son, he is appointed to rule over not simply Palestine but the entire cosmos (17:5). Jesus "leading" the disciples to a "high mountain" and a "cloud covering them" represents Jesus as dwelling in God's descending heavenly tabernacle. Peter even mentions building three "shelters" or tabernacles (17:4). According to Exodus 24 and 40, Moses and Joshua ascend upon Mount Sinai and a "cloud covered the mountain" (Ex 24:15 LXX) and the same "cloud" later "overshadowed" the tabernacle (Ex 40:35 LXX). As his Galilean ministry ends, it becomes clear that Jesus' ministry has been destined for a horrific death (14:1-12; 16:21-28; 17:11-12; 17:22-23).

JESUS' MINISTRY IN JUDEA AND JERUSALEM (19:1–28:20)

King David's first royal act was to conquer the city of Jerusalem that was originally inhabited by Jebusites (2 Sam 5:6-16). Jerusalem, known as the City of David, was also selected as the city that would eventually become the home of Israel's temple (1 Kings 5–6). But instead of embracing God's laws, Zion quickly fell into a place of rampant idolatry and wickedness (Is 47; Jer 50). Yet not all is lost, as the prophets expect that Jerusalem will serve as a rallying point in Israel and the nations' restoration in the latter days. The prophet Isaiah predicted that Israel and the nations would come and worship the Lord in Jerusalem (Is 2:2-5; cf. Mic 4:1-5; Zech 14:16-21). Jeremiah even prophesies that the entire city will blossom into an enormous temple (Jer 3:16-27; cf. Ezek 40–48). The City of David will be the central location of God's plan of redemption.

As we wade through Matthew's Gospel, we soon realize that Jerusalem in the first century is not the "mountain of the LORD's temple," where the nations worship Israel's God (Is 2:2). Zion had lapsed into the epitome of rebellion and wickedness, resembling the old city of Jerusalem the prophets railed against. Instead of welcoming her Messiah with open arms and embracing his kingdom, Israel puts Jesus to death. Yet, in the horrific death of Jesus, God indeed fulfills his promises to Jerusalem. Jesus becomes the rallying point of the nations, the end-time temple, and the beginning of the new creation.

Triumphal entry, judgment on the temple, and the Olivet Discourse (19:1–25:46). Passion Week brings Jesus' parables and

[15]Grant R. Osborne, *Matthew*, ZECNT (Grand Rapids: Zondervan, 2010), 1088.

FIGURE 4.18. DOME OF THE ROCK IN JERUSALEM

actions to a head, particularly his relationship to Israel's temple. Matthew mentions that Jesus' arrival on a donkey, as Israel's king, "took place *to fulfill* what was spoken through the prophet" (Mt 21:4; Zech 9:9). This event is a direct fulfillment of what the prophet Zechariah predicted when he wrote that Israel's king would arrive on a donkey, symbolizing a peaceful rule. But such a peaceful rule is the result of a battle previously waged by Israel's Messiah: "See, your king comes to you, righteous and *victorious*" (Zech 9:9a). Jesus has come to destroy Israel's enemy—not Rome but Satan—and lead his people out of spiritual exile (Zech 9:16). By coming on a donkey, Jesus symbolically declares that the battle has indeed already been won, a testament to the importance of Jesus' victory over Satan during the wilderness temptation (Mt 4:1-11). As the victorious ruler, Jesus targets the temple complex and proceeds to judge Israel's place of worship (21:12-13). This act of judgment on the temple takes center stage during Passion Week and will continue to be a point of contention between Jesus and the Jewish leaders (e.g., 21:23-31; 26:61; 27:39).

By singing Psalm 118, the pilgrims identify Jesus as the coming deliverer who will liberate them from bondage. Psalms 113–118 are referred to as Psalms of Hallel (*hallel* means "to praise") or the "Egyptian Hallel" (Ps 104–106; 120–136; 146–150). In general, the Hallel psalms are sung on the Feast of Tabernacles, Pentecost, and the first day of Passover. The reason why the grouping of Psalms 113–18 is called Egyptian Hallel stems from the Jewish conviction that Moses penned these psalms, recounting Israel's release from Egyptian captivity. They expect that God will repeat Israel's redemption in an even greater way at the very end of history. As was common, the Jews attending the Passover celebration in Jerusalem sing the Egyptian Hallel as they ventured to Zion. These pilgrims probably perceive Jesus as a political liberator who will lead a successful rebellion against Rome and her allies.

Jesus' actions against the temple symbolize God's utter rejection of Israel's place of worship. These actions should not be surprising, as John the Baptist anticipated this judgment by challenging Israel's identity and structure through his baptism of repentance (Mt 3:1-17). John laid the foundation for Israel, especially her temple, to be reconstituted according to different terms. Israel and her temple are now reconstituted around an individual—Jesus of Nazareth. He is the true temple and true Israel, and all those who follow him likewise become the true sanctuary and the true people of God. What is true of Jesus is true of his followers.

In driving out the money changers from the courtyard, Jesus demonstrates a concern for the nations (Mt 21:12-13). Jesus quotes Isaiah 56:7, a prophecy that the temple would become a rallying place and location of prayer for the Gentiles (Is 56:3-8). Ironically, Israel used the Father's house, intended to bless all the nations, in a way that prevented the nations from worshiping the Lord. Jesus clears the way for the end-time temple, where outcasts can gather and joyfully experience God's presence in his house (Is 56:3-8). The locus of God's presence transitions from the physical temple to the person of Jesus.

As a result, the temple's purpose in offering sacrifices for forgiveness passes away. The locus of forgiveness is now found in Jesus, the true temple, not in the sacrifices in the physical temple. Although the blind and lame were forbidden to draw near to the tabernacle as priests (Lev 21:18), they are now healed by Jesus in the temple (Mt 21:14). Jesus paves the way for the establishment of the end-time temple, where outcasts gather and rejoice in God's presence (Is 56:3-8).

FIGURE 4.19. RELIEF OF ROMANS LOOTING ISRAEL'S TEMPLE IN AD 70

Much of the Olivet Discourse (24:1–25:46) rests on God's physical judgment on Israel in AD 70, when Rome sacks Jerusalem and razes the temple. God's judgment on Israel was well founded, not arbitrary or capricious. Matthew uniquely includes a series of "woe" judgments on the Jewish leaders (Mt 23:13-39). In 23:13-39 Jesus' attention then turns from the "crowds and the disciples" (23:1) to the "teachers of the law and Pharisees," who embody the totality of Israelite leadership. These judgments, in keeping with the woe judgments found in the Old Testament (Is 3:9, 11; Jer 48:1; Ezek 16:23), condemn Israel's leaders and the nation whom they represent. Woe judgments are restricted to those whom God will judge with great finality. Judgment upon Israel's leaders turns on two foci: hypocrisy and persecution of the righteous. Woes in chapter 23 are the theological basis for the coming destruction of Israel's temple outlined in chapter 24. In short, "Israel has rejected its

> ***The Passover lies deep within the heart of the Jewish nation, symbolizing God's redemption and deliverance. It recalls how God vanquished Pharaoh and the Egyptians and anticipates what God will do in the future.***

prophets, and that by rejecting them Israel has failed to obey the law of Moses."[16]

Last Supper and betrayal (26:1–27:31). The anointing at Bethany (Mt 26:6-13) sets the tone for the events that unfold in the coming days. Little did Mary know that she was anointing Jesus for burial. Unlike John who places Jesus' anointing in Bethany at the beginning of Passion Week (Jn 12:1-8), Matthew and Mark delay the event until right before the Passover Celebration (Mt 26:17-35; Mk 14:3-9). In doing so, they tie Jesus' betrayal at the hands of Judas (26:14-16; Mk 14:10-11) to what transpires at the anointing and deftly link the (messianic) anointing to the Passover Celebration. There is no contraction between the accounts, only emphasis.

The Last Supper celebrates the annual Passover meal. The institution of Passover finds its roots in the Exodus narrative. Each year, an Israelite family must find a perfect male lamb and slaughter it at twilight. It is an atoning sacrifice. Then the families are to eat it a certain way and dress accordingly. They are to take blood from the lamb and apply it to the doorframes of their houses (Ex 12:1-50; *Pesah.* 10:5). Remarkably, Jesus typologically identifies himself as the ultimate Passover lamb and the Lord who promised to liberate Israel from slavery (Mt 26:26). In other words, Jesus is both the sacrificial lamb *and* Israel's God in the flesh.

FIGURE 4.20. MODEL OF JERUSALEM

[16]David L. Turner, *Israel's Last Prophet: Jesus and the Jewish Leaders in Matthew 23* (Minneapolis: Fortress, 2015), 284.

Crucifixion and empty tomb (27:32–28:20). Following Jesus' betrayal and arrest, he appears before the Sanhedrin, the official political representatives of Israel (Mt 26:57-68). The legal interrogation climaxes in Jesus' identification with the "Son of Man," who "[sits] at the right hand of the Mighty One and [comes] on the clouds of heaven"—a clear reference to his deity (Mt 26:64; Dan 7:13). Although innocent, Jesus remains guilty in the eyes of the Jewish leaders (Mt 26:60). The next step is to hand him over to the Roman authorities since by law the Jews are unable to employ the death penalty (see Jn 18:31). Matthew mentions two trials before Pilate (Mt 27:11-14; 27:17-26), the latter of which entails Jesus' official sentencing.

With mockery the Roman soldiers garb Jesus in royal clothes, complete with a crown of thorns and a staff in hand (Mt 27:28-30). Rife with irony, these soldiers fail to recognize that Jesus is indeed the true king of Israel. But Jesus' kingship is not limited to a particular plot of land; it stretches to the farthest reaches of the cosmos. Each of the Gospel writers connects Jesus' suffering with his kingship. At the moment of his suffering, physical defeat, and death, Jesus executes his supreme rule as Israel's king. The Old Testament generally expected Israel's Messiah to liberate Israel from political and spiritual oppression (e.g., Gen 3:15; Num 24:17). But Jesus' kingship and reign are marked not by physical triumph but by death and persecution. Through his defeat, Jesus will emerge physically victorious not only over the spiritual realm but will, at his second coming, emerge consummately victorious over the political realm.

Throughout Matthew's narrative, Jesus experiences occasional suffering and tribulation, climaxing with final tribulation of death on the cross. Taken together, these experiences directly fulfill the Old Testament anticipation that great suffering and tribulation would befall Israel in the latter days (e.g., Ezek 38:10-16; Dan 7–12). The Old Testament predicted the nation of Israel would suffer first and then be restored in the kingdom of God through a purified remnant. Now, however, these eschatological two strands are intertwined at the cross. The ideas of tribulation and kingdom, discussed separately in the Old Testament, have been surprisingly merged into a unified, ironic concept in the crucifixion.

FIGURE 4.21. JUDAS'S BETRAYAL

Matthew recounts strange phenomena accompanying the crucifixion: "From noon until three in the afternoon darkness came over all the land. . . . The curtain of the temple was torn in two from top to bottom. The earth shook, the rocks split and the tombs broke open. The bodies of many holy people who had died were raised to life" (Mt 27:45, 51-52). This seemingly bizarre occurrence of events falls very much in line with the Old Testament; the rending of the veil symbolically represents the destruction of the temple.

The curtains (including the veil before the holy of holies) found in Israel's temple are constructed of the variegated colors resembling the sky (blue and purple and scarlet material) and decorated with figures of flying cherubim (winged bird-like creatures; Ex 26:1, 31; 36:8, 35).[17] The scarlet color symbolizes the fiery color of lightning and perhaps of the sun, with the blue and purple resembling the sky and dark clouds. So also the screen for the courtyard and the entrance to the tent are manufactured out of blue and purple and scarlet material (Ex 26:36; 27:16; 36:37; 38:18). Even the loops on the edge of some of the curtains was to be of blue (Ex 36:11). Josephus and Philo, early Jewish commentators in the first century AD, observe that the outer veil of the Holy Place and curtains of the tabernacle and temple were

FIGURE 4.22. ARCH WHERE PILATE DECLARES, "THIS IS THE MAN"

Even the "tapestry" hanging over the outer entrance into the temple "typified the universe," and on it "was portrayed a panorama of the heavens" (Josephus, J.W. 5.210-14).

made to symbolize the four elements of the cosmos: earth, air, water, and fire (Philo, *Quaest. Exod.* 2.85; *Mos.* 2.87-88; Josephus, *J.W.* 5.212-14; *Ant.* 3.183). The Old Testament and Judaism graphically describe both curtains of the temple, the outer and inner veils, as small-scale portrayals of the entire universe, particularly the visible and invisible heavenly dimensions. Therefore, the rending of the veil in Matthew 27:51-52 symbolizes the beginning destruction of the temple and the cosmos. Jesus' death sends shockwaves through the cosmos. The destruction of the old age commences with his death, while the new heavens and earth dawn at his resurrection (27:53).

Mary Magdalene and the "other Mary" travel to the tomb to anoint Jesus' body (Mk 16:1) a few days later, on Sunday. Following a "violent earthquake" (Mt 28:2; cf. 8:24), an angel descends from heaven, pushes the stone away from the tomb, and sat on it (28:2). The angel commands the women to relate to the disciples that Jesus, in keeping with his promise, has risen from the dead (cf. Mt 16:21). As the women run to the disciples to tell them the news, they encounter Jesus and worship him (28:9)—a demonstration that Jesus is Israel's God incarnate. He commissions the women to tell the disciples that Jesus will meet them in Galilee (28:7, 10; cf. 26:32). Like the women, when the disciples saw Jesus, they "worshiped him" (28:17; cf. 28:9). But, "some" of the disciples still wavered in their faith and "doubted," apparently lacking a full understanding of the

[17]This discussion on the cosmic dimension of the curtain is taken from G. K. Beale, *The Temple and the Church's Mission: A Biblical Theology of the Dwelling Place of God*, NSBT 17 (Downers Grove, IL: InterVarsity Press, 2004), 38.

nature of the kingdom and Jesus' full identity. Such insight will be ultimately be grasped at Pentecost.

On a mountain in Galilee, Jesus claims that "all authority in heaven and on earth has been given to me" (Mt 28:18). In contrast to the religious authorities who commission the soldiers to spread lies and deceit (28:13), Jesus, as the faithful Son of Man commissions the disciples to spread the message of salvation (28:19-20). This well-known statement continues to fulfill Daniel 7:13-14, a prophecy about the "son of man" receiving "authority, glory and sovereign power" forever. As the Son of Man, Jesus charges the disciples with the so-called Great Commission: "Go and make disciples of *all nations* . . . teaching them. . . . And surely *I am with you* always" (Mt 28:19-20). This edict to the disciples renews the Genesis 1:26-28 commission to Adam. All of humanity, Jews and Gentiles, will now experience God's presence.

In addition to Daniel 7:13-14, Jesus' Great Commission to his disciples also appears to allude to the words of Cyrus, the king of Persia, in 2 Chronicles 36:23: "The Lord, the God of heaven, has given me all the kingdoms of the earth and he has appointed me to build a temple for him at Jerusalem in Judah. Any of his people among you may go up, and may the Lord their God be with them." This passage has three things in common with Matthew 28:18-20: (1) the authority that Cyrus and Jesus assert over the entire earth, (2) the commission to "go," and (3) the assurance of God's presence to fulfill the commission.

Jesus' commission, however, goes beyond the commission of Cyrus. Although Jesus' commission also has authority over heaven and earth, he refers to his own presence accompanying the disciples. Where the decree of Cyrus focused on the city of Jerusalem, the Great Commission applies to all the nations throughout the earth. Lastly, the

FIGURE 4.23. GARDEN TOMB

decree of Cyrus largely concerns the rebuilding of Israel's temple, a decree that may be preserved in the Cyrus Cylinder (see fig. 4.24). So it is likely that the theme of temple building is retained in Matthew 28. Jesus' followers are to fulfill the Genesis 1:26-28 commission by reconstructing the new temple, comprising true worshipers throughout the earth. It is no coincidence that Jesus' temple-building commission occurs on a mountain, for the three prominent mountains are all associated with God's sanctuary—Eden, Sinai, and Mount Zion. Indeed, the commission of Genesis 1:28 is given on the mountain of Eden.

FIGURE 4.24. CYRUS CYLINDER

First Chronicles begins with a genealogy and 2 Chronicles ends with the decree of Cyrus. Matthew, who likewise begins his gospel with a genealogy and concludes it with the divine commission, may partly model his gospel after the beginning and ending of 1 and 2 Chronicles. But the commission in Matthew 28 is not spoken by an unbelieving king to theocratic Israel. The Great Commission is proclaimed by the true, divine king Jesus to true Israel, the disciples. Second Chronicles 36:23 should be understood as indirect fulfillment or a case of typology, in which Jesus' commission far exceeds the commission of Cyrus.[18]

The promise to the disciples that Jesus would be "with" them indicates how the disciples will be empowered to carry out the original commission. Where Adam and Eve, the patriarchs, and Israel failed to spread God's glory to the ends of the earth, Jesus succeeds. The promise to be "with" them indicates *how* the disciples will be empowered to carry out the commission. The same divine presence that accompanied the patriarchs (Gen 26:24; 28:15) and Israel (1 Chron 22:18; Hag 2:4-5) will now go with the disciples. As the prophet Isaiah predicted, "Immanuel" or "God with us" has come in the person of Jesus (Mt 1:22-23; Is 7:14). The glory that descended in Jesus and now dwells in the disciples will soon reach the nations.

[18]This discussion of 2 Chronicles 36:23 is based on G. K. Beale, *The Temple and the Church's Mission*, 176-77; and, above all, on A. B. Vance, "The Church as the New Temple in Matthew 16:17-19: A Biblical-Theological Consideration of Jesus' Response to Peter's Confession as Recorded by Matthew," Th.M. thesis, Gordon-Conwell Theological Seminary, 1992.

5

THE GOSPEL OF MARK

AUTHORSHIP

Our Bibles bear the name Mark at the heading of the Second Gospel, yet Mark was not one of the original Twelve.[1] The problem especially comes to a head when we consider the Gospels as eyewitness testimony. How could Mark write a Gospel if he did not bear witness to Jesus' earthly ministry (cf. Acts 1:21-22)? The answer probably lies in the comment made by the early church leader Papias when he recollected comments made by John the Presbyter:

> This also the presbyter [John] said,
>
> "Mark, having become the interpreter of Peter, wrote down accurately, *though not indeed in order*, whatsoever he remembered of the things said or done by Christ. For he neither heard the Lord nor followed him, but afterward, as I said, *he followed Peter*, who adapted his teaching to the needs of his hearers, but with no intention of giving a connected account of the Lord's discourses, so that Mark committed no error while he thus wrote some things as he remembered them. For he was careful of one thing, not to omit any of the things which he had heard, and not to state any of them falsely." (Eusebius, *Hist. eccl.* 3.39.15)

From this quotation we gain two key insights: (1) an individual named Mark wrote this Gospel and (2) Mark did not witness these events firsthand but received eyewitness testimony through the apostle Peter. We may gain further insight from the book of Acts and Peter's firsthand account of the life of Jesus. Peter's speech concerning Jesus' words and deeds is remarkably similar to what we find in the Synoptics, especially the Gospel of Mark:

> Then Peter began to speak: "I now realize how true it is that God does not show favoritism but accepts from every nation the one who fears him and does what is right. You know the message God sent to the people of Israel, announcing the good news of peace through Jesus Christ, who is Lord of all. You know what has happened throughout the province of Judea, beginning in Galilee after the baptism that John preached—how God anointed Jesus of Nazareth with the Holy Spirit and power, and how he went around doing good and healing all who were under the power of the devil, because God was with him.

[1]This chapter is an adaptation of Benjamin L. Gladd, "Mark," in *A Biblical-Theological Introduction to the New Testament: The Gospel Realized*, ed. Michael J. Kruger (Wheaton, IL: Crossway, 2016), 61-91.

"We are witnesses of everything he did in the country of the Jews and in Jerusalem. They killed him by hanging him on a cross, but God raised him from the dead on the third day and caused him to be seen. He was not seen by all the people, but by witnesses whom God had already chosen—by us who ate and drank with him after he rose from the dead. He commanded us to preach to the people and to testify that he is the one whom God appointed as judge of the living and the dead. All the prophets testify about him that everyone who believes in him receives forgiveness of sins through his name." (Acts 10:34-43)

FIGURE 5.1. ST. PETER THE APOSTLE

Mark's Gospel appears to follow the broad outline of Peter's sermon in Acts 10:34-43, "thus creating a story of the ministry of Jesus that constitutes the core of the gospel of God."[2]

Although Mark was a companion of Paul and Peter, he was not one of the original Twelve. This Mark is mostly likely John Mark in the book of Acts (12:12, 25; 13:5, 13; 15:37), who had close interaction with several apostles (Col 4:10; Philem 24; 2 Tim 4:11; 1 Pet 5:13). Internally, there may be a few hints at Markan authorship. For example, the enigmatic figure in Mark 14:52 that flees naked could be a legitimate reference to the unnamed author. While many modern scholars doubt that John Mark authored the Second Gospel, there is simply not enough evidence to overthrow the traditional view. Internal clues within Mark's Gospel and the external witness of the early church suggest that John Mark wrote this Gospel.

DATE

The dating of Mark largely hinges on how we understand the relationship between the Synoptic Gospels and the nature of prophecy. Several scholars date Mark to the late 50s and early 60s, allowing enough time for Matthew and Luke to use Mark while composing their Gospels before the fall of Jerusalem (all three Synoptics predict the fall of Jerusalem in AD 70). Keeping in mind Nero's persecution in the mid 60s, it is possible that Mark was written around that time since his Gospel particularly highlights suffering and persecution.

PURPOSE

Mark's Gospel presents Jesus of Nazareth as an enigmatic figure, shrouded in mystery at times. The disciples often struggle with his identity and his mission. Jesus appears to be Israel's Messiah, yet his reign differs from expectations. His kingdom is marked not by political triumph but by suffering and defeat. Israel's king is also Isaiah's suffering servant,

[2]Peter Stuhlmacher, *Biblical Theology of the New Testament*, trans. Daniel P. Bailey (Grand Rapids: Eerdmans, 2017), 561 (cf. 69-70, 126, 180, 187, 560-62).

who will redeem captive Israel from the clutches of sin and death.

OUTLINE

The Synoptics tend to progress geographically from Jesus' baptism in the Jordan to his ministry in Galilee and then on to Jerusalem. In Galilee, Jesus is welcomed by the populace, both Jews and Gentiles. Jerusalem, though, is ironically the place of suffering and death. Instead of the City of David embracing her Messiah, she scorns him, eventually nailing him to a cross. One of the most distinctive features of Mark is his three-part drama. R. T. France persuasively argues that Mark's Gospel falls into three "dramatic acts," corresponding to Mark's geography:[3]

- I. Introduction to Jesus and His Galilean Ministry (1:1–8:26)
  - A. Prologue (1:1-13)
  - B. Beginning of Jesus' Galilean Ministry (1:14–3:6)
  - C. Second Phase of Jesus' Galilean Ministry (3:7–6:6)
  - D. Last Phase of Jesus' Galilean Ministry (6:7–8:26)
- II. From Galilee to Jerusalem: The Path to Suffering (8:27–10:52)
  - A. Peter's Confession and the Transfiguration (8:27–9:13)
  - B. Instruction Concerning the Kingdom and Further Healing (9:14–10:52)
- III. Jerusalem: The Passion and Empty Tomb (11:1–16:8)
  - A. Temple Judgment, Prediction of the Fall of Jerusalem, and Passover (11:1–14:31)
  - B. Betrayal, Crucifixion, and Resurrection of the Messiah (14:32–16:8)

BIBLICAL-THEOLOGICAL THEMES

Second exodus. One of Mark's unique characteristics is his use of Isaiah, particularly his theme of a second exodus.[4] Israel's original exodus from Egypt is of considerable importance; it was Israel's defining moment in the nation's history when the Lord glorified himself, redeemed Israel from bondage, vanquished their enemies, covenanted with them, and safely led them to the Promised

FIGURE 5.2. LION OF ST. MARK

Land. Israelites were not only to gain comfort from the Lord's past dealings with them in the exodus but were also to expect that he would one day repeat that momentous event. Throughout the Old Testament, especially in the Prophets, God promised to deliver Israel out of bondage at the very end of history and bring them to the Promised Land (e.g., Jer 31:7-11, 31-34; Hos 11:10-11; Mic 5:3).

The book of Isaiah, perhaps more than any other Old Testament book, portrays the restoration of Israel from Babylon as a second exodus. The Lord will manifest his glory (Is 40:5; Ex 16:7, 10; 24:16) and repeat the mountaintop experience at Sinai (Is 64:1-3; Ex 19).

[3]R. T. France, *The Gospel of Mark*, NIGTC (Grand Rapids: Eerdmans, 2002), 11-15.

[4]See Rikki Watts, *Isaiah's New Exodus in Mark*, WUNT 2:88 (Tübingen: Mohr Siebeck, 1997; repr., Grand Rapids: Baker, 2000).

God, just as in the first exodus, will lead Israel through water: "When you pass through the waters, I will be with you; and when you pass through the rivers, they will not sweep over you" (Is 43:2a; cf. 51:9-11; Ex 13:17–14:31). He even promises to guide Israel through the wilderness as he originally did in a cloud, both in front and at the rear of the caravan: "But you will not leave in haste, or go in flight; for the LORD will go before you, the God of Israel will be your rear guard" (Is 52:12; cf. 40:11; Ex 13:21-22). As the Lord provided food and water in the first exodus, so too in the second: "They will feed beside the roads and find pasture on every barren hill. They will neither hunger nor thirst, nor will the desert heat or the sun beat down on them. He who has compassion on them will guide them and lead them beside springs of water" (Is 49: 9b-10; Num 10:11–32:42).

The famous servant of Isaiah will be instrumental in delivering Israel from Babylonian captivity (Is 42:1-9; 49:1-6; 50:4-9; 52:13–53:12). One major difference remains between the first and the second exodus: the Old Testament expects the second exodus to be a consummate event when the Lord will deal with sin with great finality, forge a faithful remnant, and create a new heavens and new earth (65:17; 66:22). All of these events take place when God executes the second exodus.

Mark draws on Isaiah's framework, and many of Jesus' actions fit nicely with the prophet Isaiah's expectations of a second exodus. Isaiah's enormous influence on Mark's Gospel fits quite well with the observation that it is taken from Peter's speech in Acts 10:34-43. A chorus of Old Testament allusions, especially from Isaiah, permeate the narrative of the Acts 10 passage.[5] As we read Mark's narrative in light of the book of Isaiah, we soon conclude that Jesus is Israel's God incarnate.

Jesus' words and deeds are identical to the Lord's. Jesus has come to deliver Israel from Babylonian captivity, an enslavement marked primarily by spiritual rather than physical bondage. As a mighty warrior, Jesus vanquishes Israel's true spiritual enemy—Satan. Jesus guides his people through the wilderness; drives out Israel's spiritual enemies from the Promised Land, not only by defeating Satan but also by casting out his demonic forces; and establishes the end-time kingdom. The Lord's glory, now residing in

FIGURE 5.3. MOSES SPLITTING THE SEA, AN EVENT THAT ANTICIPATES ISRAEL'S FINAL, FUTURE REDEMPTION

[5]Stuhlmacher, *Biblical Theology of the New Testament*.

the person of Jesus, dwells with his people in the initial stages of the new creation. Yet Jesus also identifies with Isaiah's suffering servant (Mk 10:45), who suffers on behalf of the Israelites and bears their curse. Mark's picture of Jesus is complex, even enigmatic at times, in that he is simultaneously Israel's sovereign Lord and Israel's suffering servant. He is Lord and servant.

The Messiah and the messianic secret. Within the Synoptics, especially in Mark, Jesus insists that his disciples and others conceal his identity. Commentators label this phenomenon the "messianic secret." For example, Jesus exorcises demons but prohibits them from divulging his identity: "And Jesus healed many who had various diseases. He also drove out many demons, but he would not let the demons speak because they knew who he was" (Mk 1:34). Again, we can make a similar observation in Mark 8:30, which immediately follows Peter's accurate confession that Jesus is indeed the Christ (i.e., the "Messiah"): "Jesus warned them *not to tell anyone about him*" (cf. 9:9). Why would Jesus forbid his disciples from telling others his identity as Israel's long-awaited king? Does Jesus not want Israel to know that he is their savior who has come to liberate them from spiritual oppression? The answer rests on Jesus' fulfillment of Israel's expectations of the long-awaited Messiah. For us to grasp the significance of the messianic secret, we must briefly survey a few key Old Testament texts that describe the coming Messiah.

Many Old Testament passages speak or at least hint at a coming messianic figure who will deliver Israel and redeem her from her plight. The term *Messiah* means "anointed one." To be anointed connotes being set apart for a distinct purpose. We find the word *anointed* used in contexts such as the tabernacle and the altar (Ex 40:9-11). The noun form is applied to priests (Lev 4:3; 1 Sam 2:35) and kings (e.g., 1 Sam 24:6; 26:11), in particular the current and future rulers of Israel (e.g., Ps 2:2; 18:50). The book of Daniel anticipates an end-time ruler who will judge the pagan nations and usher in God's eternal kingdom (Dan 7:13-14; cf. 2:35, 44-45). Taken together, the Old Testament collectively speaks of an individual who is anointed for a specific purpose—ruling over Israel and the nations and redeeming all of creation.

FIGURE 5.4. ANOINTING OF SOLOMON

Genesis 3:15 sets the stage for the development of a messianic figure, albeit in seed form: "And I will put enmity between you and the woman, and between your offspring and hers; *he will crush your head, and you will strike his heel.*" One of the promises God makes to the original couple is that their descendants will form two lines of progeny, a godly and an ungodly seed, and these two will continually wage war with one another. One of their descendants,

FIGURE 5.5. TRIUMPH OF KING DAVID

though, will eventually "bruise" or "crush" the "head" of the serpent.

At the end of Genesis, Jacob blesses his twelve sons, and Judah receives a particularly special blessing: "Judah . . . your hand will be on the neck of your enemies. . . . The scepter will not depart from Judah, nor the ruler's staff from between his feet, until he to whom it belongs shall come and *the obedience of the nations* shall be his" (Gen 49:8-10). According to this passage, in the latter days (49:1) a future ruler will descend from the tribe of Judah and conquer Israel's enemies. As a result of this decisive victory, the nations and Israel will pay obeisance to him. In Numbers 24:17, a "star" will come from Jacob who will "crush the foreheads of Moab"—a longtime enemy of Israel.

God makes a covenant with David in 2 Samuel 7, wherein he promises to maintain a Davidic ruler in Jerusalem: "I will raise up your offspring to succeed you . . . *and I will establish his kingdom.* He is the one who will build a house for my Name, and *I will establish the throne of his kingdom forever*" (2 Sam 7:12-13). This ruler will not only establish God's eternal kingdom but also build God's temple or "house."

The book of Isaiah prophesies that a latter-day ruler of Israel will eliminate Israel's enemies and rule with righteousness and wisdom. Isaiah 11:1-5 describes this messianic figure, the "branch," in some detail: "A shoot will come up from the stump of Jesse; from his roots a Branch will bear fruit. . . . With righteousness he will judge the needy. . . . *He will strike the earth with the rod of his mouth*; with the breath of his lips *he will slay the wicked*" (cf. 9:6-7). This end-time ruler will restore the remnant of Israel (11:11-16) and draw the nations to himself (11:10-12). It is likely that this ruler should be identified with the suffering servant in the later portions of Isaiah, who brings about the release of Israel from Babylonian captivity and restores the righteous remnant (Is 42:1-9, 49:1-6, 50:4-9, 52:13–53:12).

That the Messiah should suffer persecution in some capacity is mentioned in two passages. Daniel 9:25-26 seems to suggest that the Messiah will be eventually put to death: "From the time the word goes out to restore and rebuild Jerusalem until the Anointed One, the ruler, comes, there will be seven 'sevens,' and sixty-two 'sevens.' . . . After the sixty-two 'sevens,' *the Anointed One will be put to death and will have nothing*" (cf. Zech 12:10). In summary, the Messiah will be instrumental in the destruction of Israel's enemies, the new exodus, forgiveness of sins, pouring out of the Spirit, and the dawn of the new creation.

According to the Old Testament and Judaism, the Messiah refers above all to the coming "king of Israel." The Lord promises to restore and reign over his people through his Messiah. In 2 Samuel 7, God promised David that his descendants would rule over Israel. The Old Testament traces this promise and its fulfillment in the former and latter prophets. The Messiah, a descendant of David, would be instrumental in bringing about the establishment of God's eternal kingdom and destruction of Israel's enemies. Bound up with this phenomenon is the arrival of the new exodus, making possible forgiveness of sins, pouring out of the Spirit, the dawn of the new creation, and so on. Regarding the suffering aspect of the Messiah, a few passages seem to hint that he would suffer to some extent, but this suffering is not a cardinal aspect of his ministry; nevertheless, messianic suffering is the means by which God will restore his people.

We are now in a better position to answer why in Mark's Gospel Jesus commands individuals to stay quiet: he must alter and refocus their understanding of the Messiah (and the kind of kingdom he establishes). The end-time kingdom and Jesus' kingship is marked not by political, earthly, and physical triumph but by suffering and death. Jesus does not want people to think that his first task is to overturn the political landscape of Roman domination. Rather, his kingdom is initially expressed through domination of spiritual enemies and his own victory through suffering and defeat during his ministry. Jesus' suffering, death, and triumph fulfill Old Testament expectations, yet the manner in which he fulfills them differs from expectations.

FIGURE 5.6. KING DAVID AND THE PROPHET NATHAN

According to the Old Testament, the Messiah will arrive climactically in the latter days. Jesus fulfills these prophecies but only initially. At his second coming he will completely fulfill the Old Testament predictions of his victory over all opposition. The disciples eventually come to grips with this truth after the crucifixion and the resurrection. Only then do they understand the true nature of Jesus' ministry as Isaiah's suffering servant and his defeat of invisible spiritual enemies.

INTRODUCTION TO JESUS AND HIS GALILEAN MINISTRY (1:1–8:26)

The early church, taking cues from Ezekiel 1 and Revelation 4, depicted Mark's Gospel as a fierce lion. As Richard Burridge points out, the imagery of a lion can be "uncomfortable" since lions in the Old Testament are viewed negatively and often found as vehicles for God's judgment and enemies of Israel (e.g., Num 23:24; Ps 22:13; Is 5:29).[6] Upon opening the Gospel of Mark, we are immediately struck with the sobering reality that Israel's God has come to judge those who are unwilling to repent. Lions are also known for their agility and action. One of the most remarkable features of Mark is his fast-paced narrative, even unrelenting at times. Lions in the Old Testament are often associated with royalty and Israel's end-time king (Gen 49:9; Num 24:9). The Gospel of Mark plucks at this string from beginning to end—Israel's long-awaited king has arrived on the scene. But, as Mark makes clear, Israel's king differs somewhat from expectations. His rule is not confined to a plot of land but pushes the boundaries of the cosmos, and his rule is not marked by military triumph but by physical defeat.

FIGURE 5.7. THE SYMBOLS OF THE FOUR EVANGELISTS

Mark begins his Gospel with John the Baptist calling for Israel to repent of her sins and identify with the renewed people of God (Mk 1:1-6). Unlike in Matthew and Luke, Jesus arrives on the scene as a full-grown man, perhaps reflecting the creation of Adam in the garden. Jesus' baptism at the Jordan River by John recalls Israel passing through the sea at the exodus and the second generation passing through the Jordan to enter the Promised Land (1:9-11). Israel's restoration is at hand through the person of Jesus.

Much of the first half of Mark's Gospel takes place in Galilee, where Jesus is largely successful in his proclamation of the kingdom. Yet his message remains scandalous to some. As the paradigmatic parable of the soils clearly demonstrates, his message will be accepted by some but rejected by others (Mk 4:1-25). Near and around Galilee, the kingdom grows as many respond to Jesus' kingdom pronouncement. His identity, however, remains veiled. Who is this Jesus of Nazareth?

Prologue (1:1-13). The Second Gospel opens with "The beginning of the good news

[6]Richard A. Burridge, *Four Gospels, One Jesus? A Symbolic Reading*, 2nd ed. (Grand Rapids: Eerdmans, 2005), 36.

ROMAN AND HERODIAN PALESTINE

about Jesus the Messiah, the Son of God" (1:1). By opening his Gospel with two theologically loaded titles—the Messiah and the Son of God—Mark expects his readers to reflect upon them as he sharpens, even reworks, their long-held beliefs. It may not be a stretch to suggest that every chapter, every verse of Mark's Gospel is dedicated to explaining *how* Jesus is Israel's long-awaited messiah and the unique, divine Son of God. Here the "good news" or the "gospel" highlights the role of the prophet, John the Baptist, and Jesus' temptation in the wilderness (1:1-13). Two key Old Testament quotations (Ex 23:20/Mal 3:1; Is 40:3) are cited as direct fulfillments, setting the tone for the entire narrative. Mark thoughtfully pairs these Old Testament quotations, whereas Matthew and Luke separate them and place them in different contexts (Mt 3:3; 11:10; Lk 3:4; 7:27).

The reference to "Isaiah the prophet" in verse 2 further explains verse 1, "The beginning of the good news about Jesus the Messiah, the Son of God." Many English translations put a period after verse 1 and begin verse 2 as a new sentence (HCSB; NASB; ESV; NRSV), but there is little reason to do so. Mark intends his audience to read the first two verses together: "The beginning of the good news about Jesus the Messiah, the Son of God, *as* it is written in Isaiah the prophet."[7] So, the "gospel" of Jesus, as told by Mark, is largely dependent upon and explained by the book of Isaiah. Therefore, much of the Second Gospel concerns Israel's second exodus from spiritual exile.

FIGURE 5.8. THE PROPHET MALACHI

FIGURE 5.9. ELIJAH IN THE DESERT

[7]See also Stuhlmacher, *Biblical Theology of the New Testament*, 560-61.

Why does Mark mention only the book of Isaiah by name and not Malachi, which is clearly quoted in 1:2? One unique feature of the Second Gospel is Mark's tendency to "sandwich" events together (e.g., Mk 3:20-35; 5:21-43; 11:12-25). This technique appears to be employed with the Isaiah quotation.[8] Mark first mentions Isaiah but then cites Exodus 23:20/Malachi 3:1: "As it is written in *Isaiah the prophet*: 'I will send my messenger ahead of you, who will prepare your way' [Ex 23:20/Mal 3:1]—'*a voice of one calling in the wilderness, "Prepare the way for the Lord, make straight paths for him* [Is 40:3]"'" (Mk 1:2-3). The order is as follows: Isaiah-Exodus/Malachi-Isaiah. The significance of this "Isaiah sandwich" is that the reader ought to understand Exodus 23:20/Malachi 3:1 through the lens of Isaiah 40:3.

FIGURE 5.10. SPIES CARRYING THE GRAPES OF CANAAN

According to Exodus 23:20-33, the "messenger" will protect Israel along the way to the Promised Land: "I am sending an angel ahead of you to guard you along the way and to bring you to the place I have prepared" (Ex 23:20). The messenger promises to wage war against the pagan nations since they are idolatrous and wicked. If Israel obeys the covenant, God promises to bless them, but if they commit idolatry by conforming to pagan practices, they will be punished. Malachi 3 reworks the messenger of Exodus 23 in its application. Israel has not maintained justice within the community and has broken God's law. Malachi declares that a messenger figure will again arise and prepare the way for the Lord to judge his people: "I will send my messenger, who will prepare the way before me" (Mal 3:1). In Exodus 23, Israel's enemies, the idolatrous nations, are on the receiving end of judgment. According to Malachi 3:1-6, however, the messenger is paving the way for the Lord to wage war against Israel! Like their neighbors, Israel has become entrenched in idolatry and social injustice (e.g., Mal 1:6-10, 12-14). The wicked Israelites who refuse to repent are judged by God (3:5; 4:1-4), yet those within Israel who turn to the Lord will escape his coming judgment. Malachi's messenger must prepare Israel for the Lord's coming by sparking repentance among the remnant (4:6).

[8]Stuhlmacher, *Biblical Theology of the New Testament*, 77, 560-61.

Isaiah 40 serves as a transitional point in the book of Isaiah. As anticipated in the first half of the book (e.g., Is 2:2-5; 24:1–25:12), chapters 40–66 describe Israel's release from Babylonian captivity as a second exodus (40:10-11; 51:9; 52:10). God will guide his people from Babylon to the Promised Land (49:9) and create a new heavens and earth upon their arrival (65:17-25; 66:22-23), all of which will take place through Isaiah's "servant" (42:1-9, 49:1-6, 50:4-9, 52:13–53:12). Isaiah 40:3 prophetically depicts God restoring his people from Babylonian captivity by leading them through the desert to the Promised Land: "A voice of one calling: 'In the wilderness prepare the way for the LORD; make straight in the desert a highway for our God.'" A few verses later, Isaiah provides the result of Israel's return to her land: "*And the glory of the* LORD *will be revealed*, and all people will see it together. For the mouth of the LORD has spoken" (Is 40:5). The return to the Promised Land will eventually give way to God's decisive act of the destruction of evil and the consummate restoration of all things. Those redeemed from Israel and the nations will dwell fully with God in the new creation (65:17; 66:22).

> ***John's appearance in Mark 1:6 brings to mind Elijah's prophetic attire in 2 Kings 1:8: "He [Elijah] had* a garment of hair *and had* a leather belt *around his waist." Such apparel symbolizes Israel's wretched spiritual condition and their need for urgent repentance.***

Since the "messenger" is tasked with "purifying" Israel in preparation for the Lord's coming (Ex 23/Mal 3), Mark must convince his readers that Israel is in need of such purification. At nearly every major turn in the narrative, Mark explains how Israel, the Gentiles, and all of creation are stained with idolatry and wickedness. God is determined to purify humanity and the created order so that, as Exodus 23/Malachi 3 and Isaiah 40 predict, he can dwell fully with his people in the new creation. In each major phase of Mark's Gospel, then, we will discover that Jesus cleanses humanity and creation with the ultimate purpose of dwelling with them as Israel's God incarnate.

These Old Testament quotations in Mark 1:2b-3 are applied to John the Baptist. He fulfills the messenger of judgment (Mal 3:1) and the voice that announces the arrival of Israel's restoration from captivity (Is 40:3). The messenger has a twofold agenda: he must prepare rebellious Israel, lest they be annihilated at God's coming. He pleads with Israel to repent and identify with a new wilderness community through baptism. John also announces the end of Israel's spiritual captivity by heralding the fulfillment of Isaiah's long-awaited new exodus of God's people. As Stuhlmacher notes, "For Mark the long-awaited coming of Yahweh as King and Warrior has begun, and with it, the inauguration of Israel's eschatological comfort: her deliverance from the hands of the nations, the journey of her exiles to their home and their eventual arrival at Jerusalem, the place of Yahweh's presence."[9] Israel's history is on the brink of reaching its climax of the new

[9]Stuhlmacher, *Biblical Theology of the New Testament*, 90.

creation. All who identify with John's baptism will experience the long-awaited new exodus.

Another unique dimension of Jesus' identity in Mark 1 is evident in light of the two quotations from Malachi 3 and Isaiah 40. In Malachi 3, God follows the messenger and judges Israel: "Then suddenly the Lord you are seeking will come to his temple" (Mal 3:1b). According to Mark 1, Jesus comes on the heels of the messenger—a clear identification with Israel's God. The same can be said for the Isaiah text. Isaiah 40:3 announces that the Lord has come to redeem his people from captivity and begin the process of the new creation, whereas in Mark 1 Jesus serves in this identical capacity. As Richard Hays affirms, "Jesus is in fact to be identified with the *Kyrios* [Lord] of whom Isaiah speaks."[10] Mark, from the very beginning of his Gospel, identifies the role of Jesus with the God of Israel, affirming that Jesus is God in the flesh.

Mark records that John's ministry was somewhat successful: "The whole Judean countryside and all the people of Jerusalem went out to him. Confessing their sins, they were baptized by him" (Mk 1:5). This tidbit signifies that some Israelites are identifying themselves with John's baptism and turning their backs on Israel's long-standing (and now idolatrous) institutions, such as the temple and its sacrifices. Ritual washings in the Old Testament and Judaism related, in some way or another, to the temple (e.g., Lev 15:5-27; CD-A X, 10-14). Israel had to be "clean" for God to dwell in their midst. By offering baptism for renewal, John the Baptist is indirectly challenging Israel's national identity and religious structure. He is laying the foundation for Israel to be reconstituted according to different terms, particularly Israel's temple.[11] As Mark's narrative unfolds, we learn that Israel will now be reconstituted in a person—Jesus of Nazareth, the new temple.

FIGURE 5.11. JOHN THE BAPTIST IN THE WILDERNESS

According to Mark 1:9, John baptizes Jesus in the Jordan River. At Jesus' baptism, the Spirit descends on Jesus "like a dove." The presence of the Spirit triggers the fulfillment of several Old Testament passages that

[10]Richard B. Hays, *Reading Backwards: Figural Christology and the Fourfold Gospel Witness* (Waco, TX: Baylor University Press, 2014), 20.

[11]Nicholas Perrin, *Jesus and the Temple* (Grand Rapids: Baker, 2010), 17-45.

predict the descent of the Spirit at the very end of history when Israel is redeemed (e.g., Joel 2; Ezek 37:4-14). Jesus, in some sense, experiences a personal Pentecost (cf. Acts 1–2). The Spirit's descent "like a dove" also recalls Noah's flood when God recreated the world (Gen 8:8-12). Jesus is thus viewed as the restored people of God, true Israel, in the initial stages of the new creation. A voice breaks through the clouds and declares, "You are my Son, whom I love; with you I am well pleased" (Mk 1:11). God's words echo Psalm 2:7 and 2 Samuel 7:14, which predict the arrival of Israel's king.

Since Jesus is righteous, he does not need to receive John's "baptism of repentance" (Mk 1:4). Yet, like the first generation of Israelites passing through the Red Sea and the second generation of Israelites marching through the Jordan River, Jesus graciously identifies with corrupt Israel. As the long-awaited king, Jesus typologically repeats the history of Israel to lead them out of spiritual exile and deliver them into the Promised Land of the new creation. Once Jesus has identified with John's renewal and is installed as King (1:9-11; cf. Ps 2:7), the Spirit propels him to the wilderness to conquer Satan (Mk 1:12-13). Although only one verse, Jesus' wilderness temptation for forty days has considerable implications for the remainder of his ministry. His victory as true Israel over Satan enables him to vanquish the ultimate satanic prince of all wicked nations and to conquer the land in a way that Israel had not been able. As R. T. France notes, "He [Jesus] not only wished to be seen, but saw himself, as Israel, tested and taught in the desert as God's 'son' Israel had been. . . . The antitype, as always, is greater than the type. Old Testament Israel had failed; Jesus must succeed."[12]

At the end of the temptation, only Mark mentions Jesus being with "the wild animals," perhaps recalling Adam's fellowship with the animals in the garden (Gen 2:18-20). Jesus brings reconciliation between God and creation, and he is thus seen as a new Adam who has begun to recapture the harmony that was lost in the fall.

Beginning of Jesus' Galilean ministry (1:14–3:6). The first phase of Jesus' ministry in Galilee sets the tone for the remainder of the book. Mark makes use of a narrative device sometimes translated "immediately" (*kai euthys*). This phrase is found approximately twenty-fives times in Mark's Gospel, especially in ch. 1 (1:10, 12, 18, 20, 21, 23, 29, 30, 42). Most English versions do not always translate this phrase, so it's difficult to discern upon a cursory reading. The point of the literary device is to keep up the pace of the narrative and join all of the events together as a whole. Jesus doesn't speak much in Mark's gospel and especially in chapter 1 in particular. Mark, therefore, identifies who Jesus is through action.

[12]R. T. France, *Jesus and the Old Testament: His Application of Old Testament Passages to Himself and His Mission* (London: Tyndale, 1971), 51-53.

After John is imprisoned, Jesus flees north to Galilee, probably avoiding persecution in Judea. Jesus proclaims the arrival of the kingdom of God (Mk 1:14-15) and begins his successful public ministry by calling four disciples, three of which constitute the "inner three" (Peter, James, and John [Mk 1:16-20; cf. 3:13-19]). This initial phase culminates in a dispute between Jesus and the Jewish leaders (3:1-6), an ominous sign of things to come.

Jesus summons Simon (Peter), Andrew, James, and John to follow him at the beginning of his public ministry (Mk 1:16-20). The theme of discipleship plays a key role in this Gospel as Mark seeks to answer the all-important question: What does it take to follow the Messiah? The unequivocal answer, according to Mark and the remainder of the New Testament, is that true disciples must be willing to sacrifice their life and ambitions for the sake of the kingdom. Uniquely, Old Testament prophets never call others to follow them; instead, they charge others to follow the Lord. Jesus may therefore be tacitly acknowledging a divine prerogative by commanding others to follow him.

Jesus confronts the disciples while they are fishing in the Sea of Galilee. His call for the disciples to be "fishers of men" may be more than simply a pithy statement. Jeremiah 16:16 uses similar language: "'But now I will send for many fishermen,' declares the Lord, 'and *they will catch them [Israelites in exile]*.'" On the one hand, the fishermen are to search out the scattered Israelites who are in Babylonian exile. God, in verse 15, promises to restore captive Israel and bring them back to the Promised Land. Yet God will also send "hunters" who will seek out the exiles and judge the wicked Israelites (vv. 16b-18).

A large part of the mission of the twelve disciples, analogous to Jeremiah's hunters, is to pronounce judgment on rebellious Israel. Here is a case of abiding authority. What was true in the Old Testament is true in the New. The disciples are God's emissaries who herald judgment to those who reject the kingdom message, yet they also bring mercy and restoration to those who believe in Jesus. He promises to deliver those Israelites who, despite their dwelling in the Promised Land, still remain in spiritual captivity to sin.

FIGURE 5.12. THE TWELVE APOSTLES

Second phase of Jesus' Galilean ministry (3:7–6:6). As this section makes clear, Jesus' ministry continues to gain popularity around Galilee (Mk 3:7-12). He finally assembles all twelve disciples, though he summoned four in Mark 1:16-20. Symbolically, the Twelve constitute true Israel, and Jesus charges them with the authority to proclaim the kingdom message and cast out demons (3:14-15). The exorcisms by Jesus and the disciples in the first few chapters of Mark's narrative, as Graham Twelftree notes, "were not preparatory for the coming of the kingdom, but were themselves the kingdom of God in operation."[13]

Isaiah 49:25-26 identifies the Lord as one who conquers the strong man, yet Mark identifies Jesus as Israel's redeemer. Jesus is Israel's Lord incarnate who liberates Israel from spiritual slavery.

With much symbolism, Jesus assembles the twelve disciples "on a mountainside" (Mk 3:13-19). A first-century Jew would doubtless make the connection between the number of the disciples and the twelve tribes of Israel. This explains why the apostles are so intent on preserving the number twelve in Acts 1:15-26 and elect Matthias to replace Judas Iscariot. The twelve tribes are derivative of Jacob's twelve sons (Gen 29:32–30:24; 35:18). Each tribe is apportioned a plot of land in Canaan (save the tribe of Levi [Deut 18:1-2; Josh 13:14, 33]) and is to adhere to the covenant stipulations made at Sinai. Moses charges the twelve tribes to function as priests to the pagan nations by converting them and bringing them into the covenant community (Ex 19:6). This charge corresponds to Adam and Eve's commission to be "fruitful" and "increase in number" (Gen 1:28), thus extending God's glory to the ends of the earth. Exodus 19:5-6 states, "Now if you [Israel] obey me fully and keep my covenant, then out of all nations you will be my treasured possession. Although the whole earth is mine, you will be for me a kingdom of priests and a holy nation." Yet Israel failed on both counts: they not only repeatedly broke the covenant but also refused to bring the nations into the covenant community. The stage is set for the arrival of one who will fulfill both of these obligations.

Jesus constitutes true Israel. He typologically repeats Israel's story (baptism through water, wilderness temptation, etc.) and succeeds where they failed. He reorganizes Israel in himself by assembling the twelve disciples. Just as Moses gathered Israel on Sinai and commissioned them to reach the nations, so Jesus appoints the Twelve and charges them to proclaim the message of the kingdom. This appointment involves establishing a new people group to live in the new creation, where it will grow exponentially in fulfillment of the original Genesis 1:28 commission.

Following the appointment of the twelve disciples, Jesus enters a house and begins to teach the crowds (Mk 3:20). The remainder of chapter 3 focuses on the interplay between Jesus' family and the Jewish leaders. Mark once again uses his unique sandwich technique in presenting the material: rejection by Jesus' family (3:20-21), rejection by the Jewish leaders (3:22-30), rejection by Jesus' family (3:31-34). In arranging the two episodes in this manner, Mark wants his audience to

[13]Graham H. Twelftree, *Jesus the Exorcist: A Contribution to the Study of the Historical Jesus*, WUNT 54 (Tübingen: J. C. B. Mohr [Paul Siebeck], 1993), 218.

interpret Jesus' interaction with his family in light of the debate between Jesus and the Jewish leaders. From the narrative's perspective, the unbelief of Jesus' own family, at least at this point in the narrative, is analogous to the unbelief of the Jewish leaders—both parties fail to perceive the identity of Jesus and are hostile to his ministry.

Mark subtly adds that the scribes arrive "from Jerusalem" (3:22). He slips this reference into the narrative so that the reader may anticipate Jesus' utter rejection and suffering in Jerusalem. The scribes accuse Jesus of being possessed by the spirit of Beelzebul (3:22). We are unsure as to what exactly the name means, but we can be confident that they deem Jesus to be allied with Satan. The Jewish leaders not only reject Jesus and his message but also attribute his miraculous power to Satan!

Jesus prefaces a parable of a kingdom with the question, "How can Satan drive out Satan?" (Mk 3:23). If a kingdom is riddled with division, it will not endure (3:24). It must be unified to withstand an attack. Jesus then uses the analogy of a strong man guarding a house (3:27). One must first overcome the guardian of the house to pillage its treasures.

The clearest Old Testament example of the strong man is found in Isaiah 49:24-26.[14] In this passage, Isaiah describes the return from exile. God has not forgotten Zion, and he will inhabit her once again. Verses 22-23 speak of the exiles returning with the help of the foreign nations, which will submit. Then verse 24 begins with the question, "Can plunder be taken from warriors, or captives be rescued from the fierce?" The obvious answer to this is an emphatic no. Captives cannot be released, because the mighty man

FIGURE 5.13. PARABLE OF THE SOWER

[14]Watts, *Isaiah's New Exodus*, 146-52.

would need to be vanquished. But the text responds to this situation, "Even the captives of the mighty shall be taken, and the prey of the tyrant be rescued" (Is 49:25 ESV).

The Lord, as Israel's divine warrior, will fight for his people once again and bring his people out of the possession of the strong man. By the time we get to the New Testament, we discover that the true tyrant, the strong man, is not Babylon but Satan and his demonic forces. David Garland states, "For Mark, the demonic realm represents a real power that invades the human realm. It seeks to take human minds and lives captive and to destroy them. The human realm therefore needs a divine power to be liberated from this satanic captivity."[15] Satan has held the people in spiritual exile for long enough, so now Jesus comes and "binds" the strong man, releasing his prisoners.

Chapter 4 signals an important turn in Mark's narrative and is critical to understanding the nature of Jesus' teaching on the kingdom and how his disciples and others receive his message. Functioning paradigmatically, the parable of the sower (Mk 4:1-20) answers a pressing question: If Jesus is the long-awaited Messiah and his kingdom fulfills Old Testament expectations, then why do most reject Jesus? In the immediate context, even Jesus' own family lacks understanding (3:20-21, 31-35)!

After Jesus delivers the parable of the seeds to the audience, "the Twelve and the others around him" come to Jesus privately and ask him to account for them the meaning or interpretation of the parable (Mk 4:10). Jesus responds cryptically: "The mystery of the kingdom of God has been given to you, but to those on the outside everything is said in parables" (4:11; our translation). Here Jesus claims that he will indeed give the meaning of the parable to the disciples (4:13-20) but not to the "outsiders." In the Second Gospel, a distinction exists between outsiders and insiders. Those on the inside have grasped Jesus' kingdom message and, by all appearances, will continue on in their faith. The outsiders, however, lack insight and the willingness to embrace his message. As David Garland points out, even the disciples "are at risk of moving from 'insiders' to outsiders'" throughout Mark's narrative.[16]

Jesus quotes Isaiah 6:9-10 toward the outsiders of Mark 4:11, a group that includes the Jewish leaders, Jesus' own family for the time being (3:20-21, 31-35), and generally those who have rejected Jesus' message. According to Isaiah 6, Israel is corrupt at its very core. In Isaiah 6:9-10, Israel is blind and deaf, just like the idols they worship (cf. Deut 29:3-4; Jer 5:21; Ezek 12:2; Ps 115:4-8; 135:15-18). Since Israel is on the receiving end of God's latter-day judgment, she will now be reconstituted around King Jesus. Those who rally around him separate themselves from idolatrous Israel and become part of true Israel, Jesus. The nation of Israel in the first century, as represented by the Jewish leaders, reject Jesus' message because they, like their ancestors in Isaiah's day, commit idolatry, probably by worshiping Torah and the oral tradition (Mk 7:1-23). Jesus stands in continuity with Isaiah by iterating the prophet's words. Isaiah's prophetic act remains valid into the first century!

A great deal of Jesus' parables and deeds are veiled or characterized by some form of

[15]David E. Garland, *A Theology of Mark's Gospel: Biblical Theology of the New Testament* (Grand Rapids: Zondervan, 2015), 266.
[16]Garland, *Theology of Mark's Gospel*, 408.

FIGURE 5.14. THE PROPHET ISAIAH

hiddenness or inability to understand. Those who have "eyes to see" comprehend Jesus' message, but those who are "blind" are unable to penetrate the full meaning of the revelation. In Mark's Gospel, the disciples oscillate between comprehension and inability to perceive. At times they understand, though not fully, Jesus' identity and mission (e.g., Mk 8:29), while at other times they lack insight (e.g., 8:31-33). Similar to the disciples, the crowds are oftentimes viewed as unable to comprehend Jesus' mission, although occasionally they have insight. The Jewish leadership, however, appears hardened and unable to perceive. Consequently, for some, understanding the nature of the kingdom is only temporarily hidden, while for others it is permanently hidden.

Chapter 4 ends with Jesus stilling the chaotic waters of the Sea of Galilee (Mk 4:35-41). Identifying himself as Israel's divine warrior, Jesus calms the storm. The stormy conditions on the sea symbolize the hostile forces that have arrayed themselves against Jesus and the disciples. Mark's description of this event is replete with details not found in Matthew and Luke. Mark mentions only that "other boats" accompanied Jesus and his followers (4:36b) and that he was "in the stern, sleeping on a cushion" (4:38a). Compared to Matthew and Luke, the Second Gospel also demonstrates more awareness of Galilee's geography, especially as it relates to the Sea of Galilee. These details and others affirm our suggestion that Peter, a fisherman by trade

(1:16), stands behind the Gospel of Mark. Peter was quite familiar with the Sea of Galilee, so his experience of fishing on the water for most of his life would have informed how he communicated the event to Mark. But this is not the only event in which this Gospel includes details not found in Matthew and Luke. On the whole, Mark's portrayal of the life of Jesus includes a more rich and colorful recollection of events than what is found in Matthew and Luke.

Last phase of Jesus' Galilean ministry (6:7–8:26). The last portion of Jesus' ministry in Galilee amplifies the first two phases—more miracles and greater opposition. It begins with the commissioning of the Twelve and their authority over the demonic forces (Mk 6:7-13). John the Baptist's fate is recalled, perhaps in anticipation of Jesus' eventual death. Beginning in Mark 6:45, Jesus reaches the Gentiles. To the east of the Jordan River lay Decapolis, a region influenced greatly by Greco-Roman culture. His engagement with the Gentiles climaxes with the faith of the Syrophoenician woman in 7:24-30. Since true defilement does not originate from the outside (7:15, 18-19), journeying to a Gentile area will not defile Jesus and his disciples. The dispute between Jesus and the Jewish leaders reaches a boiling point in 7:1-23, especially when he declares "all foods clean" (7:19). Ironically, the Jewish leaders have made an idol of their traditions that interpreted and applied the Torah. This phase of Jesus' career sounds off with the obstinacy of the disciples (8:11-21). Their continual lack of understanding is symbolized in the miracle of the blind man at Bethsaida (8:22-26). Like the blind man, the disciples are cured of their blindness in two stages: Peter finally acknowledges that Jesus is indeed the Messiah (8:29), but a robust understanding of Jesus' identity will come only after the resurrection.

FIGURE 5.15. MOSES, AARON, AND HUR

FROM GALILEE TO JERUSALEM: THE PATH TO SUFFERING (8:27–10:52)

On the plains of Moab, Moses predicts that in the distant future God would "raise up for you a prophet like me. . . . *You must listen to him*" (Deut 18:15). Moses' prophecy is a response to Israel's plea in Deuteronomy 5:23-27, in which the Israelites ask the Lord for a mediator who will stand before his glorious presence and faithfully communicate God's law to them. At Sinai, the nation of Israel is ghastly afraid of God's presence, so they plead for a mediator (Ex 20:19). At the transfiguration, Mark alludes to Deuteronomy 18:15 when he records God's words piercing through the clouds: "A voice came from the cloud: 'This is my Son, whom I love. *Listen to him*!'" (Mk 9:7). The transfiguration recalls Israel's experience at Sinai when God graciously gave them his law. By commanding the disciples to listen to Jesus, God is setting forth Jesus as the direct fulfillment of the end-time prophet who faithfully proclaims God's law and functions as Moses' successor.

The teachings of Jesus are hard to swallow at times (Mk 4:1-20), and his kingdom is marked not by political triumph but suffering and death. Nevertheless, the disciples must continue to trust that Jesus is faithfully proclaiming the word of God. Chapters 8–9 comprise the path of suffering. It is a time of preparation and further revelation of Jesus' identity. The narrative reaches a zenith in chapter 8: the Messiah will indeed suffer and die (8:31). This is apparent from the second and third passion prediction in 9:31 and 10:33. As Jesus approaches Jerusalem, Jewish opposition will intensify and eventually culminate in his death in Jerusalem.

Peter's confession and the transfiguration (8:27–9:13). Mark's Gospel strikes a high note in Peter's confession at Caesarea Philippi that Jesus is indeed the long-awaited Messiah: "He [Jesus] asked them, 'Who do people say I am?" After the disciples offer their list of prime candidates, Jesus pointedly asks Peter, "Who do you say I am?" The bell rings, and Peter hits the nail on the head when he declares, "You are the *Messiah*." The word for Christ is the Greek term *christos*, meaning the "anointed one" or the "Messiah." Peter claims that Jesus is indeed the highly anticipated Messiah who has come to liberate Israel. But Jesus' messiahship breaks the mold as he is a

FIGURE 5.16. CAESAREA PHILIPPI

suffering Messiah who ushers in a kingdom marked by persecution and suffering (Mk 8:31–9:1). Verse 31 is the first of three passion predictions that occur in the second portion of Mark's narrative, shifting the tone from here onwards (8:31; 9:31; 10:33). Jesus is then remarkably transformed or "transfigured" before the disciples' eyes. This event demonstrates, above all, that Jesus is the long-awaited Messiah and the *divine* Son of God. The disciples must therefore obey King Jesus (9:2-13).

> ***When Jesus heals the blind, the lame, and the mute, he resembles God in the Old Testament and signals the inbreaking of the new creation.***

Instruction concerning the kingdom and further healing (9:14–10:52). Immediately following the transfiguration, Jesus makes final preparations before entering Jerusalem. Many of Mark's themes progress, particularly Jesus' frustration with the disciples and their lack of understanding (Mk 9:18-19; 10:35-45) and his impending death (9:30-36; 10:32-34). The healing of blind Bartimaeus receives a good deal of prominence in Mark's drama (10:46-52). The healing immediately precedes Jesus' march into Jerusalem (11:1), and Bartimaeus' words are especially insightful when he declares, "Son of David, have mercy on me!" (10:48). Even before Bartimaeus is healed, he affirms what has been moving in and out of the background for several chapters—Jesus is the long-awaited Messiah. Bartimaeus's declaration sets the stage for Jesus' entrance into Jerusalem in the following chapter.

Unlike the other three Gospels, Mark describes the healing of only two blind men in his Gospel (8:22-25; 10:46-52). In the first instance, the blind man plays an important role in Mark's narrative as he symbolizes the two-staged healing of the disciples' blindness. Mark's inclusion of the healing of Bartimaeus is important to his narrative as it is the final event before Jesus' entrance into Jerusalem.

The Old Testament oftentimes uses blindness to describe Israel's inability to discern God's revelation. That is, the Israelites are unable to grasp God's actions and verbal revelation. For example, Deuteronomy 29:4 says, "But to this day the Lord has not given you a mind that understands or eyes that see or ears that hear." Israel became blind because they had conformed to their spiritually blind idols that had eyes but could not see (Ps 115:5-8; 135:16-18). When we come to the Gospels, we learn that Israel remains in a state of blindness. Why would Israel be in a state of blindness? Were they still bowing down to idols? Physically, no. By the first century, Israel knows better than to manufacture and worship idols. Instead of constructing physical idols, however, they have manufactured figurative ones. They bow down not to golden images but to oral tradition instead of God's word in Old Testament Scripture; they are guilty of worshiping human traditions and law instead of the Lawgiver.

Jesus' identity as king is central to our passage since Bartimaeus twice exclaims "Son of David" (Mk 10:47-48). But why is Jesus' kingdom on display here? What is the relationship between healing the blind and the inbreaking of the kingdom? Isaiah 35:5-6 states that the blind, the deaf, and the lame are restored because they are citizens now in God's end-time kingdom; they have been brought out of Babylonian captivity and restored through the second exodus (cf. Is 61:1-2; Mt 11:2-5). The restored people of God are spiritually and physically whole, part of the new creation and fit for the new heavens and earth. According to the Old Testament, only God, the creator of all things, possesses the ability to heal and restore (e.g., Ex 4:11; Hos 6:1-2; Ps 146:8). Although these healings are not physically permanent, they symbolize the reversal of Adam's fall and the inbreaking kingdom of the new creation. They express the consummate physical healing in the eternal, new creation. The *spiritual* healing that takes place in Jesus' ministry, though, is irreversible and will be perfected when Jesus returns a final time.

JERUSALEM: THE PASSION AND THE EMPTY TOMB (11:1–16:8)

Jesus in Mark 10:45 subtly discloses a key aspect of Mark's Gospel and his overall ministry: "For even the Son of Man did not come to be served, but to serve, and *to give his life* as a ransom for many." Jesus' wording is drawn from Isaiah 53:10-12: "Yet it was the LORD's will to crush him and cause him to suffer, and though the LORD makes his life an offering for sin. . . . My righteous servant *will justify many*, and he will bear their iniquities. . . . *He poured out his life unto death*, and was numbered with the transgressors. For *he bore the sin of many*." We may have here a case of the blueprint or prototypical use of the Old Testament. The allusion to Isaiah 53:10-12 is, like the tip of an iceberg, part of several prominent "servant songs" within the book of Isaiah (42:1-9; 49:1-6; 50:4-9; 52:13–53:12). According to Isaiah, the servant figure embodies the nation of Israel and suffers unjustly for many. The servant vicariously bears Israel's curse so that God's people might receive covenant blessings. Isaiah's servant is God's instrument in redeeming his people in the second exodus.

The final act of Mark's three-part drama leaves the reader with a clearly defined portrait of Jesus in his role as Isaiah's servant. He is the *suffering* Messiah and directly fulfills Isaiah's expectations. All aspects of his ministry must be interpreted through his death and resurrection. Knowing the end of the story brings clarity to the beginning and middle portions. The series of Jewish confrontations in act one of Mark climax with an ultimate confrontation that leads to Jesus' death. But through suffering and defeat, Jesus is, in reality, executing his messianic rule. There is victory in the midst of defeat; glory in the midst of suffering; and power in the midst of weakness. In the words of Isaiah, at his death he "divide[s] the spoils with the strong" (Is 53:12).

Temple judgment, prediction of the fall of Jerusalem, and Passover (11:1–14:31). Chapter 11 begins with Jesus entering the place of suffering and death. He journeys to Jerusalem and performs one of the most public displays of his messiahship—the triumphal entry (Mk 11:1-10). In light of the symbolism of the event, Mark could not be any clearer—the Messiah, the king of Israel, has indeed arrived!

Taking place on Sunday of Passion Week, the event commonly referred to as the triumphal entry is the clearest public demonstration that he is Israel's long-awaited Messiah. In preparation for his entry into Jerusalem, he commands his disciples to find him a specific colt, an unbroken, "tied" colt that has one mission only—to carry the kingly Messiah (11:2-3). Surprisingly, the Old Testament speaks of a tethered colt in Genesis 49:10-11: "The scepter shall not depart from Judah, nor the ruler's staff from between his feet, until he to whom it belongs shall come and the obedience of the nations shall be his. *He will tether his donkey to a vine*, his colt to the choicest branch." The fulfillment of Jacob's prophecy to his son Judah finds its ultimate fulfillment in Jesus, particularly at the triumphal entry. Jesus is publicly announcing his messianic prerogative to rule over Israel, just as Genesis 49 predicted. Jesus' abnormal request that the colt remain unbroken tightens the connection to the Greek translation of the Old Testament of Zechariah 9:9, which states that the latter-day king will come on a colt.

> ***By coming on a donkey, Jesus symbolically declares that the battle has initially been won and a time of peace has arrived.***

Chapter 9 marks a new section in the book of Zechariah that pertains to God's sovereignty over the nations, giving hope to the captive Israelites. Verses 1-7 are a judgment oracle against the pagan nations who have continually threatened Israel's existence. Yet God promises to protect his people, Israel, from the surrounding nations. Verse 9 continues this theme of a secure and sovereign rule: "Rejoice greatly, Daughter of Zion! . . . *See, your king comes to you, righteous and victorious, lowly and riding on a donkey*, on a colt, the foal of a donkey" (Zech 9:9). The manner in which the king arrives in Jerusalem is unique: "lowly and riding on a donkey." Though seemingly odd, a similar event occurs in 1 Kings 1:32-33: "When they [Zadok, Nathan, and Benaiah] came before the king, he said to them: 'Take your lord's servants with you and *have Solomon my son mount my own mule* and take him down to Gihon.'" In both contexts (Zech 9 and 1 Kings 1), riding on a donkey does not refer to a weak or incompetent ruler but to a *peaceful* one (Zech 9:10).

Jesus' identification with the messianic king of Zechariah 9 is particularly important for his career: Jesus has come to destroy Israel's enemy—not Rome but Satan—and lead his people out of spiritual exile (Zech 9:16). Even the laying of palm branches and garments before Jesus (Mk 11:8) recalls previous instances of Jewish behavior in the presence of royalty (2 Kings 9:13; 1 Macc. 13:51; 2 Macc. 10:7).

The first course of business for Israel's king is to judge the fig tree. The fig tree symbolizes the hypocrisy of the nation of Israel, much like the portrayal of the nation as a fig tree did in the Old Testament (Jer 24:5; Hos 9:10). As Rikki Watts notes, "Flourishing in appearance but lacking even a single bud . . . it [the fig tree] symbolizes both the hollow reality behind the imposing religious structure and, as in the prophets, to the extent that the temple represents unrepentant Israel, the nation itself."[17] By cursing the fig tree and forbidding it to yield fruit, Jesus is, in effect, claiming that the nation of Israel has come

[17]Rikki E. Watts, "Mark," in *Commentary on the New Testament Use of the Old Testament*, ed. G. K. Beale and D. A. Carson (Grand Rapids: Baker Academic, 2007), 209.

FIGURE 5.17. THE PROPHET ZECHARIAH

under God's wrath. Using his "sandwich" technique, Mark splits the cursing of the fig tree (Mk 11:11-14, 19-21) with the temple judgment (Mk 11:15-19), urging his readers to connect the two events. The cursing of the fig tree and the cleansing of the temple are intertwined. Jesus curses the nation of Israel because they have idolized the temple and prevented the nations from worshiping there (11:17; Is 56:7; Jer 7:11).

As a result, he "drives out" the money changers from the courtyard (11:15). The verb *drive out* is a favorite term in Mark and about two-thirds of its occurrences refer to exorcisms (e.g., 1:34, 39; 3:23; 6:13). Perhaps Jesus' expulsion of the money changers on a physical level is really an expulsion of demons on a spiritual level. Jesus' ministry began with an exorcism in Galilee and ends with an exorcism in Jerusalem. Recall that a chief aim of Jesus is to prepare the created order so that God may dwell with humanity and creation.

Jesus also "would not allow anyone to carry merchandise through the temple courts" (Mk 11:16). By forbidding the sale of sacrifices that offer ritual cleansing to the Israelites, Jesus is denouncing a basic function of the Jerusalem temple—to bring about God's forgiveness through the sacrificial system. Jesus goes on to quote Isaiah 56:7, a prophecy that the temple would become a rallying point for the nations (Is 56:3-8). Ironically, the temple, a house intended to bless all the nations, is used to prevent the nations from worship. John Paul Heil points out that "Just as the fig tree was condemned for failing to fulfill its purpose, so also conducting the commerce of sacrifice in the temple . . . renders the temple worthy of condemnation for failing to fulfill its true purpose."[18]

In judging Israel's physical temple, Jesus clears the way for establishing the end-time temple, where outcasts are gathered and made joyful in God's presence in his house (Is 56:3-8). Instead of dwelling partially in a building, God's glory has descended in his Son. Those who join themselves to Jesus

FIGURE 5.18. PARABLE OF THE WORKERS IN THE VINEYARD

[18]John Paul Heil, "The Narrative Strategy and Pragmatics of the Temple Theme in Mark," *CBQ* 59 (1997): 78.

become part of this latter-day temple. Mark 11:27–12:44 is a lengthy interaction between Jesus and the Jewish leaders in the temple complex. Each of these seemingly disparate conversations asserts the legitimacy and the presence of the end-time temple in the person of Jesus and his followers.[19] The physical temple has come under divine judgment and the disciples must trust in the establishment of the end-time temple in his ministry. For example, forgiveness of sin is now found only in Jesus, not the Jerusalem temple (Mk 11:22-25).

Chapter 12 opens with the parable of the tenants, summarizing much of what takes place during Passion Week. The parable consists of a man who plants a vineyard and leases it to tenant farmers (Mk 12:2). The owner sends servants to collect the fruit as a form of payment, but the tenants abuse and persecute them (12:2-5). Finally, the owner decides to send his "son, whom he loved," believing that the tenants would show respect (12:6). The tenants, however, kill this son, casting him outside of the vineyard (12:7-8). The owner's patience has worn out; he will return to the vineyard and kill the tenants because of their wicked behavior (12:9). The parable climaxes not only in the sending of the beloved son but also in handing over the vineyard to others (12:9).

The Old Testament often metaphorically portrays Israel as a vineyard (Ps 80:8-18; Is 27:2-6; Jer 2:21; 12:10; Ezek 19:10-14; Hos 10:1), but Isaiah 5 is one of the most detailed accounts of God planting a vineyard. The Lord, the owner of the vineyard (Is 5:7), prepared the soil, "planted" Israel, and "built a watchtower" (Is 5:2). Although the vineyard is equipped to produce "good grapes," it bears only "bad fruit" (Is 5:2). Why did Israel, the vineyard, fail to produce "good grapes"? Isaiah lays the blame at the feet of her leaders: "your guides lead you astray. . . . The LORD enters into judgment against the elders and leaders of his people" (Is 3:12-14; cf. 1:10, 23-26). The vineyard in Isaiah 5 includes not only the leaders but also the entire nation (Is 5:7). We see, then, that the leaders guided the people astray, leaving the entire group to suffer judgment (Is 5:18-24). God must "make it a wasteland" (Is 5:6) and allot judgment to the unfaithful vineyard, even though God had extensively provided for the vineyard (Is 5:1-2; cf. Jer 5:17; Mic 1:6; Zeph 1:13; Amos 4:9).

Like the vineyard in Isaiah 5, the parable of the tenants asserts that God lovingly established and blessed the vineyard, yet the vineyard fails to produce the desired result. Jesus' parable to the Jewish leaders is a symbolic use of the Old Testament, providing the theological basis for God's destruction of the temple—the unfaithfulness of Israel's leaders to obey the covenant and heed the warning of the prophets. Instead of repenting of their wicked ways, the Jewish leaders rejected the prophetic voice, culminating in the rejection of the "beloved son" (Mk 12:6 NASB). As a result, God will judge Israel and her leaders and hand the vineyard over to the Gentiles, the "others" (12:9). The end-time covenant community, the true Israel of God, will now consist largely of Gentiles. This newly reconstituted people of God makes up the new temple and houses the glory of God.

Jesus' interaction with the Jewish leaders climaxes in Mark 12:41-44 and the offering of the poor widow.[20] The disciples must

[19]Heil, "Narrative Strategy and Pragmatics," 81-89.
[20]Heil, "Narrative Strategy and Pragmatics," 88-89.

embody the faith of the widow, who tithes "only a few cents" (12:42). Like the widow, the followers of Jesus must give all that they possess for the advancement of the kingdom and believe wholeheartedly that Jesus is the true sanctuary. Only then will the disciples participate in the kingdom of God and his end-time temple.

Chapter 13 largely concerns God's impending judgment on Jerusalem, an event fulfilled in AD 70, though some this chapter's prophecies are fulfilled at the very end of time. Since Israel has continually rejected the prophetic voices through the centuries, culminating in the rejection of Jesus, God promises to pour out his judgment on Israel and Jerusalem. The mood darkens in chapter 14 when an unnamed woman prepares Jesus for burial and anoints him with expensive perfume (Mk 14:1-10). Note, though, that John names the woman as Mary (John 12:3). This section ends with Jesus and his disciples celebrating Passover (14:12-26) in anticipation of Jesus' upcoming death as the Passover sacrifice. As God redeemed Israel from Egyptian bondage, Jesus' death will release those in spiritual exile.

Betrayal, crucifixion, and resurrection of the Messiah (14:32–16:8). On the heels of celebrating the Passover meal (Mk 14:12-31), Jesus and the disciples travel to Gethsemane, where Jesus dramatically struggles with his destiny on the cross (14:32-42). Even here the disciples once again fail to display a confident faith in Jesus (14:34, 37, 39). Jesus is arrested at the hands of Judas and taken before the Sanhedrin—Israel's political body of representatives (14:53-65). This trial before the Sanhedrin (that only Mark and Matthew report; see Mt 26:57-68) was most likely preliminary in nature. Notably, during the interrogation, Jesus claims to be the Son of Man from Daniel 7, a divine figure that represents Israel (Mk 14:62; Dan 7:13). The "son of man" in Daniel 7:13 comes into the presence of the "Ancient of Days" by "coming with the clouds of heaven." Riding on the clouds throughout the Old Testament is reserved only for the Lord (e.g., Ps 68:4). The son of man figure in Daniel 7:13 is, therefore, a divine, enigmatic figure.

FIGURE 5.19. SACRIFICIAL LAMB

The Jewish leaders then accuse Jesus of blasphemy and deem him "worthy of death" (Mk 14:64). The next morning the Jewish leaders take Jesus before Pilate and attempt to have him put to death for sedition against Rome, although at the core of their accusation is Jesus' claim to be divine (Jn 19:7). Despite Pilate's ambivalence, the Jewish leaders remain steadfast in their resolve to put Jesus to death (Mk 15:1-15).

Mark highlights Jesus' identity as Israel's long-awaited king by mentioning several royal features during his mocking and crucifixion —a purple robe, a crown of thorns, the Roman soldiers' taunt "Hail, king of the Jews," and the soldiers' sarcastic genuflecting (Mk 15: 16-20). A careful reader of Mark's narrative is left with a poignant irony—in mocking Jesus, the soldiers reveal his true identity as king. The crucifixion occupies a central place in Mark's Gospel in that the entire narrative has been anticipating this event from the very beginning. Jesus' identity as God's royal Son is on display at the crucifixion (15:21-41). It is here where Jesus refashions Israel's expectations of a coming messiah.

> ***Jesus executes his kingly rule, not by conquering the Romans with a sword but by dying on a cross—the symbol of bearing God's covenant curse and sedition against the Romans.***

Throughout the Gospel of Mark, Jesus faces portions of end-time suffering and tribulation, climaxing with the absolute tribulation of death on the cross. These experiences initially fulfill several Old Testament passages that predict great suffering and tribulation would befall Israel in the latter days (e.g., Ezek 38:10-16; Dan 7–12). Peter Bolt gets to the heart of the matter:

> The cross was the great distress promised by Daniel before the resurrection day (Dan. 12:1). It was the culmination of all the beastly struggles for power that have afflicted the world with so much pain. The Messiah came into this world, and the Jewish people went out to meet him with the swords and clubs that have so often been wielded in our world as kingdom rises against kingdom.[21]

Mark 15:37-38 says that when "Jesus breathed his last" the "curtain of the temple was torn in two from top to bottom." The curtain separates the outer parts of the temple from the holy of holies, and, as we saw in our discussion of Matthew 27:51, represents the beginning destruction of not only the temple but also the cosmos. Mark 15:37-39 focuses on the death of Jesus replacing the sacrificial function of the temple. Mark sandwiches the tearing of the curtain in 15:38 with Jesus' death in 15:37 and 39. The reader is expected to interpret both events together. In contrast to the physical temple in Jerusalem, where temporary atonement is available (cf. Lev 16:12-15), Jesus' death serves as the once-for-all, end-time atonement.[22] The cross becomes the true holy of holies where Jesus as high priest offers himself as a permanent atonement (cf. Mk 15:39).

Mark ends his Gospel with a brief, even abrupt, account of Jesus' resurrection (Mk 16:1-8). Whereas Matthew, Luke, and John devote considerable space to the resurrection, Mark's account includes only a handful of verses. The two Marys, Mary Magdalene and Mary the mother of James and Salome, intend to anoint the body of Jesus at the close of the Sabbath (16:1). Yet, the stone is rolled away (16:4), and the women are unexpectedly greeted by an angel "dressed in a white robe" (16:5). The angel's words surprise them: "You are looking for Jesus the Nazarene, who was crucified. He has risen! He is not here" (16:6). Jesus' death and resurrection, seemingly

[21] Peter Bolt, *The Cross from a Distance: Atonement in Mark's Gospel*, NSBT 18 (Downers Grove, IL: InterVarsity Press, 2004), 113.

[22] Stuhlmacher, *Biblical Theology of the New Testament*, 217-21.

oxymoronic for the expected messianic king, are very much in keeping with divine design. Even within Mark's Gospel, Jesus repeatedly warns his disciples that he will eventually be put to death and then subsequently rise from the dead three days later (8:31; 9:31: 10:33-34). Yet at the crucifixion, the majority of the disciples fled in disbelief; they could not comprehend how Israel's king, the long-awaited deliverer of the covenant community, could fall into the hands of the Jewish and Roman authorities.

Jesus' resurrection is clearly a fulfillment of Old Testament expectations (1 Cor 15:4), yet it contains some remarkable new elements. The Old Testament teaches that the resurrection will occur at the very end of history, when wickedness is abolished and the new creation has dawned. Righteous individuals will be physically restored in the new creation, and the unrighteous punished (Job 19:26-27; Is 25:7-8; 26:19; Ezek 37:1-14, 26-35; Dan 12:2-3). Strangely, Jesus is raised individually and not with the rest of God's people. The saints must await their physical resurrection when he returns, but with Jesus' own resurrection the great expected general resurrection of all God's people has been set in motion (see 1 Cor 15:20-23). This may explain why the women at the tomb are "bewildered" and "afraid" (Mk 16:8) and the disciples are slow to believe. "Fear" in Mark's gospel is often associated with the disciples' reaction to Jesus exceeding expectations; he is the divine Son of God who has the power to still the storm (4:41), cast out demons (5:15), heal the woman with the issue of blood (5:33), walk on water (6:50); he is also a messiah who is characterized by suffering (9:32; 10:32). So, perhaps the women are "afraid" because he once again exceeds the expectations of his followers. By

FIGURE 5.20. WOMEN AT THE TOMB

ending his Gospel with the resurrection, Mark deems Jesus' ministry as victorious over Satan, sin, and the world. Jesus' life, death, and resurrection liberate the covenant community from sin and estrangement from God. Mark beckons his readers to believe this message and thereby join the redeemed and the new creation.

The ending of Mark's Gospel is remarkably complex since we have inherited four different endings; we will entertain only two of these. In modern English translations of the Gospel of Mark, the translators typically set off 16:9-20 with an editorial comment about how the earliest manuscripts do not contain that section. The manuscript evidence of the shorter ending (those manuscripts that omit 16:9-20) is particularly early and strong (see manuscripts א B). Second, scribes have a tendency to expand, elaborate, and smooth out difficulties. The rather abrupt ending of Mark's Gospel in 16:8 ("Trembling and bewildered, the women went out and fled from the tomb. They said nothing to anyone, because they were afraid.") certainly lends itself to further subsequent scribal elaboration and clarification. Moreover, within the expanded ending of Mark (16:9-20), several words and themes are peculiar and do not resonate within Mark's Gospel. For these reasons and others, the vast majority of scholars doubt the authenticity of 16:9-20.

6

THE GOSPEL OF LUKE

AUTHORSHIP

The Gospel of Luke is part of a two-volume work: the first "book," the Gospel of Luke, describes the person and work of Jesus, whereas the second, the book of Acts, relates how apostles continued to spread the message of Jesus to the "ends of the earth" (Acts 1:8). Since Luke–Acts is a literary unit, the authorship of Luke is identical with that of Acts. Like Mark and Matthew, the early church suggested that Luke was indeed the author of this Gospel. Similar to Mark, Luke is not one of the Twelve, and although he is not an official "apostle," he gathers his material from eyewitness testimony (Lk 1:1-3). Luke is also most likely a Gentile (Col 4:10-11, 14). Internally, the author of Luke–Acts claims to have been written by somebody who walked alongside of the apostle Paul. In the book of Acts, several passages include the first-person plural *we*, probably referring to eyewitness testimony (Acts 16:10-17; 20:5-15; 21:1-18; 27:1–28:16). Several passages in the New Testament place Luke and Mark in the same location, possibly suggesting that Luke gathered information from Mark (Col 4:10, 14; 2 Tim 4:11; Philem 24).

DATE

Since Luke probably depends on Mark's Gospel, we must date the book sometime after the publication of Mark. In Luke 21 Jesus predicts the fall of Jerusalem and the destruction of the temple, a series of events that happened in AD 70. Since chapter 21 appears to be a prophecy, even from the perspective of Luke, the Third Gospel must have been published before these events. Moreover, according to the book of Acts, the last event takes place in AD 62. These two observations suggest that the Gospel of Luke is published in the mid to late 60s.

FIGURE 6.1. LUKE THE EVANGELIST

PURPOSE

Luke publishes his gospel so that his audience "may know the certainty of the things" they "have been taught" (1:4). That is, Jesus is the long-awaited Messiah and the fulfillment of Old Testament expectations. As the Spirit-anointed king, Jesus overthrows Satan and his minions that enslave Israel and the nations in bondage of sin. Jesus of Nazareth is also the savior and Lord of Israel, who comes to liberate Israel and welcome the nations into the community of faith. Jesus offers hope to all walks of life, especially those destitute and marginalized. All who trust in Jesus inherit salvation and stand on equal footing.

OUTLINE

Similar to Mark and Matthew, Luke also presents his material geographically. Jesus is born in Judea (Bethlehem), baptized in the Jordan, and then ministers in Galilee. Both Jews and Gentiles welcome Jesus in Galilee. The journey from Galilee to Jerusalem is remarkably longer in Luke as it occupies nearly one-third of the Gospel. Jesus' ministry climaxes in Jerusalem, where he is condemned, crucified, and raised from the dead.

I. Prologue and Introduction to John the Baptist and Jesus (1:1–4:13)
  A. The Birth of John the Baptist and Jesus (1:5–2:51)
  B. The Ministry of John the Baptist and Jesus' Testing in the Wilderness (3:1–4:13)
II. Jesus' Ministry in Galilee (4:14–9:50)
  A. The Conquering Yet Rejected King (4:14-37)
  B. Following the Suffering King (4:38–9:50)
III. On the Road to Jerusalem (9:51–19:27)
  A. Hostility Toward Jesus' Ministry (9:51–13:9)
  B. The Paradoxical Nature of the Kingdom (13:10–19:27)
IV. Jesus' Ministry in Judea and Jerusalem (19:28–24:53)
  A. The Triumphal Entry and God's Judgment on Israel's Temple (19:28–21:38)
  B. The Last Supper and Jesus' Death and Resurrection (22:1–24:12)
  C. Jesus as the Fulfillment of the Old Testament (24:13-53)

BIBLICAL-THEOLOGICAL THEMES

Wilderness temptation. The wilderness temptation in the Synoptics is critical to all three narratives. The basic plot is retained in all three: Jesus is baptized as Israel's king in the Jordan River and then successfully defeats the devil in the wilderness. Once the devil is initially vanquished, Jesus has the authority and power to exorcise demons and establish the kingdom of God on earth. While all three Synoptics include the temptation narrative, only Luke and Matthew develop the event in some detail. In Mark and Matthew, the wilderness temptation immediately follows the baptism, whereas Luke includes this event after the genealogy. Jesus appears to have been tempted over the course of a forty-day fast (Mt 4:2; Lk 4:2). The qualification that this occurred in the wilderness together with the forty days recalls Israel's temptation in the wilderness. Numbers 14:34 explains why God's punishment of Israel lasted forty years in the wilderness: "For forty years—one year for each of the forty days you explored the land—you will suffer for your sins and know what it is like to have me against you." Jesus' forty-day wilderness experience of faithfulness is a typological microcosm of Israel's forty-year experience of unfaithful wandering in the desert.

FIGURE 6.2. ILLUSTRATION OF PSALM 91

According to Luke, the devil first attempts to break Jesus' trust in God's provision: "If you are the Son of God, tell this stone to become bread" (4:3-4). Satan wants Jesus to relinquish his trust in the Father and act independently of him. Jesus responds to this temptation by quoting Deuteronomy. The Old Testament context of this verse is illuminating:

> [Israel,] Remember how the Lord your God led you all the way in the wilderness these forty years, to humble and test you in order to know what was in your heart, whether or not you would keep his commands. He humbled you, causing you to hunger and then feeding you with manna, which neither you nor your ancestors had known, to teach you that *man does not live on bread alone but on every word that comes from the mouth of the Lord*. (Deut 8:2-3)

The purpose of quoting from Deuteronomy 8 is to demonstrate that Israel is to trust solely in God for all provision and care, both spiritual and physical. When Israel takes things into her own hands, she fails miserably (e.g., Num 11:1-9). In the same way, Jesus is tested to live independently of his Father, but he, unlike Israel, remains faithful by trusting in the Father's provision.

The devil then takes Jesus to a place where they could see "all the kingdoms of the world" in a moment of time, perhaps indicating that Jesus experienced this temptation in the form of a vision (Lk 4:5-8; cf. Rev 4:1; 17:3; 21:10). The devil claims to have "authority" over the kingdoms of the earth and vows to give the earthly kingdom over to Jesus if he worships him. The devil's exhortation to Jesus refers to a perpetual state of submission to and ruling alongside of Satan. The type of worship that Satan desires is identical to the worship that God deserves and requires. Jesus responds to the devil's request with a second quotation from Deuteronomy: "*Fear the Lord your God, serve him only* and take your oaths in his name" (Deut 6:13). Deuteronomy 6:13 requires Israel to maintain allegiance to God alone, despite pressure from the surrounding nations. Unfortunately, Israel repeatedly succumbs to idolatry by worshiping other gods alongside of the Lord. This results in the Lord punishing and eventually exiling Israel to Babylon. Jesus recapitulates the same testing but, despite the enticements of the devil, remains faithful to God.

For the last temptation, the devil takes Jesus to the "highest point of the temple," again, probably while Jesus experiences a vision (Lk 4:9-12). The devil tempts Jesus to cast himself from the temple's ledge so that God will send his angels to protect him. The devil supplements his attack by quoting from Psalm 91:11-12: "For he will command his angels concerning you to guard you in all your ways; they will lift you up in their hands, so that you will not strike your foot against a stone." The devil desires to control God's provision by forcing his hand to protect the Son. In other words, Satan tempts Jesus to *manipulate* God. As a response, Jesus quotes one more text from Deuteronomy: "Do not follow other gods, the gods of the peoples around you; for the *Lord* your God, who is among you, is a jealous God and his anger will burn against you, and he will destroy you from the face of the land. *Do not put the Lord your God to the test* as you did at Massah" (Deut 6:14-16). This refers to Exodus 17:1-7, where Israel demands water from God instead of trusting his provision. In the same way, Satan wants Jesus to demand that God save him from the fall from the temple. Ironically, Psalm 91 goes on to say, "You will tread on the lion and the cobra; you will trample the great lion and the serpent" (v. 13). Psalm 91 further unpacks Genesis 3:15: "And I will put enmity between you and the woman, and between your offspring and hers; *he will crush your head, and you will strike his heel.*" In his temptation, Jesus initially and decisively overthrows Satan and "crushes his head," thus fulfilling Genesis 3:15 and Psalm 91:13! As Pao and Schnabel note, "The use of this psalm [Ps 91] by Satan in the temptation narrative is striking because the divine power offered to Jesus is actually one to be used against the evil one."[1] Jesus' victory over temptation appears to have prepared him to conquer the ultimate satanic prince of all wicked nations and to conquer the land in a way that Israel had not been able. His resistance to these satanic allurements began the defeat of the devil, and his ministry of casting out demons continues the establishment of his victorious kingdom.

FIGURE 6.3. THE TOWER OF BABEL

The seventy-two disciples. Luke–Acts displays a marvelous concern for the redemption of the nations. At the presentation of baby Jesus in the temple, Simeon predicts that Jesus will be a "light for revelation to the Gentiles, and the glory of your people Israel" (Lk 2:32). By quoting Isaiah 49:6, Simeon is aware that Jesus will fulfill the Old Testament expectations of Gentiles participating in the restoration of Israel. Luke begins his two-volume project with a prediction that the kingdom will extend to the Gentiles, and he concludes with Paul preaching the gospel in Rome (Acts 28:16-31). From start to finish, the Gentiles are at the heart of Luke's message.

Another concrete example of Luke's concern for the nations is the commissioning of the seventy-two disciples. He is the only evangelist to include this narrative (Lk 10:1-24). These seventy-two disciples recall Genesis 10, in which God divides humanity into

[1]David W. Pao and Eckhard J. Schnabel, "Luke," in *Commentary on the New Testament Use of the Old Testament*, ed. G. K. Beale and D. A. Carson (Grand Rapids: Baker Academic, 2007), 285.

seventy-two people groups at the tower of Babel: "These are the clans of Noah's sons, according to their lines of descent, within their nations. *From these the nations spread out over the earth after the flood*" (Gen 10:32). In Genesis 10, the nations gather together with "one language and a common speech" (11:1) and decide to construct a grand edifice to boast in their accomplishments and manipulate God (11:3-4). Instead of the people spreading God's glory to the ends of the earth in accordance with his commission to Adam and Eve, they come together and attempt to boast in their own glory. As a result, God came down in judgment and "scattered" the nations throughout "all the earth" (11:8). God's people are supposed to spread over the face of the earth to glorify God, but now they are scattered in judgment. James Scott rightly perceives the significance of the Table of Nations in the book of Genesis when he states, "The Table of Nations is thus seen as the fundamental point of orientation for describing Israel's place among the nations of the world and the basis for envisioning world geography and ethnography in the eschatological future."[2]

Genesis 10 forms the backdrop for Jesus' commission to the seventy-two. These disciples symbolize the seventy-two nations of the world, the new people of God who have been reconstituted around one person—King Jesus. If we keep an eye on the unity of Luke–Acts, the sending of the seventy-two disciples may also prefigure the sending of the church to the nations in the book of Acts.[3]

Through the person of Jesus, the disciples are empowered to heal (Lk 10:9), judge (10:10-15), and cast out demons (10:18-20), all indications that the kingdom has arrived. The second half of the passage focuses on the success of their mission: "The seventy-two returned with joy and said, 'Lord, even the demons submit to us in your name'" (10:17). They readily acknowledge the effects of the inbreaking of the kingdom of God.

Jesus responds in a seemingly unusual manner: "'*I saw Satan fall like lightning from heaven.* I have given you authority to *trample on snakes and scorpions* and to overcome all the power of the enemy; nothing will harm you'" (Lk 10:18-19). Jesus' claim that Satan fell "like lightning from heaven" recalls Isaiah 14:12: "How you *have fallen from heaven*, morning star, son of the dawn! You have been cast down to the earth, you who once laid low the nations!" The Babylonian king attempts to elevate himself to the level of God, but God will cast him down (Is 14:15-21). Luke 10 therefore presents the seventy-two disciples as continuing the overthrow of Satan's kingdom. Jesus' victory over Satan in the wilderness invests the disciples with power to continue the expansion of God's eternal kingdom and the overthrow of Satan, thereby directly fulfilling the Old Testament expectation that the great antagonist of God's people would be finally defeated (Gen 3:15; Num 24:17-19).

PROLOGUE AND INTRODUCTION TO JOHN THE BAPTIST AND JESUS (1:1–4:13)

Central to the story line of the Bible is God's intention to dwell with humanity, not only with Israelites but with people from all walks of life. Abraham's descendants are to be a blessing to the pagan nations, and Israel is

[2]James Scott, *2 Corinthians*, NIBC (Peabody, MA: Hendrickson, 1998), 9.
[3]John Nolland, *Luke 9:21–18:34*, WBC 35B (Grand Rapids: Zondervan, 1993), 550.

FIGURE 6.4. THE VISITATION OF MARY TO ELIZABETH

to be a nation of priests that mediates God's presence to the far reaches of the earth. The Old Testament, however, recounts a pattern of failure to obey God and extend his glory to the nations. The Gospel of Luke presents Jesus' resurrection from the dead as the inauguration of a new order, with Jesus as the new temple, from whom flow the rivers of life and through whom the temple veil is opened, so that peoples from all nations might enter in. God's original purpose for the temple in Eden, that it would expand and fill the whole earth, begins to be fulfilled in Jesus. The nations participate in the people of God, not by adhering to Israelite commandments but by faith in Jesus of Nazareth. These precious themes also echo throughout the chambers of Luke–Acts.

The birth of John the Baptist and Jesus (1:1–2:51). After connecting his Gospel to other written accounts of Jesus (Lk 1:1-2), Luke begins differently from the other two Synoptics by stating the purpose of his work and a key figure of his audience: "I myself have carefully investigated everything from the beginning, I too decided to write an orderly account for you, most excellent *Theophilus, so that you may know the certainty of the things you have been taught*" (1:3-4; cf. Josephus, *Ag. Ap.* 1.1-3; 2:1-2). We know nothing of Theophilus. He very well could be the patron or financial backer of Luke's Gospel, as writing in the ancient world was costly. Although Luke mentions only one individual in 1:1-4, a wider audience is in view. Luke's emphasis on the incorporation of Gentiles into the covenant community has led many scholars to conclude that Luke's audience largely consists of Gentile Christians. In any case, he sets forth the purpose of writing the Gospel: to affirm the message of Jesus' life, death, and resurrection that Theophilus and the wider audience had received previously. Keep in mind that Luke desires to write another account of "things that have been fulfilled among us" (1:1). What "things" have been fulfilled? The entire sweep of the Old Testament anticipates the person and work of Jesus (see Lk 24:27).

Unlike Matthew's account that narrates Jesus' birth through Joseph's perspective, Luke depicts the birth narrative primarily through the eyes of Zechariah, Elizabeth, and Mary, opening with two angelic visitations. The first focuses on John the Baptist, who will "go on before the Lord . . . to turn the hearts of the parents to their children and the disobedient to the wisdom of the righteous—to make ready a people prepared for the Lord" (Lk 1:17). Like Matthew and Mark, Luke connects John the Baptist with the messenger figure from Malachi, who prophesies that in the latter days the messenger will prepare Israel for the arrival of the Lord (Mal 3:1-2; 4:5-6). Since Israel is in a state of unbelief, the messenger's task is to call the people to repentance, lest they be annihilated at the Lord's coming.

Following the angelic announcement concerning John, the angel Gabriel visits Mary and promises that she will bear a son (Lk 1:26-38). Although the third Evangelist is quick to highlight the uniqueness and importance of the person of John in the story of Israel's redemption (1:13-17; 1:67-80), the highest praise is reserved for Jesus. In the span of a few verses, Luke piles on several key descriptions that originate in the Old Testament: "Jesus" (lit. Joshua [1:31]), "Son of the Most High" (1:32), "holy one" (1:35), and "Son of God" (1:35). Each of these descriptions speaks to a specific aspect of Jesus' identity and mission, particularly his identity as the *divine* Son of God and true Israel as well as his prerogative to rule over Israel and the nations (e.g., 2 Sam 7:12; Is 9:6). We discover a chief goal in Jesus' career in 1:32-33: "The Lord God will give him the throne of his father David, and he will reign over Jacob's descendants forever; his kingdom will never end."

When Mary enters Elizabeth's house, Luke narrates that "the baby [John] leaped in her womb" (1:41). Later, Elizabeth recounts that "the baby in my womb leaped for joy" (1:44). The reason for John's sudden outburst, even within the womb, stems from the arrival of the new creation in the person of Jesus. Since the early chapters of Genesis, the Old Testament has waited for the arrival of the new age, and now that it has come, exuberant joy is the only fitting response (see Is 49:13; 51:11; 60:15; 61:10-11; 65:18-19; Luke 1:14, 58; 10:17, 21; 15:5; 19:37; 24:41, 52).

Another peculiar feature of Luke is his emphasis on hymns or songs, especially in the first two chapters (1:46-55; 1:68-79; 2:14; 2:29-32). Encased within each of these songs are prominent themes that run throughout Luke's Gospel. After Jesus is born and Mary and Joseph present him at the temple, a righteous individual named Simeon takes Jesus in his arms, declaring that Jesus will be a "light for revelation to the Gentiles, and the glory of your people Israel" (2:32). Simeon, filled with the Spirit (2:25), alludes to a few prominent passages in Isaiah where the servant will restore God's people and will reach out to Israel's neighbors. Isaiah 49:3-6 reads, "You are my servant, Israel. . . . It is too small a thing for you to be my *servant to restore the tribes of Jacob* and bring back those of Israel I have kept. I will also make you *a light for the Gentiles*, that my salvation may reach to the ends of the earth" (cf. Is 42:6). Isaiah identifies the servant (a single individual) as Israel, who will trigger the restoration of a Jewish remnant and usher Gentiles into the covenant community. By recalling Isaiah 49 and other similar texts, Simeon predicts that baby Jesus will directly fulfill Old Testament expectations in his ministry and restore the remnant within the nation of Israel. But God's restoration reaches beyond Israel and incorporates the nations. Simeon's words ring throughout Luke–Acts as Jesus is presented as the one who heralds salvation to Israel and the nations (e.g., Lk 3:6; Acts 1:8; 9:15, 13:7).

Luke is the only Evangelist to mention an event between Jesus' birth and the beginning of his public ministry (Lk 2:41-52). The story takes place when twelve-year-old Jesus is in Jerusalem with his parents to participate in the Passover celebration (2:42). The

Passover is prominent in this narrative as it anticipates the final Passover during Passion Week. But the difference between the two celebrations is pronounced. David Garland notes, "Jesus has been identified and presented as the firstborn (2:7, 23), but in the next recorded celebration of Passover at the end of the gospel, the destroyer will not pass over this firstborn Son, who will die on a cross. His death will lead to a greater liberation."[4]

> ***John stands within the Old Testament tradition of prophets who summon Israel to return to the Lord. He proclaims a "baptism of repentance," revealing that Israel remained in a calloused state against God.***

Once the feast is over, his parents begin the journey home, only to realize that Jesus is missing (Lk 2:44). After three days of looking, they finally find him "in the temple courts, sitting among the teachers" (2:46). Jesus justifies his actions by claiming that he "had to be in [his] Father's house" (2:49). Although his public ministry officially begins at his baptism (3:21-23), Jesus demonstrates, even as a boy, his unique role in Israel's redemption. He is the true "house" of God that mediates God's glory to the whole world.

The ministry of John the Baptist and Jesus' testing in the wilderness (3:1–4:13). Following Jesus' encounter with Israel's leaders at the temple (Lk 2:39-52), Luke transitions from Jesus as a boy to John the Baptist's public ministry in Judea (3:1-20). Remarkably, instead of asking Israel to seek forgiveness through sacrifices and the temple, John beckons Israel to assemble in the wilderness and identify with a baptism that will enable these individuals to gather as a new community, a new Israel. Israel's temple and national structures are riddled with idolatry (3:7-18), so God establishes Israel on a new foundation—the person of Jesus. N. T. Wright correctly unpacks the significance of John's baptism when he claims,

> Anybody offering water-baptism for the forgiveness of sins was saying: you can have, here and now, what you would normally get through the Temple cult. Anybody inviting those who wished to do so to pass through an initiatory rite of this kind was symbolically saying: here is the true Israel that is to be vindicated by YHWH.[5]

Recall that John the Baptist's parents are from the priestly tribe of Levi, and his father, Zechariah, was a priest (1:5). John is attuned to the significance of his baptism in the Jordan and the purification rites that are found within the context of the temple.

Luke's depiction of Jesus' baptism (Lk 3:21-22) also typologically recalls Israel's passing through the sea at the exodus and the second generation's crossing through the Jordan to enter into the Promised Land. Israel's redemption from spiritual captivity takes place through the person of Jesus. Luke's quotation of Isaiah 40:3-5 differs from Mark and Matthew in that he cites two additional

[4]David E. Garland, *Luke*, ZECNT (Grand Rapids: Zondervan, 2011), 143.
[5]N. T. Wright, *Jesus and the Victory of God* (Minneapolis: Fortress Press, 1996), 160.

verses from Isaiah, so the inclusion of Isaiah 40:5 is noteworthy: "And *all people* will see God's salvation" (Lk 3:6). The emphasis is clear—Jesus, who has already been identified as "salvation" (1:71, 77; 2:11, 30), is the object of the hope of all nations. Isaiah 40 describes God restoring his people from Babylonian captivity by leading them through the desert to the Promised Land. John the Baptist's ministry is preparation for God to carry Israel from spiritual Babylon and lead them to the Promised Land.

Luke then squeezes Jesus' genealogy between two key events: Jesus' baptism (3:21-23) and wilderness temptation (4:1-13). By doing so, the genealogy sheds light on both of these events. Luke's genealogy differs from Matthew's in two significant ways: it occurs immediately following Jesus' baptism (3:21-22) and goes beyond Abraham all the way to Adam (3:38). Jesus is portrayed as the second Adam who has come to do what Noah, Abraham, and Israel failed to do. Also, by reaching back to Adam, Luke illustrates "the universal scope of God's salvation that comes through Jesus."[6] The story of Adam and Eve, the patriarchs, and Israel has not been forgotten but rather climaxes in the person of Jesus. As the perfect last Adam, Jesus inherits the blessings promised to Israel and her ancestors—the same blessings that Adam and Eve and the patriarchs were to inherit upon successfully completing their mission.

Luke claims that Jesus left the Jordan River "full of the Holy Spirit" and was "led by the Spirit into the wilderness" (Lk 4:1). Central to Luke–Acts is the role of the Spirit in the person of Jesus and the proclamation of the gospel to Israel and the nations. One of the hallmarks of the new age is the arrival of the Spirit. According to the Old Testament, God's promise to establish an end-time people that enjoys his presence in a new creation, the original intention of Genesis 1–2, is actualized through the coming of the Spirit in the latter days. The Holy Spirit plays a central role in achieving God's purpose of redemption, climaxing in the restoration of all things in a new heavens and earth. The Spirit is associated with God's great act of creation (Gen 1:2; Ezek 37:12-14), the end-time temple (Hag 2:5-9; Zech 6:4-10), the new covenant (Is 59:21; Ezek 36:26-27), the restoration of Israel (Is 32:15; 44:3; 59:21), the final resurrection (Ezek 37:1-14), and the establishment of the eternal kingdom of God (Is 11:1-4). As Luke narrates the life of Jesus and the spread of the gospel in Acts, he is quick to point out the arrival and role of the Spirit, and with it the new age.

FIGURE 6.5. CROSSING OF THE RED SEA

As Jesus is led "by the Spirit into the wilderness," he repeats the story of Israel, on whom God also sent his Spirit as they came out from Egypt and went into the wilderness

[6]Garland, *Luke*, 172.

(Neh 9:20-21;[7] Is 63:10-14). Upon entering the Promised Land, God charges Israel to eradicate their enemies, the Canaanites, yet they fail to expunge them from the land (e.g., Judg 2:14). Jesus, however, faithfully resists the temptations during his forty-day testing that defeated Adam and Eve. His victory during his wilderness temptation is the initial defeat of the devil. Once Jesus is baptized, he enters the Promised Land, beginning his mission of establishing the new creation. Jesus quotes Deuteronomy three times during his temptation (Deut 6:13, 16; 8:3). "With the appearance of Jesus as the fully obedient Son of God," writes Brandon Crowe, "we encounter a new day in the history of redemption—a day of eschatological salvation secured by the Messiah."[8] Repeating the story of Adam and Eve and Israel, Jesus drives out Israel's true enemy, Satan, from the world and inaugurates the new creation.

FIGURE 6.6. JUDEAN DESERT

JESUS' MINISTRY IN GALILEE (4:14–9:50)

Leviticus 25:8-55 instructs the Israelites to observe the Year of Jubilee. Not only are the Israelites to rest on the Sabbath one day a week but the land is to "rest" every seventh year (Lev 25:4). On the seventh Sabbath rest of the land (forty-nine years in total), a Year of Jubilee is declared on the Day of Atonement (Lev 25:9). The fiftieth year is a celebration of God's gracious provision, and the entire year is considered holy (Lev 25:12). Land is to be returned to its original owner (Lev 25:13); debts are to be forgiven, allowing the downtrodden within Israel to be restored. The Year of Jubilee is picked up later in the Old Testament and cast as a prophecy associated with the release of the Israelites from Babylonian captivity. According to Isaiah 61, the servant heralds "freedom for the captives" and announces the "year of the Lord's favor" (Is 61:1-2; cf. Ezek 46:16-17). The Year of Jubilee corresponds with the release of captive Israelites since Israel has been in a state of destitution in Babylon. All hope of restoration seems lost. But Isaiah prophesies that the coming Messiah will herald the victory of God's people. He envisions the return of Israel from Babylon as an end-time Year

[7]Note that Neh 9:20-21 says that God "gave" his "Spirit to instruct them. . . . For forty years . . . [he] sustained them in the wilderness."

[8]Brandon D. Crowe, *The Last Adam: A Theology of the Obedient Life of Jesus in the Gospels* (Grand Rapids: Baker, 2017), 81.

of Jubilee. In Luke 4:18-19, Jesus quotes Isaiah 61:1-2 while attending worship in the synagogue and claims that this eschatologically charged passage is directly fulfilled at that moment. In Luke's Gospel, the poor and outcast are given hope. Although his readers may be economically poor and marginalized in their communities, they can rest assured that Jesus has liberated them from spiritual poverty and led them into the Promised Land of the new creation, where they enjoy incalculable wealth.

The conquering yet rejected king (4:14-37). Jesus opens his public ministry in Galilee by visiting the synagogues, resulting in "everyone prais[ing] him" for his unrivaled teaching (4:15). As is Jesus' custom, he attends the synagogue on the Sabbath to worship. Jesus stands up and reads from the Isaiah scroll a very specific text: Isaiah 61:1-2. Where the Evangelists Mark and Matthew quote from the Old Testament and weave the quotations into the narratives "in overt authorial commentary," Old Testament quotations in Luke's Gospel are found on the lips of his central characters.[9] Here in Luke 4 Jesus cites a quotation from the second half of Isaiah (chaps. 40–66). The first section of Isaiah generally concerns the eventual destruction of Judah, exiled in Babylon. But Isaiah 40–66 largely refers to the time of restoration, the return of Israel from Babylon. Isaiah 61:1-2 takes place within a prophet's vocation: "The Spirit . . . is on me . . . the Lord has anointed me. . . . He has sent me." These prophetic oracles from Isaiah refer to a time when God will send a prophet in the latter days who will announce the end-time Year of Jubilee and the restoration of Israel from Babylonian captivity (cf. Is 42:1-9; 49:1-6;

FIGURE 6.7. GREAT SYNAGOGUE AT CAPERNAUM

[9]Richard B. Hays, *Reading Backwards: Figural Christology and the Fourfold Gospel Witness* (Waco, TX: Baylor University Press, 2014), 58.

50:4-9; 52:13–53:12). The thrust of his message is a reversal of covenant curses that were brought on Israel for heinous idolatry (Lev 26:14-39; Deut 28:15-68).

After reading this passage from the scroll, Jesus identifies himself as the fulfillment of the prophetic figure from Isaiah: "Then he rolled up the scroll, gave it back to the attendant and sat down. The eyes of everyone in the synagogue fasten on him. He began by saying to them, '*Today this scripture is fulfilled in your hearing*'" (Lk 4:20-21). Jesus views himself as the long-awaited herald who proclaims the restoration of Israel and the inbreaking of the new creation.

The crowd stands amazed but then soon points out, "Isn't this Joseph's son?" (Lk 4:22). Jesus responds by expressing the contents of their hearts: "'Surely you will quote this proverb to me: "Physician, heal yourself!' And you will tell me 'Do here in your hometown what we have heard that you did in Capernaum'"" (4:23). The crowd desires for Jesus to prove his kingship, but he refuses. No matter what Jesus says or does, he will be rejected (4:24). Verses 25-27 state two examples of prophets who were not welcome in their native homeland: Elijah (1 Kings 17:1-24) and Elisha (2 Kings 5:1-14). Through a handful of allusions, conceptual parallels, and explicit connections, Luke intends his readers to read portions of Jesus' career through the prophetic lens of Elijah and Elisha (see 1 Kings 17; 2 Kings 4/Lk 7:11-17). Both Old Testament prophets are zealous for God's law, confront idolatry, minister to Gentiles, and perform extensive miracles. At the outset of Jesus' ministry in Nazareth, Jesus consciously weds his ministry to Elijah and Elisha. As Luke's narrative unfolds, we should expect history to repeat itself—Israel is once again worshiping idols, so she will continue to reject God's prophetic voice, making room for the Gentiles to become part of the true people of God.

Luke rounds out this section by recalling an incident in another synagogue, where a hostile demoniac confronts Jesus: "Go away! What do you want with us, Jesus of Nazareth? Have you come to destroy us? I know

FIGURE 6.8. SCROLL OF ISAIAH FROM QUMRAN

who you are—the Holy One of God!" (Lk 4:34). Jesus commands the demon to depart from the man, and the demon immediately complies (4:35). Since Jesus gained the decisive victory over Satan in his wilderness temptation, the demons are now subject to him. The result of demonic expulsion is utter surprise by the crowd in the synagogue: "All the people were amazed. . . . News about him spread throughout the surrounding area" (4:36-37).

Following the suffering king (4:38–9:50). Luke then includes several passages that focus on understanding the nature of the kingdom and what it means to participate within it. Jesus' summons to follow him and participate in the end-time kingdom entails radical commitment and devotion. The first crop of Jesus' disciples emerges in Luke 5:1-11 and 5:27-38. He soon assembles the twelve disciples on a mountain, an event that recalls God assembling Israel at Mount Sinai (6:12-16). The appointment of the Twelve also entails establishing a new people group to live in the new creation, where it will grow exponentially in fulfillment of the Genesis 1:28 commission given to Adam and Eve.

The question of discipleship is bound up with the larger topic of Jesus' identity, particularly his identity as Israel's King and his relationship to the Mosaic law. Luke 6:1-11 probes this connection, particularly with his actions on the Sabbath. If Jesus is the climax of the Old Testament and the Mosaic administration, then Israel's covenant with its stipulations, including the Sabbath, is affected.

One Sabbath day, Jesus and his disciples travel through a field, and his disciples "began to pick some heads of grain, rub them in their hands and eat the kernels" (Lk 6:1). The Pharisees determine that Jesus and his disciples are breaking the Sabbath. Although we are unsure which law or laws in particular the Pharisees have in mind (see Ex 20:8-11; 23:12; Deut 5:12-15), the Jewish leaders are certainly convinced that he and the disciples stand guilty (6:2).

Jesus replies to these accusations with an enigmatic Old Testament precedent about King David eating the consecrated bread from the temple while fleeing from Saul (Lk 6:3-4; 1 Sam 21:1-8). The issue in 1 Samuel 21 is that according to Leviticus 24:5-9, only the Levites may partake, and the bread must

> ***The Sabbath is one of the key commandments God gave to the Israelites that demarcate them as his covenant community.***

be eaten in the Holy Place. David is not a Levite, but he does demonstrate concern for holiness. But why does Jesus use this Old Testament incident to validate his actions on the Sabbath? David's actions in 1 Samuel 21 may not even have taken place on the Sabbath. The answer lies in David's status as king of Israel. He has the authority to partake of the consecrated bread in the temple (cf. 1 Sam 20:31; 21:11). There may also be another reason why Jesus' actions on the Sabbath are justified. The Sabbath is originally intended to give the Israelites rest from labor and nourishment to their bodies. Jesus has every right to claim that it is lawful to "save life" on the Sabbath (Lk 6:9). The abiding authority of the Old Testament carries over to the New.

FIGURE 6.9. KING DAVID PLAYING THE HARP

Therefore, Jesus, as the royal "Son of Man" (Lk 6:5), possesses the authority to "break" the Sabbath because the Sabbath ultimately anticipates his reign. Jesus is not so much breaking the Sabbath as he is bringing its observance to its ultimate intention. Jesus has come and conquered Satan, repossessing God's kingdom on earth in fulfillment of these expectations. The first Adam was to gain control over the environment and bring it into subjection, but he failed. Now Jesus, as the second Adam, the Son of Man, has defeated Satan and possesses authority over all creation.

By Jesus' fulfillment of the Old Testament laws that physically separate Israel from her pagan neighbors, entrance into the covenant community becomes far more accessible to Gentiles. Luke continues this important theme with his narrative of the centurion soldier (Lk 7:1-10). Upon hearing the centurion's faith in Jesus' ability to heal his servant, Jesus "was amazed at him [the centurion], and turning to the crowd following him, he said, 'I tell you, I have not found such great faith even in Israel'" (7:9). This declaration illustrates the ease with which Gentiles are now joining true Israel, the covenant community that is reorganized around the person of Jesus. Instead of having to convert to the Israelite faith—the Old Testament pattern (e.g., Ex 12:48)—the centurion simply believes in Jesus. In addition, the centurion, who is a proselyte to Judaism (Lk 7:5), represents Gentiles in general and their willingness to believe in Jesus' message in contrast to the rebellious nation of Israel (6:37-42; 7:29-35).

Following the centurion's conversion, Jesus raises a widow's son from the dead (Lk 7:11-17), an act that signifies the inbreaking of the new creation, recalling several Old Testament texts that speak of God giving life in the latter days (e.g., Is 25:8, 26:19, 65:17, Dan 12:1-2). Jesus' unique identity and kingdom message are brought to the fore with John the Baptist's interaction with his disciples (Lk 7:18-23). He reassures his cousin John that he is indeed Israel's long-awaited Messiah by quoting several texts from Isaiah that predict Israel's end-time restoration from Babylon (Is 29:18; 35:5-6; 61:1). These passages from Isaiah express how God will, through his servant, the Messiah, restore Israel (Is 42:1-9, 49:1-6, 50:4-9, 52:13–53:12). Jesus claims not only to be Isaiah's servant but the very source of restoration—a claim to his unique identity as Israel's God incarnate. Jesus of Nazareth is both Israel's Lord and servant.

Luke includes an account of a sinful woman who anoints Jesus at the house of a Pharisee (Lk 7:36-50). Jesus not only shares a meal with this unclean woman but also forgives her (7:47). Only the Lord can grant forgiveness, a status that was previously granted through cultic rituals at the temple (Lev 17:11). Here forgiveness is found in the person of Jesus, who replaces Israel's corrupt temple and, as Israel's God, offers forgiveness to those who trust him (Lk 7:48). Jesus' actions are so astonishing that some respond, "Who is this who even forgives sins?" (7:49).

Jesus' interaction with this woman segues into a wonderful summary of his successful ministry of "proclaiming the good news of the kingdom of God" in Galilee (Lk 8:1), where many prominent women follow him—Mary Magdalene, Joanna, Susanna, and others (8:1-3). The next several paragraphs

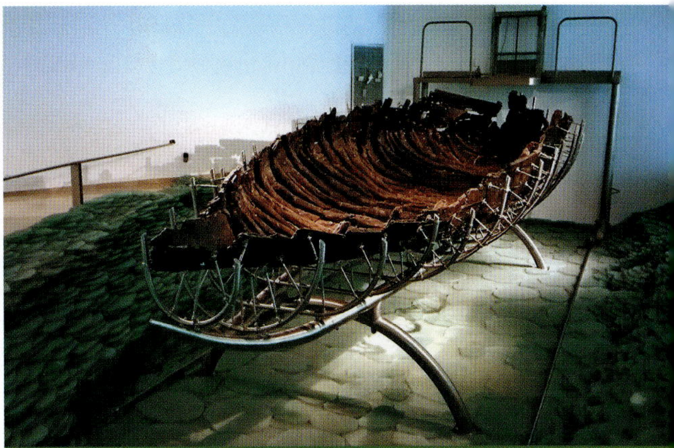

FIGURE 6.10. GALILEAN BOAT

detail the nature of the paradoxical kingdom and how it entails both victory and suffering (8:4-25). Chapter 8 concludes with three remarkable events that highlight Jesus' identity as Israel's God, starting with his authority over the spiritual and physical world in the stilling of the storm on the Sea of Galilee (8:22-25). Jesus possesses sovereign authority to silence the onslaught of "demonic forces," symbolized by the chaotic waters. In the Old Testament, the sea is the embodiment of rebellion and hostility to God's creation (e.g., Ezek 32:2; Dan 7:2). This end-time judgment that Jesus passes on the demonic

> *The Sabbath largely entails a commemoration of God's cosmic kingship and looks forward to his reign extending decisively on earth.*

realm continues in the following narrative with the Gerasene demoniac (8:26-39). The last event of chapter 8 climaxes with two miracles: an account of Jesus healing an unclean woman and raising a dead girl (8:40-56). By healing the unclean woman with menstrual bleeding (8:43-48), Jesus demonstrates his identity as the true temple, where such purification of uncleanness typically took place (Lev 15:25-30). In raising Jairus's daughter from the dead, Jesus declares that he is the author of life, heralding the long-awaited new creation (Is 65:17; 66:22).

FIGURE 6.11. ANGEL FEEDING ELIJAH

Chapter 9 is a turning point within Luke's Gospel as Jesus' ministry begins to come to a head. The chapter opens with the commissioning of the Twelve to have "power and authority to drive out all demons and to cure diseases" (Lk 9:1). The disciples are charged to continue Jesus' ministry of establishing the kingdom of God and driving out his enemies (9:1-9). The feeding of the five thousand, the only miracle recorded in all four Gospels, recalls the Passover celebration (Ex 12). John's account even frames the miracle by mentioning that the "Jewish Passover Festival was near" (Jn 6:4). The Passover lies deep within the heart of the Israelite nation and characterizes God's redemption and deliverance. It is a symbolic memorial that *recalls* God vanquishing Pharaoh and his army and *anticipates* God delivering his people out of exile once more in a second exodus of sorts. Jesus, as God incarnate, feeds this group of five thousand men plus their families, signifying God's care of Israel. He not only recreates the Passover ceremony but does so in fulfillment of Israel's long-awaited promise of redemption. Jesus is claiming, in effect, that he is the one bringing about Israel's redemption. The Passover ultimately points to him. Luke's remark that "twelve basketfuls of broken pieces" remained (Lk 9:17) possibly symbolizes this multitude as the reorganized twelve tribes of Israel.

The feeding of the five thousand brings Jesus' identity to the surface in the following section. Peter (representing the disciples) finally declares that Jesus is indeed "God's Messiah" (Lk 9:20), the long-awaited savior of Israel. But this declaration, with all its political aspirations, is immediately qualified with Jesus' explicit prediction that he will "suffer many things and be rejected by the elders, the chief priests and the teachers of the law . . . and on the third day be raised to life" (9:22).

The transfiguration, probably occurring on Mount Hermon, is one of the more eye-opening events in Jesus' ministry. The Old Testament background to the transfiguration lies in Israel's assembly at Sinai, where God covenants with Israel (Ex 19). The event at Sinai typologically functions as the blueprint for Jesus' transfiguration, where all the key visual elements of a typical theophany are present—cloud, thunder, lightning, trumpet blast, smoke, and the "voice of God."

Jesus is transfigured before Peter, James, and John, displaying his magnificent glory (Lk 9:28). The description of Jesus' clothing is described in detail: "The appearance of his face changed, and his clothes became as bright as a flash of lightning" (9:29). In the same way, Moses' face shone with God's glory when he encounters the Lord in the tabernacle (Ex 34:33-35; cf. Num 6:22-27; Ps 104:1-2). Instead of merely reflecting God's glory, though, divine glory emanates from the person of Jesus—a clear indication of his identity as Israel's God. Lightning and thunder accompany the Sinaitic theophany (Ex 19:16), and, similarly, a cloud overshadows the disciples (9:34). On Sinai Yahweh speaks out of a cloud (Ex 19:19). Likewise, God speaks to the disciples with a "voice" (9:35). Jesus takes with him Peter, James, and John (9:28), paralleling Moses taking three individuals up on the mountain in addition to the seventy elders (Aaron, Nadab, and Abihu; Ex 24:9-11). As we saw in discussing the same scene in Matthew 17, Jesus "leading" the disciples "to a high mountain" and a "cloud covering them" recalls Exodus 24 and 40. According to Exodus 24 and 40, Moses and Joshua ascend upon Mount Sinai and a "cloud covered the mountain" (Ex 24:15 LXX) and the same "cloud" later "overshadowed" the tabernacle (Ex 40:35 LXX). Peter even requests to build three "shelters" or "tabernacles" (Lk 9:33). The point of all this symbolism is that Jesus is the descending heavenly tabernacle.

In all three Synoptic accounts, Elijah and Moses join Jesus on the mountain (Lk 9:30). It is likely that these two Old Testament saints refer to the totality of the Old Testament corpus. Jesus is greater than both the law and the prophets. He is a greater Moses (lawgiver) and a greater Elijah (prophet). Furthermore, both Moses and Elijah experienced theophanies on Sinai (Ex 19; 1 Kings 19:8-18). Luke is the only Evangelist to mention what Moses and Elijah discusses with Jesus: "They spoke about his [Jesus'] departure" (Lk 9:31). Curiously, the Greek word here for "departure" is unique and could even be rendered as "exodus." The topic of conversation appears to concern the new exodus that Jesus is initiating through his death and resurrection.

> ***According to the Old Testament, Moses is renowned for giving the Torah, and Elijah is renowned for his prophetic acts.***

In the Old Testament God often appears to people on mountains to communicate a particular message, and he manifests himself in an astonishing way to the disciples, telling them, "This is my Son, whom I have chosen; listen to him" (Lk 9:35). God's declaration echoes texts such as 2 Samuel 7:14, Psalm 2:7, and Isaiah 42:1 that express the end-time establishment of Israel's king, who will usher in the eternal kingdom. The idea of Jesus being God's "Son" is also reminiscent of Israel being God's "firstborn son" (Ex 4:22), who is to obey God's law perfectly, subdue rebellion, and spread his glory to the ends of the earth. The transfiguration demonstrates that Jesus is the long-awaited yet divine Messiah, who has come to obey his Father perfectly, subdue his enemies, and spread God's tabernacling presence to the ends of the earth.

ON THE ROAD TO JERUSALEM (9:51–19:27)

One prominent theme woven throughout the Old Testament is God's care for the poor, marginalized, and foreigners. The poor have always been relegated to society's fringes, whereas wealth commands authority, respect, and the ear of the populace. Culture, ancient and modern, idolizes the wealthy and talented but marginalizes the weak, even the ordinary. The Old Testament, though, always displays a concern for the oppressed and outcast. The Lord watches over and provides for widows and orphans (Deut 10:18; 14:28; Prov 23:10; Ruth 4:13-17; 1 Kings 17). For example, Exodus 22:22-24 states, "Do not take advantage of the widow or the fatherless. If you do. . . . I will kill you with the sword; your wives will become widows and your children fatherless." Sojourners, that is, non-Israelites who temporarily live in Israel, are granted many rights within the Mosaic covenant (Ex 22:21; 23:9). They are to be treated as native Israelites (Lev 19:33-34) and allowed access to fields and vineyards (Lev 19:10; Deut 24:19-21).

One of the most extraordinary features of Jesus's kingdom message is its counterintuitiveness—a teaching that flies in the face of cultural expectations. It flips society's values on their heads. The kingdom is characterized not by wealth and talent but by humility and service to those caught in the fringes of society. The four Gospels demonstrate a constant concern for Gentiles, the weak, and the marginalized, but Luke's Gospel is exceptional. At every turn in the Third Gospel, Jesus ministers to the outsiders and welcomes them into the kingdom. As Mary sings in Luke 1:52-53, God "brought down rulers from their thrones but has lifted up the humble. He has filled the hungry with good things but has sent the rich away empty."

Hostility toward Jesus' ministry (9:51–13:9). As Jesus turns south toward Jerusalem, resistance to Jesus and his ministry comes to a head. One can detect an ominous tone in Luke's words: "As the time approached for him to be taken up to heaven, Jesus resolutely set out for Jerusalem" (Lk 9:51). Since many stand in opposition to the end-time kingdom, Jesus' followers can expect resistance and eventual martyrdom. If Jesus suffers, so too will his disciples (9:51-62), even at the hands of the Jewish leaders (11:37-12:59). Joel Green writes that "the journey [to Jerusalem] concerns not only the formation of disciples, but also the growing hostility Jesus attracts. Even the disciples resist Jesus' message. In fact, so fully have they failed to identify themselves with Jesus that, by journey's end, they have all but disappeared from view."[10] While the Old Testament expects tribulation to precede the establishment of the end-time kingdom (e.g., Dan 2; 7), Jesus installs the kingdom amid suffering and affliction. Not only does the end-time persecution of God's covenant people occur concurrently with the advent of the kingdom, but Jesus claims that suffering is a hallmark of the latter-day rule of God.

The seventy-two disciples in Luke 10 symbolize the seventy-two nations of the world, a community of disciples that reverses the dispersion of the nations in Genesis 10–11. As the new humanity, this group has been reconstituted around King Jesus, who empowers them to heal and to eradicate the demons (Lk 10:17-19). The seventy-two disciples are surprised at their power over the demons, so Jesus responds rather cryptically: "He replied, '*I saw Satan fall like lightning*

[10]Joel B. Green, "Luke, Gospel of," in *Dictionary of Jesus and the Gospels*, 2nd ed., ed. C. S. Green, Joel B. Green, Jeannine K. Brown, and Nicholas Perrin (Downers Grove, IL: InterVarsity Press, 2013), 544.

from heaven. I have given you authority to trample on snakes and scorpions and to overcome all the power of the enemy; nothing will harm you'" (10:18-19). This statement recalls Isaiah 14:12: "How *you have fallen from heaven*, morning star, son of the dawn!" In the immediate context of Isaiah 14, the king of Babylon boasts in his greatness (14:13-14) and attempts to elevate himself to the level of God, but God promises to cast him down (14:15-21). Jesus alludes to Isaiah 14 to demonstrate the defeat of Satan that began at his wilderness temptation and continues throughout his ministry, even extending to his followers (Lk 10:19; Gen 3:15; Ps 91:13).

The unification of humanity is on display in the well-known parable of the good Samaritan (Lk 10:25-37). A band of thieves attacked and robbed a Jewish man, "leaving him half dead" on the side of the road (10:30). Astonishingly, the man on the road is rebuffed by a priest and a Levite. Ordinarily, Jews and Samaritans remain at a distance from one another (cf. Jn 4:1-26), but in this instance a Samaritan went out of his way to aid this man. This parable highlights the unity that is now found in the kingdom. Whereas division marked humanity in the old age, genuine unity in Jesus is the hallmark of the new age.

The paradoxical nature of the kingdom (13:10–19:27). After expressing the Jewish leaders' general hostility toward Jesus and his followers (9:51–13:9), Luke drills down into the nature of Jesus' kingdom message and participation within it (13:10–19:27). Throughout the narrative, the nature of the kingdom and discipleship has surfaced, but Luke reserves 13:10–19:27 for a more detailed and robust description. Up to this point, Jesus has primarily explained the nature of the kingdom through symbolic events and miracles, whereas he now transitions to parabolic teaching on the end-time kingdom.

FIGURE 6.12. THE GOOD SAMARITAN

Although only a few verses in length, two crucial parables are given on the nature of the kingdom in Luke 13:18-20: the parable of the mustard seed and the parable of the yeast. Both communicate the strange idea that the end-time kingdom of God will not occur all at once, as the Old Testament generally expected, but will grow slowly, even at a snail's pace at times. Luke 19:11 even illustrates this point: "He went on to tell them a parable, because he was near Jerusalem and the people *thought that the kingdom of God was going to appear at once*." Daniel 2:44, a prominent text on the nature of the kingdom, claims on the surface that the end-time kingdom will apparently arrive in its fullness at once: "In the time of those kings, the God of heaven will set up a kingdom that will never be destroyed. . . . It will crush all those kingdoms and bring them to an end."

FIGURE 6.13. MUSTARD SEEDS

But Jesus argues that the latter-day kingdom will not arrive in a consummate manner in the present as the Old Testament and first-century Jews believed. Its fulfillment is mysterious (Lk 8:10).

God's end-time kingdom will not only entail slow growth throughout the world but will remain available to all, even the poor and outcast. Luke has woven this theme from the beginning of his Gospel and continues to do so in this section. For example, chapter 14 begins with a discourse on healing a diseased individual on the Sabbath (cf. Mk 3:1-6), and Jesus' words affirm this observation: "Is it lawful to heal on the Sabbath or not?" (Lk 14:3). The Jewish leaders are unable to give a response, and they refrain from speaking (14:6). Then, in 14:7, Jesus transitions into a parable about a wedding celebration (14:7-11), which is tied to the healing episode in 14:1-6 by an individual with dropsy. The man with an "abnormal swelling" would, to a certain degree, remain on the fringes of society (14:2). In the following parable (14:7-11), Jesus tugs on this thread and relates it to the nature of the kingdom, demonstrating how it relates to the pariahs of society.

Jesus claims that even though the Jewish leaders deserve (at least according to the cultural norms of the day) to sit in seats of honor, they are to choose the "lowest place" (Lk 14:10). Jesus' kingdom message inverts what the religious authorities cherish. The paradoxical nature of the kingdom corresponds to the paradoxical nature of Jesus' kingdom ethics: "All those who exalt themselves will be humbled, and those who humble themselves will be exalted" (14:11). Much of the remainder of this section in Luke discusses this theme from a variety of angles (14:15–17:19; 18:1–19:27). The journey to Jerusalem climaxes with Zacchaeus, the chief tax collector and the epitome of an outsider (19:1-9). As Mark Strauss points out, "Zacchaeus is the ultimate of Israel's outcasts—not just a tax collector but a chief tax collector, the worst among the worst. Yet Jesus reaches out and offers salvation even to him."[11]

JESUS' MINISTRY IN JUDEA AND JERUSALEM (19:28–24:53)

One tangible demonstration of trusting in God's wisdom and power is the act of prayer. At its core, prayer is an evidence of complete dependence on God as creator and provider. Old Testament saints and prophets often prayed to the Lord for help and provision.

[11]Mark L. Strauss, *Four Portraits, One Jesus: A Survey of Jesus and the Gospels* (Grand Rapids: Zondervan, 2007), 275.

Oftentimes, the nation of Israel requires intervention and deliverance from their enemies, so Israel's leaders petition to the Lord (e.g., Judg 6:36). Other expressions of prayer are found in situations wherein Old Testament saints yearn for God's blessing. One example of this is Hannah, who pleads for God to grant her a son who would be devoted to him "all the days of his life" (1 Sam 1:11). Confession of sin, both individual and corporate, is another key element of prayer. King David prays to God asking for forgiveness from his sin with Bathsheba (Ps 51), and prophets are seen praying for God to forgive Israel's transgressions (e.g., Dan 9; Ezra 9:5-6).

More than Matthew and Mark, Luke stresses Jesus' humanity and his utter dependence on the Father. One concrete expression of Jesus clinging closely to his Father is through prayer. Luke records Jesus praying approximately ten times at key events throughout his ministry. Jesus is found praying at his baptism (Lk 3:21), the appointment of the twelve disciples (6:12), Peter's confession (9:18), the transfiguration (9:28-29), the appointment of the seventy-two disciples (10:21), the discourse on the Lord's Prayer (11:1-4), the Last Supper (22:32), the garden of Gethsemane (22:41), and at the crucifixion (23:46). According to Luke's narrative, as his betrayal and death approaches, Jesus is found praying all the more. He is, according to Luke, the model "pray-er."[12] As the perfect Adam, Jesus trusts in the Father's sovereign hand guiding every step of the way.

The triumphal entry and God's judgment on Israel's temple (19:28–21:38). Jesus approaches two towns, Bethany and Bethphage, and makes final preparations for the triumphal entry. Jesus' arrival into Jerusalem for the Passover celebration is, thus far, the culmination of his ministry. All the major elements of his ministry relate to one another in this event. Although Luke does not explicitly link the event to Zechariah 9, as Matthew does, the connection is undeniable. Zechariah prophesied that Israel's king would arrive on a donkey, symbolizing peaceful rule. But such a peaceful rule is the result of a battle previously waged by Israel's Messiah: "See, your king comes to you, righteous and *victorious*" (Zech 9:9a). By coming on a donkey, Jesus symbolically declares that the battle has *already* been won, a testament to the importance of Jesus' victory over Satan during the wilderness temptation.

> ***The Old Testament and Judaism anticipated that God's end-time kingdom would arrive in its fullness and all at once, in contrast to Jesus inaugurating but not consummating the kingdom.***

Luke ties the crowd's citation of Psalm 118 to "the miracles they had seen," presumably on the journey from Galilee to Jerusalem (Lk 19:37). The "whole crowd of disciples" (19:37) identifies Jesus as the coming deliverer who will liberate them from bondage. Psalms 113–118 are referred to as Psalms of Hallel or the Egyptian Hallel (cf. Ps 104–6; 120–36; 146–50). In general, the Hallel psalms are sung on the Feast of Tabernacles, Pentecost, and the first day of Passover. This particular grouping of Psalms 113–118 recount Israel's release from

[12]David M. Crump, "Prayer," in Green et al., *Dictionary of Jesus and the Gospels*, 690.

MAP OF JERUSALEM AT THE TIME OF CHRIST

Egyptian captivity and anticipate a second and greater deliverance. As was common, the Jews attending the Passover celebration in Jerusalem sing the Egyptian Hallel as they venture to Zion (Zech 14:16).

The Third Gospel uniquely rounds out the triumphal entry with a heated exchange between Jesus and the Jewish leaders. Some Pharisees find fault with Jesus' disciples attributing politically charged Old Testament passages to Jesus of Nazareth (Lk 19:39). Jesus responds with a sobering prophecy about Israel's destruction in AD 70, an event that focuses on the ruin of the temple (19:41-44). The destruction of the temple will be unpacked in greater detail in chapter 21. The irony between Jesus' prediction of Israel's destruction and the Old Testament texts fulfilled in the triumphal entry cannot be missed: Zechariah 9 and Psalm 118 anticipate the Messiah defeating the pagan nations and restoring Israel, yet at the triumphal entry Jesus heralds the destruction of Israel and the restoration of the nations (Lk 20:16).

Jesus displays a concern for the nations to worship at Israel's temple by ridding the temple of those selling the sacrifices in the courtyard (Lk 19:45-46). The purpose of Israel's temple is to be "a house of prayer" (19:46). Jesus quotes Isaiah 56:7, a prophecy that the end-time temple would become a rallying place and location of prayer for the Gentiles (Is 56:3-8). Corrupted by Israel's wickedness, the temple prevented the nations from worship and has become a "den of robbers" (Lk 19:46; Jer 7:11). Jesus' actions pave the way for establishing the end-time temple, where the outcasts and Gentiles can assemble for worship.

The parable of the wicked tenants plays a central role in Passion Week, providing Jesus with the theological rationale for the destruction of Israel's physical temple and the installation of the new temple (Lk 20:9-19). Just as the wicked tenant farmers are destroyed because they do not tend the vineyard and murder the landowner's son, so Israel is destroyed because it fails to tend its vineyard and murder God's Son (20:16). As a result, God will destroy Israel's physical temple and establish a new temple through Jesus.

Jesus quotes Psalm 118:22, claiming to be the cornerstone of a new temple: "The stone the builders rejected *has become the cornerstone*" (Lk 20:17). By applying the cornerstone metaphor to himself, Jesus demonstrates his commitment to replacing Israel's physical structure with a new temple. Instead of dwelling in the confined room in a physical temple, God will now dwell in the midst of people through his Son. God's presence in the old, physical temple continues by dwelling in a more intimate way in the person of Jesus.

> ***According to Isaiah 2:2-3, Israel's temple is to be a rallying point for the Gentile nations to worship Israel's God in the latter days.***

Once Jesus quotes Psalm 118:22, he enigmatically declares, "Everyone who falls on that stone will be broken to pieces; anyone on whom it falls will be crushed" (Lk 20:18). The crushing stone highlights Jesus as the beginning of a new sanctuary since this graphic imagery comes from Daniel 2:34-35: "A stone was cut without hands, and it struck the statue . . . and crushed them" and they

FIGURE 6.14. MODEL OF THE SECOND TEMPLE

"became like chaff from the summer threshing floors; and the wind carried them away" (NASB). In Daniel 2 this stone is expected to destroy evil kingdoms and become "a huge mountain [that] filled the whole earth" (Dan 2:35). This latter-day stone in Daniel 2 grows into a mountain (Dan 2:28, 35), much like the growing temple in Isaiah 2:2.[13] Through his death and resurrection, Jesus, as the cornerstone, begins constructing God's end-time temple that will eventually encompass the entire earth in the new heavens and earth.

The triumphal entry (Lk 19:28-44) is the catalyst for Jesus' judgment on Israel's idolatrous temple (19:43-44; 21:1-38). As the Messiah and Israel's God incarnate, Jesus has come to judge the nation's idolatrous temple and establish the new end-time sanctuary. Much of Luke 21 concerns the destruction of the Jerusalem temple by the Romans in AD 70. Jesus predicts that "there will be signs in the sun, moon and stars. . . . The heavenly bodies will be shaken" (21:25-26; see fig. 6.15). The figurative depiction of cosmic destruction refers to the historical end of a sinful nation's existence through divine judgment and the emerging dominance of a victorious kingdom (e.g., Is 13:10-13; 34:4; Ezek 32:6-8; Hab 3:6-11). The conflagration of heavens mirrors the chaos on earth. One historical epoch is giving way to another. The language is appropriate here, where the nation of Israel has reached its end, giving way to a community of believers that finds its sole identity in Jesus.

[13]See G. K. Beale, *The Temple and the Church's Mission* (Downers Grove, IL: InterVarsity Press, 2004), 144-53.

Verse 21:27 explains that "they [the Israelites] will see the Son of Man coming in a cloud with power and great glory." This is a partial quotation of Daniel 7:13: "In my vision at night I looked, and there before me was one like a son of man, coming with the clouds of heaven." The reference to Daniel 7:13 in Luke 21:27 signals the direct fulfillment of the Son of Man's end-time judgment on the "fourth beast" (Dan 7:7, 11-12, 26), which is not a pagan nation, as Daniel envisions, but the nation of Israel. She has become as unfaithful and disobedient as faithless Gentile nations! The Son of Man's arrival ushers in the realization of the latter-day kingdom on earth and the restoration of the true people of God (Dan 7:22, 27). All those who follow Jesus of Nazareth, Jew or Gentile, rich or poor, will emerge victorious in AD 70 and be recognized as the restored Israel of God.

The Last Supper and Jesus' death and resurrection (22:1–24:12). The second major section of Passion Week concerns the celebration of the Passover meal and the culmination of Jesus' ministry in his death and resurrection. The institution of Passover finds its roots in the Exodus narrative, signifying God's redemption and deliverance (Ex 12). It is a reflection on God's defeat of Pharaoh and his army and an expectation of what he will do in the future. Jesus identifies himself as the ultimate Passover lamb who provides atonement for sin and as the Lord incarnate who will bring about Israel's redemption. Jesus is both the sacrificial lamb *and* Israel's God in the flesh (Lk 22:17-23).

At the tail end of the Passover celebration, Jesus predicts that Peter will indeed betray him (Lk 22:31-34). He assures Peter and the disciples that his imminent death accords with the Old Testament: "It is written: 'And he was numbered with the transgressors'; and I tell you that this must be fulfilled in me. Yes, *what is written about me is reaching its fulfillment*'" (22:37). In quoting Isaiah 53:12, Jesus identifies himself with Isaiah's suffering servant. Isaiah predicted that a servant, who embodies Israel, would suffer vicariously for Israel's sins and trigger the second exodus from captivity (Is 52:13–53:12). Jesus views himself as Isaiah's servant, knowing that he would bear the sin of others. Through death he will redeem those enslaved to spiritual bondage.

FIGURE 6.15. SIEGE AND DESTRUCTION OF JERUSALEM IN AD 70

Jesus takes his disciples to the Mount of Olives to pray in the garden of Gethsemane. Throughout Luke's narrative, Jesus prays at critical junctures of his ministry (e.g., Lk 3:21; 5:16; 6:12). As his death looms, he once again entrusts his life to the Father. Luke even records that an angel "appeared to him and strengthened him" (22:43). Shortly thereafter, Jesus is betrayed by Judas, arrested, and disowned by Peter (22:47-62).

Luke briefly narrates Jesus standing trial before the Sanhedrin, the official representative body of Israel. In response to a question concerning his kingship, Jesus responds with

FIGURE 6.16. GARDEN OF GETHSEMANE

an allusion to Daniel 7:13 and Psalm 110:1: "But from now on, *the Son of Man* will be *seated at the right hand* of the mighty God" (Lk 22:69). The council interprets Jesus' words as a claim to divinity (22:70) and accuses him of blasphemy (22:71; cf. Jn 19:7). The council hands him off to Pilate with the charge of sedition against Rome and deceiving Israel (Lk 23:2). After weighing the evidence, both Pilate and Herod determine that Jesus is innocent (23:4, 15). But, eventually, Pilate gives in to the demands of the Jewish leaders and the crowd (23:18-25).

Jesus is then mocked, beaten, and affixed to a cross between two criminals (Lk 23:26-43). Two strange events occur while Jesus hangs on the cross—the tearing of the veil and cosmic disturbance: "It was now about noon, and darkness came over the whole land until three in the afternoon, for the sun stopped shining. And the curtain of the temple was torn in two" (23:44-45). The rending of the veil symbolizes a cosmic and cultic reality: the initial destruction of the old creation and the beginning of the new creation. Now all believers, Jews and Gentiles, can enjoy God's glorious presence that was restricted to the backroom of Israel's temple. Immediately following Jesus' death and the tearing of the veil, a centurion—a Gentile—confesses, "Surely this was a *righteous man*" (23:47; cf. Mk 15:39). The soldier's words are reminiscent of Luke's emphasis on Jesus as the righteous and innocent servant of Isaiah throughout Passion Week, climaxing at the cross (Lk 22:37; Is 53:12). The prophetic vision of the nations streaming into the end-time temple (Is 2:2-3; Mic 4:1-3; Zech 14:16), led by God himself (Is 56:7), begins fulfillment in this Roman centurion's confession.

Jesus is soon buried (Lk 23:50-54). On the first day of the week, women visit the tomb. To their surprise, the stone is rolled away from the tomb, and Jesus' body is missing (24:1-3). Two angels greet the women, reminding them that Jesus told them repeatedly about his resurrection from the dead

FIGURE 6.17. PSALM 68

(24:4-8). The women believe and inform the eleven disciples about what they experienced, yet the disciples refuse to believe their report (24:9-12).

Jesus as the fulfillment of the Old Testament (24:13-53). Luke is the only Evangelist to narrate the story of Jesus talking with two of his followers on the way to Emmaus (Lk 24:13-27). Their interaction climaxes with Jesus castigating the two disciples for not expecting his crucifixion and resurrection (24:25-27). Jesus could have drawn their attention to his repeated predictions that he would die and come back to life (9:44; 18:33); instead, he brings the Old Testament to bear: "'How foolish you are, and how slow to believe *all that the prophets have spoken*! Did not the Messiah have to suffer these things and then enter his glory?' And beginning with *Moses* and all *the Prophets*, he explained to them what was said *in all the Scriptures concerning himself*" (24:25-27).

The Old Testament and Judaism symbolically depict the curtains of the temple, the outer and inner veils, as small-scale portrayals of the entire universe, particularly the visible and invisible heavenly dimensions (e.g., Ex 26:36; Philo, Quaest. Exod. 2.85).

From the beginning of his Gospel, Luke has recalled portions of the Old Testament to demonstrate that every aspect of Jesus' ministry corresponds to all of Israel's story. When examined in light of the Old Testament, Jesus and his ministry contain some surprising elements—Jesus is Israel's God incarnate; his kingdom is marked not by political rule but by suffering; he, as Israel's Messiah, comes under God's curse; he rises from the dead, apart from the corporate resurrection of the saints, and so on. Although somewhat different from expectations, Jesus still expects these two disciples to anticipate his death in resurrection by meditating on the Old Testament.

As Luke draws his narrative to a close, Jesus dines with the two disciples (Lk 24:28-32) and then with the eleven (24:36-43). Jesus reminds the eleven that "Everything must be fulfilled that is written about me in the Law of Moses, the Prophets and the Psalms" (24:44). Luke ends his Gospel with a brief summary of Jesus' ascension and with the disciples worshiping him as Israel's God incarnate (24:52). As C. Kavin Rowe notes, "The narration of the life of Jesus is thus for Luke the revelation of God, as story and revelation are woven together in the reading of the Gospel."[14] Luke opens his Gospel with a promise to reveal how the Old Testament is fulfilled in the person of Jesus (Lk 1:1). By the end of the Gospel, we can agree that Luke has indeed made good on his promise.

[14]C. Kavin Rowe, *Early Narrative Christology: The Lord in the Gospel of Luke* (Berlin: Walter de Gruyter, 2006; repr., Grand Rapids: Baker, 2009), 218.

7

THE GOSPEL OF JOHN

AUTHORSHIP

Determining the authorship of the Fourth Gospel is particularly complex. It claims to be written by the "disciple whom Jesus loved" (Jn 13:23; 19:26; 20:2; 21:20) who "testifies to these things and who wrote them down" (21:24). The difficulty lies in identifying this individual with one of the Twelve or with another member of the early church. When we examine the evidence within John's Gospel, the beloved disciple appears to be an insider, a member of the twelve disciples, an apostolic eyewitness of Jesus' deeds and miracles (21:24).

FIGURE 7.1. ST. JOHN

The beloved disciple participates in the Passover celebration during Passion Week (Jn 13:23), and the three Synoptics mention only the twelve disciples (Mt 26:17-30; Mk 14:12-26; Lk 22:7-23), thus limiting our investigation to the Twelve. Key to identifying the beloved disciple is to distinguish him from Peter and the other disciples. As D. A. Carson and Douglas Moo note, "That he is one of the seven who go fishing in chapter 21 and, by implication, is not Peter, Thomas, or Nathanael, suggests he is one of the sons of Zebedee or one of the other two unnamed disciples (21:2)."[1] James and John are the "sons of Zebedee" (Mt 10:2; Mk 1:19; Lk 5:10), and since James is martyred in Acts 12:1-2, John the apostle is the only remaining option. Taking a look at the evidence external to the Fourth Gospel, many within the early church identified the author as John, the son of Zebedee (e.g., Irenaeus, *Against Heresies* 3.1.1). Therefore, the author of the Fourth Gospel is most likely the apostle John, the son of Zebedee.

[1]D. A. Carson and Douglas J. Moo, *An Introduction to the New Testament*, 2nd. ed. (Grand Rapids: Zondervan, 2005), 237.

DATE

Since Peter's death is assumed in John 21:18-19, John must have been written after AD 64–65, the approximate time of Peter's death. The destruction of the temple in AD 70, a momentous event in Israel's history, receives little or no discussion, meaning that it either remains in the future or that significant time has passed since its destruction. Lastly, if we read John's Gospel alongside the Johannine epistles, it is possible to interpret the three epistles as a response to an aberrant interpretation of this published Gospel. Taken together, these observations suggest that the Fourth Gospel was probably published in the 80s or perhaps later.

PURPOSE

In John 20:30-31, the author explicitly mentions the purpose of his Gospel: "These [accounts of Jesus' signs] are written that you may believe that Jesus is the Messiah, the Son of God, and that by believing you may have life in his name." The Gospel of John is intended to deepen the faith of Jewish Christians and reach unbelievers by setting forth Jesus of Nazareth as Israel's Messiah and the divine Son of God, who has come to redeem humanity and creation.

OUTLINE

John's broad outline differs from the Synoptics on a number of levels. Whereas the Synoptics generally organize Jesus' ministry according to geography (Galilee, the road to Jerusalem, and the city of Jerusalem), John breaks down Jesus' ministry into two halves: the Book of Signs (1:19–12:50) and the Book of Passion (13:1–20:31). The first half demonstrates Jesus' identity as Israel's Messiah and the divine Son of God, and the second half brings both of these identities to bear on the cross and resurrection. John also devotes far more material to Passion Week, nearly half of his Gospel. By doing so, we learn much more about Jesus' interaction with his disciples, his relationship to the Father and the Spirit, and the crucifixion and resurrection.

- I. Prologue (1:1-18)
  - A. Jesus as the Spoken Word (1:1-5)
  - B. Jesus as the Light and the Temple (1:6-18)
- II. The Book of Signs (1:19–12:50)
  - A. Jesus' Public Ministry in Judea, Galilee, and Samaria (1:19–4:54)
  - B. Jewish Hostility Toward Jesus and the Triumphal Entry (5:1–12:50)
  - C. Anointed for Burial and the Triumphal Entry (12:1-50)
- III. Book of the Passion (13:1–20:31)
  - A. The Final Passover Celebration (13:1–17:26)
  - B. Jesus Is Tried, Crucified, and Buried (18:1–19:42)
  - C. Resurrection and Disbelief (20:1-31)
- IV. Epilogue (21:1-25)

BIBLICAL-THEOLOGICAL THEMES IN JOHN'S GOSPEL

Jewish festivals and holy days. One theme running through John's Gospel is his emphasis on the annual, symbolic feasts and holy days of the Jewish calendar (e.g., Jn 2:13; 5:1; 6:4; 7:37; 12:12; 13:1). These events emblazon God's past provision and his future promises on the hearts of the Israelites. Israel's festivals and holy days contain within them, to a varying degree, a prophetic pattern. That is, the symbolic elements prophetically anticipate a future time when God will liberate Israel at the very end of the age.

Three pilgrim festivals and the Day of Atonement constitute the more prominent ones. Each year, adult males are required to attend three festivals in Jerusalem—Passover, Weeks, and Booths. Each of these feasts is tied to Israel's land and livestock.

Passover begins at sunset on the fourteenth day of the first month of the Jewish calendar (Nisan 14) and is intimately bound to Israel's exodus from Egypt (Ex 12–13; Num 9:1-15). The festival celebrates the time when God redeems Israel from slavery and "passed over" those who applied the blood of a lamb to their doorposts. The feast of Weeks (also called Pentecost or Firstfruits) takes place seven weeks after the first harvest of barley (Deut 16:9). The feast becomes known as Pentecost since it occurred roughly fifty days after Passover (Acts 2:1). This festival highlights God's gracious provision of food from the land. By the time of the first century, this feast develops into a celebration of God giving the law to Moses (Jub. 6:17-22). The Feast of Booths (or Tabernacles), known as "the feast," is celebrated for seven days (plus a day of rest) in the autumn. The Israelites rehearse the wilderness wanderings by living in booths (*sukkot*) and offering up a great deal of sacrifices (Lev 23:34-43; Deut 16:13).

As time progressed, these feasts take on more significance and become more elaborate. In the first century, although Israel dwells in the Promised Land, the Israelites yearned for complete independence and renewal. These feasts symbolically look back and look forward. John's Gospel highlights these Jewish festivals more so than the Synoptic writers. Why does John go out of his way to mention the Jewish festivals? The answer lies in how they connect to the person of Jesus.

FIGURE 7.2. ISRAEL ENSLAVED IN EGYPT

We may take a cue from John 6, in which Jesus relates the feeding of the five thousand to the Passover and the manna in the wilderness wanderings (Jn 6:4, 32-58). In 6:4, John states that the "Passover Festival was near." As Jesus feeds the five thousand, he rehearses a Passover celebration with true Israel. But this meal also recalls Israel's wilderness wanderings when the Lord nourished his people. Jesus claims to be the ultimate bread and drink that give life (6:48-51, 53-58). Jesus here places himself as the ultimate fulfillment of the Passover celebration and manna of the wilderness wanderings: "My flesh is *real* food and my blood is *real* drink" (6:55). Israel expects the Lord to deliver them from Rome through the Messiah. Jesus not only claims to be the Messiah who will liberate Israel but also God incarnate (6:40-42). Andreas J. Köstenberger notes that "John taps deeply into the matrix of OT traditions in his effort to show Jesus as the fulfillment and replacement of the major institutions of Judaism. This includes holy days such as the Sabbath as well as festivals like Passover and Tabernacles."[2] As the Fourth Gospel unfolds, John simultaneously presents Jesus as the typological fulfillment of Israel's feasts and holy days and the God of Israel who promised to do so.

The Son of Man. The title *Son of Man*, found approximately eighty-two times in the Gospels, thirteen of which are found in John, is Jesus' favorite way of explaining his mission and identity. The enigmatic title should be understood against the Old Testament background of Adam and Israel deemed to be God's "son." The Gospel writers even quote, on a few occasions, Daniel 7:13 in conjunction with the expression "Son of Man" (e.g., Mt 24:30-31; Mk 13:26; 14:62; Lk 21:27). According to Daniel 7, four beasts, representing four hostile empires, emerge and wage war with one another and persecute God's people. The sea is the embodiment of evil and rebellion. Four kingdoms consume one another sequentially—Medo-Persia, Babylon, Greece, and Rome (Dan 7:3-8). These kingdoms are grotesque, symbolizing their arrogance and destructive nature.

The vision in Daniel 7 then shifts to heaven, where God is depicted as the "Ancient of Days" with white hair, sitting on a heavenly throne with wheels. God then metes out judgment on the four beasts (Dan 7:11-12). One like a "son of man" (i.e., a human being) comes up to the Ancient of Days on a cloud and is granted the eternal kingdom (7:13-14). Throughout the Old Testament, riding on the clouds is reserved for God alone (Ex 19:9; Ezek 1:4; Ps 18:11; 68:4; 104:3). Thus, the son of man is an enigmatic divine figure who approaches the Ancient of Days.[3] The son of man then receives a royal inheritance: "He was *given* authority, glory and sovereign power; all nations and peoples of every language worshiped him. His dominion is an *everlasting dominion* that will not pass away, and his kingdom is one that will never be destroyed" (Dan 7:14).

FIGURE 7.3. DANIEL AND THE WRITING ON THE WALL

Perhaps the reason why the heavenly figure is described as a "son of man" stems from the close identification this figure has with Israel. The son of man receives "authority,

[2]Andreas J. Köstenberger, *A Theology of John's Gospel and Letters* (Grand Rapids: Zondervan, 2009), 422.

[3]Seyoon Kim, *"The Son of Man" as the Son of God: A Selection*, WUNT 30 (Tübingen: J. C. B. Mohr [Paul Siebeck], 1983; repr., Eugene, OR: Wipf & Stock, 2011), 22-25.

glory and sovereign power," "an everlasting dominion," and a "kingdom" (Dan 7:14). According to the second half of the vision, the figure of the son of man is replaced by the righteous remnant of Israel, which will "receive the kingdom and will possess it forever" (7:18; see 7:22, 27). In other words, the son of man and the remnant of Israel are to be identified with one another. The second portion of the vision identifies the son of man as the "holy people" of Israel.

Often in the Old Testament, kings or prominent figures represent the nation or a large group (Josh 7:1-5; 1 Chron 21:1-17; 2 Sam 21:1). Here the son of man represents the righteous Israelites (hence the phrase "son of *man*"). When he conquers the fourth and final beast, his actions are transferred to the group. The remnant is in a position to receive the kingdom since the son of man, their representative, has vanquished their enemy. Conversely, what is true of the righteous Israelites is also true of the son of man. For example, Daniel 7:21 says, "As I watched, this horn was *waging war against the holy people and defeating them.*" Here the remnant is coming under severe persecution, suggesting that the son of man will also suffer.

The background of Daniel 7 illuminates Jesus' favorite self-designation in the four Gospels. The title *Son of Man* may also refer to Jesus' relationship to Adam. The expression in Greek could also be rendered as "the Son of *the* Man."[4] By bridging his ministry to Adam, Jesus consciously repeats Adam's life and succeeds where he failed. Adam failed to subdue creation, but now the Son of Man will succeed. Jesus' declaration that "now is the time for judgment on this world; now the prince of this world will be driven out" (Jn 12:31) fulfills the son of man's judgment on the beasts in Daniel 7 and Adam's failure to subdue the serpent in the garden.

PROLOGUE (1:1-18)

The Gospel of John not only weaves Jesus into the story of Israel's redemption, promises, and expectations but also places him at the center of a cosmic drama. Matthew and Luke introduce Jesus through genealogies, and Mark remains nearly silent about Jesus' origin. John, however, rereads Genesis 1–2 and situates Jesus squarely in the narrative as the agent of creation. As the divine Son of God, Jesus has come to deliver humanity from "darkness" and usher in the new creation. John goes out of his way to connect Jesus to Israel's institutions, especially her temple and the festivals. Those who believe in Jesus as the climax of Israel's history and the divine Son of God are granted eternal life in the new creation, the same life that the Old Testament prophets predicted would happen at the end of the age, when God resurrects all the saints.

John introduces Jesus of Nazareth by identifying him with the "Word" (*logos*) and with the eternal God ("and the Word was with God"; Jn 1:1). Jesus, as the Word, was not only with God "in the beginning" (1:1-2) but was also instrumental in creating all things (1:3). Since Jesus has the ability to create, he possesses the ability to save and give life to those in darkness (1:4-5). John the Baptist testifies that Jesus is indeed the light who has come to redeem humanity (1:6-8). The God of the patriarchs who revealed himself in a remarkable way now reveals himself

[4]Joel Marcus, "Son of Man as Son of Adam," *RB* 110 (2003): 38-61.

more fully in Jesus (1:18). Jesus is preeminently set forth in John's Gospel as revealing the Father in word and deed.

Jesus created all things, including Israelites who remain hostile to him and reject his identity and ministry (1:9-11). Although the majority of Israel will forsake him, Jesus grants the status of true Israel to those who believe in him (1:12-13). As the eternal Word (1:1), Jesus houses God's glory, the same glory that dwelled with the Israelites in the wilderness and the Promised Land (1:14). The Old Testament, especially, the Mosaic covenant, anticipates Christ (1:16-17). The God of the Old Testament has now come down in the person of Jesus Christ (1:18). These three dominant themes in the prologue—Jesus as creator, temple, and fulfillment of the Old Testament—set the stage for John's depiction of the life of Christ.

Jesus as the spoken Word (1:1-5). Compared to the Synoptics, John's Gospel begins very differently. Matthew and Luke begin with Jesus as an infant, whereas Mark moves right into Jesus' adulthood. Within John's prologue, Jesus, as the "Word," is immediately identified with God "in the beginning." In John 1:1-5, two aspects of Jesus are highlighted: his identification with the eternal God and his role in creation. John's prologue begins with an explicit recollection of the creation narrative:

> *In the beginning* God created the heavens and the earth. Now the earth was formless and empty, darkness was over the surface of the deep, and the Spirit of God was hovering over the waters.
>
> And God *said*, "Let there be light," and there was light. God saw that the light was good, and he separated the light from the darkness. God *called* the light "day," and the darkness he called "night." And there was evening, and there was morning—the first day.
>
> And God *said*, "Let there be a vault between the waters to separate water from water." So God made the vault and separated the water under the vault from the water above it. And it was so. God *called* the vault "sky." And there was evening, and there was morning—the second day.
>
> And God *said*, "Let the water under the sky be gathered to one place, and let dry ground appear." (Gen 1:1-9; cf. 1:11-30)

Throughout the creation narrative, God is often found "speaking." It is no coincidence that John labels Jesus as the Word, the revelation of Israel's God. As the ultimate expression of life and the creator of it, Jesus has now come into the world to establish the new creation and offer life to those who trust in him. John's prologue reveals that Jesus is the commencing of another creative act—the "new" creation. Jesus is the source of life and the creative light (Jn 1:4) that "shines in the darkness." And just as the first light in Genesis 1 is not swallowed up by the darkness, so Jesus as the light is not dimmed by the surrounding darkness (1:5).

Jesus as the light and temple (1:6-18). In John 1:5-13, Jesus is figuratively portrayed as the light. This designation is generally unique to John's gospel (cf. Mt 4:16) and anticipates the remainder of the narrative (Jn 3:19-21; 8:12; 9:5; 11:9; 12:35-36, 46). The strong dualism between light and darkness are Old Testament (e.g., Gen 1:3; Ex 13:21) and Jewish concepts (e.g., 1QS I, 9; II, 16; 1QM I, 11). The term *light*, referring to the revelation of salvation to *all* of humanity, is applied to Jesus as the antithesis of darkness, symbolizing humanity's plight and satanic opposition.

FIGURE 7.4. MODEL OF ISRAEL'S TABERNACLE IN THE WILDERNESS

John transitions from depicting Jesus as the light to the house of God's glory, the temple: "The Word became flesh and *made his dwelling among us*. We have seen his glory, *the glory of the one and only Son*, who came from the Father, full of grace and truth" (Jn 1:14). The term *dwelling* is peculiar and could be rendered as *tabernacled*, a term that is used in the wilderness wanderings.

As the glory of God filled Israel's tabernacle (Ex 40:34-35), so too the glory of God tabernacles in Jesus. The tabernacle typologically corresponds to the person of Jesus. The presence of God, formerly contained in the holy of holies, has begun to burst forth into the world in the form of Jesus incarnate. Jesus reveals to Nathanael that "you will see 'heaven open, and the angels of God ascending and descending on' the Son of Man" (Jn 1:51). He recalls God's appearance to Jacob at Bethel and the building of the altar, a temporary sanctuary of sorts. Jacob's stairway fused heaven and earth (Gen 28:12). Jesus claims to be the stairway of Genesis 28, asserting that he, not the Jerusalem temple, is the true link between heaven and earth. Jacob's small sanctuary in Genesis 28 pointed forward to the permanent temple of the new creation with Jesus as the centerpiece. The locus of God's presence has shifted away from the Jerusalem temple to the person of Jesus. John's Gospel does not include an account of Jesus' transfiguration, one of the most theologically rich events in Jesus' ministry, perhaps because "Jesus' entire ministry was a transfiguration, a revelation of God's glory."[5]

> ***When Israel left Sinai, God commands Israel to build the mobile tabernacle so that his glorious presence would continue to dwell in their midst during their wilderness wanderings (Ex 25:8).***

THE BOOK OF SIGNS (1:19–12:50)

Adam and Eve's fall necessitates that humanity's image be cleansed to dwell in God's presence. Ezekiel 36:25-27 explains, "I will sprinkle *clean water on you*, and you will be clean. . . . I will give you a new heart and put a new spirit in you. . . . And *I will put my Spirit in you* and move you to follow my decrees and be careful to keep my laws." According to these verses and to the wider context of Ezekiel 36–37, the prophet predicts that Israel will experience a future spiritual resurrection when they return from Babylonian exile at the end of the age. The Israelites must be renewed not only in spirit but also in body to experience God's glory in the new creation.

Nicodemus, a member of the Jewish ruling council, asks Jesus about becoming "born

[5]Craig S. Keener, "John, Gospel of," in *Dictionary of Jesus and the Gospels*, ed. C. S. Green, Joel B. Green, Jeannine K. Brown, and Nicholas Perrin, 2nd ed. (Downers Grove, IL: InterVarsity Press, 2013), 430.

again" (Jn 3:3-4). Jesus declares that only those who are "born of water and the Spirit" can "enter the kingdom of God" (3:5). He then reprimands Nicodemus for his ignorance in the matter: "You should not be surprised at my saying, 'You must be born again'" (3:7; cf. 3:10). Nicodemus should have recognized Jesus' signs that testify to the initial fulfillment of Ezekiel's end-time prophecies, when Israel would be sprinkled with water and given the Spirit (Ezek 36:25-27; cf. Jn 3:2).

The first half of the Fourth Gospel, the Book of Signs, demonstrates Jesus' identity as the divine Son of God and Israel's Messiah through miracles and exchanges with the disciples, crowds, and Israel's elite. John's prologue establishes Jesus' identity, whereas the Book of Signs works out this initial identification in more detail. John's emphasis on Jesus as the fulfillment of God's promises, the culmination of Israel's history, is striking. Like the Synoptics, John connects Jesus with the story of Israel. Yet the Fourth Gospel fleshes out these connections to the Old Testament in greater detail and makes explicit what the Synoptics imply. Jesus has come to restore humanity and creation.

John also keeps track of the sequence of events from John 1:19–2:1. He is careful point out the timing of these events in using the expression "the next day" (1:29, 35, 43) or "on the third day" (2:1). If we tally up the days, we arrive at the number six. Why would John frame these initial events within six days? As Edward Klink points out, John probably does so to present the beginning of Jesus' ministry as the beginning of the new creation.[6] God creates the heavens and earth in six days according to Genesis 1–2, and now his Son begins to establish the new heavens and earth in six days.

Jesus' public ministry in Judea, Galilee, and Samaria (1:19–4:54). Following the prologue, John works out the relationship between John the Baptist and Jesus. John the Baptist is not the Messiah but merely the one who testifies to Israel's King (Jn 1:19-28). Yet John the Baptist recognizes that Jesus is not only Israel's King but also the Passover sacrifice who will liberate those Israelites who are captive to sin (1:29). John the Baptist said, "A man who comes after me has surpassed me because *he was before me*" (1:30, emphasis added). In light of John 1:1-2, it is possible that John the Baptist could be tacitly acknowledging Jesus' preexistence.

After denying his identity as Israel's Messiah to the Jewish rulers (Jn 1:19-22), John

FIGURE 7.5. MOSES DISPLAYS SIGNS BEFORE PHARAOH

[6]Edward W. Klink III, *John*, ZECNT (Grand Rapids: Zondervan, 2016), 161-62.

identifies his ministry with the "voice" of Isaiah 40:3. John views himself as the herald of the Lord's restoration of Israel from Babylonian captivity. Isaiah 40–66 describes Israel's release from Babylonian captivity as a second exodus (40:10-11; 51:9; 52:10), the journey to the Promised Land (49:9), and the creation of a new heavens and earth (65:17-25; 66:22-23), all of which will take place through Isaiah's servant (42:1-9, 49:1-6, 50:4-9, 52:13–53:12). John, as the "voice," bears witness to Jesus. A few verses later, John the Baptist declares Jesus to be the "Lamb of God, who takes away the sin of the world" (Jn 1:29). The phrase "Lamb of God" evokes the Passover celebration, whereby the Israelites sacrifice a lamb and smear its blood on the lintels of their doors, so that the Lord would "pass over" them (Ex 12:46; cf. Jn 19:36). "Lamb of God" also echoes Isaiah 53:7-12, in which the servant figure is a "lamb [led] to the slaughter" in order to bear "the sin of many." As the God of Israel incarnate, Jesus comes to rescue Israel from spiritual bondage as the supreme Passover lamb (Jn 1:29-34).

Throughout the Old Testament and Judaism, wine and feasting celebrate the establishment of the new creation.

Chapter 1 focuses on the first crop of disciples, climaxing in Jesus' declaration that he is the gateway to heaven: "He then added, 'Very truly I tell you, you will see "heaven open, and the angels of God ascending and descending on" the Son of Man'" (Jn 1:51). Jesus has in mind Genesis 28:12: "He had a dream in which he saw a stairway resting on the earth, with its top reaching to heaven, and *the angels of God were ascending and descending on it*." Jacob dreams about angels ascending and descending on a stairway, serving as a point of access to God. Genesis 28:17 states, "He was afraid and said, 'How awesome is this place! This is none other than the house of God; this is the gate of heaven.'" By referencing Genesis 28:12, Jesus claims that he is indeed the locus of God's glory, the new temple, and gateway to God.

Jesus and several of his disciples attend a wedding at Cana, just west of the Sea of Galilee (Jn 2:1-2). Once notified that the wine had run out, Jesus tells the servants to fill up six pots with water (2:3-8). The sheer volume of these pots is staggering: twenty to thirty gallons each! When Jesus tells these servants to fill the jars with water, they "filled them to the brim," a subtle acknowledgement to the abundance of the water/wine. The headwaiter tastes the water miraculously turned into wine (2:9-10). But this wine is unlike what had come earlier during the wedding feast—it is far better.

The Old Testament often speaks figuratively of wine served at a great banquet. For example, Isaiah 25:6 says, "On this mountain the Lord Almighty will prepare a feast of rich food for all peoples, a banquet of aged wine—the best of meats and the *finest of wines*" (cf. also Jer 31:12-14; Hos 14:7; Joel 3:18; Amos 9:13-14). This banquet is to occur when God restores Israel at the end of the age and create a new heavens and earth.

Jesus symbolically uses this miracle to affirm that the new creation and the restoration of all things have indeed dawned in his ministry (cf. Mk 2:19-22). Recall that John

1:19–2:1 presents the events occurring in six days. Just as God created the cosmos in six days, so now Jesus begins the creation of a new cosmos in his first six days. Turning water into wine with six stone jars is therefore the climactic event of Jesus' first week of ministry and the richest expression of the arrival of the new creation.

John parenthetically adds that this miracle in Cana is the beginning of his signs (Jn 2:11). The Gospel of John contains seven signs: turning water into wine (Jn 2:1-12), the healing of the official's son (4:43-54), the healing at the pool (5:1-45), the feeding of the five thousand (6:1-15), walking on water (6:16-24), the healing of the blind man (9:1-12), and raising Lazarus (11:1-44). One could also make a good case for an eighth and final sign—the crucifixion and resurrection of Jesus. A "sign," according to the Fourth Gospel, therefore, is a symbolic demonstration of Jesus' identity as God's Son.

Such signs elicit two responses: belief and further unbelief. In the exodus, God poured out his ten plagues or "signs" upon Egypt. These signs clearly demonstrated God's incomparable power and unique character. For example, Exodus 7:3-5 reads, "I will harden Pharaoh's heart, and though I multiply my *signs and wonders* in Egypt, he will not listen to you. Then I will lay my hand on Egypt and with mighty acts of judgment I will bring out my divisions, my people the Israelites. And the Egyptians will know that I am the Lord when I stretch out my hand against Egypt and bring the Israelites out of it" (cf. Ex 4:9, 17; 10:1-2; Deut 4:34; see fig. 7.5).

Despite God displaying his might through the signs, the majority of Israel fail to understand their significance and trust in his promises. Deuteronomy 29:2-4 is critical in

FIGURE 7.6. JACOB'S LADDER AS THE GATEWAY TO HEAVEN

this regard: "Your eyes have seen all that the Lord did in Egypt to Pharaoh, to all his officials and to all his land. With your own eyes you saw those great trials, those *signs and great wonders*. But to this day the Lord has not given you a mind that understands or eyes that see or ears that hear." True perception of signs and wonders operates on a spiritual level. Jesus, as Israel's God incarnate, is once again bringing his people out of bondage through signs and wonders. Like the first exodus, the majority of the Israelites perceive that Jesus is unique yet fail to trust his message. Only a few will truly perceive their meaning and trust his claims.

Chapter 1 could be understood as a lengthy testimony to the person of Jesus—his identity and his mission. John the Baptist testifies to Jesus (1:6, 15, 19, 23, 32, 34), followed by the testimony of Andrew, Philip, and Nathanael (1:41, 45, 49). The miracle at Cana could thus be viewed as Jesus' self-affirmation of his identity. Signs, in other words, are tangible expressions of Jesus' own testimony to his person and mission.

FIGURE 7.7. TYRIAN SHEKELS

Since Jesus has ushered in the new age and God's presence is among his people, there is no need for the physical temple, despite Herod's resplendent renovation. Indeed, the temple itself has become a place of rampant idolatry. The time is ripe for God to judge the temple. While in Jerusalem to celebrate Passover (Jn 2:13), Jesus enters the temple complex. The Fourth Gospel places Jesus' "cleansing" of the temple at the beginning of his ministry, whereas the Synoptics narrate the event during Passion Week. Whether this event occurs twice or John decided to place it at the beginning of Jesus' ministry makes little difference. The point is that Israel's temple is riddled with idolatry, and Jesus intends on meting out judgment. Instead of serving as a place to worship the Lord and welcome the Gentile nations (Mk 11:17), the temple has become a bastion of pride and financial gain.

John tells us that Jesus is "in the temple courts" when he discovers people selling cattle, sheep, and doves (Jn 2:14). This is called the "court of the Gentiles." The Jews are to bring their sacrifices to the temple, but since these pilgrims travel great distances to celebrate the Passover, it was permitted that they could purchase them at the temple. It was often too much trouble to bring them on the journey. Diaspora Jews also needed to exchange their currency to Tyrian currency, which is accepted by the temple authorities because of its purity (silver). The currency exchange came with a price, so they taxed the exchange. In a word, the Jewish authorities exploited these pilgrims.

The financial side of the temple is more pronounced in John than the accounts in the Synoptics: "To those who sold doves he said, 'Get these out of here! Stop turning my Father's house into a market!'" (Jn 2:16). Jesus' actions are highly symbolic, intended to disrupt the function of the temple. As N. T. Wright notes, "Without the temple-tax, the regular daily sacrifices could not be supplied. Without the right money, individual worshipers could not purchase their sacrificial animals. Without animals, sacrifices could not be offered. Without the sacrifice, the Temple had lost its whole reason for existing."[7] Either during or immediately after this event, the disciples remember an Old Testament text: "Zeal for your house will consume me" (Jn 2:17). This Old Testament text, Psalm 69:9, describes the persecuted King David and his passion for righteousness and the temple (Ps 69:4, 14-19). It is possible that "zeal" could refer to the idolatrous "zeal" for the temple expressed by the religious

[7]N. T. Wright, *Jesus and the Victory of God* (Minneapolis: Fortress, 1996), 423.

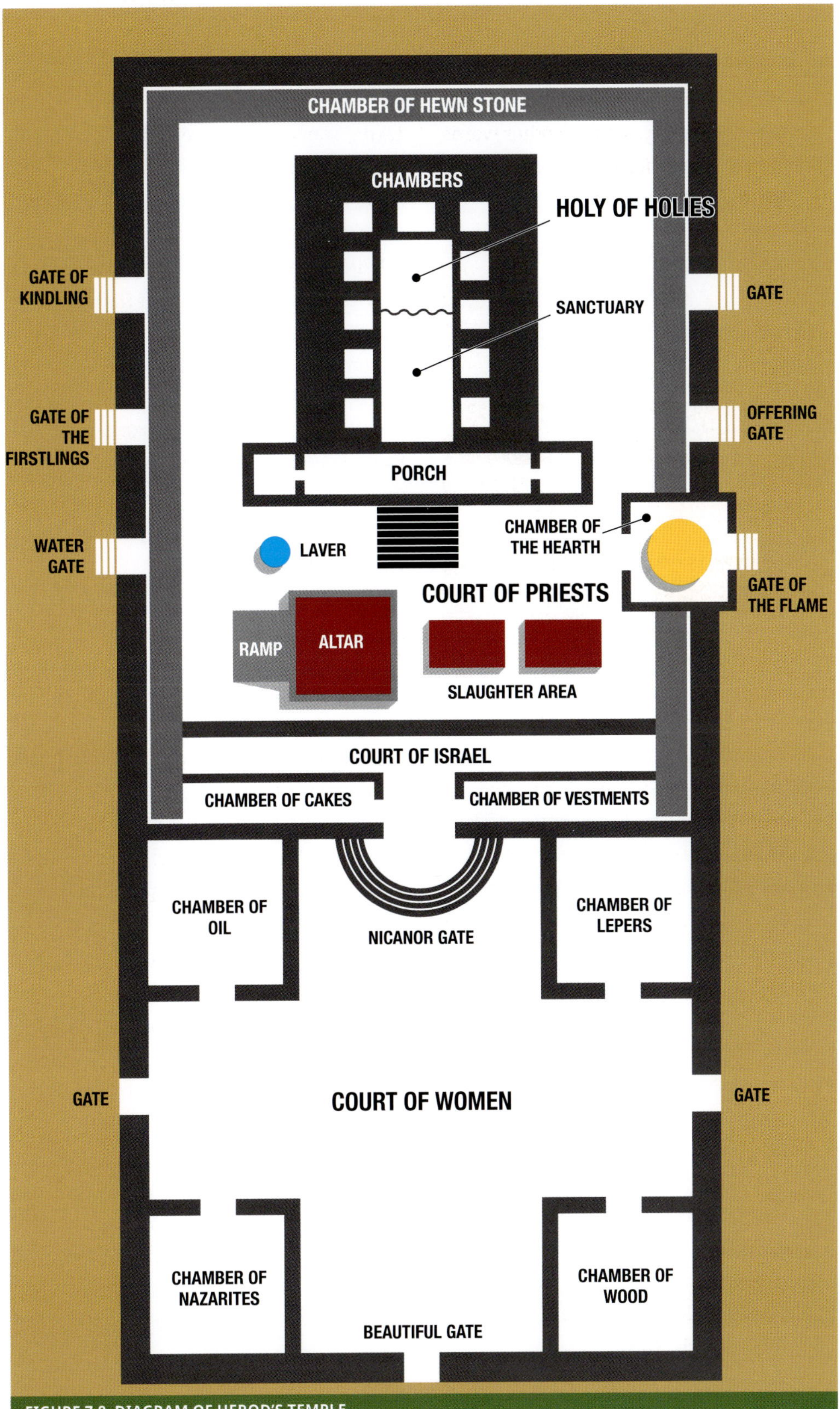

FIGURE 7.8. DIAGRAM OF HEROD'S TEMPLE

authorities who are responsible for putting Jesus to death.[8] David's actions typologically anticipate Jesus' actions in the temple. As a greater David, Jesus possesses the authority to judge the temple and render it defunct.

At the very end of history, God promises to pour out "water" and the "Spirit" on his people in order to create them anew (Ezek 36:25-27).

Aghast at Jesus' actions, the Jewish authorities demand to see a sign from Jesus that gave him the right to judge the temple (Jn 2:18). Jesus tells them that his death and resurrection will give him the authority to overthrow the temple and inaugurate a new one (2:18-21). He explicitly claims to be God's end-time temple: "'Destroy this temple, and I will raise it again in three days.' . . . *But the temple he had spoken of was his body*" (2:19-21). The Old Testament expectation for God to dwell with people in the new creation has now begun to be remarkably fulfilled in Jesus, the epicenter of God's tabernacling presence on earth.

FIGURE 7.9. LIFTING UP THE BRAZEN SERPENT

Now that John has established Jesus' identity in the first two chapters—his unique, divine relationship with Israel's God; the Passover sacrifice; Israel's Messiah; and the end-time temple—he expounds on the universality of Jesus' message. Jesus has come to save those in darkness.

John 3 and 4 demonstrate the need for all to believe in Jesus, including Israel's ruling class (Nicodemus), a Samaritan woman, and political royalty (Jn 3:1–4:54). The new creation and God's presence do not discriminate; all that is required is belief in Jesus' message and identity. Chapter 3 largely details Jesus' interaction with Nicodemus, a "member of the Jewish ruling council" (3:1). Nicodemus comes to Jesus at night, perhaps a symbolic reference to his current state of living in darkness (1:5). Much of the interaction concerns the new life that rests on the person of Jesus—a doctrine that squares with the Old Testament (3:10, 14-15). Jesus explains that being "born again" fulfills the resurrection prophecy from Ezekiel 36–37.

On his way back to Galilee, Jesus travels through Samaria, a region undesirable to the Jews, who deem the Samaritans unclean, particularly the women: "Samaritan women are deemed menstruants from their cradle" (m. *Nid.* 4.1). Samaritans also believe that the

[8]See Steven M. Bryan, "Consumed by Zeal: John's Use of Psalm 69:9 and the Action in the Temple," *BBR* 21 (2011): 479-94.

temple should be located at Mount Gerizim, not Jerusalem. On the whole, Jews and Samaritans despise one another and limit their interaction as much as possible. Despite these cultural issues, Jesus approaches the woman at the well. His offer of redemption even extends to the Samaritans. By offering living water to the Samaritan woman (Jn 4:14), Jesus is beginning to construct the new temple from which true life in God's presence dwells. Later on in John's Gospel, "living water" is tied to God's presence that is now found in Jesus (7:38). Jesus shifts the discussion from a place of worship ("neither on this mountain nor in Jerusalem" [4:21]) to a manner of worship ("true worshipers will worship the Father in the Spirit and in truth" [4:23]). God's presence will no longer be located in the holy of holies of Israel's temple but instead will break out of its architectural shackles and spread throughout the earth.

Jewish hostility toward Jesus and the triumphal entry (5:1–11:57). John 5 opens with the healing of an invalid (5:1-15), but this particular healing episode is more about Jesus' actions on the Sabbath than a disabled individual. Verses 9-17 are the heart of the discourse, and verse 9b introduces the problem: "The day on which this took place was a Sabbath." Evidently a handicapped man had violated Sabbath regulations after Jesus healed him, because he did work by taking up his bed and walking. According to the Jews, this man had broken the Sabbath—an action that incurs the gravest of penalties.

The Jews persecute Jesus, because he is doing these things on the Sabbath (Jn 5:16). Jesus, as the Lord of the Sabbath, possesses authority over it (Mk 2:23-28). He places his actions on par with God by claiming that he works as his Father works (Jn 5:17). The Fourth Gospel is unique in its developed and nuanced understanding of the special relationship between Jesus and his Father. John 5 presents Jesus as equal with the Father, yet Jesus willingly submits to him (5:18-19; 8:29). Central to this chapter and the Fourth Gospel as a whole is John's insistence that one can know the Father only through the Son since Jesus is the definitive revelation of the Father.

> ***The resurrection is to occur at the very end of history, when God would establish his kingdom, create a new heaven and earth, and dwell intimately with humanity.***

One of the ways in which Jesus is equal with God lies in his prerogative to raise the dead (5:21). Daniel 12 is one of the most explicit texts in the Old Testament that portrays the resurrection: "Many of those who sleep in the dust of the ground will awake, these to everlasting life, but the others to disgrace and everlasting contempt" (Dan 12:2 NASB; cf. Job 19:26-27; Is 25:7-8; 26:19; Ezek 37:1-14). Admittedly, resurrection in the Old Testament lacks a central role, but such is not the case in Judaism. Although Judaism at this time is exceedingly diverse, many sects significantly develop the concept of a resurrection (e.g., *4 Ezra* 2:16).

When John 5:21 says that the "Father raises the dead," we learn that God remains committed to restoring creation. Verse 21 ends with the Son also giving life and implicitly raising the dead. Verse 24a states that those believing in Jesus will receive "eternal life," and verse 24b says the one who believes also "will not be judged but has crossed over from death to life." Eternal life, then, is the transfer from one's dead existence to the new creation. The language "life" or "eternal life" in the Fourth Gospel is believers' initial experience of the new heavens and earth (e.g., Jn 1:4; 3:15-16, 36; 4:36; 6:47; 8:12; 10:28; 11:25; 17:3; 20:31).

The phrase "eternal life" is found in the Old Testament only in Daniel 12:2, in which the saints receive eternal life as they are raised from the dead at the very end of time. Now, Jesus claims that Daniel's resurrection to eternal life has begun to be directly fulfilled: "Very truly I tell you, a time is coming and *has now come* when the dead will hear the voice of the Son of God and those who hear will live" (Jn 5:25). This initial resurrection is a spiritual resurrection that will be followed by a physical one at the very end of the age: "Do not be amazed at this, for a time is coming when all who are in their graves will hear his voice and come out—those who have done what is good will rise to live, and those who have done what is evil will rise to be condemned" (5:28-29; cf. Is 26:19).

Verse 25 begins with a strange yet salient description: "a time is coming and has now come." The term *hour* or *time* plays a prominent role in John (4:21, 23; 12:23; 16:25, 32; 17:1) and originates from the book of Daniel (8:17, 19; 11:6, 35, 40; 12:1-2).[9] The hour or timing of the resurrection has now begun in the person of Jesus. Obtaining life or eternal life does not primarily mean to live forever but to be joined to God's future redemption in the new heavens and earth. "Eternal" here has more to do with the quality (new creational) than quantity (everlasting). Of course, these are not mutually exclusive, but the point is that God's promise to create a new heavens and earth at the very end of history has broken into the *present*.

As one might expect, Jesus' claim to divinity incenses the Jewish leaders: "This is why *the Jews began trying all the more to kill Him* . . . He [Jesus] was even calling God His own Father, making Himself equal with God" (Jn 5:18; HCSB). Here the label *the Jews*, found a handful of times in the Synoptics, occurs often in John's Gospel and takes on somewhat of a technical meaning. The Jews often, though not always (e.g., 2:23), stand in direct opposition to Jesus and the truthfulness of his message (7:1, 19; 8:37; 10:31; 11:53). According to John 8:23, the Jews are said to be "of this world," which stands in direct opposition to Jesus, the "true light" (1:9), and represents the "created order . . . in rebellion against its Maker."[10] Thus, the Jewish leaders in John's Gospel generally embody the hostility of the fallen world and are allied with their "father, the devil" (8:44).

Chapter six narrates the feeding of the five thousand, the only miracle repeated in all four Gospels (Mt 14:13-21; Mk 6:32-44; Lk 9:10-17). Much of the chapter draws out two items: Jesus' relationship to Passover and the repeated failure of Israel to trust God's promises of provision. One of the Fourth Gospel's points of emphasis is Jesus' concern for the Jewish feasts, particularly the Passover celebration (Jn 2:13; 5:1; 6:4; 11:55).

Taking a cue from John 6, we learn that Jesus relates the feeding of the five thousand to Passover and the manna in the wilderness

[9]Stefanos Mihalios, *The Danielic Eschatological Hour in the Johannine Literature*, LNTS 436 (New York: T&T Clark, 2011).
[10]D. A. Carson, *The Gospel According to John*, PNTC (Grand Rapids: Eerdmans, 1991), 123.

wanderings (Jn 6:4, 32-58). Jesus claims to be the ultimate bread and drink that give life (6:48-51, 53-58). Here he places himself as the ultimate fulfillment of the Passover celebration and manna of the wilderness wanderings: "My flesh is *real* food and my blood is *real* drink" (6:55). Israel expected the Lord to deliver them from Roman oppression through the Messiah. Jesus claims to be not only the Messiah who will liberate Israel but also God incarnate (6:40-42). The feeding of the five thousand "not only accomplishes the restoration of the nation for which pilgrims at the annual festival longed, but also displays the divine identity of Jesus, who provides what only God can for his people."[11]

John 6 opens with the feeding of the five thousand, an act or sign (6:14) that displays Jesus' identity as the Son of God. Like Israel's failure to trust in God's provision in the wilderness, Philip and Andrew fail to believe in Jesus' ability to provide (6:5-9). Nevertheless, he miraculously multiplies bread and fish to feed five thousand men plus women and children, resulting in an abundance of food (6:10-13). So great is the miracle that the crowd "intended to come and make him [Jesus] king by force" (6:15).

The narrative then shifts to Jesus' walking on the chaotic waters while the disciples are in a boat, a few miles off shore (6:19). Jesus' ability to walk on the water recalls Old Testament texts such as Job 9:8: "He [the Lord] alone stretches out the heavens and *treads on the waves of the sea*." Even the brief statement to the disciples, "It is I" (6:20) alludes to several Old Testament passages where the Lord is described (e.g., Ex 3:14; Is 41:4). The significance of this enigmatic event is that Jesus identifies himself with God who has come to judge Israel's enemies. Jesus is certainly Israel's king (Jn 6:15), but he is a far greater king than the crowd imagines; he is the king of the cosmos.

Much of the remainder of chapter six resumes the discussion of the miraculous feeding. Jesus interprets the feeding of the five thousand and claims to be the "real food" and "real drink" (6:55) and likens the crowd to the "grumbling" wilderness generation (Jn 6:41-43), who will die spiritually if they fail to feast on Jesus (6:57).

FIGURE 7.10. MOSAIC OF THE BREAD AND FISH

Chapter 7 continues the discussion of Jesus' relationship to Jewish feasts and the people's unbelief in response to his teaching. The Feast of Booths is at hand (Jn 7:2; see fig. 7.12), and Jesus is expected to journey to Jerusalem. But the Jewish leaders have taken note of Jesus' troublesome words and deeds (e.g., 5:18), so Jesus delays his pilgrimage despite his brothers' protestations (7:2-5). Jesus eventually attends the feast and teaches in the temple courts.

The Jewish crowd that attends the festival remains divided at Jesus' teaching. As he

[11]Gerry Wheaton, *The Role of Jewish Feasts in John's Gospel*, SNTSMS 162 (Cambridge: Cambridge University Press, 2015), 186.

FIGURE 7.11. ISRAELITES GATHERING MANNA

teaches in the temple, he mysteriously declares, "Whoever believes in me, as Scripture has said, *rivers of living water will flow from within them*" (Jn 7:38).[12] Jesus references the prophecy of water flowing from the temple in Ezekiel, Joel, and Zechariah. Rivers of living water flow from Jesus, the new holy of holies. Jesus claims to be that same presence on earth. John 7:37 divulges that Jesus spoke the words "on the last and greatest day of the festival," the time of a special water-drawing and pouring ritual in the temple (m. *Sukkah* 4:9-10).

Jesus and the Jewish leaders spar with words once again in John 8, climaxing in Jesus' stunning declaration, "Before Abraham was born, I am!" (8:58). One unique feature of John's Gospel is seven "I am" statements (cf. Mk 6:50), often occurring with a predicate: "I am the bread of life" (Jn 6:35, 41, 48, 51); "I am the light" (8:12); "I am the gate" (10:7, 9); "I am the good shepherd" (10:11, 14); "I am the resurrection" (11:25); "I am the way and the truth and the life" (14:6); "I am the true vine" (15:1, 5). Each of these statements can be traced back to portions of the Old Testament, but the expression "I am" without a predicate is most peculiar. It recalls the prominent text of Exodus 3:14: "God said to Moses, '*I am who I am*. This is what you are to say to the Israelites: '*I am* has sent me to you.'" Exodus 3 describes God's identity as covenant Lord, the one who delivers Israel from slavery and conquers Pharaoh and his army. By recalling Exodus 3, Jesus bridges his ministry to the God of Israel. Jesus is the Lord incarnate who will deliver his people from spiritual slavery and conquer a far more oppressive Pharaoh—Satan. The Jewish leaders respond rather predictably to Jesus' claim: "They picked up stones to stone him" (8:59).

In the Old Testament, the waters clearly flowed from the innermost part of the temple (i.e., the holy of holies), where the Lord's presence had dwelt in the past and would dwell again in the latter-day temple.

John 9 further explains the wide gulf between Jesus and the Jewish leaders. This time, however, a man born blind takes center stage. Jesus' ability to heal the blind throughout the Gospels demonstrates his identity as Israel's God. Certainly, many Israelites are healed by Old Testament prophets, yet such healings are rare and dependent on God's power (2 Kings 5:1-14). Jesus' healings flow from his identity as the Lord of Israel.

The Old Testament asserts that the Lord alone can ultimately restore the blind: "The Lord said to him [Moses], 'Who gave human

[12]An alternate translation renders 7:38 as follows: "As Scripture has said, rivers of living water will flow from him." It is somewhat unclear if Jesus is the focus of 7:38 ("him" or those who trust in him ["them"]).

beings their mouths? Who makes them deaf or mute? *Who gives them sight* or makes them blind? Is it not I, the Lord?'" (Ex 4:11; cf. Hos 6:1-2). Healing is bound up with God's unique prerogative to create. Jesus' ability to heal this blind man in John 9 demonstrates his identity as Israel's God. The Jewish leaders are unable to deny the miracle (Jn 9:18-34), so they remain perplexed (9:30-31), and many even deem him as demon possessed (10:19-21).

Jesus claims to be the "good shepherd" in chapter 10—a metaphor that goes back to Ezekiel 34, where God condemns Israel's leaders or "shepherds" for their lack of care. Instead of modeling their behavior on God's shepherding, they use their position for selfish reasons (Ezek 34:1-10). In contrast to their unfaithfulness, God promises to shepherd the flock of Israel personally (Ezek 34:16-19) and appoint a Davidic figure who will faithfully take care of God's people (Ezek 34:20-24). Jesus directly fulfills this promise and considers the current Jewish leaders to be analogous to the unfaithful leaders in Ezekiel's day.

John 11 outlines the death of Lazarus and Jesus asserting his role as the giver of life, a theme already developed in chapter 5. Jesus comforts Martha in John 11:23: "Your brother will rise again." Martha affirms this truth in the following verse: "Martha answered, 'I know he will rise again in the resurrection at the last day.'" Martha, a typical Jew, expects that Lazarus will participate in the resurrection at the very end of the age. Yet Jesus

> ***One of God's characteristics in the Old Testament is the ability to heal and give life, which Jesus does.***

responds to her in 11:25-26: "*I am the resurrection and the life*. The one who believes in me will live, even though they die; and whoever lives by believing in me will never die." Jesus declares himself to be the locus

FIGURE 7.12. FEAST OF BOOTHS

of resurrection life in the present and demonstrates this reality symbolically by raising Lazarus from the grave (11:43-44). The raising of Lazarus is the final sign that Jesus performs in the first half of the Gospel, eliciting belief from many Jews (11:45; 12:9). All of this shows that the prophesied resurrection of the dead begins to occur through Jesus ministry; although those he physically raises from the dead will die again, such resurrections point to his resurrection and the great, final resurrection of the dead at the very end of time.

Anointed for burial and the triumphal entry (12:1-50). The final stage of Jesus' ministry commences with his anointing and public appearance at the triumphal entry. John opens chapter 12 connecting the triumphal entry to Bethany, where "Lazarus lived, whom Jesus had raised from the dead" (12:1). While dining, Mary anoints Jesus with costly perfume, an act that anticipates Jesus' death (12:7). The following day Jesus enters Jerusalem, where pilgrims celebrate the arrival of Israel's king by quoting Psalm 118. In direct fulfillment of Zechariah 9:9, Jesus rides a colt into the city. John parenthetically remarks that the disciples did not grasp the significance of these events in light of the Old Testament: "Only *after* Jesus was glorified did they realize that these things had been written about him" (12:16). As Jesus fulfills the Old Testament, he does so, at times, in unexpected ways.

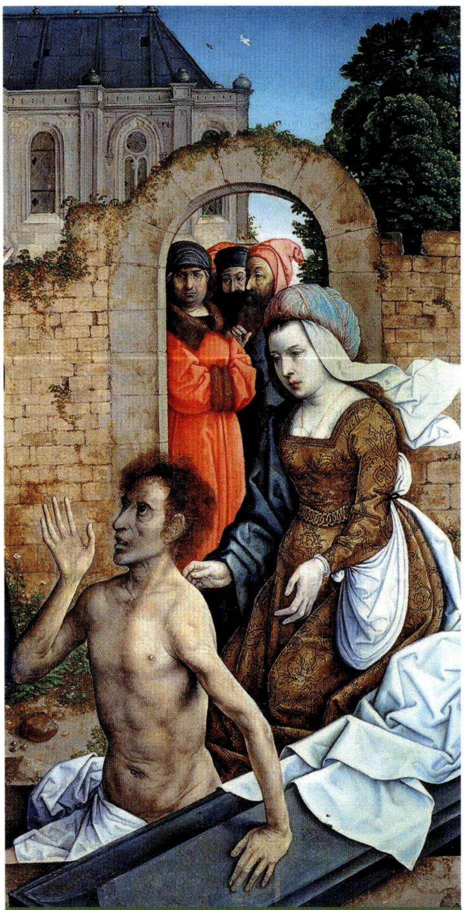
FIGURE 7.13. RAISING OF LAZARUS

The next section narrates Jesus predicting his death (12:20-36). Jesus repeatedly uses the title *Son of Man* in this section, particularly as it pertains to vanquishing the "prince of this world" (12:31). Surprisingly, in contrast to the many recorded in the Synoptics, John's Gospel does not include a single exorcism. This may reflect John's understanding of the utter pervasiveness of the hostile "world" and "darkness," as Satan and his demons are inseparably bound up with it.

John 12 climaxes with a clash between Jesus and the Jewish leaders. Despite Jesus performing many signs, the majority of Israel's leaders refuse to believe (12:37). The Fourth Gospel adds that their unbelief fulfills Isaiah's predictions (Is 53:1; Jn 12:38; Is 6:10; Jn 12:40). John then claims that "Isaiah said this because he saw Jesus' glory and spoke about him" (12:41). Jesus, the Fourth Gospel asserts, is to be identified with the Lord in Isaiah's vision (Is 6:1-4). As Daniel Brendsel notes,

> For John, Isaiah "saw" one possessing true "glory" (John 12:41). Isaiah saw a Servant whose humiliation is his glory, whose suffering reveals the identity of Yahweh, and whose death becomes the means whereby Israel and the nations might experience the eschatological second exodus for their good.[13]

BOOK OF THE PASSION (13:1–20:31)

One theme unique to John's Gospel is Jesus being "lifted up." We first encounter this language in John 3:14, when Jesus predicts that he will be lifted up in the same way "Moses lifted up the snake in the wilderness" (Num 21:8-9). Later on, Jesus claims that the Jewish leaders will lift up the Son of Man (Jn 8:28). The last statement occurs in John 12:32: "And I, when *I am lifted up* from the earth, will draw all people to myself" (cf. 12:34). Jesus is obviously talking about his crucifixion at the hands of the Jewish leaders, but the language is thick with irony. At the end of Passion Week as Jesus is physically lifted up on the cross and put to death, he is also lifted up in a spiritual sense in that he is glorified. Richard Bauckham puts it aptly:

> Other early Christian writers thought of the death and exaltation of Jesus as a sequence: suffering followed by glory, humiliation followed by exaltation. . . . John did something theologically remarkable when he collapsed this sequence into what he can speak of as a single event of Jesus's exaltation ("lifting up") or glorification.[14]

At the moment of pain, death, and darkness, Jesus is exalted in victory. He truly is the "king of the Jews" (Jn 18:33, 39; 19:3, 19, 21).

The final Passover celebration (13:1–17:26). In keeping with his Gospel's emphasis on Israel's festivals, John narrates in some detail Jesus' final hours with his disciples before his arrest. John places the final meal in the context of the Passover celebration (Jn 13:1-2). The feast anticipates a second exodus in which God will once again deliver his people out of exile. Jesus' actions during the final meal must be understood in light of Israel's general expectation that God promised to liberate his people from captivity in the latter days.

> ***The Passover meal celebrates God's redemption and deliverance, a reflection on God triumphing over Pharaoh and his army.***

Jesus' discourse in 13:1-17:26 contains some broad similarities to a "testament" genre that is rooted in the Old Testament and is subsequently developed in Judaism. Prominent figures, whose death is at hand, gathers their followers together and gives them a final word of comfort and exhortation (Gen 49; Josh 24; 1 Chron 28-29). One unique detail of John's narrative is Jesus' symbolic gesture of washing the disciples' feet (Jn 13:5-17), a task that is reserved for servants. By washing the feet of the disciples, Jesus identifies with Isaiah's servant, who will suffer on behalf of Israel. In Isaiah 40–53 the term *servant* is found nineteen times, describing, on the one hand, the nation of Israel collectively. The

[13]Daniel J. Brendsel, *"Isaiah Saw His Glory": The Use of Isaiah 52-53 in John 12*, BZNW 208 (Berlin: Walter de Gruyter, 2014), 213.

[14]Richard Bauckham, *Gospel of Glory: Major Themes in Johannine Theology* (Grand Rapids: Baker, 2015), 73.

nation is unfaithful in carrying out the divine commission to obey God perfectly and to bring his glory to the ends of the earth. On the other hand, an individual servant successfully and faithfully obeys God and bears the guilt of Israel (Is 42:1-9; 49:1-13; 50:4-11; 52:13–53:12). Isaiah 55–66 switches to the plural *servants* to designate an obedient group within Israel that identifies with the one faithful servant.[15]

In washing the disciples' feet, Jesus directly fulfills Isaiah's expectation of a suffering servant. As Isaiah's servant, Jesus suffers on behalf of Israel and establishes a community of faithful servants. "I, your Lord and Teacher, have washed your feet, *you also should wash one another's feet*. I have set you an example that *you should do as I have done for you*" (Jn 13:14-15). When we connect John's statement in 12:41, that "[Isaiah] saw Jesus' glory," a reference to the Lord's throne, with the suffering servant figure in chapter 13, Jesus is simultaneously the God of Israel incarnate *and* Isaiah's suffering servant.

Jesus continues to weave the Old Testament's story line, particularly as it relates to the temple, into his discussion with the disciples in John 14, which opens with Jesus declaring "My Father's house has many rooms; if that were not so, would I have told you that I am going there to prepare a place for you?" (14:2). While it is tempting to understand Jesus' promise as a reference to heaven, he is most likely referring to the construction of the end-time, heavenly temple, as Steven Bryan affirms: "In Jesus' going to the Father through death and resurrection, preparation is made for the dwelling place of God to be the dwelling place of Jesus' followers."[16] Jesus is beginning to remove the great gulf that separates humanity from God's glorious presence.

The Fourth Gospel then develops the Spirit's coming on the disciples and the covenant community much more than the Synoptics. Much of John 14 and 16 focus on Jesus' promise that the Father will "give [the disciples] another advocate . . . the Spirit of truth" (Jn 14:16-17). The Spirit is "Jesus' successor"[17] and the presence of Jesus among the disciples and the community. Toward the end of chapter 14, Jesus discloses the goal of the Spirit's coming: "The Holy Spirit . . . will teach you all things and will remind you of everything I have said to you" (Jn 14:26; cf. 15:26-27; 16:1-15). The mission of the Spirit parallels the mission of Jesus, as both persons are rejected by the world (1:10-11; 14:17) and teach the truth of God's revelation (14:6; 16:13). The Spirit will also testify to the truth of Jesus' works and deeds to the community (15:26). In a word, the Spirit binds the person of Jesus to the covenant community on earth.

The seventh and climactic "I am" statement is found in 15:1: "I am the true vine." Jesus' metaphor of constituting the "true vine" in John 15 echoes several Old Testament texts that depict Israel as a vine (e.g., Is 5:1-7; Jer 8:12-14). When Jesus claims to be the true vine, he identifies himself as true Israel in contrast to unfaithful Israel. According to Isaiah 5, despite God's gracious care in establishing Israel as a vineyard (Isa 5:2a), the nation responds in unfaithfulness toward his covenant (Isa 5:2b-4) and is

[15]Brendsel, *"Isaiah Saw His Glory,"* 56-60.
[16]Steven M. Bryan, "The Eschatological Temple in John 14," *BBR* 15 (2005): 195.
[17]Keener, "John," 432.

FIGURE 7.14. SYNAGOGUE AT BAR'AM

deserving of punishment and exile (Is 5:5-6). Jesus, though, claims to be the "true vine," that is, true Israel. He responds faithfully to his Father's provision. Only those who believe in him, whether Jew or Gentile, are considered part of the true vine, namely, end-time Israel: "No branch can bear fruit by itself; it must remain in the vine. Neither can you bear fruit unless you remain in me" (Jn 15:4). But the disciples must anticipate "pruning" or persecution, even though they abide in Jesus (Jn 15:2).

Continuing Jesus' discussion of the Spirit's coming, John 16 opens with a warning of unavoidable persecution: "*They will put you out of the synagogue*; in fact, the time is coming when anyone who kills you will think they are offering a service to God" (16:2). John mentions expulsion from the synagogues two other times in his Gospel (9:22; 12:42). Some of John's reader, Jewish Christians, will inevitably be expelled from their places of worship and civil life, the synagogues. The Jewish readers of the Fourth Gospel are encouraged to hold fast to the teaching of Jesus in the midst of coming persecution.

One of the most peculiar features of John's narrative of Passion Week occurs in chapter 17 and is commonly referred to as the High Priestly Prayer. At the beginning of the prayer, Jesus states, "I have brought you [the Father] glory on earth *by finishing the work you gave me to do*" (Jn 17:4). Part of the task that the Father gave to Jesus was to live as Adam and Israel by perfectly obeying, subduing evil, and spreading God's glory to the far corners of the earth. The priestly prayer primarily contains three petitions: that God would glorify the Son in the crucifixion and resurrection (17:5), protect the disciples from spiritual harm (17:15-16), and unify the covenant community (17:21-23).

Jesus is tried, crucified, and buried (18:1–19:42). Once the prayer is finished, Jesus and the disciples venture to Gethsemane. Judas betrays Jesus by leading Roman soldiers and the Jewish leaders to the garden (18:2-3). Peter, refusing to surrender, cuts off the ear of Malchus (18:10). John juxtaposes Peter and Jesus in the next sequence of events: Peter lies three times under pressure (18:15-18, 25-27), whereas Jesus faithfully speaks the truth (18:19-24). The first interrogation by the Jewish leaders takes place at night, where Annas (the former high priest of Israel) finds Jesus guilty and sends him to Caiaphas, the current high priest (18:19-24).

FIGURE 7.15. INSCRIPTION IDENTIFIES PILATE AS PREFECT OF JUDEA

John's retelling of Jesus' interaction with Pilate is far more detailed than the Synoptics' account (18:28-32). The first trial before Pilate comes on the heels of Jesus' trial before the Sanhedrin at dawn (Mt 26:57-68; Mk 14:53-65). The Jews are not allowed to put to death another Jew (18:31); that privilege belongs to the Romans. Pilate, the governor or prefect of Judea, had to give his stamp of approval.

John reminds the reader that these events "took place to fulfill what Jesus had said about the kind of death he was going to die" (18:32). Outwardly, it appears that Jesus' mission is spiraling out of control, but these horrendous events are ultimately God's intention. Pilate and Jesus retreat inside the Praetorium, the military palace (18:33-38a). Pilate's first question to Jesus is direct: "Are you the king of the Jews?" The Jewish authorities probably told Pilate of Jesus' claim to kingship. Jesus claims that his kingdom is not part of this world; it is not a plot of land or territory in its initial stages. Rather, Jesus, in keeping with his message, redefines the meaning of *kingdom* by describing it as a spiritual reign or rule. His kingdom is of an entirely different order and origin. Pilate responds to Jesus' description, saying, "You are a king, then!" (18:37). Jesus, after redefining the nature of his kingdom, does acknowledge that he is indeed a king.

John's Gospel continues the scene, whereas Luke splits the account with an interrogation from Herod (18:38b–19:7; cf. Lk 23:6-12). Pilate returns outside to the Jews and announces that he does not deem Jesus guilty; perhaps Pilate thinks Jesus is a little confused but not a political threat to Rome. Pilate could have released Jesus immediately, but he decides to give the Jews a say in the matter. Galvanized in their conviction to kill

Jesus, the Jews seek to release Barabbas, a well-known seditionist, instead of Jesus (Jn 18:40). The irony is palpable at this point in the narrative.

Although convinced of Jesus' innocence, Pilate has him flogged (Jn 19:1). The Roman soldiers craft a crown of thorns and dress Jesus in a purple robe. Both of these gestures were intended to mock him for being a purported king, hence their repeated assertion: "Hail, King of the Jews!" In biting irony, Jesus was indeed the King; his rule is not primarily over a limited territorial piece of land, though, but the entire cosmos! Even after Pilate's indirect plea that the Romans refrain from inflicting more suffering, the Jewish leaders are adamant that he be put to death because Jesus "claimed to be the Son of God" (19:7). They reveal their true motivation behind Jesus' arrest—Jesus committed blasphemy by claiming equality with God (see Jn 5:19-29; Mk 14:54-64).

After interviewing Jesus once more, Pilate firmly remains convinced of Jesus' innocence (Jn 19:12-16). But the Jews will not take no for an answer. They attempt to manipulate Pilate by coming back to the issue of Jesus' purported acts of sedition. The Jews know full well that Pilate is already in a precarious position with Tiberias Caesar. Pilate fears that the Jews will report back to Rome that he failed to punish a famed seditionist. Pilate, after hearing the Jews' response, directs Jesus to the official place of judgment—the "Stone Pavement." Pilate officially passes judgment on Jesus. John time stamps this event: "It was the day of Preparation of the Passover; it was about noon" (19:14a). The horrific events that unfold are therefore connected to the Passover celebration in which God promises to release Israel from captivity. God will pass over the faithful within Israel by slaying his own Son (cf. 3:16).

Pilate taunts the Jews by declaring, "Here is your king" and "Shall I crucify your king?" (Jn 19:14b-15a). John makes it clear that Pilate knew that Jesus is not a king. The Jews make the audacious claim that "We have no king but Caesar" (19:15b). They would rather align themselves to a pagan king rather than submit to Jesus.

FIGURE 7.16. KING DAVID

The soldiers lead Jesus out to the "place of the Skull" or Golgotha (Jn 19:17-22). John says that the Roman soldiers cast lots to determine who should keep Jesus' garment, unaware that "scripture might be fulfilled that said, 'They divided my clothes among them and cast lots for my garment'" (19:24). By quoting Psalm 22:18, the Fourth Gospel stresses that Jesus of Nazareth is indeed the long-awaited King of Israel. In the throes of death and defeat, Jesus is simultaneously the supreme ruler over all expressions of authority, both physical and spiritual. David's experiences of suffering, especially in Psalm 22, typologically foreshadow Jesus' own experiences throughout his earthly ministry, especially here at the crucifixion. As David ruled over Israel *while* undergoing persecution from those around him, so too Jesus rules in the midst of defeat and despair by his own countrymen.

> ***The Old Testament expects the nation of Israel to suffer first and then be restored in the kingdom of God through a purified remnant.***

The Passover theme is picked up once more in John 19:36, which describes Jesus' death: "These things happened so that the scripture would be fulfilled: 'Not one of his bones will be broken.'" This is a quotation of Exodus 12:46 (see also Num 9:12),[18] which describes how the Passover lamb is to be sacrificed at the time of the Exodus and in subsequent Israelite generations. The historical description of the ordinance that the Passover lamb's bones not be broken typologically foreshadows the ultimate Passover lamb, Jesus Christ. The Roman soldiers' decision to break the bones of the two criminals on either side of Jesus but not to break his bones is viewed as a fulfillment of what the Passover lamb's preparation prefigured.

Jesus experiences moments of end-time suffering and tribulation during his ministry, and then absolute tribulation on the cross. His suffering directly fulfills several Old Testament passages that anticipate Israel undergoing end-time tribulation and persecution (e.g., Ezek 38:10-16; Dan 7–12). Now, however, these two eschatological strands are intertwined at the cross—tribulation and kingdom, discussed separately in the Old Testament, are surprisingly merged into a unified, ironic concept.

Resurrection and disbelief (20:1-31). Upon discovering that the stone to the tomb had been removed, Mary Magdalene runs to Peter and "the other disciple" (John) and informs them of the news (Jn 20:1-2). The two disciples make haste and likewise discover an empty tomb (20:3-8). The Fourth Gospel parenthetically adds, "They still did not understand from Scripture that Jesus had to rise from the dead" (20:9). The disciples were slow to connect Jesus' resurrection with the Old Testament, and for good reason. The Old Testament expects all of God's people together to be resurrected as part of one event (e.g., Dan 12:2-3), yet the Gospels record only Jesus rising from the dead preceding the resurrection of the saints at the eschaton. The resurrection of Jesus is indeed a fulfillment of Old Testament prophecy, but the manner of fulfillment differs from expectations. The Old Testament prophecies of resurrection are not fulfilled at the same time but are fulfilled progressively: *first* Jesus is raised from the dead and *then* all those who believe in him.

Mary peeks into the tomb and discovers two seated angels (Jn 20:11-17). Turning around, she notices an individual thought

[18]It is also possible that allusion to Ps 34:20 (21, MT) is included with the Exodus and Numbers texts.

to be a gardener. Jesus had been transformed into a new body, so Mary fails to recognize him immediately (20:15-18). A few hours later, Jesus appears to the disciples, where they are hiding "with the doors locked for fear of the Jewish leaders" (20:19). Jesus breathes on the disciples, exclaiming "Receive the Holy Spirit" (20:22). The seemingly odd account of Jesus "breathing" on the disciples echoes Genesis 2:7, in which God breathes into Adam "the breath of life."

Jesus says, "As the Father has sent me, I am sending you" (20:21), resembling the Great Commission in Matthew 28:18-20. Jesus empowers his followers not with physical life but with spiritual might to do what Adam and others had failed to do. The apostles are commissioned as the representative bridgehead of the new humanity, the new creation, and the new Israel.

Once Jesus convinces Thomas of his resurrection (Jn 20:24-29), John discloses the purpose of his gospel: "But these [signs] are written that you may believe that Jesus is the Messiah, the Son of God, and that by believing you may have life in his name" (20:31). John presents the life, death, and resurrection of Jesus with the purpose of eliciting belief among his readers. Of all the signs that Jesus displays, his greatest is the resurrection—the defeat of sin and the beginning of the new creation.

EPILOGUE (21:1-25)

The epilogue describes Jesus' third and final postresurrection appearance to the disciples. All three appearances are designed to attest to the sign of Jesus' bodily resurrection. The disciples miraculously catch an extraordinary amount of fish and haul the net to shore (Jn 21:1-8), and, echoing the feeding of the five thousand (6:5-13), Jesus distributes bread and fish to the disciples (21:13).

After the meal, Jesus engages Peter to ensure his commitment to the nascent community of faith (Jn 21:15-17). Peter's death is even disclosed when Jesus exclaims, "'When you [Peter] are old you will stretch out your hands, and someone else will dress you and lead you where you do not want to go.' Jesus said this to indicate the kind of death by which Peter would glorify God" (21:18-19). Just as Jesus glorifies God by being lifted up on the cross (3:14), so too Peter will follow suit and be lifted up and crucified at the hands of Nero.

The Fourth Gospel ends with the apostle John's eyewitness testimony, assuring readers that his account is indeed trustworthy: "This is the disciple who testifies to these things and who wrote them down. We know that his testimony is true" (Jn 21:24). The audience can be confident that Jesus is indeed the long-awaited King of Israel and Israel's God incarnate, who has come into a dark world to deliver people from the plight of sin.

ACTS

AUTHORSHIP

Luke–Acts ought to be considered a two-volume work (Lk 1:1-4; Acts 1:1-2). The first book describes the person and work of Jesus, whereas the second narrates, in some detail, how Jesus and the apostles serve as the foundation of the early church. Like the Gospel of Luke, the early church suggested that Luke was indeed the author of Acts. The Muratorian Canon (ca. AD 170–80) explicitly identifies Luke, the companion of Paul, as the author. Irenaeus (ca. AD 200) also claims that Luke is the author of the Third Gospel and, indirectly, states that he likewise penned Acts (*Against Heresies* 3.14.1).

When we examine some of the internal evidence, the book of Acts itself hints at Lukan authorship. Several passages, for example, narrate Paul's journeys by including the first-person plural *we*. These "we sections" may indicate the eyewitness testimony of specific events (Acts 16:10-17; 20:5-15; 21:1-18; 27:1–28:16), comporting well with Paul's assertions concerning his intimate friendship with Luke. While under house arrest in Rome (or Ephesus), Paul sends his greetings to the Colossian church: "Our dear friend Luke, the doctor, . . . send[s] greetings" (Col 4:14; cf. Philem 24; 2 Tim 4:11). The early church's explicit identification and the implicit evidence within Acts lead us to conclude that Luke, the travel companion of Paul, is the author.

DATE

Dating Acts is tied to the complex relationship between the Synoptics. It seems that Luke is dependent on Mark, so Luke–Acts must have been completed sometime *after* the Second Gospel. According to the book of Acts, Paul's arrest took place around AD 62 (28:14-31). Luke–Acts likely was completed while Paul is in his first Roman imprisonment or shortly thereafter, giving us a date sometime in the mid to late 60s.

GENRE

The book of Acts falls into the category of ancient historiography, wherein authors narrate events in accordance with a particular set of aims or biases. This is not to say that Luke had little interest in historical particulars, such as geographical details and dates; he very much did. Many scholars have concluded that Luke was familiar with Roman culture, geography, and politics and that his portrayal of them was accurate. What makes Luke's portrayal of historical events different from our modern conception of historical telling of events is his theological shaping of his narrative. We as twenty-first-century Westerners largely desire to know the "bare

FIGURE 8.1. THE ACROPOLIS IN ATHENS

facts" of history. The book of Acts, however, is profoundly theological in its retelling of the origins of the church. Each character and event is purposefully included for a particular reason that contributes to Luke's overall intention of the book. Like the Gospels, the book of Acts weds theology with history and makes no qualms about it. Luke's theological shaping of his book does not distort the history that he records.

PURPOSE

When read alongside of Luke's Gospel, Acts remains moored to Jesus' ministry and teaching. The kingdom has indeed arrived, and Acts narrates the outworking of this end-time reality in the early church. The book was probably also written to convince recently converted Gentiles that they are genuinely part of the latter-day people of God, true Israel.

AUDIENCE

Both prologues of Luke–Acts explicitly list Theophilus as the intended audience, although we are not exactly sure who this individual is or where he is located. It is possible, perhaps even probable, that he is the patron or sponsor of Luke's undertaking of this two-volume endeavor. Producing a two-volume work was notoriously expensive, so its production may have required outside funding. Whatever the case may be, Theophilus certainly is not the only intended audience, since Luke has a broader readership in mind. Luke–Acts circulated throughout the eastern Mediterranean, targeting Jewish Christians and especially Gentiles.

OUTLINE

I. God's Glory Arrives in Jerusalem (1:1-6:7)
   - A. Prologue and the Commissioning of the Twelve (1:1-26)
   - B. Pentecost and the Advent of the Spirit (2:1-40)
   - C. The Apostles in Jerusalem (3:1–6:7)

II. God's Glory Expands to Samaria (6:8–9:31)
   - A. Stephen's Speech (7:2-53)
   - B. The Regathering of Estranged Israelites (8:1-40)
   - C. Paul on the Damascus Road (9:1-31)

III. God's Glory Expands Through the Witness of Peter (9:32–12:24)
   - A. Peter and the Gentiles (10:1–11:18)

- B. Paul and Barnabas in Antioch and the Famine Relief Visit (11:19-30)
- C. Herod's Persecution of the Church (12:1-24)

IV. God's Glory Expands Through the Witness of Paul (12:25–18:22)

- A. Paul's "First Missionary Journey" (12:25–14:28)
- B. The Jerusalem Council (15:1-35)
- C. Paul's "Second Missionary Journey" (15:36–18:22)

V. God's Glory Expands to the "Ends of the Earth" (18:23–28:31)

- A. Paul's "Third Missionary Journey" (18:24–21:16)
- B. Paul's Journey to Rome and Imprisonment (21:17–28:31)

FIGURE 8.2. DESCENT OF THE SPIRIT AT PENTECOST

BIBLICAL-THEOLOGICAL THEMES

Joel's prophecy of the Spirit and Pentecost. The outpouring of the Spirit at Pentecost is a supremely important event for the early church. It is the establishment of the church as the true people of God. What began in seed form in the person of Jesus and the disciples in the Gospels comes to full bloom at Pentecost in Acts 2 and the chapters that follow. Peter explains that the events taking place at Pentecost are the beginning fulfillment of Joel's prophecy that God would "pour out [his] Spirit on all people" and that all classes of people in the covenant community would prophesy (Joel 2:28-29). At the beginning of the Joel 2:28 quotation, Peter substitutes the phrase "in the last days" in place of Joel's "afterward." The substitution comes from Isaiah 2:2: "*In the last days* the mountain of the Lord's temple will be established as the highest of the mountains; it will be exalted above the hills, and all nations will stream to it." Peter blends the Spirit's coming at Pentecost with Isaiah's prophecy about the end-time temple and Gentiles streaming into it. The pouring out of the Spirit on the covenant community in Acts 2 signals God's heavenly presence descending on his people and incorporating them into his end-time temple. Heaven and earth are collapsing, and the expectation set forth in Genesis 1–2 is finally coming to fruition.

Under the old covenant, the Spirit's power enabled prophets, priests, and kings to perform their specific duties. The prophet Joel foresaw a time, though, when *all* within Israel will receive the end-time Spirit and serve in the capacity of prophets, priests, and kings. But Joel 2 is part of a larger expectation that began in the early stages of Israel's career. According to Numbers 11, Moses pleads with God to furnish him with leaders to share in the burden of the people (Num 11:11, 17 [cf. Ex 18:13-27]). God orders Moses to gather "seventy men from the elders" and "bring them to the tent of meeting, and let them take their stand there with you. Then I will come down and . . . will take of the Spirit who is upon you, and will put Him upon them" (Num 11:16-17 NASB). Moses obeys God: "He gathered seventy men of the elders . . . and stationed them around the tent. Then the LORD came down in the cloud . . . and took of the *Spirit* who was upon him [Moses] and placed Him upon the *seventy elders*. And when the *Spirit* rested upon them, they *prophesied*" (11:24-25 NASB). They then stopped prophesying, but two elders at another location continued doing so. When Joshua heard about this, he asked Moses to stop them. Moses declined, replying, "Would that *all the LORD's people* were *prophets*, that the LORD would put *His Spirit upon them*" (11:29 NASB). What began with a wish from Moses is transformed into a formal prophecy by the prophet Joel. The Spirit's gifts, formerly limited to prophets, kings, and priests, is universalized to all of God's people from every race, young and old, male and female.

At Pentecost, the Spirit empowers God's people to testify about the risen Christ to the nations. The church is on the precipice of being a "kingdom of priests" (Ex 19:6) that mediates God's glory to the nations. The promise of Acts 1:8 that the apostles will be "witnesses in Jerusalem, and in all Judea and Samaria, and to the ends of the earth" is a virtual repetition of Israel's commission in Exodus 19:6. As Moses assembled Israel at Sinai and commissioned them, so too Jesus assembles the twelve disciples on the Mount of Olives (Acts 1:12) and commissions them. The difference between Exodus 19:6 and Acts 1:8 lies in the presence of the Spirit, who will ensure that Adam and Eve's and Israel's mission will be accomplished and that the apostles will respond in obedience. God's glory is on the move.

The "Word of God."[1] The expression "word of God" or "word of the Lord" occurs over twenty times in the book of Acts, clearly indicating its importance. Drilling down a bit deeper, we learn that the phrase is often paired with terms such as *growth* and *multiplication*. For example, Acts 6:7 reads, "And the word of God continued to *increase*, and the number of the disciples *multiplied* greatly in Jerusalem" (ESV). The unique wording alludes to Genesis 1:28, where Adam and Eve are to "be fruitful and increase in number; fill the earth and subdue it. Rule over the fish in the sea and the birds in the sky and over every living creature that moves on the ground." Here God commands Adam and Eve to reproduce and create a godly community that spreads his glory to the ends of the earth.

FIGURE 8.3. EXPULSION OF ADAM AND EVE

At strategic junctures within the narrative, the book of Acts picks up on this language of growing and multiplying to mark key events during the first decades of the early church (Acts 6:7; 9:31; 12:24; 16:5; 19:20).[2] Unlike

[1]Part of the discussion of the "Word of God" is from G. K. Beale and Mitchell Kim, *God Dwells Among Us: Expanding Eden to the Ends of the Earth* (Downers Grove, IL: InterVarsity Press, 2014), 36-37.
[2]David G. Peterson, *The Acts of the Apostles*, PNTC (Grand Rapids: Eerdmans, 2009), 32-34.

Genesis 1:28, the Word of God, not people, bears fruit and multiplies in Acts. Just as Adam and Eve were to "be fruitful and increase in number" (Gen 1:28), so now the gospel is "bearing fruit and growing" and filling the earth (Col 1:6, 10). Spiritual progeny are multiplying to fill the earth through the gospel. Why does the Word of God increase and multiply in Acts through spiritual progeny instead of physical progeny itself being multiplied, as in Genesis 1:28? In fact, Genesis 1:28 likely has in mind not only physical children but also children who were to be spiritual image bearers of God.

We must recall that even in Genesis 1:28 the Word of God is essential since Adam and Eve were to subdue the earth through obedience to God's Word (Gen 2:16-17). Adam and Eve fail to subdue the serpent because they did not remember and obey God's Word properly (Gen 3:1-7). The genealogy of Genesis 5 traces the initial stage of the proper fulfillment of Genesis 1:28, and the "likeness of God" in Adam is passed down to Seth, who is in Adam's "likeness, in his own image" (Gen 5:3). Here the image of God in Adam is passed down through Seth, who keeps God's Word, unlike the murderer Cain. Images of God multiply as a vanguard movement, beginning to spread out over the earth with the goal of filling it with divine glory bearers. The book of Acts focuses on the spiritual children of Christ, the last Adam, who are multiplied by means of the Word.

GOD'S GLORY ARRIVES IN JERUSALEM (1:1–6:7)

Central to the story of the Bible is God's desire to dwell intimately with the created order. Although Adam and Eve were created perfectly and God dwelled with them in the Garden of Eden, his full presence was only partial and restricted to the invisible heavens. But God's plan to dwell intimately with his creation remains unchanged throughout the Old Testament. The patriarchs and Israel experienced glimpses of the divine presence, but the prophets reaffirm that humanity and creation will one day house the glory of God. Jeremiah 3:16-17 even suggests that God's presence will expand to such a degree that the Israelites will not "remember" or "miss" the ark of the covenant. The four Evangelists testify that Israel's God has remarkably descended in the person of Christ (Jn 1:14). As the full expression of God on earth, Jesus beckons his disciples to follow him and participate in the temple of God he establishes through his death and resurrection.

The book of Acts narrates the descent of the end-time temple on earth. God is now dwelling with his people! What began in the person of Jesus and the twelve disciples has now encompassed the outskirts of Israel and the Gentiles. The first six chapters of Acts introduce the major themes of the book—the church as the temple of God and the apostles as witnesses of Jesus' work of redemption (Acts 1:8). But as the invisible temple expands through the gospel, pushing outward from Jerusalem, persecution and affliction set in. As the kingdom thrives, so does hostility.

PROLOGUE AND THE COMMISSIONING OF THE TWELVE (1:1-26)

The prologue stresses the importance of the kingdom, the primacy of the Spirit, and the expansion of the gospel to the ends of the earth. According to Acts 1:4, Jesus commands the disciples to remain at Jerusalem and to wait for the "promise"—that is, the baptism of the Spirit. After some time, the disciples come together in Jerusalem and ask Jesus, "Lord, are you at this time going to restore the kingdom to Israel?" (1:6). Already in 1:3 Jesus is discussing the various facets and nature of God's kingdom. But in 1:6 the disciples, knowing that aspects of the kingdom of God have already come, wonder if the *theocratic nation* of Israel will be restored right then and there. The disciples consider if Jesus is going to establish his physical kingdom by judging the pagan Romans and releasing Israel from physical and spiritual bondage. But Jesus' reply is nothing short of astounding: "It is not for you to know the times or dates the Father has set by his own authority" (1:7).

Even though the disciples do not have the prerogative to know *when* the kingdom will be set up, Jesus answers their question, albeit indirectly: "You will receive power when the Holy Spirit comes on you; and you will be my witnesses in Jerusalem, and in all Judea and Samaria, and to the ends of the earth" (Acts 1:8). He asserts that the outpouring of the Spirit will demonstrate the presence of the end-time kingdom. G. B. Caird is right to suggest that the "Spirit is always an eschatological gift, a portent of 'the last days.'"[3] The Twelve are to be his witnesses by taking the gospel to the "ends of the earth." Acts 1:8 is a fitting summary of the book of Acts—God's glory will be taken to the far corners of the known world as the fulfillment of the Genesis 1:28 commission.

Acts 1:8 recalls a few prominent passages from restoration prophecies in Isaiah: "till the *Spirit is poured on us* from on high" (Is 32:15); "*You are my witnesses*, . . . and my servant whom I have chosen" (Is 43:10); "I will also make you a light for the Gentiles, that my salvation may reach *to the ends of the earth*" (Is 49:6). The point of weaving these references from Isaiah into Acts 1:8 is to signal the direct fulfillment of Isaiah's prophecies concerning Israel and the nations. Christ's death and resurrection and the pouring out of the Spirit spark the initial fulfillment of Israel's restoration.

FIGURE 8.4. TWELVE DISCIPLES AND MARY IN THE UPPER ROOM

Immediately following the commissioning of the disciples, Jesus ascends into heaven in a "cloud" (1:9). Though only one verse, Luke underscores a critical dimension to the role of Jesus in the book of Acts. Here we perceive the enthronement of Jesus, whereby he rules and reigns over the cosmos with the Father (cf. Rev 3:21). The death and resurrection of Jesus qualify him to be the exalted Lord of the cosmos, to establish the kingdom, fill the earth with God's glory, and judge the enemies of God. As the book of Acts unfolds, we must not lose sight of this reality. Jesus

[3]G. B. Caird, *New Testament Theology*, ed. L. D. Hurst (Oxford: Oxford Press, 1995), 205.

governs all the affairs of the early church and pours out his Spirit upon them at Pentecost. It may not be a stretch to retitle the book of Acts as "Acts of the Risen Lord Jesus."[4]

After receiving their commission, Jesus ascends into heaven, while the disciples descend the Mount of Olives (Acts 1:12) and immediately make plans to a replace Judas. The apostles are compelled to preserve the symbolism of their number (1:13-22), so they cast lots, and Matthias is eventually chosen to replace the betrayer (1:23-26). True Israel remains symbolically intact.

Pentecost and the advent of the Spirit (2:1-47). Acts 2 narrates the influx of thousands of Diaspora Jews into Jerusalem to celebrate Pentecost. The feast of Pentecost, known also as the Feast of Weeks, refers to the completion of the barley harvest (Lev 23:15-21). The Israelites celebrate fifty days after the firstfruits of the harvest are offered to God, giving thanks for the Lord's provision (Ex 34:22; Num 28:26-31; Deut 16:9-12). During the intertestamental period, this feast also served as a reminder of the Lord's redemption in Egypt. As time went on, the Jews celebrated Pentecost to commemorate God's giving of the law at Sinai.

The Spirit appears to have been poured out in two phases: first on the apostles and the group of 120 in the upper room of a private house (2:1-4; see fig. 8.4) and then on the Diaspora Jews in the temple (2:5-41). In both accounts, the effect of the Spirit's descent is speaking in tongues, which appear to have been known languages from different parts of the ancient world (2:8).

The list of the nations represented by Diaspora Jews at Pentecost in Acts 2:9-11 alludes

FIGURE 8.5. TOWER OF BABEL AND THE DISPERSION OF THE NATIONS

[4]Alan J. Thompson, *The Acts of the Risen Lord Jesus: Luke's Account of God's Unfolding Plan*, NSBT 27 (Downers Grove, IL: InterVarsity Press, 2011), 49.

to the Table of Nations in Genesis 10. According to Genesis 10, Noah's sons multiplied into the "seventy nations," spreading out over various regions in Mesopotamia. Genesis 11:1 states that the whole earth had "one language and a common speech." A large number of people that represented the seventy nations attempt to construct a city and a "tower that reaches to the heavens" (Gen 11:4) so that they could make a name for themselves and not be scattered throughout of the earth. This purpose diametrically opposes the Genesis 1:28 commission. According to Genesis 1, God commands Adam and Eve to spread God's glory to the ends of the earth, but here in Genesis 11 mankind assembles together. Instead of making a name for God, humans make a name for themselves (Gen 11:4). By confusing their language, humanity is unable to function as one and achieve selfish inclinations and ambitions. Humanity is now permanently divided—separated by various languages.

God's judgment at Babel is finally reversed at Pentecost: representatives from the scattered nations find true harmony by the power of the Spirit in Jerusalem. Equipped with a unified language, the church can now bear witness to Jesus' death, resurrection, and enthronement to his heavenly throne to reign as cosmic king (Acts 1:8). Under the kingship of Jesus and through the power of his Spirit, the representatives of these nations will scatter once more and subdue the powers of evil by filling the earth with God's presence (cf. Lk 10).

The appearance of "tongues of fire" demonstrates the advent of the Spirit (2:3), recalling God's unique presence that is found throughout the Old Testament in a series of theophanies, or manifestations of God. The phrase "tongues of fire" occurs in Isaiah 30:27-30, in which God descends from his heavenly temple in judgment (cf. Is 5:24-25; 1 En. 14:9-10, 15, 22). Taking these clues together, we learn that God's heavenly tabernacling presence descends on the church.

> ***At Sinai God appears in the midst of loud voices, torches, a thick cloud, and fire (e.g., Ex 19:16-20; 20:18). God's coming at Sinai stands in the background of the Spirit's coming at Pentecost (cf. Is 5:24-25; 30:27-30).***

The crowd in Jerusalem consists of Jews and Jewish proselytes, but those present at the temple are not all from Jerusalem. Many of them are from the far reaches of the Diaspora. When the Assyrians enslaved the Israelites in the eighth century BC and the Babylonians exiled them in the sixth century BC, many of the Israelites migrated throughout the eastern Mediterranean. For centuries, these scattered or Diaspora Jews lived outside of Palestine, yet they often made a pilgrimage to Jerusalem to celebrate three feasts (Passover / Unleavened Bread, Pentecost, and Booths).

The list of Diaspora Jews in Acts 2:9-11 betrays an intentional geographic order. Beginning with those living in the East and then moving counterclockwise with Jerusalem as its center, Luke demonstrates that God, at Pentecost, is restoring Diaspora Jews, with Jerusalem functioning as its center. God has regathered his people Israel and filled them with his glorious presence. Now that the people at Pentecost have received the Spirit, these Jewish converts in Jerusalem are now the end-time people of God—true Israel. The book of Acts presents the city of Jerusalem functioning as the hub of Christianity for the next several decades, where the apostles will serve as the pillars in this newly established temple (cf. Gal 2:9).[5]

Unique to Acts is the use of several speeches and dialogues throughout the book (e.g., 1:4-8, 16-22; 2:14-40; 3:12-26; 5:35-39; 6:2-4; 7:2-53; 10:1–11:18; 13:16-41; 15:1-35; 28:23-28). As in Greek and Roman historical books, speeches in Acts help drive the narrative and "interpret the story for the reader."[6] In one of the most well-known speeches in Acts, Peter quotes a lengthy portion of Joel 2 (Acts 2:17-21). In the original context of Joel 2, the prophet transforms Moses' wish into a formal prophecy. According to Numbers 11, Moses wishes that all of God's people were prophets and "that the Lord would put his Spirit on them" (Num 11:29). Joel 2 applies Moses' wish to Israel. Peter traces a line from Joel 2 to the events of Pentecost, asserting that Joel's prophecy has begun its fulfillment. The Spirit's gifts, formerly limited to prophets, kings, and priests often for service in connection with the temple, are now universalized to all of God's people from every race, young and old, male and female.

One of the most puzzling aspects of Peter's sermon is his quotation of Joel 2:30-31: "I will show wonders in the heavens and on the earth, blood and fire and billows of smoke. The sun will be turned to darkness and the moon to blood" (see Acts 2:19-20). The use of the Old Testament here in Peter's sermon is probably a combination of the symbolic use and direct prophetic fulfillment. This seemingly bizarre cosmic language from Joel 2 is found elsewhere in the Old Testament (e.g., Is 13:10-13; 24:1-6, 19-23; 34:4; Jer 4:23-28; Ezek 32:6-8). Such cosmic language figuratively refers to the historical end of a sinful nation's existence and the emerging dominance of a victorious kingdom. It captures the downfall of one nation and the rise of another. According to Acts 2, the kingdom under divine judgment is Israel, but this time it is her definitive end as a theocratic nation (cf. 1 Thess 2:16). The nation of Israel will pay dearly for executing God's Son on a cross.

The people group that emerges victorious at Pentecost is the remnant of Israelites who identify with the risen Christ and receive the end-time Spirit. The outpouring of the Spirit leads to the conversion of three thousand individuals (Acts 2:41). These newly minted converts meet daily in the temple complex, indicating that God's glory has begun to fill Jerusalem (2:46).

The pouring out of the Spirit takes place in multiple stages. Jesus first receives the latter-day Spirit at his baptism (Acts 2:33a). Once he is resurrected, he breathes on the disciples, giving them an initial experience of Pentecost (Jn 20:21-23). Finally, at Pentecost, the risen Christ pours out the Spirit on the apostles and on thousands of Jewish believers, fashioning them as the end-time Israel of God (Acts 2:33b).

The apostles in Jerusalem (3:1–6:7). For the next several chapters, the narrative continues to focus on the apostles as they minister

[5]Richard Bauckham, "James and the Jerusalem Church," in *The Book of Acts in Its Palestinian Setting*, ed. R. Bauckham, BAIPS 4 (Grand Rapids: Eerdmans, 1995), 423.
[6]Luke Timothy Johnson, "Luke-Acts, Book of," *ABD* 4:408.

FIGURE 8.6. MODEL OF THE SECOND TEMPLE

in Jerusalem and in the confines of the temple. The first half of Acts 3 centers on Peter and John in the temple, where a lame beggar is healed "in the name of Jesus Christ of Nazareth" (3:6; cf. 3:16; 4:10; 16:18; 19:13; Lk 9:49), illustrating that the end-time kingdom flourishes through the apostles by the work of the Spirit. The healing prompts another one of Peter's sermons, in which he outlines the Old Testament's expectation of Jesus' death and resurrection (Acts 3:13-26). The Jews should not have been surprised at the Messiah's death, since the Old Testament itself predicts that he would suffer, die, and rise from the dead. Luke exhorts his audience to embody the same faith of the beggar and trust "in the name of Jesus" (3:16). Peter's sermon is soon interrupted by the Jewish authorities at the temple. They drag him and John off to jail, prompting another conversion of thousands of Jews. The total conversions have now reached five thousand (4:4). Persecution once again leads to the growth of the gospel. The two apostles find themselves standing before the Sanhedrin, the ruling political body of the nation of Israel (4:5-6). The perceived affront was the healing of the lame man, and the authorities demand to know how the apostles performed such a marvelous act. Peter responds by insisting that it was done through the "name of Jesus Christ of Nazareth" (4:10), who is the very cornerstone of the true temple (4:11). The council, knowing the legitimacy of the miracle (4:14-16), lets Peter and John go with a stern warning with the hope that the two apostles would remain quiet (4:17-21). The second half of Acts 4 details the response of the other apostles and Jewish believers. They ask that God would continue to "stretch out [his] hand to heal and perform signs and wonders" (4:30). Their prayer is answered in the "filling" of the Spirit shortly thereafter (4:31).

Acts 5 begins with a seemingly odd event concerning Ananias and Sapphira (5:1-11). The couple's deception and God's subsequent judgment on them demonstrates that sin within the covenant community, the newly established temple of God, will not be tolerated. Unclean and wicked behavior has no business in the holy sanctuary of the church.

> ***The Mosaic covenant dictated in detail how the priests should keep the temple free from defilement so that God may dwell with Israel. Now that God dwells intimately with his people, sin must be avoided at all cost.***

The next section narrates the success and persecution of the apostles. They increase their missionary efforts, yet it comes with a steep price—rejection and persecution (Acts 5:12-42). After miraculously escaping from jail, the apostles are brought before the Sanhedrin to answer why they refuse to keep quiet (5:27). An important Pharisee named Gamaliel intervenes and persuades the council to release the apostles. He argues that if God is truly behind their ministry, then they "will not be able to stop these men" (5:39; cf. 22:3). As the book of Acts unfolds and the gospel is spread throughout the known world, we soon learn that such will be the case.

GOD'S GLORY EXPANDS TO SAMARIA (6:1–9:31)

The next major section of Acts introduces the audience to the apostle Paul. On his journey to Damascus to persecute the church, he encounters the risen Christ in a vision (Acts 9:1-3). Once the vision concludes, Paul is immediately stricken with blindness (9:8-9). Paul's experience on the Damascus Road is reminiscent of Israel's blindness. Moses exhorts the Israelites in Deuteronomy 29:2-4, saying, "Your eyes have seen all that the Lord did in Egypt to Pharaoh, to all his officials and to all his land. With your own eyes you saw those great trials, those signs and great wonders. But to this day the Lord has not given you *a mind that understands or eyes that see or ears that hear.*" This passage affirms Israel's perception of God's mighty deeds yet without understanding. Israel clearly comprehended the Lord's unique status but was calloused toward God's purposes in redeeming his people from Egypt and leading them through the wilderness (cf. Ps 106:7; Is 42:18-20; 64:3-4). By becoming blind like the nation of Israel, Paul discovers firsthand that Israel was ignorant of God's wisdom and design in the death of Jesus.

Stephen's speech (7:2-53). Luke introduces his readers to Stephen in chapter 6, when the twelve apostles choose seven men to assist in ministering to the widows in the church (6:1-6). At this point in the narrative, Luke tells us that the "word of God spread" and that the "number of disciples . . . increased rapidly" among the priests (6:7). Stephen is then deemed an individual "full of God's grace and power" who performs "great wonders and signs among the people" (6:8). Such a display of the inbreaking of the kingdom incenses the Jews within the neighboring regions (6:9), and Stephen soon finds himself before the Sanhedrin (6:12–7:60)

The martyrdom of Stephen at the hands of the Jews recalls Jesus' own suffering and death by Israel's leaders (Acts 7:54-60). Luke demonstrates that the followers of Jesus will likewise share his fate. Stephen's martyrdom not only functions retrospectively but also anticipates further conflict between the early church and the Jewish community in Jerusalem and the surrounding regions of the Mediterranean (Acts 8:1-8). Stephen's speech in 7:2-53, one of the longest speeches in Acts, taps into a key story line that is prominent throughout the book—God's desire to dwell with his redeemed people.

After discussing God's promise to Abraham and his offspring (Acts 7:2-8), Stephen summarizes Israel's rejection of Joseph and Moses (7:9-44). Israel rebelled against God during Egyptian captivity, committing idolatry during their wilderness sojourn. The establishment of the tabernacle and its entrance into the Promised Land led to David's desire to construct a permanent dwelling place of God (7:44-46). But this would be realized only in his son, Solomon. The statement that "Solomon . . . built a house for him [God]" is the climax of Stephen's historical recollection (7:47).

In response to the climax of Solomon building a temple for God, Stephen says, "However, the Most High does not live in houses made by human hands" (Acts 7:48). He supports this idea by quoting Isaiah 66:1-2: "Heaven is my throne, and the earth is my footstool. Where is the house you will build for me? Where will my resting place be?" The reference to Isaiah indicates that Stephen remain unconvinced that King Solomon completely fulfilled the divine promise that a son of David would build God a temple.[7] God never intended to dwell fully in the mobile tabernacle or Solomon's temple. He ultimately desired his glory to take up residence among his people (cf. Is 63:15; 64:1-2).

Stephen catches a glimpse of the new heavenly temple immediately before he is executed by stoning. He "looked up to heaven and saw *the glory of God*. . . . He said, 'I see *heaven open* and the Son of Man standing at the right hand of God" (Acts 7:55-56). Perhaps the prophet's plea from Isaiah 64:1 ("Oh, that you would rend the heavens and come down") is answered in Stephen's vision.

FIGURE 8.7. MARTYRDOM OF ST. STEPHEN

Stephen envisages Jesus as the "Son of Man standing at the right hand of God." Luke's wording suggests that Daniel 7:13 is uppermost in mind: the "son of man, coming with the clouds of heaven" (cf. Ps 110:1). In Daniel 7, the divine son of man is granted

[7]F. F. Bruce, *The Book of Acts*, NICNT (Grand Rapids: 1954), 158.

authority to rule over God's everlasting kingdom because he waged war against hostile rivals. By stating that Stephen perceived Jesus as the "Son of Man standing at the right hand of God," Luke discloses an important truth to his readers: Jesus, as the exalted Son of Man, is the supreme judge who vindicates his servants and condemns their enemies.[8] In the eyes of the Sanhedrin, Stephen stands condemned, but in the eyes of the Son of Man, Stephen is a faithful servant. Stephen's martyrdom is paradigmatic for all who harm and inflict persecution on the church. What is true of Stephen is true of all God's people. As the message of the gospel goes forth in the book of Acts, persecution against the church rapidly increases. But the church is to take comfort in the Son of Man's heavenly position, for he will vindicate the righteous and wage war against the persecutors of the church.

Stephen's tragic death becomes the catalyst for the scattering of the Jewish believers "throughout Judea and Samaria" (Acts 8:1). These believers will not run and hide; they will herald the gospel wherever they go. As the believers go forth, so does the gospel: "Those who had been *scattered* preached the word *wherever they went*" (8:4). The Jewish leaders attempted to quell the proclamation of the gospel by killing Stephen, but their actions led only to its growth.

The regathering of estranged Israelites (8:1-40). The stoning of Stephen results in the multiplication of the gospel in Samaria, a clear fulfillment of the promise made in Acts 1:8. The region of Samaria lies in Palestine, to the north of Jerusalem. Jews living in

FIGURE 8.8. SOLOMON RECEIVES THE PLANS OF THE TEMPLE

[8]Eckhard J. Schnabel, *Acts*, ZECNT (Grand Rapids: Zondervan, 2012), 390.

the region are at odds with their fellow Israelites since they were convinced that the temple should be located at Mount Gerizim, not Jerusalem. Jews and Samaritans despise one another and limit their interaction as much as possible.

Acts 8 largely concerns Philip, one of the seven chosen men from 6:5, and his role in the conversion of these estranged Jews. The Old Testament foretold the restoration and unification of the twelve tribes of Israel in the latter days (e.g., Is 11:13; 49:5-6; Ezek 37:16-17), so the conversion of the Samaritans and the Ethiopian eunuch symbolizes the direct fulfillment of those promises. In particular, Samaria was located where northern Israel had been, so the preceding chapters record the beginning fulfillment of the restoration of southern Israel, and the gospel extending to Samaria represents the fulfillment of the restoration promises to northern Israel (cf. 1:8:). The end-time people of God are beginning to fan out beyond the city of Jerusalem.

The first half of Acts 8 narrates Philip's successful journey to Samaria and his encounter with a sorcerer named Simon (8:4-25). Once the Samaritans believed Philip's message, Peter and John immediately traveled to the region (8:14). Luke states that the "Spirit had not yet come on any of them [the Samaritans]" (8:16). They had not yet experienced their own Pentecost. When the apostles laid their hands on the Samaritans, they "received the Holy Spirit" (8:17). The Spirit's descent on the Diaspora Jews in chapter 2 signals their identity as the true Israel of God. In the same way, the Samaritans' reception of the Spirit demonstrates their status as true Israel.

The second half of chapter 8 retells the interaction between Philip and the Ethiopian eunuch. This foreigner appears to be a Jewish proselyte (8:27). The odd detail that he is a eunuch may recall the prophecy of Isaiah 56:3-7 that predicts foreign eunuchs participating in end-time Israel and worshiping in the temple (cf. Ps 68:31; Zeph 3:10). Philip explains to the Ethiopian eunuch that the servant song of Isaiah 53:7-8 is indeed fulfilled in the person of Jesus (Acts 8:30-35). The seemingly odd inclusion of this event in Luke's narrative illustrates the arrival of the gospel even to nations of Africa.[9]

FIGURE 8.9. PHILIP BAPTIZING THE EUNUCH

Paul on the Damascus Road (9:1-31). Luke uses Stephen's martyrdom to introduce Saul (Paul's Jewish name) to his audience. Saul is, in some way, responsible for Stephen's murder (Acts 7:58; see 8:1-3). Such an unflattering introduction to one of the early church's greatest leaders illustrates the transforming power of the gospel of the risen Christ. Luke includes three separate accounts of Paul's conversion: the first one is given from the narrator's perspective (9:1-30), whereas the latter two are given from the

[9]I. Howard Marshall, "Acts," in *Commentary on the New Testament Use of the Old Testament*, ed. G. K. Beale and D. A. Carson (Grand Rapids: Baker Academic, 2007), 573.

mouth of Paul before Jews (22:1-21) and before Agrippa (26:9-19). Paul's conversion is a high point in the narrative of Acts. Instead of dismantling the church through horrific persecution, Paul will play a crucial role in its establishment. God commissions the apostle Paul to reach the Gentiles, a role that continues to fulfill the role of Isaiah's suffering servant (Acts 13:47).

FIGURE 8.10. CONVERSION OF PAUL ON THE WAY TO DAMASCUS

When Paul travels to Damascus to persecute Christians, he encounters a "light from heaven [that] flashed around him" (9:3). Where God manifested himself to individuals and Israel in the Old Testament, Christ manifests himself to Paul. His encounter with the risen Lord shapes his understanding of the Old Testament, God's covenant with Israel, and his expectations of the long-awaited Messiah. In short, Paul's understanding of the history of redemption arises from his Damascus Road experience.[10]

At the Damascus Road encounter, Paul quickly grasps that Christ is the Messiah, the one who has begun to redeem Israel. But Christ is more than a messiah; he is the divine Son of Man who has conquered and sits enthroned at the right hand of the Father ruling over the cosmos. Two Old Testament texts were probably in Paul's mind as he beheld Christ in a vision—Ezekiel 1:26-28 and Daniel 7:13. Both of these prominent Old Testament texts enigmatically present a human figure as divine.

With a new understanding of Christ and how he fits into God's plan of redemption, Paul then discovers his role. By tracing Luke's description of Paul's conversion and commission on the Damascus Road, we discern that Paul, in some way, embodies Isaiah's suffering servant. The apostle Paul is commissioned to bring the good news to the Gentiles (Acts 9:15; Is 49:1-6), suffer for the sake of his people (Acts 9:16; Is 52:13–53:12), and experience blindness and restoration of sight (Acts 9:8, 18; Is 42:18-20). It is no coincidence that Paul closely resembles Isaiah's famed suffering servant and Israel.

Jesus is the ultimate servant who fulfills God's mission to Israel and to the Gentiles. While the Old Testament expects the servant to reach the Gentiles, Jesus never substantially fulfilled this part of the prophecy (Lk 2:32; Acts 26:23). The New Testament broadens

[10]Seyoon Kim, *The Origin of Paul's Gospel*, WUNT 4 (J. C. B. Mohr [Paul Siebeck], 1981; repr., Grand Rapids: Eerdmans, 1981).

this direct fulfillment by affirming that the apostles who identify with Jesus, the Isaianic servant, are charged with taking on the servant's commission and fulfilling the expectation of reaching the nations (Acts 26:18, 23; 2 Cor 6:1-2; Gal 1:20). Paul's ministry, therefore, resembles Jesus' role as the servant. Paul, too, will embody the mission of Isaiah's servant by suffering and restoring Israel. Jesus never significantly becomes a light to the Gentiles, so Paul more fully fulfills the servant's role in converting the Gentiles. As David Peterson notes, "It is implied in Acts that there are aspects of the ministry of the Servant of the Lord that must be carried out by the disciples of Jesus [which were not fully carried out by Jesus himself]. His 'fulfilment' of the Servant's role in his death and resurrection does not exhaust the meaning and application of the Servant Songs in the messianic era."[11]

Several chapters later, Paul even quotes Isaiah 49:6 in Acts 13:47, applying the prophecy to himself and Barnabas: "For this is what the Lord has commanded us: '*I have made you a light for the Gentiles, that you may bring salvation to the ends of the earth*'" (see Acts 26:18, 23). Paul's quotation of Isaiah 49:6 is even more significant in the book of Acts since chapter 1 alludes to the very same text: "You will be my witnesses . . . *to the ends of the earth*" (1:8). Paul, the great persecutor of the church, is now undertaking the servant's directive and fulfilling the Acts 1:8 commission.

The commission of Paul on the Damascus Road underscores his prophetic authority, equivalent to that of Old Testament prophets. The major prophets of the Old Testament all began their prophetic careers through a divine commission (e.g., Isaiah, Jeremiah, Ezekiel), so Luke couches Paul's commission as continuing the task of the prophesied Isaianic servant, a mission that was initially fulfilled by Jesus. Taking Luke–Acts together, Christ and Paul inaugurate the second exodus of God's people that was predicted so long ago.

GOD'S GLORY EXPANDS THROUGH THE WITNESS OF PETER (9:32–12:24)

The Old Testament discusses the role of the Gentiles and how they become part of God's people in the latter days. Much of the discussion is found in the Prophets, especially Isaiah, Jeremiah, and Zechariah. According to Zechariah 14:1-15, the surviving Gentiles will trek to Jerusalem to worship the Lord and celebrate the Feast of Booths. The nations will not only join with the Jews in their worship of the Lord but will also participate in the celebration of certain Jewish festivals. The general Old Testament expectation is that Gentiles in the end times, who desire to become part of the nation of Israel, will take on physical, covenantal badges that identify them as true Israelites. But when we turn to the Gospels and Acts, we learn that Gentiles gain admittance into the covenant community by faith in the risen Christ. It was not fully revealed in the Old Testament that Gentiles would become part of true Israel by faith alone without adhering to Israel's national badges or signs—external indicators that demarcate them as part of God's chosen people group. Gentiles now identify with Jesus, not Israel's law, to become true Israelites. It is precisely at this point where Acts narrates

[11]David G. Peterson, "Acts," in *New Dictionary of Biblical Theology*, ed. David G. Peterson, D. G. Alexander, T. Desmond, and Brian S. Rosner (Downers Grove, IL: InterVarsity Press, 2000), 288.

FIGURE 8.11. CAESAREA MARITIMA

Peter's struggles with how the nations become part of true Israel.

Peter and the Gentiles (10:1–11:18). In light of Paul's conversion (9:1-31) and good news reaching "Judea, Galilee and Samaria" (9:31), Luke turns his attention to the apostle Peter, who ventures west to Lydda and Joppa, healing and evangelizing many (9:32-43). To the north in Caesarea lives a prominent Roman centurion (10:1). This figure remains important for Luke's purposes, as he will become a hinge in the narrative. Although Gentile inclusion has been anticipated up to this point in the narrative (1:8b; 8:26-40), especially in the Gospels, Peter's interaction with Cornelius sets the stage for the overwhelming acceptance of the gospel among the Gentiles.

Peter's interaction with Cornelius in Acts 10 may serve as a paradigm for Paul's travels among the Gentile churches throughout the remainder of the book. With the great reception of the gospel in the Gentile world, the apostles (and the Jerusalem church) are confronted with a difficult problem: What is the relationship between Gentiles and the Torah? Are Gentiles required to keep all the covenant stipulations that God gave to Moses at Sinai? Peter's vision in 10:9-17 and his engagement with Cornelius in 10:24-35 answer these pressing questions. Peter has a vision of a "large sheet" with unclean animals—four-footed animals and reptiles and birds (10:12). God tells Peter that he should partake of the unclean food, but Peter responds with a hearty "By no means, Lord!" Peter refuses to participate in what the Torah forbids.

Although the vision is repeated three times, the precise meaning of the vision escapes Peter (10:16-17). It is not until Peter meets with Cornelius that he grasps its meaning (10:34). The vision of unclean food in 10:9-16 symbolizes the state of the

Gentiles: God regards the Gentiles as "clean" through his Son (10:15, 28). The geography of Israel is broken down into three gradations: holy (the temple precinct), clean (Israel's territory), and unclean (beyond the boundaries of Israel). God forbade the Israelites from partaking of unclean food, since certain foods are associated with imperfection and idolatry (Lev 11:4-8, 13-20; 20:25; Deut 14:3-20; Ezek 4:14). Gentiles, too, are deemed unclean, so they are not permitted to join the covenant community unless they become clean by adhering to certain stipulations of the Torah, such as circumcision, celebration of feasts, and the offering of sacrifices.

Peter experiences a vision wherein God declares certain types of food that had previously been forbidden to be clean or permissible to consume. Israelite distinctives or national emblems are no longer required to join the covenant community; faith in the risen Christ is the only requirement. Acts 10 finishes on a high note with the Gentiles experiencing a "mini Pentecost" and fulfilling the Joel 2 prophecy about the Spirit to Israel (Acts 10:44-48). God truly admits the Gentiles into his Israelite family through faith in Jesus. Peter's speech in Acts 10:34-43 underscores the "good news of peace" that takes place through the person of Christ and is a direct fulfillment of the promised end-time peace that the Old Testament anticipated (see Is 52:7; Nah 1:15).[12]

Paul and Barnabas in Antioch and the famine relief visit (11:19-30). After Stephen's martyrdom, Jewish Christians from Jerusalem flee north to Syrian Antioch, where a large number of Gentiles are converted (Acts 11:20-21; cf. 8:1). The church in Antioch had grown so significantly that the Jerusalem church decides to send Barnabas in order to maintain a healthy relationship with it. Traveling north to Tarsus, Barnabas recruits Paul to assist his ministry in this newly founded church in Antioch (11:25). Paul then stays in Antioch with Barnabas for a whole year ministering to the local assembly (11:26).

While Paul and Barnabas are residing in Antioch, prophets from Jerusalem predict that there would be a severe famine in the region of Jerusalem (11:27-28). This would, of course, affect the Jerusalem church, particularly the poor. The Antiochean community and neighboring churches send gifts and money with Paul and Barnabas as they visit Jerusalem (11:29-30).

Herod's persecution of the church (12:1-24). Acts 12 focuses on Herod's persecution of James, the son of Zebedee (Mt 4:21), and Peter in Judea. Like the Synoptics, Jerusalem and the surrounding territories are fraught with opposition to the gospel. James's arrest and martyrdom symbolize the Jewish aggression toward the apostles as a whole (Acts 12:3). Slowly but surely, the apostles retrace the steps of Jesus, who likewise suffers under Herod and Israel's leaders (e.g., Lk 23:8-12). The narrative then quickly progresses to Peter's imprisonment and miraculous release (Acts 12:3-19). Luke finishes the chapter with a graphic description of Herod's death. Verse 23 says that Herod was struck down by the angel of the Lord because he "did not give praise to God." God kills Herod for murdering James and attempting to kill Peter. Yet the chapter ends on a high note:

[12]Peter Stuhlmacher, *Biblical Theology of the New Testament*, trans. Daniel P. Bailey (Grand Rapids: Eerdmans, 2017), 180, 560, (cf. 61-62, 69-70).

"But the word of God continued to spread and flourish" (12:24; cf. 2:47; 6:7; 13:49; 19:20). The more God's people are oppressed, the more the gospel grows. Herod's commitment to exterminate the proclamation of the gospel ironically led to its promulgation.

The "angel of the Lord" figure is found in the Old Testament and Jewish texts fighting on behalf of the Lord and annihilating God's enemies (2 Kings 19:35; 1 Macc. 7:41; Sir 48:21). God wages war on those who wage war on his covenant community.

GOD'S GLORY EXPANDS THROUGH THE WITNESS OF PAUL (12:25–18:22)

One important thread woven throughout the Old Testament is the global concern of God's message of salvation. Adam, Noah, and the patriarchs are charged with sharing God's message to others. At Sinai God declares that Israel should be a "kingdom of priests" (Ex 19:6). What does this mean for the nation? Israel, as a corporate Adam, must evangelize the surrounding nations and mediate God's presence. But the Old Testament narrates the sad tale of Israel's reluctance to bring the nations into the covenant community. Instead of Jerusalem and the temple becoming a beacon of light to the darkened nations, the nation of Israel shut out the Gentiles and barred the doors.

With the coming of Jesus, Gentiles join the covenant community by identifying themselves with him. Jesus mediated God's presence to the nations, fulfilling God's directive in Exodus 19:6. The twelve apostles then take up the evangelistic mantle and pursue the salvation of the nations. But it is not until the apostle Paul arrives on the scene that the Gentiles begin to emerge fully into the spotlight. Paul, armed with the saving message of Christ, embarks on a series of missionary journeys to bring the Gentiles into the community of faith.

Paul's "first missionary journey" (12:25–14:28). The phrase "first missionary journey," although often used, is somewhat of a misnomer; Paul has already been a missionary for roughly twelve years! After ministering to the Jerusalem church, Paul, Barnabas, and Titus bring John Mark with them back to Antioch (Acts 12:25). Shortly thereafter, Paul ventures on his "first missionary journey": "While they were worshiping the Lord and fasting [at Antioch], the Holy Spirit said, 'Set apart for me Barnabas and Saul for the work to which I have called them.' So after they had fasted and prayed, they placed their hands on them and sent them off" (13:2-3). In Cyprus, Paul, Barnabas, and John Mark enjoy a fruitful ministry and appear to have even converted the proconsul Sergius Paulus (13:4-12).

Paul and Barnabas venture north, evangelizing the southern portion of Galatia (Acts 13:14–14:23). Upon arriving in Perga, John Mark, for an unknown reason, abandons his comrades and heads for Jerusalem. Paul and Barnabas leave for Pisidian Antioch and convert a number of Jews on the Sabbath (13:13-52). Not unexpectedly, the Jews eventually reject Paul's gospel; he and Barnabas

PAUL'S FIRST MISSIONARY JOURNEY

turn to the Gentiles, thus fulfilling the mission of the Isaianic servant (13:47; see Is 49:6). They traverse Iconium (Acts 14:1-7), Lystra (14:6-20) and Derbe (14:20-21), establishing many churches that they will later visit during other missionary journeys. The first missionary journey ends when Paul and company return from the province of Galatia to Perga (14:24-25).

The Jerusalem Council (15:1-35). The relationship between Jews and Gentiles comes to a head in Acts 15, where "certain people" from Judea argue that Gentile Christians at Syrian Antioch must be circumcised to gain admittance into the covenant community (15:1). In light of the previous encounter with a similar (or same) group at Jerusalem (cf. Gal 2:4), Paul and Barnabas put up quite a fight (Acts 15:2). According to Paul, Gentile Christians must not submit to circumcision, thereby undoing the cross of Christ (cf. Gal 5:13-15).

The church at Antioch decides to send Paul, Barnabas, and "some other believers" to Jerusalem to resolve the debate (15:2). The two parties are unable to come to an agreement, so the local church decides to appeal to the Jerusalem church for an official ruling. Upon arriving at Jerusalem, Paul, Barnabas, and the others are warmly greeted by the apostles and elders. In addition to the two groups, a third and distinct group enters the picture—the "party of the Pharisees" (15:5). Nearly identical to the conflict at Galatia, this group of converted Pharisees thought it necessary for Gentiles to be circumcised to join to the covenant community. Like Paul's experience at Antioch, the meeting sparks off a great debate—Paul in one corner and, presumably, the Pharisees in another (15:6). Hearing enough of the debate, restless Peter speaks his mind. Peter, like Paul, believes that God used him to reach the Gentiles *as* Gentiles and bring them into the covenant community and, therefore, that they should not be forced submit to the "yoke" of the law (15:7-11). The Jerusalem Council draws up a letter and entrusts it to Judas (Barsabbas)

FIGURE 8.12. ST. PETER AND ST. PAUL

and Silas. They are to journey with Paul and Barnabas back to the church at Antioch (Syria) and deliver the letter. The church at Antioch would then submit to the council's decree that Gentiles are not required to adhere to the particulars of the Torah.

After the testimonies of Peter and Paul (15:7-12), James summons the council in Jerusalem. The apostle James affirms Peter's testimony, and obviously Paul's by implication, that God has indeed been working among the Gentiles (15:14). James then cites Scripture at length in support of Peter's testimony. This extended quotation consists of three Old Testament texts: "After this I will return and rebuild David's fallen tent. Its ruins I will rebuild, and I will restore it, that the rest of mankind may seek the Lord, even all the Gentiles who bear my name, says the Lord, who does these things'—things known from long ago" (15:16-18; see Jer 12:15; Amos 9:11; Hos 3:5). Gentiles *as* Gentiles are now incorporated into the end-time people of God. Although the Old Testament generally expected Gentiles to embrace Israelite distinctives in the latter days, James sees within the Old Testament itself a reference to the inclusion of Gentiles as Gentiles into the people of God. James's quotation also suggests that Gentiles are clean to enter into and worship within the end-time temple, the church, without keeping the old covenant purity laws (cf. Acts 10:1-48).

With the descent of the Spirit in Acts 2 that forges the church as the dwelling place of God, the Jerusalem Council is concerned to maintain the purity and holiness of the temple. The council decrees that Gentiles are not required to adhere to the external commands in the Torah that demarcate Israel from the surrounding nations, such as circumcision, food laws, and civil law; however, Gentiles *are* required to "abstain from *food polluted by idols*, from *sexual immorality*, from the *meat of strangled animals* and from *blood*" (15:20; see 15:29). Although the specifics of the Mosaic law that demarcate the Israelites no longer apply to God's people, they are still expected to avoid any behavior that relates to idolatry and immoral sexual practices. The portion of the law prohibiting idolatry continues to apply, in some form, to God's people in the new age even as it did in the Mosaic age. A good case can be made here for the abiding authority of the Old Testament, especially as it applies to Gentiles in the new covenant community.

Paul's "second missionary journey" (15:36–18:22). Paul and Barnabas do not return to Antioch but decide to return to the newly founded churches and "visit the believers in all the towns where we preached the word of the Lord and see how they are doing" (Acts 15:36). Barnabas desires to take John Mark, but Paul thought otherwise because John Mark had previously abandoned them in Pamphylia. The two are unable to resolve their dispute, so Barnabas and John Mark head for Cyprus, while Silas accompanies Paul through Syria and Cilicia (15:41). After passing through Derbe, they arrive in Lystra, where they pick up Timothy —the son of a Jewish mother and a Greek father (16:1-2). For Paul to be more effective among the Jews, Timothy is circumcised (16:3-5). The three of them venture west through Galatia intending to arrive eventually at Asia Minor (16:6a). Perhaps they desire to minister in one of the prominent cities, such as Colossae or Laodicea. The Spirit, however, prevents them, so the team heads north toward the province of Bithynia (16:6b). Once more, the Spirit thwarts their attempt and they make their way northwest

> ***Just as Gentile "foreigners" in Israel worshiped at the tabernacle while abstaining from idolatry, so Gentile worshipers in the church are now to worship as the new end-time temple and avoid idolatry.***

through Asia Minor into Troas (16:8-9). Apparently, Luke joins Paul, Silas, and Timothy in Troas (16:10-17; cf. 20:5-21; 18; 27:1-28).

Paul then receives a vision in which he is instructed to head west and minister in the region of Macedonia (16:9-12). They arrive in Philippi and enjoy a fruitful stint (16:12-40), where they convert a Jewish woman—Lydia, a seller of purple cloth. They even exorcise a demon from a young fortune-telling girl. But the girl's owners become so

PAUL'S SECOND MISSIONARY JOURNEY

outraged that they bring Paul before the city magistrates. According to her owners, Paul and company are advocating an illegal religion (16:21). Since they are Roman citizens, Paul and Silas are eventually released from prison. After leaving Luke at Philippi, Paul, Silas, and Timothy venture to Thessalonica, where many Gentiles and some Jews believe in the gospel (17:1-9). But, like most of Paul's experiences, the majority of the Jews reject him and his message. Fleeing for his life, Paul heads to Berea where he meets up with Silas and Timothy (17:10-12).

Hostile Jews locate Paul in Berea, so he and his travelling companions flee south to Athens (Acts 17:15-34). Speaking before the Athenian city council, the Areopagus, Paul contends that he is not introducing a new deity into the pantheon of gods; rather, he argues that his God should be identified with the "UNKNOWN GOD" (17:23). Paul then heads south to Corinth, where he meets up with Timothy. Paul then sends Timothy back to Thessalonica to determine the health of the budding Thessalonian church (1 Thess 3:5). Luke records that Paul's stint at Corinth lasted a lengthy eighteen months (Acts 18:11). At first, Paul ministers to the Jews in Corinth, as is his custom, but this does not last long (18:6). The Jewish rejection of the gospel forces Paul to focus his attention on the Gentiles in Corinth. Hostile Jews in Corinth mount a uniform attack against Paul and bring the matter before the proconsul of Achaia, Gallio (18:12-13). Rome officially recognizes Judaism, allowing the religion to practice as long as it does not become a public disturbance. Several Jews from Corinth drag Paul before Gallio and contend that he is practicing a religion incompatible with Judaism and thus with Roman law itself. Gallio, however, rules in Paul's favor so the gospel takes root among the Gentiles in Corinth (18:14-17).

After ministering in Corinth (Acts 18:1-18), Paul departs for Jerusalem with Priscilla and Aquila. Apparently, Paul makes a vow and cuts his hair at the local port, Cenchreae (18:18). No information is given pertaining to the precise nature of this vow; it could be a Nazirite vow (Num 6:1-21), a vow of thanksgiving

FIGURE 8.13. THE VIEW OF THE ACROPOLIS FROM THE AREOPAGUS

(m. *Naz.* 3.6; 5.4), or a Greco-Roman practice of shaving after a difficult journey. More likely, it is a private vow of thanksgiving.[13] Paul then arrives in Ephesus and reasons with the city's Jews that Jesus is indeed the Messiah (Acts 18:19). From all appearances the meeting goes well, as the Ephesians desire for him to stay longer. Paul intends to return to Ephesus (18:21), leaving behind Priscilla and Aquila to assist the newly founded churches there (18:24-28; 1 Cor 16:19). Paul arrives at Caesarea and travels south to Jerusalem, perhaps to celebrate Passover. Whatever the case, he finally returns to the base of his operations in Antioch (Acts 18:22).

GOD'S GLORY EXPANDS TO THE "ENDS OF THE EARTH" (18:23–28:31)

Acts 1:8, as many commentators agree, summarizes the entire book of Acts: "But you will receive power when the Holy Spirit comes on you; and you will be my witnesses *in Jerusalem, and in all Judea and Samaria, and to the ends of the earth.*" Jesus promised that the disciples would testify about him, beginning in Jerusalem and climaxing in the "ends of the earth," echoing Isaiah 49:6: "I [the Lord] will also make you [the servant] a light for the Gentiles, that my salvation may reach *to the ends of the earth*" (cf. Is 48:20). According to Isaiah 49:6, the servant will play a key role in the redemption of Israel and the conversion of the surrounding nations. In Luke, Simeon prophesies in the temple that Jesus will be a "light for revelation to the Gentiles" (Lk 2:32). By recalling this key passage of Isaiah, Luke applies a messianic text to the apostles. Jesus' mission becomes the apostles' mission. The last portion of Acts taps into this grand Isaiah theme of reaching the Gentiles in the ends of the earth. Paul finds himself in Rome under house arrest, thus directly fulfilling Isaiah's promise: "He proclaimed the kingdom of God . . . with all boldness and without hindrance!" (Acts 28:31).

Paul's "third missionary journey" (18:24–21:16). After briefly staying in Antioch, Paul starts his "third missionary journey." He returns to the well-traversed region of Galatia and Phrygia (Acts 18:23). Paul enters Ephesus and remains there for two and a half years (19:8-10). While there, he encounters some followers of John who had not yet received the Holy Spirit (19:2). Apparently, this group, like the Samaritans (8:14-17), is unfamiliar with Jesus' ministry and had not yet experienced the pouring out of the Spirit that began at Pentecost. The narrative ends with Luke's comment that "there were about twelve men in all," implying that these Gentiles are becoming part of the true twelve tribes of Israel (19:7). Paul's fruitful ministry in Ephesus ends with a riot that is part of a larger "disturbance about *the Way*" (19:23).

According to Acts, believers are viewed as belonging to a group called "the Way": "But some of them [unbelieving Jews] became obstinate; they refused to believe and publicly maligned *the Way*" (19:9); "About that time there arose a great disturbance about *the Way*" (19:23; see 24:14; 24:22). The description of "the Way" echoes Isaiah 40–66, in which God leads his people out of Babylonian exile and into the Promised Land: "There will be *a highway* for the remnant of his people that is left from Assyria, as there

[13]Darrell L. Bock, *Acts*, BECNT (Grand Rapids: Baker, 2007), 586.

PAUL'S JOURNEY TO ROME

was for Israel when they came up from Egypt" (Is 11:16); "In the wilderness prepare *the way* for the LORD; make straight in the desert *a highway* for our God" (40:3); "I am making *a way* in the wilderness" (43:19). According to Isaiah, this expression is shorthand for the restoration of Israel from Babylonian captivity (cf. 1QS 9.16-20). Luke capitalizes on Isaiah's language and labels the early Christian movement as participating in the Way. God is, indeed, spiritually leading his people, the new Israel composed of Jews and Gentiles, out of exile and into the Promised Land.[14]

The proclamation of the gospel always entails a response—obedience or disobedience. Paul's ministry in Ephesus was not all roses. At Ephesus an entire economy of manufacturing idols existed (19:24). One silversmith named Demetrius convinces his fellow craftsmen that their business would collapse, resulting in the temple of Artemis being "discredited" if Paul continues to proclaim the gospel about the one true God (Acts 19:27). Demetrius's words create an uproar in Ephesus (19:32-34). The city clerk quiets the people and pleads with them to take legal action instead (19:35-40). Paul leaves Ephesus and heads west to visit the churches in Macedonia and Achaia and secure a collection for the church in Jerusalem (20:1). Once Paul collects all the funds, he intends to deliver the collection to the church in Jerusalem. The apostle travels through Macedonia and stays in Greece for three months and in Philippi and Troas for a week (20:2-6). At Troas, Paul revives Eutychus, who apparently fell asleep during Paul's speech and then tumbles out of the window of the building (20:7-12). On his way to Jerusalem, Paul says farewell to the congregations in Ephesus and pleads with them not to succumb to false teaching (20:28-31).

[14]David W. Pao, *Acts and the Isaianic New Exodus*, WUNT 130 (Tübingen: J. C. B. Mohr [Paul Siebeck], 2000; repr., Grand Rapids: Baker, 2002), 66.

Paul's journey to Rome and imprisonment (21:17–28:31). Arriving at Tyre and then Ptolemais (Acts 21:1-7), Paul enters Caesarea and is greeted by the prophet Agabus, who predicts that Paul would be imprisoned if he continues on to Jerusalem (21:10-14). The news does not deter Paul's ambition to reach Jerusalem. While in Jerusalem, Paul meets with the apostles there. From all accounts, it appears that the collection is well received by the Jerusalem church. Nothing in Acts leads us to believe otherwise (see 24:17). The collection is an essential part of Paul's program, giving the predominantly Gentile church around the Mediterranean Sea an opportunity to serve the Jewish church's needs in Jerusalem. But while Paul is in Jerusalem, some "Jews from the province of Asia" stir up the crowd in the temple and rally against him (21:27-29). They beat Paul violently (21:30-32) and charge him with breaking purity rules. These Jews are convinced that Paul illicitly brought Gentiles into the temple precinct, though he did no such thing: "'He [Paul] has brought Greeks into the temple and defiled this holy place.' (They had previously seen Trophimus the Ephesian in the city with Paul and *assumed that Paul had brought him into the temple*.)" (21:28-29; cf. 24:10-16). Fortunately, Roman soldiers intervene and prevent Paul's death; they bind him "with two chains" and attempt to send him to the barracks (21:30-34).

Before his imprisonment, Paul asks the commander for permission to address the Jewish crowd (Acts 21:37–22:2). He then recounts his conversion experience but to no avail; the hostile crowd wants blood. The soldiers seize Paul and begin to flog him, but, surprisingly, Paul claims to be a Roman citizen deserving a fair trial. He is taken to the Sanhedrin on the following day to determine the legality of his actions. It quickly becomes evident that Paul will be imprisoned for

FIGURE 8.14. PAUL ARGUING FOR THE VALIDITY OF JESUS' RESURRECTION BEFORE THE JEWISH LEADERS

some time, but the purpose of his imprisonment is disclosed in 23:11: "The Lord stood near Paul and said . . . 'As you [Paul] have testified about me in Jerusalem, so *you must also testify in Rome.*'" Paul's arrest was the means by which the gospel would come to Rome. In order to evade the Jewish conspiracy to kill Paul, the Romans place Paul in prison in Caesarea (24:23-25). Governor Felix leaves Paul imprisoned in Caesarea for two years in order to placate the Jews (24:27), and when Porcius Festus replaces Felix, Paul stands trial once again. This time he appeals to Caesar and asks that the trial be moved to Rome (25:10-12). While in Caesarea, Paul also appears before King Herod Agrippa I and his wife Bernice (25:23–26:32). After sharing his Damascus Road experience with Agrippa, Paul is finally sent to Rome. His trip will prove just as tumultuous as his legal proceedings: he encounters a severe storm (27:1-26) and a shipwreck at Malta (27:27–28:10). Finally, after several months of strenuous travel, Paul arrives in Rome, where he will spend two more years under house arrest (27:1–28:31). The end of Acts makes clear that the nation of Israel, by and large, has rejected the gospel in direct fulfillment of Isaiah's prophecy (28:25-28). Their rejection of the gospel and, by extension Paul's ministry, has paradoxically led to the promulgation of the gospel in Rome. Through persecution, imprisonment, and shipwreck, God's glory has indeed reached the ends of the earth in fulfillment of Old Testament expectations and Acts 1:8.

ROMANS

AUTHORSHIP

Few letters in the New Testament are so readily considered Pauline as Romans. Examining the internal witness of the book, this epistle bears all the hallmarks of Pauline authorship—its opening, closing, vocabulary, style, and theology. Romans 1:1 explicitly identifies the apostle as its author, and 15:23–16:27 contains a host of historical information related to Paul's ministry and personal contacts. Even externally the authorship of Romans stands on solid historical ground since Pauline authorship has rarely been in doubt in the early church or even today. A related problem, however, is the question of literary integrity. Some manuscripts end the epistle at 15:33 and others cut the book off at 16:24. But the lack of overall manuscript evidence for the shorter version and internal considerations militate against the abbreviated ending.

FIGURE 9.1. PAUL WRITING HIS EPISTLES

DATE

Dating Romans rests on the sequence of events in Paul's missionary career. Once he leaves Ephesus on his third missionary journey, he visits the churches in Macedonia and Achaia to tie up the loose ends regarding the collection for the Jerusalem church (Acts 20:1; Rom 15:25-27). The apostle treks through Macedonia and remains in Greece for three months (20:2-3) and in Philippi and Troas for a week (20:6). Before he arrives in Corinth, where he writes his epistle to the Romans, he appears to have ventured into the province of Illyricum (Rom 15:19). Paul pens this letter at the end of his third missionary journey in Corinth, probably around AD 56 or 57.

OCCASION

We know little about the occasion of Romans since Paul divulges scarcely any information regarding the impetus for the letter. Commentators generally focus on either Paul's own circumstances for writing the letter or the situation with the church at Rome. If Paul's personal ministry remains in view, then the ultimate purpose of the letter concerns Paul's collection for the Jerusalem church and the expansion of the gospel to Spain (Rom 15:24). In that case, Paul desires to convince the church at Rome to support his trip to Spain, and the letter to the Romans functions as a doctrinal apology. He feels it necessary to outline his theology about the gospel in order to earn their personal trust and commitment. Conversely, if Romans ultimately targets the immediate circumstances of the church in Rome, the focus is shifted to the church's situation in Rome and the Jew/Gentile relationship there. With the edict of Claudius in AD 49 that expelled many Jews from Rome (Acts 18:2), Gentile membership in the Roman church likely increased exponentially. The influx of Gentiles into the church at Rome invariably changed the composition and dynamics of the church. Upon the death of Claudius in AD 54, Jews and Jewish Christians began trekking back to Rome. Paul writes this letter in the wake of Jewish Christians returning to the church, so that Jewish and Gentile Christians may pursue genuine unity in the gospel. These two approaches are not necessarily mutually exclusive, and both are probably in mind. Therefore, Romans is primarily a defense and articulation of the gospel and, secondarily, a letter relating to the harmony between Gentile and Jewish Christians within the church at Rome.

PURPOSE

Determining the overall purpose of Romans affects one's interpretation of the book as a whole. In recent decades, some scholars have been primarily concerned with the Roman church's interaction with the culture, Jews/Jewish Christians, and the empire. Although these investigations shed some light on Romans, they ought not to dictate the overall purpose of the epistle. Paul's concern, above all, is to articulate the nature of the gospel and how it relates to the human condition (chaps. 1–8) and, secondarily, how the gospel relates to social interaction and the unity of ethnically diverse believers (chaps. 9–16; Jews/Gentiles, "strong"/"weak").

FIGURE 9.2. THE ROMAN COLOSSEUM, ONE OF THE SEVEN WONDERS OF THE ANCIENT WORLD, HELD OVER FIFTY THOUSAND PEOPLE

OUTLINE

I. Letter Opening and Paul's Thesis Statement (1:1-17)
  A. Letter Opening (1:1-15)
  B. Paul's Thesis: The Gospel as Justification by Faith (1:16-17)
II. Justification by Faith Alone (1:18–4:25)
  A. The Universal Reign of Sin (1:18–3:20)
  B. Justification by Faith in Christ and the Example of Abraham (3:21–4:25)
III. Results of Justification by Faith (5:1–8:39)
  A. Justification Offers Hope (5:1-21)
  B. Justifications Offers Freedom from Sin and the Law (6:1–7:25)
  C. Justification Offers Security Through the Spirit (8:1-39)
IV. Israel and the Gospel (9:1–11:36)
  A. God's Sovereign Election of Israel (9:1-29)
  B. Israel's Disobedience in Unbelief (9:30–10:21)
  C. The Salvation of True, Ethnic Israel (11:1-36)
V. Living the Gospel (12:1–14:23)
  A. Serving the Church (12:1-21)
  B. Submitting to Authorities (13:1-14)
  C. The Weak and the Strong (14:1-23)
VI. The Gospel to the Nations (15:1–16:27)
  A. Paul's Plan to Bring the Gospel to Spain (15:1-33)
  B. Personal Greetings and Letter Closing (16:1-27)

BIBLICAL-THEOLOGICAL THEMES

Righteousness and justification by faith. According to Romans 1:17, Paul declares, "in the gospel the *righteousness* of God is revealed." The term *righteousness* is central to the book of Romans and Paul's thought in general. What does this term mean, and how does the Old Testament inform its meaning? To begin to answer these questions, we must turn to the beginning of the Bible's story with Adam and Eve in the garden. Immediately following Adam and Eve's fall, the first couple "sewed fig leaves together" because they "realized they were naked" (Gen 3:7). Garments in the Old Testament symbolize one's inheritance (Gen 37; Num 20:24-28; 1 Kings 11:30-31; 19:19-21; see fig. 9.3). This

FIGURE 9.3. JOSEPH'S COAT OF MANY COLORS

feeble attempt demonstrates a desire to be reconciled to God on their own inadequate terms. They were, at some level, attempting to repair their relationship with God through their own autonomous efforts. After the giving of the covenant curses to Adam and Eve, God "made garments of skin for Adam and his wife and clothed them" (Gen 3:21). These divinely fashioned garments of skin symbolize God's initiative in restoring humanity to himself. It also reveals the need for a proper inheritance or righteousness to dwell in God's presence.

According to the Old Testament, the "righteousness of God" refers primarily to God's judicial actions over creation rather than his covenantal relationship with Israel or God's saving actions (though they are in mind on occasion). The entire created order is held accountable to God's character, words, and deeds. The Lord's covenant faithfulness is merely a subset of his relationship with creation in general. God is the supreme ruler and judge over the entire cosmos. Psalm 9:8 illustrates this point precisely: "He rules the world in righteousness and judges the peoples with equity" (cf. Ps 48:10; 50:6; 72:1-3). The biblical conception of righteousness is intimately connected with the metaphor of a law court and thus includes a forensic notion. God is seen to be right or just over against the world's false claims to be right. However, God acts on behalf of individuals in the face of their enemies. In Psalm 37:6, God comes to the rescue of those who trust him: "He will make your righteous reward shine like the dawn, your vindication like the noonday sun." Much of the remainder of Psalm 37 reminds the Israelites that God will protect them in the midst of trouble and vanquish their enemies (Ps 37:9-40; cf. 143:1-3). Again, in Psalm 98, God promises to come and reveal his righteousness "to the nations" (Ps 98:2). The psalmist takes comfort because God will "judge the world *in righteousness* and the peoples with *equity*" (Ps 98:9). The wicked will perish, but those who fear God will be counted as righteous. God's plan is to come and establish righteousness or justice in the world. His judgment and righteousness is not only for people (both believers and unbelievers) but also for creation (Ps 98:7).

Several key texts in Isaiah prophesy that God will one day pour out his righteousness on creation, a reference to God's action in the end times whereby he brings final judgment on the wicked and full restoration to faithful Israelites. Isaiah 1:26-27 says, "Afterward you will be called *the City of Righteousness*, the Faithful City. Zion will be delivered with justice, her penitent ones with *righteousness*." Isaiah 45:8 figuratively portrays this identical phenomenon of God pouring out his righteousness: "Heavens, sprinkle from above, and let the skies *shower righteousness*. Let the earth open up so that salvation will sprout and *righteousness will spring up* with it. I, Yahweh, have created it" (HCSB; cf. Is 32:16; 33:5).

God executes his righteousness by pouring out his wrath on these enemies and reckoning his servants as "just," or in the right. Mark Seifrid concludes, "When God works salvation for his people, he establishes justice for them (and for himself) over against their enemies and his. Saving righteousness and wrath parallel one another, since they are different aspects of the same event."[1] So, when God justifies an individual, he declares or considers that person to be in a right standing before him. Throughout the book of Romans, the apostle Paul argues that God hands down a favorable verdict on those who trust in Christ's work. These individuals have been saved from God's wrath and, just as Adam and Eve received the "garments of skin" (Gen 3:21), believers inherit the righteousness of Christ. Those justified contribute nothing to their right standing, since they receive it through

[1]Mark Seifrid, *Christ, Our Righteousness: Paul's Theology of Justification*, NSBT 9 (Downers Grove, IL: InterVarsity Press, 2001), 43.

faith alone. But faith itself is also a gift from God (e.g., Rom 4:16; 9:16; Eph 2:8-9). The ultimate cause of justification is not from within individuals but rather rests in God's grace.

Israel and the plan of redemption. One of the more difficult themes in Romans is the nation of Israel's role in the story line of the Bible. God graciously cut a covenant with Abraham and promised that he would make him "into a great nation" and that "all the peoples on earth [would] be blessed" through him (Gen 12:2-3; cf. 17:4-22; 18:18). God keeps his covenant with Abraham and fashions Israel at Sinai to be a "kingdom of priests and a holy nation" (Ex 19:6). God's supreme desire is for his glory to invade every square inch of the world so that every nation will worship and honor him. God intends for Israel, a kingdom of priests, to mediate his glory to the nations. But they fail to become a light to the nations and worship and cherish idols instead of their Creator. God, however, fulfills his promise to Abraham and the patriarchs in the person of Jesus (Mt 2:15; Hos 11:1). Jesus embodies the true Israel of God by perfectly obeying his law and mediating his glory to the Gentiles.

Romans 9–11 probes several critical questions regarding the nation of Israel in God's plan. Will God restore the nation of Israel or only a remnant? And what is the relationship between the Gentiles and the Jewish people? These are particularly pressing questions to the church at Rome, which has recently witnessed the expulsion of many Jews. Paul answers the first question in Romans 9–11 and explains that "not all who are descended from Israel are Israel" (9:6). In fulfilling the many promises of the Old Testament (e.g., Is 11:16; 37:32; Jer 23:3; 31:7; Mic 5:7-8; Zeph 2:7-9), God has decreed that only a remnant will be saved during the overlap of the ages (Rom 11:5). God poured out his wrath with great finality on the nation of Israel when they crucified Christ (1 Thess 2:16), so the theocratic nation of Israel has come to an end. God's people are no longer defined by ethnicity or physical structures or a standing army but by the person of Jesus. All of Israel's theocratic institutions find their ultimate fulfillment in him.

The second pressing question Paul probes is the relationship between ethnic Jews and Gentiles. In the Gospels, the Gentiles often respond well to Jesus' kingdom message and are eager to follow him (e.g., Mt 15:21-28), and the book of Acts witnesses an explosion of Gentiles coming to faith through the apostle Paul (e.g., Acts 9:16; 10:45; 11:1). By the time the book of Romans is written, the covenant community largely consists of Gentiles. Paul declares that he has a "mystery" to share with the church in Rome: "Israel has experienced a hardening in part until the full number of the Gentiles has come in" (Rom 11:25). This verse states *how* Israel will be

FIGURE 9.4 MOUNT SINAI

redeemed—when the "full number of the Gentiles" has occurred. According to Romans 11:11-12, this fullness is already under way and God is presently restoring Israel. Verse 26 then adds, "And *in this way* all Israel will be saved." The salvation of Gentiles is currently provoking some ethnic Jews to come to the Lord. Indeed, Paul's ministry to the Gentiles is fueled with the hope that he might "arouse [his] own people to envy and save some of them" (11:13-14). The "all" in 11:26 refers to a remnant of ethnic Jews between the first and second comings of Christ.[2] According to Old Testament expectations, Israel would first be restored and then the Gentiles would follow their lead (e.g., Is 2:2-4; 60:1-14; Mic 4:1-5). But the pattern Paul outlines in Romans 11 somewhat differs from this Old Testament anticipation: Gentiles are first saved and then the ethnic Jews. As the Gentiles in Rome and elsewhere come to faith in Christ, their belief in the gospel mysteriously stimulates the faith of unbelieving ethnic Jews.

LETTER OPENING AND PAUL'S THESIS STATEMENT (1:1-17)

According to Romans 1:2, the Old Testament anticipates the gospel: "The gospel he promised beforehand through his prophets in the Holy Scriptures." The gospel focuses on Christ's death and resurrection, which the Old Testament anticipates through verbal prophecies, patterns, and types woven throughout Israel's story. As horrific and stunning as Christ's death is, the crucifixion is in line with the Old Testament's expectation (Is 53; cf. 1 Cor 15:3). The same can be said for Christ's resurrection. Despite the disciples' apprehension, Jesus' resurrection and ascension to the right hand of the Father stands in continuity with the Old Testament (Dan 12:2-3; cf. 1 Cor 15:4). The gospel, the centerpiece of the book of Romans, remains tethered to the Old Testament's story line; indeed, it is the climax of the story. Christ came to save sinners from their plight and usher them into the presence of God.

Letter opening (1:1-15). Paul opens the letter by reinforcing his apostleship, prophetic office, and Damascus Road experience (Rom 1:1). The focus lies squarely on Jesus and the gospel (1:3-5), and his mission is to "call all the Gentiles to the obedience that comes from faith" (1:5; cf. 16:26). Paul describes the nature of the gospel by listing four notable characteristics: the gospel is anticipated in the Old Testament (1:2), and centers on Jesus the Messiah (1:3). Christ, the long-awaited Messiah, presently rules in heaven because of his resurrection (1:4). Although he already enjoyed the status of "Son of God," the resurrection demonstrates his identity climactically and definitively, signaling the beginning of the new age. An effect of the gospel also includes the incorporation of the Gentiles into the people of God, true Israel (1:5).

The Gentiles in the Roman church play an integral role in that mission: "*You also are among those Gentiles* who are called to belong to Jesus Christ" (1:6). After mentioning the importance of the gospel, Paul proceeds to discuss his love for the church at Rome and his desire to be with them (1:8-15). The gospel, he claims, is a demonstration of God's power by saving those who have faith in Christ (1:16-17). Apparently, the Roman

[2]Though many commentators understand Romans 11:26 to refer to the final coming of Christ, when "all" in ethnic Israel will be saved (e.g., Douglas J. Moo, *The Epistle to the Romans*, NICNT [Grand Rapids: Eerdmans, 1996], 724).

church enjoys a vibrant faith that is celebrated "all over the world" (1:8). Paul gives thanks to God for their faith and witness by constantly praying on their behalf (1:8-10). He even wishes to visit the church at Rome (1:11; cf. 15:22-29). Assuming that he will indeed arrive, he desires to do three things for the church: "impart . . . some spiritual gift," "have a harvest among you," and "preach the gospel" (1:11-15).

Paul's thesis: The gospel as justification by faith (1:16-17). Romans 1:16-17 succinctly states God's justification of sinners. He deems those righteous who have faith in his Son. Faith in Christ is what saves a person from God's wrath and grants them end-time life, which is secured in the new heavens and earth. Faith is not a work (Eph 2:8-9). It is simply a response to or trusting in God's promises. According to its usage in Romans, the term *faith* or *belief* often lacks an object, but this is not to say that it has no object; rather, "faith has become so tied to what God has done in Christ that further specification is not needed."[3]

Paul adds a unique double preposition in Romans 1:17: "from faith to faith" (NASB). This phrase highlights the importance of faith and its natural relationship to righteousness (see 2 Cor 2:16). In verse 17, Paul quotes Habakkuk 2:4, in which righteous individuals *already* possess faith in God's promises. But Paul's point in 1:17 is not far from the context of Habakkuk 2:4. The abiding authority of the Old Testament surfaces here. Genuine faith trusts in God's promises in all of life and in every circumstance apart from human merit.

Faith is the *means* by which an individual receives a righteous standing before God. When discussing the term *faith*, Paul tends to avoid the preposition *because* and instead employs ones that denote instrumentality (e.g., *from, through*).[4] For example, he claims in Galatians 3:26, "In Christ Jesus you are all children of God through faith" (cf. Rom 3:25, 30; 2 Cor 5:7; Gal 2:16; 3:14, 26; Eph 2:8; 2 Tim 3:15). Faith in Christ appropriates his saving righteousness. Paul argues that the "*righteousness* of God is revealed" (Rom 1:17). According to the Old Testament, the "righteousness of God" refers to his judicial actions over creation. God is the supreme ruler and judge over

FIGURE 9.5. COMMENTARY ON HABAKKUK AS PRESERVED IN THE DEAD SEA SCROLLS

the entire cosmos. When Paul claims that God's righteousness is revealed, he means that only those who have faith can access this saving righteousness. God intervenes on behalf of those who possess faith in Christ and pours out his righteousness by declaring them to be in the right. The Old Testament longed for the day when, at the end of time, God would pronounce his people as righteous. Paul declares that the day has indeed arrived. But believers still await Christ's second coming, when God will *publicly* declare to all the world that believers are in the right. Justification, like all the major doctrines of the New Testament, is an "already but not yet" reality.

[3]Moo, *Epistle to the Romans*, 67.

[4]D. A. Carson, "The Vindication of Imputation: On Fields of Discourse and Semantic Fields," in *Justification: What's at Stake in the Current Debates*, ed. Mark Husbands and Daniel J. Treier (Downers Grove, IL: InterVarsity Press, 2004), 46-78.

JUSTIFICATION BY FAITH ALONE (1:18–4:25)

Adam and Eve's transgression in Eden plunged humanity and creation headfirst into sin. As a result, God banishes them from the garden sanctuary and drives them out and places cherubim "on the east side of the Garden of Eden . . . to guard the way to the tree of life" (Gen 3:24). Adam and Eve now find themselves exiled from God's presence. When Cain murders his brother later in the narrative, he too is driven from the land and becomes a "restless wanderer on the earth," away from the Lord's presence (Gen 4:14, 16). The remainder of Genesis narrates the story of God's people moving farther away from his garden sanctuary heading eastward (Gen 13:11; 25:6). As the effects of the fall begin to take root within the created realm, humanity repeatedly fails to obey God, resulting in increased estrangement from him. Sinful individuals cannot dwell in God's holy presence and survive. Sin must be punished and God alone must restore humanity.

FIGURE 9.6. CAIN SLAYING ABEL

Romans 1–4 confronts this issue of estrangement without mincing words. Sin's tyranny affects both Gentiles *and* Jews. Both groups must grasp that, because of their rebellion and idolatry, they deserve physical and spiritual death. Paul must also convince Gentiles that, although they do not have the Mosaic law in written form, they remain culpable. Gentiles, according to Paul, have a clear knowledge of God. They have natural law to convict them of idolatry and unrighteousness (Rom 2:15). Conversely, Jews contend that since they have the Mosaic law they are righteous, without blame, and surely not idolaters. Paul must convince them that although they possess the law, they are still unrighteous before God because they grievously break it. All people stand guilty before God, but faith in Christ saves humanity from their sinful plight.

The universal reign of sin (1:18–3:20). We noted that in Romans 1:17 the positive side of God's righteousness comes to the fore. It is righteousness that comes to the aid of believers and is credited to their account. Romans 1:18-3:20, however, concerns the other side of God's righteousness. He pronounces judgment on all those who are idolaters: "The *wrath of God is being revealed* from heaven against all the godlessness" (1:18). Romans 1:18-32 concerns pagan Gentiles who stand condemned before a holy God. They remain condemned because they have access to a "law of God" that is evident from creation and their conscience (2:12-16). Since all Gentiles have "exchanged the glory of the incorruptible God for an image" (1:23 NASB), they rightly deserve judgment.

The result of this heinous idolatry is that God "gave them over" to their own wickedness and lusts (1:26-32). Paul's words recall Psalm 106:20, in which the Israelites exchange the object of true worship, or "their glory," for an idolatrous image. This psalm alludes to the episode of the golden calf at Sinai. By referring to idolatry, Paul taps into the first formal sin in Israel's existence as a nation. Exodus 32 portrays Israel's idolatrous worship of the molten calf in language describing rebellious cattle to convey the idea that the people have become like the object of its worship. Israel is called a "stiff-necked people" who are "running wild" and "out of control" (Ex 32:9, 25). Because the nation has become as spiritually lifeless as the inanimate golden calf, God mocks Israel by depicting them as rebellious cows running amok.

The language of exchanging "the glory of the incorruptible God for an *image* in the form of corruptible man and *of birds and four-footed animals and crawling creatures*" (1:23 NASB) also echoes Genesis 1–3. Instead of worshiping God and giving him glory, Adam and Eve worship themselves and commit idolatry. As Morna Hooker notes, "Adam has not only failed to exercise his rightful dominion over creation, but, by placing himself in subservience to a creature (a serpent), has opened up the way to idolatry."[5] Paul therefore concludes that Adam and Israel sinned by committing heinous idolatry, and such behavior continues to be recapitulated among all sinful individuals.

But Gentiles are not the only people group deserving of God's wrath: unbelieving Jews also stand in judgment before God. Paul switches to the second-person singular ("you") as a dialogue partner, often referred to as an interlocutor (Rom 2:1-5, 17-29). This type of rhetoric is known as a diatribe, whereby a teacher converses with and rebukes the conversation partner. Although

> ***According to Romans 1:18, the behavior of the Gentiles is indistinct from the behavior of idolatrous Israelites at Sinai. They, too, have failed to worship the creator and have turned to worshiping figurative idols.***

the interlocutor is hypothetical, the individual still represents real debates and controversies. The Jews, like the Gentiles, are deceived because they think that by having the law of Moses and God's national election they are immediately part of God's family (2:3). Like the Gentiles, they too possess a clear knowledge of God through the Torah. But possession of the law does not immediately translate into a right standing before God (2:1-16). Those who are "under" or are in possession of the Mosaic law are judged by that same law (2:12). The same can be said of circumcision. Simply because a male Jew

[5] Morna D. Hooker, *From Adam to Christ* (Cambridge: Cambridge University Press, 1990), 78.

receives circumcision, an external sign of the covenant, does not preclude God's wrath (2:25-29). Like the Gentiles, the Jews are just as sinful and idolatrous. Both groups have broken God's righteous commandments, whether it is the Mosaic law or the law manifested in nature and conscience.

Therefore, Jews, who possess the law and are circumcised but lack faith in Jesus, stand condemned just like the Gentiles. In Romans 3:9-20, Paul consigns all of humanity, Jews and Gentiles, under God's wrath because they are guilty before him: "Jews and Gentiles alike are all under the power of sin" (3:9). This thesis is supported by numerous texts from a variety of Old Testament passages (Ps 5:9; 10:7; 14:1-3; 36:1; 53:1-3; 140:3; Is 59:7). These Old Testament texts clearly affirm that all humanity transgresses God's laws and deserve his judgment.

FIGURE 9.7. MOSES AND THE GOLDEN CALF

Justification by faith in Christ and the example of Abraham (3:21–4:25). Although all of humanity is guilty before God (as Paul has articulated in detail), there remains a solution for avoiding his wrath: faith in Christ. In Romans 3:21-31, God's righteousness comes into play once more, saving and acquitting those who have faith in Christ—a concept that repeats Paul's thesis in 1:16-17 of God's righteousness in declaring righteous those living by faith. God remains just or righteous because his Son pays the price of sin as an atoning sacrifice in the stead of sinners. God must maintain his holy character and perfect justice must be upheld.

Paul begins this section with the phrase "but now," referring to the two-age schema or the overlap of the ages. The old age is filled with sin, rebellion, and idolatry (Rom 1:18–3:20), but the new age—the "now"—has dawned with Christ's work on the cross and resurrection. Here Paul claims that righteousness has been more fully revealed in the gospel in the new age. Douglas Moo writes that "As the 'wrath of God' dominated the old era (1:18), so the 'righteousness of God' dominates the new."[6]

The apostle explains that "in [God's] forbearance he had left the *sins committed beforehand unpunished*" (Rom 3:25). According to the Old Testament, God promises to punish sin at the very end of history (e.g., Is 40:2; Ezek 44:29). God executes this great end-time judgment on his Messiah on behalf of his people (Rom 3:25). Zechariah 3:9 is not far from Paul's thinking: "'I will engrave an inscription on it [a stone],' says the Lord Almighty, 'and *I will remove the sin of this land in a single day*.'" Similarly, Zechariah 12:10 says, "And I will pour out on the house of David and the inhabitants of Jerusalem a spirit of grace and supplication. They will

[6]Moo, *Epistle to the Romans*, 222.

look on me, the one they have pierced, and they will mourn for him as one mourns for an only child, and grieve bitterly for him as one grieves for a firstborn son." Despite delaying judgment of intractable unbelievers for a time, God does punish sin and is vindicated as righteous. The latter-day judgment has begun in Jesus but will be consummated in the judgment of unbelievers at the very end of the age.

According to Rom 3:25, God "presented Christ as a *sacrifice of atonement*." Although many translations render this word as "sacrifice" (NIV, NJB), "expiation" (RSV), or "propitiation" (NASB, ESV), the word refers to the "mercy seat" (NET). The mercy seat is located in the holy of holies and occupies a central role in the Day of Atonement. Exodus 25:17-22 describes the construction of the mercy seat: it was to be fashioned out of gold (Ex 25:17), and two gold cherubim were to flank both sides facing inward (Ex 25:18-19). The cherubim overshadow the cover or the mercy seat with their wings spread upward. The cover sat on top of the ark that contains the two tablets from Sinai. Exodus 25:22 explains that God will "meet" with Israel "between the two cherubim that are over the ark of the covenant law" (cf. Num 7:89). Leviticus 16 also details the high priest's role on the Day of Atonement, in which the mercy seat features prominently. The high priest casts incense on the fire so that he will be shielded from God's presence in the holy of holies (Lev 16:12-13). He then takes blood from a bull and a goat and sprinkles it on the top of and at the front of the mercy seat (16:14-15). The purpose of this exercise is to "make atonement for the Most Holy Place," so that God may dwell with Israel (16:16). Israel is unclean with sin, and her temple/tabernacle has become contaminated. The Day of Atonement purifies Israel and makes the sanctuary once again holy to the Lord.

FIGURE 9.8. CARRYING THE ARK OF THE COVENANT

The mercy seat is a type of Christ, the very location of the sacrifice and God's dwelling place. At the cross Jesus' blood is sprinkled on the true mercy seat in God's invisible but true heavenly temple, and there he bears God's end-time wrath on behalf of believers. He suffers as the ultimate punishment of sin and as the substitute for sinful people. Paul can now declare that believers will be "saved from God's wrath through him [Christ]" (Rom 5:9; cf. 1 Thess 1:10). Further, through his resurrection, he is also the means by which God dwells with his people.

Because God's gracious righteousness is given to believers through faith, there is no opportunity to boast before God (Rom 3:27-31). The theme of boasting bridges Paul's discussion of works of the law and Abraham, the father of Israel. If Abraham, the great patriarch, could not boast in his works, how much more should Jews and Gentiles not boast? The apostle provides an example of an ungodly and uncircumcised individual—namely, Abraham—who trusts in God's promises and is justified apart from works (4:5). Abraham believes that God would keep his promises by making him the father of a mighty nation despite external circumstances (4:18-22). Faith serves as the instrument by which God appropriates righteousness (4:3, 5, 17-22). Abraham's faith also prepares the way for Gentile inclusion into the people of God, fulfilling God's promise to him (Gen 12:1-3). His justification in God's sight takes place before his circumcision (Rom 4:9-10; Gen 17:10-11). Since Abraham has faith apart from the law, this paves the way for others to have similar faith. Abraham is thus deemed the father of all who have faith in Christ, whether Jew or Gentile (Rom 4:11-12).

Through Christ, believers are no longer unclean with sin. He is both the sacrifice and the mercy seat; his body is the location that bore God's wrath.

Romans 4:13 reads, "It was not through the law that Abraham and his offspring received the promise that he would be *heir of the world*, but through the righteousness that comes by faith." Here the word *world* refers to the entire earth, perhaps even the starry heavens. Paul's statement universalizes the Abrahamic land promises that appear throughout the Old Testament (cf. Ps 2:8; 72:8; Is 26:19; 27:6; 54:2-3) and ultimately originate in Genesis 1:28. Through Christ, then, believers have begun to inherit these sweeping promises of the land.

Later in the chapter Paul claims that Christ was "*delivered over to death for our sins* and was raised to life for our justification" (Rom 4:25). Paul has Isaiah 53:12 (LXX) in mind here: "He [the servant] was delivered over because of their sins" (Brenton). Isaiah 53 speaks of the servant vicariously suffering the punishment of the Israelites so that he may redeem and justify them (Is 53:4-11). Christ dons believers with his own righteousness, a status that his own resurrection demonstrates.

RESULTS OF JUSTIFICATION BY FAITH (5:1–8:39)

In the ancient world, it was common for an individual to represent a community or even a nation. In the Old Testament and the ancient Near East, kings represent their nations. Often a king or leader's action either positively or negatively affect the group or nation as a whole (e.g., Ex 20:6; Josh 7:1-5; 1 Chron 21:1-17; 1 Sam 21:1; Is 49:1-6). John Reumann notes that "there is a constant oscillation between the individual and the group—family, tribe, or nation—to which he belongs, so that the king or some other representative figure may be said to embody the group, or the group may be said to sum up the host of the individual."[7] Here in Romans 5 the first

[7]John Reumann, "Introduction to the First Edition" in H. Wheeler Robinson, *Corporate Personality in Ancient Israel* (Philadelphia: Fortress, 1964), v.

Adam's failure in the garden is typologically contrasted with the last Adam's success. That success, the "one righteous act" (Rom 5:18), likely refers not only to Christ's act of obedience by dying on the cross but also includes his obedient suffering in the hours preceding his crucifixion and even extends to his earthly ministry (Mt 4:1-11; Mk 1:12-13; Lk 4:1-13). The first Adam's act of disobedience is not merely the one act of eating the fruit of the tree but is preceded by his disobedience of allowing the serpent to remain in the garden while conversing with Eve and not casting him out or calling down judgment on him in the name of the Lord.

Romans 5–8 is the result of justification. This section reveals how believers are caught between two ages: the old, sinful age and the new creation, an age dominated by righteousness and the life of the new creation. The overlap of the ages, or what is often regarded as "inaugurated eschatology," is a somewhat novel idea to some people. For the most part, the "already but not yet" framework of the New Testament is largely unexpected in the Old Testament, which anticipated the day when believers would be fully delivered from their sinful bodies and ushered into the new creation. The New Testament writers contend that believers already exist as a new creation (2 Cor 5:17) but are not yet fully and physically restored in the new heavens and earth. Paul's teaching in Romans 5–8 outlines how believers are spiritually identified with the new creation but remain physically tethered to the old age. Although believers have been spiritually resurrected and participate in the new creation, indwelling sin remains until the final resurrection (cf. Gal 5:13-26).

Justification offers hope (5:1-21). All believers, like Abraham (Rom 4:1-25), have been justified through faith in Christ. A result of justification is a robust "hope of the glory of God" (5:2). Such hope reaches into the future despite present conflict and trials (5:3) and expects God's full redemption (5:9-11). The latter portion of chapter 5 details the actions of the two Adams and their effects on humanity. Paul hangs all of redemptive history on the shoulders of two individuals—the first Adam and the last Adam. Although the story of Israel includes a number of important

FIGURE 9.9. ABRAHAM TRUSTS GOD EVEN IN SACRIFICING ISAAC

people and institutions (Israel, the Davidic monarchy, etc.), they remain secondary to these two figures. Here in Romans 5 and in 1 Corinthians 15, Paul tells the story of two Adams and how all of humanity and creation flows from them. Adam's disobedience in the garden spun creation and humanity downward (Rom 5:12). Sin reigns over these spheres and so began what is often characterized as the old age—rebellion, death, and condemnation (5:12-14, 16, 18). As a foil to the first Adam's disobedience stands Christ's success, who establishes the new age of righteousness, forgiveness, and eternal life (5:17-18). The first Adam is a pattern of the last Adam (5:14), but the last Adam is far greater than the former. The last Adam's obedience far exceeds the disobedience of the former and blazes the way for the inheritance of the new heavens and earth that all believers will enjoy (5:15). As Richard Gaffin notes, two ages dominate Paul's thought—"creation and the new creation, the original creation and its consummation, each beginning with and determined by an Adam of its own."[8]

> ***The effect of the original Adam's sin plunged humanity into despair and estrangement, whereas the obedience of the last Adam gives life and draws individuals into the presence of God.***

For those who believe in him, Christ, the last Adam, suffers the penalty of the first Adam's conduct (5:6-10). Descendants of the last Adam now enjoy a peaceful relationship with God (5:1) and experience "righteousness to eternal life" (5:21 NASB). This eternal life was promised to the first Adam in the garden upon perfect obedience, which did not occur. But this eternal life can now be experienced through identification with the perfect last Adam.

Justification offers freedom from sin and the law (6:1–7:25). Now that God has rescued believers from the age of sin and grants them life in the age filled with end-time peace and grace, Paul cautions against rebellious conduct. It would be easy to conclude that since believers are no longer condemned and that they enjoy God's boundless grace, they are free to sin, even in abundance. "Shall we go on sinning so that grace may increase?" (Rom 6:1). Paul heads off this conclusion by demonstrating that justification brings about a new existence; believers are now dead to sin and alive to God. Paul keeps the previous chapter in mind when he tells his readers that their old self (or better, old man) has been crucified with Christ (6:6). The term *self* or *man* here evokes Paul's discussion of the first and the last Adam in 5:12-20. The church at Rome must resist and abstain from sin because they enjoy a new identity in the last Adam. Believers live in the new age of righteousness, and they are, as Paul states, "slaves to righteousness" (6:15-18). Christ died to the old world and is raised as a new man, so his followers have also died to the old world and have been raised with him as a new people.

[8]Richard B. Gaffin Jr., *By Faith, Not by Sight: Paul and the Order of Salvation* (London: Paternoster, 2006), 48.

To reinforce living in accordance with the new age rather than the age of sin and rebellion, Paul discusses the role of the Mosaic law. He passionately describes his experience being "under the law" in the old age *from the perspective of a Christian living in the new age*. In Romans 7, Paul tightens the rope and focuses on one theme in particular: sin used the Mosaic law to bring about death.

The identification of *I* in Romans 7:7-25 is the subject of tireless debate. Some identify the pronoun *I* as preconversion Paul, postconversion Paul, a God-fearing Gentile, Adam, Israel, and an unknown person lacking specificity. By citing a commandment from the Decalogue ("You shall not covet" [7:7]), Paul is probably here aligning himself with the nation of Israel at Sinai in his experience with the Mosaic law. Paul also alludes to Genesis 1–3 throughout Romans 7 and thus presents himself as recapitulating Adam's fall in the garden.[9]

Analogous to Adam becoming a "living being" (Gen 2:7), Paul was at one time "alive," though obviously not sinless (7:9). Genesis 2:16-17 also details how God commanded Adam and Eve to abstain from eating fruit from the tree of the knowledge of good and evil (cf. Gen 1:28). Paul's words "when the commandment came" (Rom 7:9) probably recalls God issuing his law in Genesis 2:16-17. In Romans 7:8, Paul comments how sin "seiz[ed] the opportunity afforded by the commandment." This unique wording, particularly the personification of sin, alludes

FIGURE 9.10. TORAH SCROLL

[9]Chris Vlachos, *The Law and the Knowledge of Good and Evil: The Edenic Background of the Catalytic Operation of the Law in Paul* (Eugene, OR: Wipf & Stock, 2009).

to the serpent (who embodies sin) abusing or seizing God's commandment and perverting it to accomplish ill intent (Gen 3:1-4). Lastly, the apostle recollects how he died spiritually because of his interaction with sin and the law: "When the commandment came, sin sprang to life and I *died*. . . . The very commandment that was intended to bring life actually brought *death*. For sin . . . put me to *death*" (Rom 7:9-11). One of the most dramatic points in the Genesis 1–3 narrative is the covenantal curse that God issues to the first couple. God curses them by consigning them both to death and exiling them from his presence in the garden sanctuary (Gen 3:19, 24). Even though Adam is largely in focus in Romans 7, the nation of Israel remains in view. The fall of Adam is recapitulated on a macro scale in the nation of Israel. Both parties are created, receive God's law, and commit the same form of idolatry that results in death (Ex 19–32).

Paul's point in retelling the story of Adam and Israel is twofold: the law, although holy and righteous, can be a tool of sin that brings about death. The problem therefore lies not with the law but with the weakness of the human condition in its indefensibility against sin and temptation. By alluding to Adam and Israel, Paul includes all of humanity in his experience. It is, in a very real sense, "the autobiography of all members of the larger Adam, humanity."[10]

Justification offers security through the Spirit (8:1-39). After formerly living as a "slave to the law of sin" (Rom 7:25), Paul emphatically declares that believers are no longer under God's end-time wrath (8:1). His reasoning rests on the presence of the end-time Spirit: "Through Christ Jesus the *law of the Spirit who gives life has set you free* from the law of sin and death" (8:2). The third person of the Trinity occupies a prominent position in Romans 8 in contrast to the lack of any mention of the Spirit in the previous context. Romans 7:7-25 depict life under the law, whereas verses 8:1-39 depict living under the power of the Spirit. The Spirit indwells all believers, imparting resurrection life to them (8:11).

All believers have begun to participate in the long-awaited resurrection of the saints. We can discern shades of Ezekiel in Paul's language here in chapter 8. Ezekiel 36 predicts that in the end times God will give Israel his "Spirit" and a "new heart" (36:26-27). The next chapter then prophesies the restoration of Israel from Babylonian exile and their resurrection: "I am going to open your graves and bring you up from them" (Ezek 37:12; cf. Dan 12:1-3). Paul reaches back to Ezekiel 36–37 here in Romans 8 and assures his readers that they have begun to return from spiritual exile and to share in the end-time resurrection of the saints.

The believers' power to defeat sin and overcome the world rests in their identity as the end-time people of God who have begun to inherit the new creation. Their spiritual resurrection has restored them from their spiritual exile and alienation from God. On the one hand, if believers do not "bear fruit," they probably have not experienced the "new way of the Spirit" within them (Rom 7:5-6). On the other, if saints "put to death the misdeeds of the body," they can be assured that they are being "led by the Spirit of God" and are obedient "children of God" (8:13-14).

[10]G. B. Caird, *New Testament Theology*, ed. L. D. Hurst (Oxford: Clarendon: 1995), 99. However, many commentators believe that in Romans 7:7-25 Paul is portraying himself as a conflicted Christian.

Since believers are indwelt with the Spirit and have been resurrected on a spiritual level, they must not falter in the midst of suffering and tribulations. Such experiences are "not worth comparing with the glory that will be revealed in us" (Rom 8:18). All of creation (like believers) is caught in the overlap of the ages. The old, fallen creation has been irreversibly altered through Christ's death and resurrection, spearheading the commencement of the new creation. But with the overlap of the ages comes the "not yet" (8:19-30). The entire created order awaits the full, consummate redemption that will arrive at Christ's second coming, and since believers are part of the new creation, God promises to preserve their faith no matter the circumstances (8:31-19).

The apostle Paul claims that "neither . . . angels, nor principalities . . . will be able to separate [believers] from the love of God" in Christ (Rom 8:38-39 NASB). Satan and his minions have maliciously treated and falsely accused the covenant community since the fall, yet their slander against the saints has begun to be nullified (Rev 12:9-11) and will be brought consummately to an end at the believers' final resurrection when Christ returns. No one, including Satan, can "bring any charge against those whom God has chosen" now or on the last day (Rom 8:33; cf. 16:20; Rev 12:7-10). The bodily resurrection of the saints vindicates them before the world. The right standing before God that believers enjoy in the overlap of the ages will be publicized to all those gathered at the final judgment.

ISRAEL AND THE GOSPEL (9:1–11:36)

One aspect of Genesis 3:15 is the prediction of a perennial conflict between the "offspring" of the serpent and the descendants of the woman: "I will put *enmity between you and the woman, and between your offspring and hers*; he will crush your head, and you will

> ***At the very end of history, when believers and unbelievers are resurrected (Dan 12:1-2), God will declare to the entire cosmos and the angels that only those who trust in Christ are just or in a right standing before him.***

FIGURE 9.11. FALL OF THE REBEL ANGELS

strike his heel." We do not wait long for these words to ring true, as Cain murders his brother Abel a few verses later (Gen 4:8). The remainder of the Pentateuch narrates the struggle between the godly seed of the woman and the ungodly seed of the serpent. But the serpent's offspring often launches attacks from within. According to Exodus 32, Aaron colluded with weary Israel to fashion a golden calf and worship it (Ex 32:1-6). As punishment for their sin, the Levites slaughtered three thousand Israelites (32:27-28). Israel's history continues to unfold, and despite God's gracious provision and blessing, only a few within Israel hold fast to God's promises. By the time we reach the Old Testament prophetic books, a clear pattern has been established: God will preserve only a remnant (e.g., Is 37:32; 49:6; Jer 23:3; 31:7; Joel 2:32; Mic 2:12; 4:7; 5:7-8; Zech 8:12). God promises Abraham that he will establish a mighty nation out of his descendants, and he eventually fulfills those promises. But he promises to preserve only a few within the nation and some outside the nation, Gentiles who join Israel much like Rahab and Ruth.

After sketching out the nuts and bolts of the gospel in chapters 1–4 and its results in chapters 5–8, Paul progresses to the relationship between Israel and the gospel. Paul must confront a pressing issue: If the gospel is the fulfillment of Old Testament promises, then why does Israel, by and large, reject it? The answer lies in how God has always dealt with Israel—only a remnant of Israelites have and will continue to embrace God's promises. Secondly, according to the Old Testament, there will come a time when God will restore Israel, and the Gentiles will stream *to* Israel and become proselytes (e.g., Is 2:2-3).

FIGURE 9.12. SEVENTH PLAGUE ON EGYPT

Now, however, Gentiles have become part of true Israel, and the majority of ethnic Jews have rejected the gospel. God's dealings with Israel in the overlap of the ages is a mystery. The faith of the Gentiles serves as the catalyst for faith among ethnic Jews.

God's sovereign election of Israel (9:1-29). In Romans 9:6, Paul establishes a crucial principle that has operated since Israel's inception: "It is not as though God's word had failed. *For not all who are descended from Israel are Israel.*" Simply because one is born into Israel's covenant community does not translate into an automatic acceptance into God's true spiritual family (2:28-29). Each ethnic Israelite is responsible to make a conscious decision to follow the Lord and trust in his promises of deliverance (e.g., Deut 29:19-21). Paul's point in Romans 9:1-6 is that God has always remained faithful despite appearances. Externally, it appears as if God has abandoned the covenant with Abraham. The nation of Israel, by and large, has not embraced the gospel, so it seems that the Abrahamic covenant is failing. But, Paul argues, the true Israel of God has indeed embraced the gospel. From Adam and Eve onward, God's people have always constituted a spiritual minority.

A theologically difficult question then arises: Why do some become part of the true people of God and others do not? The answer is that God sovereignly and mercifully decides who becomes part of his true family. Romans 9:6-13 illustrate how God chooses who becomes part of true Israel. According to the world's standards, Ishmael and Esau should have been chosen, as they were the firstborn. But God often does not work in accordance with the world's standards (1 Cor 1:26-29; cf. Is 55:9). Nevertheless, no one can accuse God of being unjust, because he is all-powerful and wise: "What then shall we say? Is God unjust? Not at all!" (Rom 9:14).

Romans 9:15-29 provides the theological rationale for God's actions. He has always acted in accordance with his wisdom and his freedom of choice. No matter what individuals say or do, nothing can thwart God's decrees: "It [salvation] does not, therefore, depend on human desire or effort, but on God's mercy" (9:16). God is ultimately the one behind salvation and election. He chose Abraham, Isaac, and Jacob but rejected Ishmael, Esau, and Pharaoh. Therefore, if God, through his sovereignty, chooses that the covenant community will be composed of mostly Gentiles, it is entirely in keeping with the Old Testament pattern. As Frank Thielman affirms, "Because the biblical God freely chooses the membership of his people, he can choose Gentiles as well as Jews, and he can exclude some Jews."[11] Paul reinforces this principle in Romans 9:18 with a text from Exodus 33:19: "I will cause all my goodness to pass in front of you, and I will proclaim my name, the Lord, in your presence. *I will have mercy on whom I will have mercy, and I will have compassion on whom I will have compassion.*" Here in the Exodus narrative God allows Moses to encounter his glory, thus having mercy and compassion on him. Moses simply did not deserve to encounter God's glory in such an intimate way.

Strengthening this principle, in Romans 9:17 Paul cites Exodus 9:16: "But I have raised you [Pharaoh] up for this very purpose, that I might show you my power and that my

[11]Frank Thielman, *Theology of the New Testament: A Canonical and Synthetic Approach* (Grand Rapids: Zondervan, 2005), 368.

name might be proclaimed in all the earth." The book of Exodus often speaks of God hardening Pharaoh's heart or Pharaoh's heart becoming hard (see Ex 8:19, 32; 9:7, 12, 35; 10:1, 20, 27; 11:10; 14:4, 8). Even at Moses' commissioning, God tells him that Pharaoh will not release the Israelites, so God will

> ***The ultimate purpose in hardening Pharaoh's heart is to display God's glory to Israel and the Egyptians (see Ex 14:15-18).***

"stretch out [his] hand and strike the Egyptians with all the wonders that [he] will perform among them. After that, [Pharaoh] will let you go" (Ex 3:20). This is the first of many references that reveal how God will let his people go. Exodus 4:21 explicitly says that God will "harden his heart *so that* he will not let the people go." God hardens Pharaoh's heart not arbitrarily but with a specific purpose in mind—to prevent the release of captive Israel. But why would God harden Pharaoh's heart to prevent Israel from returning to the Promised Land? The answer to this perplexing question occurs in Exodus 7:3-5: "But I will harden Pharaoh's heart. . . .The Egyptians will know that I am the Lord when I stretch out my hand against Egypt and bring the Israelites out of it." In citing Exodus 9:16 in Romans 9:17, Paul grounds his conviction that God has mercy on some while hardening others. God's actions in election are not whimsical or capricious but wisely orchestrated. Romans 9:22-23 explain that God elects individuals with a view to his own glory. He elects and rejects on an unconditional basis.

Israel's disobedience in unbelief (9:30–10:21). In Romans 9:30-33, Paul discusses why the Jews are still in a state of unbelief: they failed to obtain God's righteousness by doing the law. Gentiles, by contrast, have access to God's saving righteousness since they possess faith in Christ (9:30). As the quotations from Isaiah 8:14 and 28:16 illustrate in 9:33, Israel's failure to embrace Christ as their Messiah and trust him for salvation has brought divine judgment. Paul understands the tragedy of Israel in light of his own conversion: "I can testify about them that they are zealous for God, but their zeal is not based on knowledge. . . . They did not know the righteousness of God and sought to establish their own" (10:2-3). What he says here of Israel had formerly applied to himself (Phil 3:4-9).

Both the pre-Christian Paul and unbelieving Israel had a "zeal" for God's law, but such zeal was "not based on knowledge" of the Messiah and the righteousness that comes only through him by faith. When Christ appeared to Paul on the Damascus Road, he received a true knowledge of Messiah Jesus (Phil 3:8). Paul realized that Christ was the fulfillment of the Mosaic law (Rom 10:4). Israel, like preconverted Paul, remains in a state of unbelief.

Israel has also failed to realize that the story of redemption has reached its zenith in Christ—the laws of Moses that demarcated the Israelites from their neighbors are now fulfilled in Christ and are no longer in force in the new age (Rom 10:4). The Spirit that produces righteousness, not the law, is the hallmark of the new age. This end-time righteousness is available for all, both Jews and Gentiles (10:9-13). But not all Israelites have "accepted the good news" (10:16). Consequently they are "disobedient and obstinate" in fulfillment of Isaiah 65:2 (Rom 10:21).

The salvation of true, ethnic Israel (11:1-36). Despite Israel's hardened state, God has not fully rejected the Jewish people but has preserved a remnant, even in midst of dire circumstances (Rom 11:1-10). Paul uses himself (11:1) and the Old Testament story of the "seven thousand who have not bowed the knee to Baal" (11:4; 1 Kings 19:10-18) to prove that God has never failed to keep his promise to preserve a remnant within Israel. Romans 11:5 states, "So too, *at the present time* there is a remnant chosen by grace." When the Old Testament comments on how many within the nation of Israel will be restored, it speaks only of a faithful remnant. Overwhelmingly, the majority of Old Testament references about Israel's restoration anticipate the salvation of a remnant and not the majority or a nation (e.g., Is 37:32; Jer 23:3; 31:7; Joel 2:32; Mic 2:12; 4:7; 5:7-8; Zech 8:12). True Israel has always been and always will be composed of a remnant.

The next section, Romans 11:11-32, details the role of Gentiles in God's plan for Israel. Strangely, through Israel's disbelief (11:7-10), the Gentiles have become part of true, end-time Israel: "Because of their [Israel's] transgression, salvation has come to the Gentiles *to make Israel envious*" (11:11). With the Gentiles participating in the new covenant community, Jews become envious or jealous, which causes them to return to the Lord (11:11b, 14). In 11:17-24, Paul employs a tree metaphor to illustrate the relationship between three parties: Jesus, the Gentiles, and the Jewish people.

Although some view the root as a reference to Israel's patriarchs and God's promises to them, the root is likely Jesus (Rom 11:18; 15:12; cf. Rev 5:5; 22:16). The wild olive branches refer to the Gentiles (11:17), and the natural branches are ethnic Jews (11:18). The natural branches have been broken off and replaced by the wild olive branches, but the natural branches are being grafted back into their own tree. Though ethnic Jews are "broken off" (11:19-20a), the Gentiles are in no position to boast about their position before God (11:20b). Gentiles, like Jews, will

FIGURE 9.13. JEROBOAM SACRIFICING TO IDOLS

be punished for any disobedience but rewarded for belief and obedience (11:21-22). Verses 23 and 24 reaffirm the salvation (present and future) of Jews: "They [ethnic Jews] . . . will be grafted in, for God is able to graft them in again" (11:23). Verse 24, in contrasting the Gentiles' unique "grafting" into the olive tree, highlights the restoration of ethnic Jews. Paul grounds this assertion in Romans 11:25-26: "For I do not want you, brethren, to be uninformed of *this mystery*—so that you will not be wise in your own estimation—a partial hardening has happened to Israel

FIGURE 9.14. OLIVE TREE

until the fullness of the Gentiles has come in and in this manner all Israel will be saved" (our translation). The apostle informs his audience how ethnic Jews are and will be saved—Gentile inclusion acts as a catalyst for Jewish salvation. When Gentiles come to faith in Jesus, the Messiah, some ethnic Jews will become jealous and likewise embrace Christ. Paul deems this relationship between Jews and Gentiles a mystery.

The broad Old Testament expectation was the restoration of ethnic Jews first and the subsequent restoration of the Gentiles (Is 2:2-3; Mic 4:1-5; Zech 2:2-11). In line with this, the book of Acts narrates the salvation of ethnic Jews and then the subsequent salvation of Gentiles, who began to compose the majority of the church. This order of salvation is also Paul's understanding—"first to the Jew, then to the Gentile" (Rom 1:16). Romans 11 states that the order of salvation is Gentiles first and then ethnic Jews. Paul argues in Romans 11:13-26 that God will use the salvation of vastly more Gentiles than ethnic Jews to provoke some Jews to jealousy and bring them to faith in Christ. This is what Paul means by mystery—the Old Testament does not clearly anticipate the wide acceptance of the gospel among Gentiles that leads to a subsequent minority of ethnic Jews who trust in Christ.

LIVING THE GOSPEL (12:1–14:23)

After discussing how the gospel relates to Israel on a corporate level, Paul turns his attention to how the gospel affects daily living on an individual level. Now that his readers partake of the new age, Paul exhorts them to work out their new identity in every aspect of life. Justification inevitably leads to sanctification. Believers must be transformed continually into the image of Christ (Rom 12:1-2), which manifests itself through service and love (12:3-21). Christians ought to submit to the government, as the sovereign Lord has established its existence (13:1-7). Love is the hallmark of the Christian life (13:8-10), particularly in the present age (13:11-14). According to 14:1–15:13, The "strong" (Christian Gentiles) are to accept and encourage the "weak" (law-keeping Jewish Christians).

Serving the church (12:1-21). In contrast to pagan Gentiles in Romans 1:18-32, who worship creation and exchange "the glory of the incorruptible God for an image" (Rom 1:23 NASB), believers are to be conformed into the image of Christ (12:1-2). Such individuals are conformed to the false image of the world. Believers, however, are to be conformed into the image of Christ (12:1-2). Romans 12:1-2 is the antithesis of 1:18-28.

The pristine image of Christ is the opposite of the worldly image that is worshiped by unbelieving humanity (1:18-32). Whichever image one reveres (God's or the world's), one resembles, either for ruin or for restoration. Believers are exhorted to be renewed in their existence as a new creation and not deterred by the old idolatrous age. Those who have trusted in Christ and have begun to regain the image of God designed for true humanity will not ultimately succumb to idolatry, since they have been decisively delivered from the effects of a distorted divine image. They will be conformed to God's image until the resurrection, when God fully refashions their image at the end of the age.

Paul assures his audience that each member of the body is integral to the church's mission (Rom 12:3-8). The second half of the chapter is devoted to the topic of love (12:9-21), that functions as the glue for the previous discussion. Central to a healthy church is love, particularly if the church consists of diverse backgrounds, which is the case with the Roman church. The church at Rome is largely composed of Gentiles, but a small group of Jewish Christians remain. In order for them to worship harmoniously, for the "strong" to worship alongside the "weak," both groups must love and serve each other.

Submitting to authorities (13:1-14). Submitting to governing authorities (Rom 13:1) can be no easy task, particularly in a context such as Rome in the mid-50s AD and into the 60s. Paul's immediate audience will be tried and tested in the years to come, especially, during the reign of Nero (ca. 54–68). Paul makes it immediately clear that *all* authority has been established by God; therefore, believers must be subject to it (13:1). To rebel against the divinely established government is to defy God himself (13:2). A key role of government is to restrain evil: "For rulers hold no terror for those who do right, but for those who do wrong. . . . If you do wrong, be afraid, for rulers do not bear the sword for no reason" (13:3-4; cf. 1 Pet 2:13-14).

Paul then picks up the theme of love once more but relates it to the law (13:8-10). The apostle states that an individual "who loves his neighbor has fulfilled the law" (13:8 NASB). Importantly, he never uses the language of Christians *doing* the law but rather *fulfilling* the law. When believers love God

FIGURE 9.15. NERO WATCHING ROME BURN

and others, they fulfill the righteous requirements of God's law. All of God's law (both the Mosaic law and the law in the new age) is summarized in these two love commands (see Mt 7:12; 22:34-40).

Paul then roots his exhortations to the church in the already but not yet: "Do this, understanding *the present time*: The hour has already come for you to wake up from your slumber" (Rom 13:11). Since believers are living in the inauguration of the latter days, they must live as though the new creation has broken into history: "So let us put aside the deeds of darkness and put on the armor of light" (13:12b).

The weak and the strong (14:1-23). Suggesting that the relationship between Gentile and Jewish Christians is somewhat strained would not be a stretch of the imagination. Paul has been warning the Gentiles throughout this epistle to be mindful of ethnic Jews (e.g., Rom 11:20-21). In a passage reminiscent of 1 Corinthians 8:9-12, Paul beckons Gentiles (the "strong") to accept the Jewish Christians (the "weak in faith") (Rom 14:1). Gentiles are not to pass judgment on their fellow Jewish Christians. Whether it is dietary regulations (14:2-3, 6) or differences over observing Jewish festivals (14:5-6), Gentiles ought to pursue unity with their fellow believers and avoid putting obstacles in their way that cause Jewish Christians to stumble (14:13-23). Christ fulfills the food laws that differentiate Jews and Gentiles, so now all food is deemed clean (14:20). There should be no division within the church at Rome.

THE GOSPEL TO THE NATIONS (15:1–16:27)

By quoting several Old Testament passages, the last portion of the epistle reinforces the central role of the Gentiles in the history of redemption (Deut 32:43; 2 Sam 22:50; Ps 117:1; Is 11:10; 66:10). The Old Testament predicts that the Gentiles will become part of God's people and join true Israel in the latter days. The apostle Paul sees himself as instrumental to the salvation of the nations, and the church at Rome lies squarely within that program. The ultimate plan as Paul sees it, though, is to proclaim Christ crucified in Spain and continue bringing the gospel to the ends of the earth.

Paul's plan to bring the gospel to Spain (15:1-33). After assuring his Roman readers of their place in the grand story line of the Bible (Rom 15:7-13), Paul proceeds to remind them of his personal commitment to them (15:14-22). He claims to be "a minister of Christ Jesus to the Gentiles," with the "priestly duty of proclaiming the gospel of God, so that the Gentiles might become *an offering acceptable to God*" (15:16). The last part of 15:16 alludes to Isaiah 66:20, in which redeemed Israelites venture to the nations and share with them the saving message of the Lord in the end times: "They will bring all your people, from all the nations, to my holy mountain in Jerusalem *as an offering* to the LORD." The apostle eyes this latter-day promise from Isaiah and applies it to his personal ministry in proclaiming the gospel to the nations. J. Ross Wagner is right to say,

> Paul finds in Isaiah a fellow preacher of the gospel, the message that reveals God's righteousness for all who believe, for the Jew first and also for the Greek. He uncovers in Isaiah's heralds a veiled prefiguration of his own mission to proclaim the good news to those among the Gentiles who have not yet heard the news of the victory of Israel's God.[12]

The time has come for the Gentiles to become part of true Israel *as* Gentiles.

Paul's mission pushes beyond Rome, though. The long-term goal is to herald the gospel in Spain. To accomplish that feat, he plans to stop in Rome as a waypoint (Rom 15:23-24).

[12]J. Ross Wagner, *Heralds of the Good News: Isaiah and Paul in Concert in the Letter to the Romans* (Leiden: Brill, 2003), 336.

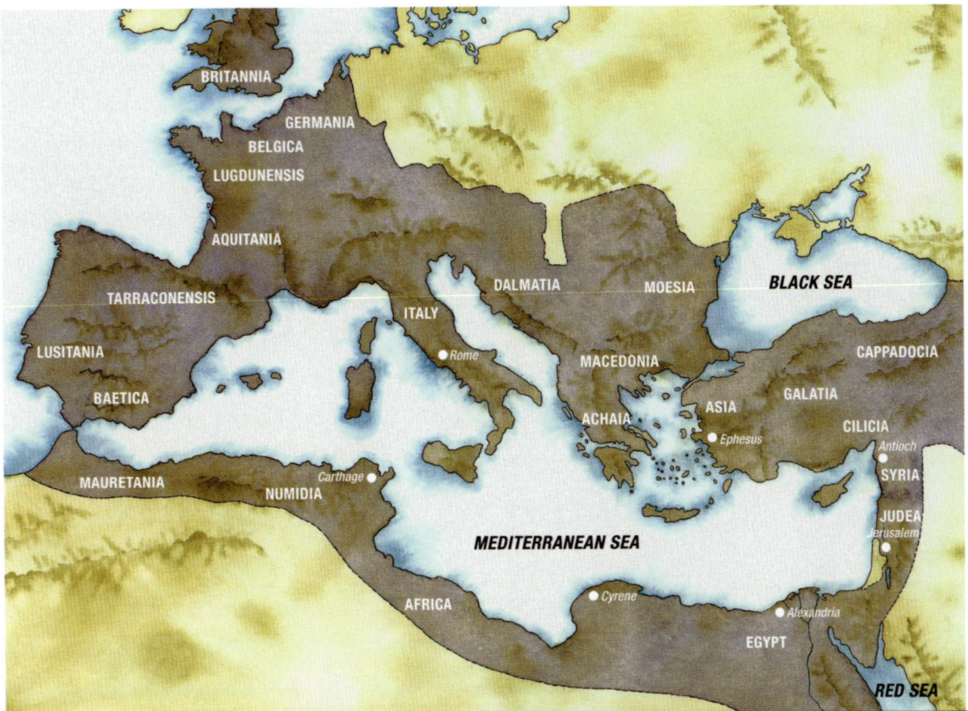

THE ROMAN EMPIRE AND THE MEDITERRANEAN WORLD

Once the apostle brings the good news to Spain, the gospel is will extend to the ends of the earth, thus continuing to fulfill the prophecy of Isaiah (Is 49:6; cf. Acts 1:8; 14:27). Before the gospel reaches Spain, Paul, though, desires to return to Jerusalem and bring financial support to the fledgling Jewish Christian community (15:27-33). The offering has been in the works for quite some time and is a critical piece of Paul's ministry, as it gives an opportunity for the largely Gentile church to support the Jewish church in Jerusalem (see 2 Cor 8–9).

Personal greetings and letter closing (16:1-27). In comparison to his other letters, Paul's greetings in Romans 16:1-16, 21-23 are lengthy. Although never having visited Rome at this point in his career, Paul had no shortage of contacts there. He warns the covenant community to avoid those who create division within the church (16:17-18). As in the first covenant community in Eden, so again in the believing community in Rome, there is deception and a need to be "wise about what is good, and innocent about what is evil" (16:18-19). If the Roman Christians continue in their faithful obedience (Rom 16:19, 26) and heed Paul's exhortation not to be deceived by the false teachers in their midst, then "the God of peace will . . . crush Satan under your feet" (16:20), Paul clearly references Genesis 3:15, a text that prophesies the crushing of the serpent's head. No doubt, Paul understands Jesus' death and resurrection to be the mortal blow on the serpent's head, but the devil has yet to be consigned to his eternal prison of punishment. He still "prowls around like a roaring lion looking for someone to devour" (1 Pet 5:8). Victory over Satan has already been achieved at the cross,

FIGURE 9.16. MICHAEL DEFEATS SATAN AS DESCRIBED IN REVELATION 12

but believers continue to wage warfare in mop-up operations. It is in this sense that the believers at Rome can directly fulfill the Genesis 3:15 prophecy. They trust in and identify with Jesus' death and resurrection. The Spirit strengthens believers to overcome the devil and sin.

Paul's assertion at the closing of the letter contains a marvelous insight concerning the gospel's relationship to the Old Testament: "my gospel and the preaching of Jesus Christ, according to the revelation *of the mystery* which has been kept secret for long ages past, but now is manifested, and by *the Scriptures of the prophets . . . made known*" (16:25-26 NASB). Certain aspects of Paul's gospel are generally "kept secret" in the Old Testament; that is, the gospel contains unexpected elements in the way the Old Testament is fulfilled (cf. Eph 6:19; Col 4:3). The manner in which some of the events are fulfilled was not so clearly seen from the Old Testament perspective. In the throes of defeat, the Messiah's death on the cross is the means by which he conquers and gives life to sinners who trust in him.

1 CORINTHIANS

AUTHORSHIP

Pauline authorship of 1 Corinthians has never been seriously questioned, for the epistle bears all the marks that it was written by Paul, such as style, vocabulary, and theology. At the beginning of the letter we read, "*Paul*, called to be an apostle of Christ Jesus" (1 Cor 1:1). And once again, at the end, we find, "I, *Paul*, write this greeting in my own hand" (16:21; cf. 16:8; Acts 19:1-41). The early church readily affirmed that Paul was indeed the author, and this conviction remains today.

DATE

The dating of 1 Corinthians depends on a complex reconstruction of the events surrounding Paul's interaction with the church at Corinth, known as the "Corinthian Correspondence." We know that Gallio was proconsul in Corinth in AD 51 and that the Jews dragged Paul before him probably in the autumn of 51. Paul is acquitted and continues to stay in Corinth (at least eighteen months [Acts 18:11]). He then sets sail for Ephesus (Acts 18:19-21) and arrives in Jerusalem shortly thereafter (Acts 18:22). Paul's second missionary journey comes to a close. On his third journey, he returns to Ephesus and ministers for two and a half years (Acts 19:1-20). It is in Ephesus where he pens his first epistle to the Corinthians (1 Cor 5:9; 16:8). A few months later, Paul writes the Corinthians once more in what we call 1 Corinthians. According to 16:8, Paul promises to remain in Ephesus "until Pentecost," a festival that takes place in the Spring (Lev 23:15-22). So, if we add two and a half years to AD 51 or 52, we arrive at the spring of AD 54 or 55.

OCCASION

Julius Caesar establishes Corinth as a Roman colony in 44 BC. The Romans refounded the city by installing Roman architecture, buildings, and temples. Strabo claims that Caesar colonized Corinth with people from the "freedman class" (*Geogr.* 8.6.23). This likely included many former slaves and military personal. Unlike Rome, where the wealthy aristocracy ruled, Corinth provided its citizens with a real opportunity to climb the social ladder. As with any growing metropolis, business owners and townspeople competed for fame, wealth, and recognition. This city was fertile ground for patrons and clients, entrepreneurs, aggressive business practices, philosophers, mystery religions, and everything in between.

Such was the climate when Paul arrived at Corinth—political and sophistic factions, moral compromises, rampant idolatry, and the pursuit of fame and wealth. Many consider factions and egotistical behavior to be an impetus, if not the root cause, for Paul's epistle. Wisdom, so treasured at Corinth, was a type of sophistic wisdom.[1] The exact contents of this wisdom are quite difficult to ascertain, but it is probably safe to assume that sophistic wisdom was alluring, philosophical, and centered on human ingenuity. Rhetorically gifted individuals paraded this wisdom, hoping to gain a following by their persuasive rhetoric. The Corinthians are jockeying with each other by aligning themselves with one sophist over another, thus, pitting the leaders (and themselves) against each other. The net result is a party-line division between the house churches. Apparently, these house churches are not divided over theological lines but rather personal rifts—a clash of ecclesiastical titans. If that were not enough, the wealthy within the church also disparage the poor members of the body, excluding them from fellowship. In the end, the Corinthians struggle mightily with living as believers in a pagan culture, as Gordon Fee argues: "Although they were the Christian church in Corinth, an inordinate amount of Corinth was yet in them."[2]

PURPOSE

Paul has received reports from "Chloe's household" and from others concerning a wide variety of problems within Corinthian community, particularly divisiveness (1 Cor 1:11; 7:1; 16:17). He writes to the Corinthians shortly thereafter to address these issues. At its most basic level, the Corinthians struggle with church unity. Because the Corinthians are a proud group of individuals, following proud leaders, division and factionalism run rampant.

OUTLINE

I. Letter Opening and Thanksgiving (1:1-9)
II. Internal Strife and Division (1:10–4:21)
  A. God's Wisdom in the Cross (1:10–2:16)
  B. Church Leaders as Servants of the Church (3:1–4:21)
III. Moral and Ethical Issues Within the Church (5:1–6:20)
  A. Expelling Immorality in the Church (5:1-13)
  B. Further Divisions at Corinth (6:1-20)
IV. Marriage and Christian Liberty (7:1–11:1)
  A. Christian Liberty and Idolatry (7:1–10:33)
  B. Issues During Public Worship (11:1-34)
V. Spiritual Gifts in Worship (12:1–14:40)
  A. The Church as Christ's Body and the Goal of Spiritual Gifts (12:1–13:13)
  B. Spiritual Gifts in Public Worship (14:1-40)
VI. Defense of Christ's Resurrection (15:1-58)
  A. The Historical Evidence of Christ's Resurrection (15:1-34)
  B. The Theological Rationale for Christ's Resurrection (15:35-58)
VII. The Collection, Greetings, and the Letter Closing (16:1-24)

BIBLICAL-THEOLOGICAL THEMES

The "mystery" of the cross. With the exception of Ephesians, no other book in the New Testament employs the term *mystery* more than 1 Corinthians. Occurring six times in the epistle, *mystery* is found in key passages

[1]Duane Litfin, *St. Paul's Theology of Proclamation: 1 Corinthians 1–4 and Greco-Roman Rhetoric*, SNTSMS 79 (New York: Cambridge University Press, 1994).
[2]Gordon Fee, *The First Epistle to the Corinthians*, NICNT (Grand Rapids: Eerdmans, 1987), 4.

FIGURE 10.1. RUINS AT CORINTH

and plays a significant role in the overall purpose of the book (1 Cor 2:1, 7; 4:1; 13:2; 14:2; 15:51). The key term *mystery* originates in the book of Daniel, especially chapters two and four. *Mystery* in Daniel concerns God's end-time kingdom and related events. We can roughly define it as the disclosure of divine wisdom, knowledge that was largely hidden but has been subsequently revealed (Dan 2:20-23). In Daniel, God primarily communicates his wisdom through dreams and visions mediated by either an individual or angel. The two-tiered structure of mystery in Daniel is a bit peculiar: an individual (Nebuchadnezzar) receives a cryptic dream followed by an interpreter (Daniel). In the book of Daniel, this structure is found in dreams (chaps. 2, 4), visions (chaps. 7, 8, 10-12), writing (chap. 5), and previous prophecy (chap. 9). The two-tiered component of mystery (cryptic vision followed by interpretation) signals the hidden nature of the term and its subsequent revelation.

The New Testament picks up and applies this word and concept to a number of prominent themes—kingdom (Mt 13:11), the crucifixion (1 Cor 2:1, 7), resurrection (1 Cor 15:51), Christ's cosmic rule (Eph 1:9), and the nature of the Antichrist (2 Thess 2:7). One prominent theme that is tied to *mystery* is the relationship between Jewish Christians and Gentile Christians (Rom 11:25). We will now examine why *mystery* is applied to the crucifixion in 1 Corinthians 2.

According to the Old Testament, the Messiah refers above all to the king of Israel. The Lord promises to restore and reign over his people through his Messiah. In 2 Samuel 7, God promised David that his descendants would rule over Israel. The Old Testament traces this promise and its fulfillment in the former and latter prophets. The Messiah, a descendant of David, would be instrumental in bringing about the establishment of God's eternal kingdom and destruction of Israel's enemies. Bound up with this phenomenon is the arrival of the new exodus, making possible forgiveness of sins, pouring out of the Spirit, the dawn of the new creation, and so on. Regarding the suffering aspect of the Messiah, a few passages seem to hint that the Messiah would suffer, to some extent, but this suffering was not yet understood as a cardinal aspect of his ministry. Messianic suffering is the means by which God will restore his people (e.g., Gen 3:15; Isa 53; Dan 9:26; Zech 12:10; 13:7).

FIGURE 10.2. DANIEL AND KING CYRUS IN BEL'S TEMPLE

With a basic grasp of the Old Testament expectations of the Messiah in the first century, we can appreciate the mystery of the crucifixion in 1 Corinthians 2. The wisdom of the cross is largely hidden in the Old Testament, but it has now been more fully made known or revealed in the New. The disclosed *mystery* is the exalted, kingly, divine Messiah affixed to the cross. While Jesus is suffering a shameful death on the cross, he is simultaneously the supreme divine ruler—"the Lord of glory" (2:8).

Although a suffering messiah was to some degree anticipated, messianic suffering does not play a central role in the Old Testament, especially in Jewish thought. Worldly wisdom could not conceive that the Messiah could be crucified, much less be seen as a glorious divine ruler actually exercising ruling power while being defeated.[3] This understanding of the Messiah develops Old Testament and Jewish expectations. Paul portrays Jesus as executing his divine *messianic* office at the moment of the horrific crucifixion.

The resurrection of Christ and the saints. Much of our understanding of the doctrine of the resurrection can be traced back to 1 Corinthians 15, in which Paul argues in some detail that the resurrection of Christ and believers is firmly rooted in the Old Testament. For example, 1 Kings 17 narrates the powerful story of Elijah raising a widow of Zarephath's son: "The LORD heard Elijah's cry, and the *boy's life returned to him, and he lived*" (1 Kings 17:22). As miraculous as this event was, the widow's son eventually died at some point in the future. This miracle is a glimmer of what will take place at the very end of time, when God raises righteous Israelites to inhabit the new creation, never to die again.

Resurrection in the Old Testament is often debated, and scholars differ on which Old Testament texts explicitly predict the end-time resurrection (e.g., Job 19:26-27; Is 25:7-8; 26:19; Ezek 37:1-14; Dan 12:2-3). Among the clearest passages predicting the resurrection of the righteous saints is Daniel 12:2: "Multitudes who sleep in the dust of the earth will awake: some to everlasting life, others to shame and everlasting contempt." Daniel 12 affirms that the resurrection will occur at the very end of history, when God will end all forms of corruption and establish the

[3]See David W. Chapman, *Ancient Jewish and Christian Perceptions of Crucifixion*, WUNT 244 (Tübingen: Mohr Siebeck, 2008).

new heavens and earth. Righteous individuals will be physically restored in the new creation, and the unrighteous will be consummately punished.

The Old Testament does not often refer to the resurrection explicitly, yet the need for the resurrection remains. The Old Testament asserts that God is deeply concerned for all of creation's spiritual and physical well-being. The fall plunged creation and humanity into sin, but God promises to redeem the created world and fallen humanity in their fullness.

Outside of the Old Testament in the ancient Near East, some discussion exists concerning the afterlife. Within these pagan worldviews, death remains the chief enemy of all, for the grave is a place of shadows, confinement, darkness, and the great unknown.[4] Certain ancient cultures held to some sort of afterlife, but only on a spiritual level—not a renewed, physical existence. The Egyptians, for example, believed that only Pharaoh, the socially elite, and other noble citizens had the opportunity to pass through death and journey through a series of steps to eternal existence. If they pass the test, they will be rewarded and transform into a star in the heavens.

Although Judaism in the first century was exceedingly diverse, many Jewish sects significantly developed the concept of a resurrection. For example, 1 Enoch 62:15 says, "The righteous and elect ones shall rise from the earth. . . . They shall wear garments of glory" (cf. 1 En. 22:13), and 4 Ezra 2:16 likewise states, "I will raise up the dead from their places, and will bring them out from their tombs."

FIGURE 10.3. THE PROPHET ELIJAH

[4]Philip S. Johnston, *Shades of Sheol: Death and Afterlife in the Old Testament* (Downers Grove, IL: InterVarsity Press, 2002), 230-39.

The New Testament places the resurrection at the core of its teachings (e.g., Mt 22:30; Lk 14:14; Rom 6:5; Phil 3:10-11; Rev 20:5). Unlike the Old Testament, the New Testament proposes a somewhat radical idea—the resurrection of the saints is a staggered event. John 5:25, in alluding to Daniel 12:2, says, "A time is coming and has now come when the dead will hear the voice of the Son of God and those who hear will live." The souls of saints are raised first (Eph 2:6; Col 3:1), and then, at the end of the age, their bodies are redeemed. The spiritual precedes the physical.

FIGURE 10.4. SOSTHENES AND OTHER APOSTLES

There is another way in which the Old Testament anticipation of the resurrection differs from its fulfillment in the New Testament: the Messiah is physically raised first, followed by his people at the very end of history. The Old Testament expected all of God's people to be resurrected *together* in a single event, yet Paul views the resurrection as initially and unexpectedly fulfilled in Christ's physical resurrection. His physical resurrection guarantees saints' resurrection (1 Cor 15). He is the initial installment or the "firstfruits" of the resurrection of all the saints (1 Cor 15:22-23). To summarize, the end-time resurrection is directly fulfilled in three stages: (1) Christ's physical resurrection, (2) believers' spiritual resurrection, and (3) believers' physical resurrection. The Old Testament does not outline these three stages with great precision, however. What the Old Testament anticipates in general, the New Testament fleshes out with greater precision.

LETTER OPENING AND THANKSGIVING (1:1-9)

Paul begins the letter with his conventional opening: "Paul, called to be an apostle of Christ Jesus by the will of God, and our brother Sosthenes" (1 Cor 1:1). This curious mention of an individual named Sosthenes (who lives in Corinth) occurs in only one other place in the New Testament, in Acts 18:17: "Then the crowd there turned on *Sosthenes* the synagogue leader and beat him in front of the proconsul."

Acts 18:12-21 details Paul's struggles with his fellow Jews at Corinth. They accuse Paul of teaching things "contrary to the law" (18:13). Eventually, Gallio deemed Paul's actions legal. The Jews violently responded by beating Sosthenes, a synagogue leader (18:17). If this Sosthenes in Acts 18:18 is to be identified with the Sosthenes of 1 Corinthians 1:1, then this opening verse contains a considerable amount of weight. Sosthenes, although at one time antagonistic toward Christianity, has enthusiastically joined Paul's ministry in Ephesus.

Paul then proceeds to identify the audience of his epistle. The standard formula is given but with an important exception: "To the church of God in Corinth . . . *together with all those everywhere who call on the name of our Lord Jesus Christ*" (1 Cor 1:2, emphasis added). Typically, Paul identifies a specific audience (Gal 1:2; Phil 1:2; Col 1:2), but here in 1 Corinthians 1:2 he addresses the Corinthian house churches and a much wider audience—*all* Christians. Paul's letter, therefore, contains principles that are universally applicable for the church at large (cf. 2 Cor 1:1; Eph 1:1).

In 1 Corinthians 1:4-9 Paul delivers his thanksgiving; the Corinthians, Paul claims, are "enriched . . . with all kinds of speech and . . . knowledge" (1:5). They are not deficient in any gift and are greatly anticipating the return of Christ (1:7-8). The apostle's words here ring throughout the epistle, especially in chapters 1–2 and 12–14, thus providing the foundation for subsequent instruction.

FIGURE 10.5. DAVID AND GOLIATH

INTERNAL STRIFE AND DIVISION (1:10–4:21)

Examples of God working against the worldly culture and blessing the humble, lowly, and seemingly insignificant are woven throughout the Old Testament.[5] In reading Israel's history, the weak and the lowly are exalted, and the proud are humbled. Take, for example, King David, who was the youngest of his brothers and lacked the physical traits to battle Goliath in his own strength (1 Sam 17:33). God blessed David and empowered him to defeat Goliath and Israel's other enemies. One verse from David's career epitomizes God's dealings with Israel: "The LORD does not look at the things people look at. People look at the outward appearance, but *the LORD looks at the heart*" (1 Sam 16:7).

That same principle is found here in 1 Corinthians 1–4, the heart of the epistle. Paul depicts two types of wisdom: divine and human. Humanity's wisdom boasts in worldly knowledge, sophistication, philosophy, and rhetoric—the sum of all human achievement. Conversely, God's wisdom is evident on a spiritual level and is manifested in the cross, the epitome of humiliation and abasement (1 Cor 1:18-31). Believers have the ability to grasp God's wisdom and the means to live in accordance with it through the agency of the Spirit (2:1-16). When we take a step back and view the first four chapters in light of the church's main issue with disunity, we conclude that if the Corinthians understand and imitate the ethics of the cross, their divisions will cease and they will function as one unified people of God. Instead of embracing a self-promoting lifestyle, the Corinthians must pursue humility and service to one another.

Church leadership is prominent in chapters 3–4, as Paul devotes a considerable

[5]This section has been adapted from Benjamin L. Gladd, *Revealing the* Mysterion*: The Use of Mystery in Daniel and Second Temple Judaism with Its Bearing on First Corinthians*, BZNW 160 (Berlin: Walter de Gruyter, 2008), 112-90.

amount of time to the role of teachers within the local church. They must promote unity in their ministry. The church should not serve the leaders, but the leaders ought to serve the church (3:1-23). The Corinthian leaders must function as conduits of God's wisdom (4:1-5) and live in keeping with the ethics of the cross (4:6-21).

> *God's wisdom is not only beyond humanity's reach but also defeats all human sophistry (1 Cor 1:19; Is 29:14), even the wise of the world (1 Cor 1:20-21). Both Jews and Greeks alike examine the message of the cross and regard it as absurd (1:22-25).*

God's wisdom in the cross (1:10–2:16). The first two chapters are complex, and Paul's logic appears a bit tangled. But once we understand the general flow of thought, everything falls into place: 1 Corinthians 1:18-31 is the *content* of God's wisdom, 2:1-5 is the *manner* in which Paul proclaimed the cross, and 2:6-16 is the *nature* of God's wisdom. The Corinthian community is riddled with strife and divisions, so, in 1:10, Paul delivers the main point of the first four chapters: "I appeal to you . . . that all of you agree with one another in what you say and that there be no divisions among you, but that you be perfectly united in mind and thought." He is greatly concerned with Corinthian elitism and the resultant factions that stem from a skewed view of wisdom (1:17-21). These factions are utterly ridiculous in Paul's eyes (1:13). After minimizing the importance of his own record of baptizing believers (1:14-16) but not the act of baptism itself, he claims that his purpose in coming to the Corinthians was to proclaim the gospel: "Christ did not send me to baptize, but *to preach the gospel*—not with wisdom and eloquence, lest the cross of Christ be emptied of its power" (1:17).

Verses 17 and 18 constitute Paul's thesis statement in this section and the thrust of 1 Corinthians: the message of the cross permanently transforms believers' behavior and worldview. The only way for the Corinthians to end their factional conduct is to embrace the message of the cross. The words "cleverness of speech" in verse 17 are a technical phrase referring to Greco-Roman rhetoric and sophistry. Paul's simple proclamation of the gospel is antithetical to the Corinthian worldview. If Paul succumbs to such rhetoric in his ministry, the cross would be emptied of its power (1:17). The content, not the form, of the message—Christ crucified—delivers people from their plight.

In contrast to the "cleverness of speech," Paul preaches the "message of the cross" (1:18). To outsiders, the message of the cross is weak and foolish, but to those who believe, the cross is salvation and power. Verses 19-25 support Paul's thesis: the world's wisdom, alluring to the Corinthians, is unable to grasp Christ's work on the cross.

True wisdom, Paul claims, is found in Christ: "Let the one who boasts boast in the Lord" (1 Cor 1:31; Jer 9:23). Paul arrived at the Corinthian church avoiding sophistic methods and rhetoric (1 Cor 2:1) because he desired "to know nothing . . . except Jesus Christ and him crucified" (2:2). Paul's method was in conformity with his message: "I came to you in weakness with great fear and trembling. My message and my preaching were . . . with a demonstration of the Spirit's power" (2:3-4; cf. 1:17).

Paul rehearses how he proclaimed the message of the cross in 1 Corinthians 2:1-5, whereas in 2:6-16 he describes the nature and accessibility of that wisdom. According to 2:7, Paul labels God's wisdom a "mystery": "We declare God's wisdom, *a mystery* that has been hidden." The biblical conception of mystery differs somewhat from the modern definition. It denotes the unveiling of a specific Old Testament doctrine that pertains to end-time events (e.g., Dan 2:28; Mt 13:11; Rom 11:25). The disclosed mystery is the exalted, kingly, divine Messiah affixed to the cross.

Although a suffering messiah was anticipated to some degree, messianic suffering does not play a central role in the Old Testament. Worldly wisdom could not conceive a crucified Messiah, much less a divine ruler who exercises power while being defeated. As Gordon Fee puts it, "One may have a Messiah, or one may have a crucifixion; but one may not have both—at least not from the perspective of a merely human understanding. *Messiah* meant power, splendor, triumph; *crucifixion* meant weakness, humiliation, defeat."[6] This understanding of the Messiah differs from Old Testament and Jewish expectations. Thus, Paul portrays Jesus as executing his divine *messianic* prerogative at the moment of the crucifixion. Though a few passages hint at such an ironic conquest (e.g., Is 53), the Old Testament generally did not expect the Messiah to rule powerfully in the midst of suffering.

Church leaders as servants of the church (3:1–4:21). Paul condemns the Corinthians' conduct because they are divisive and concerned only with glorifying themselves and their leaders. He labels such behavior as "worldly" (3:1, 3). The Corinthians, by elevating and pitting one leader over another, are embracing the philosophy of the fallen world even though they belong to the new age. Their competitive spirit and conduct are indicative of the world. "For when one says, 'I follow Paul,' and another, 'I follow Apollos,' are you not mere human beings?" (1 Cor 3:4).

Paul not only condemns their divisive behavior but refashions their perspective, giving them a biblical worldview of church

FIGURE 10.6. SOCRATES, THE WELL-KNOWN GREEK PHILOSOPHER

[6]Fee, *First Epistle to the Corinthians*, 75.

FIGURE 10.7. VINEYARD IN ISRAEL

leaders or "servants" (1 Cor 3:5-9). Apparently, the house churches are rallying around certain leaders and pitting them against each other. Instead of exalting them, the Corinthians must realize that church leaders are servants. Ministers serve the church and are not to be idolized. Paul provides three metaphors describing leaders' service and responsibility to the church. These leaders will undergo latter-day judgment and evaluation of their service.[7] Paul states, "If what has been built survives, the builder will receive a reward" (3:14; cf. 3:8). So, if the congregation bears fruit, then the church leaders will pass the test.

The first metaphor of a biblical worldview of church leaders—Paul as a planter—recalls several Old Testament texts that speak of a cultivated field or vineyard, suggesting that Paul views himself as a latter-day servant in God's field (Is 5:1-7; Jer 26:18). After this agricultural metaphor, Paul abruptly says they are "God's building" (1 Cor 3:9). Paul is not describing a generic building but the temple as a building. The sudden metaphorical shift from a field to a temple makes wonderful sense considering that the Garden of Eden and Israel's garden-like Promised Land are often associated with God's sanctuary. Paul even calls himself a "wise master builder" in laying the foundation of the church, a phrase that recalls the skilled workers who helped construct Israel's tabernacle (Ex 35:31-32).[8]

Therefore, the church is a temple/field in which Paul and church leaders serve. If they are faithful to their task, they will receive a good "wage." Conversely, if they are unfaithful, God will judge them accordingly. Church leaders are builders of God's house, the

[7]F. M. Smit, "'What Is Apollos? What Is Paul?' In Search for the Coherence of First Corinthians 1:10-4:21," *NovT* 44 (2002): 238.
[8]Jon Laansma drew our attention to the use of this word in Exodus and its noun form in 1 Corinthians 3.

temple, and each leader must "build with care" (1 Cor 3:10).

Malachi 3–4 similarly predicts that God will "come to his temple" and "refine" Israel, purifying a remnant within them. Against this background, the Corinthian church is refined and tested as a group of Israelite priests, proving whether or not the priestly leader will receive a reward or will suffer loss.[9]

Paul's third metaphor, stewardship of mysteries, is an example of a church leader that has a proper relationship to end-time revelation of the cross and understands the gravity of this responsibility (1 Cor 4:1-5). Stewardship carries with it notions of trust and faithfulness. Using a model found in the book of Daniel, Paul sees himself as a latter-day prophet like Daniel and seeks to be faithful to the mysteries God has given him (4:2; Dan 2:22-23). Only his Master—the Lord—is qualified to judge his faithfulness (1 Cor 4:3-4) and will evaluate the mysteries of Paul's heart at the end-time judgment (4:5; cf. Eph 3:2-10).

Surprisingly, Paul declares that he has been using himself and Apollos as examples all along. He rhetorically employs himself as an example so that the Corinthians would not "go beyond what is written" in the authoritative record of Old Testament revelation (1 Cor 4:6). Paul's entire purpose in this exercise is to show the Corinthians that they may not play favorites with the leaders—"You will not be puffed up in being a follower of one of us over against the other" (4:6). For the remainder of the chapter, Paul contends that his ministry is characterized by the mystery of the cross. The Corinthians are convinced they have arrived (4:7-8), whereas Paul contrasts this arrogance with his own ministry of suffering and self-understanding (4:9-21).

The language of building is here associated with the Old Testament conception of the temple (Mal 3:1-3; 4:1; 1 Chron 29:2), and Paul is portrayed as constructing the church as God's temple.

MORAL AND ETHICAL ISSUES WITHIN THE CHURCH (5:1–6:20)

The covenant community always struggles with sin in the camp. One of the most graphic stories is the sin of Achan in Joshua 7, who hid some of the items that were set apart for

FIGURE 10.8. STONING OF ACHAN

[9]For further amplification on the temple in 1 Corinthians 3, see G. K. Beale, *The Temple and the Church's Mission: A Biblical Theology of the Temple* (Downers Grove, IL: InterVarsity Press, 2004), 245-52.

destruction (Josh 7:1). His sin affected the entire nation, and the Israelites shockingly lost the battle of Ai (Josh 7:4-5). Achan (and his family) paid a dear price for his actions and was subsequently stoned (Josh 7:25). The covenant community at Corinth faces a similar issue—heinous sin has emerged within the church. But a major difference exists between the Corinthian church and ancient Israel: the believers at Corinth are part of God's end-time temple and true Israel, having begun to inherit the new heavens and earth. Sin within the camp at Corinth is all the more serious.

Expelling immorality in the church (5:1-13). In 1 Corinthians 5–7, Paul reveals one of his main reasons for writing this letter. Much of what we find in this section entails an exhortation to refrain from sexual immorality. The Corinthians must rid themselves of the member who had sexual relations with his mother-in-law (5:1-8). Paul then reminds the church once more (5:9-11) that they are not to associate with a purported Christian who "claims to be a brother or sister but is sexually immoral or greedy, an idolater or slanderer, a drunkard or swindler" (5:11). The abiding authority of the Old Testament is evident in this passage as several texts from Deuteronomy are employed to substantiate the claim that God alone has the right to judge the "outsiders" (i.e., unbelievers): "God will judge those outside. 'Expel the wicked person from among you'" (1 Cor 5:13; cf. Deut 17:7; 19:19; 21:21; 22:24; 24:7). Since the Corinthians are part of God's covenant community, they are to behave as such and eradicate all forms of wickedness. As Ciampa and Rosner put it, "If God's people in Israel expelled certain sinners, then God's people in Christ should do no less."[10] Where their Israelite ancestors failed to do so, the Corinthians must succeed (1 Cor 10:6). The greatest struggle at Corinth is not from the outside but from within.

Further divisions at Corinth (6:1-20). After admonishing the Corinthians to refrain from sexual immorality, Paul moves the discussion to the church's litigious behavior. Dragging one another to court displays further evidence of disharmony at Corinth (1 Cor 6:1-6). Instead of striving for self-validation and self-worth, the Corinthians must live for one another. Their behavior must reflect the ethics of the cross instead of the world (6:7-10). The second half of chapter six reflects, yet again, the Corinthian problem with sexual immorality. God is dedicated to restoring the entire person (not only the soul); the spirit and the body are incontrovertibly tied together. When an individual commits a sexual sin, the soul is affected. Now that the Corinthians have been re-created in the image of God, they enjoy his glorious presence through the indwelling Spirit. As the end-time temple, they are to live for God in their entire being (6:20; see 2 Cor 6:16-18).

MARRIAGE AND CHRISTIAN LIBERTY (7:1–11:1)

Most members of the church at Corinth are recently converted Gentiles. And while some of them may have known a bit about Judaism before their conversion, most probably did not. With the audience of 1 Corinthians being largely Gentile, it is extraordinary how much

[10]Roy E. Ciampa and Brian S. Rosner, "1 Corinthians," in *Commentary on the New Testament Use of the Old Testament*, ed. G. K. Beale and D. A. Carson (Grand Rapids: Baker Academic, 2007), 710.

of the Old Testament is in play. First Corinthians is brimming with Old Testament quotations, allusions, and concepts.

Perhaps even more astonishing is how Paul connects his Gentile audience to Israel in the Old Testament. He does this throughout 1 Corinthians. For example, he refers to them repeatedly as the "assembly of God" or the "church of God" (1:2; 10:32; 11:16, 22; 15:9). These references draw from Nehemiah 13:1, the only place in all the Old Testament where "church of God" appears. The phrase in Nehemiah refers to the congregation of Israel: "On that day the Book of Moses was read aloud in the hearing of the people and there it was found written that no Ammonite or Moabite should ever be admitted into the *assembly of God*." Paul repeatedly applies the phrase to the Corinthians since they are the continuation of true Israel.[11]

Israel's God is the God of the Corinthian church, and Israel's story is their story. But one important difference remains: the believers at Corinth participate in end-time Israel. Old Testament saints, with all of their privileges and experiences, never enjoyed their status as the latter-day people of God in the new creation. Paul exhorts his readers to flee from sin and remain mindful of their identity as true Israel living in the fulfillment of Israel's prophecies in the latter days.

Christian liberty and idolatry (7:1–10:33). The theme of sexuality continues into chapter 7, particularly the relationship between a husband and wife. Both partners are inseparably joined together and are obligated to meet one another's needs (1 Cor 7:1-5). Paul includes in his discussion of marriage his desire that those unmarried ought to "stay unmarried, as I do" (7:8). He then drills

FIGURE 10.9. TEMPLE OF THE GODDESS ATHENA

[11]See G. K. Beale, "The Background of ἐκκλησία Revisited," *Journal for the Study of the New Testament* 38 (2015): 1-18 for fuller analysis of the use of "church [assembly] of God" in 1 Corinthians and elsewhere in the New Testament.

down into the theme of divorce (7:10-16, 39-40): the believing spouse must remain married if the unbelieving spouse decides to remain. But if the unbelieving spouse leaves the marriage relationship, the believing spouse is able to remarry (a believer). Those from other walks of life are also exhorted to live worthy of the gospel—Gentiles (7:17-20), slaves (7:21-24), and virgins (7:25-38).

Chapter 8 focuses on Christian liberty, particularly how it relates to cultic practices that may be offensive to "weaker" believers—that is, those who have not fully grasped the freedom that exists in Christ. The chapter begins with a problem among some of the Corinthians: eating food that had been sacrificed to idols in the local temple. Supporting the principle that "an idol is nothing at all in the world" (8:4) is a quotation from Deuteronomy 6:4, one of the most notable texts in all the Old Testament.

FIGURE 10.10. JEWS WEAR TEFILLIN PHYLACTERIES ON THE ARM OR HEAD

At the beginning of Deuteronomy 6, Moses discloses the reason he is reminding the Israelites of God's law: "So that you, your children and their children after them may fear the Lord your God as long as you live by keeping all his decrees and commands that I give you, and so that you may enjoy long life" (6:2). Obeying God's law is the means by which Israel will flourish in the Promised Land.

We once again find this central theme here in Deuteronomy 6:3: "Obey so that it may go well with you and that you may *increase greatly* in a land flowing with milk and honey, just as the Lord, the God of your ancestors, promised you" (see Gen 1:28). This connects Israel's identity and mission to Adam and Eve and the patriarchs. When viewed in the wider context, Moses' words take on additional significance. The divine commission for Adam and Eve to rule over and fill the earth with God's glory progresses from the patriarchs to the nation of Israel, which is, in some sense, a corporate Adam (Gen 5:3; Ex 4:22). Like Adam and Eve, Israel is to rule over the earth, imitate God's character by obeying the law, and serve as priests by converting the pagan nations (Ex 19:6).

In 1 Corinthians 8:4, Paul refers to the heart of the law from Deuteronomy 6:4-5: "Hear, O Israel: *The Lord our God, the Lord is one*. Love the Lord your God with all your heart and with all your soul and with all your strength." Verse 4 discloses God's identity as "one," standing in stark contrast to the polytheistic convictions of the pagan nations (cf. Deut 4:35, 39). The Shema (named after the first word of Deut 6:4, *hear*) was regarded in Judaism as central to the Israelite belief system. According to the Mishnah, Jews were to recite the Shema in the morning and evening (m. *Ber*. 1.1-2). Later Judaism included Deuteronomy 6:4-9 within the *tefillin* (phylacteries), small boxes that contain four prominent scriptural passages and are worn daily on the arm and the head (*b. Men.*

34a; 36a). Jews were to mediate on these truths, especially the divine command that Israel reflect often on the Lord's unique existence in contrast to polytheistic tendencies of the surrounding cultures.

Paul's use of Deuteronomy 6:4 reinforces Israel's long-held conviction that the God of the Old Testament is indeed the only God. The Corinthians must not embrace the pagan understanding of gods standing behind idols. Paul then, keeping Deuteronomy 6:4 in mind, goes on to make a startling claim in 1 Corinthians 8:6: "For us there is but one God, the Father, from whom all things came and for whom we live; and there is but *one Lord, Jesus Christ, through whom all things came and through whom we live.*" As Richard Bauckham notes, "The unique identity of the one God *consists of* the one God, the Father, *and* the one Lord, his Messiah."[12]

The remainder of chapter 8 further unpacks Paul's teaching on Christian liberty and food. If a weak believer, an individual who does not have correct insight or knowledge into the nature of idols, is offended by the actions of a strong believer, then the strong Christian must refrain from eating (8:7-13).

Now that Paul has cracked the door open on the topic of Christian liberty, he uses himself as an example to the Corinthians as one who understands his freedom, as an apostle, in Christ. The heart of this chapter is found in 1 Corinthians 9:22: "To the weak I became weak, to win the weak. I have become all things to all people so that by all possible means I might save some." Although Paul has the right not to follow all the prescriptions of the Mosaic law that separate the Jewish people from their neighbors, he does so at times to "win" the Jews (9:19-22). Above all, Paul's behavior is always constrained by the gospel (9:23).

> ***Paul draws a direct line beginning with the Israelites, who came out of the exodus, all the way to the Gentile church at Corinth.***

Chapter 10 returns to the theme of idolatry, but this time Paul confronts the topic directly and unpacks the Old Testament teaching on the issue. The chapter begins with a riveting description of the Corinthians: "I do not want you to be ignorant of the fact, brothers and sisters, that *our ancestors* were all under the cloud and that they all passed through the sea" (10:1). The Corinthian congregation, a church filled primarily with *Gentile* Christians, is aligned with the nation of Israel, so much so that Paul includes the Corinthians in the lineage of Israel when he tells them the first generation of Israelites are their ancestors. "The story of Israel," as Richard Hays points out, "is for the Gentile Corinthians not somebody else's story; it is the story of their own authentic spiritual ancestors."[13] Although the Corinthians are not ethnically part of Israel, they enjoy complete identification with Israel through their position in Christ, the embodiment of true Israel (cf. Gal 3:16, 26, 29).

After recounting the wilderness experience of the Israelites, Paul discloses his reason

---

[12]Richard Bauckham, *Jesus and the God of Israel: God Crucified and Other Studies on the New Testament's Christology of Divine Identity* (Grand Rapids: Eerdmans, 2008), 101 (emphasis original).

[13]Richard Hays, *First Corinthians*, Interpretation (Louisville: Westminster John Knox, 1997), 160.

for doing so—the failure of the Israelites in committing idolatry is an example to the Corinthians. Paul's message is clear: do not repeat the sin of your ancestors! First Corinthians 10:7-22 continues the discussion of idolatry with an eye on Israel's incident concerning the golden calf. Here Paul understands that to sacrifice to an idol is to sacrifice to a demon (10:19-20). Such a sacrifice entails worshipers becoming "participants with demons" who are active behind the idol (10:20). The idolatrous behavior at Corinth runs parallel to Israel's idolatry in the wilderness. Within this section, Paul explicitly quotes Exodus 32:6 and alludes to Deuteronomy 32:17, 32:16, and 32:21.

FIGURE 10.11. VOTIVE PLAQUE DEPICTING THE ELEUSINIAN MYSTERIES

Exodus 32:6 says, "Afterward they sat down to eat and drink and got up to indulge in revelry." This is a description of the Israelites in their raucous worship of the calf. Exodus 32 portrays the people as wild calves or untrained cows because they transformed into the very object of their worship. The rebellious Israelites became "stiff-necked" (Ex 32:9; 33:3, 5; 34:9) and disobedient, as they "were running wild" (Ex 32:25). The people lost their way and had been "quick to turn away" (Ex 32:8), needing to be gathered together again at the camp's entrance (Ex 32:26). Just as the first generation of Israelites spiritually transformed into the image of the golden calf they worshiped, the Corinthians are in danger of being transformed into or participating in the image of the demons (1 Cor 10:20).

Issues during public worship (11:1-34). Chapter 11 divides roughly into two sections, and both concern the Corinthian worship service: head coverings (11:1-16) and the Eucharist or the Lord's Supper (11:17-34). The first section on head coverings is, at the core, a discussion of gender roles during worship. Paul roots his discussion in the Genesis 1–3 narrative. Genesis 3:16 is alluded to in 11:3, and Genesis 1:26-27 is also in mind in 11:7. First Corinthians 11:8-9 mentions the sequence of creation as set forth in Genesis 2:21-23. Paul attempts to return the Corinthian church to its creational intention, particularly as it is applied to head coverings. By wearing a head covering in worship, a woman symbolizes her submission to the man, who is also under submission to God (1 Cor 11:7; cf. Eph 5:25-33).

The second portion of the chapter is devoted to the problem of divisions during the Lord's Supper (1 Cor 11:17-34). The first half of this section outlines the pernicious problem taking root in the church. The nub of the issue is found in 11:20-21: "When you come together, it is not the Lord's Supper you eat, for when you are eating, some of you go ahead with your own private suppers." The church at Corinth, like many churches in the

FIGURE 10.12. ATRIUM IN POMPEII

first century, probably assembled in house churches (see Rom 16:3-5; 1 Cor 16:19; Col 4:15; Philem 2). Wealthy Christians in Corinth hosted the worship gatherings in their private homes, and some of these homes consisted of many rooms and a dining room (triclinium) and an atrium. Larger homes could host fifty or so,[14] whereas smaller ones hosted far less. Here, though, in 1 Cor 11 it appears that the entire church has come together in a single home (11:18), possibly the home of Gaius (cf. Rom 16:23). When the church at Corinth assembled in a single house place, the rich within the congregation probably feasted in the dining room and relegated the poor during the Lord's Supper to outside in the atrium. When the Corinthians come together and participate in the Lord's Supper but divide according to one's social standing, then they are turning back the redemptive-historical clock. In Christ, the Corinthians are true Israel and all barricades have been torn down. They are one people group in Christ. But by shunning the poor, though, the wealthy at Corinth have fallen out of step with a cardinal eschatological reality—absolute unity within the covenant community.

SPIRITUAL GIFTS IN WORSHIP (12:1–14:40)

The pouring out of the Spirit at Pentecost signals a new chapter in the Bible's grand story line. God's people now enjoy a unique Spirit-filled experience, an experience that was previously limited to only prophets, priests, and kings in the Old Testament. The Spirit's ministry enables believers to bear witness to the risen Christ to those outside the church and serve one another within the church. To unbelievers, Spirit-enabled gifts

[14]Jerome Murphy-O'Connor, *St. Paul's Corinth: Texts and Archaeology* (Collegeville, MN: Liturgical Press, 1983), 156-58.

testify to the risen Christ. Such gifts, when properly employed, also promote unity and harmony within the covenant community.

The church as Christ's body and the goal of spiritual gifts (12:1–13:13). Paul begins his discussion of spiritual gifts with the ultimate goal of unity (12:4-6). Whether a message of wisdom, special knowledge, healing, prophecy, or different kinds of tongues, the Spirit distributes each gift for the well-being and unity of the church (12:11). Each member, whether Jew or Gentile, equally participates in the "one Spirit." Believers are "the body of Christ, and individual members of it" (12:27 HCSB). Gifts promote unity among the church members, even those from various social backgrounds and ethnicities. In the following chapter, Paul tempers the role of gifts with love. Without love, any gifting becomes unfruitful because it fails to edify the church (13:1-13). Paul uses himself as a hypothetical example to show that even his gifts would be worthless without love (13:1-3).

FIGURE 10.13. TEMPLE SCROLL AT QUMRAN

Spiritual gifts in public worship (14:1-40). After instructing the congregation on the goal of the gifts and the motivation that propels their use, Paul highlights some trouble spots within the Corinthian congregation's worship. Speaking in "tongues"—that is, personal revelations—is a private endeavor and edifies only the individual. Unless tongues are interpreted in a public gathering (14:5, 13-17), they ought to remain private (14:2, 4). Prophecy, however, is designed for the public consumption since it edifies the church as a whole and unifies the entire congregation (14:3, 6, 18-19).

One of the more remarkable aspects of 1 Corinthians is Paul's discussion of speaking in tongues. In 13:1-2, Paul associates tongues, angels, and mysteries: "If I speak in the tongues of men or of *angels*. . . . If I have the gift of prophecy and can fathom all *mysteries*." Once again, Paul states, "Anyone who speaks in a *tongue* does not speak to people but to God. Indeed, no one understands them; they utter *mysteries* by the Spirit" (14:2). In several early Jewish texts, we find the visionary joining the angels in their heavenly veneration of God. One passage in the Dead Sea Scrolls is strikingly similar to Paul's discussion: "And the offering of their *tongues* . . . *seven mysteries of knowledge* in the wonderful *mystery* of the seven regions of the hol[y of holies]. . . . The *tongue* of the first will be strengthened seven times with the *tongue* of the second to him" (4Q403 1 II, 26-28). Angels and Jewish worshipers at Qumran jointly praise God with their "tongues" in God's heavenly sanctuary, celebrating deep knowledge or mysteries. If part of Paul's understanding of tongues resembles this Jewish outlook, then the worshipers at Corinth are participating in the angelic praise of God in heaven (cf. Rev 4:4; 5:8).[15] The final section of chapter 14 regulates how the spiritual gifts operate during worship (1 Cor 14:26-40). Paul places great emphasis on the proper order of the speakers and prophets since "God is not a God of disorder but of peace" (14:33).

FIGURE 10.14. WOMEN AT THE TOMB OF JESUS

DEFENSE OF CHRIST'S RESURRECTION (15:1-58)

The final block of teaching turns on the most detailed description of resurrection in the New Testament, perhaps in all of early Christianity.[16] Chapter 15 breaks down into two large sections: the historical evidence for Christ's resurrection (15:1-34) and the theological rationale for it (15:35-58). Why Paul decides to expound on this doctrine may stem from some members of the Corinthian congregation denying the resurrection (15:12, 35). As the apostle argues, Christ's resurrection was anticipated in the Old Testament, attested to by hundreds, and was necessary for the restoration of all things. Christ's resurrection also affects believers since he is the "firstfruits" (15:20, 23) or beginning of their renewal.

The historical evidence of Christ's resurrection (15:1-34). God's commitment to all of creation is evident in every page of the Bible. He is committed to dwelling with humanity and creation in the new heavens and earth for eternity. Central to his plan of redemption is the complete restoration of the person—soul and body. In 1 Corinthians 15, the apostle Paul argues for the necessity of the resurrection of Christ and believers. Of all the various doctrines Paul taught his churches, the most important message is the gospel itself—Christ's death and resurrection (15:3). These twin events were not outside God's plan but occupied a central place in the history of redemption. Paul states that Christ was crucified "according to the Scriptures" (15:3), possibly alluding to Isaiah 53:5:

[15]See Markus Bockmuehl, *Revelation and Mystery in Ancient Judaism and Pauline Christianity*, WUNT 36 (Tübingen: J. C. B. Mohr [Paul Siebeck], 1990; repr., Grand Rapids: Eerdmans, 1997), 169-70.

[16]The discussion of 1 Cor 15 has been adapted from Benjamin L. Gladd, *Revealing the Mysterion: The Use of Mystery in Daniel and Second Temple Judaism with Its Bearing on First Corinthians*, BZNW 160 (Berlin: Walter de Gruyter, 2008), 223-61.

"He was pierced for our transgressions" (cf. Is 53:8). Christ was also "raised on the third day according to the Scriptures" (1 Cor 15:4). The phrase "on the third day" alludes to the discovery of the empty tomb and recalls Hosea 6:2, which predicts God raising Israel from the dead: "He will raise us up on the third day" (NASB). The raising of Christ from the dead inaugurates the end-time resurrection of Israel. The Old Testament explicitly and implicitly expected Christ's death and resurrection. Adam and Israel's failure to subdue their enemies and spread God's glory to the ends of the earth anticipates Christ's obedience and victory, climaxing in his death and resurrection.

Christ appeared to the disciples (15:5, 7) and five hundred more (15:6). Even Paul testifies to his resurrection on the road to Damascus (15:8). To deny the resurrection, like some at Corinth, is to deny the very received traditions of the apostles, even Paul himself. Since Christ has been raised, believers will follow suit (15:9-34). Christ is the "firstfruits" of the resurrection (15:20, 23) who guarantees the resurrection of all believers.

The theological rationale for Christ's resurrection (15:35-58). In 15:35, Paul poses the question, "But someone will ask, 'How are the dead raised? With what kind of body will they come?'" Paul dedicates the remainder of the chapter to answer this key question (cf. 15:12). In 15:35-57, Paul uses a type of rhetoric that would have been familiar to the Corinthians. This type of argument adapts or accommodates the audience's currently held beliefs, which is then followed by a correction.[17] In 15:36-38, Paul condemns his audience for denying God's power in creation: "When you sow, you do not plant the body that will be. . . . *God gives it a body* as he has determined" (15:37-38). God is able to transform a dead seed to a living plant or tree.

Building on the principle that God creates and transforms in 15:39-41, Paul introduces two spatial polarities: earth (people, animals) and heaven (sun, moon). The next section, 15:42-44a, brings together these two points—God can transform things from death into life (15:36-38), from earth to heaven (15:36-41). Paul finally relates these observations to the nature of the resurrection: "*So will it be* with the resurrection of the dead. . . . It is sown a natural [earthly] body, it is raised a spiritual [heavenly] body" (15:42-44a). Paul has, in effect, now made room for a doctrine of the resurrection within his established framework. God can transform a terrestrial, earthly body (15:36-38) to a heavenly one (15:39-41).

Moving beyond spatial polarities in 15:39-44a, he now typologically argues for a temporal polarity: "If there is a natural body, there is also a spiritual body. So it is written: The first man Adam became a living being; the last Adam became a life-giving Spirit. However, the spiritual is not first, but the natural, then the spiritual" (15:44b-46 HCSB). The terms *first* and *last* set a chronological distinction, whereas *natural* and *heavenly* reveal a spatial one. Paul's interpretation of Genesis 2:7 fuses the temporal and spatial polarities, providing the basis for such a claim. The pre-fall Adam of Genesis 2:7, from Paul's perspective, is still considered a "natural" or earthly being, even though he had not yet sinned. Christ, however, has a *different* body of glory. Before the resurrection, Christ

[17] Jeffrey R. Asher, *Polarity and Change in 1 Corinthians 15: A Study in Metaphysics, Rhetoric, and Resurrection*, HUT 42 (Tübingen: Mohr-Siebeck, 2000), 48-90.

identifies with the earthly body of the pre-fall Adam. At the resurrection, the Spirit transforms Christ's body into a heavenly one that is the beginning of the end-time new creation, fit to inhabit the heavens and the earth.

First Corinthians 15:50-53 answers the initial question posed in 15:35. Paul explicitly states what has been implicit thus far: "Flesh and blood cannot inherit the kingdom of God, nor does the perishable inherit the imperishable" (15:50). The apostle contends, probably in agreement with the Corinthians, that earthly bodies are unable to dwell in a heavenly environment. But unlike those in Corinth, Paul believes that God possesses the ability to refashion and transform those in their earthly bodies into heavenly ones, a point he previously made in 15:36-38. The answer, Paul emphatically declares, is a mystery—the transformation of all believers, both dead *and* alive, into the heavenly image of the last Adam (15:51-52). Although the Old Testament writers probably assumed some sort of transformation of the body (e.g., Is 26:19; Dan 12:2-3), they were probably not expecting the physical transformation of those living at the time of the final resurrection of all saints. In addition, Paul does not argue for the restoration of believers into the image of the first Adam's body (an Old Testament and Jewish expectation) but the transformation of the body into the image of the last Adam (2 Cor 5:1-5; Phil 3:20-21; 1 Jn 3:2), a teaching that was not clearly anticipated in the Old Testament.

At the consummation of the age, Christ will discard the believers' clothes of the old, fallen Adam and clothe them with the end-time attire of the last Adam (1 Cor 15:53-54). Therein lies the key that was hidden from the Corinthians. Believers are transformed from their earthly existence to a heavenly one, reconciling the spatial polarity with Paul's Adam framework, the temporal polarity. Paul concludes with results of the resurrection in 15:54-55, the main point of 15:35-55.

THE COLLECTION, GREETINGS, AND THE LETTER CLOSING (16:1-24)

The final chapter of the letter transitions into a pragmatic discussion concerning the collection. Paul asks the church to save a portion of their income "on the first day of every week" (1 Cor 16:2). Christ's resurrection, having occurred on Sunday, alters not only how the covenant community worships but also *when* they worship. The gift is intended to support the church in Jerusalem (16:3). This particular heartfelt offering crops up in a few prominent places within Paul's epistles (e.g., 2 Cor 8–9; Rom 15:25-28). At this time, the Jewish church in Jerusalem is struggling on many fronts (Acts 24:17), and the apostle Paul takes it on himself to serve them in a tangible way.

Paul intends on collecting the offering on his way through the churches of Macedonia, which, apparently, are also contributing to the collection (Rom 15:26). In addition to meeting the Jerusalem church's physical needs, the collection unites Jewish and Gentile Christians. Ultimately, Paul's gospel remains to the "Jew first" and for the eventual and continual salvation of a Jewish remnant (Rom 11:25). Paul may view the collection as bringing about the direct fulfillment of Isaiah 2:2-3; 60:5-6; and Micah 4:1-2—passages that predict the conversion of the nations in the latter days and their support of the Israelites.

The second half of the chapter addresses the Corinthians and their reception of several of the saints (16:10-18). The church at Corinth must also "stand firm in the faith" (16:13). The network of churches in Asia Minor, where Paul resides while writing the epistle, sends its greetings (16:19-20). The letter ends with Paul's greeting the church with his "own hand," the typical way for Paul to authorize his letters (Gal 6:11; Col 4:18).

2 CORINTHIANS

AUTHORSHIP

Second Corinthians claims to be written by the apostle Paul, and few today dispute that claim. The letter opens with the typical Pauline designation: "Paul, an apostle of Christ Jesus" (2 Cor 1:1). The epistle is filled with personal touches and insights from Paul's plans and journeys (e.g., 1:16). The early church heartily agreed that this letter should be attributed to Paul. His authorship of this epistle has not been an issue, but the unity of 2 Corinthians remains problematic for some scholars (see below).

DATE

What we now refer to as 2 Corinthians appears to be the fourth letter that Paul wrote to the church at Corinth. The first letter to the Corinthians is written while Paul ministers in Ephesus on his third missionary journey and dates to AD 54–55 (1 Cor 5:9; Acts 19:1-22). The second letter, commonly known as First Corinthians, is also written from Paul's stint in Ephesus in the spring of AD 54 or 55 (1 Cor 16:8). After making a short visit to Corinth, Paul pens his third letter to the church once more from Ephesus (2:3-9; 7:8-12). The fourth and final letter, what we label 2 Corinthians, is written shortly thereafter, probably from Macedonia in AD 55–56.

OCCASION

By the time we turn from 1 Corinthians to 2 Corinthians, Paul's relationship to the church of Corinth has changed drastically. Paul writes 1 Corinthians and sends Timothy to deliver it to the church, knowing that this congregation is filled with strife and division. Paul plans to visit Corinth after he passes through Macedonia and takes the collection to Jerusalem (1 Cor 16:1-7). But when Timothy arrives at Corinth with the letter of 1 Corinthians, the church is rife with deep-seated division. A few church leaders have turned against Paul, and the church is now even more splintered. Neither Timothy nor Paul's letter (1 Corinthians) is able to correct the systemic problem. Paul desires to venture to Corinth immediately and visit with the church a second time before heading to Jerusalem. He journeys to Corinth, but before he arrives, some individuals from outside of Corinth, known as the super apostles, enter the congregation (2 Cor 11:13-15).

These super apostles attack Paul's character, contending that since he is weak and unsophisticated, he cannot be a true apostle. Great opposition arises against him and his apostleship (2 Cor 2:1, 5-8; 7:8-13; 11:4). These outsiders have swayed the majority of the church in Corinth, resulting in many of the Corinthians nearly abandoning the gospel.

Paul leaves the situation in Corinth unresolved. He returns to Ephesus and writes another letter, called the "tearful letter" or "severe letter." Instead of Timothy delivering the letter, Titus does so. According to 2 Corinthians 2:3-9 and 7:8-12, this letter asks the church to repent from their worldly views and reprove the Corinthian leader. After Titus gives the letter to the church, things take a turn for the better. Eventually, Paul decides to leave Ephesus, probably because of persecution (2 Cor 1:8-10), to meet up with Titus in Macedonia. He receives news that the Corinthian church is doing much better. The breach between the Corinthians and Paul is beginning to mend. What remains is a handful of church members who still cling to the false teaching of the super apostles.

Such is the situation when Paul writes 2 Corinthians. The worst is over; Paul needs only to affirm repentance of the majority and correct the rebellion of the minority. The few who reject his apostolic authority remain active within in the Corinthian congregation and have the potential to influence the majority. From somewhere in Macedonia, Paul writes 2 Corinthians ("Corinthians D") in AD 55 or 56.

To summarize the sequence of the correspondence, Paul writes "Corinthians A" (1 Cor 5:9) and then pens "Corinthians B" (1 Corinthians) a few months later. "Corinthians C" is the "tearful letter" Paul issues after hearing of the church's abandonment of the gospel (2 Cor 2:3-9; 7:8-12). Finally, Paul sends his fourth letter to the church at Corinth, "Corinthians D" (2 Corinthians) to encourage their stance in the gospel and admonish the unrepentant minority.

PURPOSE

Paul's opponents accuse him of being unsophisticated, weak in appearance, and without the proper credentials, thus damaging his apostolic message. Paul responds by claiming that he is a genuine apostle because he lives and ministers in light of the cross. His apostleship must be authentic because it embodies the death of Christ. Paul writes 2 Corinthians so the church will embrace the ethics of the cross, resist the opponents' teaching, and accept his apostolic authority.

FIGURE 11.1. RUINS OF CORINTH

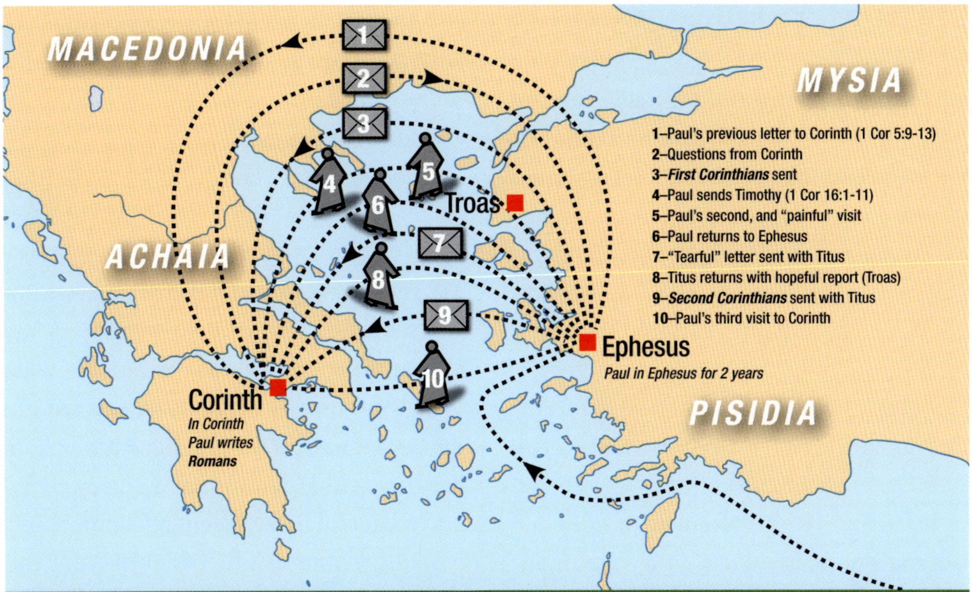

PAUL'S VISITS AND LETTERS TO CORINTH

INTEGRITY OF 2 CORINTHIANS

Although all extant manuscripts attest to the unity of the book, several modern scholars contend that a few sections are stitched together to form 2 Corinthians. Typically, the epistle is divided into two sections: 1–9 and 10–13 (though there are several other alleged interpolations). Some consider chapters 10–13 to be letter "C," or Paul's tearful letter, thus explaining the shift of tone from positive to negative. Others suggest that Paul wrote 10–13 after 1–9, constituting letter "E."

Taking into account the external textual witnesses and the internal argumentation, the best explanation is that the epistle forms a unity, all written from the same time and place. Accounting for the change in tone, Paul simply turns his attention to the rebellious Corinthian minority in chapters 10–13.[1] The first seven chapters of the letter concern the past events at Corinth, chapters 8–9 refer to the present situation with the collection, and chapters 10–13 anticipate Paul's third visit to Corinth. The epistle could thus be considered as a chronological progression—past, present, and future.[2]

OUTLINE

I. Defense of Paul's Apostleship (1:1–7:16)
   - A. Change of Plans but Not of Heart (1:1–2:17)
   - B. The Nature of the New Covenant (3:1-18)
   - C. Believers as a New Creation (4:1–5:21)
   - D. Paul as Isaiah's Servant (6:1–7:16)

II. Concern for the Collection (8:1–9:15)

III. An Appeal to the Rebellious Minority (10:1–13:10)

IV. The Letter Closing (13:11-14)

[1]Scott J. Hafemann, *2 Corinthians*, NIVAC (Grand Rapids: Zondervan, 2000), 32-33.
[2]James M. Scott, *2 Corinthians*, NIBC (Peabody, MA: Hendrickson, 1998), 208-9. See also Hafemann, *2 Corinthians*, 390.

BIBLICAL-THEOLOGICAL THEMES

End-time suffering and the people of God. Beginning with Cain and Abel and culminating in the end-time persecution of righteous Israelites, the Old Testament bears witness to the oppression of God's people. Suffering and unjust persecution are a staple of Israel's story. The Israelites suffer at the hands of their enemies for hundreds of years—Egyptians, Philistines, Moabites, Assyrians, Babylonians, and the Greeks to name a few (see figs. 11.3 and 11.4). Israel is no stranger to suffering, yet the prophets predict that the nation, particularly those righteous Israelites within the nation, will undergo severe testing in the latter days. Deuteronomy 4:30 predicts that Israel will be "in distress" in the "later days." Jeremiah even asserts that Israel will be forced to endure a "time of trouble" (30:7), and Zechariah pointedly declares that "two-thirds [of Israel] will be struck down and perish" (13:8; cf. Ezek 38–39). But by far the most detailed account of Israel's tribulation is narrated in Daniel 10–12.

FIGURE 11.2. ST. PAUL

These chapters constitute Daniel's final vision, and those who are wise will instruct many and undergo severe affliction (11:33-35). According to 12:1, a great persecution will set in—"a time of distress such as has not happened from the beginning of nations until then." But in the midst of this tribulation, a remnant of faithful Israelites will be delivered (12:1). They will eventually be resurrected, and those who have understanding will "shine like the brightness of the heavens" (12:2-4).

Daniel 11:36-45 expects a final opponent of God to besiege the covenant community. The end-time attack against Israel will manifest itself on two levels. An opponent will persecute righteous Israelites: "Forces will rise up to desecrate the temple fortress and will abolish the daily sacrifice. Then they will set up the abomination that causes desolation" (11:31). Here the enemy will wage war against the temple precinct and defile it by setting up "the abomination of desolation." Verses 33-35 further describe the attack against the wise within the covenant community: "Those who are wise will instruct many . . . they will fall by the sword or be burned or captured or plundered" (11:33). Nevertheless, the righteous will persevere under pressure (11:32), though they will "stumble" and be "refined" and "purified" (11:35).

Daniel 12:10 describes the conduct of two groups in the latter days. The righteous Israelites will possess great discernment in the end times. From the outside, it seems as though the wicked have the upper hand, especially in light of grave persecution, but those who have insight into God's plan (the wise) will grasp the significance of the end-time turmoil. God has decreed that the wicked become increasingly hostile to those

FIGURE 11.3. DESTRUCTION OF JERUSALEM

within the covenant community ("Many will be purified, made spotless and refined"). The wicked or the lawless ones from 11:29-34 have been deceived by the end-time opponent. These lawless ones spiral into greater wickedness and deception: "The wicked will continue to be wicked" (Dan 12:10).

Turning to the Gospels, we learn that the latter days have commenced and the end-time tribulation of Israel has begun in the person of Jesus. He experiences tribulation throughout his ministry, climaxing with the tribulation of his death on the cross. But the inbreaking of the great tribulation does not stop there. It continues on in Jesus' followers. The "body of Christ" also suffers tribulation during the church's ministry before Christ's second coming. At the very end of history, before Christ returns, believers will endure a heightened, universal tribulation and persecution (see Rev 11:7-14).

Second Corinthians springs from this intense period of tribulation that began in Jesus' ministry and continues until he returns. At center stage in 2 Corinthians lies Paul's legitimacy as a true apostle of Christ. One of his adamant appeals to the Corinthians is his insistence that his apostleship is patterned after the cross, from which Christ rules in the midst of end-time affliction and tribulation. By virtue of his union with Christ and his personal commission by the risen Christ, Paul possesses the legitimate office of an apostle. The Corinthians can discern tangible marks of the end-time tribulation through Paul's hardships—marks that bear witness to Christ's crucifixion and display power in weakness. In addition, the false teachers in the Corinthian church (the so-called super apostles) are a manifestation of the deceivers from Daniel 7–12. All who stand in opposition to Paul and his message are representatives

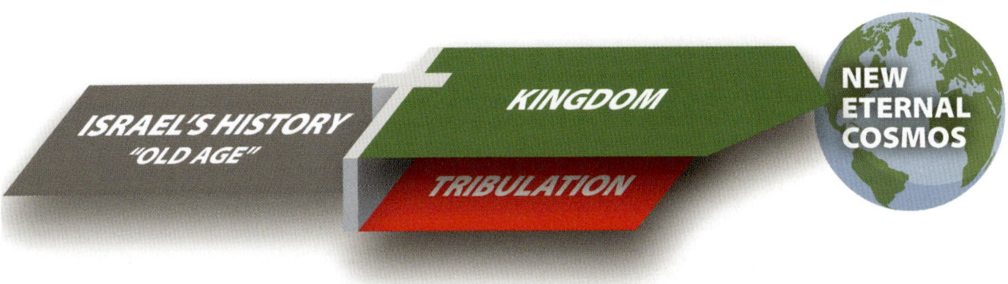

FIGURE 11.4. TRIBULATION IN THE OVERLAP OF AGES

of Satan (2 Cor 11:13-15), an expression of the end-time deceivers of Daniel.

Isaiah's promise of the new creation.[3] The fall of Adam and Eve in Genesis 3 brought about dire consequences for humanity and creation. Mankind and the created order are no longer able to enjoy intimate communion with the Lord. But God promises to undo the harmful effects of sin and recreate the world. This theme of full and final redemption runs throughout the Old Testament, and Isaiah 40–66 discusses this more than any other section of the Old Testament.

In the immediate context of Isaiah, the nation of Israel finds herself in exile and under the thumb of the Babylonian Empire. Isaiah 40–66 portrays the exile as an expression of divine wrath (Is 51:20; 51:17, 22), anger (Is 47:6; 60:10), forsakenness (Is 49:14; 54:6-7; 62:4), rejection (Is 54:6), hiddenness (Is 54:8; 57:17; 59:2; 64:7), and consequent "separation" between God and the nation (Is 59:2). God promises to redeem Israel's inhabitants, "blot out [their] transgressions" (Is 43:25), and free them from the bondage resulting from sin (Is 42:6-9; 49:8-9) by the sacrificial death of the servant (Is 53:4-12).

FIGURE 11.5. ALEXANDER THE GREAT CONQUERS PALESTINE, FURTHER EXPANDING HIS EMPIRE

Israel's return from exile is a period in which there is a cessation of anger and in which peace is reestablished between the nation and its God (cf. Is 48:18; 52:7; 57:19). This is a peace that results from and is characteristic of the new creation, modeled on the original garden of Eden. The Lord's role as Israel's creator (Is 43:1) is accentuated in his portrayal as the one who "created," "formed," and "made" the nation for his glory (Is 43:7). The Israelites are exhorted to reflect not on their former condition of exile, when they experienced divine wrath (Is 43:18; cf. 65:16b-19), but rather on God's imminent new creation of them as his chosen people whom he forms for himself (Is 43:19-21). This coming restoration is further highlighted as a new creation through describing Israel's return with imagery of paradise: "wild animals . . . jackals and the owls" glorify God because the wilderness now gushes forth with abundant water (Is 43:19-20).

According to 2 Corinthians 5:14-22, Paul delivers a message of reconciliation and declares that all those who identify with Christ are a "new creation" (5:17, 19). In light of Isaiah 40–66, reconciliation in Christ is Paul's way of signaling that Isaiah's promises of restoration from the alienation of spiritual exile have initially been fulfilled by Christ's work on the cross. The results of sin—separation and alienation from God—have been overcome through the divine grace expressed in Christ. Since the Corinthians participate in the new creation (5:14-19), they must behave as those reconciled to God (5:20) and accept Paul's apostolic authority.

[3]The discussion of Isaiah in 2 Cor 5 is taken from G. K. Beale, "The Old Testament Background of Reconciliation in 2 Corinthians 5–7 and Its Bearing on the Literary Problem of 2 Corinthians 4:14–7:1," NTS 35 (1989): 550-81.

He alludes to Isaiah 43:18-19 and 65:17 to wed the promises of Isaiah with the work of Christ. Jesus' death and resurrection fulfill Isaiah's promise, resulting in restoration of an estranged people to their God. The effect of Christ's work can be aptly summarized as a "new creation" (2 Cor 5:17). The Old Testament's expectation that God would one day re-create the world and establish a new creation has begun in the person of Christ. When individuals join themselves to him through faith, they initially participate in the new heavens and earth.

DEFENSE OF PAUL'S APOSTLESHIP (1:1–7:16)

The Old Testament awaited the day when God would make a new covenant with Israel (e.g., Jer 31:33-34). The first covenant is intrinsically temporary and designed only for the Israelite nation. The sacrificial and civil laws are established for a specific time and for a specific people group, anticipating Christ's work. The old covenant too can be broken (Jer 31:32). The new covenant, however, is eternal and unable to be broken (Heb 13:20). It will never cease but will remain in the new heavens and earth for eternity.

The prophet Jeremiah explains a key aspect of the new covenant: *all* Israelites in the end times will have access to God's revelation and will be in a position to teach one another (Jer 31:34). Within the Mosaic administration, only prophets and priests are appointed to teach the Israelites. Teaching God's law also presupposes a deep knowledge of it. Jeremiah claims that the Israelites under the new covenant will "all know me" (31:34). Righteous Israelites will possess a more robust understanding of God's law and be in a position to teach their neighbors.

The first half of the epistle is intended to sway the Corinthians to embrace Paul's apostolic ministry of the new covenant, an administration that is principally dependent on Christ's death and resurrection. Paul works systematically, moving from one topic to another while tethering each discussion to the significance of the new covenant. His proclamation of the gospel, apostleship, and actions fall in line with the superior nature of the new covenant.

> ***The Old Testament expects that in the latter days Israel will undergo severe persecution at the hands of their enemies (e.g., Dan 12:1). God promises to send his Messiah to deliver the Israelites and vanquish their enemies.***

Change of plans but not of heart (1:1–2:17). The letter is addressed to the local church at Corinth and to "all his holy people throughout Achaia" (2 Cor 1:1). Although 2 Corinthians is exceptionally occasional, Paul envisions his epistle circulating to other house churches and Christian assemblies in the province of Achaia. The apostolic teaching contained herein remains relevant for the other churches in the region.

Paul labels God the "Father of compassion and the God of all comfort" (2 Cor 1:3). God promises to comfort Paul in his "troubles" (or better, "every tribulation") so that he can comfort the Corinthians in their own tribulations

(1:4). Every tribulation that Paul and the Corinthians are experiencing is part of this great end-time tribulation. Paul's reasoning is based on their union with Christ: "We share abundantly in the sufferings of Christ" (2 Cor 1:5). Since Christ suffers great tribulation during his ministry, especially on the cross, those who follow him will suffer in the same manner.

FIGURE 11.6. DESCENT OF THE HOLY SPIRIT AT PENTECOST

But just as believers share in Christ's tribulations, so they also share in his comfort. In the throes of death and anguish, the Father comforts the Son assuring him that he will rescue him in his resurrection. The Corinthians must recognize their hardships in light of the Bible's grand story line. Their tribulations are difficult yet temporary. God has made them a new creation (5:17) and promises to usher them fully into the new heavens and earth in the future at the resurrection. As Richard Hays wonderfully puts it,

> The vocation of God's people entails suffering. . . . The apparent tension between Paul's suffering and his claim that the new creation has already arrived is not a sign of contradiction in Paul's thought. It is, rather, a consequence of his conviction that the church lives in the time between the times. Those who stand at the collision point of the two ages live under the sign of the cross.[4]

Paul then relates how he (and probably Timothy) had a brush with death and experienced end-time suffering in Asia (1:8). What strengthens Paul in the midst of such hardship is depending on God, "who raises the dead" (1:9). Paul's confidence and hope rests on his knowledge that God will one day fully redeem him in the new creation. Eschatology is the bedrock of his hope.

Chapter 1 shifts into a defense of Paul's ministry. His conduct is blameless before God and the world (2 Cor 1:12). Paul's opponents may have surmised that he could not be a true apostle, since he changed his plans several times. Paul intends to visit the Corinthians twice: once on the way to Macedonia and once on the way back to Jerusalem, enabling the Corinthians to give twice for the collection (1:15-16). Paul's travels are certainly not out of selfish ambition but for the Corinthians and the saints in Jerusalem. The

[4]Richard Hays, *The Moral Vision of the New Testament: Community, Cross, New Creation: A Contemporary Introduction to New Testament Ethics* (New York: HarperCollins, 1996), 25.

FIGURE 11.7. TITUS VENERATES THE ROMAN GENERAL FOR HIS VICTORY OVER ISRAEL

apostle keeps his promises and remains faithful, just as God does. Second Corinthians 1:20 asserts, "no matter how many promises God has made, they are 'Yes' in Christ." These Old Testament promises are directly fulfilled in Christ's first coming. The "many promises" likely refer to all the end-time promises God made to his people in the Old Testament. Uppermost in Paul's mind, though, are the promises related to the Spirit (1:22; 3:6), new covenant (3:1-6), new creation (5:17), restoration from exile (5:17-6:18), and temple (6:16).

Paul then states that God "makes both us and you stand firm in Christ . . . and put his Spirit in our hearts as a deposit" (1:21-22). The presence of the Spirit in the heart of believers signals the beginning direct fulfillment of latter-day Old Testament promises. The entire sweep of the Old Testament points to and is fulfilled in Christ. God genuinely fulfills his Old Testament promises in the hearts of all believers. But fulfillment does not stop there—even the gift of the Holy Spirit itself is one of the great promises God made to restored Israel in the latter days (e.g., Is 32:15; 44:3; 59:21; Ezek 39:29; Joel 2:28; Zech 12:10).

Chapter 2 opens with Paul's decision to avoid another "painful" journey to Corinth (2 Cor 2:1). After writing 1 Corinthians, he travels to Corinth, but upon arrival, outsiders enter the congregation, and one key member of the church becomes antagonistic toward Paul (2:5). The apostle hastily retreats and pens what scholars call the "tearful letter" (see 2:4). This letter is effective, spurring the leader at Corinth to repent. Paul asks the church to forgive him and "reaffirm your love for him" (2:8). After arriving in Troas and being unable to rendezvous with Titus, he departs for Macedonia (2:12).

The last bit of chapter 2 details some of Paul's ministry at Troas, a period filled with adversity and persecution: "Thanks be to God, who always leads us as captives in Christ's triumphal procession and uses us to spread the aroma of the knowledge of him everywhere" (2 Cor 2:14). Paul recalls the popular Roman procession whereby they lead their defeated enemies into a city. The general or Caesar would lead such a procession, an attempt to bring glory and honor to the Roman leader. At the end of the procession, the Romans would kill representative slaves and offer them up as a sacrifice to their gods (Josephus, *J.W.* 7.5.5-6). But here Paul claims that God is "leading" him in a "triumphal procession," an act that is repulsive to the world but wise and powerful to God. Paul's afflictions and tribulations throughout his ministry appear foolish to the world but glorious in the sight of God. Just as Christ ruled in the midst of suffering, so does Paul.

> ***This new community is not marked by outward, physical signs that demarcate them from the surrounding nations; rather, they are internally set apart as the people of God. Faith in Christ is what defines them as end-time Israelites.***

The nature of the new covenant (3:1-18). In the previous section, Paul articulated *why* he is qualified to be an apostle: he is living a life consistent with the ethics of the cross (2 Cor 2:14-17). In the next several verses, Paul further explains his qualifications as a legitimate apostle. In contrast to the false teachers, Paul does not need a formal letter of recommendation (cf. Acts 9:2), because he produces letters of recommendation *for himself*. Paul's opponents are claiming that their letters of recommendation meet all the proper requirements. Perhaps a church in Judea wrote letters of recommendation for the opponents (cf. Gal 1:22). Whatever the case may be, Paul claims that his letters of recommendation are the Corinthians themselves. Why should they require a commendatory letter when their own hearts bear witness to Christ's work? Instead of Paul carrying around a physical letter of commendation, he carries around the Corinthians' commendation in his heart (2 Cor 3:2). But it is not merely their Christian existence that composes such a "letter"; it is their identity as spiritually resurrected believers that commends Paul's ministry.

The "Spirit of the living God" wrote this letter "not on tablets of stone but on tablets of human hearts" (2 Cor 3:3). These phrases are reminiscent of Jeremiah 31:33: "I will put my law in their minds and *write it on their hearts*. I will be their God, and they will be my people" (cf. Ex 31:18; Jer 17:1; Ezek 11:19; 36:26). The allusion to Jeremiah 31 signals the direct fulfillment of this prophecy, implying that the Corinthians are part of the new covenant community.

In 2 Corinthians 3:4, Paul places his apostolic commission in the same tradition as the commissioning of Old Testament prophets (e.g., Ex 4:10; Judg 6:11-24; Is 6:1-8). He asserts that he is a genuine minister or mediator of a new covenant that is not "of the letter but of the Spirit" (2 Cor 3:6). He grounds this statement with another proposition: "The letter kills, but the Spirit gives life." He draws a contrast between the role of the Mosaic law and the Spirit. In tandem with sinful human nature, the Mosaic law produces death (cf. Gal 3:10, 23; Rom 8:3, 8), whereas the Spirit produces life (cf. Rom 8:2; 1 Cor 15:45). The overall point of Paul's discussion in 2 Corinthians 3:3-6 reveals that the long-awaited new covenant is "marked preeminently by inward divine enablement to carry out God's will."[5]

The Spirit, not the Mosaic law, gives life to believers. The phrase "the Spirit gives life" evokes Ezekiel 37:14: "I will put *my Spirit* in you and *you will live,* and I will settle you in your own land." Paul asserts that the Spirit's work in the hearts of the Corinthians is the beginning fulfillment of Ezekiel 37 (cf. Ezek 11:19; 36:26-27), a prophecy that anticipates the day when Israel will be resurrected and ushered into the Promised Land (cf. 1 Cor 15:49-54).

Making use of a rhetorical technique called *a fortiori* or *qal wahomer* (the lesser to the greater), Paul proceeds to argue for the superiority of the new covenant in 2 Corinthians 3:7-18. The dominant Old Testament background for this passages rests squarely on Exodus 34:29-35, in which Moses descends from Mount Sinai after encountering Israel's God. As a result of his intimate experience with the Lord, Moses' face exuded God's glory (Ex 34:30). But that glory is temporary and succumbs to fading (2 Cor 3:7). Paul capitalizes on this description of Moses' glorious face and argues that even the old covenant, an agreement that resulted in death, is accompanied with glory. As Murray Harris notes, "The dispensation of the Law pronounced a curse on people who failed to carry out the Law's regulations (Deut. 27:26), yet that era or ministry was 'glorious' since that Law and those regulations expressed the sovereign will of God."[6] Therefore, if the old covenant is attended by glory, how much

FIGURE 11.8. MOSES BREAKING THE TABLETS

[5]Murray J. Harris, *The Second Epistle to the Corinthians: A Commentary on the Greek Text,* NIGTC (Grand Rapids: Eerdmans, 2005), 274.
[6]Harris, *Second Epistle to the Corinthians,* 287.

more glorious is the new covenant (2 Cor 3:11)! The old covenant glory "did not just peter out like a battery-powered flashlight; rather it was done away by the greater glory of the new covenant."[7]

> ***The image that believers are being transformed into is none other than the image of the last Adam (see 1 Cor 15:45-50; Rom 5).***

Paul explains that when people turn to the Lord, "the veil is taken away" (2 Cor 3:16). When this occurs, "all, who with unveiled faces contemplate the Lord's glory, *are being transformed into his image with ever-increasing glory*, which comes from the Lord, who is the Spirit" (3:18). Those who trust in Christ experience a tight-knit relationship with God and begin to reflect the glory of his image. The argument of chapter 3 climaxes in believers being transformed into the glorious image of Christ (3:12-18). When the Corinthians gaze on the image of Christ, they become fashioned into his same image (3:16-18). Such transformation is wrought by the Spirit, who accompanies the new covenant and ministers in the hearts of believers (3:3, 6).

Believers as a new creation (4:1–5:21). The believers' transformation into the last Adam continues into 2 Corinthians 4:1-6, where Paul's ministry is also the means by which their transformation takes place. The Spirit applies what Paul proclaims. The transformation of the Corinthian believers into Christ's image encourages Paul to press on as a faithful minister of God's Word (4:2). He commends his ministry because God shines the light of the new creation through Paul's message (4:6). Verse 6 quotes Genesis 1:3: "For God, who said, *'Let light shine out of darkness,'* made his light shine in our hearts." Just as God caused light to flood into the darkness of the first creation, so he gives light to those lost in darkness (4:4). God uses his creative might to transform blind individuals into his image and glory, the same glory that the first Adam lost in Genesis 3. Paradoxically, transforming into the image of the last Adam takes place through suffering. Just as Jesus' own life is characterized by suffering climaxing in his final physical resurrection, so it is the case with his people (4:7-18). What is true of God is true of his people.

The "earthly tent" in 2 Corinthians 5:1 refers to the believer's mortal body that will eventually suffer corruption (be torn down). After death, Christians will "have a building from God, an eternal house in heaven, not built by human hands" (5:1). This statement refers to their participation in the new heaven and earth as the end-time temple of God. N. T. Wright captures the essence of the passage when he claims, "A Christian in the present life is a mere shadow of his or her *future* self, the self that person will be when the body that God has waiting in his heavenly storeroom is brought out, already made to measure."[8]

Although the Corinthians will be "swallowed up by [resurrection] life" at the end of

[7]Richard Hays, *Echoes of Scripture in the Letters of Paul* (New Haven, CT: Yale University Press, 1989), 135.
[8]N. T. Wright, *Surprised by Hope: Rethinking Heaven, the Resurrection, and the Mission of the Church* (New York: HarperOne, 2008), 154.

the age (2 Cor 5:4), such life is already at work in them (4:12). The Spirit is the down payment of the new creation (5:5), so the Corinthians must be courageous by not being discouraged and groaning at the bodily decay that has set in (5:2, 4). They have to "live by faith, not by sight" in order to act on the unseen reality of the initial form of their resurrection life (5:7). An expression of such trust in unseen things results in tremendous confidence (5:8).

Paul concludes this first paragraph with another reference to the future, final resurrection: "For we must all appear before the judgment seat of Christ, so that each of us may receive what is due us for the things done while in the body, whether good or bad" (2 Cor 5:10). There must be a bodily resurrection of both the believing and the unbelieving. Both groups must be resurrected in bodily form to receive their due for what they had committed in their physical bodies.

Because Paul is compelled by the love of Christ to preach the gospel, he regards no one "from a *worldly point of view*" (2 Cor 5:16). The Greek phrase behind "worldly point of view" often occurs in the context of discussing the old age and its behavior (e.g., Rom 8:4-5, 12-13; 2 Cor 1:17; 10:2-3). Paul and his associates have a different worldview that embraces the cross and its effects. Before Paul's conversion, he evaluated Christ according to the ethics of the "old age," explaining why he persecuted the church. Now that Paul has a worldview in keeping with what God has done through Christ, he evaluates Christ and believers according to a different standard (2 Cor 5:16b). All of life must be viewed through the lens of Christ and his work.

Coming on the heels of Paul's declaration that he now views Christ differently, he claims that "If anyone is in Christ, the *new creation* has come: The *old* has gone, the *new* is here!" (5:17). The wording brings to bear several key passages from Isaiah that speak of Israel's restoration from exile, a second exodus from Egypt—that is, Babylon. (Is 43:18-19; 65:17; 66:22). The prophet Isaiah calls this deliverance the "new heavens and a new earth" since the Promised Land will be a place of peace, righteousness, joy, and the installation of God's kingdom (cf. Is 65:18-25). Just as God created the cosmos in Genesis 1–2, so he will once again create a new

FIGURE 11.9. ONE HUNDRED AND TWENTY LIONS DECORATE THE ENTRANCE TO BABYLON SYMBOLIZING STRENGTH AND PROSPERITY

heaven and earth (Is 65:17; 66:22). The Israelites are to forget their previous behavior that resulted in Babylonian exile (the "former things") and embrace what God will be doing by recreating Israel in the Promised Land.

If an individual is found in Christ, that person is a "new creation" (lit. "there is new creation"). The promised restoration of Israel into the Promised Land is *now* fulfilled in Christ. The same can be said for the long-awaited peace, forgiveness of sins, pouring out of the Spirit, return from "exile," joy, righteousness, and, finally, new creation! This restoration from exile takes place through God reconciling believers through Christ (2 Cor 5:18-21). Paul uses the idea of *reconciliation* to refer to the inaugurated promises of Israel's return to God from exile. Christ's work on the cross and his resurrection radically changes Paul's understanding of the world around him. The apostle acknowledges that he treats people differently now that the new age is a reality. Paul instructs the Corinthians to live in light of the new age by regarding others in accordance with the overlap of the ages. According to Ralph Martin, "In the new creation this is how he views all other people according to their standing in him, in the new eschatological situation . . . this is how he expects the Corinthians to view him and his ministry."[9] The Corinthians must realize that the world's values and ethics are completely different from God's. If the Corinthians continue to evaluate Paul's ministry according to worldly standards, then they are "playing into the hands of the spirit of the [old] age."[10]

> ***Before conversion, individuals were "exiled in spiritual Babylon," enemies of God and enslaved to sin. But when individuals are joined to Christ through faith, God brings them into a right relationship with himself by creating them anew.***

Paul as Isaiah's servant (6:1–7:16).[11] In 2 Corinthians 6:2, Paul appeals to Isaiah 49:8 in order to validate his claim as an apostle of reconciliation. Isaiah 49:8 explicitly references Israel's restoration: the first part of the verse runs parallel to the second. That is, the "time of my favor" and the "day of salvation" (Is 49:8a) are explained to be the time of coming restoration: "I will keep you and will make you to be a covenant for the people, to restore the land and to reassign its desolate inheritances" (Is 49:8b). Isaiah 49:8 repeats of the promise of restoration mentioned only two verses earlier, in which the role of the servant was not only "to restore the tribes of Jacob and bring back those of Israel" but also to extend salvific restoration "to the ends of the earth" (Is 49:6). The majority of Israel will reject the servant's efforts (Is 49:4-6a, 7a), so God promises to save only a remnant of Israelites and Gentiles (Is 49:6b).

Paul applies the prophecy of Isaiah's servant to himself, directly fulfilling the promise of the righteous "servant, Israel" (Is 49:3).

[9]Ralph P. Martin, *2 Corinthians*, WBC 40 (Grand Rapids: Zondervan, 1986), 151.
[10]C. Marvin Pate, *The End of the Age Has Come: The Theology of Paul* (Grand Rapids: Zondervan, 1995), 90.
[11]The discussion of Isaiah in 2 Cor 6-7 is taken from G. K. Beale, "The Old Testament Background of Reconciliation," 550-81.

Although Paul heralded reconciliation to the Corinthians, some in the church continue to question the legitimacy of his apostleship. The church in Corinth claims to partake of the end-time promises of restoration to God, but they are in danger of forfeiting these blessings if they continue to reject Paul as God's ambassador. To reject Paul is to reject the risen Lord (2 Cor 5:18-20).

Paul continues tapping into Isaiah's servant expectations when he furnishes a list of hardships that validate his apostolic calling (2 Cor 6:4-10). In stark contrast to the impeccable resume of his opponents, he boasts about his participation in the end-time tribulation: "We commend ourselves . . . in troubles, hardships and distresses; in beatings, imprisonments and riots" (6:4-5). Paul's afflictions stand in continuity with the sufferings of Isaiah's servant since he is united to Christ, the ultimate servant, and identified with his sufferings (Is 52:14–53:12).

Chapter 6 ends with a series of commands to the Corinthians to avoid being "yoked together with unbelievers" (6:14). These exhortations are grounded in a pastiche of several Old Testament texts in 2 Corinthians 6:16-18 that refer to God's promise to redeem and return Israel to the Promised Land (Lev 26:11-12; 2 Sam 7:14; Ezek 11:17; 20:34, 41; 37:27; Is 43:6; 49:22; 52:11; 60:4). These Old Testament passages prophesy the rebuilding of the temple when Israel returns from Babylonian captivity. The church must embrace their identity as redeemed Israel and the end-time temple of God by applying these precious truths to their lives. As Peter Balla notes, "The Corinthians are the beginning of the prophesied end-time tabernacle or temple, and they are part of the dawning fulfillment of Israel's restoration prophecies."[12] The church's participation in this new temple provides the basis for personal holiness. Priests in the Old Testament are required to maintain a holy lifestyle because they ministered in Israel's sanctuary. Their holy conduct falls into step with their holy, priestly identity. In the same way, the Corinthians must avoid all forms of immortality. Unclean behavior has no business in a holy congregation that houses God's glory. This explains why Paul quotes Isaiah 52:11 (a restoration prophecy about priests separating form the uncleanness of Babylon), "Therefore, "Come

FIGURE 11.10. ST. PAUL IN PRISON

[12]Peter Balla, "2 Corinthians," in *Commentary on the New Testament Use of the Old Testament*, ed. G. K. Beale and D. A. Carson (Grand Rapids: Baker Academic, 2007), 773.

FIGURE 11.11. SHOPS IN CORINTH

out from them and be separate, says the Lord. Touch no unclean thing, and I will receive you" (2 Cor 6:17). The Corinthians are beginning to fulfill Isaiah's prophecy.

The climax of the Corinthians' identity occurs in 7:1: "Therefore, *having these promises*, beloved, let us cleanse ourselves from all defilement of flesh and spirit, perfecting holiness in the fear of God" (NASB). What promises does Paul have in mind here? The same ones he has discussed up to this point: Israel's restoration, the rule of the messiah, the rebuilding of the temple, the arrival of the Spirit, new covenant, and the resurrection. Chapter 7 also contains a few historical bits, particularly the success of Paul's "tearful letter" delivered by Titus (7:7-9). The majority of the Corinthians appear to have responded positively to Paul's difficult letter (7:9-13). The worst is over.

CONCERN FOR THE COLLECTION (8:1–9:15)

The following two chapters are devoted to what scholars call "the collection." The Jerusalem church is experiencing significant economic distress, but it is not clear why. It could have been due to persecution (Acts 11:19) or a famine (Acts 11:27-30). This is not the first time that Paul has been concerned for the Jerusalem church. Several years prior, while Paul and Barnabas were in Antioch, a few prophets from Jerusalem predicted that a severe famine would occur in the region. This would, of course, affect the Jerusalem church, particularly the poor. The Antiochean community and probably neighboring churches sent gifts and money with Paul and Barnabas as they visited Jerusalem (Acts 11:27-29).

This "second" attempt to support the church is several years in the making. We first find reference to it in Galatians 2:10: "All they asked was that we should continue to remember the poor, the very thing I had been eager to do all along." Writing from Ephesus, Paul asks the Corinthians to take up a collection weekly for the Jerusalem church: "On the first day of every week, *each one of you should set aside a sum of money* in keeping with your income, saving it up, so that when I come no collections will have to be made. Then, when I arrive, I will give letters of introduction to the men you approve and *send them with your gift to Jerusalem*" (1 Cor 16:2-3). Paul intends to collect the offering on his way down through the churches of Macedonia, which, apparently, are also contributing to the collection (Rom 15:26).

Perhaps Paul's urgent request stems also from his understanding of the Old Testament. In light of the Bible's story line, the collection unites Jewish and Gentile Christians. By rallying the Gentile churches to give to the churches in Jerusalem, Paul's gospel remains to the Jew first (cf. Rom 11:25). Paul may even view the collection, to some degree, as bringing about the fulfillment of texts such as Isaiah 60:5-6: "The wealth on the seas will be brought to you [true Israel], to you the *riches of the nations will come*. Herds of camels will cover your land, young camels of Midian and Ephah. And all from Sheba will come, bearing gold and incense and proclaiming the praise of the Lord" (cf. Is 2:2-3; Mic 4:1-2).

Those repentant at Corinth are given an opportunity to demonstrate their reconciliation to Paul and ultimately to Christ. The collection, according to Scott Hafemann, "was the means by which God's work of sanctifying grace would continue in their lives. . . . The Gentiles' sharing willingly with Jews from the abundance of God's provision was a tangible demonstration of the new covenant of the new creation."[13] The Corinthians must give out of their plenty so that the Jewish Christians in Jerusalem could enjoy financial equality (2 Cor 8:14). Paul had been encouraged with the Corinthians and their initial pledge to support the collection (9:1-5), so he trusts that they will fulfill their promises. The Corinthians are assured that God will meet their needs and bless their sacrificial gifts (9:6-11). The collection would preserve the unity Jews and Gentiles enjoy in Christ. In a word, "hand in hand with providing aid, Paul was motivated to demonstrate to Jerusalem that, just as there was one Lord and one gospel, so there was one church. That church was comprised of both Gentiles in the Diaspora and Jews in Judea."[14]

AN APPEAL TO THE REBELLIOUS MINORITY (10:1–13:10)

Paul's tone changes drastically in the last section of the book (2 Cor 10–13), as he narrows his audience to the minority at Corinth who remain incalcitrant and continue to succumb to false teaching. Once again, Paul is forced to validate his apostleship and critique the false teachers. The entire point of this section of the letter is that when Paul arrives at Corinth, he wants to avoid being "harsh" with the rebellious minority, so that they would repent and be "fully restored" to him (13:9).

Chapter 10 begins with a personal appeal to the Corinthians that they hold fast to his apostolic teaching (2 Cor 10:1). The rebellious minority at Corinth must soon confess their sin to prevent a face-to-face encounter with Paul (10:2-11). At the end of the chapter, Paul is reluctant to compare himself to the false teachers: "We do not dare to classify or compare ourselves with some who commend themselves" (10:12). For Paul, boasting

[13]Hafemann, *2 Corinthians*, 330.

[14]Scot McKnight, "Collection for the Saints," in *Dictionary of Paul and His Letters*, ed. Scot McKnight, Gerald F. Hawthorne, Ralph P. Martin, and Daniel G. Reid (Downers Grove, IL: InterVarsity Press, 1993), 145.

FIGURE 11.12. CHAPEL OF ST. PAUL IN DAMASCUS

is ultimately grounded not in personal accomplishments but in the gospel (10:16-17). The object of the proclamation, the crucified Christ, is the reason for commendation.

Chapter 11 is a balancing act and, on the face of it, appears to be at odds with Paul's claims in the previous chapter. Here Paul dabbles into "foolishness," stooping to the level of the false teachers by comparing his credentials to theirs (11:1). The Corinthians must resist Satan's deft attempts to deceive them in believing the false teaching that has taken root within the minority of the church.

> ***Satan's ploy to beguile the Corinthians echoes his behavior in the garden when he tempted Adam and Eve (2 Cor 11:3).***

If an individual preaches "another Jesus," the Corinthians must recognize this satanic ploy and utterly reject the message and the messenger (11:4, 13-14 HCSB).

The second half of the chapter recounts Paul's credentials, wherein he demonstrates the validity of his apostleship and therefore his message. But Paul's boasting is probably not what the Corinthians expect. Instead of highlighting his Jewish accolades, he spends the bulk of the time underscoring various aspects of suffering (2 Cor 11:16-33). Since Paul endures end-time tribulation, thus imitating the crucified Christ, his apostleship remains valid. His ministry embodies the cross—glory in weakness, triumph in affliction, power in persecution.

As God's apostle, Paul is privy to unique revelations and visionary experiences. On the Damascus Road, his life is radically changed when the risen Christ appears and reveals to him the particulars of the gospel and the manner in which Gentiles would join Israel (Acts 9:1-43; 22:1-21; 26:9-19). A similar apocalyptic experience is found here in 2 Corinthians 12:1-10, and traces of the Damascus Road encounter are discernible.

Paul does not divulge the precise details of the experience, only that it took place "fourteen years ago" (2 Cor 12:2). What is important is *what* was revealed to him—"he [Christ] said to me, 'My grace is sufficient for you, for my power is made perfect in weakness'" (12:9). Paul pleaded with Christ for him to remove a "thorn" in his flesh, but to no avail. Instead of the thorn hindering his ministry, Paul discovers that it provides the opportunity for God to display the power of the cross. The apostle walks away from these revelations with a greater understanding of how Christ is glorified in the midst of suffering. The Corinthians must embrace Paul's message because his ministry and message flow from the cross. Paul longs to see the Corinthians once more, and he promises to not be a burden to them (12:14). The church at Corinth must realize that Paul and his associates are ministering for the church's welfare (12:15-19). Yet, Paul is hesitant to see some at Corinth for fear that they have not repented of their sinful behavior (12:21).

The final chapter ratchets up the stinging exhortation. Paul asserts that he will "not spare those who sinned earlier or any of the others" (13:2). The minority within the church must accept the legitimacy of Paul's ministry and message. These members must test themselves and determine whether Christ truly resides in them (13:5).

FIGURE 11.13. ST. PAUL

THE LETTER CLOSING (13:11-14)

The last few verses of the letter appear to be addressed to the entire church at Corinth: "Rejoice! Strive for full restoration, encourage one another, be of one mind, live in peace" (2 Cor 13:11). Both groups, the rebellious minority and the repentant majority, must embrace Paul's apostleship and message. They are to love one another and, in particular, yearn for unity in the gospel. Paul and his associates in Macedonia send their greetings to the Corinthians (13:12). The epistle ends with all three members of the Godhead mentioned: "The grace of the *Lord Jesus Christ*, and the *love of God*, and the fellowship of the *Holy Spirit* be with you all" (13:13 NASB). The hallmark of the covenant community in the new age is robust unity that is found only in the gospel message.

GALATIANS

AUTHORSHIP

The apostle Paul undoubtedly wrote this epistle. The letter bears his name (1:1), and a number of personal touches and recollections of events are stamped on the epistle (1:12-24; 2:1-14; 6:11). The early church wholeheartedly believed that Paul authored the book (e.g., Eusebius, *Hist. eccl.* 1.12.1; Irenaeus, *Haer.* 3.7.2; Clement of Alexandria, *Paed.* 1.9), and modern scholars follow suit.

DATE

Dating the book of Galatians is a bit tricky because it depends on the epistle's audience. The North Galatian theory identifies Galatia as the area where ethnic Gauls dwelt in the northern portion of the Roman province. Those who hold to this theory claim that Paul is writing to the churches he visited later in North Galatia in Acts 16:6 and 18:23 on his second missionary journey (AD 49–51). The South Galatian theory identifies Galatia as a Roman province. During Paul's first missionary journey he visited cities in south Galatia, such as Pisidian Antioch, Iconium, Lystra, and Derbe in approximately AD 45–47 (Acts 13:13–14:23). If Paul wrote to these churches in south Galatia, then we could peg a date around AD 48 or later.

Another key element is the Galatians' relationship to the Jerusalem Council in Acts 15. Since the apostles in Acts 15 discuss the identical issue we find in Galatians, it seems strange that Paul would not have mentioned this official decree if it had already taken place. Therefore, we believe that the epistle to the Galatians is written to the churches in south Galatia, prior to the Jerusalem Council, and should be dated somewhere around AD 48.

FIGURE 12.1. THE APOSTLE PAUL

OCCASION

After Paul spread the gospel to the churches in southern Galatia, he and Barnabas return to Syrian Antioch (Acts 14:26-28). While Paul and Barnabas are in Antioch, some Jewish Christians came into the nascent Galatian churches and begin preaching a message contrary to Paul's proclamation. This group, known as the "troublers" or "agitators" (Gal 1:7; 5:10, 12), may have arrived from Jerusalem. Their teaching resembles Acts 15:1: "Unless you are circumcised, according to the custom taught by Moses, *you cannot be saved.*"

They attempt to persuade the Galatian Gentiles to keep aspects of Mosaic legislation, especially circumcision (Gal 5:12; 6:12-13). Jewish Christians, perhaps in Jerusalem, are alarmed at the startling rate of Gentiles trusting in Jesus as the Messiah. In order to preserve Israelite culture, some of these Jewish Christians think it necessary for Gentiles to adopt aspects of the law of Moses. For Gentiles to enjoy a relationship with God and become part of end-time Israel, they must adopt a Jewish way of life. The false teachers argue that Galatians must take on the yoke of the Torah, particularly circumcision, if they desire to become part of God's true people and receive deliverance from their sin.

Paul's message to the Galatians stands in stark relief to the message of the Judaizers. The two views are mutually exclusive. The Judaizers eventually convince many within the Galatian church that Gentiles are indeed obligated to adhere to certain national aspects of the law, such as circumcision and dietary regulations, so that they might receive forgiveness of sin.

PURPOSE

Paul writes this epistle to convince the Galatian church that they are in danger of abandoning Christ if they continue to supplement their faith in Jesus with the law of Moses. Faith in Christ alone delivers individuals from sin and death, not obedience to the law.

OUTLINE

I. Letter Opening (1:1-5)

II. Paul's Apostolic Authority (1:6-24)
   - A. The Genuine Gospel (1:6-10)
   - B. Paul's Apostolic Commissioning (1:11-24)

III. Examples of Paul Proclaiming the Gospel (2:1-21)
   - A. The Famine Relief Visit (2:1-10)
   - B. Paul Confronts Peter (2:11-21)

IV. The Mosaic Law in the Economy of Salvation (3:1-29)
   - A. The Reception of the Spirit (3:1-5)
   - B. The Faith of Abraham and the Inclusion of the Gentiles (3:6-14)
   - C. The Role of the Law in the Plan of God (3:15-29)

V. Deliverance from the Evil Age (4:1-31)
   - A. Law as a Tutor (4:1-7)
   - B. The Apostle's Heartfelt Desire for Restoration (4:8-20)
   - C. Hagar and Sarah (4:21-31)

VI. The Law and Freedom in Christ (5:1-26)
   - A. Freedom and the Golden Rule (5:1-12)
   - B. Bearing Fruit in the New Age (5:13-26)

VII. Preserving One's Identity as the New Creation (6:1-18)
   - A. Dealing with False Teaching (6:1-10)
   - B. Identity as the New People of God (6:11-18)

BIBLICAL-THEOLOGICAL THEMES

Paul's gospel and the new perspective. For the past few decades, several notable scholars have argued for an overhaul of the traditional understanding of Paul, particularly Galatians and Romans. This reappraisal, known as the New Perspective, begins with a reevaluation of God's relationship to Israel in the Old Testament. Israel, the New Perspective argues, understood itself to be elected graciously by God at Sinai. Israel did nothing to enter the covenant. The Israelites did not attempt to earn salvation but performed law-sanctioned works in order to preserve and maintain their covenantal relationship with God. Judaism in the first century, they contend, is not works-based, as has been traditionally understood. The New Perspective claims that scholars have been in the wrong for centuries in their misreading of Jewish literature, particularly the Pauline epistles.

FIGURE 12.2. JEWISH PRAYER BOOK FOR THE SABBATH

According to the New Perspective, when we turn to Galatians and Romans, we discover that Paul is not objecting to the Gentiles' legalistic understanding of the law. The Gentiles are not trying to earn their way to heaven by embracing the requirements of the Mosaic law. Instead, Paul is attempting to overturn the Gentiles' obedience to certain particulars of the Torah because they are embracing specific Mosaic legislation that physically demarcated Gentiles from Jews (circumcision, dietary laws, and Sabbath observance). Now that Christ has come and ushered in a new age, Jews and Gentiles constitute one entity, and obeying such external requirements of the old covenant unravels what Christ has done on the cross. According to the New Perspective, the doctrine of justification is not so much tied to how an individual relates to God but how an individual identifies with true Israel. Justification is not about how a person enters into the true community of faith but how a person continues to be identified with that community through faithfulness (faith plus good works). When God justifies a person, he declares that an individual has been persevering in the end-time community of Israel.

At the heart of the dispute between the traditional understanding of Paul and the New Perspective is whether Paul is *primarily* concerned for the individual's posture before an almighty God. Before the advent of the New Perspective, the majority of scholars understood Paul's conception of justification as entailing a sinner's stance before a just and righteous God. That is, those who trust in Christ's work on the cross are "declared righteous" from their sin and guilt before God's tribunal. But now New Perspective scholars are convinced that Paul's gospel is primarily concerned with the social dimension of the covenant community. They ask how believing Jews and Gentiles can be unified. Such unity comes by believing in and giving allegiance to Jesus Christ as the greatest revelation of God, a revelation to which the Old Testament law pointed. Therefore, the New

Perspective argues that one should not give ultimate allegiance to the nationalistic distinctives of the law (circumcision, dietary laws, etc.) as God's final revelation but to Christ as God's eschatological revelation.

A key weakness of the New Perspective is its lack of integrating Paul (and other New Testament authors) with the grand story line of the Bible. Paul's message must be understood as it relates to the broad contours of the biblical story, beginning with the creation of Adam and Eve, their fall, and God's promise to overcome their failure (Gen 3:15). Adam and Eve's failure in the garden profoundly affects the story of the cosmos, Israel, and all of humanity.

At the most basic level, all of humanity, Jews and Gentiles, is tethered to either Adam and Eve's failure in the garden or to the success of the last Adam on the cross. Possessing faith in Christ is the means by which a person is identified with the last Adam (Rom 5:12-21; 1 Cor 15:45-57). Focusing on how one continues to be identified with the covenant community puts the cart before the horse. Our identity with the first or last Adam must remain primary.[1] If one believes in the last Adam's justifying work, that individual's guilty and sinful identity with the first Adam is erased. That person subsequently enters into the true covenant community and continues to be identified with the community by faith, inevitably producing good works.

Faith in Christ is the means by which God justifies an individual (Rom 4:1-25; Gal 2:15-16; Eph 2:8-9). When someone is declared right in God's sight, that person is admitted into true Israel. Becoming part of Israel is the effect or *result* of being justified in God's sight. The two are not synonymous, and the vertical dimension of the gospel—that is, an individual's stance before a holy and just God—remains paramount. The Galatians fail to recognize that their disobedience to the national laws of Israel threatens their vertical relationship with God.

Although the New Perspective is inherently flawed, it has refocused our attention to the social dimension of the Mosaic law and how aspects of it stand as a barrier between Jews and Gentiles. This is a good thing when properly understood. Traditionally, scholars often overlooked the social implications of Paul's gospel in his writings. The New Perspective is wrong to collapse the horizontal implications of the gospel with the vertical dimensions of the gospel itself but right to put its finger on an important social aspect of Paul's message.

The New Perspective is also right to contend that horizontal Jewish-Gentile unity occurs by faith in and giving allegiance to Christ as the supreme revelation of God, to which the Old Testament law pointed. Consequently, the New Perspective argues that one should not give their greatest allegiance to the nationalistic distinctives of the law (circumcision, dietary laws, etc.) as God's final revelation but to Jesus as God's decisive end-time revelation. Despite this, the New Perspective errs in not emphasizing that one must first come into a vertical saving relationship with Christ by affirming that he died for the penalty of sin and rose again from the dead.

When we turn to the book of Galatians, we learn that the Galatian Gentiles are indeed trying to gain entrance into true Israel by adhering to particular national aspects of the Mosaic law. These national

[1]Richard B. Gaffin Jr., *By Faith, Not by Sight: Paul and the Order of Salvation* (London: Paternoster, 2006), 47-48.

laws are social and political in orientation (see below). But these national laws that pertain to the nation of Israel are a subset of the entire law of Moses, which is a subset of law in general. Any form of works that precedes faith stands in opposition to faith in Christ. Faith, as the biblical writers contend, is the fountainhead of good works and precedes all forms of works.

The Galatians are wrong on two counts: (1) They fail to realize that by preserving the national laws of Moses, they promote obedience to *all* of the Torah (Gal 2:15-16) and law in general, an impossible task since no one can perfectly obey (5:3; so also Jas 2:10). In this errant framework, faith *plus works* justifies. But that is not a correct understanding of justification, as Paul argues. Faith in Christ justifies, not works. The Galatians are jeopardizing their vertical relationship with God, because their lives are not first and foremost characterized by faith in Christ. (2) The Gentile Galatians are also wrong in their appraisal of the Mosaic law in light of the new age. Now that Christ has begun to establish the new creation, the old covenant, as an administrative entity, is no longer in force, and certain aspects of the Mosaic law are fulfilled. Christ, for example, is the true circumcision, the true temple, and all find ritual purity in him. The Old Testament instructions about circumcision, the temple, and cleansing are part of the old age and no longer required in the new age since they are fulfilled in Christ. The Galatians are attempting to obey laws that are, quite simply, out of date (see fig. 12.3).

The end-time conversion of the Gentiles. The book of Galatians engages one of the most pressing issues in the early church—the relationship between Christian Gentiles and the law of Moses. When Gentiles are converted to Christianity, are they required to keep the Torah's requirements? Must the Gentiles keep all of the commandments or only some of them? According to the Old Testament, the question is not if the Gentiles become part of God's people but how.

We are concerned with the way in which the Old Testament addresses Gentiles joining Israel in the latter days. This brief survey has profound implications for how we understand Paul's message to the Galatian church and his other writings. Are Gentiles expected to embrace certain aspects of the Israelite faith when they join themselves to Israel in the end time? This issue has some overlap with the issues surrounding the New

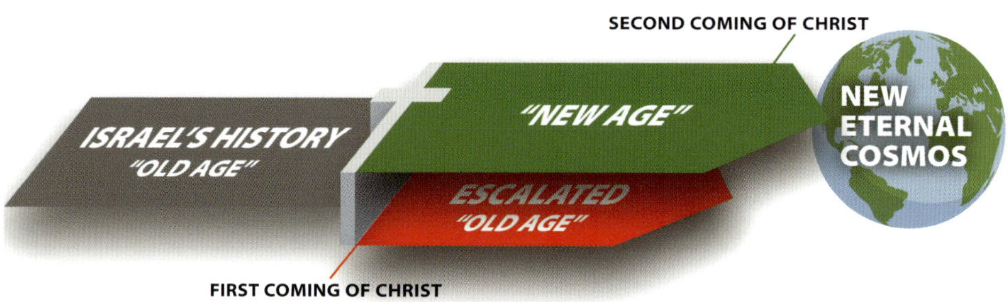

FIGURE 12.3. THE OVERLAP OF AGES

Perspective's view about how the Old Testament law relates to the New Testament.

Isaiah 56:3 mentions that the foreigner "is bound to the LORD," and 56:6 further describes how the foreigner does so. Foreigners "minister to him [the Lord]," "love the name of the Lord," and, importantly, "keep the Sabbath without desecrating it." The last description is the most telling in that God requires foreigners to maintain one of the most distinctive features of the covenant community—keeping the Sabbath (e.g., Ex 20:8-11; 31:14-16; Lev 23:3, 11, 15). The same conduct is required of the eunuch in Isaiah 56:4-5: "to the eunuchs who keep my sabbaths . . . to them I will give within my temple and its walls a memorial and a name."

In addition to covenant keeping, God expects foreigners and eunuchs to offer sacrifices at the temple: "I will bring to my holy mountain and give them joy in my house of prayer. Their burnt offerings and sacrifices will be accepted on my altar" (Is 56:7). Apparently, at the end of the latter-day pilgrimage (see Is 2:2-3; Mic 4:1-2), Gentiles will bring sacrifices to the temple, an act that further separates the covenant community from the pagan nations. The Gentiles are also to serve in the temple as Israelite priests: "And foreigners who bind themselves to the LORD to minister to him . . . in my house of prayer" will offer "burnt offerings and sacrifices" (Is 56:6-7; cf. Is 66:18-21).

According to Zechariah 14:1-15, the surviving Gentiles will go up to Jerusalem to worship the Lord and celebrate the Feast of Booths. Gentiles will not only join the Jews in their worship of Yahweh but will also participate in the celebration of certain Jewish festivals, particularly the Feast of Booths. In Zechariah 14, "all the nations" celebrate this feast.

FIGURE 12.4. RITUAL BATH AT QUMRAN FOR PURIFICATION

Standing alongside these important texts are a few Old Testament passages that indicate Gentiles will join Israel *apart from the law*. For example, Abraham, even before being circumcised, "believed the Lord, and he credited it to him as righteousness" (Gen 15:6). Abraham's faith leads to justification *before* he receives the Israelite sign of circumcision (Gen 17:23-27, see Rom 4:9-10). This key event in Abraham's life anticipates God justifying Gentiles in the latter days through faith alone and, consequently, admitting them into the covenant community without requiring them to adhere to the nationalistic signs of old Israel (cf. Gen 17:5).

The above survey of various Old Testament passages indicates that converted Gentiles in the end times will join themselves to Israel by taking on national badges or signs—external indicators that demarcate them as part of God's chosen people group. These Old Testament examples suggest that the general Old Testament expectation is that Gentiles in the latter days are required to take on physical, covenantal badges that identify them as Israelites.

When we arrive at the book of Galatians, we learn that Gentiles gain admittance into the covenant community by faith in Christ. It was not *fully* revealed in the Old Testament that Gentiles would become part of true Israel by faith alone without adhering to Israel's nationalistic identification tags of the Mosaic law. According to Galatians 1:11-12, Paul receives a revelation from Christ. It is precisely this revelation or "newness" that Paul is proclaiming. Gentiles can identify with and become true Israel only by faith in Christ and not having to identify with the national marks of an Israelite of the old epoch (whether that be circumcision, Sabbath laws, dietary laws, etc.). Gentiles identify with Christ, not Israel's law, to become true Israelites. Gentiles do not have to move to Palestine to become Israelites; they only have to move to Jesus.

> ***Now that Christ has inaugurated a new age, the age of the new creation, the role of the Mosaic legislation within the covenant community has changed.***

LETTER OPENING (1:1-5)

The history of redemption, from the creation of Adam and Eve to Israel's return from exile in the new creation, centers on God's supreme desire to dwell with humans as his glorious image-bearers and to glorify himself through that dwelling. But the fall inhibits God's program since a holy God is unable to dwell in the presence of sin. Humanity must be delivered from its plight, and sin eradicated from all of creation. Christ's death and resurrection do just that. The crucifixion assuages God's anger and the resurrection overcomes sin's penalty. God is now in a position to redeem those estranged from him. In a book that focuses on some of the gritty details of the Galatians' interaction with the Mosaic law, it is easy to lose sight of the gospel and how it affects all of life. Though only a few verses, Paul wastes no time setting the tone for the entire book in Galatians 1:4-5. First and foremost, the Galatians must understand that they were once alienated from God.

Many typical elements are present in the letter's opening, but two notable features stand out in 1:1: Paul draws attention to his apostolic authority and to Christ as the beginning of the new creation: "who raised him [Christ] from the dead." Christ's resurrection affects Paul's understanding of the gospel and the role of the law in salvation history. Paul's authority as an apostle, commissioned by the risen Messiah, is the basis for his message to the Galatians.

Whereas in 1:1 Paul underscores Christ's role in establishing the new creation, in 1:4 Jesus lays down his life as an atoning sacrifice. The apostle alludes here to Isaiah 53:6,[2] in which the Lord offers up his suffering servant as an atoning sacrifice. Paul says that Christ "gave himself for our sins." Paul presents Christ as both the God of Israel incarnate and the suffering servant who will redeem the covenant community by bearing their sin. Christ's work, in direct fulfillment

[2]Douglas J. Moo, *Galatians*, BECNT (Grand Rapids: Baker, 2013), 72.

of Isaiah's expectation, releases the Galatians from captivity and shepherds them into the Promised Land of the new creation.

Paul goes on to contend that Christ came to deliver the Galatians "from the present evil age" (Gal 1:4; cf. Rom 12:2). As Richard Hays observes, Christ's selfless work on the cross is "an apocalyptic rescue operation."[3] The resurrected Christ inaugurates the new eternal cosmos, and his work as an atoning sacrifice constitutes the core of the gospel. By taking on the yoke of the Torah, the Galatian Gentiles' relationship with God is at stake. If they add any type of works to their faith in Christ, they nullify what Christ came to do—namely, deliver them from the evil age. Paul rules out a works-plus-faith-equals-salvation scheme.

PAUL'S APOSTOLIC AUTHORITY (1:6-23)

Israel's story is filled with prophet after prophet pleading with the covenant community to repent of their sinful ways and embrace the Lord. For example, the prophet Elijah pleads with Israel and her wicked king, Ahab, to abandon their allegiance to Baal (1 Kings 18). Despite these prophetic confrontations, Israel, by and large, refuses to heed Elijah's words. Old Testament prophets generally follow suit, pleading with Israel and her kings to return to the Lord. The New Testament apostles are the mouthpiece of God on earth, instructing, correcting, and encouraging the covenant community. Paul's letter to the Galatians falls very much in line with the Old Testament tradition of a prophet exhorting and correcting God's people.

The first portion of Galatians largely rests on Paul's commissioning on the Damascus Road as a genuine apostle of Christ. By asserting that he received a "revelation from Jesus Christ" (Gal 1:12) and was set apart from his mother's womb (1:15; Is 49:1), Paul firmly establishes himself as an apostle and prophet who embodies the mission of the risen Christ. Paul's gospel, then, contains the unvarnished message of God himself. The Old Testament is filled with prophets speaking on behalf of God to Israel, and Paul places himself squarely in the prophetic tradition. But with the coming of Christ, God has spoken more fully in his Son (Jn 1:17; Heb 1:1),

FIGURE 12.5. THE PROPHET ELIJAH

[3]Richard Hays, "The Letter to the Galatians: Introduction, Commentary, and Reflections," in *The New Interpreter's Bible*, ed. L. E. Keck (Nashville: Abingdon, 2000), 202.

increasing the prophetic role of the twelve apostles and Paul. Much of the book of Galatians hinges on the veracity of Paul's legitimacy as an end-time, apostolic prophet of God speaking to the covenant community gathered throughout Galatia.

The genuine gospel (1:6-10). When Paul begins his letters, he typically expresses his gratitude for the church's faith and perseverance (e.g., Rom 1:8; 1 Cor 1:4-7), but here in Galatians 1:6-9 Paul is vehemently opposed to their behavior. He pulls no punches in his honesty with the Galatians and is taken aback that the churches in Galatia have been so "quickly deserting the one who called [them] to live in the grace of Christ and are turning to a different gospel" (1:6). Jewish Christians have successfully convinced the Galatian Gentiles that they must obey key portions of the law of Moses, particularly those regulations that physically distinguish Jews from Gentiles. But for Paul, this aberrant teaching is not a mere addition to the faith or hybrid gospel; it is "another gospel" entirely and has nothing to do with the gospel Paul proclaims (cf. 2 Cor 11:4). The penalty for preaching such a message results in covenant cursing and judgment, the receiving end of God's wrath (Gal 1:8-9). The word *curse* (1:8-9) occurs in a number of contexts in the Old Testament. It can refer to items that are consecrated or set apart to God (Lev 27:28a; Josh 7:13), in which case the term is positive. But it can also designate items that are "set apart for destruction." Joshua 6:17 states: "The city and all that is in it are to be devoted to the Lord" (cf. Num 21:3; Deut 7:26). When Paul claims that someone proclaiming a false gospel is to be "set apart" for God's destruction, it entails God's end-time wrath that is initially applied to the individual at the present and then fully applied at the end of history.

FIGURE 12.6. THE CONVERSION OF ST. PAUL

Paul's apostolic commissioning (1:11-24). The second half of Galatians 1 largely constitutes Paul's status as an authentic apostle, converted and commissioned by the risen Christ. Paul's message is intimately bound up with his apostleship. In order to persuade the Galatians to believe the gospel, he must first convince them of his genuine apostleship. The message was revealed to him by Christ himself (1:12, 16). Paul's message bears the stamp of Christ and his approval. To reject Paul and his gospel is to reject the risen Christ! When the resurrected Messiah appears to Paul on the Damascus Road (Acts 9:1-19; 22:3-16; 26:9-18), Paul is immediately convinced of several important insights, one of which is the overlap of the ages. According to Seyoon Kim, "Since both the revelation of the Messiah and resurrection from the dead were expected in Judaism to be God's eschatological act signaling the end of this aeon and the beginning of the new, Paul was convinced [on the Damascus Road] that the *eschaton* had broken in with God's saving act in Jesus Christ."[4]

Persuaded that the latter days have broken into history, Paul becomes convinced that the gospel contains a few new and surprising elements that focus on the cross and resurrection—Christ's rule in the midst of death and the staggered fulfillment of the resurrection (see Rom 16:25-26). The gospel not only includes some new components but also contains surprising *consequences*. The manner in which Gentiles and Jews stand on equal footing in the person of Christ is chief among these surprising consequences (cf. Eph 3:1-6). The Old Testament expected Gentiles to become part of true Israel in the latter days by becoming proselytes (e.g. Ps 87:4; Is 56:2-8; 66:19-21); that is, they were expected to adhere to the Mosaic commandments (e.g., Zech 14:16-19). But when Christ appears to the apostle Paul on the Damascus Road and commissions him to reach the Gentiles, Paul concludes that Gentiles are not required to keep certain aspects of the Torah, because they have met these obligations through faith in Christ, who obeyed and fulfilled the law's requirements.

After recounting his former life as a radical Jew who persecuted the church (1:13-14), Paul alludes to Isaiah 49:1: "Before I was born the Lord called me; from my mother's womb he has spoken my name" (Gal 1:15; cf. Jer 1:5). The allusion to Isaiah is significant on several levels. Isaiah 49:1 is part of the book's larger servant program (42:1-9; 50:4-11; 52:13–53:12). According to Isaiah 49, the servant's mission (as true Israel [49:3]) is to restore the remnant within Israel (Is 49:5) and then to convert the Gentiles in the latter days (Is 49:6). This last dimension of the servant's task is particularly important to Paul's overall mission and his desire to spread the gospel to the Gentiles within the latter days. As Moisés Silva writes, "Paul must have seen his own ministry as integrally related to the work of the OT prophets, and in some sense even as its culmination. Now at last the message of salvation is breaking all national barriers. Light has fallen on the lands of the Gentiles, of whom the Galatians are part."[5] Paul's desire to travel to Arabia after his conversion on the Damascus Road (Is 1:16-17) may also reflect the book of Isaiah's expectation that nations will travel from the East to Jerusalem in the eschaton (Is 60:6-7).[6]

Three years later after the Damascus Road event, he finally meets with a few of the key apostles to "get acquainted with," them (Gal 1:18-20). Paul's ministry, particularly his gospel, is not outside the bounds of Christianity but fits squarely in the middle.

[4]Seyoon Kim, *The Origin of Paul's Gospel*, WUNT 4 (Tübingen: J. C. B. Mohr [Paul Siebeck], 1981; repr., Grand Rapids: Eerdmans, 1981), 72 (emphasis original).

[5]Moisés Silva, "Galatians" in *Commentary on the New Testament Use of the Old Testament*, eds. G. K. Beale and D. A. Carson (Grand Rapids: Baker Academic, 2007), 786-87.

[6]Richard Bauckham, *The Jewish World Around the New Testament*, WUNT 233 (J. C. B. Mohr Siebeck, 2008; repr., Grand Rapids: Baker, 2010), 261.

EXAMPLES OF PAUL PROCLAIMING THE GOSPEL (2:1-21)

One of the most pressing issues in the early church was the nature of the new covenant. Were Gentiles in the covenant community expected to obey *all* aspects of the Mosaic law under the new covenant that Christ inaugurated? This critical question is part of a larger question regarding Christ's relationship to the Mosaic law. Consider Christ as a hermeneutical filter through which the entire law passes. He filters out those aspects of the law that are designed for national Israel and do not relate to the new covenant community in the new age. But the portions of the law of Moses that are more moral and less ethnic in nature pass through the filter (e.g., the Ten Commandments). National laws under the old covenant that regulate civil relationships in the land cease to function once Christ comes because he fulfills the Old Testament land promises. Christ's kingdom extends over the whole creation and is not confined to a parcel in the Middle East. Laws that regulate life in the Promised Land are now defunct. The Mosaic law as an administration that operates in the old age is no longer in force in the new. Jesus is the beginning fulfillment of the temple, the throne of David, the new Jerusalem, and the new Israel, all of which correspond to major features of real estate in the old theocratic nation of Israel. In the same way, the ritual laws regulating temple worship and its sacrifices are fulfilled in Christ. He is the typological fulfillment of all to which the temple pointed. Those aspects of the Mosaic law that regulate Israel in the old age as a nation are now laid aside. God's covenant people are no longer a theocratic nation but a community of saints. So, in the end, God's people living in the new age are only responsible to obey those aspects of the law of Moses that primarily focus on moral issues.

FIGURE 12.7. PASSOVER HAGGADAH OR RITUAL FROM THE CAIRO GENIZAH

Much of Paul's argumentation in Galatians, especially in chapters 2–3, is concerned with how Jewish Christians and Gentiles relate to one another. Race and ethnic distinctions are here to stay and will exist in the new heavens, but former *national* identifications pass away and are completely fulfilled in Christ. People groups in the old age are identified with particular idols and false tribal or national deities, but in the new age these same people groups are now identified with the risen Christ—unity in Christ, yet diversity in race and ethnicities.

As an end-time prophet of God, Paul must ensure that his conduct remains consonant with his message. Chapter 2 comprises two examples of Paul proclaiming the same gospel but in different contexts. In order for Paul to prove that he did not change or truncate his message, he furnishes two specific events that demonstrate his long-held conviction that Gentiles are saved from God's wrath through faith in Christ and that they are not required to keep the old national prescriptions of the Torah in the new age. Gentiles will remain Gentiles in the new age, yet they stand on equal footing with Jewish Christians through Christ, the true Israel.

The famine relief visit (2:1-10). Scholars are not in agreement about the precise timing of the event outlined in 2:1-10. It is possible that Paul is describing his visit to the Jerusalem Council in Acts 15. More likely, though, Paul is referring to Acts 11:27-30, known as the famine relief visit. While Paul and Barnabas are in Antioch, some prophets from Jerusalem predicted that a severe famine would transpire in the area (Acts 11:28). The church in Jerusalem would certainly feel its effects, so the Christian communities in the surrounding area pitched in and sent gifts and money with Paul and Barnabas as they visited Jerusalem (Acts 11:29-30). While Paul and Barnabas (and Titus) are providing for the Jerusalem church, Peter, James, and John met with them, and a private discussion ensued concerning circumcising believing Gentiles (Gal 2:2-3). It appears that a "circumcision party," distinct from Peter and John, is attempting to force Titus (a Gentile) to be circumcised (2:4). Paul would have none of it, and he immediately condemned the act. The leaders of the church agreed with Paul that Gentiles must not be required to maintain the national prescriptions of the Torah (2:6-10).

Paul confronts Peter (2:11-21). Though the basic message of Galatians 2:11-21 is clear enough, it is difficult to reconstruct the particulars behind this event, especially Peter's motivation in deserting the Gentiles at Antioch. We have two general options in reconstructing this complex event: the first option suggests that Peter is in Antioch (Syria) eating non-kosher meals with Gentiles, but when the "circumcision group" or the "men from James" arrive, Peter withdraws and keeps the dietary restrictions with the Jewish Christians. According to this view, three groups thus exist in Antioch: law-free Gentiles, law-keeping Jewish Christians,

FIGURE 12.8. EMPEROR CLAUDIUS

and the "circumcision group"/"men from James." Peter simply collapses under pressure from the circumcision group and withdraws from the Gentiles. The central problem with this first view is how Peter can be so capricious. According to Acts 10–11, Peter understands that "all foods are clean" and is convinced that Gentiles are not required to keep the dietary restrictions (see Acts 10:9-15, 27-28, 34-35). How can Peter receive a notable revelation and lapse into his former behavior because of some pressure by the circumcision group?[7]

The second option solves some of the tension between Galatians 2 and Acts 10–11. While Peter is in Antioch (Acts 11:19-26), persecution breaks out in Jerusalem during the reign of Claudius, under the governors Tiberius Julius Alexander and Ventidius Cumanus. Apparently, the Jerusalem church endures heavy persecution, so James sends a delegation to Peter (the "men from James") pleading with him to stop eating with the Gentile Christians. Since the Jewish religion is "official" and recognized by the Roman government, the early church believes that they too should fall under this legal umbrella (cf. Acts 18:12-16). The sending of "men from James" represents James and the Jerusalem church's attempt to survive and remain legal in the eyes of Rome. The early church must stay within the broad bounds of Judaism, and Peter's intimate association with the Gentiles is provoking persecution.[8] By Peter's close association with Gentiles, Christianity appears to be at odds with Judaism.

A group of Jews located in Jerusalem, the "circumcision group," had been persecuting the church there. Peter, under pressure from the Jerusalem church, collapses and withdraws from Gentile fellowship. In addition, the rest of the Jews joined Peter and began keeping the kosher laws. Even Barnabas followed suit (Gal 2:9)!

Despite Peter's good motives, the net result is a complete bifurcation of the church in Antioch: one church that obeys all aspects of the law (Jewish Christians) and the other church that does not (Gentiles). Peter and the apostles at Jerusalem fail to see the long-term theological and ecclesiastical consequences of their actions. For Paul, reinforcing obedience to the national prescriptions of the Mosaic law that separate Jews and Gentiles strikes at the heart of the gospel itself and undermines his mission (Gal 2:14).

In Galatians 2:15-16, Paul gets at the core of the debate with Peter by saying that "a person is not justified by the works of the law, but by faith in Jesus Christ." Three main options exist for understanding the key phrase "works of the law": general legalism, boundary markers that separate Gentiles from Jews, and any deed that pertains to the Mosaic legislation. We prefer the last option—works that fall under the umbrella of the law of Moses (see Gal 5:3). Observing the Mosaic law does not declare one right before God. In the case at Galatia, obeying the dietary regulations, Sabbath commands, and circumcision does not count for anything. But the theological point is far deeper: any human works, in keeping with the Mosaic covenant or otherwise, are unable to justify or declare one righteous before God. As Thomas Schreiner notes, "Paul reminds Peter that he

[7]D. A. Carson, "Mirror-Reading with Paul and Against Paul: Galatians 2:11–14 as a Test Case," in *Studies in the Pauline Epistles: Essays in Honor of Douglas J. Moo*, ed. Matthew S. Harmon and Jay E. Smith (Grand Rapids: Zondervan, 2014), 105-6.

[8]Carson, "Mirror-Reading with Paul and Against Paul," 109.

must not impose the law on Gentiles, for both he and Peter already recognize that human beings will not be vindicated before the divine tribunal on the basis of their obedience of the law, but only through faith in Christ Jesus."[9]

Within the last section of chapter 2, Paul heads off the Judaizers in Galatia who claim that such a lifestyle leads to sin. In their estimation, if the Gentiles are not required to keep all aspects of the Mosaic law, they will inevitably live a life of licentiousness and rampant sin. That is simply not the case, because faith in Christ brings about a relationship with him, which in turn unites us with Christ: "I have been crucified with Christ *and I no longer live, but Christ lives in me*. The life I now live in the body, I live by faith in the Son of God, who loved me and gave himself for me" (Gal 2:20). Far from living a sinful and reckless lifestyle, the Gentiles embody a lifestyle that is in accordance with the ethics of the cross (cf. 1 Cor 1–2).

THE MOSAIC LAW IN THE ECONOMY OF SALVATION (3:1-29)

The remainder of Galatians focuses on three dimensions of Paul's gospel in contrast to his opponents: the chronological dimension, the anthropological dimension, and the ethical dimension.[10] The next four chapters in Galatians are largely configured in light of the "already but not yet" of the inbreaking of the latter days. Now that the new age has arrived, the national prescriptions of Mosaic law are fulfilled in the centerpiece of this new age—the person of Christ. The Old Testament's covenants, laws, and institutions anticipate him.

The reception of the Spirit (3:1-5). According to Galatians 3:1-5, this community apparently enjoys charismatic experiences in the Spirit: "Does God give you *his Spirit and work miracles among you* by the works of the law, or by your believing what you heard?" (3:5). Paul affirms that the experience of the Spirit depends not on doing the national prescriptions of the Mosaic law but on believing in Christ's work on the cross and resurrection (3:2). The apostle maintains that the Christian life must be characterized by faith from start to finish. It simply will not do to begin the Christian life by faith and finish with works: "After beginning by means of the Spirit, *are you now trying to finish by means of the flesh*?" (3:3).

> ***If God justifies Abraham, the great patriarch, by faith apart from the law (the Mosaic law comes after Abraham), then it should not surprise us that Gentiles are not required to keep the law.***

The faith of Abraham and the inclusion of the Gentiles (3:6-14). The next section (Gal 3:6-14) is riddled with Old Testament quotations in support of Paul's line of argumentation. He begins with an example of "living by faith and not by works" in his use of the great patriarch Abraham (3:6; Gen 15:6). Paul may even be portraying Abraham as a Gentile who has been justified by faith

[9]Thomas R. Schreiner, *Galatians*, ZECNT (Grand Rapids: Zondervan, 2010), 166.
[10]Frank Thielman, *Theology of the New Testament* (Grand Rapids: Zondervan, 2005), 266-74.

(cf. Deut 26:5). This interpretation of the Abraham narrative deals a deathblow to the opponents' insistence on the Gentiles obeying the Torah. Paul even goes on to claim that the Old Testament itself anticipates the day when Gentiles will become members of the covenant community without obeying the national laws of the old covenant (Gal 3:8-9; Gen 12:3; 18:18).

God promises Abraham that he would be the father of a nation and that Gentiles will one day be included. That promise is initially fulfilled in Isaac and then ultimately Christ, the "seed" (Gal 3:16). Those who have faith and believe in Christ partake in the fulfillment of the promise made to Abraham (Gen 12:3; 18:18; 22:18). With great clarity, Paul argues that Gentiles become "children of Abraham" by possessing faith in Christ (Gal 3:7). God graciously bestows upon the Galatian Gentiles the right to become full-blown citizens of true Israel (the Israelite-Abrahamic seed) by joining themselves to Christ, the true seed of Israel (3:16, 19).

After explaining that the Galatian Gentiles enjoy the full benefits of joining Israel, Paul further clarifies why keeping the requirements of the Torah is so costly: "All who rely on the works of the law are *under a curse*" (Gal 3:10). The Galatians are convinced that by following the prescriptions mandated by the Mosaic law they were receiving God's blessings. But the opposite is true. When the Galatian Gentiles hold fast to dietary regulations, circumcision, Sabbath, and so on, God ironically puts them under a covenantal "curse."

FIGURE 12.9. ABRAHAM MEETS STRANGERS

Why would God do such a thing? The answer lies in Israel's (and all of humanity's) inability to keep God's law (Gal 3:10; Deut 27:26). No matter how hard the Galatians try to keep God's law, they inevitably fail to do so perfectly, so God puts them under a covenantal curse. The same principle is at work in the garden with Adam and Eve, when God gives them his "law" (Gen 2:16-17). When the original couple disobeys, God curses and bans them from his presence (Gen 3:16-19). Stephen Westerholm rightly expresses Paul's thought here:

> To Paul's mind they [the Galatians] had not rightly grasped the significance of Christ's death. That death was not to be understood as atoning for the inevitable shortcomings of those who, because of their basic commitment to observe the law, were otherwise righteous; rather, it showed that there can *be* no righteousness based on the law's observance—for otherwise Christ would not have had to die.[11]

The Mosaic law indeed offers eternal life, but it is predicated on perfect obedience (Gal 3:12; Lev 18:5). Christ's work on the cross affords individuals the opportunity to be set free from God's covenantal curse. Christ becomes a curse to release those under the curse (Gal 3:13; Deut 21:23). Since no one can

[11]Stephen Westerholm, *Perspectives Old and New on Paul: The "Lutheran" Paul and His Critics* (Grand Rapids: Eerdmans, 2004), 373 (emphasis original).

perfectly keep the Mosaic prescriptions, one must possess faith in Christ to be declared right before God. The effect or result of being justified by faith is entrance into true Israel and the reception of the end-time Spirit (Gal 3:14).

The role of the law in the plan of God (3:15-29). The general theme of Galatians 3:15-22 is a proper perspective on how the Mosaic law fits into the big picture of the Old Testament story line. Paul's approach to the law here rests on a redemptive-historical vantage point. God makes a promise to Abraham and to his seed (3:16), so the Mosaic law comes *after* that promise (3:17). The law does not invalidate the promise that God made but rather anticipates the promise he would bring—the gospel and the blessings that follow. Even the entire Old Testament consigns people under sin so that the gospel could liberate humanity from the law's curse (3:22).

An important aspect of the law is to lay bare humanity's rebellion. One of the reasons God gives the Israelites his perfect law is to reveal their sinful condition and promote trust in his promises of redemption. By disclosing the big picture of what God is trying to achieve in the course of redemption, the Galatians can now understand how the Mosaic law fits into God's grand design. The Mosaic administration contains national prescriptions that were inherently temporal; they are designed for a certain people group at a certain time and place.

According to Galatians 3:22, Scripture "locks up" individuals under the dominion of sin, as demonstrated by Jews under the law in the old covenant. The Mosaic law operates as a key component in redemptive history by revealing Israel's sin and depravity (3:19). Because Paul and his contemporaries were imprisoned under the law until faith is revealed, i.e., faith in Christ (3:23), the law served as a "guardian" or "pedagogue" to lead them to Christ (3:24-25). The result of dwelling in Christ is profound unity within the covenant community and membership in the kingdom (3:26-29). Whether Jew or Gentile, all believers constitute true Israel and are

> ***The Mosaic law, the economy that "locked up" and "supervised" Israel, gives way to Christ. The law has ended now that "this faith has come" (Gal 3:25).***

FIGURE 12.10. PEDAGOGUE AND BOY

clothed with the garments of the last Adam—namely, Christ (3:26; cf. 1 Cor 15:49, 53).

DELIVERANCE FROM THE EVIL AGE (4:1-31)

The Old Testament demonstrates an awareness of evil spirits harassing and attempting to seduce the Israelites toward idolatry. Leviticus 17:7 explicitly forbids the worship of demons associated with idols: "They must no longer offer any of their sacrifices to the goat idols[a] to whom they prostitute themselves," and Deuteronomy 32:17 reveals that demons lie behind all forms of idolatry: "They [the Israelites] sacrificed to false gods, which are not God—gods they had not known" (cf. 2 Chron 11:15; Ps 106:37). Since the fall of Adam and Eve, the created order becomes infested with evil spirits. Instead of worshiping the true and living God, humanity worships demons through idolatry and subsequently become imprisoned.

Chapter 4 refers to the Galatians' behavior in obeying portions of the Mosaic law that enslave them once again. Before they turned to Christ, they were under the control of the old age (4:8-11)—characterized by sin, demonic forces, and the "flesh"—which opposes God (4:3). But Jesus delivers the cosmos and humanity from this bleak situation. Through the cross and resurrection, Christ abolishes the old age and inaugurates the new creational order. If the Galatians desire to be delivered from the "present evil age" (1:4), they must cling to Christ by trusting solely in him.

Law as a tutor (4:1-7). Almost rehearsing his previous argument about the tutor (3:23-25), Paul again discusses Israel as a young minor in 4:1-2. The "heir [Israel] is subject to guardians and trustees" (4:2). Paul uses a cultural metaphor in 4:1-7 to reinforce the idea that the Mosaic law is temporary. Typically, in the Greco-Roman environment the wealthy would employ a guardian or tutor who managed a child. But when the child becomes of age, the tutor is no longer needed. In the same way, since Israel "has come of age," there is no need for the old covenant. As Guy Waters writes, "Now that Christ has come (4:4-5), God's people have fully entered, in Christ, into all that our sonship and inheritance entails (4:6)."[12]

In Galatians 4:3, Paul interprets his own metaphor concerning the heir: "So also we, while we were children, were held in bondage *under the elemental things of the world*" (NASB). As the heir is under the supervision of a guardian or tutor, so individuals also are under "elemental things." Of particular interest is the phrase "the elemental things of the world" (4:3). The word *elemental* refers to something that is a principle, describing the most basic structure of a given topic. For example, the term can mean a letter of the alphabet or elementary teachings, but Paul weds the term with *world*. The most natural interpretation of "elemental things of the world" is the basic elements of the cosmos, such as earth, wind, and fire. Some interpreters champion a demonic interpretation for "elemental things of the world," making good sense in the immediate context and elsewhere in Paul. It seems likely that both meanings are in mind here. Elemental things consist of demonic forces that are intertwined with the fallen physical cosmos.

[12]Guy Prentiss Waters, "Galatians," in *A Biblical-Theological Introduction to the New Testament: The Gospel Realized*, ed. Michael J. Kruger (Wheaton, IL: Crossway, 2016), 261.

Creation and humanity are under God's curse, under sin, and slaves to corruption, longing for the day of full redemption (cf. Rom 8:18-25). Being enslaved to the elementary things of the world (as well as sin) is living according to the old world and its demonic forces and coming under the universal curse. Adam and Eve's sin reverberated throughout the cosmos and all subsequent generations of humanity. In Galatians 3–4, Paul's alignment of certain aspects of the Mosaic law and elementary things of the world is striking. In 4:3 the Jewish people continue to live in slavery under the demonic realm and identify with the fallen cosmos. The Galatian Gentiles' former predicament of enslavement to elemental things is probably in Paul's mind in 4:8-9.

The apostle warns the Galatians that if they adhere to the Mosaic law as the essential basis of their salvation, they retreat back to the old age and undo what Christ has done through the cross and his resurrection. As a grave consequence, they will "[fall] away from grace" (5:4).

The apostle's heartfelt desire for restoration (4:8-20). The next section of chapter 4 is especially personal, as Paul recounts his initial interaction with the Galatians and his apparent illness that eventually led to their conversion (4:13-14). The apostle remains shocked that the Galatian Gentiles are obeying various calendrical commandments (Sabbath, feasts, etc.) required by the law that are only designed for the nation of Israel (4:10). The Galatians fail to grasp that Christ is the hermeneutical filter who sifts out all the laws of the old covenant pertaining to Israel and her land. Paul begs the Galatians to imitate his own life of embracing Christ apart from these national particulars (4:12).

The false teachers (Jews or Jewish Christians who assert that *all* believers must obey the national prescriptions of the Mosaic law) infiltrated the community to win over the Galatians. Rather than being zealous for Christ, these agitators' supreme desire is to receive flattery from the Galatian church, resulting in the community being zealous for them (4:17). Although Paul is the Galatians' "mother" (4:19) and longs to speak tenderly to them, he maintains a stern tone throughout letter (4:20).

> ***Israel's sin problem was not just confined to the period of the Mosaic economy but has been a universal predicament since Eden (Gal 3:22).***

Hagar and Sarah (4:21-31). The final section of chapter 4 depicts life under the overlap of the ages. The consideration of Hagar and Sarah falls on the heels of Paul's discussion of the Galatians and their apparent desire to follow the zealous Judaizers (4:17). Recall that the metaphor of birthing begins in 4:19: "My dear children, for whom I am again in *the pains of childbirth*." Resuming his argument in 4:8-11 about the Galatians "turning back to those weak and miserable forces," Paul gives these believers an Old Testament example of why the Mosaic law enslaves and the gospel offers freedom (4:21-31).

Verse 21 casts the direction of the passages by comparing those who are "under the law" with those who are not. Those who are under the law are children of Hagar and

FIGURE 12.11. SARAH OFFERS HAGAR TO ABRAHAM

are of the "flesh," while those who are not under the law are children of Sarah (4:23). Paul illustrates this paradigm by showing how the two women represent two types of covenants (4:24).

The first covenant is from "Mount Sinai" and identified with the earthly Jerusalem (4:25). The covenant of freedom is identified with the heavenly Jerusalem (4:26). Paul wants the Galatians to identify with the heavenly Jerusalem that frees its citizens instead of the earthly Jerusalem that enslaves its citizens. Isaiah 54:1 demonstrates that the Galatians must identify with the heavenly Jerusalem that has an abundance of children (Gal 4:31).

The prophet Isaiah identifies Jerusalem as a "barren woman" who is later restored from exile in the latter days: "'The Lord will call you back as if you were a *wife* deserted and distressed in spirit—a *wife* who married young, only to be rejected'" (Is 54:6). This woman is not identified until 54:11-12: "Afflicted *city*, lashed by storms and not comforted, I will rebuild *you* with stones of turquoise, *your* foundations with lapis lazuli. I will make *your* battlements of rubies, *your* gates of sparkling jewels, and all *your* walls of precious stones." According to Isaiah 54, God will restore Jerusalem, who is barren because of her exile in Babylon. Surrounding Isaiah 54 are a few depictions of Israel as a "mother" (Is 49:14-26; 50:1-11). In addition to being a barren mother, Israel lies estranged from her husband, the Lord. But God promises to return to his wife and restore her, producing offspring for her in the new creation. Isaiah goes on to claim that Sarah is Jerusalem's mother: "'Look to Abraham, your father, and to *Sarah, who gave you birth*. When I called him he was only one man, and I blessed him and made him many'" (Is 51:2).

In the next verse, we learn that Sarah is identified with Zion or Jerusalem (Is 51:3).

Isaiah depicts two women—one barren and exiled in Babylon, the other woman fruitful and ushered into the Promised Land. In his portrayal, the prophet also identifies these women as two "Jerusalems." One has been ransacked and destroyed, whereas the other is rebuilt and restored in the new creation. Isaiah reads the story of Abraham, Hagar, and Sarah (Gen 16:1-16; 21:1-21) as a prophecy of what God will do once again with his people when they come out of Babylon. Paul picks up on Isaiah's understanding of the Genesis narrative and ties it to the situation in Galatia. If the Galatians hold fast to Christ, then they will, in direct fulfillment of Isaiah, come out of spiritual exile and become citizens in the "heavenly Jerusalem" and offspring of the matriarch Sarah.[13]

THE LAW AND FREEDOM IN CHRIST (5:1-26)

Embedded within the Old Testament is God's promise to protect and preserve his saints. For example, in Numbers 6:24-25 Aaron and his descendants bless the Israelites with the benediction, "The Lord bless you and keep you; the Lord make his face shine on you and be gracious to you." God's presence gives life to those who are near to him. The often-quoted Psalm 1:3 also promises great blessing to those who trust in the Lord: "That person is like a tree planted by streams of water, which yields its fruit in season." In contrast to the wicked who are blown away (Ps 1:4), the faithful are upheld by God's presence. Living in exile from God inevitably leads to death and destruction, whereas strength and life are found in abundance in his presence. In the last half of Galatians 5, Paul lists the well-known "fruit of the Spirit" (Gal 5:22-23). Only those who trust in Christ enjoy the Spirit's presence and fulfill the long-awaited blessings of the fruit of the new creation (Is 32:15-20; 44:1; 57:15-19). God's promise to draw near to his saints and shine on them in a new and special way has now been set in motion through Christ's work.

FIGURE 12.12. STATUE OF MOSES

[13]For a similar line of argumentation of this difficult passage, see Silva, "Galatians," 808-9.

Freedom and the Golden Rule (5:1-12). The beginning of chapter 5 sets forth a clear dichotomy between attempting to obey the law of Moses as an essential step for one's salvation and embracing Christ by faith. Being united to Christ through faith leads to freedom, whereas obeying the national prescriptions of the Torah, as a crucial aspect of salvation, inevitably results in slavery (Gal 5:1). One of the most succinct statements about Paul's understanding of the law occurs in Galatians 5:2: "If you let yourselves be circumcised, *Christ will be of no value to you at all.*" Only two options exist for the Galatian Gentiles—obey the Mosaic law or embrace Christ. There is no middle road. Supporting this thesis, Paul astoundingly argues, "Again I declare to every man who lets himself be circumcised that he is *obligated to obey the whole law*" (5:3). It is all or nothing for the apostle. To keep one requirement of the Torah obligates an individual to obey *perfectly* all of its commandments.

If obeying the Torah is not what regulates the Christian life in the new age, what does? Paul answers this pressing question, "The only thing that counts is *faith expressing itself through love*" (5:6). Faith in Christ is *always* accompanied by works, specifically love toward God and one's neighbor (cf. Jas 2:14-26). Love must be seen as a necessary byproduct of faith in Christ and not as an essential basis for salvation *together with faith in Christ*. Galatians 5:14 explicitly claims that "the entire law is fulfilled in keeping this one command: 'Love your neighbor as yourself.'" By quoting Leviticus 19:18, Paul reaffirms a central commandment contained within the Torah itself.

Loving God and loving one another are concretely expressed in the Ten Commandments (Ex 20:1-17; Deut 5:6-21). Jesus himself says that loving God and loving one another are the greatest commandments (Mk 12:20-31 and par.), and he quotes two Old Testament texts from the Torah to support this claim (Deut 6:4; Lev 19:18). Although the covenant community in the new age is not required to keep the civil and cultic portions of the Mosaic law that preserved Israel's identity, Christians are still obligated to obey the moral commandments of God's law, those commands that began in the garden of Eden and flow through the Mosaic covenant. The abiding authority of the Old Testament carries over to the new covenant community.

According to Galatians 5:7-10, a specific individual (the leader of the agitators?) has been rhetorically persuading the Galatian Gentiles to obey the national laws of Moses. But Paul declares that this enemy "will have to pay the penalty" for upending the Galatians' faith (5:10).

Bearing fruit in the new age (5:13-26). In stark contrast to living under the "yoke of slavery" (5:1), the Galatian Gentiles are to "walk by the Spirit" (5:16). What follows is one of the richest depictions of Christians living in the new age. Paul begins by arguing what life looks like when individuals live in accordance with the old age (5:19-21). Their lives are marked by "sexual immorality, impurity and debauchery," and so on. Living in accordance with the old age entails patterning oneself after the first Adam. Paul's understanding of "flesh" here is not primarily a description of physicality but a description of an individual's fallen condition (e.g., Rom 7:5, 18, 25). Adam and Eve's sin results in humanity being cast into a state of "fleshly" living. But the work of Christ achieves victory over the fallen state of humanity and the cosmos. He succeeds in conquering sin and death, yet his victory remains to be executed in its fullness. Believers await the return of Christ, when he will eradicate and punish sin fully, completely establish the new heavens and earth, and don believers with a new body that is free from sin.

After describing what fleshly living entails, Paul sketches what "walking by the Spirit" involves: "The fruit of the Spirit is love, joy, peace, forbearance, kindness, goodness, faithfulness, gentleness and self-control" (5:22-23). The wording recalls two prominent texts from the book of Isaiah. In the coming end-time kingdom, Isaiah prophesies that the Spirit will descend on Israel and create abundant fertility and spiritual fruitfulness:

> Till the *Spirit* is poured on us from on high, and the desert becomes a fertile field, and the fertile field seems like a forest. The LORD's justice will dwell in the desert, his *righteousness* live in the fertile field. The fruit of that *righteousness* will be *peace*; its effect will be quietness and confidence forever. My people will live in *peaceful* dwelling places, in secure homes, in undisturbed places of rest. (Is 32:15-18)

Another passage from Isaiah predicts the Spirit going forth and producing spiritual fruit (Is 57:16, 19) in the godly Israelites. In the immediate context of Isaiah 57, this fruit is explicitly identified as the fruit of peace (Is 57:19) and the byproduct of patience (Is 57:15 LXX) and joy (cf. Is 57:21 LXX) among God's restored people in the new age.

Paul's description of the fruit of the Spirit evokes Isaiah's promise that the Spirit would usher in abundant fertility in the coming new age. Isaiah proclaims that in the new creation the Spirit will generate bountiful fruitfulness—righteousness, patience, peace, joy, holiness, and trust in God.

> ***The apostle pleads with the Galatian Gentiles to embrace their status as the restored people of God, Israel, in the new creation, who are part of the dawning of the new heavens and earth (Is 65:17; 66:22).***

By trusting in Christ, the Galatians are the true people of God, playing a significant role in God's redemption of the cosmos. If the church of Galatia is genuinely part of this redemptive, cosmic drama, then they must heed Paul's exhortations to embrace Christ by faith alone and abandon any attempt to curry God's favor through good works (Gal 2:16; 3:3, 5, 10).

PRESERVING ONE'S IDENTITY AS THE NEW CREATION (6:1-18)

Chapter 6 divides into roughly two halves—protection against false teaching and maintaining one's identity as the new creation. These twin themes remain tethered throughout the New Testament, and the Galatians must fortify themselves against the onslaughts of the devil through these false teachers. If they hold fast to the gospel and understand their position in Christ (6:1-10), they will affirm their membership in the new heavens and earth (6:11-18).

Dealing with false teaching (6:1-10). Paul finishes the last chapter with the practical way in which the Galatians "keep in step with the Spirit" (Gal 5:25b) and demonstrate their identity as the redeemed people of God who have been restored from spiritual Babylon (5:22-23). Those who "live by the Spirit" must "restore" an individual who has been ensnared in sin (6:1). It is not crystal clear whether Paul has a specific sin in mind (namely, false teaching) or if he is referring to sin in general. A strong case can be made for the former since Paul targets false teaching throughout the letter. The Galatians are to be on guard or watchful for false teaching and, when it arrives, "carry each other's burdens" (6:2; cf. Rom 15:1; Jude 22-23). The thrust of Galatians 6:1-6 is that Spirit-led believers participating in the new age are marked by their willingness to weed out false teaching within the local church and restore those who have succumbed to it. Once the Galatians overcome their issue with the false teaching of the agitators, they will possess the tools to prevent such an event from occurring again.

The apostle then outlines the consequences of righteous and unrighteous behavior, particularly as it relates to the false teaching. Those who give into and remain in false teaching will reap what they sow (6:7). This language is reminiscent of Job 4:8, in which those who "plow evil" and "sow trouble" will "reap it" (cf. Prov 22:8). In the same way, the Galatians must avoid acquiescing to or sowing false teaching, lest they "reap destruction" (Gal 6:7-8a). But if the church sows the fruit of the Spirit, they will "reap eternal life" (6:8b; cf. Hos 10:12). The church at Galatia must continue to manifest their identity as a new creation in all their actions, resulting in a great harvest when Christ returns with great finality and establishes the new heavens and earth in all their fullness (Gal 6:9).

Identity as the new people of God (6:11-18). Emphatically, Paul states, "See what large letters I use as I write to you with my own

FIGURE 12.13. SYNAGOGUE FLOOR

hand!" (6:11). Paul appears to have physically taken the reed pen from the unnamed secretary and written these words to authenticate the letter to the Galatians. Such an act is not uncommon in the ancient world and appears to be commonplace for Paul (1 Cor 16:21; Col 4:18; 2 Thess 3:17; Philem 19).

One of the Mosaic laws that the agitators are forcing on the Galatian Gentiles, if not the preeminent one, is the prescription to be circumcised (Gal 6:12). Circumcision is one of the most distinguishing traits of the Jewish people in the pagan world (e.g., Gen 17:10-14). By compelling these Galatian Gentiles to be circumcised, the false teachers are trying to preserve the physical traits of the Jewish people. They desire the Galatians to look and act like Jews. But Paul declares that even these false teachers, who are probably Jews, cannot "keep the law" (6:13).

His opponents make circumcision compulsory in order that they would not be "persecuted for the cross of Christ" (6:12). They would rather boast in and be identified with the law (e.g., circumcision) than boast in and be identified with Christ (6:13). Paul prefers to boast in the cross since he no longer has a place in the old world. Through Christ's work, the world has been destroyed or crucified to him, and he has been crucified to the world (6:14).

In Galatians 6:15-16, Paul explains that he boasts only in the cross because "neither circumcision nor uncircumcision means anything" to God since they are part of the old world that is passing away (6:15a). What does matter, though, is the inbreaking of the new creation (6:15b). Hans K. LaRondelle writes, "Reborn Christ-believers—from both Israel and the Gentiles—are . . . in Paul's theology, the only *faithful* Israel of God."[14] The expression in 6:16, "peace and mercy to all," recalls once more Isaiah 54:1-10 (see 4:27). In Isaiah 54:10 (LXX) God proclaims to Israel, "Neither shall my *mercy* fail you, nor shall the covenant of your *peace* be at all removed." Isaiah 54:7-8 further underscores this theme: "With great *mercy* I will have *compassion* upon you. . . . With everlasting *mercy* I will have *compassion* upon you." By faith in Christ, Gentile *and* Jewish believers fulfill the Isaiah 54 prophecy about peace and mercy falling on the true people of God.

[14]Hans K. LaRondelle, *The Israel of God in Prophecy: Principles of Prophetic Interpretation* (Berrien Springs, MI: Andrews University Press, 1983), 111 (emphasis original).

EPHESIANS

AUTHORSHIP

Ephesians claims to have been written by Paul (Eph 1:1; 3:1), and the letter ends with a few historical assertions regarding his ministry (6:18-24). The early church readily affirmed Pauline authorship. For example, Irenaeus asserts "Even as the Blessed Paul declares in his Epistle to the Ephesians" (*Haer.* 5.2.3; cf. 5.8.1; 5.14.3; Clement of Alexandria, *Paed.* 1.5; *Strom.* 4.8.). Some today, however, doubt that the apostle Paul authored the epistle. It has been fashionable in recent years to argue that someone under the guise of Paul penned Ephesians and other New Testament letters that bear his name, such as Colossians, 2 Thessalonians, and the Pastorals. Paul himself did not write the letter, they claim, but an individual(s) deliberately imitated him. Certainly, pseudonymity (that is, writing under a fictitious name) existed within Judaism (e.g., 1 Enoch, 2 Baruch, 4 Ezra). But the question remains whether the early church embraced this literary technique. Little evidence exists that the early church condoned pseudonymity. Indeed, the church explicitly denounced it.[1] In the midst of discussing heresy that crept in within the early church, Eusebius records, "We . . . receive both Peter and other apostles as Christ; but *we reject intelligently the writings falsely ascribed to them*, knowing that such were not handed down to us" (*Hist. eccl.* 6.12.3).

Some scholars argue that Ephesians falls under the category of pseudonymity or a Deutero-Pauline form of literature (a disciple of Paul wrote on behalf of Paul) for a few reasons: the vocabulary, style, and theology are considered different from Romans, 1–2 Corinthians, and Galatians. But the differences between Ephesians and Paul's letters are not as pronounced as many claim. Many of the themes found in Ephesians are found elsewhere.[2] Moreover, one has to take into account the style and vocabulary of Paul's secretary. All in all, there is no substantive reason why we should doubt that Paul wrote this letter.

DATE

According to 3:1 and 4:1, Paul claims to be writing from prison, but *which* imprisonment is in mind? Acts mentions a few: Philippi (16:22-40), Caesarea (23:23–26:32), and Rome (27:1–28:31). But in 2 Corinthians 11:23 (which is probably written before Paul's trip to Jerusalem to deliver the famine

[1]D. A. Carson, "Pseudonymity and Pseudepigraphy," in *The Dictionary of New Testament Background*, ed. Craig A. Evans and Stanley E. Porter (Downers Grove, IL: InterVarsity Press, 2000), 857-64.

[2]For further argument in favor of Pauline authorship, see Harold W. Hoehner, *Ephesians: An Exegetical Commentary* (Grand Rapids: Baker, 2002), 2-61.

relief) Paul claims to have endured far more imprisonments. Luke has thus not furnished a complete list of Paul's imprisonments in the book of Acts, so this letter may have been written from an unknown imprisonment. Nevertheless, a Roman imprisonment is preferred. Ephesians, Philippians, Colossians, and Philemon are all probably written from the same place, hence their traditional designation as the Prison Epistles. If Paul writes while under house arrest in Rome (Acts 28:30-31), it is likely that this epistle is composed in the early 60s.

OCCASION

Unlike Paul's other epistles, this one is uncharacteristically "impersonal." Typically Paul greets his audience, gives thanks for what God has done on their behalf, and outlines the general contents of the letter. Letters are also occasional by nature, so we often discern within the letter why it was written. In Ephesians, however, we have only a few of these features. As we sift through the message of the letter, it is unclear why Paul wrote it. In addition, in 1:1 several early manuscripts lack the phrase "in Ephesus," meaning it would read, "To God's holy people, the faithful in Christ Jesus." By removing "in Ephesus," the epistle concerns the saints at large and not one particular congregation. Even if "in Ephesus" is original, the very fact that the location of the audience was debated in the early church demonstrates the largely general nature of the letter. In the end, we should deem Ephesians to be a general letter that targets many if not all of the churches in Asia Minor.

FIGURE 13.1. LIBRARY IN EPHESUS

PURPOSE

Paul writes to encourage the churches in Asia Minor to persevere in their faith, grasp their "calling" as the end-time people of God, and, most importantly, recognize their deep-seated unity in the gospel.

OUTLINE

I. Letter Opening (1:1-2)
II. Christ's Work as Cosmic King (1:3-23)
  A. Blessings in Christ (1:3-14)
  B. Paul's Prayer and Thanks for Christ's Kingship (1:15-23)
III. Spiritually Resurrected and Unified in Christ (2:1-22)
  A. Raised with Christ (2:1-10)
  B. Jews and Gentiles as True Israel (2:11-22)
IV. Gentiles as True Israel in Christ (3:1-21)
  A. The "Mystery" of the Gentiles (3:1-13)
  B. The Content of Paul's Prayer (3:14-21)
V. End-Time Realities Applied (4:1-32)
  A. The Spirit and the Distribution of Gifts (4:1-16)
  B. The Church as the New Adam (4:17-32)
VI. Harmony in the New Creation (5:1–6:20)
  A. Children of the Light (5:1-20)
  B. Living in God's House (5:21–6:9)
  C. Waging Warfare in the Latter Days (6:10-20)
VII. Letter Closing (6:21-24)

BIBLICAL-THEOLOGICAL THEMES

Angels and the fracturing of humanity. The book of Ephesians could be summarized in one word—unity. Chapter 1 outlines the cosmic unity in Christ, chapter 3 highlights the ethnic unity between Jews and Gentiles, and chapter 5 underscores unity within the family and vocation. Paul's vigorous commitment to unity is firmly grounded in his understanding of the story line of the Old Testament. The splitting of humanity at the Tower of Babel had a ripple effect throughout the cosmos (Gen 11:1-9). God divided humanity according to language and angelic overseers. He charges these angels to rule over the nations on his behalf. Deuteronomy 32:8 asserts, "When the Most High gave to the nations their inheritance, when he divided all mankind, he set up boundaries for the peoples according to the number *of the sons of Israel*." The meaning of the last phrase of this verse is notoriously difficult to pin down in the Hebrew text, but the Septuagint (LXX) is explicit: "according to the number of the angels of God." Apparently, these angelic overseers report to God and manage the nations' affairs. An early Jewish commentary, the Targum on Deuteronomy 32:8-9 (*Pseud Jon*) is explicit in this regard:

> When the Most High made allotment of the world unto the nations which proceeded from the sons of Noah, in the separation of the writings and languages of the children of men at the time of the division, He cast the lot among the *seventy angels, the princes of the nations with whom is the revelation to oversee the city*, even at that time He established the limits of the nations according to the sum of the number of the seventy souls of Israel.

God appoints these angels to keep the unbelieving nations separate from one another. Israel, however, does not have such evil angels over them. The nation enjoys an intimate relationship with God and does not require angelic mediators (though Michael is their angelic protector). Instead of ruling well on God's behalf, the fallen angels sought to become powerful by attempting to be the source of power and authority. They cause further division between nations by giving them idolatrous traditions and customs (Ps 82; cf. Deut 4:19; Judg 11:24; Dan 10:13, 20; Acts 17:26).

Division and fracture among the nations will not prevail, though. The Old Testament longs for the day when people groups will live in harmony (e.g., Is 2:3; 56:3-8; Zech 2:11; 8:20-23). Creation, too, is expected to dwell in harmony: "The wolf and the lamb will feed together, and the lion will eat straw like the ox, and dust will be the serpent's food. They will neither harm nor destroy on all my holy mountain" (Is 65:25).

Now that Christ has come, all of creation has found its end-time unity in Christ. Babel has been reversed and the divisive work of Satan's evil angelic powers has been thwarted. This doctrine is most apparent in Colossians 1:19-20: "For God was pleased to have all his fullness dwell in him, and *through him to reconcile to himself all things, whether things on earth or things in heaven,* by making peace through his blood, shed on the cross." Unity in Christ extends to the various people groups, social structures, and angels. Ephesians 1:10 says that Christ sums up all things to heal discord and disharmony within humanity and the cosmos at the fullness of the time. Jesus Christ, as a "household manager," restores fractured people groups, particularly the strained relationship between Jews and Gentiles. Ephesians tells us that Christ has come to repair the fractured relationships of *all* believers—people groups, families, and employers and employees.

Israel's Promised Land and the new creation. At every turn in Ephesians, Paul reminds his readers of the rich blessings they enjoy in Christ. One particular theme running throughout the book is the idea of their "inheritance" (1:14, 18; 5:5), which is part of a larger discussion of Israel's Promised Land. From Abraham to Israel's return from Babylonian captivity, one of the most pressing issues of Israel's narrative is her land. Moses conveys to Israel God's promises to them: "He will bring you *to the land* that belonged to your ancestors, and *you will take possession of it.* He will make you more prosperous and numerous than your ancestors" (Deut 30:5; cf. Jer 29:14). But to grasp the nature of Israel's land, we must begin not with Abraham in Genesis 12 but Adam and Eve in Genesis 1–2.

FIGURE 13.2. TEMPLE OF HADRIAN IN EPHESUS

Temples in the ancient world contained images of the god placed in them. Adam is that image, placed in the garden temple. As a divine image bearer, God tasks him to fill the earth with his glory along with Adam's progeny. He must expand the borders of the land of Eden, wherein God's glory dwells, and Adam and his progeny are to expand these geographical borders until they circumscribe the entire earth.

FIGURE 13.3. AL KARNAK IN EGYPT

The mantle of Adam's responsibility is placed on Abraham and his seed, Israel, a "corporate Adam." God never intended Israel's land to be confined to a parcel in the Middle East but to expand to the farthest corners of the earth (Is 11:9; Hab 2:14). He desires his presence to burst forth to the very ends of the earth. Although the initial form of the Abrahamic promise relates only to the land of Canaan, it is placed in a global context: "All peoples on the earth will be blessed" (Gen 12:1-3). The next restatement (Gen 13:14-17) still has the boundaries of Canaan in view, but it adds that God will make "[Abraham's] offspring *like the dust of the earth*, so that if anyone could count *the dust*, then *[his] offspring* could be counted" (13:16). Because the promise looks toward the very end of time, it refers to a number of Israelites so large that they are unable to fit in the land. Israel's Promised Land is also deemed precious because it is the place where God dwells with his people (cf. Is 49:20-21; 54:1-3). As Israel's land expands, so does God's glorious presence.

This expansive temple-land theology undergirds other prophecies of the universal expansion of Israel's land as depicted in other parts of the Old Testament. For example, at the final resurrection of the dead that will coincide with resurrected people inhabiting the new creation, Isaiah 26:15 prophesies, "You have *increased* the nation, O Lord, You have *increased* the nation, You are glorified; You have *extended all the borders of the land*" (NASB). The allusion to Genesis 1:28 ("Be fruitful and increase" and "fill the earth") leads to the expansion of Israel's land. This cosmic expansion of Isaiah 26 is wedded to Israel's end-time resurrection, suggesting that the fulfillment of the Genesis 1:28 commission to expand occurs through the resurrection of people.

FIGURE 13.4. AERIAL VIEW OF THE TEMPLE MOUNT

As we wade into the New Testament, we learn that Christ is true Israel and the end-time temple (Jn 2:21). Christ began to fulfill the Old Testament prophecies of "Jerusalem," "Zion," the "temple," and the "throne of David," all of which are to be significant pieces of real estate in the coming new land of Israel (Mt 5:5; Rom 4:13; Heb 11:8-16). Christ fulfills these promises in a physical manner through his resurrection, but there is also a sense in which these Old Testament promises are fulfilled in the overlap of the ages on a spiritual level.

One example of an initial, spiritual fulfillment of the Old Testament land promises lies in Ephesians 1:13-14, in which the Spirit is described as "a deposit guaranteeing our inheritance." Paul likely echoes the inheritance of the Promised Land that Israel never fully possessed. The word here for "inheritance" is repeatedly used in the LXX of the Pentateuch to refer to Israel's land of inheritance (e.g., Num 26:56; 32:18). The Spirit, who will dwell in his fullness throughout the future new cosmos, has entered into believers in the present. All who identify with the risen Christ acquire an initial inheritance of the new earth. Oren Martin concludes,

> The New Testament presents the land promised to Abraham and his offspring as finally fulfilled in the (physical) new creation, as a result of the person and work of Christ. At this time in salvation history, however, the fulfillment is focused primarily on Christ, who himself has inaugurated a new creation through his resurrection and has made new creations out of those united with him.[3]

Yet, in the new heavens and earth, all the land promises that God made to his people

[3]Oren Martin, *Bound for the Promised Land: The Land Promise in God's Redemptive Plan*, NSBT 34 (Downers Grove, IL:

will be completed with great finality. At the very end of history, the Promised Land will climax in a new cosmos with its rich soil and abundant life and house the veritable glory of God (Rev 21:1–22:5).

LETTER OPENING (1:1-2)

Paul opens his letter with the standard introduction—he introduces himself, identifies his audience (1:1), and ends with "grace and peace" from God and Christ (1:2). The line "to God's holy people in Ephesus," however, contains an abnormality. Several early manuscripts lack the prepositional phrase "in Ephesus" (1:1b), and a good case can be made that it should be omitted. The upshot of this peculiarity is that the epistle was intended not only for the church in Ephesus but for all the churches in the western portion of Asia Minor (cf. Rev 2–3). This geographic omission may explain why the epistle contains general Christian instruction that can be applied to a wide audience throughout the region of Asia Minor.

CHRIST'S WORK AS COSMIC KING (1:3-23)

Kings and prominent leaders in the Old Testament often represent their community or nation. What is true of the king is true of the nation. Faithful representatives secure blessings for their people. One example of this idea is found in Ephesians 1:17, in which Paul implores God to give the saints "the Spirit of wisdom and revelation." The same wording occurs in Isaiah 11:2 describing the Spirit's role during the Messiah's reign: "The Spirit of the Lord will rest on him [the Messiah] —the Spirit of wisdom and of understanding . . . the Spirit of the knowledge and fear of the Lord." Isaiah predicts that the Spirit will guide the Messiah's ministry, especially as it relates to upholding "justice . . . for the poor" (Is 11:4). The Gospels make it clear that Isaiah's prophecy is fulfilled in the per-

InterVarsity Press, 2015), 119.

SEVEN CHURCHES IN ASIA MINOR

son of Jesus (Mt 3:16; Jn 1:32-33), but Paul takes a passage about the Messiah and applies it to the church. As Clinton Arnold notes, "The Spirit who came upon the Messiah is the same Spirit who now rests upon his people and provides knowledge, wisdom, and power."[4] The apostle argues that believers are, in some tangible way, enjoying the same experience of the Spirit that Jesus himself enjoyed.

Blessings in Christ (1:3-14). Verses 3-14 are normally labeled a *berakah* or extended praise that extols God for his great acts of redemption (cf. 2 Cor 1:3-7; 1 Pet 1:3-9). This common Old Testament practice is often labeled a blessing (Gen 14:20; 24:27; 1 Kings 8:15, 56; Ps 41; 72). In Ephesians 1:3-14, Paul praises God for what he has accomplished in Christ on behalf of the church and, most of all, for God's glory. There are three high points in 1:3-14: the Father's election of the saints (1:6), Christ's redemption securing the saints' salvation (1:12), and the sealing of the Spirit preserving the saints' salvation (1:14).

Paul reminds the church of their inheritance and position in Christ (1:3), referring to the spiritual blessings that every believer receives in the heavenly realm of the new creation. Believers can be confident that no matter what will befall them, they are currently enjoying the initial benefits of the new heavens and earth in Christ. Verses 4-8a speak of God's election of the saints and the benefits that follow, all of which takes place in Christ.

According to 1:8b-9, God revealed "the mystery of his will" to the saints. The term *mystery* refers to God's previously hidden wisdom that is now revealed with the help of his Spirit (Dan 2:27-30, 47). The remainder of the chapter outlines in some detail what Paul means by the "mystery of his will." Ephesians 1:10 says, "to bring unity to all things in heaven and on earth under Christ." Christ's work restores a lost unity and harmony between heaven and earth that had been plunged into disintegration because of sin (cf. Col 1:20-22). God's cosmic household had fallen into disorder, wrecked and fragmented. Christ came as a household manager to put God's cosmic house back into order. Christ reintegrates and restores the cosmic unity and harmony that had been lost at the fall of humanity. The mystery contained in 1:20-23 consists of three related components essential to Christ's regathering

> ***Although Christians do not enjoy the benefits of the new creation in their fullness (their resurrected body, an environment free of sin, etc.), they have begun to enjoy the spiritual benefits of the new heavens and earth.***

"all things" under himself (Eph 1:10): the scope (1:20-23), instrumentation (1:7), and result of Christ's rule (1:9-10).[5]

Paul's prayer and thanks for Christ's kingship (1:15-23). After thanking God for what he has done (1:3-14), Paul prays and

[4]Clinton E. Arnold, *Ephesians*, ZECNT (Grand Rapids: Zondervan, 2010), 104.

[5]For further explanation of "the mystery" in Ephesians 1, see G. K. Beale and Benjamin L. Gladd, *Hidden but Now Revealed: A Biblical Theology of Mystery* (Downers Grove, IL: InterVarsity Press, 2014), 148-59.

gives thanks for the church's faith (1:15-23). His knowledge of the church's firm belief in Christ propels him to give thanks constantly (1:16a). Paul also gives thanks for the church's love for others (1:15b). The apostle then requests that the Father furnish the church with a healthy dose of "wisdom and revelation" (1:17).

Verses 1:20-23 outline what Paul means by the expression "mystery of his will" already stated in 1:9. In the Old Testament, one of the core elements of the coming Messiah is his role in ruling over Israel and the surrounding nations (e.g., Gen 49:8-10; Num 24:17; Dan 2:35, 44-45). The Messiah is to come and defeat Israel's enemies in the latter days, resulting in the reconciliation of the pagan nations to the Lord. But the Old Testament does not develop in significant detail how the end-time Messiah would rule on a *cosmic* level. According to Ephesians 1:20-22, God "raised Christ from the dead and seated him at his right hand in the heavenly realms, far above all rule and authority, power and dominion. . . . And God placed *all things* under his feet and appointed him to be head over *everything*." Christ executes his messianic prerogative as cosmic ruler over the heavens as well as the earth (Phil 2:9-11; Col 1:15-18; Rev 1:5-18).

> ***Christ's coming, rule, and exaltation to the right hand of the Father signaled not only Christ's reign over earthly rulers but also over hostile spiritual rulers in the heavenly regions.***

In this vein, Paul directs readers' attention to Daniel 7:14 and 24, which reads, "And to him [the son of man] was given *the rule* . . . *His authority is an everlasting authority*, which will not pass away, and his kingship will not be destroyed . . . he [God] shall give to the holy people of the Most High, to reign over an everlasting kingdom, and *all authorities* will be subjected to him."[6] Although the Old Testament generally expects the coming Messiah to rule on an earthly level, Daniel 7 suggests that the Messiah's rule extends to earth *and* heaven.

Adam should have defeated the satanic serpent in Eden but failed to do so. The last Adam succeeds where the first fails. In Ephesians 1:22, Paul quotes Psalm 8:6: "God placed all things under his feet." Psalm 8 depicts what Adam should have accomplished in the garden and how he was to expand God's glory to the far corners of the earth (Gen 1:28). For Adam to achieve this aim, he needed to rule over the serpent (Gen 1:26-27). Psalm 8 expresses what Adam should have accomplished and looks forward to the end of history when another Adam will arrive on the scene. By recalling Daniel 7 and Psalm 8, Paul claims that the resurrected and enthroned Christ has achieved Adam's and the Son of Man's rule over the earthly and heavenly realms.

SPIRITUALLY RESURRECTED AND UNIFIED IN CHRIST (2:1-22)

God deeply cares for our souls *and* our bodies. Job 19:26-27, for example, states, "And after my skin has been destroyed, yet in my flesh

[6]The Dan 7:14 quotation is taken from the LXX (Theodotion), and 7:24 is from the LXX (Old Greek).

I will see God; I myself will see him with my own eyes—I, and not another." When God promises to deliver or redeem us from sin, his promises entail complete deliverance from the fall. Our entire beings will be restored and placed within the new creation. The Old Testament expects the bodily resurrection of the saints to occur in the latter days (e.g., Is 26:19; Dan 12:1-2), yet the latter days have begun in the person of Christ and his resurrection. Paul and other New Testament writers argue that the saints are first raised with Christ on a spiritual level and await their full, physical resurrection at some point in the future when Christ returns a second time (e.g., Jn 5:24-25; Col 3:1-2). Paul's discussion of believers being raised and made alive in Christ (Eph 2:5-6) taps into this broader theme of redemption. Saints still hope with Job, though, and await the day when they can see God with their own physical eyes.

Raised with Christ (2:1-10). The beginning of chapter 2 graphically describes the former life of his Gentile audience, a life lived in the "old age." Such a life is characterized by spiritual death, an inevitable result of sin, the inability to do the law, and an allegiance to the devil (2:1-2). As a grave consequence, unbelievers are currently under God's wrath and alienation (2:3). Old Testament prophets anticipate God to pour out his wrath in the distant future (e.g., Is 51:22; 63:3). But with the arrival of Christ, God's wrath has pushed into the present.

While unbelievers are under the control of the devil and in a state of peril and death, God graciously and freely rescues some (Eph 2:5). God raises the saints and seats them in heaven (2:6). As Christ was raised and seated at the right hand of the Father (1:20), so too believers are raised and seated. The purpose of God spiritually resurrecting believers is to demonstrate the graciousness of God in Christ (2:7). Salvation is completely external to believers: "It is by grace you have been saved, through faith—and this is not from yourselves, it is the gift of God—not by works, so that no one can boast" (2:8-9).

Jews and Gentiles as true Israel (2:11-22). The result of Christ spiritually resurrecting believers is their identity as true Israel. Identity flows from spiritual renewal. Before belief in Christ, Gentiles were "separate from Christ, excluded from citizenship in Israel and foreigners to the covenants of the promise, without hope and without God in the

FIGURE 13.5. JOB AND HIS WIFE

world" (Eph 2:12). But because of Christ's work, Gentiles are now able to participate in the covenant community. The cross restores humanity's relationship to God (2:1-10) and provides the means for Gentiles to become part of true Israel (2:11-18). Christ "destroyed

FIGURE 13.6. TEMPLE WARNING INSCRIPTION

the barrier" between Jews and Gentiles (2:14), by abolishing the national laws that long divided Jews from Gentiles.

Reconciliation to God through the blood of Christ (Eph 2:1-10) makes reconciliation possible with one another (2:11-22), Christ's sacrifice offers peace and access to God's presence (2:17-18). Paul quotes a key text from Isaiah that prophesies the restoration of Israel: "He [Christ] came and preached *peace to you who were far away and peace to those who were near*" (Eph 2:17; Is 57:19). The wider context of Isaiah 56–57 pictures the reconciliation of Jesus and Gentiles enjoying God's presence at the temple (e.g., Is 56:6-8; 57:14-19; 66:18-21). Christ's work inaugurates the fulfillment of this anticipated reconciliation. Since the church is the "holy temple in the Lord" (2:21), reconciliation is now possible even between deeply antagonistic groups.

In the Old Testament, peace for the Israelites came through sacrifices, but for Paul peace comes from God through the sacrificial work of Christ. Part of the point in Ephesians 2:17 with Christ preaching peace to those who are far away and those who are near is that Jews and Gentiles fulfill the Isaiah prophecy by moving not to geographical Israel but to Christ, the true Israel, the true temple, the zenith of the law, and the true circumcision.

The last bit of chapter 2 fits naturally within the Gentiles playing a significant part in establishing true Israel in the new age (Eph 2:19-22). In Christ, the Gentiles are "members of his [God's] household, built on the foundation of the apostles and prophets, with Christ Jesus himself as the chief cornerstone" (2:19-20). The entire structure is considered a holy temple that grows (2:21 NASB). The church, as a growing temple, fulfills God's original intention that his glory will eventually fill the earth (Gen 1:28).

God charges his people to expand the borders of Eden and all subsequent temples until his presence fills every nook and cranny of the earth. It is not until the coming of Christ when his intention is finally enacted. Here in Ephesians 2:19-22, the temple begins to expand as its boundaries include Gentiles from around the world. As history marches forward, the temple will continue to incorporate more and more people until his glory climactically invades the entire cosmos at the end of the age (4:13).

GENTILES AS TRUE ISRAEL IN CHRIST (3:1-21)

The apostle Paul argues that Gentile believers are "heirs together with Israel, members together of one body, and sharers together in the promise in Christ Jesus" (3:6). The Old Testament contains a few examples of Gentiles becoming Israelites and partaking of all the benefits of a fully-fledged Israelite. For example, Caleb, one of twelve sent to spy out Canaan, descended from an Edomite clan (Gen 36:15; Num 32:12) yet was granted a full allotment of the Promised Land (Num 13:1–14:10). Although ethnically a Gentile, Caleb assimilated into the Israelite culture and faith and is considered a full-blown Israelite.

The Old Testament generally expected Gentiles to embrace all the particulars of the Mosaic covenant, but Christ's death has changed how people groups now define themselves, especially with respect to the Mosaic laws that formerly defined Israel as a peculiar ethnic nation. Key to understanding how Gentiles relate to Jews is Jesus' identity as true Israel. Jesus sums up in himself all that true Israel is to be, both in terms of his faithful obedience and in terms of being the true temple, truly clean (not cleansed by Israel's food laws), the true circumcision, the true Sabbath (rest is found only in Christ), and all the beginning fulfillment of the promises of the worldwide extension of Israel's land. All of these end-time promises find their direct fulfillment in Christ (2 Cor 1:20; Gal 3:16; Rev 2:12). Paul argues that Gentiles, together with Jews, become true Israelites by submitting to and identifying with Christ as true Israel rather than sub-

> ***What the Old Testament sacrifices temporarily and partially achieved has been completely accomplished by Christ's peacemaking sacrifice.***

FIGURE 13.7. TWENTY-FOUR ELDERS CASTING CROWNS

mitting to and identifying with the national particulars of Israel's land and her law. Finally, "God's people will now be identified by their togetherness in a multiethnic loving group endowed by the Spirit of God rather than by circumcision, ritual purity, and bloody sacrifices."[7]

The "Mystery" of the Gentiles (3:1-13). Paul begins his intercessory prayer in Ephesians 3:1 and finally resumes it in 3:14-19. He prays that his audience may have a robust relationship with Christ (3:16-17) and experience spiritual insight into God's plan of salvation in Christ (3:18-19). Because Jews and Gentiles constitute a single community (3:2-13), they are to have a deep relationship with Christ and rich insight into his plan of redemption (3:14-19).

> *Gentiles can now become true Israel by identifying with Christ.*

The unveiled mystery in 3:3-13, although it is applied to the way Gentiles relate to Jews, is so tethered to the Messiah that Paul can label it the "mystery of Christ." Paul declares that the mystery "was *not made known to people in other generations* as it has now been revealed by the Spirit to God's holy apostles and prophets" (3:5). The focus on the contrast between these two generations is probably not so much on the two parties themselves (the Old Testament and New Testament writers) but the age in which they live. The "people in other generations" lived in the old age, wherein God partially hid this mystery. The apostles and prophets are part of the new age in which God has revealed the mystery.

What is the content of this mystery? Paul discloses the answer in Ephesians 3:6: "Through the gospel *the Gentiles are heirs together with Israel*, members together of one body, and sharers together *in the promise in Christ Jesus*." Christ's identity as true Israel is the key to the mystery: Gentiles identify with him, not Israel's law, to become true Israelites. The Old Testament prophecies of the end-time salvation of the Gentiles expected the nations to travel to the land of Israel, become circumcised, worship at Israel's temple, submit to clean and unclean laws, and so on. But now Gentiles become true Israelites by moving to Jesus, in whom they are circumcised and are declared clean and in whom is the true temple. This New Testament teaching is not clearly seen in the Old Testament, hence the term *mystery*.

According to 3:10, the unity that Jews and Gentiles enjoy in Christ is set on display on a cosmic level: "Through the church, the manifold *wisdom of God* should be made known *to the rulers and authorities in the heavenly realms*." Fallen angels in the Old Testament play a role in God's management of the nations, and each nation possesses a corresponding angel. Instead of ruling well, angels selfishly govern the nations, deepening the divisions between them. But now that Christ has come, previously estranged nations are beginning to be reconciled in God's cosmic household (Eph 1:10, 20-23). The church is commissioned to be a beacon of unity to unbelievers on earth and to the fallen angels (the rulers and authorities in

[7]Arnold, *Ephesians*, 190.

the heavenly realms). When believers seek unity across ethnic lines (2:11–3:6), within the family (5:21–6:4), and in matters of employment (6:5-9), the church heralds Christ's work of unity to the world around them and declares to the evil angelic authorities that Christ's death and resurrection broke their divisive work among the nations.

The content of Paul's prayer (3:14-21). In the last portion of chapter 3, Paul resumes his prayer from 3:1 and finally provides its content. Paul makes a handful of critical requests: that the church may be strengthened and Christ would dwell in their hearts (3:16-17), be empowered to grasp the love of Christ (3:18), and be filled with the fullness of God (3:19). The heart of Paul's prayer rests on the church's deep understanding of their position within God's great plan of redemption (3:2-13). The churches in Asia Minor and beyond largely comprise Gentiles, so Paul pleads with God that the churches understand their position within God's larger plan of redemption. The apostle goes to great lengths to explain that they are not second-class citizens, watching God's plan unfold as mere observers. Gentiles in the new age enjoy full citizenship in God's covenant community. The Old Testament saints—Noah, Abraham, Isaac, Jacob, Joseph, David, and others—are the Gentiles' forefathers in Christ (Gal 3:7; 1 Cor 10:1)! Israel's history is their history.

The prayer ends with a doxology, demonstrating that God's plan of redemption is headed toward the ultimate goal of giving God glory (Eph 3:20-21; cf. Rom 11:36). The church must embrace their position within the story line of the Bible and understand that the history of redemption, from the Garden of Eden to the new heavens and earth, is designed ultimately to bring God glory.

END-TIME REALITIES APPLIED (4:1-32)

The second half of Ephesians applies the great truths that Paul labors to explain in the first half of the epistle. Chapters 1–3 largely entail the saints' position in Christ, particularly the unity that the saints enjoy with one another. Chapters 4–6 outline how these rich, end-time truths affect their behavior in a concrete fashion. The saints must actively preserve their newfound unity in Christ, which is fostered when the church's leaders serve one another so that "we all reach unity in the faith and in the knowledge of the Son of God and become mature, attaining to the whole measure of the fullness of Christ" (4:13).

As a result of the fall, the Old Testament is characterized by disharmony between people groups and families, but the New Testament changes course. A cursory read through the Old Testament's portrayal of Israel's kings and their fractured relationships with their nation, their children, and their wives gives us the impression that Israel is divided at its core. Even David was hunted by his son Absalom (2 Sam 15)! Something had to be done. In the New Testament, however, discord and division have given way to peace and unity. The New Testament saints rally around King Jesus and discover long-awaited unity within the eternal kingdom. As Paul argues forcefully in the second half of the epistle, believers must "make every effort to keep the unity of the Spirit

FIGURE 13.8. DAVID AND HIS SON ABSALOM

through the bond of peace" (Eph 4:3).

The Spirit and the distribution of gifts (4:1-16). Right out of the gate, Paul charges the congregation to "live a life worthy of the calling you have received" (4:1). Since the church is the end-time people of God and a growing temple (2:21-22), believers must vigorously pursue humility and love (4:2). Paul then explains how the Spirit plays a key role in the life of the church. Although the church is unified, the Spirit enables its individual members to perform a variety of functions—prophets, evangelists, pastors, and teachers (4:11). The goal of the Spirit's work in the church is to "reach unity in the faith and in the knowledge of the Son of God and become mature" (4:13).

In Ephesians 4:8, Paul cites Psalm 68:18 to introduce the spiritual gifts allocated to believers. According to this psalm, God defeats Israel's enemies and dwells in his temple in Zion (Ps 68:17-19). Paul reads Psalm 68 as prophetically anticipating Christ's work of redemption. As Frank Thielman notes, "Acting in the role of God himself in Ps. 68:17–18, Christ had triumphed over the cosmic forces arrayed against God's people. From his lofty and newly-won position in the temple on the eschatological Zion, he distributed gifts to God's people."[8] Believers are equipped to serve one another in the end-time temple of God.

According to the Gospels, the Spirit enables Jesus to perform the three roles of prophet, priest, and king. At his ascension and enthronement, Christ sends forth the Spirit on all his people to gift them to be prophets, priests, and kings. All the saints have some gifts, but not all have the same gifts (Rom 12:6-8; 1 Cor 12–13; 1 Pet 4:9-11). All gifts, to one degree or another, are ways that believers function as a collective body through their offices of a prophet, priest, and king.

The result of the Spirit's work in distributing prophetic gifts to the church, especially that of prophets, evangelists, pastors, and teachers (4:11), is the means by which false teaching is eradicated: "We will no longer be infants, tossed back and forth by the waves, and blown here and there *by every wind of teaching and by the cunning and craftiness of people in their deceitful scheming*" (Eph 4:14). When the church faithfully proclaims God's truth, his people successfully suppress doctrinal error. False teaching tears the church apart, but sound doctrine stitches believers together in love (4:15-16).

The church as the new Adam (4:17-32). The second half of the chapter describes how the church is *not* to live: "You must no longer live as the Gentiles do, in the futility of their

[8]Frank Thielman, "Ephesians," in *Commentary on the New Testament Use of the Old Testament*, ed. G. K. Beale and D. A. Carson (Grand Rapids: Baker Academic, 2007), 824.

thinking" (Eph 4:17). Unbelievers are "darkened in their understanding and separated from the life of God" (4:18). The contrast between believers and unbelievers remains stark, and the lines must not be blurred.

Paul reminds his readers what they learned when placing their faith in Christ (Eph 4:20-21). At that time they were instructed to put off their "old self . . . and to put on the new self" (4:22-24). The commands to "put off . . . be made new . . . put on" are not present commands for those who have already become Christians. These phrases are descriptions of what Christians were taught to do when they became believers (4:21).

Some translations of 4:22 and 24 read "the old self" and "the new self," but this obscures the Old Testament background. The phrases are better rendered as "the old man" and "the new man," making sense of the contrast of the former old age with the new age. Since believers are joined to *the* last Adam, they are now considered to be a "new man" or corporate last Adam.

The wording of 4:22 and 24 recalls and develops 2:15, in which Paul says that Christ abolished "the Law of commandments contained in ordinances, so that in Himself He might make the two into one new man, thus establishing peace" (NASB). Jew and Gentile were two distinct groups, estranged from each other, but since their creation in Christ they are now "one new man" because Christ himself is "the one new man," the new or last Adam. They now stand in wonderful unity as a new, corporate Adam.[9]

Paul progresses from the identity of his readers in 4:22-24 to the series of commands in 4:25-32 by the transitional word *therefore*, indicating in that the preceding argument is the foundation for what follows. Since believers are a "new man," breaking the power of sin from the old age, they are empowered to obey God's commands in the new age. Without the power of the new creation, there is no ability to obey God and please him. The expression "put off falsehood" in 4:25 continues the "put off your old self man" in 4:22. Once the old man has been cast aside, its characteristic sins are as well.

> ***The Spirit enables the church to assume the ministry that had been carried out by prophets, priests, and kings in the Old Testament.***

HARMONY IN THE NEW CREATION (5:1–6:20)

Ephesians 6:10-17 is a well-known passage that draws the curtain back on believers engaging the world and the devil. Paul argues that the saints' struggle is "not against flesh and blood, but against the rulers, against the authorities, against the powers of this dark world and against the spiritual forces of evil in the heavenly realms" (6:12). Daniel 12:1 anticipates this battle within the spiritual realm: "At that time Michael, the great prince who protects your people, will arise. There will be a time of distress such as has not happened from the beginning of nations until then" (cf. Dan 10:13, 20). Accord-

[9]Herman Ridderbos, *Paul: An Outline of His Theology*, trans. John Richard De Witt (Grand Rapids: Eerdmans, 1975), 393.

ing to Daniel's vision, Michael is the great angel appointed to represent God's people. The archangel Michael is subordinate to and fights with the son of man (Dan 7:13) against all the demonic forces arrayed against Israel. The devil and his forces have always actively opposed God, but their rebellion will culminate in one last ferocious battle. Although Christians are characterized by peace, Paul summons them to conduct spiritual warfare before the final battle at Christ's second coming. Paul reminds Christians that the battle against the devil and his demons is an ever-present reality, but believers can be confident that they will emerge victorious because of Christ's triumphant work on the cross.

FIGURE 13.9. THE THREE ARCHANGELS

Children of the light (5:1-20). According to Ephesians 5:8, saints are said to have been in "darkness" but now exist as "light in the Lord," themes that recall Genesis 1. The church must embrace their identity as the new creation in a dark world that lives in rebellion against God. The next several verses extend Paul's discussion of the new creation, culminating in the quotation in 5:14, "This is why it is said: 'Wake up, sleeper, rise from the dead, and Christ will shine on you,'" language that recalls Isaiah 26, 51, and 60.

Isaiah 26:19 prophesies the resurrection of Israel; Isaiah 51 prophetically exhorts God's people to come out of exile; and Isaiah 60 commands end-time Israel to be restored from exile by mirroring God's light of the new creation that breaks forth into the darkness of the old. The restored Israelites will shine on the Gentiles, who are ensconced in the gloom of the old cosmos. According to Ephesians 5:8-14, God's people are shining brilliantly into the darkness of the old creation. Believers, who have already experienced the risen Christ, are to "wake up" and "rise from the dead" (5:14) so that they may evangelize the unbelievers who dwell in deep gloom.

Eschatology continues to fuel Paul's admonitions in Ephesians 5:16: "making the most of every opportunity, because *the days are evil*." Paul's exhortation to make the most of every opportunity turns on the beginning of the deceptive evils of the end times, and believers must not fall prey to such deception. Instead of being deceived by the world, the church is to be "filled with the Spirit" (5:18) and worship the risen Christ and the Father (5:19-20).

Living in God's house (5:21–6:9). The second half of chapter 5 begins with a section called a "household code" that occupies a key block of material in the letter (cf. Col 3:18–4:4; 1 Pet 2:11–3:7). This section is intimately bound up with the gospel and believers' relationship to it (Eph 5:1-21). Ephesians 1:10 states, "when the times reach their fulfillment," Christ, as a cosmic household manager, restores the fragmented relationships of individual family households—husbands and wives, parents and children, and slaves and masters.

After detailing the responsibilities of the wife (5:22-24), Paul progresses to the responsibilities of the husband (5:25-33). The mandate in 5:25 for husbands to love their spouses is strengthened by a comparison to Christ and the church. Husbands are to love their wives as Christ loves the church, and Paul spends the next few verses elaborating on Christ's selfless love for his bride (5:25b-27). In 5:28, another comparison is made between the husband's love for his wife—self-love. Paul then quotes Genesis 2:24 in Ephesians 5:31 to demonstrate that the church finds its unity in Christ.

The Old Testament conception of marriage finds its roots in Genesis 2:24, the prototype of the Israelite model of marriage. The primeval couple's marriage is the template for all future marriages, and Genesis 2:24 undergirds the marriage metaphor between the Lord and Israel (Deut 10:20; 31:16-17; Mal 2:15). Just as Adam makes a covenant with his wife, Eve, the Lord cuts a covenant with his wife, Israel (Is 54:6; Jer 2:29–3:25; Hos 1–3; Amos 7:17). Israel is to model her behavior after Eve and remain faithful to her Adamic husband, the Lord.

The mystery in Ephesians 5 refers to Paul's perception that Adam and Eve's union in marriage typologically corresponds to Christ and the church. The Old Testament contains historical patterns that foreshadow or prophetically anticipate corresponding events at a later time. The nation Israel's kings, prophets, priests, and significant events constitute the essential ingredients of sacred history. For Paul and the other New Testament authors, the "former historical realities [of the Old Testament] were actually orchestrated by God himself to set patterns and provide foretastes of his wider agenda, which would come to its climax centuries later in Jesus the Messiah."[10] Within this framework, Adam and Eve's marriage plays a prominent role as it looks forward to Christ's marriage to the church.

> ***God's people must always recall Adam and Eve's marriage in the garden as the fountainhead of all Israelite marriage.***

Once Paul wraps up his discussion of the responsibilities of husbands, he progresses to children (Eph 6:1-4). Children must obey and honor their parents "so that it may go well with you and that you may enjoy long life on the earth" (6:3). Paul draws from Exodus 20:12, in which obedient children are told they will "live long in the land" of Israel's promised inheritance in Canaan. The reference to the earth here in Ephesians 6:3 probably refers to the new earth. The fifth commandment, originally referring to long life in the Promised Land, is applied to Christians living long on the new earth.

[10]Dennis E. Johnson, *Walking with Jesus Through His Word: Discovering Christ in All the Scriptures* (Phillipsburg, NJ: P&R, 2015), 74.

Children, therefore, are to prepare for inhabiting the new creation by obeying their parents.

Paul then takes up the issue of slaves obeying their "earthly masters with respect and fear, and with sincerity of heart" (6:5). Paul commands some within the church to be "slaves of Christ" and serve the Lord because he will reward them for their faithful obedience (6:6-8). Slavery in Paul's day differs from its modern expression. Some owners in the ancient world were cruel to their slaves and treated them without respect. But there remains one key principle that was alive and well in the Greco-Roman world and continues into the present: slaves were *owned*. Although the apostle here does not protest against slavery, he begins to remove its underpinnings. Slaves are not ultimately responsible to their earthly masters but to Christ, their supreme master and Lord.

FIGURE 13.10. THE GODDESS ARTEMIS OF EPHESUS

Waging warfare in the latter days (6:10-20). Paul rounds out the household codes with a discussion of Christian armor that protects believers against the end-time attack of Satan and his minions. Satan attempts to divide and breach the unity that believers enjoy with one another, so believers must "put on the full armor of God" (6:11). The following section on the believer's armor contains a bevy of points of contact with the Old Testament (Eph 6:14-15, 17), chief among them the book of Isaiah. According to Isaiah 59:17, the Lord "put[s] on *righteousness as his breastplate* and the *helmet of salvation* on his head." The Lord promises to wage war against his enemies so that "people will fear the name of the Lord" (Is 59:19). Similar language is also found earlier in Isaiah, where the prophet predicts that the Messiah will wear a belt of justice (Is 11:5). This end-time king will lay waste to God's enemies and judge Israel with faithfulness (11:4). One last prominent text is Isaiah 52:7, in which the feet of the Lord's prophets are beautiful because they "proclaim peace" and "bring good tidings." These prophets herald the news that God has conquered Israel's enemies and established his end-time kingdom (Is 52:9-10).

By applying these texts from Isaiah to the church, Paul argues that believers participate in the end-time battle that began with the person of Christ. Jesus won a "D-day" victory over the devil, and Christians fight in the wake of that decisive victory in skirmishes against Satan and his allies. Just as Christ's resurrection gave him the "mighty strength" to defeat his enemies (Eph 1:19-22), believers are called to be "strong . . . in his mighty [resurrection] power" (6:10). The devil and his minions continue to resist, although the final outcome of "V-day" is inevitable at Christ's second coming. Though believers wage end-time warfare, they declare "peace" to the world that Christ has already achieved victory.

Christians must be prepared to fend off "the devil's schemes" in the "day of evil" (Eph 6:11, 13). In this respect, they are to "[make] the most of every opportunity, because the days are evil" (5:16). Satan's end-time deceptive schemes have been around since the first century, and believers remain on alert (cf. Eph 4:14). According to the Old Testament, false teaching blossoms in the latter days, and many within the covenant community fall prey to such teaching (e.g., Dan 11:32). Equipped with the armor of God, saints are empowered to overcome such devilish practices.

LETTER CLOSING (6:21-24)

The letter closes with Tychicus carrying the letter to the church to inform them of Paul's situation in Rome and to encourage the church (Eph 6:22). It is possible that Tychichus is responsible to visit several churches in Asia Minor (see introduction) with this general letter and explain its contents to them. The last verse reminds the church of their status as an "incorruptible" new creation in Christ: "Grace be with all who love our Lord Jesus Christ in *incorruption*" (6:24; our translation). Paul's final word encourages the saints to identify with the incorruptible new eternal cosmos. When Christ returns, believers will experience the incorruptible physical resurrection in all its fullness.

PHILIPPIANS

AUTHORSHIP

Peeking inside the epistle to the Philippians, we discover the traditional elements of Pauline authorship. The letter opens with the typical formula, "Paul and Timothy, servants of Christ Jesus" (1:1), and also contains a few details related to Paul's ministry (1:12-14; 3:4-6). The letter even ends with a strong personal appeal (4:14-23). The early church never doubted the authenticity of the book (e.g., Polycarp, *Phil.* 11.3; Irenaeus, *Haer.* 18.4), and modern scholars scarcely doubt Paul's authorship.

FIGURE 14.1. THE PRAETORIAN GUARD

DATE

The date of the letter depends on where Paul is imprisoned (1:7, 13). Like the other Prison Epistles, there are typically three possibilities: Rome, Caesarea, and Ephesus. If Paul were imprisoned in Caesarea, there is hardly enough time for the Philippian church to communicate with Paul; the church is simply too distant from Caesarea. Ephesus lies much closer to Philippi, so many commentators opt for this location. The only problem is that there is no explicit evidence that Paul was ever in jail in Ephesus. Rome seems to be the best option since he makes reference to the "praetorian guard" and "Caesar's household." Despite the long distance between Rome and Philippi, it is possible for several trips to have been made during his stint at Rome and for his messengers to pass each other on the way. Therefore, we should date the epistle to Paul's imprisonment in Rome in the early 60s.

OCCASION

Like most of Paul's epistles, this letter was written for several reasons. The church at Philippi had been integral in Paul's ministry, for he first traveled to Philippi on his second missionary journey (Acts 16:12-40). Somehow, probably through a messenger, the Philippian church learned of Paul's Roman imprisonment. They then sent

Epaphroditus bearing gifts to Paul (Phil 4:18). But once Epaphroditus arrives at Rome, he is stricken with an illness, even to the point of death (2:25-30), so Paul writes to the Philippians to assure them that Epaphroditus is recovering and to express his thanks for their gift.

All was not well in Philippi, however. Opponents of Paul surfaced on two fronts: some at Philippi are proclaiming the gospel as a means of self-promotion and envy (1:15-17, 28); others, probably Judaizers of some stripe, are attempting to force the Gentile church at Philippi to embrace national prescriptions of the Mosaic law (3:2-11). Division also runs deep at the church at Philippi (4:2), and false teaching may play some role in their factious behavior. Much of the letter is devoted to remedying the divisions within the community by encouraging the Philippians to serve one another.

PURPOSE

Paul pens this epistle to thank the Philippians for their gift, assure them that Epaphroditus is well, confront the false teachers, and remind the church to remain unified and steadfast in the face of hostility.

OUTLINE

- I. Letter Opening (1:1-2)
- II. Paul's Ministry in Roman Imprisonment (1:3-30)
  - A. Prayer and Thanksgiving (1:3-11)
  - B. Suffering and the Expansion of the Gospel (1:12-30)
- III. Discovering Unity in Christ's Service (2:1-30)
  - A. Embodying Christ's Humility (2:1-11)
  - B. Obedience Leads to Life (2:12-30)
- IV. Avoiding False Teaching and Imitating Paul (3:1-21)
  - A. False Teaching at Philippi (3:1-14)
  - B. Transformation into the Last Adam (3:15-21)
- V. Concluding Admonitions in Light of Christ's Return (4:1-20)
  - A. Unity in Heaven and on Earth (4:1-2)
  - B. Ethics and the Return of Christ (4:4-9)
  - C. The Philippian Gifts (4:10-20)
- VI. Letter Closing (4:21-23)

BIBLICAL-THEOLOGICAL THEMES

Suffering and multiplication. Intimacy between the Lord and humanity is not the only privilege lost when Adam and Eve sinned in the garden. Their charge to fill the earth with God's glory is also affected. Despite the fall, the original commission remains intact, but Adam and Eve will fulfill this charge under a far more difficult set of circumstances. The couple will indeed fill the earth, but they will do so through pain and suffering. Part of the curse that Eve receives in light of the fall demonstrates a tight relationship between suffering and multiplication: "To the woman he said, 'I will make your *pains in childbearing very severe; with painful labor you will give birth to children*" (Gen 3:16). The curse recalls Adam and Eve's commission to fill the earth with godly individuals who will subdue it and spread God's glory (Gen 1:28). The curse ironically reaffirms the Genesis 1:28 commission—God will ensure that Adam and Eve will have a godly progeny, but this process will entail great pain and affliction.[1]

On account of Joseph's enslavement and eventual rise to power, the Israelites find

[1]Mitchell Kim, "The Blessing of the Curse: Fulfilling Genesis 1:28 in a Context of Suffering," PhD diss., Wheaton College, 2011.

FIGURE 14.2. JOSEPH SELLING CORN IN EGYPT

themselves in the foreign land of Egypt. In fulfillment of the Genesis 1:28 commission, the Israelites "were exceedingly *fruitful*; they multiplied greatly, *increased* in numbers and became so numerous that the land was *filled* with them" (Ex 1:7). As time passed, they fall out of favor with the Egyptians, and a new Pharaoh, "to whom Joseph meant nothing," arrives on the scene (Ex 1:8). This Pharaoh oppresses the Israelites by ramping up their workload and forcing them to labor in difficult conditions. Remarkably, the Israelites respond to such oppression in a positive manner: "The more they [the Israelites] were oppressed, the more they *multiplied and spread*" (1:12). Genesis 1:28 is recalled but in the context of suffering.

As we journey into the New Testament, we trace this theme through Christ and the early church. On the cross, God's glory bursts forth through the horrific death of his Son and fills the earth. The narrative of Acts weds suffering and the expansion of the gospel in the early church. For example, according to Acts 6:7, "the word of God *spread*. The number of disciples in Jerusalem *increased rapidly*, and a *large number* of priests became obedient to the faith." Immediately following this episode is the first martyr of Acts—Stephen (Acts 6:8–7:60; cf. 9:31; 12:24; 16:5; 19:20). The gospel multiplies in the midst of great pain and suffering.

Philippians taps into this theme when Paul encourages the church with news that "what has happened to me has actually resulted in the advance of the gospel, so that it has become known throughout the whole imperial guard, and to everyone else, that my imprisonment is in the cause of Christ" (Phil 1:12-13 HCSB). As Paul suffers under house arrest in Rome, the gospel multiplies and Christ is magnified. The same principle of growth amid suffering holds true. The church at Philippi must hold fast to Christ in the midst of difficulty so that the gospel may flourish throughout Macedonia and beyond.

Grumbling in the wilderness. Paul portrays the saints at Philippi as Israelites wandering through a metaphorical wilderness and enduring difficult trials. In the Old Testament, the wilderness is often depicted as treacherous, a place of sin, evil, and unbelief (Lev 16:10; Is 13:20-22; Jer 9:10-12; 12:10-12). It symbolizes barrenness and hostility. God tests the Israelites in the wilderness as they wander for forty years. Grumbling in the wilderness is the tangible expression of a lack of faith in God, even when he graciously provides for his people (e.g., manna). Exodus 15:24, for example, says, "The people *grumbled* against Moses, saying, 'What are we to drink?'" (cf. Ex 16:2; 17:3; Deut 1:27). But for those who remain faithful to the Lord, the onslaught of evil and temptation can be resisted, as God promises to shield them with his invisible presence.

Jesus wanders in the Judean wilderness for forty days and resists Satan's sly attempts to undermine his faith in the Lord's promises. He withstands the devil's schemes by trusting in God's provision (Mt 4:1-11 and par.). The New Testament writers assert that all the saints are metaphorically wandering, in some form or another, through the wilderness on their way to the new creation. Only those who trust in the Lord's promises of redemption will enjoy his protective presence in the wilderness (Rev 12:1-6). But those who disbelieve, complain, and grumble will forfeit their inheritance of the new creation.

Paul commands the church at Philippi to avoid "grumbling or arguing" (Phil 2:14). As Moisés Silva points out, the wording here is "reminiscent of the experience of the Israelites in the wilderness."[2] According to 1 Corinthians 10:10, the church at Corinth must "not *grumble, as some of them [the first generation of Israelites] did*—and were killed by the destroying angel." Paul recalls a difficult time in Israel's history when she wanders in the desert for forty years before entering into the Promised Land. Like Israel, the church faces temptations of idolatry and grumbling in the wilderness. If those grumbling at Philippi continue to do so, their entrance into the Promised Land of the new creation is at risk.

FIGURE 14.3. ISRAELITES GATHERING MANNA IN THE WILDERNESS

LETTER OPENING (1:1-2)

The epistle opens with a salutation from Paul and Timothy to the saints in Philippi (1:1; cf. Acts 16:1). Although Timothy is paired with Paul as playing some role in the letter's authorship, the apostle Paul's voice is dominant throughout. Paul and Timothy are also labeled "servants of Christ Jesus" (1:1). By highlighting the metaphor of a servant, Paul draws a close connection between his (and Timothy's) ministry and *the* servant of 2:6-11—Christ himself. Paul's ministry is modeled

[2]Moisés Silva, "Philippians," in *Commentary on the New Testament Use of the Old Testament*, ed. G. K. Beale and D. A. Carson (Grand Rapids: Baker Academic, 2007), 837.

after Christ's ministry as the servant spoken of in Isaiah, particularly his exaltation in the midst of suffering and defeat.

While Paul addresses the entire church gathered at Philippi, he singles out the overseers and deacons. The church has been assembled around the risen Christ for only a few decades, but the apostles are quick to establish church government (Acts 20:28; 1 Tim 3:1; Titus 1:7). The apostles primarily install elders and deacons to protect the flock from the invasion of false teaching. According to Philippians 3:2-21, false teaching is threatening Paul's congregation, so the leadership of the church must act quickly and decisively.

PAUL'S MINISTRY IN ROMAN IMPRISONMENT (1:3-30)

The Old Testament contains many examples of saints offering prayers to God on behalf of and for his people. Some prayers are petitions for miraculous interventions, healing, and requests for unique knowledge (e.g., Gen 15:2; 2 Sam 15:31). One can hardly forget Hannah's urgent request to the Lord to provide her with a son (1 Sam 1:10-11). In the Psalms, prayers become even more elaborate and are oftentimes mixed with thanksgiving, praise, petitions, and lament (e.g., Ps 22; 88; 130).

Considerable geographic distance exists between Paul and the church at Philippi, yet he remains in solidarity with them. Following in the tradition of Old Testament saints, one of the ways Paul ministers to the church is through prayer and thanksgiving. Transformation of the human heart is utterly dependent on God's creative work (Ps 51:10). Only God has the power to convert, transform, and glorify his saints, a theme that runs throughout the story of redemption. Philippians 1:9-11 reveals the focus of his prayer, in which Paul pleads with God to increase their love toward one another and to protect them from false teaching.

The latter half of chapter 1 outlines Paul's difficult situation in Rome. As a consequence of Adam and Eve's fall, suffering and the multiplication of God's people go hand in hand (Gen 3:16; Ex 1:7, 12). Christ's crucifixion embodies this principle of suffering. As Christ hangs on the cross, the end-time kingdom begins to multiply, and, slowly but surely, it will reach the ends of the earth (Acts 1:8).

Prayer and thanksgiving (1:3-11). The first several verses of the body of the letter are a prayer for the Philippians, the basis of which rests on the church's "partnership" in the gospel (Phil 1:5). He tells the church that God promises to finish what he started (1:6). Individuals who have been initially fashioned into a new creation will fully transform into the image of Christ at the resurrection.

FIGURE 14.4. HANNAH PRAYS IN THE TEMPLE

Verses 9-11 disclose the content of Paul's prayer to God: "that your love may abound more and more in knowledge and depth of insight" (1:9). The emphasis on love in the knowledge of the truth is critical for their survival. The church must overcome false teaching so that they can be blameless at Christ's second coming (1:10). At the end of the prayer, Paul divulges the goal of his prayer for the

Philippians—"to the glory and praise of God." The church at Philippi must persevere in their faithfulness to the gospel and love toward one another, demonstrating tangible "fruit" so that God receives all the glory (1:11).

Suffering and the expansion of the gospel (1:12-30). Instead of impeding Paul's message, his Roman imprisonment has led to the advance of the gospel (Phil 1:12). Although he is confined in Rome, Paul enjoys some level of freedom. It is quite possible to imagine Paul "shut up with his guard in an apartment at night and, during the day, able to divide his time between his rooms and the precincts of his tenement—perhaps wandering about the courtyard if such was a part of his dwelling."[3] The apostle ministers a great deal to the church at large during this two-year imprisonment in Rome.

Nevertheless, Paul recognizes that he is suffering for the sake of the gospel, a theme that pulls together two critical themes of the story line of the Bible—persecution and affliction advance the presence of God. Paul's Roman imprisonment continues this redemptive-historical theme of expanding God's presence on the earth in the midst of hardship. Paul's suffering leads to the gospel ringing out "throughout the whole palace guard" (Phil 1:13). As Morna Hooker writes,

> His imprisonment "has actually helped to spread the gospel," since the whole imperial guard is talking about his case, and so learning about the Christian faith, while fellow Christians are emboldened to make a similar stand. Paul's own experience of opportunity through suffering is thus a proclamation of the gospel.[4]

Some appear to proclaim Christ "out of selfish ambition" and "from false motives" (1:17-18). Outside of this passage, we know little about this minority at Rome. At the very least, we should distinguish this group from the false teachers in 3:1-11.[5] The message of the gospel, not the messenger, transforms individuals (cf. 1 Cor 1:18-31). Paul's attitude remains positive as he anticipates his full, spiritual "deliverance" (Phil 1:19; cf. Job 13:16). It is a salvation that is eagerly expected and hoped for (Phil 1:20), a deliverance that will occur at the very end of time when God ushers him into the new heavens and earth.

> ***The goal of redemptive history can be summed up in the last sentence: "to the glory and praise of God" (1:11b).***

The "provision of the Spirit of Jesus Christ" (Phil 1:19) empowers the apostle to be a vessel through which Christ can be magnified, whether through his physical life or death. For Paul, "to live is Christ" means that Christ's resurrection life dwells in and enlivens Paul (1:21; cf. Gal 2:20). The Spirit is the agent who appropriates Christ's life-giving power (cf. Rom 1:4; 8:11, 14). Yet, Paul determines that "to die is gain" because death is a heightened spiritual existence, when the nonmaterial soul or spirit departs from the old, fallen body and is translated into the heavenly presence of Christ. Paul expresses anxiety about which to choose, preferring death in order to

[3]Brian Rapske, *The Book of Acts and Paul in Roman Custody* (Grand Rapids: Eerdmans, 1994), 239.

[4]Morna Hooker, "Philippians," in *The Cambridge Companion to St. Paul*, ed. James D. G. Dunn (Cambridge: Cambridge University Press, 2003), 110.

[5]Ralph P. Martin, *Philippians: An Introduction and Commentary*, TNTC 11 (Downers Grove, IL: InterVarsity Press, 1987), 81.

be closer to Christ, but he recognizes that God wills for him to remain a little longer on earth to minister to God's people (Phil 1:23-26).

FIGURE 14.5. THE PROPHET ISAIAH

DISCOVERING UNITY IN CHRIST'S SERVICE (2:1-30)

Chapter 2 is the key that unlocks the entire book. Paul relates to the church at Philippi *how* they are to overcome division within the church—they must embody Christ's service and humility. When examining the "hymn" (2:6-11), we discern shades of Adam.[6] Although we lack an explicit reference to Genesis 1–3 in the hymn, Adam probably reverberates through Paul's mind. Christ is the one who undoes Adam's fall by becoming a servant (2:7). Christ must bear the human image of God to redeem those with a fallen and distorted image and restore them to the pristine, perfected image of God.

Embodying Christ's humility (2:1-11). The church is to be "like-minded, having the same love, being one in spirit and of one mind" (2:2). The Philippians, like most churches, ancient and modern, struggle with unity (cf. 4:2). Paul describes how unity is possible in the overlap of the ages: "Do nothing out of selfish ambition or vain conceit. Rather, in humility value others above yourselves" (2:3). The exhortation reaches its climax in 2:5: "Have the same mindset as Christ Jesus," the ultimate example of humility and service.

Verses 6-11 describe in some detail what Jesus' humility tangibly entails. Scholars agree that these verses constitute a hymn that can be divided into two sections, with the first stressing Christ's status as a servant (2:6-8) and the second underscoring Christ's heavenly enthronement at the right hand of God (2:9-11).

Instead of enjoying the incalculable benefits as the object of worship and adoration by the angels in heaven, Christ becomes flesh in service to others.[7] The suffering servant of Isaiah stands behind the language of 2:7-9: "*He made himself nothing* by taking the very nature of a *servant*. . . . He humbled himself by becoming obedient to *death*—even *death* on a cross! Therefore God *exalted him*." The idea that a servant would die for others and then be exalted recalls Isaiah 52–53: "See, my servant will act wisely; *he will be raised and lifted up and highly exalted*" (Is 52:13); "I will give him a portion among the great, and he

[6]Hooker, "Philippians," 112.

[7]Richard Bauckham, *God Crucified: Monotheism and Christology in the New Testament* (Grand Rapids: Eerdmans, 1999), 58.

will divide the spoils with the strong, because *he poured out his life unto death*. . . . For he bore the sin of many" (Is 53:12). Christ, the preexistent one, gave up the advantages and privileges of heaven to become a servant. Instead of being served, he served the many by dying on a cross (cf. Mk 10:45).

The second half of the hymn evokes the book of Isaiah once more: "At the name of Jesus *every knee should bow*, in heaven and on earth and under the earth, and *every tongue acknowledge* that Jesus Christ is Lord" (Phil 2:10-11). Isaiah 45:23b reads, "Before me *every knee will bow*; by me *every tongue will swear*." The context of Isaiah 45:23 is insightful and underscores God's exclusivity. The passage indicates that the nations will one day publicly decry their idols and acknowledge the one true Lord (Is 45:18-23).

With Isaiah 45 in mind, Paul contends that all of humanity, both Jews and Gentiles, will declare at the very end of history that Christ is indeed unique and that no other gods exist. According to 2:9, God rewards Christ because he has fulfilled the mission of the suffering servant. Christ's incarnation and then exaltation is, as I. H. Marshall describes, a "V-shaped career (from God 'down' to earth and back 'up' again)."[8] God bestows on Christ the honorific title of *Lord*, and because Christ humbled himself and served others, he is now ruling at the right hand of the Father. The servant is truly exalted.

Obedience leads to life (2:12-30). The exalted and resurrected Christ sits at the right hand of the Father, giving life to those who trust him and bringing them into the new creation. Christians now have the power to obey God's commands and please him. In Philippians 2:12-13 Paul says, "continue to work out your salvation with fear and trembling, for it is God who works in you to will and to act in order to fulfill his good purpose." He exhorts his readers to continue "working out" their salvation and then asserts that they are able because God is willing and ultimately working in them (cf. Phil 1:6, 29).

> ***By applying Isaiah 45:23 to Christ, Paul identifies him with Israel's God at his glorious ascension into heaven.***

As faithful followers of the exalted Lord and as "children of God," readers are to shine as stars in the world, holding fast the word of life so that at Christ's second coming, Paul will have a reason to glory (2:15-16). The phrase "word of life" likely conveys the idea of "the word that leads to life"; that is, the message about the gospel leads to a new, resurrected existence in Christ. His death and resurrection transform individuals from darkness to light, death to life, and old age to the new age.

Paul recalls the transition from an old existence to a new existence when he alludes to Daniel 12:3: "Those who are wise will *shine* like the brightness of the heavens, and those who lead many to righteousness, *like the stars* for ever and ever."[9] Believers have initially experienced the promise of Daniel 12:2, and because they still live in a dark

[8]I. H. Marshall, "Philippians," in *New Dictionary of Biblical Theology: Exploring the Unity and Diversity of Scripture*, ed. T. Desmond Alexander and Brian S. Rosner (Downers Grove, IL: InterVarsity Press, 2000), 321.

[9]F. F. Bruce, *Philippians*, NIBC (Peabody, MA: Hendrickson, 1995), 62.

FIGURE 14.6. MARTYRDOM OF ST. TIMOTHY

world of "warped and crooked" people (Phil 2:15), they are compelled to shine as stars by holding firmly "to the word of life" (2:16). Matthew Harmon rightly argues, "What was revealed to Daniel hundreds of years before has begun to be experienced by new covenant believers in anticipation of the fullness of the promise that culminates in resurrected/glorified bodies living in a new heaven and earth."[10]

In the last section of chapter 2, Paul discusses Timothy and Epaphroditus (2:19-30). Always a thoughtful pastor, the apostle intends to send Timothy soon to Philippi so that he can "receive news about you" (2:19). Paul desires to keep tabs on the church's spiritual health and determine if his epistle has indeed been successful to quell division. Epaphroditus then comes to the fore, and Paul is eager to send him back to Philippi. Apparently, Epaphroditus became "ill, and almost died" (2:27). By returning him to his church, the Philippians will rejoice and Paul will "have less anxiety" (2:28).

AVOIDING FALSE TEACHING AND IMITATING PAUL (3:1-21)

In a passage reminiscent of certain passages from Romans and Galatians, Paul confronts the false teaching at Philippi. At its heart lies the misguided and deceptive message that Philippian Gentiles must physically resemble Jews in many key aspects of life. In the Old Testament, Gentiles enter into the covenant community by embracing the Torah. For example, regarding the Passover celebration, Exodus 12:49 says, "The same law applies *both to the native-born and to the foreigner* residing among you" (cf. Num 15:16, 29). The Old Testament also predicts that in the latter days Gentiles would join themselves to Israel by adopting certain aspects of the Torah (Is 2:2-3; 56:3-7; Zech 14:1-15).

Gentiles are expected to conduct themselves in accordance with Israel's teachings, particularly as it relates to the national prescriptions of the law (sacrifices, Sabbath observance, and festivals). But the apostle Paul declares that Gentiles are not required to keep

[10]Matthew Harmon, *Philippians* (Fearn, Scotland: Mentor, 2015), 259.

such commandments when they become part of true Israel, because they are joined to Christ, the embodiment of true Israel (Eph 3:6). The Philippian Gentiles need not move to Palestine to become part of true Israel, because they receive their land inheritance in Christ. They need not obey the food laws that separate the Israelites from their pagan neighbors, because they are now ritually clean in Christ (cf. Acts 11:9). All the requirements of the law, especially those that regulate Israel's unique theocratic and geographical status among the nations, are satisfied in the person and work of Christ (Phil 3:9).

The true danger of this false teaching, however, lies in the relationship between these works of the Torah and the Philippians' faith in Christ. If they take on the yoke of the Torah, the Philippians jeopardize their relationship with God, a covenant bond that is fundamentally based on Christ's work on their behalf. God justifies the members of the church of Philippi through their faith in his Son. Any attempt to earn a relationship with God through works of the Torah or otherwise strikes at the heart of the gospel.

False teaching at Philippi (3:1-14). The Philippians appear to be undergoing some form of persecution and pressure from a group of unbelieving Jews who are forcing them to embrace national aspects of the Mosaic law. This teaching is remarkably similar to what the agitators were doing in Galatia. These Judaizers in Philippi are probably attempting to foist Mosaic regulations on the Gentiles in the church so that they would look outwardly like the nation of Israel. Above all, by convincing the Philippian Gentiles to obey these external rules, the false teachers are attempting to sway the Philippians to merit their own standing before God. Paul calls this group of opponents "dogs," "evildoers," and "mutilators of the flesh" (Phil 3:2).

For the apostle, joining true Israel solely rests on faith in Jesus and the work of the Spirit in the heart of the believer: "For it is *we who are the circumcision*, we who serve God by his Spirit, who boast in Christ Jesus, and who put no confidence in the flesh" (Phil 3:3). Paul declares how fruitless boasting is in the flesh. If anyone could boast, it would be Paul, who was "circumcised on the eighth day, of the people of Israel, of the tribe of Benjamin, a Hebrew of Hebrews . . . a Pharisee; as for zeal, persecuting the church; as for righteousness based on the law, faultless" (3:4-6). Physical circumcision is meaningless unless one's heart is circumcised (cf. Rom 2:25-29).

Paul possesses outstanding Jewish credentials and hails from the tribe of Benjamin.

FIGURE 14.7. FORUM AT PHILIPPI

He likely speaks Hebrew in addition to Greek, Latin, and Aramaic. Before his conversion, he was a Pharisee—an ultraconservative who bristled at Hellenism. To demonstrate his allegiance to the Torah and Pharisaism, he even persecuted the church. He desired to purge Israel of Gentile uncleanness and destroy those blasphemers who worship a cursed messiah.

Determining the precise meaning of his statement "as for righteousness based on the law, *faultless*" remains difficult (3:6). It is troubling, even seemingly contradictory, to Paul's exposition of his relationship to the law in Romans 7. The key, however, is to recognize Paul's differing perspectives of his relationship to the law. In Romans 7, Paul, as a Christian living in the new age, examines his pre-Christian relationship with the law—he was unable to do the law. In Philippians 3:4-6, Paul puts himself back in his shoes as an unbeliever living in the old age ("in the flesh" and "persecutor of the church") and reflects on his previous relationship with the law. At that time, he thought performing acts of righteousness together with his faith would earn him salvation.

In Philippians 3:7-14 Paul switches back to the present, as a believer, and appraises what he formerly considered to be righteousness. Paul's zealous accomplishments through doing Torah (that is, "righteousness") is, in reality, merely "garbage" (3:8). As George Ladd notes, "What he as a Jew had thought was righteousness, he now realizes to be the very essence of sin, for his pride in his own righteousness (Phil. 3:9) had blinded him to the revelation of the divine righteousness in Christ."[11] Righteousness does not come from doing Torah or any form of works but is instead appropriated through faith in Christ (3:9).

According to 3:10, Paul wants to "know the power of his resurrection" before participating in his sufferings. The Spirit who raised Jesus from the dead indwells believers, energizing them to persevere through difficult trials. As Christians persevere, they experience the fellowship of Christ's sufferings and are "becoming like him in his death." The result of persevering through difficulties is attainment of the final, physical resurrection of the dead (3:11). Although Paul has not obtained the physical resurrection, he desires to press on so that he may "take hold" of it, since Christ first took hold of him on the Damascus Road (3:12). The apostle has not yet experienced this final resurrection but strains toward it as a runner right before the finish line (3:13). The metaphor of running comes into focus in 3:14: "I press on toward the goal to win the prize for which God has called me heavenward [to the resurrection] in Christ Jesus." The reward is the ultimate possession of the resurrection body, stirring Paul to please the Lord in his earthly ministry.

Transformation into the last Adam (3:15-21). The last part of chapter 3 concerns Paul as a model who has "live[d] up to what we have already attained" (3:16-17). This exhortation probably includes imitating Paul's identity as one who participates in eschatological suffering and in the inaugurated form of resurrection (3:10). The Philippians must continue to persevere in their faith and eradicate false teaching.

[11]George Eldon Ladd, *A Theology of the New Testament*, rev. ed., ed. Donald A. Hagner (Grand Rapids: Eerdmans, 1993), 545.

The false teaching at Philippi is first and foremost concerned with earthly things, probably manifesting itself in imposing idolatrous dietary regulations on the Gentiles ("their god is their stomach" [3:19; cf. Mk 7:19; Rom 16:18]). Since the Christians at Philippi have been spiritually raised with Christ, they must "eagerly await a Savior *from there*" (Phil 3:20; cf. Eph 2:6; Col 3:1). The believers at Philippi must be so attuned to their resurrected identity in Christ that they eagerly await their physical resurrection that will occur at Christ's second coming at the very end of history.

When Christ returns, he promises to "bring everything under his control" and "transform our lowly bodies" to a body "like his glorious body" (Phil 3:21). The language of a "lowly body" or "humble state" (NASB) is nearly identical to 2:8, in which Christ is said to have "humbled himself." At the end of the age, Christ will complete the process of creating his people in his end-time image, when he will transform believers into his image as the last Adam (cf. Rom 8:29). The followers of Christ become conformed to the image of their Lord on an initial, spiritual level when they trust in him and then on a consummate, spiritual and physical level at the resurrection.

CONCLUDING ADMONITIONS IN LIGHT OF CHRIST'S RETURN (4:1-20)

The final section of the epistle entails a blend of admonitions to the church at Philippi. Once again, unity is discussed (4:1-3), demonstrating the importance of this theme in the local church. Unity is a central teaching in Paul's letters since it is a critical result of the gospel. Faith in Christ produces unity between hostile people groups. Humanity has found its end-time unity in Christ. What is true on a spiritual level now will one day become fully realized in the new heavens and earth, where all of God's people will enjoy perfect harmony with one another. But the church now, although caught in the overlap of the ages, must embrace unity in service to one another. In a very real sense, the believers at Philippi display heartfelt unity with Paul. The Philippians exceled at caring for him and ensuring his physical needs were met (4:10-20), yet the church lacks internal unity between some of its members.

> *In contrast to the false teachers who treasure earthly things, Christians must embrace their heavenly identity in Christ (3:20).*

Unity in heaven and on earth (4:1-2). The beginning of chapter 4 begins with "Therefore," probably indicating that Paul's exhortation in 4:1-3 rests on the church's identity "in heaven" with Christ now and in

FIGURE 14.8. ANCIENT ROMAN STREET

the future (3:20). *Because* the church is united to Christ in heaven, they are to pursue unity on earth. We have no indication of the nature of the fissure within the community, only that they are not "of the same mind" (4:2). The language of being "of the same mind" recalls 2:2, in which Paul reminds the church of their unity in Christ: "Make my joy complete by being like-minded, having the same love, being one in spirit and of *one mind*." He then goes on to demonstrate what having the proper attitude entails when he discusses Christ's humility and exaltation: "In your relationships with one another, have the *same mindset* as Christ Jesus" (2:5). The two women, Euodia and Syntyche, must follow in the footsteps of Christ by overcoming their division and sharing the "same mindset" of Christ, who is faithful in his obedience. The Philippians are "little Adams" in all their conduct since they identify with the last Adam in the present and will be conformed to his image in the future at their resurrection (3:21).

FIGURE 14.9. ALTAR AT TEL BE'ER SHEVA

Ethics and the return of Christ (4:4-9). Verses 4-9 consist of various exhortations that relate to the church's position in Christ and their future resurrection. The basis of Paul's admonitions is the appeal to Christ's second coming: "Rejoice! Let your gentleness be evident to all. *The Lord is near*" (4:4b-5). The phrase "the Lord is near" recalls the general theme of Christ coming to his saints and transforming them into their resurrected bodies (e.g., 1 Cor 16:22; Heb 10:24-25; Rev 1:7). All of Paul's appeals in this section—"rejoice," "let your gentleness be evident," "do not be anxious," "present your requests to God," "think about such things," and "put it into practice"—likely spring from the church's conviction that Christ will return and transform their bodies into a consummate new creation, renewed individuals that are fit for the new heavens and earth. But such end-time transformation has already broken into the present (Phil 3:20), further energizing these exhortations. The church of Philippi must fall into the rhythm of the new creation.

The Philippian gifts (4:10-20). Before Paul closes the letter, he takes a moment to thank the believers for their graciousness. It is not clear, though, what specifics Paul has in mind when he says that the Philippians were previously not in a position to help him (4:10b). What is clear is that the church has come to his aid and renewed their concern for him (4:10a). Paul is well acquainted with the transient nature of material possessions. At points in his ministry, he has experienced plenty and being well fed. But more often than not, Paul finds himself hungry and living in want (4:12). No matter which end of the spectrum Paul finds himself in, he affirms, "I can do all this through him who gives me strength" (4:13). Such empowerment is not merely psychological but eschatological (cf. Eph 6:10). God's creative work of transforming individuals into the new creation enables God's people to withstand difficult circumstances.

Paul recounts his early ministry with the church at Philippi, particularly the church's graciousness (Phil 4:14-16). Acts 16 spends more time narrating Paul's imprisonment in Philippi (Acts 16:16-40) than the details of Paul's ministry to the Philippians (Acts 16:12-15). Apparently, his converts at Philippi aided Paul's missionary efforts, even "more than once" (Phil 4:16). They continued to assist Paul's ministry, despite his imprisonment, when they sent Epaphroditus to him bearing gifts. These gifts, Paul claims, "are a fragrant offering, an acceptable sacrifice, pleasing to God" (4:18). Such a description of the gifts resembles several Old Testament texts that concern sacrificial offerings (e.g., Gen 8:21). The gifts also bear remarkable similarity to Isaiah 56:7: "These [Gentiles] I will bring to my holy mountain and give them joy in my house of prayer. Their *burnt offerings and sacrifices will be accepted on my altar*; for my house will be called a house of prayer for all nations." According to Isaiah 56:6-7, Gentiles are expected to stream to Jerusalem in the latter days, where they will join themselves to Israel and participate in Israelite worship (cf. Ezek 20:41). In a similar vein, Isaiah 60:5-6 reads, "The riches of the nations will come. . . . bearing gold and incense" (cf. Is 61:6).

The promises of Isaiah are in mind, then Paul interprets the church's tangible gift as the direct fulfillment of Isaiah's prophecy that Gentiles would worship God in the end time. The members of the Philippian church function as priests in God's temple, offering up spiritual sacrifices (cf. Rom 12:1). The Philippians stand on equal ground with Israel, inheriting the riches and glory that are found only in Christ Jesus (Phil 4:19). The members of the church, who serve as priests before God, do not dwell physically in the earthly Jerusalem but dwell spiritually even now in the heavenly Jerusalem (cf. Heb 12:22).

LETTER CLOSING (4:21-23)

Paul ends his epistle in the traditional way by sending along his greetings on behalf of those who are with him in Rome. The apostle also mentions a group from "Caesar's household" (4:22). The identity of this group remains elusive. It may very well refer to Roman guards or others who have been converted during Paul's imprisonment. According to 1:13, the gospel has advanced "throughout the whole palace guard and to everyone else." In any case, Paul attempts to draw solidarity between the people of God in Rome and in Philippi.

15

COLOSSIANS AND PHILEMON

COLOSSIANS

AUTHORSHIP

The letter of Colossians internally claims to have been written by the apostle Paul (1:1, 23; 4:18), and the early church never seriously questioned its authenticity (Irenaeus, *Haer.* 14.1; Clement of Alex, *Strom.* 1.1).[1] Until recently, there had been little doubt that the apostle Paul wrote the letter. Those who argue against Pauline authorship claim that the letter differs significantly from Paul's other epistles, particularly in its theology and language. Its textual relationship to Ephesians has also led to serious doubt. Here the issue of pseudonymity once again comes to the fore. Yet, when understood correctly, the theology contained in Colossians sits well with Paul's other books. The grammar, syntax, and vocabulary, although different in some portions of Colossians, are not enough to unseat the Pauline authorship, especially considering that Paul may have used a secretary who had his own particular style. Moreover, all of Paul's letters are directed to unique situations, probably requiring different vocabulary, content, and style well-suited for the specific occasion. Since Paul combats a specific heresy at a specific time in Colossae, he probably tailors the letter accordingly.

DATE

That Paul writes Colossians while in prison seems obvious enough (4:18), but it is unclear which imprisonment is in mind. Colossians is often grouped with Ephesians, Philippians, and Philemon, and for good reason. Since Ephesians and Colossians share more textual parallels than any other Pauline letters and both were written in prison, they are likely written at the same time and place (see discussion of the dating of Ephesians). We should therefore date this letter sometime in the early 60s, probably while Paul is under house arrest in Rome awaiting trial (Acts 28:30-31).

OCCASION

The close relationship between Colossians and Philemon, based on the names mentioned in the two letters, is readily affirmed.

[1]This chapter is an adaptation of Benjamin L. Gladd, "Colossians," in *A Biblical-Theological Introduction to the New Testament: The Gospel Realized*, ed. Michael J. Kruger (Wheaton, IL: Crossway, 2016), 301-19; and G. K. Beale, "Colossians," in *Commentary on the New Testament Use of the Old Testament*, ed. G. K. Beale and D. A. Carson (Grand Rapids: Baker Academic, 2007), 841-71.

Their textual similarities are also striking. Epaphras apparently planted the congregation at Colossae (Col 1:7-8): "You learned it [the gospel] *from Epaphras*, our dear fellow servant, who is a faithful minister of Christ on our behalf, and who also told us of your love in the Spirit." Yet Paul takes it on himself to communicate with this church. Many within the church at Colossae have fallen prey to false teaching, a system that incorporates aspects of Judaism and paganism. Although we cannot reconstruct the precise details of this heresy, it appears that much of it rests on a desire to experience God's presence in a heightened and more intimate way.

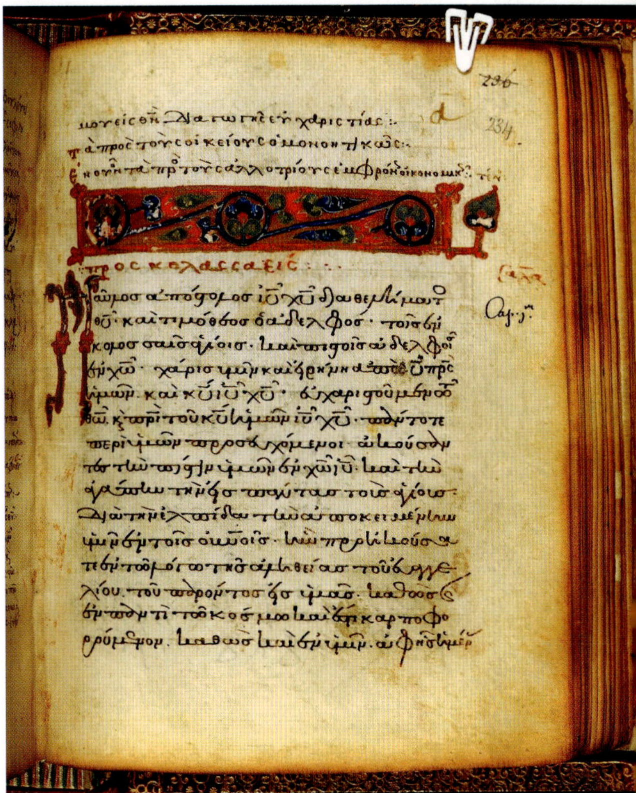

FIGURE 15.1. GREEK MANUSCRIPT OF COLOSSIANS

PURPOSE

The church at Colossae desires to know and experience not only the crucified Christ but also deeper spiritual truths and realities. They dabble in Jewish philosophy and pagan practices. In their eyes, Christ's work could meet some of their spiritual needs but was not sufficient to meet all their needs. Paul writes Colossians to correct the local heresy and affirm the priority of Christ and the gospel.

OUTLINE

- I. Letter Opening (1:1-2)
- II. Thanksgiving and the Propagation of the Gospel (1:3-14)
  - A. Fulfillment of the Adamic Commission (1:3-12)
  - B. Christ's Kingdom of Redemption and Forgiveness (1:13-14)
- III. The Exalted Christ (1:15-23)
  - A. Christ's Supremacy over the First Creation (1:15-17)
  - B. Christ's Supremacy over the New Creation (1:18-20)
  - C. Christ's Work of Reconciliation (1:21-23)
- IV. Christ and the Unveiled Mystery (1:24-29)
  - A. Sharing in Christ's Suffering (1:24-25)
  - B. Christ and the Unveiled Mystery (1:26-29)
- V. Admonition to Denounce False Teaching (2:1-23)
  - A. The Superiority of Christ (2:1-15)
  - B. The Folly of Wisdom Outside of Christ (2:16-23)
- VI. Life as Resurrected Beings (3:1-25)
  - A. The Believers' Identification with the Risen Christ (3:1-11)
  - B. Living in Light of the Believers' Resurrection (3:12-25)
- VII. Gospel Proclamation and the Letter Closing (4:2-18)
  - A. Paul's Request for Evangelism (4:2-6)
  - B. Personal Requests and the Letter Closing (4:7-18)

FIGURE 15.2. ROMAN TEMPLE

BIBLICAL-THEOLOGICAL THEMES

Colossian heresy and the temple of God. Paul somehow discovers that the church at Colossae is under the threat of false teaching. Nuancing the precise content of the heresy is notoriously difficult, so we ought to remain cautious here. The heresy appears to be an amalgam of Greco-Roman and Jewish beliefs.[2] The stress on wisdom, knowledge, and "elemental spiritual forces of this world" betrays a Greco-Roman belief system (Col 2:8, 18-19). The mention of Sabbath observance, religious festivals, and food regulations also resonate within a Jewish context (Col 2:11, 20-23). But Sabbath and dietary observance is part of the old age and a shadow of the believer's inheritance in Christ. The new age is at hand, so to continue to affirm such practices is to revel in the old age.

One tenet of the false teaching at Colossae is the strong belief in evil spirits and their activity within the world. "The advocates of the new teaching," as Clinton Arnold notes, "emphasized a rigorous asceticism with a variety of taboos, ritual observances, and dietary regulations. These practices were motivated at least in part by a desire to gain ritual power over the harmful and malignant forces."[3] Some members of the Colossian church perform various rituals in order to gain power over spiritual forces. Paul combats this belief system by arguing that Christ is not just a powerful being but is completely supreme over spiritual forces. Christ defeated these cosmic forces, so there is no need to cower in fear or perform magic for personal deliverance.

Another key tenet of the false teaching is the strong desire to experience God's presence in a unique and heightened manner.

[2]For a well-balanced understanding of the Colossian heresy, see Douglas J. Moo, *The Letters to the Colossians and to Philemon*, PNTC (Grand Rapids: Eerdmans, 2008), 46-60.

[3]Clinton E. Arnold, *The Colossian Syncretism: The Interface Between Christianity and Folk Belief at Colossae*, WUNT 77 (Tübingen: Mohr Siebeck, 1995; repr., Grand Rapids: Baker, 1996).

Colossians 2:18a says that the false teaching at Colossae promotes "false humility and the worship of angels by *entering into the innermost sanctuary*" (our translation). The same Greek wording is found in pagan inscriptions of individuals near Colossae "entering into" the sanctuary of the temple of a deity. One of the clearest inscriptions reads, "Under the rule of Apollo . . . there came—in order to see a revelation from the gods—Crispus Trypone and Poplius Pupius Callacles, who underwent an initiation and *walked within the holy place*."[4] The false teachers at Colossae promise the church members a more intimate experience with God. Through various rituals, the Colossians could enter into the sanctuary of heaven and enjoy God's resplendent glory.

The false teachers at Colossae who promised a heightened, ecstatic experience of enjoying God's presence stand in direct opposition to Paul's teaching throughout the letter. Paul alludes to Genesis 1:28 in Colossians 1:6 and 10 and considers the church at Colossae as blessed with the favor of God's end-time presence. Through Christ's work and the Spirit's presence, God genuinely dwells in their midst. According to 1:9-10, the Colossians are skilled temple builders who imitate the work of tabernacle craftsmen in Exodus 31. The church at Colossae performs good works by or producing the fruit of faith. Those who have placed their trust in the risen Christ have been "raised" with him and now find their complete identity in him as the true temple and have their spiritual existence in heaven (Col 3:1). What the false teachers promise through ritual, the Colossians enjoy by faith in Christ.

Return from exile. As God expelled Adam and Eve from the garden on account of their disobedience, he also expels Israel from the Promised Land on account of their idolatry. Yet he promises to bring Israel back into the land and restore them to their rightful place of inheritance. The Lord redeems the Israelites from Babylonian captivity through the decree of Cyrus, but the Israelites remain under the political thumb of the Persians. Despite being back in the Promised Land, Israel remained in spiritual exile. Jesus identified with sinful Israel by going into spiritual exile on the cross and bearing God's wrath. At his resurrection, Jesus participates in the new heavens and earth (i.e., the Promised Land) in his transformed, new creational body. All those who identify with Christ's work are released from exile and enter the Promised Land of the new creation.

Paul latches on to this spiritual return from exile when he utters his words of thanksgiving in Colossians 1:12-14: "and giving joyful thanks to the Father, who has qualified you to share in the inheritance of his *holy people* in the kingdom of light. For he has *rescued* us from the dominion of darkness and brought us into the kingdom of the Son he loves, in whom we have *redemption*, the forgiveness of sins." Just as God delivered Israel, redeemed them from Egyptian slavery, and gave them the Promised Land as an inheritance (Ex 6:6; 14:30; Deut 7:8), so too he delivers the church from spiritual bondage. The Colossians now enjoy their inheritance of the new creation, which will arrive in its fullness when Christ returns and establishes the new heavens

[4]M. E. Boring, K. Berger, and C. Colpe, *Hellenistic Commentary to the New Testament* (Nashville: Abingdon, 1995), 485-86.

and earth. Despite being granted entrance into the new creation, the Colossians have not arrived fully into the new age; they still struggle with indwelling sin and remain in exile to some degree, both spiritually (since they are not perfectly set apart from the old age) and physically (since they still have corruptible bodies).

LETTER OPENING (1:1-2)

Paul begins this epistle with his standard introductory features—he identifies himself (and his coworker) and the audience of the letter (cf. Gal 1:1-2; Eph 1:1-2; Phil 1:1). Paul anchors his apostleship in the will of God, providing the basis for his authority to write the letter. The audience is identified as "the saints and faithful brethren in Christ who are at Colossae" (1:2 NASB). Although Paul did not establish the church at Colossae (1:7), he possesses the authority to admonish and encourage this faithful church.

> *God is now beginning to dwell with his people in an unprecedented way, and God's glory is indeed beginning to fill the earth.*

THANKSGIVING AND THE PROPAGATION OF THE GOSPEL (1:3-14)

In typical Pauline fashion, the thanksgiving section comes on the heels of the letter's opening. Paul subtly places the Colossian church in God's overarching story line of the Bible and reveals how they are playing a crucial role within it. The divine commission that Adam and Eve are given in Genesis 1:28 has now blossomed in Christ (Col 1:6, 10).

Since the gospel is "bearing fruit" and "growing" at Colossae, Paul has been fervently praying that the church would persevere and reach a state of maturity (1:9-12). Paul's thankful spirit flows from Christ's work on the Colossians' behalf: "He has rescued us from the dominion of darkness and brought us into the kingdom of the Son he loves, in whom we have redemption, the forgiveness of sins" (1:13-14).

Fulfillment of the Adamic commission (1:3-12). Paul thanks God for his audience's warm acceptance of the gospel. He further claims that the gospel is "bearing fruit and growing throughout the whole world" (1:6; 1:10). Paul's wording alludes to Genesis 1:28: "God blessed them and said to them, '*Be fruitful and increase* in number; fill the *earth* and subdue it." According to Genesis 1, Adam and Eve are commanded to have children, forming a community that would enjoy perfect fellowship with God and keep the created order under their subjection and dominion (Gen 1:28b). Not only are Adam and Eve to bring the earth under their subjection, they are to extend God's presence, originally limited to the Garden of Eden, to the ends of the earth. Adam and Eve failed to obey God, so their commission is passed on to succeeding generations—Seth, Noah, the patriarchs, and, finally, Israel. But Israel, like the original couple, fails to bring the earth under subjection and extend God's glory to the ends of the earth. God's plan to fill the earth with his glorious presence and subject it to his rule reaches a decisive point of fulfillment during Jesus' ministry. God's glorious presence has begun to descend from heaven to earth. By applying Genesis

1:28 to the church at Colossae, Paul claims that the divine commission to Adam is beginning to be fulfilled in Christ.

Paul yearns for the Colossians to be "*filled* with the *knowledge* of His [God's] will in all *spiritual wisdom and understanding . . . in every good work*" (1:9-10 NASB). The language here closely follows Exodus 31:3: "I have *filled* him with the divine *Spirit of wisdom, and understanding, and knowledge in every work*" (cf. Is 11:2; our translation). Exodus 31:1-11 asserts that God empowers Israelites with the Spirit to construct the tabernacle. Accordingly, Paul sees God filling Christians with his Spirit so that they can live skillful, godly lives in helping to build God's spiritual sanctuary and shine brightly in a world of gloom. The Colossians are analogous to Old Testament temple builders in that they "contribute to the process of constructing the church as God's temple."[5] By heralding and embodying the gospel, believers carry forth the message of salvation that inevitably leads to the conversion of others (Col 1:6-7, 28-29; 4:3-6) and the growth of the invisible temple. Saints are, at their core, missional in all their behavior.

Christ's kingdom of redemption and forgiveness (1:13-14). The last half of the thanksgiving section ends on a high note, with the focus not so much on who Christ is (that will come later) but on what he has accomplished. Verse 13 describes, in graphic detail, the believer's transfer from one realm to another: "He [God] has rescued us from the dominion of darkness and brought us into the kingdom of the Son." Through faith in Christ's redemptive work (1:14), Christians are no longer identified with the "dominion of darkness" but with the "kingdom of the Son." This transfer entails the forgiveness of sin and the new life that is found only in

FIGURE 15.3. MODEL OF ISRAEL'S TABERNACLE IN THE WILDERNESS

[5]T. Desmond Alexander, *From Eden to the New Jerusalem: An Introduction to Biblical Theology* (Grand Rapids: Kregel, 2008), 66.

Christ, a new creational existence that is nothing short of astounding. Believers can be assured that if they have robust faith in the gospel (1:10-11), they presently enjoy spiritual life in the new heavens and earth.

Jesus, as God's perfect image, fulfilled the original charge to Adam by bringing all of creation under God's reign.

THE EXALTED CHRIST (1:15-23)

Throughout the Old Testament, God's unrivaled sovereign rule over the cosmos is on display. Psalm 103:19 echoes this theme: "The Lord has established his throne in heaven, and his kingdom rules over all." God creates Adam and Eve to mediate this rule over the earth and extend it to the ends of the earth. Although the fall corrupted the first couple's capacity to mediate the divine rule, God overcame this dilemma by restoring humanity's image. This deliverance culminates in the life, death, and resurrection of his Son. Since Christ is in the perfect image of his Father even before the creation, he rules alongside him over the cosmos. But Christ is not only in the perfect image of the Father; he also re-creates the image of God's people so that believers may join Christ in his redemptive-historical cosmic reign and extend that rule on earth. The book of Colossians strikes this chord loudly.

What follows is one of the most treasured portions of Colossians. This unit is typically referred to as a hymn since it is a distinct unit and poetically arranged. We are unsure whether Paul authored this hymn or if he simply adapts it for his purposes. In any case, the hymn focuses on the person and work of Christ and primarily develops two facets, reverberating throughout the entire epistle:[6] (1) the chronological priority of Christ (his preexistence), Christ's supremacy over the first creation (Col 1:15-18a), and (2) the creational priority of Christ, his supremacy over the new creation (1:18b-20).

Christ's supremacy over the first creation (1:15-18a). Within the first portion of the hymn (1:15-18a), Christ is the preincarnate Adam, after whom the first Adam was patterned. Colossians 1:15 recalls Genesis 1:27: "God created mankind *in his own image*, in *the image of God* he created them; male and female he created them" (cf. 1 Cor 11:7; 2 Cor 4:4). Paul has taken the language of the first Adam and used it to describe the preincarnate Christ.

Sonship is intimately tethered to bearing one's image. God's relationship to Adam illustrates this relationship. Since Adam is created in God's image, he is deemed to be God's son. Adam's son, Seth, was said to be in his Adam's image: "When Adam had lived 130 years, he had a *son* in his own likeness, *in his own image*; and he named him Seth" (Gen 5:3). The first Adam, existing in the image of God, must rule over the created order on behalf of God. But, as we know all too well, Adam fails. So God raises up others and creates them in his image (Seth, Noah, Abraham, Isaac, etc.). They are fashioned to rule over the created order and spread God's glorious presence. Finally, God sends his own Son to earth, who is in his pristine image. But in

[6]David W. Pao, *Colossians & Philemon*, ZECNT (Grand Rapids: Zondervan, 2012), 84.

Colossians 1:15 Paul focuses on Christ's preincarnate divine rule. Jesus is God's divine Son, which means he is also in the image of his Father (Col 1:13). But again, we must remember that this language of the first Adam as a son in God's image is taken by Paul to describe Christ as the eternal Son of God in God's image before creation.

Paul also calls Christ "the firstborn": "The Son is the image of the invisible God, *the firstborn* over all creation" (1:15). While some argue that Christ being the firstborn reflects a creaturely state, this is both theologically and exegetically problematic (cf. Jn 1:3). Christ's status as the firstborn is not to be taken as a literal depiction (i.e., Christ is literally the first one born) but as a figurative expression. This particular concept resonates with the Old Testament.[7] "Then say to Pharaoh, 'This is what the Lord says: Israel is my *firstborn* son" (Ex 4:22; cf. Ps 89:27; Heb 1:6). These texts do not refer to a literal or physical firstborn but to relational priority. Christ is the firstborn because he is the most supreme being, not because he is created. The prophesied messianic king in Psalm 89:27 is firstborn because he is the supreme sovereign over all. Paul's point in Colossians 1:15 is quite clear—Christ is preexistent and sovereign over the created order.

Christ's supremacy over the new creation (1:18b-20). The second portion of the hymn is stunningly majestic, focused on Christ and how he relates to the new order of creation (1:18b-20). Christ, as a resurrected being, has begun the end-time renewal of the cosmos ("and through him to reconcile to himself all things" [1:20]). He also embodies God's glorious presence as the end-time temple. Colossians 1:19 alludes to Psalm 67:17-18 (Ps 68 in English translations): "God was *well-pleased to dwell* in it [Zion] . . . the Lord will dwell [there] forever . . . *in the holy place*" (our translation). The temple on Zion in which God dwells according to Psalm 67 is now applied to Christ in Colossians 1:19.[8] This is the same divine presence that is partially housed in Israel's mobile tabernacle and temple. In the new age, God's unfettered presence descends to earth in Christ (cf. Mt 1:22-23). The expectation in Genesis 1–2 that heaven and earth would be joined together is finally being realized.

FIGURE 15.4. ADAM AND EVE

[7]Craig S. Keener, *The IVP Bible Background Commentary: New Testament*, 2nd ed. (Downers Grove, IL: InterVarsity Press, 2014), 571.

[8]For further discussion of this psalm allusion, see G. K. Beale, *Colossians and Philemon*, BECNT (Grand Rapids: Baker, 2019), 108-9.

Christ's work of reconciliation (1:21-23). Following hard on Paul's description of Christ as the supreme ruler and God's divine, preexistent Son, the apostle highlights his role as the great reconciler: "Once you were alienated from God and were enemies in your minds because of your evil behavior. But now he has reconciled you by Christ's physical body through death to present you holy in his sight" (Col 1:21-22a). Here is the very heart of the gospel: God accepting wretched sinners through the death of his righteous Son (cf. 2 Cor 5:21). Paul carefully discloses the intended effect of God's great act of reconciling sinners: "to present you holy in his sight, without blemish and free from accusation" (Col 1:22b). God desires that humanity exist in a restored condition, a state that is initially promised to Adam and Eve if they obey perfectly (Gen 1:28; 2:15).

FIGURE 15.5. MOSAIC OF DANIEL AND THE LIONS

CHRIST AND THE UNVEILED MYSTERY (1:24-29)

The last portion of chapter 1 largely entails Paul's relationship to the gospel and his role in the promulgation of a mystery. He is a servant, commissioned to proclaim the mystery to the church of Colossae (Col 1:25). On a conceptual level, this passage resembles the book of Daniel, in which the prophet is charged with mediating mysteries to king Nebuchadnezzar (Dan 2:24-47; 4:19-27). Daniel acquires mysteries or end-time revelations (Dan 2:17-18, 28-29) and gains great insight into the rise and fall of nations (e.g., Dan 2:36-45; 4:19-27; 5:13-28; 7:14-27). In a similar way, the apostle Paul received end-time revelations (Eph 3:2-13) and is tasked with mediating them to the nations for their benefit.

Sharing in Christ's suffering (1:24-25). Verse 24 is notoriously difficult to understand on several levels: "Now I rejoice in what I am suffering for you, and *I fill up in my flesh what is still lacking in regard to Christ's afflictions*, for the sake of his body, which is the church." Is Paul suggesting that Christ's work on the cross is somehow incomplete? Does Paul suffer the same way as Christ suffers on the cross?

Paul's language here refers generally to his living a "cruciform lifestyle" (cf. 2 Cor 4:7-12; 12:9-10). That is, the apostle embodies the paradox of the cross—strength in weakness, victory in defeat, wisdom in foolishness. His discussion of wisdom in 1 Corinthians 1–2 is his longest exposition of the nature of the cross and believers' understanding of it. At the heart of those two chapters is this concept of power in weakness. To state it succinctly, while Jesus is suffering a shameful death on the cross, he is simultaneously the supreme ruler. He rules while undergoing defeat. Jesus is King at the very moment that he appears to be defeated and at the very time he is accursed.

When Paul suffers for the sake of Christ, he is conforming to the pattern of Christ. Just as Jesus displayed power in the midst of defeat, so does Paul. Christ executes his messianic prerogative to rule while dying, and Paul rules alongside Christ when he suffers. Paul's ministry, therefore, is, brought into conformity with Christ's work on the cross, not with reference to sin but with reference to ruling over the hostility of the world (cf. Rev 2:7, 11, 17). In particular, Paul is uniquely suffering in the way Christ suffered (and will continue to so suffer until his own death) in order to complete Christ's ministry of carrying the gospel to the nations.[9] But other passages in the Pauline epistles, tell us that Paul is not alone in embodying the cross. All believers, as N. T. Wright suggests, "are not merely imitating him [Christ]. They are incorporated into his life, his paradoxical new way of life."[10]

Christ and the unveiled mystery (1:26-29). Paul shifts his attention to the content of his message to the Gentiles:

> I have become its servant by the commission God gave me to present to you the word of God in its fullness—*the mystery that has been kept hidden for ages and generations, but is now disclosed to the Lord's people.* To them God has chosen to make known *among the Gentiles* the glorious riches of *this mystery,* which is Christ in you, the hope of glory. (Col 1:25-27)

Although only three verses, this section is packed with great significance. Why would Paul claim that a particular aspect of the relationship between Jews and Gentiles was previously hidden? Something about the way in which Jews and Gentiles relate to one another in the New Testament age is not crystal clear in the Old Testament.

When we examine Colossians 1:25-27 in light of Ephesians 3, we conclude that both passages are remarkably similar. Helpfully, Paul's discussion of the relationship between Jews and Gentiles in Ephesians is far more developed than his brief words in Colossians 1:25-27. What remains implicit in Colossians 1:27 ("Christ in you") becomes explicit in Ephesians 3:6: ("Gentiles are heirs together with Israel, members together of one body, and sharers together in the promise in Christ Jesus").

The mystery is not that these two groups are merely one covenant community, since that had already been clearly prophesied in the Old Testament (e.g., Ps 87; Is 19:18-24; 49:3-6; 66:18-21); rather, they are one in the person of Christ. Gentiles have now become true Israelites through faith in Christ, the embodiment of true Israel, without having to identify themselves with the various national laws formerly required by the Mosaic covenant for those living in geographical Israel. Simply put, the mystery comprises how Gentiles become true Israelites in the end-time without taking on the national markers of Israel.

ADMONITION TO DENOUNCE FALSE TEACHING (2:1-23)

The Old Testament saints pined to experience God's glorious presence. Moses, for

[9]For elaboration, see Beale, *Colossians and Philemon,* 139-43, where Paul's non-atoning sufferings are seen as a completion of Christ's sufferings, as the Isaianic Servant, whose mission was to bring salvation to both Jews and Gentiles; Christ begins to fulfill the mission to Jews but does not complete the full mission since he did not go to the Gentiles. It is Paul that continues and completes the Isaianic Servant's mission of saving the Gentiles through his suffering ministry.

[10]N. T. Wright, *Colossians and Philemon,* TNTC 12 (Downers Grove, IL: InterVarsity Press, 1986), 92.

example, pleads with God, "Show me your glory" (Ex 33:18). But God grants Moses partial access to his glory by exposing only his "back" (Ex 33:23). The Old Testament yearned for the day when heaven will descend and humanity will experience God in his fullness in the eternal new cosmos. In the New Testament, we learn that God's presence in the Old Testament temple is manifested on earth in the person of Christ. God grants those who believe in the risen Christ access into his tabernacling presence.

The false teachers at Colossae claim that believers can experience a heightened, more intimate experience with God. Chapter 2 confronts this heresy head on, and most of what we know about this false teaching stems from this chapter. The first half of the chapter (2:1-15) entails Christ's work on believers' behalf—that is, his victory over the inimical spirits and his great act of spiritually resurrecting believers. The second half of chapter 2 asserts that Christ is far better than any Jewish or pagan ritual (2:16-23).

The superiority of Christ (2:1-15). Paul never met the Colossians personally (Epaphras founded the church [Col 1:7; 4:12-13]), but he strives earnestly for them and holds a special place in his heart for this church. The main point of Colossians 2:1-5 occurs in 2:4: "I say this *so that no one will delude you with persuasive argument*" (NASB). One of the central reasons Paul penned this letter is because of the presence of false teaching in Colossae. Some in the church are advocating the use of pagan rituals, magical incantations, and Jewish teachings in conjunction with the apostolic message of Christ.

Colossians 2:6 moves the argument along by further unpacking 2:1-5. In the following section of 2:6-15, the main point exposes the problem with the false teaching: "hollow and deceptive philosophy, which depends on human tradition and the elemental spiritual forces of this world *rather than on Christ*" (2:8). Instead of embracing a teaching that is focused on Christ, the Colossians are faced with the threat of believing a message that is void of the gospel and Christ.

Paul's imperative to "continue to live your lives in him [Christ]" (2:6a) is spelled out in the following verses and expresses a major theme that continues up through, at least, Colossians 4:6. In the immediate context, the Colossians must conduct themselves by resisting false teaching and being "rooted and built up in him as [they] were taught" (2:7). Colossians 2:8a further unpacks Paul's statement in 2:6a that the church must walk in Christ by first telling them what to not do: "See to it that no one takes you captive through hollow and deceptive philosophy." The spiritual health of the Colossians hinges on their denial of false teaching and their embrace of sound doctrine.

The second part of 2:8b gives us the specifics of the false doctrine: "which depends on human tradition and the elemental spiritual forces of this world." The first part of this description probably describes the origin of the false teaching. Instead of having its origin in the triune God, the false teaching is, from start to finish, characterized by a human worldview (whether Jewish or pagan). That is, the Colossians are confronted with a teaching that is opposed to the worldview of God as it is manifested in the apostolic teaching. The second part ("the elemental spiritual forces of this world") is a most peculiar phrase in 2:8b and 2:20.

The phrase "elemental spirits" (ESV) is one Greek word (more literally, "elements" or "elemental things") and generally refers to something that is the most basic structure of a given topic. Paul also qualifies the word with another key term—*world.* The combination of these two words appears several times outside of the New Testament, most of which come from a first-century AD Jewish author, Philo. One of his most pertinent texts comes from *On the Life of Moses* I, 96, 3: "The chastisement was different from the usual kind, for *the elements* of the universe—earth, fire, air, water—carried out the assault. God's judgment was that the materials which had served to produce *the world* should serve also to destroy the land of the impious."[11] The phrase "elements of the world" has the same meaning of "the entire world" elsewhere in other contemporary Hellenistic writings.

Thus, the phrase in 2:8b and 2:20 refers to the "elements of the old world." The phrase may also include a spiritual or demonic element since angels are intertwined with this physical cosmos. This spiritual and physical dimension to the phrase makes much sense in light of Paul's use of the term *world* elsewhere (e.g., Rom 3:6, 19; 5:12-13; 11:12, 15). According to the New Testament, the world is part of the two-aged schema, whereby the old age has begun to be destroyed and the new age has broken in. When we define *world* according to this pervasive New Testament framework, we learn that the term encompasses not only the physical particulars of the cosmos but also the spiritual. To summarize, elemental things consist of demonic forces that are fused with the fallen physical world (cf. Gal 4:3, 9). When Paul states that the heresy is that "which depends on human tradition and the elemental spiritual forces of this world," he claims that the false teaching is the product of and aligned with the fallen angels and cosmos.[12]

FIGURE 15.6. ANCIENT GREEK INCANTATION

The false teaching at Colossae is the product of a corrupt, old-age worldview that has come under divine judgment.

The folly of wisdom outside of Christ (2:16-23). Colossians 2:16 and 2:21 describe what appears to be a Jewish teaching: "Therefore do not let anyone judge you by what you *eat or drink*, or with regard to a religious *festival, a New Moon celebration or a Sabbath day. . . . 'Do not handle! Do not taste! Do not touch!'*" In the Old Testament, God forbids the Israelites to eat certain types of food, as they are associated with the pagan nations and idolatry (Lev 11; Deut 14). God also requires the Israelites to celebrate several annual feasts and rest on the Sabbath

[11]See also *Mos.* I, 155, 5; II, 267, 4; *Abr.* 162, 6; *Opif.* 52, 5; *Cher.* 127, 3; cf. 2 Pet 3:10, 12.
[12]Moo, *Letters to the Colossians and to Philemon*, 191-92.

(e.g., Ex 10:9; 12:14, 17; 20:8; Lev 23:34). The point of these requirements is that they demarcate the Israelites from the surrounding pagan nations. God is holy, void of sin, and requires his people to act accordingly (e.g., Lev 11:44-45; 20:26). Apparently, some of the false teachers at Colossae are requiring the church to keep these national particulars of the Mosaic law.

FIGURE 15.7. JERICHO SYNAGOGUE MOSAIC

Paul responds vigorously to this errant teaching and labels these Jewish regulations as shadows: "These [Jewish laws] are a *shadow* of the things that were to come" (Col 2:17a). These Jewish rules, often expressed in the synagogue, are not an end in and of themselves. They typologically point beyond themselves and expect something greater and permanent.

Paul discloses the very object to which these laws pointed: "the reality, however, is found in *Christ*" (2:17b). These Jewish rules that were being required by the false teachers find their fulfillment in Christ—nothing more, nothing less. Now that Christ has come, why are they continuing to embrace old shadows (cf. Heb 10:1)?

The second characteristic of the false teaching is much more difficult to ascertain: "Let no one keep defrauding you of your prize by delighting in self-abasement and the worship of the angels, *taking his stand on visions* he has seen" (2:18 NASB). The key phrase "taking his stand on visions he has seen" is better translated as "which things he has seen [visions of angels] when entering into the innermost sanctuary." Inscriptions near Colossae use the same Greek word for "entering" to refer to entering into a god's temple. For example, one reads, "There came in order to seek a revelation from the gods—Crispus Tryphone and Poplius Pupius Callacles, who underwent an initiation and *walked within the inner holy place*."[13] The false teachers, then, encouraged church members at Colossae to experience God's glorious presence in a new and more intimate way. This explains why Paul dedicates so much attention in this epistle to God's end-time temple in Christ (Col 1:9-10, 19; 2:9-10). The Colossians must condemn this false teaching and understand that all the divine fullness they need dwells in Christ and their union with him. Believers must patiently wait until they are transformed into their resurrected bodies in the new heavens and earth to experience a heightened, consummate state of God's presence.

The main point of Colossians 2:16-23 falls here in 2:18: "Do not let anyone . . . disqualify you." The verb *disqualify* carries with it the sense of condemning or judging. Paul forbids the Colossians from being in a position of

[13]Boring, Berger, and Colpe, *Hellenistic Commentary to the New Testament*, 485-86.

subordination to these false teachers and thus being judged by them. The criteria (i.e., the false teaching) that these teachers used to condemn the church are utterly baseless. Verses 22-23 explain why the church should not fear coming under judgment of the false teachers:

> These rules, which have to do with things that *are all destined to perish* with use, are *based on merely human commands and teachings*. Such regulations indeed have an appearance of wisdom, with their self-imposed worship, their *false humility* and their harsh treatment of the body, but *they lack any value in restraining sensual indulgence*.

Paul exposes the false teaching for what it is: the result of human invention and devoid of Christ and the gospel.

LIFE AS RESURRECTED BEINGS (3:1–4:1)

After confronting the Colossian heresy, Paul unveils the key motivation for Christian living: the spiritual resurrection of the saints. The resurrection not only imparts new life to believers but also serves as the basis for Christian ethics. A guiding principle to this section is found in Colossians 3:14: "And over all these virtues put on love, which binds them all together in perfect unity." Unity between all personal relationships (3:18–4:1) is the climax of this chapter and the entire book. It can be achieved only by identifying with the risen Christ.

Believers' identification with the risen Christ (3:1-11). Paul views the resurrection as already begun in the lives of believers. Christian ethics rest firmly on the believers' resurrected status. Note Colossians 3:1-2: "Since, then, *you have been raised with Christ*, set your hearts on things above, where Christ is, seated at the right hand of God. *Set your minds on things above, not on earthly things.*" Believers must view all of reality through their heavenly position in Christ. Although believers still wrestle with indwelling sin, they enjoy an inaugurated resurrected status with the risen Christ.

Colossians 3:5-11 is the natural implication of believers' current and future resurrected status: "Put to death, therefore, whatever belongs to your earthly nature: sexual immorality, impurity, lust, evil desires and greed, which is idolatry" (3:5). In typical fashion, Paul refrains from naming every single sin under the sun but simply mentions a few representative sins (cf. Gal 5:19-20). The imperative in Colossians 3:9a receives quite a bit of emphasis in this section: "*Do not lie to each other*." The church must resist all forms of false doctrine and refrain from promulgating it.

The last portion of 3:9-10 details why the Colossians must not lie to one another: "Do not lie to each other, *since you have taken off your old self* with its practices and *have put on the new self*, which is being renewed in knowledge in the image of its Creator." The wording reads literally: "Do not lie to one another, because you have taken off *the old man* . . . and have put on *the new man*." English translations render this wording of man as *self*. Unfortunately, the translations miss a crucial biblical-theological link. Paul's wording reflects believers' identity as fashioned in the image of Christ, the last Adam or new man (1 Cor 15:45).[14] Paul often expresses the same redemptive-historical conviction in his

[14]Thomas R. Schreiner, *New Testament Theology: Magnifying God in Christ* (Grand Rapids: Baker, 2008), 308.

writings—namely, every individual is either in union with the first Adam or the last Adam (Rom 5:18; 1 Cor 15:22).

In Colossians 3:11, Paul lists a concrete example of how they are to live in light of their new identity: "Here there is no Gentile or Jew, circumcised or uncircumcised, barbarian, Scythian, slave or free, but Christ is all, and is in all."

Living in light of believers' resurrection (3:12–4:1). The last half of Colossians 3 details how the resurrection life in Christ operates within the church. As is typical of Paul, he moves from the indicative (believers' union with Christ) into the imperative (how believers are to function now that they have been united to Christ). The second half of chapter 3 continues the imperative of the Christian life.

> ***An effect of resurrection life is the complete equality between all members of humanity: all are equally in the renewed image of God. Life in the first Adam is characterized by division and fracture, whereas life according to the last Adam is genuine unity.***

The beginning of verse 12 is crucial to the entire section of 3:12-17: "Therefore, as God's chosen people, holy and dearly loved, clothe yourselves with compassion, kindness, humility, gentleness and patience." Paul anchors the command to "put on" in the Colossians' status "as God's chosen people." This expression is reminiscent of 1 Peter 2:9: "But you are a *chosen people*, a royal priesthood, a *holy* nation." Interestingly, in the immediate context of 1 Peter 2:9, Peter alludes to an Old Testament text that establishes Israel's status and mission at Sinai before God: "Now if you obey me fully and keep my covenant, then out of all nations you will be my treasured possession. Although the whole earth is mine, you will be for me *a kingdom of priests and a holy nation*" (Ex 19:5-6). This Old Testament text and others like it remind the Israelites of their commission to be a godly community that evangelizes the surrounding nations so that the entire earth will be filled with God's glory (cf. Gen 1:26-28; Ps 8). This commission is originally given to Adam and Eve, but they fail. It was then handed down to the patriarchs and Israel, but they, like the original couple, fail. Jesus, as the last Adam and true Israel, obeys where his predecessors fail. He subdues God's enemies, begins the process of building a godly community, and initiates the descent of God's glory on the earth.

All believers who identify with Christ through faith participate in God's end-time people group (i.e., true Israel). As the end-time people of God, the Colossians can rightly be called "chosen . . . holy and dearly beloved" (3:12). The same Christ who spiritually resurrects this community also forms them into the end-time covenant community.

Colossians 3:14-15 is wonderfully important to this section, as Paul gets to the core issue at stake: "And over all these virtues put on love, which binds them all together in perfect unity. Let the peace of Christ rule in your hearts, since as members of one body you were called to peace." Love is the key

FIGURE 15.8. MOSES AND ISRAEL ON MOUNT SINAI

characteristic of Christian conduct within the covenant community (cf. Mk 12:31; Rom 13:9). But love is a means to an end in this context. The purpose of love between people groups, families, and all other communities is perfect unity, which can be achieved and maintained only if all parties earnestly love one another in Christ.

The next section (3:18-21) is commonly referred to as the "household codes" and is nearly identical to those found in Ephesians 5:22–6:9. Many scholars believe that these codes stem from the wider Greco-Roman world, wherein codes were given concerning the relationship between husband and wife, master and slave, and fathers and children. Paul adopts the household codes and tethers them to Christ and the gospel. Indeed, Christ (or "Lord" or "Master") is mentioned seven times in 3:18-4:1 of the household code. In Colossians 3:1, Paul rehearses believers' identification with Christ, the last Adam, and 3:10 also mentions that believers participate in the last Adam's image ("you have put on the new man"). Immediately following both of these new creational indicatives stand two sets of new creational imperatives (3:2-9, 11-17). The household codes in 3:18–4:1, then, are the functional outworking of the Colossians existing in the image of the last Adam.

The codes progress from the relationship between husband and wife, to children and their parents, and then to slaves and masters:

> *Wives*, submit yourselves to your husbands, as is fitting in the Lord. *Husbands*, love your wives and do not be harsh with them. *Children*, obey your parents in everything, for this pleases the Lord. *Fathers*, do not embitter your children, or they will become discouraged. *Slaves*, obey your earthly masters in everything. (Col 3:18-22)

GOSPEL PROCLAMATION AND THE LETTER CLOSING (4:2-18)

Paul urgently requests that God affords him an opportunity to spread the gospel (Col 4:2-6) and then relates several personal requests (4:7-17). He finishes this letter intent on reminding the Colossians how much he and his friends love and care for them. They are to take comfort knowing that Paul's words, as contained in this epistle, are meant for their spiritual health.

Paul's request for evangelism (4:2-6). Following the household codes, the apostle turns his attention once more to conduct within the covenant community, this time with an eye on their vertical relationship with God: "Devote yourselves to prayer, being watchful and thankful" (Col 4:2). Paul asks the Colossian congregation to pray earnestly for their own lives and his (4:2). Specifically, when the Colossians pray for Paul, they are to ask that God would "open a door for [the gospel] message" (v. 3a). This will supply Paul the opportunity to "proclaim the mystery of Christ." Here the mystery of Christ appears to be synonymous with the gospel, the "word" or "message." Paul pleads with the Colossians that they pray for the proclamation of the disclosed mystery that includes the gospel going to Gentiles, a message that precludes the Gentiles obeying the national particulars of the old covenant.

FIGURE 15.9. ST. MARK AND ST. LUKE

Personal requests and the letter closing (4:7-18). After finishing the body of the letter (Col 4:6), Paul begins the formal closing section. Two individuals will accompany the epistle to the church at Colossae—Tychicus and Onesimus. Although we are unsure as to whether these two are the epistle's official letter couriers, it seems likely that this is the case.

According to Colossians 4:7-8, Tychicus and Onesimus will perform two duties: (1) inform the Colossians of Paul's Roman imprisonment and (2) encourage the hearts of the Colossians. This probably entails worshiping with the church and also some form of teaching and exhortation. This latter component is crucial for a variety of reasons. Paul's letter couriers must explain and perhaps supplement the epistle, since that was part of the typical function of both Jewish and Greco-Roman letter carriers. Tychicus and Onesimus are no doubt familiar with its contents by the time they are sent to the church. Although there are no formal quotations of the Old Testament, the book is rich with Old Testament allusions and concepts. The Gentiles at Colossae grasp varying degrees of Old Testament knowledge; some would understand most if not all of the Old Testament allusions. Others, however, might not have been able to perceive Paul's subtle references. The letter couriers could fill this gap and inform the members of what Old Testament texts and concepts Paul has in mind.

In Colossians 4:10-11, Paul highlights three key individuals who are presently with him in Rome:

> My fellow prisoner *Aristarchus* sends you his greetings, as does *Mark*, the cousin of Barnabas. (You have received instructions about him; if he comes to you, welcome

> him.) *Jesus, who is called Justus,* also sends greetings. These are the only Jews among my co-workers for the kingdom of God, and they have proved a comfort to me.

Aristarchus is described as Paul's "fellow prisoner." The second prominent individual named is Mark, who writes a Gospel bearing his name (see Acts 12:25; 13:4-12; Philem 24; 2 Tim 4:11; 1 Pet 5:13).

Epaphras, the founder of the church in Colossae, sends his greetings back to the church. Paul and his coworkers learned about the Colossians and the false teaching from Epaphras (1:4). Apparently, Epaphras does not embark on the journey back to Colossae from Rome. Mark is not the only person in Rome who will write a gospel on the life of Jesus. Luke is also with Paul and his coworkers. Paul only describes Luke as "the doctor" (4:14). When Paul is once again imprisoned in Rome, Luke stays by his side. Taken together, Mark, Luke, and Paul will write a considerable amount of the literature in the New Testament. Their theology is the result of years of ministry, personal interaction, and hardship.

PHILEMON

AUTHORSHIP

The epistle claims to have been written by Paul (v. 1), and the early church affirmed it.[15] The Muratorian Canon, for example, says, "He [the apostle Paul] wrote, besides these, one to Philemon, and one to Titus, and two to Timothy." A few, however, doubt Pauline authorship because of the letter's narrow purpose and brief remarks. Yet nothing internally or externally overthrows the traditional view that Paul wrote this letter.

DATE

Since the epistle is closely tied to the epistle to the Colossians, the book of Philemon was probably written at the same time and from the same place. Some locate the provenance at Ephesus (AD 55–56), Caesarea (AD 57–59; Acts 23:23–26:32), or Rome (AD 60–62; Acts 28:14-31). It is most probable, however, that Paul wrote Colossians/Philemon at Rome in the early 60s, as we concluded above (see discussion on Colossians).

RELATIONSHIP TO COLOSSIANS

It seems Colossians and Philemon are written from the same location and at approximately the same time. Both epistles claim to have been written from prison. In Colossians, Paul sends greetings from Aristarchus, Mark, Epaphras, Luke, Demas, and Justus (Col 4:10-14) and has Tychicus and Onesimus deliver the letter to the church (Col 4:7, 9). Philemon also mentions the greetings from Aristarchus, Mark, Epaphras, Luke, and Demas (v. 23). Onesimus and Archippus are also mentioned in Philemon (vv. 2, 10-16). In addition, Onesimus (Col 4:9) and probably Philemon were residents of Colossae.

[15]This section is an adaptation from Benjamin L. Gladd, "Philemon," in *A Biblical-Theological Introduction to the New Testament: The Gospel Realized*, ed. Michael J. Kruger (Wheaton, IL: Crossway, 2016), 401-10.

OCCASION

Scholars have traditionally maintained that Onesimus, a slave of Philemon, flees for an unknown reason. One view argues that perhaps Onesimus had robbed his master (v. 18). Coincidentally, Philemon meets Paul in Rome and embraces the gospel (v. 10). Fortunately for Onesimus, Paul already knows Philemon. As it turns out, Onesimus becomes a great asset for Paul's ministry, so the apostle writes to Philemon, the owner of Onesimus, to be reconciled with the slave. Once Philemon frees his servant Onesimus, he is able to return to Paul and assist him further. This long-standing view suffers from a few problems: How does Philemon encounter Paul in Rome, who is under house arrest? In addition, what are the chances that Paul already knew Philemon?

Another view is that Onesimus came to know Paul (or, at least, learned about him) through Philemon or the house church at Colossae. Onesimus therefore decides to flee from his master (perhaps he stole or mismanaged funds?), seeking to find a safe haven in Rome. He purposefully travels to Rome and visits the famed Paul. Onesimus is converted while in Rome (v. 10) and attempts to reconcile with Philemon through Paul. The advantage of this view is that it makes better sense of how Onesimus met Paul. Instead of happenstance, this meeting was thoroughly intentional. At the end of the day, it makes little interpretative difference how Paul and Onesimus met. What remains crucial is the conversion of Onesimus and Paul's desire for him to be reconciled with his master.

PURPOSE

Paul writes this brief letter to reconcile Onesimus and Philemon. Philemon ought to welcome his slave, Onesimus, not merely as a slave but much more as a brother in Christ. In addition, Paul wishes that Philemon return Onesimus to Paul so that they may continue to reap a great harvest of ministry in Rome.

OUTLINE

I. Letter Opening (1-3)
II. Thanksgiving (4-7)
III. Paul's Request for Onesimus (8-21)
IV. Letter Closing (22-25)

LETTER OPENING (1-3)

The letter contains the usual features (the opening, thanksgiving, body, closing). Despite the letter's brief length and "narrow" purpose, the epistle is still coauthored by Timothy. Philemon, though, is not the only intended recipient, for Paul also lists Apphia, Archippus, and the house church. Paul calls Philemon a "dear friend and fellow." We are not exactly sure how Paul came to know Philemon (Paul did not found the church in Colossae; Epaphras did).

Verse 1 explains that Philemon is the addressee of the letter, while verse 2 adds Apphia, Archippus, and the house church ("the church that meets in your [Philemon's] home"). By expanding his audience, we can probably conclude that Paul intends for his teachings, or at least the principles, contained within this brief letter to apply to the Christians within the region at Colossae. The epistle to the Colossians is primarily directed toward those house churches in Colossae, yet the letter to the Colossians is to be circulated to the church at Laodicea: "After this letter [the epistle to the Colossians] has been read to you, see that it is also read in the church of the Laodiceans and that you in turn read the letter from Laodicea" (Col 4:16). Although brief, this verse gives us some insight into how Paul's letters circulated within the early church and his desire for them to do so (cf. 1 Cor 1:2). The upshot is that Paul's letter to Philemon (and his other epistles) contains a wider intended audience, whereby an apostle communicates God's timeless truth to the church (cf. v. 8).

THANKSGIVING (4-7)

In typical fashion, Paul progresses from the opening of the letter to the thanksgiving section. As usual, he tells us why he is thankful for Philemon: "I hear about your love for all his holy people and your faith in the Lord Jesus" (v. 5). Apparently, Philemon has fully embraced the gospel and is manifesting his faith by refreshing the hearts of the saints (v. 7) and loving the Lord's people (v. 5). This was probably demonstrated by Philemon's care for the local congregation. We should also note that the church in Colossae meets in Philemon's house (v. 2; cf. 1 Cor 16:17-18; 2 Cor 7:13).

PAUL'S REQUEST FOR ONESIMUS (8-21)

Paul could, because of his apostolic authority, command Philemon to be reconciled with Onesimus and send him back to Rome (v. 8). Instead, he appeals to Philemon out of love (v. 9). Paul even gives a personal tidbit in further describing himself: "Paul—an old man and now also a prisoner of Christ Jesus" (v. 9). There may even be a tinge of sympathy here that Paul seeks to invoke. When Onesimus arrives in Rome, apparently the two soon become friends. Paul goes on to comment how he became "his son"—a strong term of endearment that most likely entails his conversion. Paul also uses this label for Timothy (1 Cor 4:17; 1 Tim 1:2, 18; 2 Tim 1:2; 2:1). It would have been easy for Paul to

FIGURE 15.10. LAODICEA ON THE LYCUS

claim that Onesimus is only useful to him; instead, Paul says that he is now useful to both Philemon and him (v. 11).

Paul sends Onesimus, his "very heart" (v. 12), back to Philemon, although Paul would rather he stayed in Rome (v. 13). But before Paul makes any decisions involving Onesimus, he requires Philemon's blessing. The apostle deeply desires Philemon to act on his own accord: "I did not want to do anything without your consent, so that any favor you do would not seem forced but would be voluntary" (v. 14). Paul explains that perhaps the reason why God intended Onesimus to flee from his master is to give him the opportunity to meet Paul and embrace the gospel (v. 15). Now, although he is still a slave, Onesimus is a brother in Christ. It simply will not do to continue to treat Onesimus strictly as a slave: "no longer as a slave, but better than a slave, as a dear brother. He is very dear to me but even dearer to you, both as a fellow man and as a brother in the Lord" (v. 16). Murray Harris rightly gets at the heart of the matter: "Here is Paul, a highly educated Roman citizen, pleading the cause of a runaway slave whose life was potentially forfeit because of his flight and theft. This indicates that Paul believed that the same brotherly love that would be shown to a free person should be expressed to a slave."[16] Philemon is a participant in God's end-time community, and he must treat Onesimus accordingly.

FIGURE 15.11. MOSAIC OF ROMAN SLAVES

Building off his previous argument, Paul asks Philemon to welcome Onesimus as he would Paul himself (v. 17). Verse 18 may give us a little insight into what was causing the rift between Philemon and Onesimus: "If he has done you any wrong or owes you anything, charge it to me." It seems as though there is some sort of financial loss or mismanagement of funds by Onesimus. Paul therefore promises to repay the debt. Notice here the reference to Paul taking over where the secretary leaves off: "I, Paul, am writing this with my own hand" (v. 19; cf. 1 Cor 16:21; Gal 6:11; Col 4:18; 2 Thess 3:17). It is not clear what Paul means when he claims that Philemon owes Paul his "very self" (v. 19). Perhaps Paul's ministry directly or indirectly led to Philemon's conversion.

Paul then comments, "I do wish, brother, that I may have some benefit from you in the Lord; refresh my heart in Christ. Confident of your obedience, I write to you, knowing that you will do even more than I ask" (vv. 20-21). If we read between the lines, it seems Paul wants Philemon not only to be reconciled with Onesimus but also to send Onesimus back to Rome for Paul's benefit (see v. 14). Paul asks that Philemon refresh his heart in the same way that he refreshed the hearts of the Lord's people in verse 7.

[16]Murray Harris, *Slave of Christ: A New Testament Metaphor for Total Devotion to Christ*, NSBT 8 (Downers Grove, IL: InterVarsity Press, 1999), 58.

LETTER CLOSING (22-25)

Paul's first Roman imprisonment affords him a considerable amount of flexibility. In Acts 28:16-31 Paul is under house arrest as he conducts a substantial amount of ministry. There he ministers to a number of people and publishes several letters. The last two verses of Acts explain, "For two whole years Paul stayed there in his own rented house and welcomed all who came to see him. He proclaimed the kingdom of God and taught about the Lord Jesus Christ—with all boldness and without hindrance!" (Acts 28:30-31).

In the letter's closing, Paul asks that Philemon prepare a guest room since he plans on visiting Colossae once he is released from Rome (v. 22). Since Paul is held wrongfully under house arrest, he expects that justice will prevail and he will be released. Epaphras, the individual who started the church Paul addresses in Colossians (Col 1:7), sends his greetings to Philemon and his house church.

Recall that Paul and his coworkers probably learned about the Colossian heresy from Epaphras (1:4). Epaphras's devotion to Paul's ministry is unwavering, as he will stay with Paul in Rome. Epaphras is not only dedicated to Paul but remains steadfastly committed to the Colossian congregation:

> Epaphras, who is one of you and a servant of Christ Jesus, sends greetings. He is always wrestling in prayer for you, that you may stand firm in all the will of God, mature and fully assured. I vouch for him that he is working hard for you and for those at Laodicea and Hierapolis. (Col 4:12-13)

A person named Demas is also mentioned, but nothing more is said. Paul will, however, reference him at the end of his career when he is once again imprisoned: "for Demas, because he loved this world, has deserted me and has gone to Thessalonica. Crescens has gone to Galatia, and Titus to Dalmatia" (2 Tim 4:10). If this is the same individual, then Demas, although at one time committed to the gospel, abandons his comrades and heads for Jerusalem.

Two other important figures, Mark and Luke, send their greetings. This is not the only time Paul mentions his close association with them (see Col 4:10, 14; 2 Tim 4:11). This is the same Mark that writes the Gospel of Mark. If we date this epistle to the early 60s, then Mark's Gospel has already been published or will be soon. We first meet him at the beginning of Paul's "first missionary journey." After ministering to the Jerusalem church, Paul, Barnabas, and Titus bring Mark (also known as John Mark) with them back to Antioch (Acts 12:25; 13:2-3). In Cyprus, Paul, Barnabas, and John Mark enjoy a fruitful ministry and appear to convert the proconsul Sergius Paulus (13:4-12). Paul and Barnabas head north, evangelizing the southern portion of Galatia (Acts 13:14–14:23). Upon arriving in Perga, John Mark, for an unknown reason, abandons his comrades and heads for Jerusalem.

Later on, however, Mark reconciles with Paul. The book of Acts never mentions this reconciliation between the two, but it can be inferred from Paul's letters (Col 4:10; Philem 24, 2 Tim 4:11). Mark not only becomes a traveling companion of Paul but also befriends the apostle Peter (1 Pet 5:13). The point is that Mark and Paul did not always get along, but in the end they worked through their issues and became key players in the expansion of the early church. This principle of reconciliation that Paul and Mark demonstrate must be brought to bear on the strained relationship between Philemon and Onesimus.

1 AND 2 THESSALONIANS

1 THESSALONIANS

AUTHORSHIP

The author of 1 Thessalonians explicitly refers to himself as Paul (1:1), and the letter contains a number of historical references to Paul's career (2:1–3:6).[1] The early church (Tertullian, *Res.* 24; Origen, *A Letter from Origen to Africanus* 9) and the majority of contemporary scholars affirm Pauline authorship, so we have no reason to doubt that the letter is written by the apostle Paul.

DATE

Paul establishes a church at Thessalonica around AD 49 or 50 during his second missionary journey (Acts 17:1-9). Unbelieving Jews instigate some Gentiles to rally against the apostles, so Paul flees to Berea, where many of the Jews in the synagogue and other Gentiles in the city respond positively to the gospel. The antagonistic Jews of Thessalonica hear about his success in Berea and travel there, stirring up animosity against Paul (Acts 17:10-15). Paul then leaves Berea for Athens (Acts 17:16-34).

While in Athens, Paul sends Timothy to determine the welfare of the church, and Timothy returns with a positive report (1 Thess 3:1-9). Leaving Athens, Paul ventures to Corinth, where his proclamation of the gospel prompts Jewish opposition once again (Acts 18:1-17). This time, some Jews brought Paul before Gallio, the Roman proconsul, on trumped-up charges. Gallio's time in office lasts from July 51 to June 52, and we can assume that Paul's year-and-a-half residence in Corinth overlaps with Gallio's tenure (although the Roman proconsul may have entered office a year or so earlier). Paul probably wrote both letters to the Thessalonians while staying in Corinth in AD 50 or 51.

OCCASION

Unbelieving Jews at Thessalonica consider Paul a false prophet who blasphemes God by calling Jesus, a crucified criminal, the Messiah. Acts 17:5 states that Thessalonian Jews become enraged after a large number of Jewish proselytes (Gentiles who converted to Judaism) believe Paul's message in the synagogue. If Paul's integrity were questioned by the new Christian flock, their young faith would begin to flounder. So, Paul responds to these false accusations that attempt to undermine his authority and ministry by

[1]This chapter is an adaptation of G. K. Beale, *1–2 Thessalonians*, IVPNTC (Downers Grove, IL: InterVarsity Press, 2003).

writing 1 Thessalonians (2:1-12). A spate of other problems also emerge within the church of Thessalonica that need addressing: discouragement due to severe trials (3:3-5), laxness in sexual morality (4:2-8), confusion over the relationship of deceased Christians to Christ's final coming (4:13-18), and an overemphasis on the second coming of Christ (5:1-11).

PURPOSE

Paul composes 1 Thessalonians to confront several issues at the church in Thessalonica. Above all, the Thessalonians must persevere in their faith in Christ despite harsh persecution from the hands of the local Jewish community.

OUTLINE

- I. Letter Opening (1:1)
- II. Thanksgiving and an Example of Effective Witness (1:2-10)
  - A. Thanksgiving Arises from Prayer, Christian Living, and Election (1:2-5)
  - B. Faithfulness in the Midst of Suffering (1:6-10)
- III. Paul's Faithful Proclamation of the Gospel in Thessalonica (2:1–3:13)
  - A. Paul's Endurance in the Midst of Hardship (2:1-20)
  - B. Thessalonian Endurance in the Midst of Hardship (3:1-13)
- IV. Living to Please God (4:1-18)
  - A. Avoiding Sexual Sin, Loving One Another, and Leading a Quiet Life (4:1-12)
  - B. The Nature of Christ's Second Coming (4:13-18)
- V. Living in Light of the Day of the Lord (5:1-24)
  - A. The Timing of the Day of the Lord (5:1-11)
  - B. Blameless at Christ's Coming (5:12-24)
- VI. Letter Closing (5:25-28)

FIGURE 16.1. THESSALONIKI, GREECE

BIBLICAL-THEOLOGICAL THEMES

In recent decades, many have been enamored with eschatology and, in particular, an event known as the rapture. According to this popular view, the church is suddenly and secretly raptured or caught up to heaven immediately preceding the seven-year tribulation on earth. Central to this view is 1 Thessalonians 4:16-17: "*The Lord himself will come down* from heaven, . . . and the dead in Christ will rise first. After that, *we who are still alive* and are left *will be caught up together with them in the clouds* to meet the Lord in the air." Accordingly, some interpret this passage in chapter 4 as a secret coming of Christ to rapture believers, and they argue that then 1 Thessalonians 5:1-11 follows chronologically, referring to Christ's final coming to judge and redeem those believers still left on earth, who came to faith after the "rapture." But this line of interpretation is problematic: chapter 4 parallels the following section in 5:1-11 and does not follow it chronologically. Paul narrates the resurrection at the end of the age in 4:14-18 and then rehearses it once more in 5:1-11. Why outline the same event

FIGURE 16.2. JOSEPH RECEIVES HIS FATHER AND BROTHERS

twice? The first passage concerns Jesus' second coming and how the resurrection of *believers* will take place, whereas the second passage (5:1-11) concerns God's impending judgment on *unbelievers* (cf. Acts 24:15). The same event is in mind in both passages, but Paul presents the second coming of Christ from two different angles. The entire discourse of 4:16–5:7 is built on the basic structure of Matthew 24. Paul interprets the whole of Matthew 24 as referring to judgment preceding the final coming of Christ.

The saints' resurrection at the very end of the age is part of a larger band of texts that mention the vindication of God's people (1 Cor 15:52; Rev 20:12-15; 21:1-4). Throughout the Bible, the cloud refers to the theophanic presence of God (or Christ) with his people (Ex 13:21-22; Num 14:14; Deut 1:33; Ps 78:14; Dan 7:13; Mt 17:5; 24:30; Mk 9:7; Acts 1:9). The significance of the church ascending to heaven in a cloud symbolizes its vindication and acceptance by God. Just as God vindicates his Son at the resurrection and ascension on a cloud (Acts 1:9-11), so Christ will vindicate his people in a similar way. As Tremper Longman and Daniel Reid explain, "The picture is that of the Lord coming to earth as the cloud-riding warrior. Like those who welcome the arrival of a deliverer to a city held under siege, the saints are taken up, not to depart to heaven, but—it seems—to meet him and escort him on his victorious 'march' to earth."[2]

First Thessalonians 4:16-17 does not teach a secret rapture of the church but the ultimate vindication of the saints by their physical resurrection at Christ's second coming. The Thessalonians are being persecuted for holding fast to and worshiping the risen Christ (1:6; 2:14). Christ's return and the promise of their future physical resurrection reassures them to persevere in their faith. Believers are to remind one another of the second coming of Christ and their final inheritance of the new creation at the resurrection (4:18).

LETTER OPENING (1:1)

Paul warmly greets the church and includes Silas and Timothy. These two individuals are his fellow workers in the ministry and perhaps his secretaries (see Rom 16:22; 1 Pet 5:12). Both Silas and Timothy accompany Paul in his travels and preach alongside him (2 Cor 1:19; Acts 15:40–20:2).

[2]Tremper Longman III and Daniel G. Reid, *God Is a Warrior*, SOTBT (Grand Rapids: Zondervan, 1995), 173-74.

THANKSGIVING AND AN EXAMPLE OF EFFECTIVE WITNESS (1:2-10)

Paul thanks God for the readers because he recognizes that they are marked with the genuine characteristics of God's end-time people. This is Paul's only letter in which the introductory thanksgiving is not limited to the opening paragraph but covers the span of the first three chapters. His opening thanksgiving extends from 1:2 to 2:12 and is picked up again in 2:13 and 3:9. Paul's thanksgiving assures Christians of the reality of their faith and his genuine apostleship. He gives thanks for the evidence of their sincere Christian experience (1:2-3) and election in Christ (1:4-5). Paul then urges them to reflect on his own apostolic calling and genuine faith that were demonstrated among them not long ago (1:5).

Although suffering is part of a fallen world, 1:6-10 explains that hardship is not accidental. An intended result of imitating the suffering of Christ and the apostles is the spread of the gospel among unbelievers. The Old Testament documents examples of individuals experiencing great affliction that outwardly seemed inexplicable. Only afterward was such suffering understood to be part of God's larger plan of redemption. One such example is Joseph's unjust treatment at the hands of his brothers and the Egyptians. Following the death of his father and the repentance of his brothers, Joseph solemnly declares, "You intended to harm me, but God intended it for good to accomplish what is now being done, the saving of many lives" (Gen 50:20; see fig. 16.2). Little did Joseph know at the time of his betrayal in Genesis 37 that God would use such an atrocity to spare the lives of thousands from all the surrounding nations. In the same way, the Thessalonians' perseverance in the face of affliction led to the promulgation of the gospel in the provinces of Macedonia and Achaia (1 Thess 1:8).

Thanksgiving arises from prayer, Christian living, and election (1:2-5). Paul gives thanks to God because of what he recalls about the Thessalonians (1:2). The characteristics marking the Thessalonians as God's true people are their "work produced by faith," "labor prompted by love," and "endurance inspired by hope" (1:3). True faith persists even through difficult trials because of the end-time hope in Christ's future coming at the very end of history. According to 1 Thessalonians 1:4-5, God, deserving all thanks, is the one who elects and ultimately inspires good works in people.

Faithfulness in the midst of suffering (1:6-10). The Thessalonians imitated the pattern of faithful living that Christ and the apostles set forth (1:6). Paul mentions the apostles first because the Thessalonians had first become attracted to them as imitators of Christ. Through these apostles, the church then imitated the risen Christ. The Thessalonians are especially influenced by how Paul reacts to suffering with faith and joy, resulting in an effective witness to others (cf. 2 Cor 4:7-16; Col 1:24). The whole Thessalonian church is faithful in proclaiming the gospel, so much so that the gospel expands throughout the surrounding territory (1 Thess 1:8).

The majority of believers in Thessalonica are Gentiles who previously worshiped in the local pagan temple. But when Paul shared the gospel with them, they abandoned their idols and clung to the crucified Christ. In contrast to their former loyalty to pagan idols, the Thessalonians now serve the "living and true God" (1:9). Behind idols lie demons who deceive individuals, causing spiritual harm and division (see Deut 32:15-18; 1 Cor 10:19-21). Paul's language here recalls Jeremiah 10:10: "But the Lord is the *true God*; he is the *living God*." The context of Jeremiah 10 is a tirade against idolatry. The authority of the Old Testament carries over to the New Testament. The church, the continuation of the true Israel to whom Jeremiah spoke, is to turn from the idols of this world and to serve God wholly and truthfully.

FIGURE 16.3. JEREMIAH LAMENTING ISRAEL'S SIN

PAUL'S FAITHFUL PROCLAMATION OF THE GOSPEL IN THESSALONICA (2:1–3:13)

Chapter 2 focuses on Paul's intimate relationship with the Thessalonians and his desire to see them once more. Despite "strong opposition," the apostle shares with the church the good news of Christ (2:2). Paul and his coworkers stood faithful and blameless in their conduct during their original stint at Thessalonica (2:7-10), so he remains concerned that they press on in their faith despite great adversity. As the churches in Judea were persecuted by the Jews, so too is the church at Thessalonica (2:14-16). Old Testament prophets were often on the receiving end of suffering, even at the hands of their own countrymen. Jeremiah, for example, was beaten and tossed into a cistern for prophesying against the Israelites (Jer 38:1-6). Jesus directs the parable of the wicked tenants toward the Jewish leaders for repeatedly persecuting Israel's prophets, culminating in Jesus' own death (Mt 21:33-46; Mk 12:1-12; Lk 20:9-19). In the same way, some within the unbelieving Jewish community are antagonistic toward the Thessalonians. As a result of such horrendous atrocities that the Jewish people committed against the Thessalonian church, the apostles, and ultimately Christ, God pours out his wrath on the theocratic nation of Israel (1 Thess 2:16).

Paul's endurance in the midst of hardship (2:1-20). Paul explains what kind of motives Christians should possess to remain holy and become effective witnesses in a dark world. Desiring to please God and longing for others to please him result in a bold and effective witness (1 Thess 2:3-12). Paul's bold speech was the reason his visit to Thessalonica had not fallen on deaf ears. His boldness, despite strong opposition, made a lasting impact on his readers (2:1-2).

On two occasions, Paul underscores God's bearing witness to the faithfulness of his ministry (2:5, 10). Although the world condemns Paul's motives in its courtroom, God vindicates him in heaven. Armed with the knowledge that he is backed by divine approval,

Paul is robustly confident in his role as God's legal ambassador (cf. 2 Cor 2:17; 4:2; 12:19). His confidence resembles the Old Testament prophets before him, whose hearts were tested by God and who go forth boldly, knowing they possessed divine approval (Ps 17:3; 26:2; Jer 11:20; 12:3; 17:10).

In 1 Thessalonians 2:13-16, Paul compares the suffering of the Thessalonians with the persecution of the Jerusalem church: "For you . . . *became imitators of God's churches in Judea* . . . You suffered from your own people *the same things those churches suffered from the Jews*" (2:14). He continues his discussion about the rejection of the Messiah by the Jews, "who killed the Lord Jesus and the prophets and also drove us out. They displease God and are hostile to everyone in their effort to keep us from speaking to the Gentiles so that they may be saved. In this way they always *heap up their sins* to the limit. The wrath of God has come upon them at last" (2:15-16). The phrase "heaping up sins" occurs in the Old Testament as a description of God dealing with his enemies. In each case, the opponents of God complete a certain amount of sin before he considers them ripe for definitive judgment. Abraham's descendants do not emerge from Egypt until the sin of the Amorites is "filled up" (Gen 15:16; our translation). Similarly, Daniel 8:23-25 states that judgment will come at the end of the age when sins have been "filled up" (our translation; cf. Mt 23:31-38; Rom 9:18; 11:7-10, 25).

The wicked behavior of first-century Jews is part of a national pattern of past generations. Their rebellion climaxes in the persecution of Christ, Christian prophets,

FIGURE 16.4. DESTRUCTION OF THE JEWISH TEMPLE IN AD 70

and apostles and in the hindering of the preaching of the gospel to Gentiles. God judges Israel by forbidding the nation to herald the message of salvation to the Gentiles. But God's judgment in 1 Thessalonians 2:14-16 does not include the righteous remnant within the nation. Instead, divine judgment falls squarely on Israel's antagonistic leaders and others in the nation who are intractable in their unbelief and refuse the original divine commission to carry God's truth to the ends of the earth.

Thessalonian endurance in the midst of hardship (3:1-13). Paul wished to be reunited to the Thessalonians, yet Satan prevents this endeavor (1 Thess 2:18). But the apostle's desire to keep tabs on the church has not waned, so he sends Timothy to Thessalonica to "find out about [their] faith" in the midst of difficult circumstances (3:5; cf. Acts 17:14-15). Would the church abandon Christianity and return to their previous lifestyle of ease, worshiping other gods and enjoying a harmonious relationship with their community? When Timothy reports back, Paul discovers that the Thessalonians have indeed maintained their newly minted faith (1 Thess 3:6-7).

Paul outlines the theological rationale for the Thessalonians undergoing such difficulties: "For you know quite well that we are destined for them [difficulties]" (3:3). These trials are not random but are part of God's grand design. History will conclude with the establishment of God's kingdom and the world's resistance to it. According to Old Testament expectation, the prophets foretold that Israel will undergo severe testing in the latter days (e.g., Dan 7, 11–12; Ezek 38:4-13; Zech 14:2). God will eventually defeat Israel's persecutors, judge her compromisers, and bequeath an eternal kingdom to Israel. These end-time trials begin during Jesus' ministry and climax in his crucifixion. Those who follow Jesus in the present age, including the Thessalonians, identify with these same trials until he returns (see, e.g., Jn 16:33; Acts 14:22; Rom 5:3; 8:35).

Even though Paul endures persecution and hardships, it is well worth the price: "In all our distress and persecution we were encouraged about you because of your faith" (1 Thess 3:7). Paul's ministry is so tethered to the Thessalonians that they are his very reason for living. He asserts, "Now we *really* live, since you are standing firm" (3:8). But the church in Thessalonica must continue to press on in their dependence on the gospel and their love for one another (3:10-11). Paul remains concerned for their endurance and personal holiness when Christ returns to mete out judgment on the ungodly and fully restore the righteous in the new creation (3:11-13).

At the end of 1 Thessalonians 3:13 Paul writes, "May he strengthen your hearts . . . when our *Lord Jesus comes with all his holy ones*," which draws from Zechariah 14:5: "You will flee. . . . Then *the Lord my God will come, and all the holy ones with him*." Instead of Zechariah's "Lord my God," Paul substitutes "our Lord Jesus." Zechariah 14:5 is part of a larger prophetic description of the final judgment, through which Israel's enemy and God's own people must pass through (Zech 13:9; 14:16-19). Paul is not bashful about identifying the risen Christ with Israel's God. The Thessalonians' successfully passing the test of the last judgment forms the climax of chapter 3 as a whole and the entire letter up to this point.

LIVING TO PLEASE GOD (4:1-18)

Paul devotes the first half of chapter 4 to three aspects of living in the new age that Christ inaugurates—avoiding sexual immorality (4:3-8), loving one another (4:9-10), and leading a "quiet life" (4:11-12). All three of these exhortations emanate from the church's identity as the new covenant people of God and his promise to strengthen them (3:13). Many of the admonitions arise from the church's calling to be holy in a defiled world. Leviticus 11–16, for example, details God's command to purify the tabernacle from defilement caused by the illicit actions of Nadab and Abihu, Aaron's sons.[3] They "offered unauthorized fire before the LORD" (Lev 10:1), thus defining the sanctuary, so God commands Moses and Aaron to rid the tabernacle of all uncleanness. In the same way, the Thessalonians must actively pursue holy living since God dwells in their midst.

Avoiding sexual sin, loving one another, and leading a quiet life (4:1-12). Paul's audience primarily includes Gentiles (1 Thess 1:9), and he must often warn them to live a holy life and free from idolatry and sexual sin. They are to be holy, a word repeated three times in the immediate context. The Old Testament concept of holiness directly relates to a central part of the Old Testament story—God's desire to dwell with humanity in the new creation. Israel's landscape is broken down into three gradations: holy (the temple precinct), clean (Israel's territory), and unclean (beyond the boundaries of Israel). Israelites are prohibited from partaking of unclean food, since certain foods were associated with imperfection and idolatry (e.g., Lev 11:4-8, 13-20; 20:25). Gentiles, too, are considered unclean, so they are not permitted to join the covenant community unless they become clean by adhering to certain stipulations of the Torah, such as circumcision, celebration of feasts, and the offering of sacrifices. The Torah prescribes a multitude of cultic laws that remove, albeit temporarily and not perfectly, the taint of sin and defilement. As Michael Morales states, "Israelite worship was a cultic journey into YHWH's heavenly abode, a journey that entailed the blood of atonement and the fires of consecration, but one that also led to joyous communion and fellowship with God."[4] The atoning sacrificial death of Christ is the way in which unclean and defiled individuals can be considered not just clean but holy, resulting in their identity as the true temple of the Holy Spirit.

God dwells intimately with the congregation at Thessalonica, so its members must rid themselves of every defilement that inhibits God's glorious presence in their lives.

Although the Thessalonians are deemed holy, they must continue to rid themselves of all defilement of sin and rebellion. At the resurrection, believers will be utterly holy, able to dwell intimately with God in the new heavens and earth. In the present overlap of the ages, the Thessalonians must embrace

[3] L. Michael Morales, *Who Shall Ascend the Mountain of the Lord? A Biblical Theology of Leviticus* (Leicester, UK: Apollos; Downers Grove, IL: InterVarsity Press, 2015), 148-49.

[4] Morales, *Who Shall Ascend?*, 141.

FIGURE 16.5. EZEKIEL'S VISION OF ISRAEL'S RETURN AND RESURRECTION

a holy lifestyle by avoiding sexual immorality (4:3), lust (4:5), impurity (4:7), and not taking advantage of others (4:6). Christians must live in a state of harmony with one another in love and demonstrate that love to unbelievers (4:9-10).

The apostle then admonishes the church to "lead a quiet life" (4:11a). Elsewhere in the New Testament, living a quiet life either before a hostile world or in the presence of an unbelieving spouse encourages unbelievers to come to faith (1 Tim 2:1-4; 1 Pet 3:1-4). Paul also tells the Thessalonians to "mind your own business and work with your hands" (1 Thess 4:11b). The Thessalonians probably refrain from daily work because of a mistaken belief that Christ will return in the near future. Why work if Christ's return is right around the corner? Some of the lazy Thessalonians may even depend on the charity of hard-working church members.

The nature of Christ's second coming (4:13-18). The last half of chapter 4 confronts the tricky issue of the resurrection: "We do not want you to be uninformed *about those who sleep in death,* so that you do not grieve like the rest of mankind" (4:13). The Old Testament generally expects one final resurrection at the very end of history (e.g., Dan 12:1-2). So when Christ individually rose from the dead, without any other saints, confusion set in. Paul resolves this tension by affirming that Christ's resurrection is the "firstfruits of those who have fallen asleep" and that when he returns a second time, "those who belong to him" will then be raised (1 Cor 15:20, 23). False teachers may have arisen within the church at Thessalonica proclaiming that the final resurrection of the saints had already occurred on a spiritual level and that the peaceful and secure conditions of the new creation had arrived (1 Thess 5:3; see Is 11:6-9; 54:10-15; 60:17-22; 66:12-22). This false teaching developed over a misunderstanding of how the Old Testament prophecies are initially fulfilled in the latter days that began with the first coming of Christ.

The remainder of 1 Thessalonians 4:15-17 elaborates on further details about Jesus' second coming and how the resurrection of Christians will take place: Christ will come and first raise the dead believers and then transform those Christians who are still alive. Even Christians who are alive at his second coming will experience a resurrection. God will transform their old bodies and renew them in the same manner as those bodies lying in the grave (4:17).

According to 4:16, Christ will "*come* down from heaven." This Greek word for "coming" is probably better understood as "presence" in this verse. Downward physical motion from heaven to earth is not what Paul has in mind. Revelation 6:14 refers to the end of the cosmos in terms of a scroll that has been split and each of the two halves rolled up. The present physical reality will disappear and the formerly hidden heavenly dimension, where Christ and God now dwell, will be revealed (Rev 11:19; 19:11; 21:1-3).

Likewise, the resurrection of the dead should not be conceived as a physical rising upward from the grave but a transformation of an old-world body into a new creational body that can inhabit the new heavens and earth where God dwells in his fullness. N. T. Wright gets to the heart of the matter: "The promise is not that Jesus will simply reappear within the present world order, but that when heaven and earth are joined together in the new way God has promised, then he will appear to us—and we will appear to him, and to one another, in our own true identity."[5] The old, fallen body is like a cocoon that will wither away, and a new body will emerge that is suited for the new earth. The last phrase of 1 Thessalonians 4:17, "so we will be with the Lord forever" is the goal of God's work of resurrection in 4:14-17. Christ's resurrection leads to our resurrection, resulting in dwelling with the Lord forever in the new eternal cosmos.

LIVING IN LIGHT OF THE DAY OF THE LORD (5:1-24)

Paul equates Christ's return in 1 Thessalonians 4:13-18 with the "day of the Lord" in 5:1-11. These two passages describe an identical event, albeit from different vantage points. Paul confronts the pressing issue of whether one can pinpoint the precise timing of Christ's return. His answer is clear: the Thessalonians must understand that the day of the Lord will come like a thief in the night (5:2; see Mt 24:36, 42-43). The Old Testament, particularly the Prophets, explains that the day of the Lord will entail two broad realities—divine judgment and restoration.

Many Old Testament texts speak of God judging the nations (e.g., Is 19:16; Jer 46:10; Ezek 30:9), but according to Amos 5:18, God will even judge Israel: "Why do you [Israel] long for the *day of the Lord*? That day will be darkness, not light." Once God pours out his wrath, judgment eventually gives way to restoration. Zechariah 2:11 describes the restoration of Israel and the nations in the day of the Lord: "Many nations will be joined with the Lord *in that day* and will become my people. I will live among you and you will know that the Lord Almighty has sent me to you" (see, e.g., Is 2:2-4; 11:10; Amos 9:11; Mic 4:6-7).

> ***The old-world reality will be ripped away and the dimension of the new, eternal reality will appear along with Christ's presence.***

The apostle argues that the day of the Lord can arrive at any moment, so the church at Thessalonica must be "sober, putting on faith and love as a breastplate, and the hope of salvation as a helmet" (1 Thess 5:8). Beginning and ending with the topic of peace (5:13, 23), the last half of chapter 5 concerns the various ways in which the covenant community manifests peace.

[5] N. T. Wright, *Surprised by Hope: Rethinking Heaven, the Resurrection, and the Mission of the Church* (New York: HarperOne, 2008), 134-35.

The timing of the day of the Lord (5:1-11). We can subdivide the first half of the chapter (5:1-11) into three smaller units: the unexpected coming of the day of the Lord, when unbelievers will be judged (5:1-3); the preparedness of believers because of who they are in relation to God (5:4-7); and the faithfulness of God's people that springs from their election (5:8-11). The "day of the Lord" (5:1), a well-known phrase throughout the Bible, refers to God's judgment and defeat of his adversaries at the very end of history. God even judges those individuals who eternally identify with the covenant community but truly are not (e.g., Joel 2:31; Zeph 1:14-16). The day of the Lord also includes the deliverance of God's people (Obad 15–21; Zech 14). Where the Old Testament claims that Israel's God will judge and restore on that day, Paul asserts that Christ will fulfill this activity (1 Thess 4:16). The implication is clear: Christ's second coming is equivalent to the Lord's coming to judge and save in the Old Testament. What is true of Israel's Lord is true of Christ.

> ***Believers can be confident that their identity is coupled with the new heavens and earth, giving them the confidence to withstand intense persecution as they await Christ's return.***

Paul merges his thief metaphor with a picture of a woman writhing in birth pangs: "While people are saying, 'Peace and safety,' destruction will come on them suddenly, *as labor pains on a pregnant woman*, and they will not escape" (5:3). Those unprepared for a thief's visit, who believe they have peace and safety, will be surprised by Christ's coming.

The church must remain vigilant and self-controlled (1 Thess 5:6) because they are "children of the light and . . . do not belong to the night or to the darkness" (5:5). The contrast of darkness and light in the Old Testament recalls the light of the first creation breaking into the darkness of the world (Gen 1:1-5). Later on in the Old Testament, the language refers to the light of the new creation that will shine into the realm of the old, fallen world of darkness (Is 60:1-3, 19-20). The New Testament employs the light/darkness contrast to illustrate the inbreaking of the new creation through Jesus and his followers (Jn 1:1-5; Eph 4:22-24; 5:8-13; Col 1:12-13).

The Thessalonians are to be "sober, putting on faith and love as a *breastplate*, and the hope of salvation as a *helmet*" (5:8). Paul's formula for genuine Christian existence is expressed through faith, love, and hope (5:8; cf. 1:3). The seemingly odd mention of a breastplate and helmet makes much sense in light of Isaiah 59:17, in which God himself will "put on righteousness as his *breastplate*, and the *helmet* of salvation on his head." The Lord promises to wage war against his enemies so that "people will fear the name of the Lord" (Is 59:18-19). Closely resembling 5:8, believers don Christ's armor, including "the breastplate of righteousness" and the "helmet of salvation" (also alluding to Is 59:17), in waging war against the devil and his minions in Ephesians 6:10-17. Those who identify with Christ's victory have already won the battle.

Although victory has been achieved, the battle continues on in mop-up operations. Consider a soldier who, after having been clothed with armor, must remain watchful to conduct battle and avoid harm. The latter days have been inaugurated, and the Thessalonians must be watchful as they wear their armor to fight and protect themselves in the midst of end-time trials and conflicts with the realm of darkness. In addition, Paul's audience "should not fear the day of the Lord, since they need only put on the armor of faith, love, and hope—virtues of which they have already amply demonstrated as their own possession (1:3)."[6]

Blameless at Christ's coming (5:12-24). Paul bookends 5:12-24 with the theme of peace (5:13, 23). This literary structure underscores the idea of peace throughout 5:12-24. The word *brethren* (NASB), found five times in 5:12-27, underscores the church as a family. If earthly families should be characterized by peace, how much more the family of God. The following section exhorts the Thessalonians to achieve peace with one another (5:14-22), climaxing in 5:23: "May your whole spirit, soul and body be kept blameless at the coming of our Lord Jesus Christ." God sanctifies the church so that it may be blameless at Christ's final coming at the very end of history.

FIGURE 16.6. STATUE OF A MAN IN ARMOR

LETTER CLOSING (5:25-28)

Paul asks the Thessalonians to pray for him and his colleagues (5:25) and encourages them to "greet all God's people with a holy kiss" (5:26). Greeting one another with a holy kiss often appears in connection with living at peace with one another (Rom 16:16-20; 2 Cor 13:11-12; 1 Pet 5:14). All people groups in Christ function as one spiritual family living in harmony with one another.

[6]Jeffrey A. D. Weima, "1-2 Thessalonians," *Commentary on the New Testament Use of the Old Testament*, ed. G. K. Beale and D. A. Carson (Grand Rapids: Baker Academic, 2007), 883.

2 THESSALONIANS

AUTHORSHIP

Although 2 Thessalonians claims to have been written by Paul (1:1; 3:17) and the early church affirms his authorship (e.g., Irenaeus, *Haer.* 3.7.2, 4.27.4; Tertullian, *Pud.* 13), some recent scholars argue that this epistle is pseudonymous, written by someone imitating Paul. Central to this claim is that 2 Thessalonians seemingly contradicts 1 Thessalonians regarding its eschatological outlook. First Thessalonians 5:1-11 suggests that Christ's coming is imminent, whereas 2 Thessalonians 2:1-12 asserts that two events preface Christ's second coming. How can both be true? Though some recent scholars find a contradiction between these two texts, the Gospels themselves contain the same perspective. A better explanation is that Paul writes 2 Thessalonians to correct a misunderstanding of 1 Thessalonians. Thus, the two letters to the Thessalonians are indeed in agreement with one another.

DATE

This epistle follows the publication of 1 Thessalonians, perhaps even by a few months. Since we date 1 Thessalonians to AD 50–51, while Paul lives in Corinth, we put the date for 2 Thessalonians around AD 50–51.

OCCASION

Paul most likely pens 2 Thessalonians to correct the Thessalonians' aberrant view of eschatology because they did not completely grasp his teaching in 1 Thessalonians. In Paul's first letter, he corrects those who elect timetables for Christ's return and explains why the Thessalonians appear lethargic (1 Thess 5:12-14). To curb their idle behavior, Paul thus warns them that the day of the Lord is imminent: "For you know very well that the day of the Lord will come like a thief in the night" (1 Thess 5:2). By the time we read 2 Thessalonians, such imminence has been overly developed: the Thessalonians believe that Christ's final coming has *already* arrived in some invisible, spiritual manner. Paul must correct their aberrant view of eschatology once more and explain why the day of the Lord has not consummately occurred. Gordon Fee captures the essence of 2 Thessalonians when he states, "Here is another Pauline moment which as a whole helps us better to understand the nature of the final outcome of the gospel itself, while at the same time giving us insight into the 'everyday' nature of living Christ in a very pagan culture."[7]

PURPOSE

Paul writes 2 Thessalonians to respond to an erroneous view of eschatology that his first epistle addressed. The aim of 2 Thessalonians is to convince the church that Christ's second coming remains a future reality and, above all, to hold fast to sound doctrine.

OUTLINE

I. Letter Opening (1:1-2)
II. Thanksgiving (1:3-12)
   A. Thanking God for Faith in Trials (1:3-10)
   B. The Goal of Christian Living—Giving Glory to Christ (1:11-12).

[7]Gordon Fee, *The First and Second Letters to the Thessalonians*, NICNT (Grand Rapids: Eerdmans, 2009), 242.

III. Standing Firm Against False Teaching (2:1-17)
   A. Do Not Be Deceived About Christ's Final Coming (2:1-12)
   B. Stand Firm in Apostolic Teaching (2:13-17)

IV. Expanding the Gospel and Resisting Disorderly Conduct (3:1-15)
   A. Prayer for the Unhindered Spread of the Gospel (3:1-5).
   B. Refrain from Disorderly Conduct (3:6-15)

V. Letter Closing (3:16-18)

BIBLICAL-THEOLOGICAL THEMES

Genesis 3:15 sets forth the broad trajectory of warfare between the godly and ungodly descendants of Adam: "And I will put *enmity between you and the woman*, and between your offspring and hers; he will crush your head, and you will strike his heel." Within the Pentateuch, God's people are often oppressed, both physically and spiritually. Cain, the first descendant of Adam and Eve, murders his brother Abel (Gen 4:6-10). Pharaoh enslaved Israel and attempts to exterminate the baby males of Israel (Ex 2:15-16). As Israel wanders in the desert, the Amorites wage war against them (Num 21:21-30). And once the nation enters into the Promised Land, they are beset with great opposition. Intertwined with physical opposition is the teaching of false prophets, who make up a considerable part of Israel's story. Deuteronomy lays out the criteria for determining whether a prophet is genuine (Deut 18:22), and false prophets often misled the nation, causing many within the nation to stumble (Num 22:1–25:18; 1 Kings 18:19-40; Jer 23:16-18; Ezek 13:3).

The idea of an end-time antagonist, a figure that will oppress and deceive the covenant community in the latter days, begins to emerge within the prophetic corpus of the Old Testament. By far, the most detailed discussion of this end-time oppressor stems from the book of Daniel, particularly, chapters 11–12. According to Daniel 11, an end-time attack on Israel will manifest itself in two ways. An opponent will persecute righteous Israelites. Daniel 11:31 says, "*His armed forces will rise up to desecrate the temple fortress* and will abolish the daily sacrifice. Then they will set up the abomination that causes desolation" (cf. Dan 2:8, 11, 25; 8:9-12; Is 14:12-14). Here the enemy will wage war

FIGURE 16.7. BALAAM, A WELL-KNOWN FALSE PROPHET IN ISRAEL'S HISTORY, AND HIS DONKEY

against the temple precinct and defile it by "setting up the abomination that causes desolation." Daniel 11:33-35 further describes the attack against the wise within the covenant community: "Those who are wise will instruct many, though for a time they will fall by the sword or be burned or captured or plundered" (Dan 11:33). Nevertheless, the righteous will persevere under pressure, though they will fall and be refined and purified (Dan 11:32, 36; cf. 12:10).

According to Daniel, Israel's latter-day enemy will also deceive some within the Israelite community by enticing speech. His deception results in some within the covenant community forsaking the holy covenant (Dan 11:30). His influence through flattery also extends to those who violate the covenant to become even more godless (Dan 11:32), to compromise, and to foster deception and further compromise among others. Verse 34 reveals that "many will join with them in hypocrisy" (NASB). Israelites will claim to be faithful to God's law but are, in reality, unfaithful.

At the Olivet Discourse, Jesus discusses end-time opponents of Israel, using language from the book of Daniel: "Many will come in my name, claiming, '*I am the Messiah*,' and will *deceive many* . . . and many *false prophets* will appear and *deceive many people*." (Mt 24:5, 11; cf. 24:23-26). Jesus envisions an antichrist figure(s) who will deceive Israel preceding the destruction of the temple in AD 70. His influence will be a sign that Israel's destruction is near. In Matthew 24:5, the oppressor will be characterized by deception, claiming to be "the Messiah" and therefore upsetting the faith of many.

In light of our brief analysis, we can now understand Paul's admonitions to the Thessalonian community more richly. Paul corrects the church's confusion over the second coming of Christ. He makes it clear that Christ's second coming has not yet occurred, since that day will be preceded by two events—apostasy and the unveiling of the "man of lawlessness" (2 Thess 2:3 NASB). Paul claims that Daniel's "man of lawlessness" has not yet arrived on the scene, but, alarmingly, there is a sense in which the end-time oppressor is *already* on the scene. This suggestion explains the language in 2:7: "The *mystery* of lawlessness is *already at work*" (NASB). Second Thessalonians 2:7 is not a general form of wickedness and persecution but a specific end-time deception and persecution that ought to be attributed to the church's end-time antagonist. Paul employs the word *mystery* here in 2 Thessalonians 2:7 to describe a unique situation with startling ramifications: according to Daniel, the end-time persecutor will appear to the covenant community in his full bodily presence in the future, yet Paul argues that the antagonist is "already at work" in the community, even though he is not present in bodily form. The church is to be on high alert for false teaching, so it must embrace the apostolic message of the gospel and its implications for daily living.

LETTER OPENING (1:1-2)

The inclusion of Silas and Timothy indicates that they are Paul's fellow workers and perhaps were formally commissioned by him to deliver the epistle (1:1). It is also possible that Silas and Timothy are his secretaries. The initial mention of Paul himself suggests that the letter ultimately represents his own apostolic authority as a representative of the divine Messiah, the "Lord Jesus Christ" (1:2).

THANKSGIVING (1:3-12)

Running through the entire Old Testament is great antagonism toward the covenant community. The enemies of God have an insatiable desire for wickedness, so when confronted by truth and righteousness, they inevitably respond with hostility. For example, much of King David's life is characterized by unjust pain and suffering at the hands of his enemies, King Saul, and even his own son Absalom! Psalm 38:19-20 expresses his deep frustration: "Many have become my enemies without cause; those who hate me without reason are numerous. Those who repay my good with evil lodge accusations against me" (cf., e.g., Ps 11:2; 37:32; 42:3, 10). The Thessalonians know this principle all too well. But despite their great persecution, the church can be confident that their oppressors will not go unpunished, since God is just (1:6) and promises to punish the church's adversaries.

Thanking God for faith in trials (1:3-10). Paul first thanks God for the Thessalonians' growing faith and love for one another (1:3). He is grateful not only that their faith produces love but that it inspires them to weather all the persecutions and trials they suffer (1:4). Their endurance is evidence that God's judgment is indeed just (1:5). Divine justice is the basis for faithful suffering leading to being counted worthy. The apostle explains why justice is upheld when God punishes unbelievers: "He will pay back trouble to those who trouble you" (1:6). Both references to trouble mirror the Old Testament conception of *lex talionis* ("an eye for an eye, a tooth for a tooth"). The unjust verdict by the world and the consequent persecution of Christians will be overturned at the final judgment when God declares his saints to be in the right and the world in the wrong.

The world's unrighteous verdict declared against God's people will be reversed in their favor when the "Lord Jesus is revealed from heaven in blazing fire with his powerful angels" (1:7). The phrase the "Lord Jesus is *revealed* from heaven" is the beginning of a flurry of allusions to Isaiah that come in the following verses. The Aramaic translation of Isaiah 66:7 says the messianic "king will be *revealed*," and the context indicates that this revelation will be from heaven (Is 64:1; 66:1).

FIGURE 16.8. THE PROPHET SAMUEL ANOINTING DAVID AS ISRAEL'S KING

The word *revealed* connotes an uncovering and, when applied to Christ's final appearance, refers not primarily to some sort of directional movement from heaven to earth but to Christ's hidden presence being unveiled from the invisible heavenly dimension (1 Cor 1:7; 1 Thess 4:16-17; 1 Pet 1:7, 13; 4:13). In 2 Thessalonians 1:8-9, God pours out judgment on unbelievers because of their rebellion of not obeying the gospel. But for the faithful, Christ's second coming is a source of hope since God will fully restore them in the new creation (1:10).

The end of chapter 1 concludes with a note of prayer as Paul asks God to make the Thessalonians "worthy of his calling" (1:11; cf. 1:5). Paul then pairs the believers' works with Christ receiving all the glory—the ultimate goal of the Christian life (1:11-12).

At the second coming, Christ will be revealed to all of creation.

The goal of Christian living—giving glory to Christ (1:11-12). In contrast to the unbelieving reaction to Christ's coming as judge, he will "be *glorified* in his holy people and . . . marveled at among all those who have believed" (1:10). The wording here in 1:10 recalls Isaiah 2, which states twice that "the Lord alone will be *exalted* in that day" (Is 2:11, 17). The word *exalted* is roughly synonymous with the repeated mention of God's glory in Isaiah 2:10, 19, and 21. The further influence of Isaiah comes into focus in 2 Thessalonians 1:12 when Paul alludes to Isaiah 66:5: "so that the name of our Lord Jesus be *glorified*." According to Isaiah 66:5, end-time judgment will befall idolaters who do not pursue God's glory: "Your own people who hate you [the faithful remnant], and exclude you because of my name, have said, '*Let the Lord be glorified*, that we may see your joy!' Yet they will be put to shame." In stark contrast, the righteous Israelites will indeed see God's glory (66:18-19).

The apostle prays in 2 Thessalonians 1:12 that "the name of our Lord Jesus may be *glorified* in you, and you in him." God creates his artwork on the Thessalonians throughout their lives (1:11), bringing them to perfection at the very end of time. At Christ's coming, the community of the saints will be pieces of art, like sculptures, perfectly reflecting God's marvelous handiwork and radiating back on Christ the glorious virtues he has bestowed.

STANDING FIRM AGAINST FALSE TEACHING (2:1-17)

Much of the second letter turns on the false teaching that the Thessalonians have embraced. But this false teaching that crept into the church at Thessalonica, like other forms of heresy in the early church, is wedded to eschatology. Apparently, the Thessalonians believed that Christ's second coming had already come in some invisible, spiritual manner. So Paul now corrects their aberrant view of eschatology and explains why the day of the Lord has *not* already occurred. False teaching is not a new phenomenon to the covenant community. For example, the false prophet Hananiah prophesies that Babylon would release the enslaved Israelites so that they may return to the Promised Land in just two years. But Jeremiah, the true prophet of God, scoffs at Hananiah and predicts that Israel's exile will be much longer and Babylon's subjugation will be far more oppressive (Jer 28:1-16). Throughout the Old Testament, false teaching threatens the health of the covenant community, and with the coming of Christ, false teaching intensifies. Paul exhorts the Thessalonians to sound the alarm for the advent of false teachers. Chapter 2 is split into two halves—the first section describes some of the precise details of Paul's corrective eschatology (2:1-12), and the second half reminds the church of the importance of sound doctrine, particularly as it pertains to eschatology (2:13-17).

Do not be deceived about Christ's final coming (2:1-12). In 2 Thessalonians 2:1-12, Paul exhorts the community not to be led astray about the timing of the day of the Lord. False teachers apparently proclaim that the final coming of Christ and the resurrection had already arrived. Paul says, "[Do not] become easily unsettled or alarmed by the teaching allegedly from us—whether by a prophecy or by word of mouth or by letter—asserting that the day of the Lord has already come. Don't let anyone deceive you in any way" (2:2-3a). These false teachers claim that the spiritual resurrection had occurred and there would be no future bodily resurrection of the saints. They also taught that Christ had already come finally to raise his people to glory (cf. 1 Cor 15:12-24; 2 Tim 2:16-18; 2 Pet 3:3-13).

Paul combats this doctrinal attack by claiming that two events must come to fruition before Christ's return: "Don't let anyone deceive you in any way, for that day will not come until the rebellion occurs and the man of lawlessness is revealed, the man doomed to destruction" (2 Thess 2:3). The rebellion or apostasy probably refers to those within the covenant community who fall away from the faith, and the man of lawlessness is the latter-day opponent of Israel—the "antichrist" (1 Jn 2:18, 22; 4:3; 2 Jn 7). Since neither of these two events has occurred in their fullness, Christ's final return remains a future event.

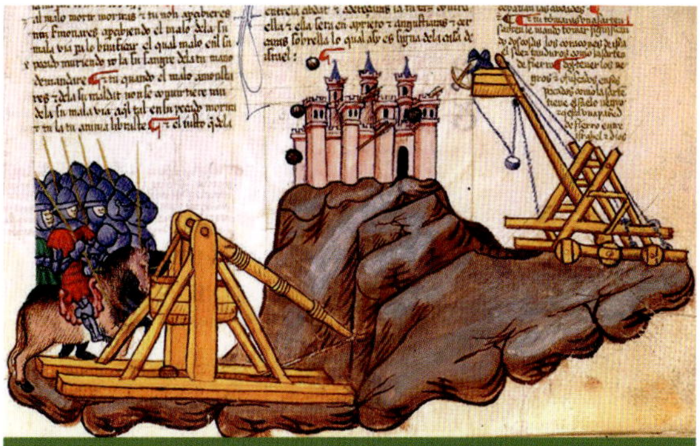

FIGURE 16.9. MACCABEAN REVOLT

The expression "man of lawlessness" recalls Daniel 11:29-36 and 12:10.[8] As we mentioned above, the book of Daniel develops this character in graphic detail. This pernicious figure will wage war against the righteous Israel in the latter days and, through his great influence as a false teacher, sway the majority of the Israelites to embrace false teaching. Paul expounds on the man of lawlessness in 2 Thessalonians 2:3-4 and claims that the Thessalonians should not be deceived into thinking that Christ's coming has already happened, since the final apostasy in the church and the final appearance of antichrist have not come to pass. According to 2:4, the antichrist will assume a position of authority in the church and thereby promulgate widespread deception. This event is a fulfillment of Daniel's tyrant setting up the abomination of desolation in the temple (Dan 11:31). The thrust of Paul's argument is that Daniel's prophecy is directly and uniquely fulfilled; although the latter-day foe has not yet come in physical form, the antagonist spiritually inspires the false teachers at Thessalonica, who deceive and persecute

[8]Keith A. Mathison, *From Age to Age: The Unfolding of Biblical Eschatology* (Phillipsburg, NJ: P&R, 2009), 526.

the church. This final antichrist figure is not the incarnation of Satan but a "pseudo-incarnation," since the man of lawlessness "sustains a kind of messianic relation to Satan."[9]

Surprisingly in 2 Thessalonians 2:7, Paul reveals that the "mystery of lawlessness is already at work" (NASB). It is not until the restrainer, probably an angel, withdraws that the end-time oppressor of Israel will be physically manifested (cf. Mt 16:18; Rev 20:1-9). Second Thessalonians 2:8-10 anticipates the demise of this end-time figure and his cooperation with Satan: "Then the lawless one will be revealed, whom the Lord Jesus will overthrow with the breath of his mouth and destroy by the splendor of his coming" (2:8). The figure will bring about a great deception within the covenant community and unbelievers (2:10-12). Individuals who succumb to the deception and "delight in wickedness" will be on the receiving end of God's judgment (2:12).

FIGURE 16.10. DEFENDING JERUSALEM'S WALL

Stand firm in apostolic teaching (2:13-17). Paul remains thankful to God for electing the Thessalonian community and maintaining sound doctrine, the latter of which is due to the protection that election affords, so that the chosen ones are not deceived (2:13). The goal of God choosing the Thessalonians is that they may "share in the glory of our Lord Jesus Christ" (2:14). While being rooted in God's sovereign power, readers must continue to live holy lives and keep the gospel free from corruption. The Thessalonians must not abandon apostolic tradition but seek to preserve it: "*Stand firm and hold fast to the teachings we passed on to you*, whether by word of mouth or by letter" (2:15).

EXPANDING THE GOSPEL AND RESISTING DISORDERLY CONDUCT (3:1-15)

The first section of chapter 3 contains Paul's plea for prayer, requesting the church to pray for the expansion of the gospel (3:1-5). The gospel took root at Thessalonica, and Paul desires that it continue to spread rapidly (3:1). The Thessalonians must pray for protection from unbelievers, as many are hostile to the apostolic message (3:2). The second section warns against unruly behavior (3:6-15). Paul tells the faithful not to associate with disorderly people, because sin can easily spread. One can hardly forget the opposition to the rebuilding of Jerusalem's walls and the temple under the leadership of Zerubbabel, Joshua, and Nehemiah (Ezra 4:1-24; 5:6-17; Neh 4:1-23; see fig. 16.10). Israel is tempted to abandon the building projects and compromise with their neighbors. In a similar manner, Paul exhorts the believers at Thessalonica to remain steadfast and persevere in the face of grave danger. The faithful within the church ought to conform to the apostolic pattern set forth by Paul and his associates (2 Thess 3:6-11). The disorderly within the church are to stop their unruly behavior (3:12). The main point of Paul's instructions is to encourage harmony and peace within the church (3:16).

[9]Meredith G. Kline, *God, Heaven, and Har Magedon: A Covenantal Tale of Cosmos and Telos* (Eugene, OR: Wipf & Stock, 2006), 181.

Prayer for the unhindered spread of the Gospel (3:1-5). The last major section of the epistle begins with a command to pray for the growth of the gospel (3:1). Literally, the verse reads, "pray . . . that the word of the Lord should be running" (our translation). God's original plan in Eden is for his glory to expand to the far reaches of the earth (Gen 1:28). This original plan is not lost in the fall but remained central to the Old Testament's message (e.g., Gen 9:1; Ex 1:7). With the coming of Christ, God begins to spread his glory in a decisive manner. God's end-time glory has come in the person of Christ and continues on in the church (Jn 1:14; 1 Cor 6:19). By asking the church to pray for the rapid spread of the gospel, Paul latches on to this central theme. The Thessalonians play a key role in God's program for the restoration of all things.

The Christian life has not been easy for the Thessalonians, and it will not get any easier. The church must pray that they "may be delivered from wicked and evil people" (3:2). The apostle is preoccupied with those who profess Christian faith but deny it by their false doctrine or rebellious lifestyle. Paul rests in God's deliverance, knowing he and his audience will be secure. God promises to strengthen and protect his people from Satan's scheme of inspiring wickedness and false doctrine (3:3), so Paul remains confident the readers will embrace his admonitions outlined in this epistle.

Refrain from disorderly conduct (3:6-15). His audience must distance themselves from unruly people within the church. These disruptive individuals are out of bounds because they break their commitment to God and to the church. They do not live according to the teaching they received (3:6). Instead of conforming to the disorderly behavior of the unruly (3:7-9), the Thessalonians must imitate Paul and his coworkers (3:10-14). They must respond to the false teaching about Christ's second coming by standing firm and adhering to the teaching Paul passed on to them.

Because they are persuaded that Christ's second coming and the final, physical resurrection have already occurred, some within the church at Thessalonica are not working. Some members believe that paradise has come and work is merely optional. Why work if the eternal Sabbath "rest" has already transpired? The theological error stems from a misguided understanding of Adam's role before the fall. God commands Adam to work the ground well before the fall (Gen 2:15). The last half of 2 Thessalonians 3:10 reads, "The one who is unwilling to *work* shall not eat." This proverb echoes Genesis 3:19: "By the *sweat of your brow* you will *eat* your food." The point of Paul's proverbial statement is that the created order of this world, even after the fall, requires all people to work in order to feed and support themselves. Paul's response is bound up with an "already but not yet" work ethic.

While it is true that Christ's first coming inaugurated the latter days, believers still possess fallen bodies and live in a fallen world as they await the final new creation and the full redemption of their bodies. According to 3:10, the prescription for all individuals to work and support others remains. Those choosing not to follow the pattern of work within the created order are considered "idle and disruptive." To maintain order, all of creation has its own job to perform, and God expects individuals to maintain order by working and supporting themselves.

LETTER CLOSING (3:16-18)

Paul rounds out his epistle with a climactic statement: "May the Lord of *peace* himself give you *peace* at all times and in every way" (2 Thess 3:16). God's peace fuels harmony within the church and outside of it, where saints persevere through suffering. The Pauline conception of peace is tied to Isaiah's end-time promises that God's people will experience peace in the future new creation when Israel comes out of exile. Isaiah describes the ungodly, who will not experience resurrection leading to life (Is 26:14-15), in contrast to God's people, who will be raised to joyous life (Is 26:19). God promises to bring peace to restored Israel in the end times: "Lord, you establish *peace* for us; all that we have accomplished you have done for us" (26:12); "Let them make peace with me, yes, let them make *peace* with me. In days to come Jacob will take root, Israel will bud and blossom" (27:5-6).

> ***As image bearers, believers are created to be productive. Such a work ethic is part of the expected moral, creational order within the overlap of the ages.***

This expected restoration did not occur in its fullness when the Israelite remnant return from Babylon. Peace did not pervade the land. But when Christ died and arose from the dead, he set the new creation in motion and, with it, genuine eschatological peace. Now that true Israel has initially come out of exile, genuine peace and reconciliation are available to all who trust in the risen Christ. By claiming that the "Lord of peace" offers peace to the Thessalonians (2 Thess 3:16), Paul asserts that Isaiah's prophecies have been directly fulfilled, at least initially, in the church at Thessalonica. Through Christ, believers now enjoy reconciliation to God and experience his glorious presence. As Leon Morris so aptly states, "Peace means the defeat of evil. Peace means breaking down the barrier between man and God. Peace means the presence of God's rich and abundant blessing."[10] As the Thessalonians hold fast to Christ in a hostile community, they must take comfort in God's glorious presence and yearn for the day when they will dwell with him for all of eternity in the new heavens and earth.

In contrast to the fraudulent letters attributed to him, Paul signs this letter to authenticate it (2 Thess 3:17; cf. 2:2). The apostle still has the false teaching of 2:2-12 in mind even at the end of the epistle. With the exception of Philemon 19, the only other epistles in which Paul explicitly mentions his signature are those that contain his opposition to false teachers (1 Cor 16:21; Gal 6:11; Col 4:18). As Paul's letters circulate in Asia Minor and beyond, so too does the threat of false teaching and spurious Pauline letters. The "secret power of lawlessness" (2 Thess 2:7) is spiritually in their midst, and the Thessalonians must be vigilant to root out all forms of false teaching. Since the hallmark of an authentic letter is Paul's signature, the Thessalonians can be confident that this letter contains genuine apostolic teaching, so they must heed its life-giving message.

[10]Leon Morris, *The Atonement: Its Meaning and Significance* (Downers Grove, IL: InterVarsity Press, 1983), 143-44.

THE PASTORAL EPISTLES

AUTHORSHIP

For a few reasons, authorship of the Pastorals remains contested. Some contemporary scholars argue that these letters were not written by Paul but were composed in the late first century or early second century. It is supposed that at least one disciple of Paul wrote the letters to a local community of believers in his own day. These commentators argue that the vocabulary, syntax, genre, and theology differ with the traditional letters of Paul, so pseudonymous authorship is the only logical explanation. Moreover, there are historical problems: according to Acts 28, we learn that Paul spends two years in Rome under house arrest, and no mention is made of his release. The Pastoral Epistles, however, claim that Paul is no longer in prison and that he continues to travel and minister to local congregations.

As a response to these protestations against Pauline authorship, we must admit that the vocabulary and syntax of the Pastorals are indeed different from Paul's other epistles. However, when comparing the three Pastorals to one another, we discover that the language of each letter differs from the others. Does this mean that there are multiple pseudonymous authors of the Pastorals? Different language does not require different authorship. Since the occasion of each letter differs from Paul's other epistles, it makes sense that his language would be unique. Paul simply tailors his letters to a specific set of circumstances. Furthermore, the use of secretaries can account for the different vocabulary and style in the Pastor Epistles. Finally, we need to keep in mind that we lack a data bank of what constitutes Paul's style and vocabulary. Each of his letters is, to some degree, occasional.[1]

FIGURE 17.1. CHRISTIAN SYMBOL

[1]For further elaboration of the points made in this paragraph, see Beale, *Colossians and Philemon*, 1-8, 439-42, the discussion of which also applies to the Pastoral Epistles.

The historical problems are not insurmountable either. It is possible that Paul pens these letters at a time not recorded in Acts. Paul made other journeys not contained in Acts, it is probable that he is eventually released from Rome since he is falsely accused (Acts 21:27-36). Clement even claims that Paul "reached the farthest limits of the west" before he was executed (*1 Clement* 5:7), and the "farthest limits of the west" probably refers to Spain.

DATE

At the end of Acts, we find Paul under house arrest in Rome for two years. Although Acts is silent about Paul's release, it appears that he is freed from his first Roman imprisonment around AD 62 and heads either east or west. First Timothy and Titus are possibly written around AD 63 65. After ministering in Asia Minor, Paul is once again imprisoned in Rome, where Onesiphorus finally finds him (2 Tim 1:16-17; cf. Philem 7, 20). This time, however, he will not be released. Paul, probably months away from death (2 Tim 4:6), writes 2 Timothy sometime before his martyrdom in AD 66.

OCCASION

Titus. After Paul is released from house arrest in Rome, he, Timothy, and Titus soon make their way to Crete. Paul plants a few churches on the island and leaves Titus there to shepherd God's people. In Titus 1:5, Paul commands Titus to complete what he had left unfinished by proclaiming sound doctrine and establishing a strong church government.

1 Timothy. Paul and Timothy then arrive in Ephesus, where they become aware that some within the church "suffered shipwreck with regard to the faith" (1 Tim 1:19). A group from within the local congregation spread false teaching, so Paul expels Hymenaeus and Alexander. Paul then leaves Ephesus for Macedonia. It is possible that he writes 1 Timothy there, although little is known for certain (1 Tim 1:3). Paul embarks for Ephesus and requests Timothy to stay in the city and to remain holy, uphold the gospel, and lead the church wisely.

2 Timothy. Paul planned on spending the winter in Nicopolis in Epirus (Titus 3:12); instead, he is once again imprisoned in Rome (2 Tim 1:16-17). His fate is sealed and he expects to be soon martyred (2 Tim 4:6). Some of his companions forsake him (2 Tim 1:15), and, tragically, Demas abandons the faith. Titus leaves Crete for Dalmatia (2 Tim 4:10), whereas Luke stands by Paul's side (2 Tim 4:11). Timothy leaves Ephesus and is close to Troas, so Paul asks him to bring Mark and some notable belongings on his way to Rome (2 Tim 4:11-12).

An important occasion for all three of letters is that of false teaching that is threatening the church in Ephesus and Crete. Paul writes in response to thwart the false teaching through Timothy (e.g., see 1 Tim 1:3-6; 4:1; 2 Tim 2:15-18; 23; 3:1) and Titus (e.g., Titus 1:10-16).

GENRE

The collection of documents known as the Pastoral Epistles comprises three books—1 Timothy, 2 Timothy, and Titus. These letters and Philemon are unique in that they are the only epistles to address a particular individual. Philemon, although a private letter, does not contain such strong admonitions as those in the Pastorals. First Timothy and Titus ought to be considered "mandate letters," wherein a senior official instructs a less experienced individual in specific responsibilities as a delegate.

The delegate is to perform a certain task and required to maintain integrity and high moral standing. Unlike 1 Timothy and Titus, 2 Timothy is not a "mandate letter" but a "paraenetic letter," whereby "an author writes to an understudy in order to encourage him to remember and follow models of good behavior, to live according to certain moral precepts, and to avoid examples of bad behavior."[2]

PURPOSE

According to 1 Timothy, Paul exhorts Timothy to remain faithful, guard apostolic traditions and the gospel, and live exemplary as an elder.

Paul writes to Titus to seek out qualified elders in Crete to occupy a position of authority within the church. Those eligible are probably few and far between, but elders must be qualified. Titus must also complete the work that Paul has done in Crete before traveling to Nicopolis.

Finally, Paul addresses Timothy once more in 2 Timothy so that he will fetch Mark and his personal belongings to Rome. More importantly, Paul pleads with Timothy not to forsake the gospel but to persevere in the midst of grave persecution and keep the gospel unsullied from corruption.

Common to all three letters is Paul's fervent concern to root out all forms of false teaching. False teachers threaten to upset the faith of God's people, so Paul responds with great conviction since the integrity of the gospel is at stake.

OUTLINE

1 Timothy

I. Preservation of Sound Doctrine (1:1–2:15)
   A. Rooting Out False Teaching (1:1-20)
   B. Guidelines for Corporate Worship (2:1-15)
II. Guidelines for Church Leadership (3:1–4:16)
   A. Ethical and Theological Requirements (3:1-16)
   B. End-Time False Teaching (4:1-16)
III. Caring for One Another in the New Age (5:1–6:21)
   A. Proper Management of the Affairs of God's People (5:1-25)
   B. Faithfulness in Ministry (6:1-21)

2 Timothy

I. Paul's Final Words (1:1–2:26)
   A. Encouragement in the Gospel (1:1-18)
   B. Entrusted with the Gospel (2:1-26)
II. Christian Unity and Perseverance (3:1–4:22)
   A. Living in the Latter Days (3:1-17)
   B. Paul's Final Charge (4:1-22)

Titus

I. The Appointment of Elders (1:1-16)
II. Living Within and Outside the Community of Faith (2:1-15)
III. Living as the New Creation (3:1-15)

BIBLICAL-THEOLOGICAL THEMES

A central reason why Paul pens the Pastoral Epistles is to stave off false teaching in the local church. Although many of these churches had been recently planted during the apostles' missionary activities, pressure from false teachers surfaced immediately from within and outside the covenant community.

False teaching has always plagued God's people. Satan's deception of Adam and Eve continues in the story of Israel. At the end of Deuteronomy, Moses predicts that Israel will turn from the Lord and become wicked

[2]Frank Thielman, *Theology of the New Testament* (Grand Rapids: Zondervan, 2005), 431.

in the latter days: "*In days to come*, disaster will fall on you because you will do evil in the sight of the LORD and arouse his anger by what your hands have made" (31:29; cf. 4:30). Earlier in Moses' appeal to Israel, he states precisely how Israel will turn away from God: "You [the present generation of Israelites] are going to rest with your ancestors, and these *people will soon prostitute themselves to the foreign gods* of the land

FIGURE 17.2. JETHRO ADVISING MOSES AND SHARING HIS ADMINISTRATIVE BURDENS

they are entering. *They will forsake me and break the covenant* I made with them. . . . Many disasters and calamities will come on them" (31:16-17). Within this period known as the latter days, Israel will succumb to false teaching and commit heinous idolatry. Since Israel breaks the covenant, God promises to pour out his wrath on them by sending them into exile (cf. 30:15-20).

The book of Daniel provides us with one of the richest and most detailed accounts of what will transpire during the latter days. Much attention is given to an end-time antagonist of Israel and how he will oppress and deceive the covenant community (Dan 7:24-25; 8:9-12, 23-25; 9:26-27; 11:29-45). According to Daniel 11:29-45, a final opponent of God besieges the Israelite community. Verse 36 characterizes the opponent in stunning terms: "Then the king will do as he pleases, and *he will exalt and magnify himself above every god and will speak monstrous things against the God of gods*; and he will prosper until the indignation is finished, for that which is decreed will be done" (NASB; cf. Dan 2:8, 11, 25; 8:9-12; Is 14:12-14). This figure will commit great blasphemy by placing himself on a pedestal above God and disparaging him.

Israel's latter-day enemy will deceive some within the covenant community through enticing speech. His deception will be accompanied with smooth words, resulting in some "forsak[ing] the holy covenant" (Dan 11:30). His influence also extends to those who act wickedly toward the covenant to become even more godless themselves (11:32), to compromise, and to foster deception and compromise further among others.

In the Gospels, Jesus claims that false prophets or messiahs have indeed arrived on the scene to deceive the covenant community. Matthew 24:23-24 reads, "If anyone says to you, 'Look, here is the Messiah!' or, 'There he is!' do not believe it. For *false messiahs and false prophets will appear and perform great signs and wonders to deceive, if possible, even the elect*" (cf. 24:10-12). Paul builds on Jesus' words and even claims that the man of lawlessness is already at work in deceiving the church (2 Thess 2:3, 7). John sharpens this language further when he claims that "many antichrists have come" and have begun to take a foothold within the church (1 Jn 2:18-19).

The apostles respond to the influx of false teaching within the church by installing elders to oversee the local congregations. In addition to church administration, the hierarchical structure must be partly understood within the context of latter-day false teaching. With the constant threat of false teaching infiltrating the church, elders or bishops (the same office) are appointed to maintain the doctrinal purity of the covenant community (e.g., Titus 1:5-16; 1 Tim 1:3-7, 19-20). The office of elder in the church continues the position of elder in Israel in the Old Testament. Elders in Israel possess civil and religious authority, whereas elders in the New Testament enjoy full religious authority over the sphere of the new Israel, the church (Acts 15:2, 4, 6, 22, 23; 16:4).

1 TIMOTHY

PRESERVATION OF SOUND DOCTRINE (1:1–2:15)

Since the Garden of Eden, Satan tempts God's people with lies and deceit. Adam and Eve fail to meditate on and commit themselves to God's law so that they might ward off the serpent. By succumbing to false teaching, humanity is plunged into darkness. The story of Israel is no different. At each turn, Israel is tempted to abandon God's law and resist the voice of Moses and their prophets. The more the people of God resisted truth, the more they became ensnared in sin. The church, however, must learn from Israel's mistakes and commit themselves to sound doctrine. As mentioned in the introduction to this section, false teaching confronts the early church on all sides. It is evident that here in Ephesus, where Paul installs Timothy as overseer. Paul wastes no time getting to the heart of the matter here in the first section of 1 Timothy; false teaching must be confronted, and Timothy must "fight the battle well" (1:18).

Rooting out false teaching (1:1-1:20). Paul exhorts his "son" Timothy to remain firm in his devotion to the gospel (1:2). Timothy must not only live in accordance with the gospel but ensure that the local churches at Ephesus do so as well. Adherence to the gospel, Paul claims, manifests itself in a variety of ways. Chapter 1 is largely devoted to Timothy weeding out heresy in the church. With the dawn of the tribulation, end-time false teaching escalates, threatening the local church (cf. 2 Pet 3:3; 1 Tim 4:1). With this in mind, Paul commands Timothy in 1:3b-4, "Instruct certain men not to teach strange doctrines, nor to pay attention to myths and endless genealogies" (NASB). One of the most difficult interpretative issues in 1 Timothy is identifying the false teaching in Ephesus. The false teaching appears to be, to some degree, syncretistic. Elements of Judaism appear to surface, for the false teachers are called "teachers of the law" (1 Tim 1:7; cf. Titus 1:10, 14; 3:9). But Greco-Roman elements are evident in 1 Timothy 4:3, in which the false teachers are said to "forbid people to marry."

Note, though the end-time opponent in Daniel 11:37 is prophesied to "show no regard . . . for the desire of women," and this prophecy could be the basis of the false teaching outlined here (NASB). According to 2 Timothy 3:8, the same false teachers are compared to Jannes and Jambres, who were magicians and "opposed Moses" (cf. 2 Tim 2:18; 3:13; Titus 1:15). Hymenaeus and Alexander are two further examples of those who fail to persevere in sound doctrine (1 Tim 1:19-20).

FIGURE 17.3. GNOSTIC GEM

Not only do these false teachers proclaim that the general resurrection has already happened, but there also seems to be an element of magic and abstention from food. Some scholars suggest that the Pastorals betray full-blown Gnosticism, but it is probably best to claim that the letters reveal incipient or *proto*-Gnosticism. Gnosticism, as a full-blown system, does not occur until the second century. The heresy spreads quickly throughout the Ephesian house churches "like gangrene" (2 Tim 2:17). Once the false teachers have a foothold within the local church, they sway many of the women (2 Tim 3:6). It is even possible that wealthy Ephesian women (cf. 1 Tim 2:9, 11-14) paid the false teachers to tutor them and then the teachers subsequently instruct the congregations that met in the women's homes.[3] Perhaps these wealthy women, a group of young widows, are also spreading false teaching from house to house (1 Tim 5:13; 2 Tim 3:7).

In contrast to the false teachers who abuse the Torah, Paul claims that the law must be used properly (1 Tim 1:8). One aspect of the Torah is to expose sins within the human heart, and Paul appears to reference that aspect here; it is "for lawbreakers and rebels" (1:9). In 1:12-16, Paul uses himself as an example of one who "acted in ignorance and unbelief" (1:13), yet God poured out grace on him (1:14). Despite Paul being the "worst" of sinners, Christ rescues sinners from their plight and ushers them into the new creation (1:15-16).

Guidelines for corporate worship (2:1-15). Proper conduct entails praying for those in authority. Churches must pray for those in key positions within the government so that the gospel may go forth throughout the world (1 Tim 2:3-7). Because Paul is an apostle to the Gentiles (2:7), he remains concerned about their conduct within the local church. Some Ephesian men are quarreling with one another, preventing orderly worship. Women, too, were dressing improperly. The heart

[3] Alan Padgett, "Wealthy Women at Ephesus: 1 Tim 2:8-15 in Social Context," *Int* 41 (1987): 19-31.

manifests itself outwardly, particularly in apparel. In the ancient world, a woman's attire reflects her attitude and occupation. Within the Roman Empire in the first century, women began demonstrating their sexual freedom through their dress; their attire reflected promiscuous and rebellious lifestyles.[4] This background may be in mind in 1 Timothy 2:9-10, in which Paul commands women to refrain from dressing immodestly, an act that reflects an ungodly lifestyle. Women must dress with virtue in mind and embrace a lifestyle in keeping with the gospel: "women who profess to worship God" (2:10; cf. 1 Pet 3:3-4).

After regulating proper dress, Paul moves on to another topic—women's role of teaching in the church. Paul first mentions that a woman should "learn in quietness and full submission" (1 Tim 2:11). In light of other relevant uses of the word *learn* (Rom 16:17; 1 Cor 4:6; 14:31, 25), we probably should attribute learning with some form of instruction or doctrine within the context of corporate worship. Paul then goes on to limit women teaching: "I do not permit a woman to teach or to assume authority over a man; she must be quiet" (1 Tim 2:12). Paul does not permit or allow a woman to teach in an authoritative capacity during corporate worship. He substantiates his claim by recalling the order of creation in the Genesis narrative (2:13-14). From Paul's perspective, the Genesis narrative not only informs his theology but serves as a template for the church's polity.

GUIDELINES FOR CHURCH LEADERSHIP (3:1–4:16)

The Old Testament often addresses the leadership of Israel and, more often than not, presents Israel's rulers and leaders in a negative light. Israel's leaders are metaphorically portrayed as shepherds, who are to model themselves after the Lord, the great shepherd of Israel (Ps 23:1). The book of Ezekiel details God's role as shepherd and his commission to other shepherds. God condemns Israel's "shepherds" for their lack of care. In contrast to their unfaithfulness, God promises to shepherd faithfully the flock of Israel (Ezek 34:16-19). He also promises to send a Davidic figure who will faithfully take care of God's people (Ezek 34:20-31). Jesus, as the Good Shepherd (Jn 10:11-14), fulfills this promise as Israel's Messiah and the Lord incarnate. That same role continues on in the apostles and, in a similar manner, in the elders of the church. Here in 1 Timothy 3:1–4:16, Paul pleads with Timothy to install elders who, like the good shepherd, live with integrity and faithfully protect the flock of Israel from false teaching.

Ethical and theological requirements (3:1-16). Paul turns to the requirements of overseers and deacons. The office of an overseer is identical with that of an elder or bishop (cf. Titus 1:5-7). First Timothy 3:1-7 has the office of an elder in mind, whereas 3:8-13 concerns deacons. With respect to both offices, Paul issues a series of ethical requirements, which touch on virtually every part of life: conduct within the church (3:2, 6), at home (3:2, 4-5), and outside the church (3:7).

Much of what is said concerning an elder is applied to deacons, save one notable detail: elders must be "able to teach" (3:2). Paul in 3:8 says that deacons are to be dignified or "worthy of respect." First Timothy 3:9 outlines how deacons are to pursue a life of dignity:

[4]Bruce W. Winter, *Roman Wives, Roman Widows: The Appearance of New Women and the Pauline Communities* (Grand Rapids: Eerdmans, 2003), 97-122.

"They must keep hold of the deep truths of the faith with a clear conscience." Just as men are to be dignified, so are the women: "Women are to be worthy of respect" (3:11). The next two verses (3:12-13) outline the requirements for deacons, who must also be upright in character and godly. Paul ends this section with one of his central purposes in penning this letter: "You will know how people ought to conduct themselves in God's household" (3:15). It is probable that Paul has in mind in these final verses the entire congregation and not simply elders and deacons.

The Old Testament portrays God's redemptive work as the object of proclamation (e.g., Ps 67:2; 98:2), whereas 1 Timothy 3:16 presents Christ's work as the very object of proclamation.

First Timothy 3:16 contains a hymn that Paul describes as a revealed mystery: "By common confession, great is *the mystery of godliness*: He who was revealed in the flesh, was vindicated in the Spirit, seen by angels, proclaimed among the nations, believed on in the world, taken up in glory" (NASB). The hymn describes in poetic form how Christ's incarnation, the act of God becoming man, is largely hidden in the Old Testament. Christ's divinity is clearly mentioned in line one ("he who was revealed in the flesh") and is probably at the core of the hymn. Like spokes protruding from the center of a wheel, several lines of the hymn are linked to Christ's divine nature. Line four describes Christ as being "proclaimed among the nations." The center of gravity shifts from the Lord's actions being declared to the nations to *Christ himself* being made known. Line five also conceives of Christ in this capacity: "[he was] believed on in the world."

The Old Testament unequivocally makes clear that Israel and humanity in general, for that matter, must rely on and trust solely in God as he has revealed himself through his promises and redemption (e.g., Gen 15:6; Ex 14:31), but in 1 Timothy 3:16, Christ is the object of faith and trust. The Old Testament does not explicitly ascribe that role to the Messiah, whereas Paul and the other New Testament writers do so without hesitation. Although the Old Testament appears to anticipate, to some degree, the arrival of a divine, preexistent messiah (e.g., Is 9:6; Mic 5:2), this doctrine is mostly hidden. It is as though the door remained barely cracked open for later interpreters to return to these Old Testament texts and discover that a "preexistent messiah" is indeed anticipated in the Old Testament.

End-time false teaching (4:1-16). Chapter 4 opens with a remarkable acknowledgement of the presence of the end-time tribulation: "The Spirit clearly says that *in later times* some will abandon the faith and follow deceiving spirits and things taught by demons" (1 Tim 4:1; cf. 2 Tim 3:1). According to the Old Testament, particularly Daniel 7–12, a hallmark of the latter-day tribulation is false teaching. Paul claims that the Ephesian church is already experiencing the latter-day tribulation of deceptive teaching and apostasy. The next verse details the specifics of the false teaching in Ephesus—forbidding people to marry and ordering them to abstain from certain foods (1 Tim 4:3).

Paul charges Timothy to "point these things out to the brothers and sisters" (4:6). To rid the church at Ephesus of false teaching, Timothy must identify and eradicate the false teaching that has wormed its way into the covenant community. Instead of being caught up with futile debates (4:7), Timothy must devote himself to godliness because it holds promise "for both the present life and the life to come" (4:8). Timothy must fall into the rhythm of the new creation in his present life and adopt habits that are in keeping with life in the new heavens and earth. The last bit of chapter 4 is a wonderful summary of pastoral guidance that Paul relays to Timothy (4:11-16). This admonition generally falls into the two categories of ethics and sound doctrine: "watch your life and doctrine closely" (4:16). Timothy must embody these twin themes and "command and teach these things" to others (4:11).

CARING FOR ONE ANOTHER IN THE NEW AGE (5:1–6:21)

The Old Testament has an incredibly rich view of humanity as being created in God's image. The way the Israelites relate to one another is always central. Deeply embedded in the Mosaic covenant is a strong concern for foreigners, slaves, children, and the elderly. The Israelites must be gracious in their dealings with each other and quick to serve. Jesus himself claims the two most important commandments are to love God and love one another (Mt 22:36-40). This same principle carries over into the church and is even intensified in the new age. The apostles are quick to admonish their congregations to care for one another in a variety of ways (e.g., 1 Cor 12:25; 2 Cor 13:11; Gal 5:13; Eph 4:2; Col 3:16; 1 Thess 4:18; Heb 3:13). The final section of 1 Timothy touches on this theme, in which Paul requires the church to care for one another intensely.

FIGURE 17.4. ST. PETER

Proper management of the affairs of God's people (5:1-25). Paul drills down into some details within the church of Ephesus and how Timothy ought to advise men and women (1 Tim 5:1-16). Most of the instruction in the first half of chapter 5 concerns widows. Those "widows who are really in need" must be supported by the local church (5:3, 9, 16). The wording recalls Leviticus 19:32, in which the Israelites are commanded to "show respect for the elderly." This abiding principle carries over into the church, and Timothy must ensure that the church at Ephesus, the true Israel of God, upholds this aspect of the Mosaic legislation. Such women in the local congregation also ought to demonstrate faithfulness to their family and the local church in all their conduct (1 Tim 5:4-8, 10). The church, however, should refuse supporting the "younger widows," who are likely to remarry and not require financial help (5:11-12; cf. 1 Cor 7:9). Embedded within these instructions is a strong warning for the church to avoid false teaching. These women are falling prey to false teaching and spreading it throughout the church: "They get into the habit of being idle and going about from house to house. . . . Who talk nonsense" (1 Tim 5:13). Strong relationships within the local body of believers and the family mitigate against false teaching and "give the enemy no opportunity for slander" (5:14).

The second half of chapter 5 ascribes certain responsibilities and privileges to elders within the local church. Elders are "worthy of an ample honorarium" because "the Scripture says: *Do not muzzle an ox while it is treading out the grain*, and, *the worker is worthy of his wages*" (5:17-18 HCSB). Here Paul quotes Deuteronomy 25:4 in the first line and possibly alludes to Leviticus 19:13 and Deuteronomy 24:14-15 in the second. Paul reinforces a general moral principle of justice—even animals enjoy the benefits of their labor. What is true in the Old Testament is true in the New. Human laborers (i.e., elders) deserve the benefits of their work within the local church (cf. Lk 10:7; 1 Cor 9:7-9).

Faithfulness in ministry (6:1-21). After reminding the slaves in the Ephesian church to deem their masters "worthy of full respect" (1 Tim 6:1-2), Paul once again enters into a discussion of false teaching (6:3-10). Here, though, the apostle weds false teaching with the malevolency of greed. False teaching within the community of faith produces division among individuals, particularly those individuals "who think that godliness is a means to financial gain" (6:5). The church must avoid letting money become the motivating factor in life (6:9-10) but should be content with simply "food and clothing" (6:8). Timothy ought to flee from trivial pursuits and remain faithful to sound doctrine and the gospel (6:11). He must "take hold of . . . eternal life" (6:12) by often recalling his present salvation in Christ and his imperishable inheritance in the new creation.

Part of the basis of Timothy's faithfulness to the gospel and the local church lies in God's sovereign and eternal authority. Thick with Old Testament wording, the hymn of praise heaps a series of titles on God (1 Tim 6:15b-16). In stressing God's sovereign power, Paul says that he is "the only Ruler, King of kings and Lord of lords" (6:15; cf. Deut 10:17; Ps 136:3; Dan 2:47; Rev 17:14; 19:16). This string of appellations highlights God's power in ushering in his end-time kingdom in the new heavens and earth. The second series of descriptions describes his eternal, glorious presence that will one day fill the new cosmos: "[He] alone is immortal and . . . lives in unapproachable light, whom no one has seen or can see" (6:16; cf. Ex 33:20; Ps 104:2). This hymn undergirds Timothy's motivation in his pursuit of eradicating false teaching and continued faithfulness to the church at Ephesus. Paul reassures Timothy that his efforts have eternal consequences because they are critical to God's original intention to dwell fully with the saints in the new creation.

2 TIMOTHY

PAUL'S FINAL WORDS (1:1–2:26)

At the end of his life, the patriarch Jacob assembles his sons and blesses each of them (Gen 49:1-28). What followed was a blessing mingled with prophecy. Early Judaism developed this type of communication into a specific genre of a testament. This type of literature contains the last words of a prominent individual given to his family before death. While not formally a testament, Paul's last words to Timothy recall such Old Testament and Jewish examples. Paul is aware that his time is short, so he spends the first half of the letter reaffirming the importance of sound doctrine and appointing elders who will uphold the primacy of the apostolic voice. The apostles bore witness to Christ's life, death, and resurrection, and Paul himself experienced the risen Christ on the Damascus Road. So, Timothy must proclaim what the apostles have passed on to him; nothing more, nothing less.

Encouragement in the gospel (1:1-18). Second Timothy opens in a similar manner to 1 Timothy but with one key difference. Paul qualifies his apostleship in 2 Timothy 1:1 using a unique phrase: "an apostle . . . in keeping with *the promise of life* that is in Christ Jesus" (cf. 1 Jn 2:25). By including the "promise of life," the apostle underscores the end-time hope that lies before him. With the imminent threat of death, Paul firmly plants his expectation of redemption in the new creation, a hope that is made available in Christ Jesus. Moving into the thanksgiving portion of the letter (2 Tim 1:3-7), he tells Timothy of his longing to see him (1:4). Paul remains thankful for Timothy's faith in the gospel and encourages him to "fan into flame" his calling at Ephesus (1:6).

Timothy's faith in Christ and his steadfastness in his calling is the basis for Paul's exhortation to "not be ashamed of the testimony" of Christ (1:8). Like Paul, Timothy's calling will entail great difficulty and suffering. The next several verses describe in some detail God's great act of redemption in the person of Christ (1:9-10). Verse 9 discloses how God saves and calls individuals, whereas verse 10

FIGURE 17.5. MARTYRDOM OF ST. PAUL

outlines the results of the gospel. According to 1:10, Christ "has destroyed death and has brought life and immortality." Both expressions are rich in eschatology and connected to the grand story line of the Bible. The Old Testament aches for the day when God will vanquish sin and death and establish the new creation. As Paul explains, these twin end-time themes are wrapped up in Christ's crucifixion and resurrection.

The end of chapter 1 exhorts Timothy to hold tightly to the sound teaching that was entrusted to him (1:13-14). Timothy's perseverance stands in stark contrast to "all the Jews and Greeks who lived in the province of Asia," particularly Phygelus and Hermogenes (cf. Acts 19:10). Several of Paul's contacts and friends left the faith and refuses to assist him. Onesiphorus, though, ministers to Paul while he is imprisoned in Rome and often refreshes him (2 Tim 1:16).

Entrusted with the gospel (2:1-26). Timothy is to proclaim sound doctrine to others, especially "reliable people who will also be qualified to teach others" (2 Tim 2:2). Timothy must reproduce himself in others in the same way Paul reproduced himself in Timothy. For the local church at Ephesus to survive the onslaught of false teaching, Timothy must establish godly men who are devoted to apostolic testimony. Like Paul, Timothy must share in suffering (2:3). The command to "join with" Paul "in suffering" probably refers to living a cruciform lifestyle, a life that embodies the cross (cf. 1 Cor 1:18–2:16; Col 1:24). When Paul and Timothy suffer for the sake of Christ, they conform to the pattern of Christ. Just as Christ displays power in the midst of defeat, so do Paul and Timothy.

Paul exhorts Timothy to "remember Jesus Christ, *raised from the dead*" (2:8). The insistence on fixing Timothy's attention on the risen Christ is remarkable because it continues Paul's emphasis on the new creation and life in the new heavens and earth (cf. 2 Tim 1:1, 10). Timothy must focus his life and ministry on Christ's end-time act of ushering in the new heavens and earth through his resurrection. When Christ rose from the grave, God began the process of creating the new heavens and earth in and through his Son. By believing in the risen Christ, believers share in that end-time act of redemption (2:11). They too are no longer identified with the present world order but with the eternal new cosmos, where they will reign with Christ (2:12).

The second half of chapter 2 reminds Timothy of his responsibility to avoid false teaching (2:14-16), especially the false teaching of Hymenaeus and Philetus, who taught that the resurrection of the saints had fully and physically taken place (2:17-18). Men who become elders must be able to teach and, when false teaching arises, instruct the false teachers with gentleness (2:24-25). Above all, Paul exhorts Timothy to "Do your best to present yourself to God as one approved . . . who correctly handles the word of truth" (2:15). Mark Thompson rightly underscores Paul's final admonitions to Timothy when he says, "It is indeed a serious responsibility that Timothy has been given. Just as clearly, this careful, sober handling of the word of truth that Paul is advocating is contrasted with the reality of false teaching: enticing but self-serving and completely at odds with the faith as Timothy has learned it."[5]

CHRISTIAN UNITY AND PERSEVERANCE (3:1–4:22)

The Old Testament expects that the latter days will initially be filled with civil chaos and disunity in the family. Malachi 4:5-6, for example, states, "I will send the prophet Elijah to you before that great and dreadful day

[5]Mark D. Thompson, *A Clear and Present Word: The Clarity of Scripture*, NSBT 21 (Downers Grove, IL: InterVarsity Press, 2006), 92-93.

of the Lord comes. *He will turn the hearts of the parents to their children, and the hearts of the children to their parents.*" Here the end-time Elijah figure will mend familial relationships within the covenant community to avoid God's wrath being poured out on them. Texts such as this demonstrate that the covenant community and society at large will be rampant with division and strife in the end times. This is precisely what Paul has in mind in the second half of 2 Timothy, especially 3:1-9. Timothy and the church must exhibit unity and service in the midst of an antagonistic culture.

Living in the latter days (3:1-17). Timothy should not expect false teaching to abate but to increase: "There will be terrible times *in the last days*" (3:1). The presence of tribulation in the form of false, deceptive teaching at the church of Ephesus is also one of the signs that the long-awaited latter days had finally come. The wording in 3:1, "in the last days," is a general echo of the repeated corresponding "in the latter days" phrases of the Old Testament. Paul is not merely referencing a distant, future time but a period that began in the first century. The Ephesian church is already experiencing the latter-day tribulation of deceptive teaching and apostasy (1 Tim 1:3-4, 6, 7, 19-20; 4:7; 5:13-15; 6:20-21; 2 Tim 1:15; 2:16-19, 25-26; 3:2-9). The next few verses sample several key manifestations of wicked conduct in the latter-day tribulation. Many of these nefarious sins can be traced back to an insatiable desire of self-worship and gratification, sins reminiscent of the conduct of Israel's antagonist in the latter days (e.g., Dan 11:36-39).

The false teachers at Ephesus would "worm their way into households and capture idle women burdened down with sins" (2 Tim 3:6 HCSB). Paul compares these false teachers at Ephesus to Jannes and Jambres, who "opposed Moses" (3:8). Although Jannes and Jambres are not named in the Old Testament, Paul has in mind Exodus 7–9. Strands

FIGURE 17.6. MOSES DISPLAYING SIGNS AND WONDERS BEFORE PHARAOH

of Judaism pick up on and develop the interaction between Moses and these two individuals (e.g., CD-A V, 17-19; T. Sol. 25:4). Within these Jewish traditions, Jannes and Jambres are prominent rivals of Moses who attempted to imitate signs and wonders by teaming up with Satan. In the same way, these false teachers at Ephesus are analogously opposing the truth of the gospel (2 Tim 3:8).

False teaching and persecution go hand in hand in the tribulation, so it is fitting that Paul touches on the latter here in 3:10-17. Paul recollects his own and Timothy's faithfulness in the face of suffering (3:10-12). To withstand end-time affliction and false teaching, Timothy and all believers must dedicate themselves to the study of the Holy Scriptures (3:15-17).

Paul's final charge (4:1-22). With a string of commands, Paul pleads with Timothy to admonish and exhort the Ephesian church with God's Word (4:2, 5). The basis for Paul's admonition lies once again in the already but not yet of the new creation and the tribulation (4:1-4). At the end of 4:1, we read, "In view of his [Christ's] *appearing* and his *kingdom*, I give you this charge." Timothy must faithfully proclaim the gospel to the church because Christ will appear at his second coming to judge the false teachers and those who have been led astray by them (4:3-4) and because the end-time kingdom has dawned.

> *The church at Ephesus can be confident that the latter days have broken into history because of the presence of false teaching and intense persecution.*

The apostle admits that he is on the cusp of dying but looks forward to receiving the "crown of righteousness," a reward that awaits all believers (4:8; cf. Rev 2:10; 3:11). Death is knocking at Paul's door, so he pleads with Timothy to come to him quickly (2 Tim 4:9). He is despondent because Demas, who "loved this present world," left Paul (4:10 NASB). An individual named Crescens retreated to Galatia. Even Titus, probably the cherished friend of Paul, departed for Dalmatia (4:10). The only one that remains with Paul in Rome is his beloved friend Luke (4:11). Timothy is to bring Mark (probably the author of the third Gospel), a cloak, and the "scrolls, especially the parchments" (4:13). One can make a good case that this is a reference to portions of the Old Testament.

In the last bit of the letter's body, Paul appears to recall the prophet Daniel: "But the Lord stood at my side and gave me strength. . . . And I was delivered from the lion's mouth" (4:17). It appears that Paul is alluding to one of the most notable events of Daniel's career—his time in the lions' den. The Greek translation of Daniel 6:20 is remarkably close to Paul's wording: "O Daniel, are you still alive, and has your God whom you continually serve saved you from the lions" (cf. 1 Macc. 2:60). The most obvious parallel between the two texts is the deliverance from a dire situation in which both figures rely completely on God's mercy. Daniel trusted that God would rescue him from the lions, and Paul is delivered from the clutches of the Roman government, probably in the context of a formal trial (2 Tim 4:16). Paul states in 4:17 that the "Lord stood at my side and gave me strength." This is similar to Daniel 6:22, in which Daniel claims that "God sent his angel." In both situations, God's presence offers safety and comfort. God's kingdom also plays prominently in both passages. Paul takes comfort in knowing that, upon his

FIGURE 17.7. GREEK FRAGMENT OF THE NEW TESTAMENT

death, he will be ushered into God's "heavenly kingdom" (2 Tim 4:18). The hymn of Daniel 6:26-27, like the other hymns in the book of Daniel (e.g., Dan 2:20-23), highlights the permanence of God's kingdom: "His *kingdom* will not be destroyed, his *dominion* will never end" (6:26). Paul's (preliminary?) defense before the Roman magistrates and their fatal verdict of punishment, the figurative lion is analogous to Daniel's situation in the lions' den. With the aid of Christ's presence (4:17a), Paul is rescued from their schemes and persecutions.

In the closing of the letter, Timothy is to greet several of Paul's friends in Ephesus—Priscilla and Aquila (cf. Acts 18:2) and the household of Onesiphorus. A few in Rome send their greetings back to Timothy (2 Tim 4:21). Appropriately, Paul's final words assure Timothy of God's gracious presence: "The Lord be with your spirit. Grace be with you all" (4:22).

TITUS

THE APPOINTMENT OF ELDERS (1:1-16)

The letter to Titus opens with Paul's identification as a "servant" and an apostle who is commissioned to proclaim the gospel (1:1). This gospel, Paul argues, was in the mind of God "before the beginning of time" but has now been "brought to light" through apostolic preaching (1:2, 3). By anchoring his position as an apostle and his message as the very word of God, Paul lays the foundation for the remainder of his exhortation to Titus.

Paul discloses the reason why Paul dropped off Titus on Crete: "that you might put in order what was left unfinished and appoint elders in every town, as I directed you" (1:5). It appears as though Paul had already ministered on the island. Paul had been to Crete on his way to Rome in Acts 27:7, yet there was hardly enough time for Paul to have an extended ministry on the island, so Titus is entrusted with Paul's mission: proclaim the gospel and establish churches that are able to withstand the pressures of the world and the devil.

FIGURE 17.8. PHAISTOS DISC FROM CRETE

Building a network of healthy churches on the island of Crete is no easy task for Titus, especially when many within the communities are hostile to the gospel. Paul quotes Epimenides, a sixth-century pagan poet in Titus 1:12: "One of Crete's own prophets has said it: '*Cretans are always liars, evil brutes, lazy gluttons*" (cf. Isocrates, *Callim.*, 8-9). The Cretans are notoriously wicked, even in the eyes of the pagans. For the church to survive in the midst of despicable living, it must heed Paul's words. He urges Titus on two general fronts: appoint worthy elders to preserve the apostolic testimony (Titus 1:6-9) and preach sound doctrine (1:10-16). Preservation and proclamation are the heartbeat of this letter.

The reference to rebirth refers to a re-enlivening of a person and is conceptually synonymous with bringing a person back to life—the equivalent of a resurrected state of existence.

LIVING WITHIN AND OUTSIDE THE COMMUNITY OF FAITH (2:1-15)

Chapter 2 turns on Paul's concern for the general health of the church and the preservation of relationships. One of the hallmarks of the covenant community in the latter days is the remarkable unity within the body. Paul insists that individuals within the end-time people of God should live harmoniously with one another and remain committed to the apostolic faith. The older men must be "self-controlled, and sound in faith" (2:2). Even the older women ought to avoid divisive behavior and "teach what is good" (2:3). Young men and slaves are mentioned, and Paul expects the same of them (2:6-10).

Such behavior is ultimately rooted in the gospel or the grace that "has appeared that offers salvation to all people" (2:11). Embracing Christ's death and resurrection naturally entails a repudiation of sin and all things related to "this present age" (2:12). Paul commands Christians to focus their attention on the second coming of Christ, an event that will take place at the end of history when God will fully judge evil and install resurrected saints in the new heavens and earth (2:13). This eschatological cornerstone strengthens Christian living and offers hope in the midst of worldly living and false teaching, both of which are present in communities that surround the nascent church of Crete. The church, although seemingly insignificant on the island of Crete, finds its ultimate identity in the covenant community that stretches into the Old Testament.

Paul says that Christ "redeem[ed] us from every lawless deed, and to purify for Himself a people for His own possession" (2:14 NASB). Labeling believers as a special people and a treasured possession recalls several passages in the Pentateuch (e.g., Ex 19:5; 23:22; Deut 7:6). The allusion to this Israelite appellation is reinforced in 2:14 when Paul prefaces it with yet another description: "to redeem us from every lawless deed," a reference to Psalm 130:8 ("he himself will redeem Israel from all their sins"). Unlike the historical description of Israel in Exodus and Deuteronomy, Psalm 130:8 is a prophecy, so Paul views the church of Crete as the beginning fulfillment of restored Israel.

LIVING AS THE NEW CREATION (3:1-15)

Titus must remind his congregation that they are to be "subject to rulers and authorities" (3:1). This is no easy task, especially in an environment such as Crete. Instead of falling prey to division, the church must promote unity and be loving toward one another (3:2, 9-11). Unity and love are emblematic of the new age, and believers must embody these twin characteristics.

In contrast to the former way of life (3:3), believers enjoy a renewed existence through the gospel. Paul asserts that God "saved us, not because of righteous things we had done, but because of his mercy. He saved us through the washing of rebirth and renewal by the Holy Spirit" (3:5). The Spirit here is the agent of the resurrection of the new creation. As so often elsewhere in Paul's writings, this resurrection begins in this life spiritually and will be consummated in the full physical resurrection life of the age to come. Titus 3:7 states that what God has done in the present will be fully realized in the new heavens and earth: that "we might become heirs having *the hope of eternal life*."

Longing for a renewed body is not simply a theological exercise but immensely practical. Paul urges Titus to "stress these things" to the congregation with the hope that they would "devote themselves to doing what is good" (3:8). Works are the inevitable result of one's end-time identity and inheritance in the new cosmos.

The brief epistle ends with a few instructions. Artemus or Tychicus is to carry the letter to Crete, and Titus is to meet Paul in Nicopolis (3:12). But Paul never arrives in Nicopolis, for he will be imprisoned in Rome in the coming months (2 Tim 1:17; 4:9-18). With the church always on his mind, Paul's desire to bring God's glory to the ends of the earth never wanes.

HEBREWS

AUTHORSHIP

The book of Hebrews comes down to us anonymously, containing only a handful of clues about its authorship. Its sophisticated style of rhetoric tells us that the author is well acquainted with Greek rhetorical conventions. Yet a cursory cataloging of the Old Testament quotations and allusions reveals that the author is also steeped in the Old Testament. According to 2:3, the author also appears, at some level, to distance himself temporally from the twelve apostles. Lastly, the end of the book mentions "brother Timothy" (13:23). Taken together, some scholars attribute the authorship of Hebrews to Paul or his companions (e.g., Barnabas, Luke). For example, Clement of Alexandria believes that Paul was the author, while Luke "translated it carefully and published it for the Greeks" (*Hist. eccl.* 6.14.2; cf. 6.25.12). The trend to ascribe authorship, in some way, to Paul continued into the sixteenth century. It is not until the Reformation that the church takes up the issue of authorship once more. Calvin proposes Clement of Rome or Luke in his comments on 13:23, whereas Luther posits Apollos. Today, options are aplenty: Barnabas, Priscilla, Silas, Timothy, Epaphras, Philip, and Mary. Therefore, it is probably best to claim ignorance and agree with Origen when he states, "Who wrote the epistle, in truth, God knows" (*Hist. eccl.* 6:25.14).

DATE

Since we are unsure of the book's authorship, we are forced to look for hints within the epistle. One popular line of argumentation is that the Jerusalem temple remains intact and the sacrificial system is still operating (9:6-7, 9, 13; 8:13; 10:1-3; 13:10). Why would the audience of Hebrews be tempted to return to offer up sacrifices if the temple has been destroyed? Thus, it seems to have been written before the destruction of the temple in AD 70.

OCCASION

In light of Hebrews 13:24, the author appears to be writing primarily to Jewish Christians and secondarily to converted Gentiles who live in or near Rome. This audience, probably meeting in a few house churches for worship, has endured some level of persecution and hardship (although they have not "resisted to the point of shedding . . . blood" [12:4]). This situation may explain why they are minimizing corporate worship (10:25). Why the congregation experiences hardships and ostracism is hard to say. It could be that these believers are being marginalized in their Jewish communities and families because they embrace Christ.

Also, the strong tone of the letter may explain its unique genre. The structure of the

FIGURE 18.1. FAMOUS ROMAN BUILDINGS

epistle and its warning sections lead many scholars to conclude that the book is a homily or a series of homilies targeting the congregation in Rome.[1] Hebrews 13:22 even asserts that the epistle is a "word of exhortation" (cf. Acts 13:15).

PURPOSE

The author of Hebrews exhorts Jewish Christians and perhaps some Gentiles through a homily to resist the temptation to revert to the old covenant with its emphasis on the sacrificial system and abandon faith in Jesus. The congregation must press on in their faith so that they may continue to enjoy access to God's throne room.

OUTLINE

I. Prologue: The Exaltation of the Last Adam (1:1-4)

II. Christ Superior to the Angels (1:5–2:18)
  - A. Superior to the Angels as the Exalted Lord (1:5-13)
  - B. Superior to the Angels as the Perfected Adam (2:1-18)

III. Christ Is Superior to the Old Covenant in His Sabbath Rest (3:1–6:20)
  - A. The Greater Moses (3:1-6)
  - B. Warning of Entering Sabbath Rest (3:7–4:13)
  - C. Jesus as the Great High Priest (4:14–5:10)
  - D. Warning of Apostasy (5:11–6:12)
  - E. The Blessing of Abraham and Jesus as Priest (6:13-20)

[1]See, e.g., William L. Lane, *Hebrews 1–8*, WBC 47A (Grand Rapids: Zondervan, 1991), lxix-lxxv.

IV. Jesus as the Great High Priest in the Line of Melchizedek (7:1–10:39)
   A. Jesus and Melchizedek (7:1–8:13)
   B. The Superiority of the Heavenly Temple (9:1-28)
   C. The Perfect Sacrifice of Christ (10:1-39)
V. The Nature of Persevering Faith (11:1–12:29)
   A. Heavenly Cloud of Witnesses (11:1-40)
   B. Persevering Faith of Christ and True Believers (12:1-29)
VI. Final Admonitions, the Benediction, and Letter Closing (13:1-25)
   A. The Results of a Heavenly Citizenship (13:1-19)
   B. The Benediction and Letter Closing (13:20-25)

BIBLICAL-THEOLOGICAL THEMES

Jesus: A better sacrifice. The Old Testament presents the Garden of Eden as the first sanctuary wherein Adam and Eve dwell with the Lord. Chapter 3 of Genesis narrates the fall of Adam and Eve, resulting in their exile and banishment from God's glory. Stained with guilt and sin, a sacrifice is required to make reparations. An animal sacrifice is offered and Adam and Eve are given "garments of skin" (Gen 3:21). The Old Testament regulates many different forms of offerings and sacrifices, and central to these rituals is God's presence among his people. The book of Leviticus outlines the way in which a holy God can dwell with sinful and unclean individuals in the tabernacle/temple. Leviticus 9 sets forth the sacrificial rituals in the following order: expiation (burnt offerings), consecration (grain offering), and fellowship with God (peace offerings).[2] Once the peace offering had been made, Leviticus 9:23 reads, "*The glory of the Lord* appeared to all the people." The temple cult climaxes in the Day of Atonement when the high priest enters the holy of holies once a year and sprinkles blood on the mercy seat (Lev 16). Sin had to be dealt with before the worshiper could enjoy fellowship with the Lord. Like the removal of dirt and grime from a window, the purpose of the temple rituals is to remove sinful contaminants that defiled the worshiper. Even before Moses prescribes the various rituals that Israel is to perform in the books of Exodus and Leviticus, the Old Testament often narrates prominent individuals presenting sacrifices to the Lord (e.g., Gen 4:4; 8:20-21; 12:6-8; 22:2-13). For Israel to enjoy the glory of her Lord, atonement for sin must be made. But two problems quickly surface as the Old Testament unfolds: sacrifices are unable to atone fully for sin (e.g., Hos 6:6), and Israel and her priests are

FIGURE 18.2. OLD TESTAMENT SACRIFICE

[2]L. Michael Morales, *Who Shall Ascend the Mountain of the Lord? A Biblical Theology of the Book of Leviticus*, NSBT 37 (Downers Grove, IL: InterVarsity Press, 2015), 122-24.

incapable of faithfully offering up sacrifices (e.g., 1 Sam 15:21-22). The book of Isaiah understands these deficiencies and predicts that a future servant figure will become "an offering for sin" and will "justify many" within Israel (53:10, 11). For complete atonement to be made, a faithful and righteous individual, not an animal, will offer himself up as the ultimate sacrifice in the latter days.

The New Testament stresses that Jesus is the ultimate sacrifice, whose death fully atones for sin. The time has come for God to deal with sin once and for all. John the Baptist without hesitation declares that Jesus is the "Lamb of God, who takes away the sin of the world" (Jn 1:29). The Son's death appeases the Father's wrath, resulting in reconciliation between God and humanity. Christ's death and resurrection pave the way for God to dwell with believers. But Jesus is not only the perfect sacrifice, he is also the perfect high priest. Where the Old Testament tends to separate these two realities, the New Testament joins them. Christ is both sacrifice and high priest (Heb 7:27; 9:12). He offers up himself!

FIGURE 18.3. THE HIGH PRIEST AARON

Jesus: A better priest. The Genesis 1–2 narrative presents Adam as a priest and king who, as the image of God, reflects God's attributes and manifests them within the created order. As a priest, God charges Adam to work and take care of the garden—the first sanctuary—that must remain free from all unclean things (2:15; cf. Num 18:7). He is also to be holy and mediate God's presence on earth by pushing the boundaries of the garden outward so that the entire world would be filled with the presence of God. Yet Adam fails in his priestly role by letting the unclean serpent into the garden (Gen 3:1), by not obeying God's command, and by not expanding the garden's boundaries. God then raises up the nation of Israel as a corporate image to serve as a "kingdom of priests" to obey his commands and mediate his glorious presence to the nations (Ex 19:5-6). Once again, the Old Testament narrates a cycle of failure. The Gospels, however, portray Jesus as a faithful priest who expels all unclean things from the created order that had been overrun with sin and unclean spirits. As a divine priest, Jesus mediates God's glory on the earth to all of humanity. Heaven descends in the person of Christ on earth (Mt 1:23; Is 7:14), yet at his ascension, Christ ushers God's people back to heaven, where he represents the covenant community before God's throne.

The book of Hebrews forcefully argues that the covenant community has begun to draw near and enjoy heaven itself (4:16; 7:25; 10:1, 22; 11:6). Through their union with Christ, all believers have "come to Mount Zion, to the city of the living God, the heavenly Jerusalem" (12:22). At the present, while believers physically remain on earth and await their final arrival into the new heavens and earth, they can be confident that Christ represents them before the heavenly throne, guaranteeing their future inheritance of eternal "Sabbath rest" (4:9).

FIGURE 18.4. THE PROPHET ZECHARIAH

PROLOGUE: THE EXALTATION OF THE LAST ADAM (1:1-4)

The prologue of the book, only four verses long, is packed with the major themes of Hebrews, focusing on the person of Christ, his identity as God and Adam, his enthronement as cosmic King, and his atoning death. In the Old Testament, God revealed his perfect plan of redemption to Moses, the patriarchs, the prophets, and many more through a variety of mediums (1:1), but in the new age God unveils further details about his plan in the person of Christ: "In these last days [God] has spoken to us by his Son" (1:2). God's identity and his plan are now brought into greater clarity in the person of Christ in the present (cf. Jn 1:17-18). But the Old Testament itself even anticipates God disclosing additional revelation at the very end of history (e.g., Joel 2:28-32; Dan 10:14; 11:35). God's revelation in Christ is, as Geerhardus Vos states, "not one new disclosure to be followed by others, but the consummate disclosure beyond which nothing is expected."[3] Until the second coming of Christ, when God's revelation will be expressed in its fullness, the revelation God gave humanity

[3]Geerhardus Vos, *Biblical Theology: Old and New Testaments* (Grand Rapids: Eerdmans, 1948; repr., Carlisle, PA: Banner of Truth, 2000), 302.

reaches its climax in the person of Jesus. The next few verses of the prologue bring into focus the precise details of God's full revelation of the exalted Christ (1:3-4).

The author explicitly frames the book of Hebrews with the phrase "in these last days" (1:2). The phrase "last days" refers to the Old Testament expectation that God will act decisively and with great finality at the very end of history (e.g., Gen 49:1; Num 24:14; Is 2:2). A few end-time events are worth mentioning: an individual ruler will emerge who will conquer Israel's enemies and establish God's eternal kingdom. In the last days, God will also offer complete forgiveness of sins so that he might dwell with Israel in the new creation. By framing the prologue with an explicit reference to the latter days, the author pleads with the churches to understand that they are living in the overlap of the ages, the final stage of history. Their faulty view of the Mosaic law is tethered to a faulty understanding of the last days.

Verses 2-3 cast Jesus as an Adam figure who has inherited the right to be enthroned over the cosmos through his perfect obedience. Verse 2 describes Jesus as the "*Son*, whom he appointed *heir of all things*." This alludes to Psalm 2:7-8, which reads, "He said to Me, 'You are My *son*. . . . Ask me, and I will make the *nations your inheritance, the ends of the earth your possession*." (cf. Heb 1:5). Christ's appointment to inherit the earth as God's Son takes place at his resurrection (cf. Rom 1:4).

The commission of Genesis 1:26, 28 to "rule over . . . the earth" is applied to Israel's patriarchs. God commands them to rule over their enemies and be a blessing to the surrounding nations (Gen 22:17-18; 26:3-4). But they, like Adam, fail. Through Christ's perfect life, death, and resurrection, he earns the right to inherit the cosmos. Hebrews 1:2-3 depicts Christ as "the radiance of God's glory and the exact representation of his being." As the cosmic, last Adam King, Christ is now in a position to bring "many sons and daughters to glory" (2:10) so they will identify with him and enjoy all the benefits of his exalted position. But Christ is not only the last Adam, he is even described as God himself: "The Son is the radiance of God's glory . . . sustaining all things by his powerful word" (1:3; cf. Jn 1:14). Christ's identity as the last Adam flows from and is rooted in his divine preexistence as the eternal Son of God.[4]

The end of Hebrews 1:3 reveals yet another dimension of Christ's right to rule over the cosmos: "*After he had provided purification for sins*, he sat down at the right hand of the Majesty in heaven." Christ deserves to rule over the cosmos because he not only fulfilled the commission given to Adam and Israel but also because he suffered as the perfect atoning sacrifice. Suffering leads to exaltation. The sacrificial system in the Old Testament only temporarily appeased God's wrath and only in part (Rom 3:25; Heb 10:1-10). It was not until the last Adam suffers and dies that God's wrath is appeased with great finality. Central to the book of Hebrews is the superior sacrifice that is found only in Christ. Only those who trust in his perfect sacrifice can receive complete forgiveness (Heb 9:14, 26, 28).

Hebrews 1:4 sets up the next two chapters of discussion: "So he became as much *superior to the angels* as the name he has inherited is

[4]Lane G. Tipton, "Christology in Colossians 1:15-20 and Hebrews 1:1-4: An Exercise in Biblico-Systematic Theology," in *Resurrection and Eschatology: Essays in Honor of Richard B. Gaffin, Jr.*, ed. Lane G. Tipton and Jeffrey C. Waddington (Philipsburg, NJ: P&R, 2008), 177-202.

superior to theirs." It is not clear why the author devotes so much space to the superiority of Christ over the angels. Does the audience have too high a view of angelic beings? Are they tempted to worship them? Although a few commentators believe so, it may stem from the angelic role in mediating the Mosaic law.[5] According to Hebrews 2:2, angels mediate the old covenant given at Sinai (cf. Gal 3:19). The audience of Hebrews must not turn back to the Mosaic law, since it was mediated through angelic beings. Instead, the congregations must embrace the new covenant that is mediated through Christ (Heb 8:6; 9:15). At the very least, the point of the discussion in chapters 1–2 is that Jesus stands in stark relief to the angels. Christ, as the divine last Adam, is better than the angels in every way.

The last Adam must pay the price for the first Adam's transgression.

CHRIST SUPERIOR TO THE ANGELS (1:5-2:18)

Nearly every square inch of the book of Hebrews is devoted to the person of Christ and his work. In particular, the first two chapters center on two aspects of Christ—his success as the incarnate Son and his authority over creation as the divine Lord. The Old Testament often makes reference to a coming Adam figure who will undo the result of Adam and Eve's sin in the garden (e.g., Gen 3:15). A true Israelite, a son of David, will arise and establish God's eternal kingdom on earth (e.g., Num 24:17; 2 Sam 7). Yet, as we make our way into the Gospels, we learn that it is Israel's Lord who comes down and becomes the last Adam and true Israel to undo the fall, bear the sins of many, and establish God's end-time kingdom. Christ is both Israel's Lord incarnate and a descendant of Adam and Israel. The author of Hebrews capitalizes on both aspects of the exalted Christ, stressing that he ushers in a new stage of redemption affecting every aspect of believers' lives. Why return to the old covenant, when Christ inaugurates the new creation and leads his people into heaven itself?

Superior to the angels as the exalted Lord (1:5-13). In 1:2b-4, Jesus "made the universe" and is the "radiance of God's glory and the exact representation of his being." The author identifies Jesus with God at every point. Angels are created, and Jesus is the creator. In light of the Old Testament quotations in Hebrews 1:5-13, Christ remains far superior to the angels *because* he is the end-time ruler over the cosmos who is also identified with Israel's God. Richard Bauckham notes that "in three key respects—creation, sovereignty and worship—the Son is related to the angels precisely as God is."[6]

Hebrews 1:5-12 fall into "three movements," and each movement is supported with a dominant set of Old Testament quotations drawn from the LXX.[7] Further, according to Hebrews 1:5-13, God addresses his heavenly council and makes a number of staggering claims about his Son. The first

[5]Thomas R. Schreiner, *Commentary on Hebrews* (Nashville: B&H, 2015), 59-60.
[6]Richard Bauckham, *Jesus and the God of Israel* (Grand Rapids: Eerdmans, 2008), 243.
[7]George H. Guthrie, "Hebrews," in *Commentary on the New Testament Use of the Old Testament*, ed. G. K. Beale and D. A. Carson (Grand Rapids: Baker Academic, 2007), 925.

movement (1:5) sounds off with God identifying his Son as directly fulfilling the messianic expectations of Psalm 2:7 and 2 Samuel 7:14. These two Old Testament passages are part of a stream of texts flowing from the fount of Genesis 1:26-28. Adam, being in the image of God, is to rule over the earthly realm in the same way God rules over the cosmos. God's enemies were to be conquered and expelled from the earth. The Lord promises David in 2 Samuel 7 that one of his offspring will fulfill Adam's original charge to rule over all God's enemies. Hebrews states that Christ has indeed decisively defeated the power of the devil and death, thus fulfilling the Old Testament anticipation (2:14-15). God informs the heavenly council that his Son is superior because he is the end-time ruler of the cosmos.

The second movement (1:6-7) is supported by three quotations (Deut 32:43; Ps 97:7; 104:4). This movement, especially in light of Deuteronomy 32:43, highlights angels' response to God's promised conquest of his enemies on behalf of his covenant people. Deuteronomy 32:43 asserts, "Let all the angels of God worship him . . . for he will avenge the blood of his sons, and he will render vengeance, and recompense justice to his enemies" (LXX [Brenton]). This promise is initially fulfilled when Israel crosses the Jordan and arrives in the Promised Land. Yet it also anticipates a time when God will avenge his enemies with great finality in Christ. Considering Christ's work, readers can be assured that they have begun to enter the Promised Land. In 1:6, God applies Deuteronomy 32:43 to his Son. When God states that the angels are to worship "him," he is referring to Christ. But, in Deuteronomy 32:43, Israel's Lord is the object of worship.

FIGURE 18.5. KING DAVID

Thus, God unflinchingly identifies Christ with himself. Both, while separate persons of the Trinity, are deemed worthy of praise and worship. Christ is better than the angels because he is identified with Israel's God who has begun to lead his people into the Promised Land.

The third movement (1:8-12) consists of two substantial quotations (Ps 45:6-7; 102:25-27) and addresses Christ's role as cosmic ruler and creator. These two psalms testify to God's unique identity as Israel's eternal ruler and creator of the universe. Once again,

God places these two psalms that speak to his uniqueness and exclusivity on the person of Christ: "But about the Son [Christ] he [God] says" (Heb 1:8). Christ is better than the angels because he is identified with the eternal God of the cosmos who created them.

> ***The audience of Hebrews must continue to embrace Christ and his work and hold fast to the teachings of the apostles.***

Chapter 1 climaxes with a quotation from Psalm 110: "To which of the angels did God ever say, 'Sit at my right hand until I make your enemies a footstool for your feet?'" (Heb 1:13). The psalmist David refers to a future priest-king who is greater than he (Ps 110:4). Guthrie comments on the use of Psalm 110:1 here in 1:13: "Christ, as exalted, will utterly defeat the enemies of God and his people (2:5-9), and this gives a struggling people hope of vindication. . . . The Son also functions as a high priest, who has made a sacrifice that has dealt with sin decisively."[8]

Superior to the angels as the perfected Adam (2:1-18). Chapter 2 begins with the first of five "warning passages" found in the book of Hebrews (2:1-4; 3:7–4:13; 5:11–6:12; 10:19-39; 12:14-29). These warning sections function as a pastoral exhortation that binds the preceding and following material. Like a preacher injecting application throughout the sermon, the writer of Hebrews administers words of exhortation to his readers to keep them on their toes and heed its instruction. Many within the congregation publicly confess their faith in Christ, yet they are tempted to return to their former way of life in Judaism. If they do so, as the author of Hebrews argues, they reject Christ and his work and become apostate. The author fills each warning passage with end-time language to spur the congregation to persevere in their present situation of conflict (10:32-39).

The exhortation of 2:1-4 comes on the heels of the robust Christology of chapter 1. If the congregations "pay the most careful attention" to what they have heard through the apostles, they will enter the promised rest (2:1a). If, however, they refuse and relapse into the sacrificial aspects of Judaism, then the audience, having been once moored to the shores of salvation, will inevitably "drift away" (2:1b).

Moving on from a lengthy discussion of Christ's exalted status as Israel's Messiah, Creator, and Lord, the author in chapter 2 robustly defends Christ's humanity. He is still more excellent than the angels in his humanity as the last Adam. The author uses Psalm 8, one of the clearest passages in the Old Testament that discusses the goal of humanity, to explain Christ's accomplishments as the end-time Adam. Psalm 8 is, in some sense, a commentary on Genesis 1–3 that looks back to the creation of all things (8:3), particularly Adam and Eve, their fall, and God's charge for them to vanquish their enemies (8:4-8). But Psalm 8 also brilliantly looks forward to the day when a descendant of the first Adam, a "son of man," will retrace the first Adam's steps and succeed where he falters (8:1-2, 9; cf. Dan 7:13). The enemy has been abolished

[8]Guthrie, "Hebrews," 943-44.

(Ps 8:2, 6-8), creation has been restored (Ps 8:6-8), and God's glory has reached the ends of the earth (Ps 8:1, 9). Hebrews then, with a tinge of enigma, states that Christ was "made complete through what he suffered" (2:10; our translation). Christ fulfills Psalm 8's expectation of a coming Adam figure by becoming an obedient "son of man" who rules with faithfulness over God's enemies, adhered to God's commandments, and suffers on behalf of others (Heb 5:6). Christ decisively overthrows the power of the devil and breaks the stronghold of death (2:14), events that are to occur at the very end of history. Christ becoming perfect means that God glorified him as a result of his end-time obedience as the last Adam.[9]

Christ's achievement as the last Adam not only displays his superiority to the angels but also extends to those who trust in him. Believers are called "many sons" led by "the author of their salvation [Christ]," and they are referred to as his "brethren" and "children whom God has given [to him]" (2:10-13 NASB). Hebrews 2:12-13 cites two Old Testament passages that demonstrate the solidarity between Christ and his people (Ps 22:22; Is 8:17-18). The point of these passages is that the audience of Hebrews spiritually participates in Christ's status as the ascended, end-time Adam of Psalm 8. Christ identifies with believers, and believers identify with him. Later in the book, the author argues that his audience has come to the heavenly realm of Mount Zion and Jerusalem, where the "church of the firstborn" exists (Heb 12:22-23). Through Christ, believers have defeated their ardent foes—death and the devil (2:14).

CHRIST IS SUPERIOR TO THE OLD COVENANT IN HIS SABBATH REST (3:1–6:20)

According to Numbers 20:12, God forbids Moses and Aaron from entering the Promised Land. Instead of striking the rock (Num 20:11; cf. Ex 17:6), God commands Moses merely to speak to the rock (Num 20:8). Upon striking the rock with Aaron's staff, Moses fails to trust in the Lord (Num 20:12). Moses and Aaron demonstrate the same lack of trust as the nation of Israel.[10] In Numbers 14:11, the Lord castigates Israel for their failure to trust in his promises: "How long will they [the Israelites] refuse to believe in me, in spite of all the signs I have performed among them?" Despite the godliness of Moses and Aaron, they, along with the first generation of Israelites, do not set foot in Canaan. Even when Israel settles in the Promised Land, the nation is later expelled on account of idolatry. When Israel does return to the Promised Land after Babylonian captivity, there is still a sense of incompleteness. Full restoration of God's people remains a future reality. It is not until Jesus faithfully enters the land, drives out Satan, and bears the sin of his people that God's people "enter" the land.

Their firstborn status as heirs of the new creation has been inaugurated through their union with the ascended Christ in heaven.

[9]Moisés Silva, "Perfection and Eschatology in Hebrews," *WTJ* 39 (1976): 60-71.

[10]Victor P. Hamilton, *Handbook on the Pentateuch*, 2nd. ed. (Grand Rapids: Baker Academic, 2005), 336.

The greater Moses (3:1-6). Hebrews 3:1-6 attests to Christ's faithfulness in establishing the new covenant community. The author typologically compares Christ's faithful obedience to Moses' faithful service to the house of Israel (3:2; cf. Num 12:7). As great as Moses was, he was never the builder of Israel, only the servant (Heb 3:5). The Lord alone is the builder or creator of the covenant community (3:4). Jesus, however, is far greater than Moses. He is not only a faithful servant to the new covenant community but also the builder or creator of the new covenant community as Israel's God. Christ's perfect obedience in his life, death, and resurrection qualifies him to be God's faithful Son (3:6). Christ is simultaneously true Israel (i.e., the house) and Israel's Creator and Lord. The section ends with a jarring condition: "And we are his house, *if indeed* we hold firmly to our confidence and the hope in which we glory" (3:6). The congregations must continue to persevere in their faith in Christ's finished work so that they can continue to be part of the true Israel, the house of God.

FIGURE 18.6. MOSES RECEIVING THE LAW

Warning of entering Sabbath rest (3:7–4:13). The threat at the end of 3:6 introduces the second warning section of the book (3:7–4:13). In a prototypical or blueprint manner, the author quotes Psalm 95 repeatedly throughout chapters 3–4 (3:7-11, 15; 4:3, 5, 7), so its importance cannot be overlooked. Psalm 95 explains that the first generation of Israelites in the wilderness failed to "enter God's rest" because they rebelled in hardened unbelief (95:10). Psalm 95 addresses later generations of Israelites, saying that the time is ripe ("Today") for them to believe and enter God's rest in contrast to their unfaithful forefathers (95:7). But neither generation was faithful, nor did they enter God's rest (cf. Heb 4:6). God commands full "rest" in the Promised Land. Although the second and subsequent generations entered the physical Promised Land, they prove to be unfaithful in it and did not enjoy the ultimate rest (4:8). True spiritual and physical rest occurs only with the complete eradication of sin, defeat of Israel's enemies, and the establishment of God's end-time kingdom. The promise of God's people participating in his rest remains unfulfilled until the coming of Christ. The author of Hebrews argues that such end-time rest remains in the future, a consummate form of rest that will occur in the new heavens and earth when Christ returns. At the second coming of Christ, the church will enter the full rest in the new creation. Certainly, believers have begun to participate in that promised rest that Christ inaugurated (e.g., Mt 11:28-29; 12:8), but here in Hebrews 3–4 the Sabbath remains a future phenomenon.[11] The entire section of 3:7–4:13 is laced with a warning to not rebel like the previous Israelite generations (3:16-19; 4:8) but to persevere at the present time or "today" (3:7, 13, 15; 4:7). The congregation must strive and "make every effort to enter that rest" (4:11).

God is the first to achieve final, consummate rest, when he finishes his creative act in Genesis 1–2. Hebrews 4:5 cites Genesis 2:2 ("On the seventh day [God] rested from all his work") to support such a claim. If Israel had been faithful, God would have brought them into perfect rest, the same rest he experienced on the seventh day of creation. But Israel rebels, so God decrees, "They shall never enter my rest" (Heb 4:5; Ps 95:11). The promise though "remains for some to enter that rest" (Heb 4:6). The believers' future Sabbath rest (4:6, 9) is a resting "from their [good] works" in the same way "as God did from his" (4:10; Gen 2:2). Christians must persevere in good works so that they can inherit rest at the end of the age (Heb 4:11). Believers will finally and fully enter the same rest that God enjoys when Christ returns at the very end of history.

At the resurrection, Christ, as the last Adam and true Israel, enters his end-time Sabbath rest and ascends to the throne in heaven. Christ represents all believers in his heavenly Sabbath rest, allowing God's people to participate in end-time rest. But the believers' rest remains incomplete in the present. The final, consummate form of rest will occur at the end of the age, when believers experience a bodily transformation into the image of the last Adam.

Jesus as the Great High Priest (4:14–5:10). Following the warning passage, the author begins to work out the significance of Christ's high priestly status. Up to this point, the author of Hebrews has argued that Jesus is far superior to the angels in his exaltation as the last Adam (1:4–2:18) and superior to Moses and Joshua because he provides a greater rest (3:1–4:13). Now the author turns his attention to another aspect of Christ's superiority: his superior priestly status. It is superior to the Levitical priesthood of the old covenant at all points (4:14–10:18). These three sections demonstrate the superiority of the new age that Christ inaugurates.[12] The new is better than the old. The discussion of Christ's priestly work is anticipated in the prologue (1:3) and at the end of chapter 2 (2:17). By far, the book of Hebrews discusses Christ's priestly dimension more than any other book in the New Testament. This section of 4:14–5:10 focuses on the audience's ability to approach the throne of God through Christ's mediatorial work.

According to Genesis 1–2, God fashions Adam in his image as a priest-king to rule over the created order and mediate his presence to the ends of the earth (Gen 1:28; 2:15). Adam and Eve's failure precipitate the success of the last Adam, who will become the perfect priest and king. After outlining Christ's superiority in his role as the last Adam throughout chapters 1–2, the writer of Hebrews discloses his superior priestly status in chapters 4–10.

Based on Christ's enthronement at the right hand of the father in the heavenly temple, the author exhorts the audience to approach God with great confidence that they would "receive mercy and find grace" (Heb 4:16). The priests of the old covenant

[11]Jon Laansma, *"I Will Give You Rest,"* WUNT 98 (Tübingen: J. C. B. Mohr [Paul Siebeck], 1997), 292.
[12]Schreiner, *Hebrews*, 150-51.

failed to offer Israel true access to the inner sanctuary of the old, physical temple (cf. 7:11, 19; 9:9). Jesus' priestly sacrifice, however, enables believers to approach God's presence and access the holy of holies in the true temple in heaven (cf. 10:1, 14). By turning back to the old covenant, the audience's access to God is threatened.

> ***Christ sits enthroned, ruling over the cosmos, and intercedes on behalf of his people before a glorious and holy God.***

Hebrews 5:1-4 details the one critical aspect of the priests' role within the nation of Israel—they represent the people of Israel before an awesome and holy God. The priest embodies the covenant community as he enters the presence of God daily and, in particular, on the Day of Atonement (Lev 16). The priesthood is a unique institution; only those from the tribe of Levi are appointed by God for representing his people and maintaining the temple (Heb 4:4; see Num 8:5-26). Hebrews 5:6-7 cites two Old Testament quotations (Ps 110:4; 2:7) to support Christ's priestly appointment to represent the people of Israel.[13] Psalm 110:4 states, "The LORD has sworn and will not change his mind: 'You are a priest forever, in the order of Melchizedek.'" This verse, found two other times in Hebrews (7:17, 21), emphasizes Jesus' eternal priesthood. Psalm 110:1 ("The LORD says to my lord: 'Sit at my right hand until I make your enemies a footstool for your feet'") also occurs in 1:13 and 10:13.

The presence of Psalm 110 throughout the book of Hebrews reveals the importance of Christ's kingly and priestly offices in the new age. Psalm 110 itself anticipates the day when both offices will be merged in a future Adam figure. Trusting in Christ's cosmic rule is not sufficient for the audience. They must also embrace his superior end-time representative role in heaven on their behalf.

Warning of apostasy (5:11–6:12). On the heels of the discussion of Christ's priestly status comes one of the most riveting warning passages in the book (5:11–6:12). The first part of the warning is a harsh confrontation between the author and the audience (5:11-14). Readers should have been teachers by this point, but they require "someone to teach [them] the elementary truths of God's word all over again" (5:12). The author desires that his congregations "move beyond the elementary teachings about Christ" and press on to deeper truths of God (6:1). The next section within the warning is notoriously difficult to interpret (6:4-8). This group had been "enlightened," "tasted the heavenly gift," and "shared in the Holy Spirit" (6:4) but eventually fell away (6:6).

There are three main views for identifying this group. (1) Some interpreters argue that the group in 6:4-8 is to be identified with true believers within the church and that the strong warning stirs their faith to continue to persevere in Christ. The warning is thus a purely rhetorical device. (2) Another view argues that the group in 6:4-8 refers to believers who lost their salvation.[14] (3) Lastly, the

[13]Guthrie, "Hebrews," 960.
[14]Scot McKnight, "The Warning Passages of Hebrews: A Formal Analysis and Theological Conclusions," *TJ* 13 (1992): 21-59.

group is composed of apostates, who experienced various end-time realities within the covenant community yet failed to persevere in their faith. The role of the Old Testament here gives us some insight into the nature of the group. The wording in 6:7-8 alludes to Deuteronomy 11:11.[15] Like the first generation of Israelites who resist God's gracious blessings in the wilderness, some within the new covenant community are following suit and disobeying. As Dave Mathewson points out,

> It appears that in analogy to the old covenant community the people depicted in 6:4-6 are not genuine believers or true members of the covenant community. Like their OT counterparts, they have experienced all these blessings (vv. 4-5), but like the wilderness generation they are hardhearted, rebellious (3:8), and possess an 'evil heart of unbelief' (3:12, 19).[16]

This third option makes the most sense considering the immediate and broad context of Hebrews and the New Testament in general. At the very least, the author of Hebrews distances his congregations from the group specified in 6:4-8 when he states, "We are convinced of better things *in your case*" (6:9). Also, the shift in language from "you" and "we/us" in 5:11–6:3 is contrasted with the "those" and "they" in 6:4-8.

The book of Hebrews asserts that judgment awaits unbelievers and apostates at the end of the age (6:2; 9:27), serving as an encouragement for true believers to persevere (10:26-31, 36-38; 12:25-29; 13:4). Saints must persevere "to the very end" (3:14; 6:11). Those who heed the warnings of judgment and the exhortations to continue in faith will

FIGURE 18.7. GATHERING MANNA IN THE WILDERNESS

receive, at the consummation of history, their full salvation (9:28), their reward (10:35; 11:26), and the complete inheritance of what is promised (6:11-12, 17-18; 9:15; 10:23, 34-35; 11:39). At the very end of history, true believers will receive the promised rest of the new creation (6:12; 11:9-16; 13:14).

The blessing of Abraham and Jesus as priest (6:13-20). The final section of chapter 6 highlights two encouraging aspects of life in the new age. The first underscores the believers' possessing the inheritance that God promised to their father Abraham. The author states, "Imitate those who through faith and patience *inherit what has been promised*" (6:12). The following verses then explain what that looks like. God pledged to Abraham that he would be a father of a mighty nation that would become a beacon of light to the surrounding nations (Gen 12:1-3; 15:1-21;

[15]Dave Mathewson, "Reading Heb 6:4-6 in Light of the Old Testament," *WTJ* 61 (1999): 209-25.
[16]Mathewson, "Reading Heb 6:4-6," 222.

17:1-22). The author of Hebrews then quotes Genesis 22:17: "'I will surely bless you and give you many descendants'" (Heb 6:14). The audience must believe that God is fulfilling his promise to Abraham through the work of his Son. In the prologue, the writer even asserts that God appointed Christ as the "heir of all things" (1:2). God's covenant promises are being realized in Christ, and all those who trust in him will also participate in them. The second characteristic of living in the new age is the surety of Christ's priestly role in heaven at the throne of God (6:16-20). The readers of Hebrews are reassured that they have a supreme advocate in heaven.

JESUS AS THE GREAT HIGH PRIEST IN THE LINE OF MELCHIZEDEK (7:1–10:39)

Genesis 1–3 portrays Adam as a prophet, priest, and king. God commands him to rule over the created order, mediate his presence on earth, and teach and obey the divine commandments. But the fall splits these three aspects of Adam's identity into three distinct offices. Deuteronomy 17:14–18:22 officially establishes the theocratic offices of king (17:14-20), priest (18:1-13), and prophet (18:14-22). Yet the Old Testament envisions the three offices coming together in God's people in the end times (e.g., Joel 2:28-29), implying that a future ruler in the latter days would unite these three offices in himself (for the combination of the offices of king and priest in a coming messianic figure, see Zech. 6:21-13). There are also several instances of Old Testament individuals combining the offices in their behavior. Moses is certainly one of the first to display qualities of all three offices (cf. Gen 14:18-20). He rules over Israel, mediates God's presence to the Israelites, and communicates God's law to them. David, who ruled over the united monarchy, speaks often about entering God's temple (e.g., Ps 63) and even dons an ephod (2 Sam 6:14) and partakes of the bread in the Holy Place (1 Sam 21), acts permissible only for priests. He writes a good portion of the book of Psalms, testifying to his prophetic role. Psalm 110 explicitly identifies a future ruler that will be a "priest forever, in the order of Melchizedek" (110:4; cf. Zech 6:13). The New Testament, particularly the book of Hebrews, asserts that all three theocratic offices are now completely united in the person of Christ, never to be split again. Hebrews 8:1 concludes, "We do have such a *high priest*, who *sat down at the right hand of the throne* of the Majesty in heaven."

Jesus and Melchizedek (7:1–8:13). Chapters 7–8 continue to discuss Christ's unique role as an eternal priest in heaven. Hebrews 7:1-10 narrates the Old Testament account of a seemingly minor figure, Melchizedek, and his role as a priest-king in the story of Abraham. According to Genesis 14, Abraham meets Melchizedek after vanquishing several kings allied against his nephew Lot (Gen 14:1-16). Once Melchizedek blesses Abraham for winning the battle, Abraham immediately gives him a "tenth of everything," a gesture that acknowledges Melchizedek's priestly status (Gen 14:20; cf. Num 18:21, 26). The author of Hebrews recounts these events and then explains three aspects of the meaning of Melchizedek's name. It means "king of righteousness," "king of Salem," and "king of peace" (7:2). Then the author makes an interesting observation about Melchizedek: "[He is] without father or mother, without genealogy, without beginning of days or end of life" (7:3).

Certainly, Melchizedek had parents and belonged to a family, but those details are not specified in the Genesis narrative. For a book that often connects its characters to genealogies (e.g., Gen 5:1-32; 11:10-32), the absence of a genealogical connection is noteworthy. Psalm 110:4 recognizes this lack of information in Genesis 14 and predicts that the end-time figure will be a "priest *forever*, in the order of *Melchizedek*." The author of Hebrews capitalizes on the insight of Psalm 110:4, claiming that Christ is an eternal priest because he identifies with the eternal order of the Melchizedekian priesthood and not from the priestly order of the tribe of Levi (Heb 7:4-10).

After furnishing the Old Testament background of Christ's eternal priesthood, the next section provides yet another reason why Christ does not minister through the line of Levi—Old Testament priests are unable to consecrate God's people to dwell in his presence (7:11-28). In the Old Testament, priests are consecrated or ordained by "completing the hands" or "filling the hands," an idiom indicating they have been ordained to serve in the temple. "These are the names of the sons of Aaron, the anointed priests, whose *hands* they have *been completed* to minister" (Num 3:3, our translation; see, e.g., Ex 29:9, 29, 33, 35). A central problem with the priests of the old covenant is that they themselves could never be fully completed or consecrated because of the stain of sin (Heb 7:11), nor could they "complete" the Israelites by allowing them unfettered access to God's presence. Jesus, however, fully consecrates believers as complete priests through his work of redemption in his resurrection (7:16), granting them access to

FIGURE 18.8. MEETING OF ABRAHAM AND MELCHIZEDEK

approach God and broach the holy of holies in heaven. All believers in the new age enjoy priestly access to God's heavenly sanctuary through Christ's identification with Melchizedek, the same access that was limited to only the high priest. Yet believers enjoy an even more intimate and more permanent experience with God since the high priests had only limited access to the holy of holies once a year (7:23-26).

Now, in chapter 8, the author states explicitly what has been implied thus far: Christ's kingship and priesthood are the result of his ascension: "The main point of what we are saying is this: We do have such a high priest, who sat down at the right hand of the throne of the Majesty in heaven" (8:1). His ascension inaugurates his cosmic priesthood as he serves in God's heavenly temple of the new creation (cf. 9:11, 24; 10:12-13). The earthly priests and the physical temple were merely shadows. According to 8:2, Christ pitches the "true tabernacle" in heaven (see Num 24:6). He is the ultimate priest-king whose resurrection signals the beginning of the latter-day temple and who continues reigning and ministering within the heavenly temple palace.

The writer then goes on to state that Christ is also mediator of a superior covenant "since the new covenant is established on better promises" (8:6). The famous prophecy of the new covenant from Jeremiah 31:31-34 is quoted at length in 8:8-12. In its original context, Jeremiah predicts that a remnant of Israelites (Jer 31:7) will benefit from two end-time blessings:

> This is the covenant that I will make with the house of Israel . . . : I will put my law within them, and I will write it on their hearts. And I will be their God, and they shall be my people. And no longer shall each one teach his neighbor and each his brother, saying, "Know the Lord," for they shall all know me, from the least of them to the greatest, declares the Lord. (Jer 31:33-34 ESV)

The prophet Jeremiah states that all end-time Israelites (1) will have intimate access to God's revelation and presence and (2) will teach one another. Within the Mosaic administration, only prophets and, above all, priests instruct the Israelites. Certainly, the Old Testament mentions parents instructing their children about God's law (e.g., Deut 4:10; 6:7), but teaching outside of the family is restricted to prophets and especially priests. Teaching God's law also presupposes a deep knowledge of it. Notice how Jeremiah claims that the Israelites under the new covenant will "all know me." The remnant will possess a more robust understanding of God's law and therefore be in a position to "teach his neighbor."

Understood this way, Jeremiah 31 is thus not so much about the qualitative difference in the internalization of God's law (although certainly the law will be more deeply emblazoned on the human heart) as it is about a democratization of the priestly and prophetic roles within the end-time community of faith (see Ps 119; Joel 2). From this perspective, one central area of discontinuity between the two covenants is the temporal nature of the Mosaic covenant. The first covenant is intrinsically temporal and designed for the Israelite nation. The sacrificial and civil laws are established for a specific time and for a specific people group. They anticipate Christ's work. The old covenant could indeed be broken (Jer 31:32), but the new covenant, as the author of the book explains, is eternal and unable to be broken (13:20).

The superiority of the heavenly temple (9:1-28). The distinction between Israel's earthly temple and the true heavenly temple takes center stage in chapter 9. Spatial and temporal eschatology are very much in the author's mind here. The heavenly temple is superior to the earthly one because it is part of the new age (temporal) and superior to the earthly temple because it is located in heaven (spatial). The author begins with explaining some physical features of the first temple—the lampstand, table of showbread, altar of incense, the ark of the covenant, and so on (9:2-5)—and then turns to the nature of the priests' service within the temple. Priests ministered daily, offering up sacrifices outside the temple in the courtyard and tending the lamps in the Holy Place (9:6). Leviticus 16 details the high priest's role on the Day of Atonement, in which the mercy seat features prominently. The high priest cast incense on the fire that he might be shielded by the cloud from God's presence in the holy of holies (Lev 16:12-13). He then took blood from a bull and a goat and sprinkled it on top of and at the front of the mercy seat (16:14-15). The purpose of this exercise is to "make atonement for the Most Holy Place" (16:16) so that God may dwell with Israel. The nation had become stained with sin, and her temple/tabernacle was unclean. The Day of Atonement "purified" Israel and allowed the temple to become holy to the Lord.

The author also explains that Israel's temple is a symbolic shadow pointing to the latter-day "greater and more perfect tabernacle" (9:11) in which Christ and the church dwell. Hebrews 9:9 asserts that the old, physical temple is a symbol or illustration for the end-time heavenly temple, where Christ now sits at the right hand of the Father (1:3; cf. 9:23-24). The earthly temple is a miniature, symbolic depiction of God's true temple.

> ***Since the Mosaic covenant is now considered old (8:13 HCSB), the audience of Hebrews must embrace the new, eternal covenant administration designed for life in the new age.***

The first temple had to give way to the more perfect temple because the priests of the old covenant could not bring God's people access to the inner sanctuary of the old, physical temple (7:11, 19; 9:9). The daily sacrifices are simply unable to "clear the conscience of the worshiper" (9:9; cf. 9:15), so that God could dwell intimately with his people. Animal sacrifices fail to appease God's wrath fully (9:12-13). But Jesus offers up himself as the ultimate and perfect sacrifice to God (9:26-28) once for all, granting believers unfettered access to the true temple in heaven. At his ascension, Christ "entered the Most Holy Place [or the heavenly temple] by his own blood" (9:12; cf. 9:24-25). The result of Christ's one-time sacrifice is that believers now enjoy forgiveness of sin, enabling them to "serve the living God" in his heavenly temple (9:14). God's plan to dwell with his people is being realized through Christ's death and resurrection.

The perfect sacrifice of Christ (10:1-39). Chapter 10 continues to explain the significance of Christ's sacrifice in the new age. Much of what the author explained in the previous chapter is further refined. The old covenant sacrificial regulations are unable to perfect the Israelites (10:1). That is, the sacrifices do not grant them access to God's full presence. Quite simply, "it is impossible for the blood of bulls and goats to take away sins" (10:4). The author goes on to quote Psalm 40:6-8 in Hebrews 10:5-7, supporting the ineffectual nature of the daily sacrifices (10:4). The psalm in its original context describes King David's thanksgiving for the Lord's intervention (Ps 40:2). David divulges that God ultimately desires obedience over sacrifice: "Sacrifice and offering you did not desire. . . . I desire to do your will, my God; your law is within my heart" (40:6, 8). By contrasting the sacrificial system and obedience, David keenly recognizes the insufficiency of Israel's sacrifices. Elsewhere in the Old Testament, obedience to God is prioritized: "To obey is better than sacrifice, and to heed is better than the fat of rams" (1 Sam 15:22; cf. Ps 51:16; Amos 5:22).

FIGURE 18.9. ELI AND SAMUEL SERVING AS PRIESTS BEFORE GOD

The author of Hebrews capitalizes on this insight in Psalm 40, demonstrating that the sacrifices of the temple are ultimately unable to cleanse the heart. Believers are cleansed only "through the sacrifice of the body of Jesus Christ once for all" (Heb 10:10). In light of Psalm 40, Jesus is not only the ultimate sacrifice but also the end-time King who perfectly obeys God's will. Hebrews 10:5 prefaces the Psalm 40 quotation: "When Christ came into the world, *he [Christ] said*." Christ is here explicitly identified with King David. Yet, as Karen Jobes points out, a key difference remains between these two individuals: "David's desire exceeded David's ability . . . What David desired, Christ accomplished."[17] Only through Christ's perfect obedience is he qualified to be an atoning sacrifice for sin. A few verses later, the author quotes Jeremiah 31:33-34 once again, underscoring the result of Christ's work as a priest-king. In direct fulfillment of the expectation of Jeremiah 31, which as we have seen prophesied that the office of priest would be democratized, believers are priests who enjoy access to God's holy presence in his heavenly temple (Heb 10:15-18).

The second half of the chapter, the fourth warning passage of the book (10:19-39), continues to highlight the priestly status of all believers. Christ is the "great priest" (10:21),

[17]Karen H. Jobes, "The Function of Paronomasia in Hebrews 10:5-7," *TJ* 13 (2002): 190.

and believers participate in his priestly status. Now that believers have begun to have access to God's heavenly temple through Christ's continual work as a mediator (10:19-21), they must "draw near to God with a sincere heart and with the full assurance that faith brings" (10:22a). Identification with Christ in the heavenly temple propels believers to rid themselves of sin and pursue righteousness (10:22b-26).

The remaining verses in chapter 10 urge the congregation to persevere in their faith. To return to physical sacrifices is to trample the Son of God underfoot (10:29). Some of the believers in their local churches endure great hardship (10:32-34), so they must not allow their suffering to be in vain. They must persevere until Christ returns, when they will be "richly rewarded" (10:35).

THE NATURE OF PERSEVERING FAITH (11:1–12:29)

God's people in the Old Testament find solidarity with one another through God's covenant with Abraham (Gen 12:1-3; 15:18; 17:1-14). Throughout the various epochs in the history of redemption, all of God's people find unity with one another and rest in a covenant relationship with him. The "hall of faith" list in Hebrews 11 displays the wonderful union between God's people. Old Testament and New Testament saints are joined together in God's covenant community. Edmund Clowney notes that "the story of the Bible is real history, wrought in the lives of hundreds and thousands of human beings. In a world where death reigned, they endured, trusting the faithfulness of God's promise."[18] The true Israelite community of faith in the Old Testament continues in the person of Christ and the church. The readers of Hebrews must embody the faith of their ancestors and push through difficult times by persevering in the gospel they have received.

Heavenly cloud of witnesses (11:1-40). Chapter 11 supplies the audience with concrete examples of "those who have faith and are saved" (10:39). In the book of Hebrews and elsewhere in the New Testament, faith is unswerving trust in God's promises that perseveres until the end, even in the face of great peril. The readers of Hebrews are being tempted to relinquish their faith in God's promises by turning back to their former lives of the old covenant. These congregations must embody the same faith that was displayed by this veritable list of who's who of Old Testament saints, including such figures as Abel, Noah, Abraham, Isaac, Jacob, Joseph, and Moses (11:4-28). If the great father Abraham is tested, the readers of Hebrews should expect nothing less (11:8-12, 17-19).

This list of Old Testament saints not only demonstrates that readers need to have the same faith as their ancestors but also reminds them about the new age in which they are living. Hebrews 11:39 summarizes the entire list: "These were all commended for their faith, yet *none of them received what had been promised*" (cf. 11:13). Old Testament saints certainly experienced God's grace in their personal deliverance from sin, but their salvation anticipates the end-time redemptive-historical epoch. Although Old Testament believers receive forgiveness and

[18]Edmund P. Clowney, *The Unfolding Mystery: Discovering Christ in the Old Testament*, 2nd ed. (Phillipsburg, NJ: P&R, 2013), 14.

are justified in God's sight, they still live in the old age, looking forward to the day when God would deal once and for all with sin in the latter days and provide them access to his glorious presence in the new eternal cosmos. According to 11:10, Abraham was "looking forward to the *city with foundations*" (cf. Rom 4:13). This is the same city that other Old Testament saints hoped for: "They were longing for a better county—a *heavenly one*. Therefore God is not ashamed to be called their God,

FIGURE 18.10. BRINGING JOSEPH'S COAT TO JACOB

for he has prepared a *city* for them" (11:16). The Promised Land, as fertile as it was, is but a shadow of what would transpire in the future. The Lord promised the Old Testament saints a citizenship in the new creation where they would dwell with him, and he has begun to deliver on that promise through his Son. All believers are now "made perfect" (11:40), meaning that Old Testament and New Testament saints have initial access to God's heavenly presence in the person of Christ.

Persevering faith of Christ and true believers (12:1-29). The writer of Hebrews reminds his audience that they are running a race, "surrounded by such a great cloud of witnesses" (12:1). The faithful ancestors mentioned in chapter 11 "surround" them, encouraging them to "throw off everything that hinders" their faith in Christ (12:1b). The audience of Hebrews must contemplate the lives of the Old Testament saints and imitate their faithfulness in dire circumstances.

The author then shifts to the ultimate example of persevering faith: "Fixing our eyes on Jesus, the pioneer and perfecter of faith. For the joy set before him he endured the cross . . . and sat down at the right hand of the throne of God" (12:2). As Christ suffered and was subsequently exalted as the preeminent priest-king in fulfillment of Psalm 110 (see Heb 1:3-4), the audience should expect to follow the same principles—suffering leads to exaltation (12:3). Suffering remains at the forefront of the author's mind in the following section (12:4-12). Apparently, though the audience has indeed suffered to some extent (10:32-35), the congregations have not yet "resisted to the point of shedding . . . blood" (12:4). As a father disciplines his children for their benefit, so the Lord disciplines those within his covenant community (12:5-11).

The fifth and final warning section spans the remainder of the chapter (12:14-29). The author exhorts his audience to "make every effort to live in peace with everyone and to be holy; without holiness no one will see the Lord" (12:14). Since all believers identify with the risen Christ in heaven, they enjoy God's heavenly glory in an "already but not yet" manner. The strong exhortation to be holy reflects the importance of this spiritual reality. Believers have already been made holy through Christ's work, but as priests they must purge every sinful and unclean contaminant from their lives (12:15-17).

The next several verses forcefully reaffirm the audience's participation in the heavenly sanctuary. The readers have already entered the heavenly holy of holies through their forerunner, Jesus (10:19-22; 4:14—16), resulting in their identification with "Mount Zion . . . the heavenly Jerusalem" (12:22; cf. Gal 4:26; Rev 3:12). The book of Revelation even identifies the heavenly Jerusalem with the new heavens and earth (Rev 21–22). They also have come "to Jesus the mediator of a new covenant, and to the sprinkled blood" (Heb 12:24). Hebrews 12:24 is the climax of verses 18-24 and perhaps the entire epistle.[19] Through persevering faith in Christ (12:25-27), believers experience the immeasurable spiritual realities that the Old Testament saints longed for. Christ's ministry, death, and resurrection set the new age in motion, and all believers begin to share in the benefits of the new creation.

FINAL ADMONITIONS, THE BENEDICTION, AND LETTER CLOSING (13:1-25)

From time to time, the Old Testament illustrates God's original intention for humanity to dwell intimately in his presence. For example, the prophet Samuel comes on the scene when Eli's house is in disorder. His two sons, Hophni and Phineas, extorted the Israelites, so God judges them (1 Sam 2:12-17; 4:10-11). In contrast to the wicked priests, Samuel obeys God's law and faithfully communicates his message to the Israelites (1 Sam 3:19-21). When Samuel is young and "ministering before the Lord," he wears a "linen ephod" (1 Sam 2:18), a sign that he is participating in the duties of the priesthood. A few verses later, we learn that "Samuel grew up in the presence of the Lord" (1 Sam 2:21), indicating that the boy spends his childhood serving the Lord in the temple. There is a sense in which this passage simultaneously looks backward and forward. Samuel's intimate presence with the Lord in the tabernacle recalls Genesis 2, in which Adam and Eve dwell in the garden temple of Eden as priests in the presence of the Lord. But Samuel's extraordinary relationship with the Lord also anticipates the day when all God's people will dwell in the Lord's presence and experience his glory in an intimate way (e.g., Is 66:1-2). The author of Hebrews argues that all believers minister as priests in heaven: "You have come to Mount Zion . . . the heavenly Jerusalem" (Heb 12:22). The prophet Samuel had only tasted what the audience of Hebrews enjoys in heaven through faith in Christ.

FIGURE 18.11. ELI'S SONS COMMITTING SACRILEGE

The results of a heavenly citizenship (13:1-19). The final chapter of the letter contains a string of various exhortations that flow from the audience's heavenly identity in Christ. Their restored, spiritual condition

[19]Paul Ellingworth, *The Epistle to the Hebrews*, NIGTC (Grand Rapids: Eerdmans, 1993), 81.

manifests itself in tangible works. Right out of the gate, the author commands readers to love one another, remember those in prison, remain pure in marriage, and avoid the love of money (13:1-5). Why become ensnared with riches, when God promises to uphold the well-being of his children (see 13:5-6; Deut 31:6; Ps 11:6-7)? The congregation must also support their church elders and "imitate their faith" (Heb 13:7; cf. 13:17). One way in which readers affirm their ministers is by holding fast to sound doctrine. The author warns to "not be carried away by all kinds of strange teachings," particularly the insistence of obeying the Jewish dietary regulations that demarcate the nation of Israel from their pagan neighbors (13:9; cf. 9:10; Col 2:16). Christ's work of redemption fulfills these requirements, so there is no need to continue to observe them.

According to 13:11-14, the author once again reminds the congregation that Christ's sacrifice as a sin offering purifies them (see Lev 16:27). Christ became ritually unclean so that they could become clean and dwell in the presence of God. Believers are looking expectantly "for the city that is to come" (Heb 13:14). This coming city is none other than the new heavens and earth, where all of God's people will dwell for all of eternity.

The benediction and letter closing (13:20-25). The famous benediction in 13:20-22 contains an allusion to the Greek translation of Isaiah 63: "The God of peace, who through the blood of the eternal covenant *brought back* from the dead our Lord Jesus, that great *Shepherd of the sheep*." Isaiah 63:11 (LXX) reads, "Where is he that *brought up* from the sea the *shepherd of the sheep*?" Jesus is cast as a greater Moses whom God delivers from death at the second exodus. Just as the first exodus is the catalyst for establishing the temporary temple (e.g., Ex 15:17; Is 63:18), so too the second exodus is the impetus for the establishment of God's permanent heavenly sanctuary on earth (Is 63:15; 64:1). Through his sacrificial work, Jesus guides his people to the true, heavenly mountain tabernacle (Heb 6:19-20; 9:11-12, 23-24; 10:19-22; 12:22-24).

The letter ends with a line about Timothy's release (13:23). Timothy, a Jewish Christian, features prominently in Acts, in which he accompanies Paul in his missionary endeavors (e.g., Acts 16:1-5; 17:1-15). In Paul's writings, he is said to be Paul's "son" and personal ambassador (1 Cor 4:17; 16:10-11; Phil 2:19-22; 1 Thess 3:1-6). Paul also directs some of his letters to him (1–2 Timothy). The author of Hebrews claims that Timothy is released (13:23), so it is probably fair to assume that Timothy was imprisoned at an unknown location and subsequently set free. The plan is for Timothy to visit the congregation and for the writer of Hebrews to meet up with him there.

Verse 24 urges the congregation to "greet all your leaders and all the Lord's people" (cf. 13:7), and the end of 13:24 the author divulges an important location: "Those *from Italy* send you their greetings." The phrase "from Italy" is found in Acts 18:2, where it refers to those living outside of Italy but have come from Italy. The point is that the author of Hebrews sends greetings on behalf of a group of Christians who are displaced from their native home of Italy.[20] We can infer that the author, like his flock, is not living in Italy and that "he

[20]William L. Lane, *Hebrews 9–13*, WBC 47B (Grand Rapids: Zondervan, 1991), 571.

prepared his homily for a group of believers in or near Rome."[21] Although his readers live in the center of the Roman Empire, they must embrace their true home on Mount Zion, the heavenly city, where they have begun to dwell for all eternity.

[21]Lane, *Hebrews 9–13*, 571.

JAMES

AUTHORSHIP

The letter claims to have been written by James or Jacob (1:1; Gr. *Iakōbos*). James is a fairly common name in the first century, and the New Testament contains approximately five individuals bearing that name: James, the son of Zebedee (Mt 4:21; Acts 15:13); James, the son of Alphaeus (Mt 10:3); James, the father of Judas (Lk 6:16); James the "Younger," the son of Mary (Mt 27:56; Mk 15:40); and James, the half-brother of Christ (Mt 13:55; Gal 1:19). In all likelihood, the half-brother of Jesus writes this epistle (Acts 12:17; 15:13; 21:18). This conclusion rests on the author's authority over the "twelve tribes scattered among the nations" (Jas 1:1). From Acts 1 to Acts 11:1, the twelve apostles constitute the leadership of the early church. The Twelve are eyewitnesses to Jesus and guardians of his tradition (Acts 1:8, 22; 5:32; 10:41-42). With Peter as their leader, they occupy a distinct authoritative role over the early church (4:35, 37; 5:2; 6:2; 9:27). But as the book of Acts unfolds, James, the half-brother of Jesus, begins to take the reins of the leadership over the early church.[1] For example, Acts 21:18-19 states, "The next day Paul and the rest of us went to see *James, and all the elders were present*. Paul greeted them and reported in detail what God had done among the Gentiles through his ministry." James assumes the position of bishop over Jerusalem, presiding over a group of twelve presbyters in the early stages of the church (Eusebius, *Hist. eccl.* 2.1.2-5). This group would have initially been made up of the twelve apostles, but as time went on and some were martyred, elders begin to replace the apostles.

DATE

Dating the book of James may, in some way, be tied to Paul's teaching on justification. The language of works, faith, justification, and the quotation of Genesis 15:6 leads some to conclude that James is reacting, to some degree, to a misunderstanding of Paul's writings or teachings. But if James's teaching on justification remains independent of Paul, then the book could be dated in the 40s. When James's teaching on faith and works in 2:14-26 is carefully examined, however, the author seems to presuppose some familiarity with Paul's teachings on justification.[2] The early church settles this issue at the Jerusalem Council (Acts 15) in AD 48, so a dating in the early to mid-40s is preferable.

[1]Richard Bauckham, "James and the Jerusalem Church," in *The Book of Acts in Its First Century Setting* (Grand Rapids: Eerdmans, 1995), 4:415-80.

[2]Douglas J. Moo, *The Letter of James*, PNTC (Grand Rapids: Eerdmans, 2000), 25-27.

OCCASION

James, probably presiding over the church in Jerusalem, addresses his audience as the "twelve tribes scattered among the nations" (1:1). James probably has in mind largely Jewish Christians and some Gentile Christians living outside Palestine in the Diaspora. These congregations, like most congregations throughout the eastern Mediterranean world, need constant attention and instruction. James, one of the key leaders of the early church, takes it on himself to minister to these dispersed congregations on a host of topics—the role of the Torah, money, faith, wisdom, wholesome speech, humility, prayer, and so on. Much like the famed patriarch Jacob, who is the father of the twelve tribes of Israel, this James (or Jacob) assumes the mantle of shepherding the twelve tribes of the church.

FIGURE 19.1. JAMES THE JUST

PURPOSE

James writes to Jewish Christians as a pastor and exhorts them to live as holy Christians, caught in the overlap of the ages and in the midst of life's pressures and trials. "Simply put," writes Karen Jobes, "the purpose of the letter was to instruct Jewish Christians how to live faithfully to Christ within their heritage as Jews."[3]

OUTLINE

- I. Letter Opening and the Testing of Faith (1:1-18)
  - A. Letter Opening (1:1)
  - B. Trials and Christian Maturity (1:2-18)
  - C. Word and Works (1:19-27)
- II. Faith and Works (2:1-25)
  - A. Faith and Works in Avoiding Favoritism (2:1-13)
  - B. Faith and Works and the End-Time Judgment (2:14-26)
- III. Christian Speech and the Wisdom of God (3:1-18)
  - A. The Power of Speech (3:1-12)
  - B. Earthly Wisdom and Divine Wisdom (3:13-18)
- IV. Coming Out of Spiritual Exile (4:1-17)
  - A. Living According to the Old World (4:1-12)
  - B. Submission to God's Law and Power (4:11-17)
- V. Concluding Admonitions (5:1-19)
  - A. Judgment on the Wealthy Oppressors (5:1-6)

[3]Karen H. Jobes, *Letters to the Church: A Survey of Hebrews and the General Epistles* (Grand Rapids: Zondervan, 2011), 166.

B. Suffering like the Prophets (5:7-12)

C. The Prayer of the Righteous (5:13-20)

BIBLICAL-THEOLOGICAL THEMES

The Old Testament contains a substantial amount of "wisdom" literature (e.g., Proverbs). Generally speaking, this type of literature concerns God's wisdom endemic *within* the created order. Such wisdom certainly has a divine origin (e.g., Job 28:1-28), but it is something that can be determined by observing the created order. For example, Proverbs 30:25 reads, "Ants are creatures of little strength, yet they store up their food in the summer." Readers are commanded to observe how ants behave and conduct themselves accordingly (cf. Prov 30:19; 27-28). One learns God's righteous decrees by observation. The Old Testament sages, like Solomon "found evidence of God's power and purposes in the rhythms of nature and urged their followers to incorporate that order into their own lives."[4]

FIGURE 19.2. SOLOMON RECEIVING THE QUEEN OF SHEBA

As the Old Testament continues to unfold in the history of redemption, God, in some sense, begins to reveal his wisdom in a different manner. In the books of Daniel and Zechariah, God communicates to his prophets through dreams and visions, requiring an angel to interpret symbolic revelations. Such wisdom is not embedded within the created order but is revealed from the throne of God. This divine wisdom is unattainable, beyond human grasp. It can be known only if God chooses to reveal it. One more unique characteristic of this type of wisdom is its rich eschatological outlook. Daniel and Zechariah largely are concerned with events that will take place at the very end of history and disclose how God's people can navigate through the rough waters of latter-day trials.

If we keep this paradigm in mind, we have a richer understanding of Jesus' message. Throughout the four Gospels, we discover Jesus teaching the disciples as the embodiment of divine wisdom. He not only lives in accordance with God's righteous principles but also mediates God's wisdom to the disciples through word and deed (e.g., Mt 13:11 and par.). He skillfully teaches them about end-time events, particularly the inbreaking of God's kingdom and the beginning of the great tribulation.

[4]Carol S. Grizzard, "The Scope of Theology in Wisdom Literature," in *An Introduction to Wisdom Literature and the Psalms: Festschrift for Marvin E. Tate*, ed. H. W. Ballard Jr. and W. D. Tucker Jr. (Macon, GA: Mercer University Press, 2000), 214.

FIGURE 19.3. JOB REBUKED BY HIS FRIENDS

The genre of the epistle is probably some form of wisdom or ethical literature that James may have delivered as a series of sermons. The letter itself could be viewed as revealed end-time wisdom pleading with the audience to acquire more of God's divine wisdom. James explicitly says that the readers are living "in the last days" (Jas 5:3). The congregations of James are enduring "trials" (1:2) and "suffering" (5:10), and they are told to expect some within their communities to "wander from the truth" (5:19). If these churches are to survive the waves of testing, they must plead with God to give them "wisdom that comes from heaven" so that they might "reap a harvest of righteousness" (3:17-18).

LETTER OPENING AND THE TESTING OF FAITH (1:1-18)

The book of Job narrates the story of God testing an individual in every facet of life. God permits Satan to take all of Job's possessions (Job 1:13-17), family members (1:18-19), and health (2:7). God knew that despite severe suffering, Job would maintain his faith and fear God and shun evil (2:3; cf. 1:8). But when we take a step back, we can connect Job's suffering to others in the Old Testament. Robert Fyall points out that "Job takes his place with Joseph in prison, with Moses in the desert, with Jeremiah in the dungeon, with the Paul of 2 Corinthians 11."[5] Central to suffering in the history of redemption is the refinement

[5]Robert S. Fyall, *Now My Eyes Have Seen You: Images of Creation and Evil in the Book of Job*, NSBT (Downers Grove, IL: InterVarsity Press, 2002), 190.

of faith, increased dependency on God, and the display of his absolute wisdom. At the end of the book, Job says, "My ears had heard of you *but now my eyes have seen you*" (42:5). Through inconceivable testing, Job confesses that he has deeply learned about God's power and wisdom. As James's congregations undergo a variety of difficult trials, they too must wrestle with their faith and cling to God's wisdom and power. The goal of such pain and difficulty is that they, like Job, may be "mature and complete" (Jas 1:4).

> ***From the outset, James, perhaps embodying the authority of the patriarch Jacob, reminds the church of their identity in Christ.***

Letter opening (1:1). James specifies his audience as the "twelve tribes scattered among the nations" (1:1). From the fourth century on, the letter of James is considered part of a collection of seven letters (1–2 Pet, 1–3 Jn, Jude) labeled the Catholic Epistles (Eusebius, *Hist. eccl.* 2.23.25). They are named as such because the audience of the seven letters tend to be general or non-specific. These seven letters target the church at large rather than individual congregations. The title *twelve tribes* in 1:1 is probably to be taken literally but with a tinge of figurative language. The congregations that receive this letter are mostly Jewish Christians and some Gentile Christians. *Twelve tribes* also refer to the churches as the true Israel of God. They are ethnically part of Israel, but more importantly they are citizens of the true end-time Israel (cf. 1 Pet 1:1). Israel in the Old Testament typologically anticipates the church in the New Testament. These Christian communities are also "scattered among the nations" (Jas 1:1). Once again, two shades of meaning are probably in mind—the physical dispersion of the Jews outside of Palestine is the background against which James portrays true Israel's absence from their home in the new creation. When properly understood, the entire exhortation contained in the letter hangs on the audience's identity as the true people of God. The Jewish and Gentile believing readership are the true Israel, scattered abroad in exile from their heavenly homeland in the new eternal cosmos. Their actions must fall in line with their identity.

Trials and Christian maturity (1:2-18). Wasting no time, James opens the body of his letter with a command: "Consider it pure joy . . . whenever you face trials of many kinds" (1:2). He does not specify what type of trials are in mind, only "many kinds." The basis for his exhortation lies in how trials affect a believer's character: "The testing of your faith produces perseverance" (1:3). But then he goes on to outline the ultimate goal of experiencing difficulties: "so that you may be *mature* and *complete*" (1:4). The testing of faith conforms individuals into the image of Christ. The more believers endure hardship, the more God fashions them into the perfect image of Christ, the embodiment of the new creation (cf. 1 Pet 1:6). Later in the chapter, James frames the admonition with an important allusion to the book of Daniel: "*Blessed is the one who perseveres* under trial because . . . *that person will receive the crown of life* that the Lord has promised to those who love him" (Jas 1:12). The wording here closely resembles Daniel 12:12-13: *"Happy [or blessed] is the one who perseveres [through "affliction"]* and attains the thousand three hundred thirty-five days. And you, come, and rest, and *you will rise for your allotment at the consummation of the days*" (LXX [Theodotion]). The passage from Daniel is found at the end of the book, where a final admonition is given to the readers. The Israelites are to expect great hardship in the latter days when an antagonist will arise, persecute God's people, and introduce false teaching. The faithful Israelites who withstand the wiles of the antagonist and hold up under persecution will be "blessed" (Dan 12:12). The last verse of Daniel shifts to the person of Daniel himself: "You will rest, and then at the end of the days you will rise to receive your allotted inheritance." The wording is not a far cry from James's promise that a faithful person "will receive the crown of life" (Jas 1:12).

By tapping into Daniel 12, James frames his entire discussion of perseverance in chapter 1 within the scope of the end-time tribulation. The epistle's readers are confronted not with generic trials but with specific end-time affliction that wages war against their faith and character (see Jas 5:11). The prophecy of Daniel is beginning to be directly fulfilled. These believers scattered throughout the Diaspora must remain steadfast in their afflictions, knowing that these end-time trials refine them and give them an opportunity to demonstrate their faith so that they, like the prophet Daniel, may inherit the new creation.

One of the peculiarities of James's letter is the constant attention to wisdom and how it plays a critical role in the daily lives of believers. Verse 5 begins with a plea to ask God for wisdom and instruction: "If any of you lacks wisdom, you should ask God, who gives generously to all." What is not immediately clear, though, is the goal of such wisdom. Why do these churches need wisdom? At one level, all of the exhortations within the epistle spring from God granting his wisdom to his children. An array of Old Testament passages come to the fore that promise life to those who are wise and live in accordance with God's precepts (e.g., Prov 2:3-6). Yet, in another sense, wisdom in James 1:5-8 is contextualized. Wisdom carefully navigates end-time trials and deception (cf. Jas 1:16-18, 22). The book of Daniel is helpful once more, particularly in chapters 11–12. In the latter days, only the wise will persevere under persecution and are subsequently "refined, purified and made spotless until the time of the end" (Dan 11:35; cf. 12:3). This is remarkably similar to James 1:2-3, where God tests the faith of his saints, a principle outlined in the book of Daniel. James, therefore, pleads with the churches to ask God to pour forth his wisdom so that they can distinguish between true and false doctrine and

FIGURE 19.4. THE FOUR BEASTS OF DANIEL 7

maintain genuine faith amid difficult circumstances (see Jas 5:19-20).

The next few verses transition to a discussion of how believers must be wise in the latter days when they face temptation. James says that God does not tempt individuals, but they are "tempted when they are dragged away by their own evil desire and enticed. Then, after desire has conceived, it gives birth to sin; and sin, when it is full-grown, gives birth to death" (1:14-15). Part of the background here is Genesis

> *As God's spoken word in Genesis 1–2 created the world, God's living, written Word creates individuals as a new creation who inevitably obey God's perfect law.*

3, in which the serpent deceives Adam and Eve and sin enters into the world. Probably through an analogous use of the Old Testament, James draws this Scripture into his argument to convince his readers that all of humanity repeats the fall of Adam and Eve for each transgression (cf. Rom 7). Believers, however, are not characterized by sinful behavior but by obedience. James 1:18 asserts that all believers are "a kind of *firstfruits* of all he created." He views Christians "as that part of creation first harvested by God as part of the new creation."[6] Those whom God has brought forth as newly created firstfruits will produce peace as the fruit of righteousness (3:18 NASB). Such creational overtones explain why James refers to God as the "Father of heavenly lights" in 1:17. This name for God recalls his creation of the lights or luminaries in the heavens (Gen 1:14-16; Ps 136:7; Ezek 32:8). The congregations are consequently reassured that the Lord, the creator of all things, executes his creative power when he gives life to the believers scattered throughout the Diaspora.

Word and works (1:19-27). Verses 19-27 of chapter 1 lay the foundation for James's extended discussion of faith and works in 2:14-26. What must be kept in mind, though, is how 1:19-27 piggybacks on the previous passage. The second half of chapter two begins with an imperative to "take note of this" (1:19). Here the command appears to draw attention to the preceding statement that God transforms individuals into the "firstfruits" of the new creation according to his will (1:18). James then issues the commands to hear and speak with a wise demeanor and be "slow to become angry" (1:19). On the basis of their new birth, they are to "get rid of all moral filth and the evil that is so prevalent and humbly accept the word planted in you, which can save you" (1:21). The Word of God transforms these congregations into the new creation (1:18), so they must continue to rely on that same life-giving Word. The "word" here in 1:21 is none other than the Old Testament Scriptures (1:25; 2:8, 11; 4:5-6). The audience's status as a new creation empowers them to rid themselves of the ways of their old decaying life (1:21a; cf. 1 Pet 1:22–2:3). The believers' identity as a new creation is the basis of James's critical admonition in the following chapter.

[6]Peter H. Davids, *The Epistle of James*, NIGTC (Grand Rapids: Eerdmans, 2013), 90.

FAITH AND WORKS (2:1-25)

The Old and New Testaments are filled with stories concerning false accusations against God's people. In 1 Kings 21, King Ahab desires Naboth's vineyard, a nearby piece of land, so that it could be used for his "vegetable garden" (21:2). But Naboth refuses Ahab's offer to pay for the vineyard, as it is part of his family's inheritance and should remain in the family (21:3; cf. Lev 25). Ahab's wife, Jezebel, arranges for "two scoundrels" to give false testimony against Naboth, resulting is his death (21:13). Naboth is unjustly executed and, although Ahab and his family would eventually be punished (21:29; cf. 22:29-40; 2 Kings 9:21-37), righteous Naboth is never truly vindicated. This is but one example of God's people suffering unjustly at the hands of wicked individuals. Both Testaments teach that the day is coming when Israel's God will vindicate his saints and condemn the wicked. At the cross, it appeared as though God's enemies had won. His perfect and righteous Son is unjustly put to death. At the resurrection, however, God vindicates or justifies his Son, declaring to the world that Jesus is right and they are wrong (Rom 1:4). James reminds his congregations that the day is coming when God will also publicly vindicate or justify them. Although believers enjoy a present justification through faith in Christ (e.g., Rom 3:24-28), they await a future, final justification. At the very end of history, when God resurrects believers and unbelievers (Dan 12:1-2), he will publicly declare to the entire cosmos that only those who cling to Christ are in the right and all others are in the wrong. The resurrection of the saints demonstrates their prior justified state in Christ.

FIGURE 19.5. STONING OF NABOTH

Faith and works in avoiding favoritism (2:1-13). The entirety of chapter 2 could be considered a large expansion of 1:22: "Prove yourselves *doers of the word*, and not merely hearers who delude themselves" (NASB). True spirituality for James (and the other New Testament writers) always manifests itself in behavior in keeping with the end-time kingdom. One cannot participate in the covenant community in word only. Faith in Christ is always expressed through works. The first half of the chapter entails a concrete discussion of a true faith that rejects all forms of favoritism (2:1-13), and the second half drills down to the theological rationale of faith and works (2:14-26).

James quickly begins with an admonition to "not show favoritism" for those who are "believers in our glorious Lord Jesus Christ" (2:1). The title *glorious Lord Jesus Christ* gives us a bit of a pause, as it is found only here in all of the New Testament. The closest expression is "the Lord of glory" in 1 Corinthians 2:8, which describes Christ as the exalted, preeminent, and supreme ruler over the cosmos (cf. *1 En* 22:14; 27:3, 5). Christ's majestic position of ruling frames much of James's discussion in 2:1-13. What binds this section together is how believers express their faith through kingdom ethics. By showing favoritism toward the rich within the congregations, the readers eclipse God's authority by becoming judges themselves (Jas 2:4). God alone determines what is right and what is wrong. He also promises that the poor who are "rich in faith" will "inherit the kingdom" (2:5).

FIGURE 19.6. PURPORTED OSSUARY OR BONE BOX OF JAMES

With Jesus' establishment of the new age, his people are called to live as citizens of his kingdom. Since all believers equally participate in the kingdom, they are now bound to a set of latter-day kingdom ethics, which pertains to living in a particular stage of redemptive history. All genuine Christians belong to the new age and are required to live accordingly. These ethics are not antithetical to those in the old covenant or Mosaic administration (Deut 6:5), but they are internalized, reaching their intended state of fulfillment (Jer 31:31-34; Ezek 36:25-27). This is probably what James is getting at when he says that believers "keep the royal law" and practice the love command—"love your neighbor as yourself" (Jas 2:8). Here he quotes Leviticus 19:18 and then goes on to quote two of the Ten Commandments two verses later (Jas 2:11; Ex 20:13, 14). The churches may be neglecting the moral law of the Torah. Christ is a hermeneutical filter through which the entire law passes through in order to arrive in the new creation (Mt 5:17). Those parts of the law that are designed for national Israel are filtered out and fulfilled in Christ, but the parts of the law that are more moral and less ethnic in nature pass through (e.g., the Ten Commandments). When individuals show favoritism by promoting the rich and marginalizing the poor, they fail to uphold the moral law and subvert a key aspect of living as the end-time people of God in the new age—the love of others.

Faith and works and the end-time judgment (2:14-26). The next section begins with a question: "What good is it . . . if someone claims to have faith but has no deeds? Can such faith save them?" (Jas 2:14). In light of the immediate context, James is primarily concerned with relating faith and works to the final judgment at the end of one's life (see 2:13; 3:1, 6; 4:12; 5:1-9). The point throughout the passage is that genuine faith will, without exception, produce good works that will demonstrate one's standing before God; otherwise such faith is considered dead (2:26). Faith without accompanying works is not genuine faith at all but like that which is held by the demons (2:19), a purely cognitive recognition of God without a desire to trust and to obey.

The reference to believers being "justified" in 2:21-24 largely has in mind this final, end-time meaning. According to the apostle Paul, justification entails two levels of vindication: one in the present and one in the future. Because of sin, an individual incurs guilt and deserves God's wrath. But, when God justifies a person based on Christ's work, that individual is vindicated from a guilty verdict *in the present age* (Rom 3:24; 1 Tim 3:16).

There lies a future dimension to justification, too. When believers are resurrected and their bodies are fashioned into a state that is fit for the new creation, they will stand before God's judgment seat at the very end of the age. God will then decree a final, public verdict to the entire cosmos, vindicating his people because of the totality of their faithful works (e.g., Mt 12:36-37; Rom 2:3-10; 2 Cor 5:10). Individuals are exclusively saved through genuine faith in Christ and his work on the cross and resurrection, but such faith will always result in works. These end-time works together with their resurrected condition will vindicate their faith in Christ, just as Christ's own perfect obedience led to his vindication through his resurrection (see 1 Tim 3:16). James's description of justification, particularly his use of the verb *to justify*, does not have in mind how to establish a right standing before God in this life. James is primarily concerned with how faith and works relate to the final judgment *at the end of one's life*. The good works done throughout a person's life will receive God's final vindicating approval at the end of the age.[7] It is in this way that works "save" a person from final condemnation (Jas 2:14). For James, "the ultimate vindication of the believer in the judgment is based on, or at least takes into account, the things that a person has done."[8]

Abraham's obedience to God's command to offer Isaac on the altar is representative of all his good works (2:21-23; Gen 22:9, 12; 15:6). The same is also true in the case of Rahab (Jas 2:25; Josh 2:4, 6, 15). James 2:24 formulates a universal principle on the basis of the example of Abraham: "You see that a man is justified by *works* and not by faith alone" (NASB). The plural *works* here confirms that it was the summation of Abraham's good works of his entire life that vindicated the genuineness of his faith. What was true in the Old Testament is true in the New.

FIGURE 19.7. ABRAHAM SACRIFICING ISAAC

James's use of the words *faith* and *works* in our passage prompts one more important discussion. He appears to be at odds with Paul's teaching on justification:

> You see that a man is *justified by works and not by faith alone*. (Jas 2:24 NASB)
>
> For we maintain that a man is *justified by faith apart from works of the Law*. (Rom 3:28 NASB)

Some scholars suggest that the church in the first century held differing and even conflicting views on justification. But the most satisfactory way to solve this pressing problem

[7]For further elaboration of justification in James 2, see G. K. Beale, *A New Testament Biblical Theology: The Unfolding of the Old Testament in the New* (Grand Rapids: Baker, 2001), 520-22.
[8]Moo, *Letter of James*, 134-35.

is to recognize James's use of the words *faith* and *works*. He insists that faith is always accompanied by works (Jas 2:17, 20, 26), but when Paul employs faith in connection with justification, he wants to highlight that it is faith alone, and not by faith plus works, that allows one *to enter* into the sphere of salvation. James, on the other hand, wants to underscore that true faith will inevitably and subsequently produce good works, both of which are necessary to enter into the final new creational kingdom. J. Gresham Machen notes that "As the faith which James condemns is different from the faith which Paul commends, so also the works which James commends are different from the works which Paul condemns."[9]

CHRISTIAN SPEECH AND THE WISDOM OF GOD (3:1-18)

One unique characteristic of the epistle of James is his emphasis on speech in the Christian life. Godly speech is often discussed in the wisdom literature of the Old Testament. Those within the covenant community are marked by speaking truth, kindness, and encouragement (e.g., Ps 15:1-3; 37:30; 145:5-7; Prov 10:11, 19-21; 11:12-14). But those who slander, deride, and cast aspersions at one another are headed toward destruction (e.g., Job 19:18; Ps 10:7; 34:13; 52:2-4; Prov 4:24; 6:16-19). One of the most graphic and bizarre illustrations of disrespect is found in 2 Kings 2:23-25, in which a pack of forty-two boys from Bethel jeer at the prophet Elisha, mocking him for being bald. In response, Elisha calls down a curse and two bears then maul the boys. God is serious about how the covenant community treats one another. Speech is always wedded to how individuals perceive one another's worth. James 3:9 claims that it is wrong to curse each other because we are "made in God's likeness." To treat one another with disrespect is to disparage the Creator himself.

The power of speech (3:1-12). After articulating the nature of true faith, James progresses to another related topic—the tongue. Genuine faith is on display when individuals speak. Jesus himself said that "the things that come out of a person's mouth come from the heart" (Mt 15:18; cf. 12:34-37). The discussion begins with a strong warning to Christians: "Not many of you should become teachers . . . because you know that we who teach will be judged more strictly" (Jas 3:1). The Old and New Testaments affirm the unique position

FIGURE 19.8. TEACHER WITH STUDENTS

[9]J. Gresham Machen, *The New Testament: An Introduction to Its Literature and History*, ed. W. John Cook (Edinburgh: Banner of Truth, 1976), 239.

of teachers within the covenant community (e.g., 1 Cor 12:28), but with that authority comes great responsibility. Teachers, James argues, will be "judged more strictly" at the very end of history. Perhaps the closest New Testament passage to James 3:1 is found in 1 Corinthians 3, in which teachers or servants will undergo latter-day evaluation that will test their service. If the congregation bears fruit, then the church leaders will pass the test. Three metaphors—gardening, building, and being a steward of mysteries—illustrate Paul's point that God takes the role of pastors and teachers very seriously. They are shepherds of the flock and are responsible for their faithfulness toward their congregations (1 Pet 5:1-4).

Two illustrations demonstrate the importance of the tongue for Christian living—horses and ships (Jas 3:3-4). As a bit controls the horse and a rudder governs a ship, so too the tongue, for good or for evil, yields a tremendous effect on the body (3:5a). The tongue has the power to make "great boasts," similar to how a small spark sets an entire forest on fire (3:5b). Verse 6 relates how God will evaluate speech at the judgment: "It [the tongue] corrupts the whole body, sets the whole course of one's life on fire, and is itself *set on fire by hell.*" The Old Testament, particularly in Psalms and Proverbs, discusses how speech reflects one's true inner character and how God will hold all individuals accountable for such behavior. Psalm 12, for example, recounts the Lord's disgust for deceptive and arrogant speech: "Everyone lies to their neighbor; they flatter with their lips but harbor deception in their hearts. May the Lord silence all flattering lips and every boastful tongue" (Ps 12:2-3; cf. 10:7-8; 34:13; 41:5-9; 52:2-4; Prov 4:24; 10:11; 12:5-6). Jesus even confronted this kind of speech on a number of occasions: "Anyone who says to a brother or sister, 'Raca' [contemptable], is answerable to the court. And any who says, 'You fool!' will be in danger of the fire of hell" (Mt 5:22; cf. 5:37; 12:34-37; 1 Cor 6:10; Eph 4:25, 29, 31; 5:4). James, therefore, admonishes his congregations to manifest true faith by bridling their tongues and ensuring that only blessing flows from their lips.

By way of analogy, James continues his exhortation with a string of allusions to Genesis 1–3: "All kinds of *animals, birds, reptiles and sea creatures* are being tamed and have been tamed by mankind, but no *human being* can tame the tongue. It is a restless evil, full of deadly poison. With the tongue we praise our Lord and Father, and with it we curse *human beings*, who have been made in *God's likeness*" (Jas 3:7-9). Why would James echo Genesis 1–3 at this juncture? He has already argued that since his churches are part of the firstfruits of a new created order (1:18; cf. 3:18), they must live in light of their new identity. In the same way that God created Adam and Eve (Gen 1–2), God has begun to refashion their divine image through his creative might so that their entire lives might be brought into conformity with the redemption of all things.

Earthly wisdom and divine wisdom (3:13-18). Having already laid the foundation for his discussion of wisdom in 1:5-7, James presses his point further on the nature of godly wisdom. Two forms of wisdom are starkly juxtaposed in 3:13-18. First stands the wisdom of the world that is deemed "earthly, unspiritual, demonic" that breeds "selfish ambition . . . disorder and every evil practice" (3:15-16). The other form of wisdom "comes from heaven" and is considered "pure; then peace-loving, considerate, submissive, full of mercy and good fruit, impartial and sincere" (3:17). The wording here resonates with passages in the Old Testament and Judaism where wisdom is hidden and then later revealed (e.g., Dan 2; 4). Oftentimes in these passages two types of wisdom are contrasted: the wisdom of the Lord and the wisdom of humanity. God's true wisdom is set in contrast to the world's wisdom. James's careful use of terms in 3:13 aligns with Daniel 1:4, which describes Daniel and his peers' superior characteristics in contrast to the Babylonians: "Young men without physical defect ... *knowledgeable* in all *wisdom* and educated and *wise*" (LXX; cf. Dan 5:11; 6:4). Throughout the book, Daniel's wisdom is contrasted with the wisdom of the "wise" Babylonians. At every point where the Babylonians falter in their wisdom, Daniel succeeds (Dan 2; 4; 5). By reaching back to the book of Daniel, James encourages his congregations to show their works "by deeds done in the humility that comes from wisdom" (Jas 3:13). The churches must demonstrate genuine faith in Christ by wisely preserving unity within their congregations, avoiding false teaching, and remaining faithful in trials. God's heavenly wisdom provides the framework for all of Christian living.

FIGURE 19.9. CROSSING OF THE RED SEA

COMING OUT OF SPIRITUAL EXILE (4:1-17)

When the Old Testament anticipates the redemption of the saints at the very end of the age, it generally predicts a radical and complete transformation of the body and spirit. But the New Testament strangely claims that God transforms the saints in two stages. Personal redemption begins with an initial, persevering trust in Christ and is completed when he returns. Although believers are indeed a new creation and have an inheritance in the promised land (cf. Heb 12:22), they are still coming out of "Babylonian exile" (what may be called "ongoing sanctification" in Pauline terms). James himself says that they remain "scattered" (Jas 1:1). As Christians continue to emerge from exile and enter the promised land, they shed their sinful baggage that weighs them down. Christians must treat believers and unbelievers in accordance with the overlap of the ages. James's audience must understand that believers are part of the new age, people who have been given a new birth through Christ's work. They are to embrace their existence as a new creation and cast off all the habits of the old Adam.

Living according to the old Adam (4:1-12). Most of chapter 4 can be summarized as living in accordance with the old, sinful characteristics of the first Adam who embodies earthly wisdom (3:15). All true believers grow in their new creational existence, but because they still physically live in the old, material world, and their new creational existence remains incomplete, sin still dogs them. Believers find themselves in the process of shaking the sinful shadow of the old man that lingers in them. Even though the old man has died and its shadow is waning, chapter 4 is a description of this shadowy old man attempting to wreak havoc and take the reins from the new man. Genuine believers will, however, eventually overcome such attempts through their "deeds" (2:14-26).

Life in the first Adam is marked by strife, division, and unfettered selfishness. Through pride the old man will attempt to overthrow God's rule and upend a community living in harmony. The first four verses contain a cluster of military terms that underscore the old man's relentless pursuit: "*battle* within you . . . so you *kill* . . . so you *quarrel* and *fight*. . . . Friendship with the world means *enmity* against God . . . anyone who chooses to be a friend of the world becomes an *enemy* of God" (4:1-4). The stakes of this battle could not be higher. If James's congregations do not fight against the fallen and ungodly world system that wages war against righteousness, then God will combat against them (cf. Rom 8:13). James, quoting from Proverbs 3:34, supports this theme: "God opposes the proud but shows favor to the humble" (Jas 4:6). Here we have a case of the abiding authority of the Old Testament.

What is true in the Old Testament is true in the New: God's gracious hand is ever extended to those who pursue humble repentance, but to those who reject God he stands opposed.

One of the most startling characteristics of chapter 4 is James's harsh appellations for his congregations. Without pulling any punches, he calls them "adulteresses" (4:4 HCSB). The term *adulteresses* is unique and gives the reader pause. It recalls several key passages within the book of Hosea, in which the prophet castigates the Israelites for breaking the covenant (Hos 2:4; 4:2, 13-14; 7:4).[10] Instead of clinging to the Lord in obedience like a faithful bride, the Israelites have embraced the false gods of the pagan nations (e.g., Hos 1:2; 2:2-13). The point of the allusion is that James's audience is "in danger of the same kind of covenant unfaithfulness" that was pervasive in Hosea's day.[11]

James even labels his audience "sinners" and "double-minded" (4:8). Why would James use such terminology? The answer lies in the already-but-not-yet aspect of their salvation as mentioned above. Douglas Moo notes that "the Christian, living in the 'overlap' of the ages, is pulled between the kingdom of Christ and the kingdom of Satan, the realm of Spirit and the realm of 'flesh.'"[12]

[10]Karen H. Jobes, "The Greek Minor Prophets in James," in *'What Does the Scripture Say?': Studies in the Function of Scripture in Early Judaism and Christianity*, ed. Craig A. Evans and H. Daniel Zacharias (New York: T&T Clark, 2012), 2:147-58.

[11]Jobes, "Greek Minor Prophets in James," 156.

[12]Moo, *Letter of James*, 194.

Although the saints are part of the "firstfruits" of the new heavens and earth (1:18), they still possess a shadow of the old man. When James calls them "sinners" and "adulteresses," he has in mind the "not yet" aspect of their redemption—the dim influence of the old Adam.

James 4:7 contains two strong commands—"submit" to God and "resist the devil." In submitting to God, believers rely on his military strength to defeat the devil. Through Christ's work, especially his defeat of the devil in his wilderness temptation and his work on the cross and resurrection, believers now have the power to resist Satan's beckoning call. The apostle Paul explains that believers have donned the "full armor of God," enabling them to take a stand "against the devil's schemes" (Eph 6:11; cf. Is 59:17). Believers participate in the end-time assault that began with the person of Christ. Jesus won a "D-day" victory over the devil, and Christians fight in the wake of that decisive victory in skirmishes against Satan and his allies.

James commands the churches to "come near to God" so that "he will come near to you" (Jas 4:8a). The Greek translation of Hosea 12:6 may be in mind here: "Keep thou mercy and judgment, and *draw near to thy God* continually" (12:7; Brenton). In the immediate context of Hosea 12, God accuses the Israelite leadership of defrauding the people through "dishonest scales" (12:7). They are commanded to turn from their unjust ways and draw near to the Lord. In the same way, James pleads with the churches, particularly the wealthy in it who are exploiting the poor (Jas 2:2-7), to pursue repentance and "come near to God" (cf. 2 Chron 15:2; Zech 1:3; Mal 3:7). Even the commands to "wash your hands" and "purify your hearts" recall the detailed Old Testament purity laws that cleanse the sullied Israelites from the stain of sin so that God may dwell with them. Now that God dwells with the church in a far more intimate way through Christ's atoning death, the churches must rid themselves of any sinful defilement (Jas 4:9-10).

Submission to God's law and power (4:11-17). The second half of chapter 4 continues James's discussion of living in accordance with the old, sinful way of thinking and acting. James 4:11-12 describes individuals judging others in a manner that only God judges, while 4:13-17 condemns those who live in utter autonomy from him. When individuals slander one another and judge others, they become the absolute arbiter of right and wrong. This type of sin is reminiscent of God's prohibition to Adam and Eve not to eat from the tree of the knowledge of good and evil (Gen 3:17; cf. 3:22). God alone possesses the right to decide what is right and what is wrong, as James himself declares: "There is only one Lawgiver and Judge" (Jas 4:12). He rebukes those within the churches for defaming one another and for speaking against the law and judging it (4:11). Believers are to submit to God's perfect law that "gives freedom" (2:12).

James's readers are tempted not only to become independent from God's law but also to usurp his sovereign power in their lives. The entire discussion of attempting to conduct business outside of God's sovereign will lies in humanity's insatiable desire to sit enthroned over the created order. He labels such independent behavior as "arrogant schemes" and "evil" (4:16). James scoffs at the idea of merchants making business arrangements outside of the Lord's will to

FIGURE 19.10. EGYPTIAN BRICK MAKERS

"go to this or that city, spend a year there, carry on business and make money" (4:13). Why is this behavior so problematic? All individuals are unaware of what tomorrow may bring: "You do not even know what will happen tomorrow" (4:14). Such language recalls Proverbs 27:1: "Do not boast about tomorrow, for *you do not know what a day may bring*" (cf. Lk 12:18-20).

James compares the transience of life to a "mist that appears for a little while and then vanishes" (4:14). In some sense, the lives of righteous and the wicked are a "mist" in that they exist only for a brief moment. But, the transient nature of the wicked is reinforced because God's end-time judgment awaits them (see *4 Ezra* 7:61). "The transience of this mortal life," as Richard Bauckham writes, "is of real consequence only for the wicked, who have set all their hopes on the worldly goods they enjoy in this life and face only judgment after death."[13] The righteous, however, will be resurrected in order to inhabit the new creation for all eternity.

CONCLUDING ADMONITIONS (5:1-19)

One constant between the Old and New Testaments is the oppression of the righteous. In order to prevent an uprising, Pharaoh enslaves the Israelites, forcing them to build the cities of Pithom and Rameses (Ex 1:11). The Israelites endure "harsh labor," causing them to undergo a "bitter" existence (1:14). Later on, the narrative relates how the Israelites could stand it no longer and "cried out" to the Lord, who "heard their groaning" (2:23-24). Israel's magnificent redemption

[13]Richard Bauckham, *The Jewish World Around the New Testament* (Grand Rapids: Baker, 2008), 216.

from Egyptian captivity answers this initial and brief request. God keeps the promises he made to the patriarchs (e.g., Gen 12:1-3; 15:1-21; 17:1-22). This line of thought can be traced to a request found in Revelation 6:10: "How long, Sovereign Lord, . . . until you judge the inhabitants of the earth and avenge our blood?" Much of the book of Revelation is a response to this cry for help from the martyred saints in heaven. God promises to vindicate and avenge his children by pouring out righteous judgment on those who unjustly judge believers. Here in the final section of James, God punishes the unbelieving rich for abusing the poor in his congregations. These individuals spent their entire lives pursuing material possessions only to have their wealth "testify against" them (Jas 5:3). The time is now ripe for God to avenge the poor and the oppressed.

Judgment on the wealthy oppressors (5:1-6). James shifts from exhorting the merchants within the church in 4:13-17 to the unbelieving rich in 5:1-6. The rich are condemned in this section not because they are wealthy but for how they became so. The section opens with a command for the rich to "weep and wail . . . because of the misery that is coming on you" (5:1). The language here falls within the Old Testament category of "woe oracles" that announce inescapable impending judgment (Is 3:11; 5:8-22; Jer 13:27; cf. Mt 23). James goes on to describe the nature of their wealth: "Your wealth has rotted, and moths have eaten your clothes" (Jas 5:2). The wording may recall the Sermon on the Mount in Matthew 6:19: "Do not store up for yourselves treasures on earth, where moths and vermin destroy." Throughout the book of James, there are a number of verbal and conceptual affinities to the Sermon on the Mount.[14] James does not possess the Gospel of Matthew, as it was probably not written at this time, but he likely learned about Jesus' life and teachings through his own experience and through the twelve apostles. James is, after all, the half-brother of Jesus and no doubt draws from his own personal encounters.

Verses 3-4 explain why the unbelieving rich are on the receiving end of God's end-time judgment for their insatiable appetite for wealth: "You have hoarded wealth *in the last days*. Look! The *wages you failed to pay the workers* who mowed your fields are crying out against you" (Jas 5:3b-4a). It is quite possible that James has in mind some within his congregation who are defrauded by these wealthy individuals. The result of such mistreatment is that the "outcry of the harvesters has reached *the ears of the Lord of Hosts*" (5:4b HCSB), which resembles the language of Isaiah 5:9: "*In my ears the* L*ORD* *of hosts* has sworn, 'Surely, many houses shall become desolate, Even great and fine ones, without occupants'" (NASB). According to Isaiah 5, Israel and her leaders are prospering: "Woe to you who *add house to house and join field to field till no space is left* and you live alone in the land (Is 5:8-9; cf. 5:12). One reason why Israel's leaders have accrued such wealth lies in their abuse of the poor: "It is you [the elders and leaders] who have ruined my vineyard; the plunder from the poor is in your houses. What do you mean by crushing my people and grinding the faces of the poor?" (Is 3:14-15; cf. Ezek 18:10-18). Isaiah decrees, then, that the wickedness of Israel

[14]Andreas J. Köstenberger, L. Scott Kellum, and Charles L. Quarles, *The Cradle, the Cross, and the Crown: An Introduction to the New Testament* (Nashville: B&H, 2009), 706.

rests on the actions of her wealthy leaders (Is 1:10, 23-26; 3:12-14), and God will exile the nation and her leaders to Babylon (Is 5:13). James employs a unique title for God in 5:4: "the ears of *the Lord of Hosts*" (HCSB). Throughout the Old Testament and in the book of Isaiah, the title refers to God as a divine warrior who fights for or against his people (1 Sam 17:45; Is 1:24; 9:7). The point is that when the unbelieving rich abuse the poor and treat them unjustly, the Lord of the angelic armies will fiercely avenge his own and wage war against the rich (cf. Jer 5:5; 12:3).

Suffering like the prophets (5:7-12). The middle portion of chapter 5 returns to the topic of endurance amid suffering. The congregations are to "be patient . . . until the Lord's coming" (Jas 5:7). Like a farmer awaiting the nourishing rains, believers must await Christ's second coming when he judges the wicked and restores the righteous (cf. Deut 11:14; Jer 5:24; Hos 6:3). While the saints await their redemption, they must avoid grumbling (Jas 5:9). God tests the Israelites in the wilderness as they wander for forty years. Grumbling in the wilderness tangibly demonstrates a lack of faith in God's provision (Ex 15:24; 16:2; 17:3; Deut 1:27). But for those who remain faithful to the Lord, the onslaught of evil and temptation can be resisted, as God promises to shield them with his invisible presence. James asserts that all the saints are metaphorically wandering, in some form or another, through the wilderness on their way to the new creation. Only those who trust in the Lord's promises of redemption will be secure in his presence in the wilderness (Rev 12:1-6). But those who disbelieve, complain, and grumble forfeit their inheritance of the new creation. As judge, Christ is "standing at the door," ready to evaluate the works of his people to determine whether they are genuine (Jas 5:9; cf. Rev 3:20).

James holds up the prophets who have gone before and remained faithful in the "face of suffering" as an example for the churches to imitate (5:10). These faithful saints withstood the mounting pressure to abandon all trust in God and give in to temptation (see Heb 11:32-38). Although countless saints are on James's mind, he mentions only Job's "perseverance" (5:11). Job is the model saint who refused to turn his back on the Lord (e.g., Job 1:21; 2:10). At the end of the book, God blessed Job and "restored his fortunes and gave him twice as much as he had before" (Job 42:10). The same promise of blessing is extended to James's congregations who are beset with end-time trials. As in 1:12, James once more alludes to Daniel 12:12 when he asserts that believers are "blessed . . . who have persevered" (Jas 5:11; see Dan. 12:12: "Happy [or blessed] is the one who perseveres [through affliction] . . ." [LXX (Theodotion)]). If they maintain their faith through fiery trials, then God will reward them, as he did with Job, in the new heavens and earth.

The prayer of the righteous (5:13-20). The letter ends with a summons for the church to pray in earnest in all circumstances: "Is anyone among you in trouble? Let them pray" (5:13; cf. Ps 50:15; 91:15). The next verse fleshes out a particular situation that requires urgent prayer: "Is anyone among you sick? Let them call the elders of the church to pray over them and anoint them with oil" (Jas 5:14). The use of oil here is reminiscent of Mark 6:13, where the disciples proclaim the message of the kingdom

FIGURE 19.11. ELIJAH RECEIVING THE WIDOW'S BREAD

and "*anointed* many sick people with *oil and healed them*" (cf. Lk 10:34). It could be that the oil is mentioned to function as a medicinal aid, but in all likelihood it is probably in line with the general Old Testament act of anointing unique individuals for a specific undertaking. Kings, priests, Israelite leaders, and even furnishings in the temple are anointed. Anointing marks an individual (or thing) for a particular use that is to be set aside, devoted only to God (e.g., Gen 28:18-22; Ex 30:30; Dan 9:25-26). James requests, then, that oil be used in conjunction with the elders' prayer so that the sick individual would be marked out in earnest devotion to God for healing. The elders of the church are to pray like Elijah, whose prayer was "powerful and effective" (Jas 5:16-17). In this vein, the section of 5:13-16 seems to contain a series of varied exhortations for the congregations to follow. They are to pray, sing, anoint the sick with oil, and confess sin to receive forgiveness. Note that in the Old Testament, these activities take place within the context of Israel's temple through the administration of the priests. Here, though, each of these aspects is performed within the local congregations. As the true temple, God's people are also priests who are to rid themselves of all impurity and offer up spiritual sacrifices of prayer and praise.

The last two verses of the epistle are seemingly misplaced: "If one of you should *wander from the truth* . . . : Whoever turns a sinner from *the error of their way* will save them from death and cover over a multitude of sins" (5:19-20). Why does James broach the topic of false teaching at the end of a book that is devoted to authentic Christian living? If we take into account the capstone of the epistle, acquiring the heavenly wisdom from God and how believers are to use such wisdom to navigate through trials at the end of days, then James's admonition makes wonderful sense. Out of deep love and concern, the apostle James desires that every aspect of life should be pleasing and honorable to God as believers are caught in the overlap of the ages. With the aid of God's wisdom, believers must be on the lookout for false teaching and wisely correct those who have succumbed to it (cf. Jude 20-23).

20

1 PETER

AUTHORSHIP

According to 1:1, Peter authors this letter, and the early church makes no qualms about it. In his discussion of the two epistles of Peter, Eusebius states that 1 Peter is the "only one of which I know to be genuine and acknowledged by the ancient elders" (*Hist. eccl.* 3.3.4). As of late, many scholars are convinced that this letter is pseudonymous, written by a "Petrine school." A common argument stems from Peter's apparent lack of schooling according to the Gospels. How can a simple fisherman pen a complex letter such as this? The problem with this conclusion is that we simply do not know much about Peter's educational background. In addition, Peter uses a secretary to compose the letter, so the vocabulary, syntax, and general style of the letter could well be attributed to the secretary, Silas (5:12). For good reason, then, we believe that the apostle Peter, one of Jesus' closest disciples, wrote this letter.

DATE

Peter writes from "Babylon" (5:13)—that is, Rome. Peter probably arrives in Rome in the 60s and is martyred a few years later around AD 65. Also, if Peter pens 2 Peter, we need to leave enough time for him to write and publish it. Thus, we should date the epistle somewhere in AD 60–62.

FIGURE 20.1. LAMENT OF ST. PETER

OCCASION

Peter writes to the largely Gentile churches in northwest Asia Minor: "Peter, an apostle of Jesus Christ, To God's elect, exiles scattered throughout the provinces of Pontus, Galatia, Cappadocia, Asia and Bithynia, who have been chosen" (1:1-2). Although we are unsure of the precise source of their suffering, it is quite clear that these churches are enduring significant social ostracism (1:6; 3:13-17; 4:12-19). It is probable that Christianity, at this time, has come under general persecution from a number of fronts—their communities, relatives, hostile Jews, and even their own family.

PURPOSE

When the audience of 1 Peter committed themselves to Christ, it came with a steep price (4:1). Inevitably, these newly minted Christians found themselves at odds with their friends, coworkers, family members, and government. Shortly after their conversion, Peter's readers clashed with the world around them. First Peter is primarily written to address this upheaval. Perhaps these Gentile Christians did not anticipate such suffering when they embraced the gospel. In any case, Peter comforts these believers in Asia Minor by reminding them that their faith will undergo severe testing, but this will give way to eternal rest in heaven. Peter not only highlights the role of persevering faith but also, like the other New Testament writers, reminds his readers of their position in Christ. By placing their faith in Christ, these Gentile Christians become part of the restored Israel of God, an event that the Old Testament prophesied about centuries before.

OUTLINE

- I. Letter Opening (1:1-2)
- II. Christ's Work of Redemption and Godly Living (1:3-25)
  - A. The Return of Christ and the Believers' Inheritance (1:3-12)
  - B. Holy Living in Light of the Latter Days (1:13-21)
- III. The Church as the Growing End-Time Temple (2:1–3:22)
  - A. Believers and the Temple of God (2:1-10)
  - B. The Temple of God in a Hostile World (2:11-25)
  - C. Believers as a Unified Community (3:1-12)
  - D. Believers as a Suffering Community (3:13-22)
- IV. Called to Godly Living (4:1-19)
  - A. Righteous Suffering (4:1-11)
  - B. Power in the Throes of Defeat (4:12-19)
- V. Leadership of the Church and Letter Closing (5:1-14)
  - A. Pastors as End-Time Shepherds of the Church (5:1-10)
  - B. Letter Closing (5:12-14)

BIBLICAL-THEOLOGICAL THEMES

Echoing Exodus 19:6, Peter identifies the largely Gentile group of Christians in Asia Minor as a "royal priesthood" who "offers spiritual sacrifices acceptable to God through Jesus" (1 Pet 2:5). The priestly status of all believers finds its point of origin in Genesis 1–2. Since God creates Adam and Eve in his image, their activities on earth are to mirror his activities in heaven. Adam's commission to cultivate and guard in Genesis 2:15 as a priest-king continues the theme of subduing and filling the earth (Gen 1:28). Adam is to be God's obedient priest in maintaining the physical and spiritual welfare of the garden sanctuary. As a faithful priest, he must protect the sanctuary of Eden and recollect, interpret, and apply God's word (Gen 2:16-17). But Adam and Eve soon fail by allowing the unclean serpent to enter (Gen 3:1). They also fail to hold fast to God's word and resist the serpent's wily temptation (Gen 3:3-5). The story is once again repeated with the nation of Israel. They, too, allow God's sanctuary to be defiled with idolatry and refuse to embrace God's law. Despite being charged with the commission to spread God's glory to the nations as a royal priesthood (Ex 19:6), they selfishly keep God's decrees to themselves and fail to evangelize the nations. The Old Testament prophets, however, anticipate the restoration of Israel and the salvation of the nations (Is 2:1-5; Mic 4:1-3). Isaiah 66:21 even states that some from the Gentiles will become priests and Levites in the end-time temple of God (so also 56:1-7).

Jesus, as the true Priest-King, faithfully mediates the presence of God to Israel and the nations. He begins to rid the earth of all things unclean (sin, wickedness, the devil, etc.) and perfectly embraces the law of God and teaches it to his people. By being joined to Christ, all New Testament saints are considered priests who serve in the temple of God. As priests in God's temple, believers offer the sacrifice of witness. First Peter states that God constructs believers into a spiritual temple that functions as a "holy priesthood, offering spiritual sacrifices acceptable to God through Jesus Christ" (2:5). As a royal priesthood living as "foreigners and exiles" (2:11), these spiritual sacrifices of praise testify to the risen Christ among their hostile communities so that "though they accuse you of doing wrong, they may see your good deeds and glorify God on the day he visits us." (2:12). Just as the Old Testament priests sacrificed on behalf of the people to bring them to God, so the New Testament priests sacrifice through suffering on behalf of the nations.

LETTER OPENING (1:1-2)

Peter opens his epistle by identifying himself as "an apostle of Jesus Christ" (1:1a). This title carries with it all sorts of rich characteristics. Peter is indeed one of the twelve apostles that walked alongside Jesus during his earthly ministry. He is even considered, along with James and John, to be part of the "inner three" who bore witness to intimate details of Christ and incredible miracles (e.g. Mk 5:37; 9:2; 14:33). The Jesus that Peter knew intimately is the same Jesus that the churches in Asia Minor confess. Since Peter bears the indelible mark of an apostle, his words carry a unique status of authority. It is with this authority that he writes to the churches in Asia Minor.

FIGURE 20.2. ADAM AND EVE IN THE GARDEN

After identifying himself as an apostle of Jesus Christ, Peter spends a considerable amount of time identifying his audience. Preceding the location of the audience, Peter calls them "elect" and "scattered exiles" (1:1b; cf. 2:11; Heb 11:13). These labels function on two levels: (1) Peter uses two labels that recall Israel in the Old Testament (e.g., Deut 7:6; 14:2; Ps 105:6) and attributes them to the largely Gentile churches in Asia Minor. The inescapable conclusion is that Peter considers his audience to be part of true, end-time Israel. (2) The churches are labeled *scattered exiles*, a term that traditionally refers to Israelites outside of the Promised Land (Neh 1:9; Is 49:6; Jer 15:7). Using this language, Peter refers to his audience on a redemptive-historical plane. The new creation that the Old Testament so often speaks about arrives only partially. Peter's audience is caught within the overlap of two ages—the age of the new creation and the old age of rebellion. He views the Gentiles as new creational "exiles" sojourning through the old age.

Verse 2 states how the church comprises the elect, "who have been chosen according to the foreknowledge of God the Father, through the sanctifying work of the Spirit, to be obedient to Jesus Christ and *sprinkled with his blood.*" The phrase "sprinkled with his blood" echoes Exodus 24:8, when Moses sprinkles the blood on the Israelites, ratifying the covenant. These Gentiles have been graciously brought into God's people through Christ's death so that they may obey his will.

FIGURE 20.3. MOSES DESCENDS FROM MT. SINAI

CHRIST'S WORK OF REDEMPTION AND GODLY LIVING (1:3-25)

At the end of chapter 1, Peter claims that his churches are "born again" through the "living and enduring word of God" (1:23). According to Genesis 1, God creates the world by his word and fashions Adam and Eve into existence. The adjective *living* appeals to God's Word as possessing life within itself and thus able to grant life. Peter supports his statement in 1:23 by appealing to Isaiah 40:8 in verses 24-25: "All people are like grass, and all their glory is like the flowers of the field; the grass withers and the flowers fall, but the word of the Lord endures forever." The believers in Asia Minor can be confident that God is in the process of creating a new, perfect world that will never perish but will last for all eternity. They must not lose heart in the midst of affliction, as their salvation is bound up with that end-time renewal.

The return of Christ and the believers' inheritance (1:3-12). Peter begins the body of the letter explaining why his audience must endure hardship and great suffering: "He [God] has given us *new birth* into a living hope through the resurrection of Jesus Christ from the dead. . . . This inheritance is kept in heaven for you, who through faith are shielded by God's power until the coming of the salvation that is ready to be revealed in the last time" (1:3-5). God forges these pagan, idolatrous, and selfish Gentiles into a new humanity through the power of Christ's resurrection (1:23). In addition, the inheritance that these churches now enjoy is none other than the initial phase of the new eternal cosmos in Christ. The nation of Israel in the Old Testament did indeed possess some inheritance in the Promised Land, but it was snatched away by the Assyrians and Babylonians. Peter's audience, though, has a secure inheritance. As Oren Martin writes, "No foreign enemies can take this inheritance, because, unlike the previous symbol of God's presence in the land, this one is kept in heaven."[1]

The last bit of this section (1:6-9) is the climax of Peter's exhortation thus far and is pivotal for the overall purpose of the book. Verse 7 is explicit: "These [trials] have come so that the proven genuineness of your faith—of greater worth than gold, which perishes even though refined by fire—may result in praise, glory and honor when Jesus Christ is revealed." The largely Gentile readers have come under great persecution and suffering from a number of fronts, but their suffering is not in vain—God receives all the glory from their hardships.

Although only a few verses, 1:10-12 is the focus of a considerable amount of discussion. Peter's words here are thick and his syntax is a bit tricky. But the thrust of the section is that his audience is presently experiencing a salvation that has been waiting in the wings for quite some time. The Old Testament prophets were searching "intently and with the greatest care" (1:10) about the precise timing of the Messiah's suffering that will result in the salvation of God's people Israel (1:11).

The churches in Asia Minor are presently participating in the end-time restoration that God promised in the Old Testament so long ago. One particular prophetic text from Isaiah is worth citing: "In the last days the mountain of the LORD's temple will be established as the highest of the mountains. . . . Many peoples will come and say, 'Come, let us go up to the mountain of the LORD, to the temple of the God of Jacob. He will teach us his ways, so that we may walk in his paths'" (Is 2:2-3; cf. Mic 4:1-2). Here in Isaiah, God promises to escort the nations to his end-time temple and Jerusalem, where they will adhere to his law and worship him there. This text and many more like it find their initial direct fulfillment in the person of Christ.

> ***Since Christ embodies true Israel, the true temple, and the new creation, the persecuted Gentiles in Asia Minor enjoy all of these benefits because of their identity in him (1 Pet 1:3).***

The Old Testament prophets searched intently for the timing of the Messiah's arrival. Although they lacked some of the finer details of the Messiah's suffering, they generally understood that he would suffer, die, and finally be exalted (e.g., Is 52–53; Dan 9:26). Yet, they did not know the precise timing of the arrival of the latter days and when the Messiah would suffer. Peter's audience lives in an exciting time—the Messiah's arrival and the establishment of his long-awaited kingdom. Christ inaugurated the

[1]Oren R. Martin, *Bound for the Promised Land: The Land Promise in God's Redemptive Plan*, NSBT 34 (Downers Grove, IL: InterVarsity Press, 2015), 150.

new age, and Peter's audience must live in accordance with it.

Holy living in light of the latter days (1:13-21). Peter first tells his readers who they are before telling them how to behave (1:1-12). Like other biblical writers, Peter's admonitions come on the basis of who they are in Christ (notice the *therefore* at the beginning of 1:13). Unless individuals have been made anew in Christ, they are unable to obey God's commandments. Conversion precedes obedience. Verse 13 first strikes the reader as a bit strange: "Therefore, *with your minds ready for action*, be serious and set your hope completely on the grace to be brought to you at the revelation of Jesus Christ" (HCSB). The KJV translates this phrase

FIGURE 20.4. ROMAN GLADIATORS

as "gird up the loins of your mind." Peter employs a military metaphor here (Judg 18:16). In the ancient world, individuals dress in long garments, and in order to prepare for battle, they pull up their garments to free themselves for quick movement. The point is that Christians must be fully alert for battle. Although they cannot see it, indeed, a war rages on between believers and unbelievers. The churches in Asia Minor may not perceive that their persecutors, whoever they might be (government, family members, etc.) are warring against them in a cosmic conflict (see 1 Pet 5:8).

The next three verses focus on how the churches must live in the midst of a hostile world: "As obedient children, do not conform to the evil desires. . . . But just as he who called you is holy, so be holy in all you do" (1:14-15). Peter shifts from a military metaphor to a cultic one. Since the congregations are the true and living temple of God (cf. 2:4-10), they must live accordingly. Holiness in the Old Testament is wedded to God's nature and his glorious presence that dwelled partially in Israel's midst. The geography of Israel is broken down into three gradations: holy (the temple precinct), clean (Israel's territory), and unclean (outside the boundaries of Israel). The Israelites are forbidden from partaking of unclean food or participating in any unclean activity. The general thrust of the holiness in the Old Testament is the strong conviction that the Israelites must not only be "clean" but progress into a state of utter "holiness," fit for God's presence. "To be holy is to be unblemished or unmarred. It is to experience life in all its fullness as God has originally intended it to be."[2]

Peter gives the basis for his exhortation that the churches "be holy" by citing a combination of texts from Leviticus (Lev 11:44-45; 19:2; 20:7, 26). While it is difficult to pinpoint exactly which one is in view, the point of these quotations is straightforward. Israel's holiness springs from their deliverance out

[2]T. Desmond Alexander, *From Paradise to the Promised Land: An Introduction to the Pentateuch*, 3rd ed. (Grand Rapids: Baker, 2012), 244.

of Egyptian bondage (Lev 11:45). Israel is God's legal heir, so sin has no business inhabiting Israel's land. God redeems Israel from Egypt to be different from the neighboring pagan nations, to imitate his holy character. By applying this text to the largely Gentile churches in Asia Minor, Peter is, in effect, claiming that these small congregations are true Israel and, as such, must behave accordingly.

First Peter 1:17-21 is rich with a variety of metaphors and Old Testament imagery. The first key metaphor is the church's identification as foreigners. Although not the same word found in 1:1, this term is often located in Old Testament and Jewish texts that describe Israel living outside of the Promised Land (e.g., Ezra 8:35; Jdt 5:9). What is remarkable about this designation is where Peter uses it in his line of argumentation: "Since you call on a Father who judges each person's work impartially, live out your time as foreigners here in reverent fear." Believers must fear God in the midst of their sojourn to the Promised Land because he judges without partiality.

According to 1:20, Christ "was revealed in these last times for your sake." Christ, Israel's long-awaited King, inaugurates the "latter days," which refer to the final phase in history when Israel will commit idolatry and God will send the nation into exile. An antagonist will arise, persecute, and deceive Israel, and the nation will be engaged in warfare with surrounding nations (e.g., Deut 31:29; Ezek 38:16; Dan 2:8, 11, 25; 8:9-12). After this, the Messiah will arrive on the scene, redeem Israel from the nations' clutches, eliminate wickedness, and install God's eternal kingdom in the new heavens and earth (e.g., Gen 49:1; Num 24:14; Dan 2:28-29). Christ's coming began the destruction of the old age and the inbreaking of the new. According to J. Ramsey Michaels, "The assumption of this epistle is not that Jesus is absent from his people, so that he must 'come.' Rather, he is present with them but invisible; therefore he must 'be revealed.'"[3] Peter's readers must grasp their relationship to God, Israel, and the surrounding hostile communities in light of living in the overlap of the ages.

> ***Christ has redeemed them from spiritual slavery and brought them into the Promised Land of the new creation. They must therefore live up to their identity.***

The final section in the chapter exhorts the church to love one another because believers have been purified and renewed through God's Word. Verse 22 recalls what has already been established in the preceding sections—Christ has purified the churches in Asia. That is, God made them alive, set them apart, and declared them righteous. Therefore they must "have sincere love for each other, love one another deeply, from the heart" (1 Pet 1:22). The next few verses express why the church must love one another: they have been "born again" (1:23a). Believers are part of the new creation, a process that began with the resurrection of Christ (1:3).

[3]J. Ramsey Michaels, *1 Peter*, WBC 49 (Waco, TX: Word Books, 1988), 32.

FIGURE 20.5. RELIEF DEPICTING DEPORTATION TO ASSYRIA, WHERE ISRAEL IS FIRST EXILED

Peter states how these believers have been converted: "through the living and enduring word of God" (1:23b). Peter then cites Isaiah 40:6-9 in verses 24-25 to support this claim: "For, 'All people are like grass, and all their glory is like the flowers of the field; the grass withers and the flowers fall, but the word of the Lord endures forever.'" In the immediate context of this Old Testament quotation, Isaiah 40 serves as a transitional point within the book of Isaiah. Anticipated in the first half of the book (e.g., 2:2-5; 24:1–25:12), Isaiah 40–66 describes Israel's release from Babylonian captivity as a second exodus (40:10-11; 51:9; 52:10), the journey to the Promised Land (49:9), and the creation of a new heavens and earth (65:17-25; 66:22-23). All of this will take place through Isaiah's servant (42:1-9, 49:1-6, 50:4-9, 52:13–53:12). Isaiah 40 describes God restoring his people from Babylonian captivity by leading them through the desert to the Promised Land. The restoration of Israel from Babylon is cast in such a way that it recalls Israel's restoration from Egyptian captivity. Just as God redeemed his people from Egyptian bondage, so he will release the Israelites from the Babylonians.

The theme of God's word enduring and humanity failing resonates throughout Isaiah. In the face of danger and unlikely events, Isaiah proclaims God's word to Israel (Is 29:4-5; 31:3). Isaiah tells Israel that God will send them into Babylonian captivity and that they will indeed return when God establishes the new heavens and earth. God's eternal word is absolutely central to Isaiah. God knows the future and tells Israel what it is! He tells Israel that they will go into exile and eventually be restored to their homeland.

Peter's use of Isaiah 40 here in 1:24-25 makes good sense on a few levels. Isaiah 40 is cast as a prophecy, and Peter quotes the prophecy as a direct fulfillment of that promise. There may also be a prototypical or blueprint use of the Old Testament, since much of Isaiah 40–66 is in view. Peter argues that "this is the word that was preached to you" (1:25b), an affirmation that these Old Testament promises from Isaiah are coming to fruition. Through the work of Christ as Isaiah's suffering servant (2:22-25), the church has been initially redeemed from Babylonian exile and has begun to live in the Promised Land of the new creation.

THE CHURCH AS THE GROWING END-TIME TEMPLE (2:1–3:22)

Peter continues to underscore his audience's identity in light of Christ's coming and the effects of the crucifixion and resurrection. Christ's work on the cross and his resurrection triggers the end-time restoration of the new heavens and earth (Is 66:22; 2 Cor 5:17). But the churches in Asia Minor must not simply contemplate these glorious truths; they must act on them by living them out daily. As the restored Israel of God in the beginning of the new creation, Peter exhorts his readers to embrace a lifestyle that is in accordance with their restoration. He devotes much of 1 Peter 2:1–3:22 to the church's status as the end-time people of God. This stands in sharp contrast to how the Gentiles probably perceive themselves living in a pagan environment. Peter's word enriches their identity and forges a common denominator between the scattered exiled communities throughout Asia Minor.

Believers and the temple of God (2:1-10). Peter begins chapter 2 with a series of exhortations. The first three verses of this chapter are tightly wrapped together with the first imperative occurring in 2:2. Verse 1 most likely explains how believers are to "crave spiritual milk": "Therefore, putting aside all evil, all deceit, hypocrisy, envy, and all slander, long for pure milk as infants [long for pure milk]" (2:1-2a; our translation). One longs for milk by putting aside wickedness. It is likely best to interpret *milk* in this passage as a reference to God's Word.[4] When believers nourish their souls in the Word, a holy conduct inevitably follows. The second half of 2:2 reveals the goal of craving God's Word: "so that by it you may grow up in your salvation" (2:2b). Peter is not content at the current state of his audience. They must press on in their faith and, like babies, "grow up" (cf. Heb 5:12-14). Verse 3 states the reason why the church must mature in their faith: "now that you have tasted that the Lord is good."

Verse 3 appears to recall Psalm 34:8: "*Taste and see that the* Lord *is good*; blessed is the one who takes refuge in him." Psalm 34 describes David's deliverance in the midst of trouble. It is noteworthy that Psalm 34:8 is an imperative whereas 1 Peter 2:3 has occurred in the past. Tasting is a past event in 1 Peter 2, so Peter is claiming that his readers, if they have persevered through affliction, have already been delivered from persecution and presently enjoy communion with God.

The next paragraph is riddled with the Old Testament. Verse 4 claims that Christ is a "living Stone," a stone that is "rejected by human

[4]However, see Karen H. Jobes, *1 Peter*, BECNT (Grand Rapids: Baker, 2005), 136, who understands the term to apply more broadly to "the ultimate reality of the new creation that the resurrection of Christ has established."

beings but chosen by God and precious to him." Several texts are in mind here. The first text, Psalm 118:22, communicates the idea that God desires what man rejects. A rejected stone that is ultimately exalted to the chief cornerstone by God carries with it traces of God constructing his temple with something or someone who is rejected by people but glorious in God's sight (Ps 118:23-29). The second part of the verse likely has Isaiah 8:14-15 and 28:16 in mind: "He will be a holy place; for both Israel and Judah he will be a stone that causes people to stumble and a rock that makes them fall. And for the people of Jerusalem he will be a trap and a snare. Many of them will stumble; they will fall and be broken, they will be snared and captured" (Is 8:14-15); "See, I lay a stone in Zion, a tested stone, *a precious cornerstone* for a sure foundation; the one who relies on it will never be stricken with panic" (Is 28:16).

The ultimate gist of these two texts (within the broader context of Isaiah) is that God will raise up a servant who will be rejected by the majority of Israelites (and the pagan nations) but will ultimately be vindicated (Is 52–53). Those who join themselves to this individual will be restored and become part of true Israel and God's end-time temple (Is 49:6) and enjoy entrance into the new heavens and earth (Is 66). But those who reject God's servant, as most will do, will be shattered by God's judgment.

After describing Christ as a rejected yet precious stone (2:4), Peter makes a staggering claim: "You also, like *living stones*, are being built into *a spiritual house* to be a holy priesthood, offering spiritual sacrifices acceptable to God through Jesus Christ" (2:5). Christ is the locus of God's presence and the restored people of God (2:4), and because believers place their faith in him, they too enjoy those same benefits (2:5). Just as Christ is a "living Stone," so are believers. Christ is the end-time temple of God (cf. Jn 2:21), and believers are "a spiritual house" (2:5a). God's design is to dwell with humanity in the new eternal cosmos (Gen 1–2; Rev 21–22), and Christ initially achieves this plan during his first advent and especially at the cross and resurrection.

First Peter 2:6 is a formal quotation of Isaiah 28:16, a text that is already in the background of 2:4 and has been applied to Christ. Peter applies this text to the church, indicating the fulfillment of Isaiah's prophecy. What has been fulfilled in Christ is now, by extension, fulfilled in God's people. In 2:7 Peter once again taps into Psalm 118:22 and applies this text to the church in Asia Minor: "Now to you who believe, this stone is precious. But to those who do not believe, '*The stone the builders rejected has become the cornerstone.*'" Those who embrace Christ through faith participate in God's end-time people, the temple, but those who reject him are crushed under its weight (Mt 21:44; Lk 20:18). This latter truth is explained in greater detail in 2:8, in which Peter formally cites Isaiah 8:14-15 (a text that surfaces in 2:4).

With direct fulfillment on his mind, Peter continues to heap up one Old Testament quotation after another. First Peter 2:9-10 is a combination of three texts: Exodus 19:6, Isaiah 43:20-21, and Hosea 2:23. The first quotation ("a chosen race") originates from Isaiah 43:20-21: "The wild animals honor me, the jackals and the owls, because I provide water in the wilderness and streams in the wasteland, to give drink to *my people, my chosen*, the people I formed for myself, that they may proclaim my praise." The thrust of the Old

FIGURE 20.6. ISRAELITES CROSSING THE RED SEA

Testament context there is that the Lord will bring his people out of Babylonian exile. Verses 18-19 are also telling: "Forget the former things; do not dwell on the past. See, I am doing a new thing!" God, by bringing his people out of exile, will usher in the new heavens and earth (cf. Is 65:17). By applying this phrase to the congregations in Asia Minor, Peter is claiming that the church is part of the new creation, the restored people of God!

Secondly, Peter quotes from Exodus 19 when he uses the phrase "a royal priesthood, a holy nation":

> Then Moses went up to God, and the LORD called to him from the mountain and said, "This is what you are to say to the house of Jacob and what you are to tell the people of Israel: 'You yourselves have seen what I did to Egypt. . . . Now if you obey me fully and keep my covenant, then out of all nations you will be my treasured possession. Although the whole earth is mine, you will be for me *a kingdom of priests and a holy nation*.'" (Ex 19:3-6)

The significance of this phrase is twofold: (1) Israel's experience at Sinai is the birth of the nation, the defining moment when Israel became God's "son." The application of this phrase to the church, comprising Christian Jews and Gentiles, indicates that the church constitutes the true Israel of God. (2) This quotation defines the missional nature of the church. Israel is supposed to be the means by which all the nations are to have a relationship with God. They are the bearers of God's glory to the world.

Lastly, 2:10 is a quotation from Hosea 1:10-11 and 2:23: "Yet the Israelites will be like the sand on the seashore, which cannot be measured or counted. In the place where it was said to them, '*You are not my people*,' they will be called 'children of the living God.' The people of Judah and the people of Israel will come together; they will appoint one leader and will come up out of the land, for great will be the day of Jezreel" (Hos 1:10-11); "I will say to those called '*Not my people*,' '*You are my people*'; and they will say, 'You are my God'" (Hos 2:23). In Hosea 1:9, God instructs Hosea to name one of his children Lo-ammi, which simply means "not my people." God will reject his idolatrous people, Israel, and deem them as Gentiles. But in Hosea 1:10-11, after God has rejected and judged his people, he will once again restore them. The same can be said of 2:23: God will restore his once-rejected people. This text is not claiming that Gentiles who were not God's people will become God's people. Instead, it is claiming that Israel will become not God's people and then be restored as God's people. The application of Hosea 1:10-11 and 2:23 in 1 Peter 2:10 is significant: God considers the mixed congregation in Asia Minor to be his people, the end-time restored people of

God. D. A. Carson puts his finger on the thrust of these Old Testament quotations:

> He [Peter] is giving his readers a distinctive identity that is bound up tightly with God's mercy to them in Christ Jesus, and with their response in obedient faith and holiness. One of the effects, of course, was to make them sufficiently different as a "people" or "race" or "nation" that first-century pagan society would not be long in resenting them.[5]

The temple of God in a hostile world (2:11-25). Peter continues to explicate how the church must live in light of the gospel—that is, Christ's life, death, and resurrection. Since the church is the true Israel of God (2:4-10), on account of Christ's work, it must resemble the covenant community in all its behavior. The section of 2:11–3:12 is the effect of the church being identified as true Israel in 2:4-10. The apostle Peter gets into the gritty details of what this behavior looks like in 2:13-25. His main focus is on how the churches of Asia Minor apply to their lives their end-time status as true Israel in their interaction with the government (2:13-17) and employers (2:18-20). Ultimately, the church must embody the pattern of living that Christ has set before them (2:21-25).

The first part of this section deals specifically with how the churches in Asia Minor are to conduct themselves before the local magistrates, who are ultimately agents of the Roman Empire. We know that these churches have come under persecution (e.g., 1:6-9; 4:12), and a good case could be made that these congregations are on the receiving end of persecution on a number of fronts—religious, familial, and political.

Verse 13a broadly commands, "Submit yourselves for the Lord's sake to every human authority," leaving 2:13b-14 to unpack what this looks like in further detail. Peter expects these churches to submit to human authority. Defining what Peter means by *submit* is not altogether clear, though. It generally carries with it the idea of subordination (in contrast to independence). Romans 13:1-7 is the closest text to 1 Peter 2:13-14, where we find believers instructed to submit to authorities. Paul admonishes the Roman church to not rebel against their political authority (Rom 13:2). At the very least, Peter requires that the churches in Asia Minor respect and obey their political authorities. The church is also required to come under the authority of the government "for the Lord's sake." Although using only a few words, Peter discloses a key motivating factor: the churches must obey the governing authorities because God has intentionally established them (cf. Rom 13:1-4). Since God wisely and sovereignly establishes these political bodies, he expects that believers recognize his wisdom in this establishment and obey.

After sketching the church's conduct with respect to the government, Peter tackles three specific relationships that are altered in light of the church's identification as true, end-time Israel. This section in 1 Peter 2:18–3:12 is known as the "household codes," which is nearly identical to those found in Colossians 3:18-21 and Ephesians 5:22–6:9. Many scholars believe that these codes stem from the wider Greco-Roman world, wherein codes were given concerning the relationship between husband and wife, master and

[5]D. A. Carson, "1 Peter," in *Commentary on the New Testament Use of the Old Testament*, ed. G. K. Beale and D. A. Carson (Grand Rapids: Baker Academic, 2007), 1032.

slave, and fathers and children. What must be kept in mind is the code's relationship to the end-time people of God as a new creational community. The household code is integrated with the gospel and the believer's relationship to it. Christ's work unites those relationships that the fall fractures. A key distinctive of the old age is division among people groups (cf. Gen 10–11; Deut 32:8) and familial relationships (Mal 4:6). Now that Christ has come, believers, as true, end-time Israel, enjoy harmony among themselves in their human and spiritual families. They should even pursue such harmony with unbelievers (cf. Eph 4–6).

Peter first outlines how the congregations relate to their employers. "Slaves, in reverent fear of God submit yourselves to your masters, not only to those who are good and considerate, but also to those who are harsh" (1 Pet 2:18). Is Peter condoning slavery within the church? It is of utmost importance to first understand the nature of slavery in the Greco-Roman world. Slaves are granted many rights, such as worshiping, marrying, and making money. They were artisans, architects, doctors, philosophers, teachers, and writers. Race is also not an issue. It is possible for slaves to gain freedom for a price (manumission), and many receive it after about thirty or so years of service. Slavery in Peter's day looks different from "old South" (Antebellum) slavery. Certainly, owners were cruel to their slaves and treated them poorly. But there remains one key principle that was alive and well in the Greco-Roman world and continues into the present: slaves are owned. The master exerts absolute control over the servant. Peter requires slaves to be submissive to their masters, but ultimately they are to seek God's approval (2:20). There may be a hint of Peter undermining slavery ownership here since he claims that God is indeed the ultimate authority. In any case, those within the churches at Asia Minor must respect and

FIGURE 20.7. MOSAIC DEPICTING A MISTRESS AND SLAVES

submit to their masters even in the face of injustice (2:18b) since God promises to reward faithfulness (2:20b).

Peter interrupts his discussion of the household codes with the supreme example of servitude: "To this you were called, because Christ suffered for you, leaving you an example, that you should follow in his steps" (2:21). The apostle Peter then cites a well-known suffering servant passage from the book of Isaiah (53:9): "He committed no sin, and no deceit was found in his mouth" (2:22). Peter proceeds to allude to other portions of Isaiah 53 in the next several verses (2:23-25; see Is 53:4-7). The servant's suffering is the means by which Israel will be restored (e.g., Is 52:15; 53:11). Jesus, as the suffering servant, suffers unjustly. Both of these points are highly relevant for Peter's overall argument in chapter 2. Jesus, as Isaiah's servant, suffers and dies so that the churches in Asia Minor might become part of true Israel. His death leads to their new birth. The slaves in the churches (and all other believers) must look to Jesus, who suffers supreme injustice. In a very real sense, all the members of the churches are little "suffering servants," who embrace the life of the ultimate suffering servant (cf. Is 49:6 in Lk 2:32 and Acts 13:47). Andrew Abernethy writes, "As Christian communities read Isaiah 52:13-53:12 in the light of its witness to Christ, the suffering servant's death does more than achieve atonement for sin. It creates a community of servants who are willing to suffer and serve like their master."[6]

> ***Jesus is the fulfillment of Isaiah's suffering servant, who suffered for the sake of true Israel.***

Believers as a unified community (3:1-12). After providing a supreme example of servitude, Peter outlines a wife's role to her husband: "Wives, in the same way submit yourselves to your own husbands so that, if any of them do not believe the word, they may be won over without words by the behavior of their wives" (3:1). The term *submit*, as we saw earlier in 2:13, refers to the general, obedient submission of one to another (e.g., Rom 13:1; Col 3:18-22). This will obviously look differently in different locales and cultures, but the principle must remain the same—wives must have a general disposition of submission to their husbands. Here, though, there is a specific goal in mind: "They [unbelieving husbands] may be won over without words by the behavior of their wives" (3:1b). It was and still is not uncommon for Christian women to be married to unbelieving men (and, of course, Christian men can be married to unbelieving women). Peter's exhortation is largely missional, requiring women to embody godly living in a pagan environment (3:2). In the Greco-Roman world, a woman's attire reflected her attitude and occupation. According to Bruce Winter, a new type of woman emerged in the first century AD. This new woman bucked the trend and was free of sexual constraints, and her attire reflected her promiscuous lifestyle.[7] You wear what

[6]Andrew T. Abernethy, *The Book of Isaiah and God's Kingdom: A Thematic-Theological Approach*, NSBT 40 (Downers Grove, IL: InterVarsity Press, 2016), 159.

[7]Bruce Winter, *Roman Wives, Roman Widows: The Appearance of New Women and the Pauline Communities* (Grand Rapids: Eerdmans, 2003).

you are. Peter may very well have this problem in mind here in 3:3-4.

Peter then roots his exhortation by looking back to the Old Testament: "For this is the way the holy women of the past who put their hope in God used to adorn themselves. They submitted themselves to their own husbands, *like Sarah, who obeyed Abraham and called him her lord*" (3:5-6). These women in Asia Minor are to be analogous to Sarah by honoring and submitting to their husbands (cf. Gen 18:12). Indeed, Peter claims, they are Sarah's "daughters" if they obey.

After dedicating 3:1-6 to wives, Peter brings husbands into the discussion in 3:7: "Husbands, in the same way be considerate as you live with *your wives*, and treat them with respect as the weaker partner and as heirs with you of the gracious gift of life, so that nothing will hinder your prayers." The word *wives* here could be rendered *women*. Peter has in mind all the women in the household (wives, daughters, mothers-in law). Although only one verse, Peter's words quickly get to the point. Husbands must be lovingly considerate of all the women in the household and treat them "as the weaker partner" (cf. 1 Thess 4:4). In so doing, they promote a restored, end-time family. The last bit of 3:7 is certainly interesting: "so that nothing will hinder your prayers." The sense is that a breach in the family relationship has deleterious effects on one's relationship with God.

Peter's discussion of the household codes reaches its main point in 3:8: "Finally, all of you, be like–minded, be sympathetic, love one another, be compassionate and humble." This captures the essence of Peter's exhortation to the church. Love for God and neighbor binds the church together, forging unity, which is the goal of the end-time people of God (cf. Rom 12:16). Verse 9 further unpacks this theme: "Do not repay evil with evil or insult with insult. On the contrary, repay evil with blessing." A key motivating factor in his command is found in the last part of the verse: "because to this you were called so that you may inherit a blessing" (3:9b). It is difficult to determine if this blessing occurs during the earthly life of the Christian or is something that will be received at the end (cf. Eph 6:2-3). In any case, a blessing is guaranteed for those who pursue love and unity.

FIGURE 20.8. DAVID FLEES JERUSALEM

Peter then cites Psalm 34:12-16 to support the idea that God rewards righteous behavior but punishes wickedness. One peculiarity is the length of the quotation. This is, by far, the largest Old Testament quotation of a single text in 1 Peter. Psalm 34 largely concerns king David. The superscription at the beginning of the Psalm reads, "When he pretended to be insane before Abimelek, who drove him away, and he left" (see 1 Sam 21:10–22:1). This historical tidbit colors the entire psalm, casting it in a particular light. In a word, the psalm details the persecution of the righteous and God's deliverance of them.

The righteous man (namely, David) earnestly seeks the Lord for help (Ps 34:4) and is subsequently delivered (Ps 34:6-7). Importantly,

David is assured that his will protect him: "The angel of the LORD encamps around those who fear him, and he delivers them" (Ps 34:7). The remainder of the Psalm continues to unpack this theme in some detail. God seeks after and fights for his righteous servants but punishes those who are wicked and attack the righteous (Ps 34:8-18). Psalm 34:19 is key: "The righteous person may have many troubles, but the LORD delivers him from them all." The righteous can expect persecution, yet they are assured of God's salvation.

Peter's use of Psalm 34 is appropriate on many levels. Like David, the churches in Asia Minor have come under persecution (1 Pet 1:6-7). As David suffers, so too these Christian communities will suffer. But, like David, they also can rest in God's deliverance. They may not be delivered physically from persecution, but they will be rescued spiritually. Also, Psalm 34 reinforces Peter's focus on the churches' conduct as the true, end-time people of God. The churches must pursue righteousness in their conduct with the governing officials (2:13-17), employers (2:18-25), and spouses (3:1-12). If they do so, then God will indeed reward them (3:9).

King David's experiences ultimately anticipate Christ's unjust suffering on the cross.

Believers as a suffering community (3:13-22). Coming on the heels of the Psalm 34 quotation, Peter states, "Who is going to harm you if you are eager to do good?" (3:13). The answer, of course, is no one. Since God preserves the faithful, no ultimate harm can come to his righteous servants. This theme is rooted in the person of David, who unjustly suffers at the hands of the wicked. Psalm 34:19-20 says, "The righteous person may have many troubles, but the LORD delivers him from them all; he protects all his bones, not one of them will be broken."[8] Peter's point is clear enough: although suffering has broken out within the community, they must, like David and Christ, trust in God's provision and their eventual deliverance. This is confirmed in 3:14: "But even if you should suffer for what is right, you are blessed. '*Do not fear their threats; do not be frightened.*'"

Again, Peter refers his readers back to the Old Testament to support this claim, quoting Isaiah 8:12. The Old Testament context of Isaiah 8 is insightful. Syria and the northern tribes of Israel form a coalition to destroy the two southern tribes. Instead of trusting the Lord for deliverance, Judah forms an alliance with their long-time enemy, Assyria. Isaiah and his family are encouraged not to follow Judah's behavior in seeking security from Assyria (Is 8:11-17). Isaiah is not to fear what Judah fears (Is 8:12). Instead of trusting in God, Judah fears that Syria and Israel will destroy them. Isaiah thus should not be alarmed (Is 8:13).

Therefore, the churches in Asia Minor should not fear persecution for their Christian beliefs. They are tempted to look around them and grow despondent, much like disobedient Israel, but they must, like Isaiah and his family, trust in God's goodness and provision. God promises that he will surely

[8]This passage is partly alluded to, together with Ex 12:46 and Num 9:12, in Jn 19:36, where Jesus' bones are not broken, as were the other two criminals on either side of him. These three Old Testament passages are "fulfilled" in Jn 19:36, so that they are a typological foreshadowing of Christ's suffering on the cross.

preserve them in the midst of all expressions of persecution and turmoil. The quotation from Isaiah 8:12-13 continues into 1 Peter 3:15. The Greek translation of Isaiah 8:13 reads, "*Sanctify the Lord* himself, and he himself will be your fear," which closely resembles 1 Peter 3:15a: "But *sanctify Christ as Lord* in your hearts" (NASB). Peter appears to be identifying Christ with the God of Israel in Isaiah 8. Since Christ is God incarnate, he is the veritable object of faith and trust who promises to deliver the church from their predicament. Christ, too, is the temple sanctuary of refuge against ultimate spiritual danger. Isaiah 8:14 refers to God as a "sanctuary," so it is implied that Peter identifies Jesus as this divine sanctuary.

Peter moves the argument forward by underscoring the importance of testifying: "Always be prepared to give an answer to everyone who asks you to give the reason for the hope that you have" (3:15b). If the churches faithfully persevere amid persecution, they will inevitably have ample opportunities to share their faith with their friends and family members. Peter may subtly have the end of Isaiah 8 in mind here in 3:15b-16. The Lord tells Isaiah to "bind up this testimony of warning" and to "seal up" the oracle of judgment against Israel (Is 8:16; cf. 8:18). It is not immediately clear why Isaiah is to seal up the vision, but it may refer to Israel's inability to understand and perceive God's word. Sealing up the vision may also refer to the fact that this prophecy is not fulfilled in the present but will be at some point in the future. "Sealing" likely refers to the lack of fulfillment, and unsealing probably represents its future fulfillment when the prophecy will be understood more fully (cf. Is 29:11-12; Dan 12:4, 9). Peter encourages the church to prepare to bear witness because the prophecy has been unsealed with the coming of Christ.

What follows in 3:18-22 is one of the more difficult texts in the New Testament. Peter weaves together several themes that appear disjointed and opaque. First Peter 3:19 asserts, "After being made alive [in the Spirit], he went and made proclamation to the imprisoned spirits." The ancient and modern church continues to struggle with the precise meaning of this statement. There are two general approaches for understanding this knotty passage: (1) this verse describes Jesus' descent into hell and his proclamation to demons that occurred after Jesus' death and before his resurrection. (2) Jesus' proclamation of his defeat of the demonic powers takes place (most likely) after the resurrection. In support of the first option, Jesus' proclamation is generally sandwiched literarily between his death (3:18) and his resurrection/ascension (3:21-22). But, the second option is to be preferred because it appears that the proclamation takes place while Jesus is in his resurrected body. At the end of 3:18, Peter claims that Jesus is "made alive" by the Spirit. This verb often accompanies the theme of the resurrection or new creation (e.g., Jn 5:21; Rom 4:17; 1 Cor 15:22). In addition, the apostle Paul alludes to a similar phenomenon in Ephesians 3:10, where the message of unity is proclaimed "through the church, the manifold wisdom of God . . . to the rulers and authorities in the heavenly realms" (cf. Eph 1:20-22; 3:1-9; Col 2:15). It is not foreign to the New Testament for Satan and his demons to be reminded of Christ's victory after his resurrection and ascension (cf. Rev 12:7-12). To paraphrase 3:19-20, Christ announces his triumph over sin and death to Satan and his demons, who had long

FIGURE 20.9. COAT OF MANY COLORS

ruled the created realm. Simply put, "at the time of his resurrection, Jesus proclaimed his victory to the imprisoned spirits, thereby sealing their doom."[9]

Peter then focuses on the relationship between water and salvation: "In it [the ark] only a few people, eight in all, were saved through water, and this water symbolizes baptism that now saves you also" (1 Pet 3:20-21). On the one hand, Peter's reading of Genesis 6 is rather straightforward: the ark preserves Noah and his family through the waters of judgment (cf. Mt 24:39). On the other, Peter goes on to claim that the flood waters prophetically anticipate the washing of one's conscience, which is made possible by Christ's resurrection. Peter reads the Genesis 6 narrative and sees its ultimate meaning tethered to the person of Christ and his victorious resurrection. Now that Christ has won the victory over sin, death, and the devil, he rules "at God's right hand— with angels, authorities and powers in submission to him" (1 Pet 3:22).

CALLED TO GODLY LIVING (4:1-19)

The story of Joseph (Gen 37–50) reminds believers that God designs and orchestrates all events of life, including grave trials and intense persecution. Joseph is sold into slavery by his brothers, wrongly accused by his master's wife, and forgotten about in jail. Yet Joseph declares to his brothers at the end of the narrative, "You intended to harm me, but God intended it for good to accomplish what

[9]Peter H. Davids, *A Theology of James, Peter, and Jude*, BTNT (Grand Rapids: Zondervan, 2014), 148.

is now being done, the saving of many lives" (Gen 50:20; cf. 45:7-8). Appearances are deceiving. It appeared that all was lost and that Joseph's life was spiraling out of control, but he rightly recognizes God's sovereign hand during great calamities. Peter, too, reminds the churches of Asia Minor that God is sovereignly at work in their lives, even when they suffer at the hands of their community. They must never lose sight that "in all things God may be praised through Jesus Christ" (1 Pet 4:11). The scattered exiles in Asia Minor exist for the purpose of recognizing God's providence and giving him the glory in all things.

Righteous suffering (4:1-11). Chapter 4 roughly breaks down into two sections (4:1-11; 4:12-19). The main point of the first section occurs in 4:2: "They [those who suffer faithfully] do not live the rest of their earthly lives for evil human desires, but rather for the will of God." Suffering, as Peter argues, must be patterned after Christ's suffering: "Since Christ suffered in his body, arm yourselves also with the same attitude" (4:1). Peter and other New Testament writers argue that one must suffer faithfully and not in vain. It is one thing to suffer as a natural consequence of one's own wrongdoing (3:17; 4:15), but it is quite another to suffer unjustly. Here Peter claims that those who suffer unjustly have "finished with sin" (4:1 HCSB). Jobes rightly interprets this tricky verse by arguing that "those who suffer unjustly because of their faith in Christ have demonstrated that they are willing to be through, or done, with sin by choosing obedience, even if it means suffering."[10] Genuine salvation that inevitably leads to suffering will always be accompanied by a holy lifestyle (Rom 6:2). Peter discloses how the largely Gentile church in Asia Minor previously lived "in debauchery, lust, drunkenness, orgies, carousing and detestable idolatry" (4:3). God will judge those pagans that continue to revel in those things (4:5-6).

The next section explicitly connects the church's behavior in light of the inauguration of the overlap of the ages: "The end of all things is near. *Therefore* be alert and of sober mind so that you may pray" (4:7). Because the latter days have begun through the person and ministry of Christ, believers now live in a unique time in the history of redemption. Peter pleads with his congregations that they would pray (4:7b) and, "above all, love each other deeply" (4:8). Love shines brightly in a world that is hostile to the church and inflicts great harm. This love manifests itself in service to others (4:10) and truthful speech (4:11). The purpose of doing such things rests in giving glory to God. Peter states the matter as follows: "If anyone serves, they should do so with the strength God provides, so that in all things God may be praised through Jesus Christ" (4:11; cf. 1 Cor 10:31). The churches in Asia Minor must understand that their actions carry great consequence.

Power in the throes of defeat (4:12-19). In 4:12, Peter appears to make reference to a specific situation that has befallen his congregation: "Dear friends, do not be surprised at *the fiery ordeal* that has come on you to test you, as though something strange were happening to you." It is not clear what this "fiery ordeal" is. It could be a conflict with

[10]Jobes, *I Peter*, 265.

the government (cf. 2:13-17) or with their community (cf. 4:4). In any case, Peter urges the churches to expect such events. What has come on them, as difficult as it may be, is inevitable and bound up with living in the latter days (4:7). Strangely, the churches are to rejoice in their suffering. But Peter drills down even further in 4:13: "rejoice inasmuch as you *participate in the sufferings of Christ.*" This statement is indeed problematic on a few levels. Is Christ's work on the cross somehow insufficient? Do Christians somehow atone for sin? We suggest that Peter's language here refers generally to living a cruciform lifestyle (cf. Jn 3:14; 2 Cor 4:7-12; 12:9-10; Col 1:24). That is, the churches must embody the paradox of the cross—strength in weakness, victory in defeat, wisdom in foolishness.

The churches' faithfulness in suffering not only displays God's power and end-time rule but also ensures that they will one day participate in Christ's consummate rule.

The apostle Paul's discussion of wisdom in 1 Corinthians 1–2 is the longest exposition of the nature of the cross and believers' understanding of it. At the heart of those two chapters is this concept of power in weakness. To state it succinctly, while Jesus is suffering a shameful death on the cross, he is simultaneously the supreme ruler. He rules while undergoing defeat. Mysteriously, Jesus is King at the very moment he is accursed (cf. Jn 3:14; 8:28; 12:32).

When the churches in Asia Minor suffer for the sake of Christ, they conform to the pattern of the Christ. Just as he displayed power in the midst of defeat, so does the church. Christ executes his messianic prerogative to rule while dying, and these churches rule alongside of Christ when they suffer. Peter connects the churches' suffering with the knowledge that they will one day physically rule with Christ at his coming. Notice the stated goal of 1 Peter 4:13: "rejoice inasmuch as you participate in the sufferings of Christ, so that you may be overjoyed *when his glory is revealed.*"

Peter affirms that the persecuted church is indeed "blessed" because "the Spirit of glory and of God rests" on them (4:14). Peter alludes to a prominent Old Testament passage that describes the Messiah's rule in the latter-day kingdom. A key element to the Messiah's reign, according to Isaiah 11, is his possession of the Spirit, and central to the Spirit's empowerment is his ability to give the Messiah wisdom and understanding (Is 11:2). The Messiah will judge impartially and with justice (Is 11:3-5). He will also be a rallying point for the restoration of the Gentiles and the scattered Israelites (Is 11:10-16).

Why does Peter allude to an overtly messianic passage and apply it to the church? We have already seen in 1 Peter how believers' lives are patterned after Christ's life. They are to suffer as he suffered, and here, Peter argues, they are to rule as he rules. Christ directly fulfills this prophecy from Isaiah 11, yet believers also fulfill this messianic prophecy since they are fully identified with the risen Christ. What is true of Christ is true of believers. The churches in Asia Minor fulfill Isaiah 11 through suffering, and they, through loving one another (1 Pet 4:8) become a blessing to the surrounding "nations."

LEADERSHIP OF THE CHURCH AND LETTER CLOSING (5:1-14)

According to the Old Testament, Satan's mission is to bring unjust accusations against the saints before the presence of the Lord (Job 1:6-11; 2:1-6; Zech 3:1-2). God protects the saints from such accusations before his heavenly throne because they are false and because God anticipates the death of his Messiah on behalf of his people. As a result of Christ's work, God excommunicates Satan from his heavenly court (Rev 12:7-13) and nullifies his ability to bring a legal charge against the saints (Rom 8:33-34, 38). God hands down a favorable verdict on behalf of his people. Still, Peter claims that the devil "prowls around like a roaring lion" (1 Pet 5:8). Satan lost his heavenly influence of falsely accusing the covenant community, yet he continues to deceive and afflict God's people, making every attempt to undermine the faith of believers.

Pastors as end-time shepherds of the church (5:1-10). The apostle Peter opens this section with two important personal qualifications: "To the elders among you, I appeal *as a fellow elder and a witness* of Christ's sufferings who also will share in the glory to be revealed" (5:1). The first qualification draws some continuity between Peter and the local leadership of the congregations. Peter appears to be drawing continuity between his pastorate and theirs. Second, Peter claims to be a personal "witness of Christ's sufferings" (cf. Lk 24:48). This likely refers to Peter's personal interaction with Jesus during his earthly ministry and his post-resurrection appearances (Acts 1). Peter employs both of these qualifications to provide the basis of his appeal to the church leaders.

First Peter 5:2a gets to the heart of Peter's appeal: "Be shepherds of God's flock that is under your care." The next verses explain what shepherding looks like: "watching over them . . . not pursuing dishonest gain, but eager to serve; not lording it over those entrusted to you, but being examples to the flock" (5:2b-3). The leaders of the churches in Asia Minor must follow Peter's exhortation since the "Chief Shepherd" will one day appear and they will "receive the crown of glory that will never fade away" (5:4). Notice how Peter labels Christ as the supreme or "Chief Shepherd" (5:4a; cf. 2:25). Christ is the ultimate example to pastors in all respects, so church leaders must model their behavior after Christ's (cf. Jn 10:11).

The Old Testament often depicts God as the shepherd of Israel. God is figuratively portrayed as a shepherd because he is a faithful caretaker. He looks out for his sheep by

FIGURE 20.10. KING DAVID IN PRAYER

providing for them. This theme highlights God's mercy, love, and faithfulness (Ps 23:1; 80:1). Although God remains faithful, his flock invariably strays. The book of Ezekiel describes God's role as shepherd and his commission to other shepherds. God condemns Israel's leaders or shepherds for their lack of care. Instead of modeling their behavior on God's shepherding, they use their position for selfish reasons (Ezek 34:1-10). In contrast to their unfaithfulness, God promises to shepherd faithfully the flock of Israel in the future (Ezek 34:16-19). He promises to send a Davidic figure who will faithfully take care of God's people (Ezek 34:20-24). This Messiah will also be the means by which God restores his people and judges the nations (Ezek 34:25-31).

When we turn to the New Testament, Jesus identifies with God's relationship to his people as their Good Shepherd who stands against the faithless shepherds of Israel (Mt 25:32; Jn 10:11-14). Like Israel's leaders in the Old Testament, the Jewish leaders in the first century lead Israel astray. As the Chief Shepherd, Jesus arrives to take care of his people. This reference identifies him as the God of the Old Testament, who predict that he would replace Israel's false shepherds and be their caring shepherd.

Peter introduces this section with a plea to the church's leaders as elders and shepherds (1 Pet 5:1-2). No doubt the prominent Old Testament texts that describe Israel's leaders as shepherds are in view, especially since Peter's emphasis is on the elder's faithfulness. He commands the church's leaders not to be like Israel's previous leaders—faithless.[11]

After exhorting the local church leaders, Peter focuses on the younger crowd within the church (5:5). This is probably a reference

FIGURE 20.11. MOSAIC DEPICTING A TIGER HUNT

[11]Timothy S. Laniak, *Shepherds After My Own Heart: Pastoral Traditions and Leadership in the Bible*, NSBT 20 (Downers Grove, IL: InterVarsity Press, 2006), 233.

to newer converts to Christianity and not necessarily to their age (although both of these could be in mind). The apostle states, "In the same way, you who are younger, submit yourselves to your elders." We do not know what specifically Peter has in mind when he says "submit" (cf. 2:13; 3:1); he simply undergirds this exhortation by focusing on humility, quoting from Proverbs 3: "God opposes the proud but shows favor to the humble." If Christians treat one another with a humble attitude and submit to God, they will be lifted up (1 Pet 5:6). The idea here is that God will promote them, but only if they do not promote themselves.

Peter delivers his last round of imperatives in 5:8-9a: "Be alert and of sober mind. Your enemy the devil prowls around like a roaring lion looking for someone to devour. Resist him, standing firm in the faith." Peter likely finishes his epistle with this exhortation because of its staggering importance. The first two imperatives (be alert and be sober minded) carry with them the idea of complete awareness. The second command to be sober minded sometimes occurs in military contexts. For example, 1 Maccabees 12:27 uses this word in a military context, "Ionathan gave orders to those with him *to be vigilant [sober-minded]* and to be ready for battle with their weapons" (cf. Mt 24:43 NETS). If Peter uses this word in a similar fashion, then his exhortation is even more forceful. The church must be prepared for battle. This suggestion fits well within the immediate context, since Peter claims that the "devil *prowls around* like a roaring lion *looking for someone to devour*" (5:8). Peter may allude to Job 1:7: "The Lord said to Satan, 'Where have you come from?' Satan answered the Lord, 'From roaming throughout the earth, going back and forth on it'" (cf. Ps 22:12-13). In both texts, Satan is on the prowl and proactively looking to conquer and afflict God's people. Peter finally pulls back the curtain and reveals the true source of the church's suffering—the devil himself. Though Satan remains culpable for the sufferings of the church, God has sovereignly and wisely ordained them (4:12-19).

If we are to understand Peter's warning to the church, we must once again grasp believers' spiritual position as citizens of the kingdom. As the Gospels make plain, the inbreaking of the end-time kingdom of God occurs through the person of Jesus. But this kingdom is somewhat different from expectations. Instead of the kingdom coming fully and all at once for the world to see, it has come partially and, for the most part, invisibly (see Mt 13).

Although the churches in Asia Minor do not physically see the kingdom, they nevertheless participate in it.

Christ conquers Satan during his forty-day period of temptation and at the cross, yet the devil and his minions remain hostile. They have lost the war, but they will fight until their consummate defeat. Peter therefore encourages the church to engage this enemy. He tells the church how they are to do so in 1 Peter 5:9: "Resist him, standing firm in the faith." Although Peter does not specify the object of their faith in 5:9, we can be sure that they are to trust earnestly in Christ's victory over Satan and believe that he has indeed vanquished evil.

The climax of chapter 5 (and arguably the entire book) occurs in 5:10-11: "And the God of all grace, who called you to his eternal glory in Christ, after you have suffered a little while, will himself restore you and make you strong, firm and steadfast. To him be the power for ever and ever. Amen." Much like the beginning of the letter, Peter reminds the church of their election in Christ and that God will preserve them until their bodily resurrection (cf. 1:3-5). God's redemption of the church brings glory to the triune God. The redeemed saints exist to give glory to God, which is made possible by Christ's work on the cross and the resurrection.

FIGURE 20.12. NERO AND HIS MOTHER, AGRIPPINA

Letter closing (5:12-14). Peter closes the letter by naming two individuals who play a prominent role in his life and ministry. The first, Silas, appears to have occupied some role in composing the letter: "With the help of *Silas*, whom I regard as a faithful brother, I have written to you briefly" (5:12). Silas (also called Silvanus) is a scribe or secretary who aids Peter in writing down his words. Peter also assures the churches that the message he proclaims in this epistle is true; he faithfully bears witness to the saving message of Christ that he learned. The last command to the church is forceful: "Stand fast in it [Peter's message]" (5:12b). The churches must believe Peter's message and act in accordance with it.

The subject of 5:13 appears, on the surface, most peculiar: "*She* who is in Babylon, chosen together with you, sends you her greetings, and so does my son Mark." The feminine pronoun is used as a reference to the church (cf. Eph 5:23-27). Peter also claims that he (and his local congregation) is in "Babylon." Although the nation of Babylon is not in existence in the first century, Jews sometimes used this as a reference to Rome since it symbolizes spiritual slavery and oppression (cf., Rev 14:8; 16:19; 17:5). While Peter's churches have begun to inherit the new heavens and earth, they physically reside in Asia Minor enduring great hardship. But the churches are not alone: Peter identifies with their hardship by referencing Babylon here at the end of his epistle. According to church tradition, Peter is martyred in Rome by Nero. It is said that he is crucified upside down in AD 64 (see Jn 21:18-19). Peter may have an inclination that he may never leave Rome and, like some within these churches, will suffer martyrdom. The apostle stands in complete solidarity with these persecuted individuals in Asia Minor.

Peter mentions a second individual: "my son Mark" (1 Pet 5:13). This may very well be the same Mark that played a key role in establishing early Christianity (e.g., Acts 12:12; Col 4:10; 2 Tim 4:11; Philem 24) and writing the Gospel of Mark. Moreover, according to early church tradition, Mark depends on Peter to write his gospel (Eusebius, *Hist. eccl.* 3.39.15). By including these two individuals, Peter reveals the tightknit relationship that the leaders of the early church enjoy with one another and the need for intimate community.

2 PETER AND JUDE

2 PETER

AUTHORSHIP

Although Peter is identified as the author in 1:1, many commentators reject Petrine authorship. Four common arguments are the following: Peter uses the book of Jude to compose his epistle. But why would Peter make use of Jude, a work written by one who is not one of the original twelve apostles? Second, 2 Peter deems Paul's writings as Scripture (3:15-16), presupposing a second-century date of authorship, since some scholars believe that Paul's writings would not be seen as holy Scripture until some point in the second century AD. Third, the content of 1 and 2 Peter differs significantly. Lastly, early attestation to the book of 2 Peter is not widespread in the early church.

Despite these opinions, none of them carry enough weight to overturn the traditional position that the apostle Peter wrote this epistle. The book explicitly claims to have been written by Peter (1:1), and 3:1-2 affirms that this was indeed the second letter to the churches in Asia Minor. Clearly 2 Peter and Jude are textually related (see discussion below), but textual dependence does not preclude Petrine authorship. Peter's use of Jude poses no problems, as Jude himself is a half-brother of Christ and a prominent leader of the early church. Moreover, treating Paul's epistles as Scripture resonates well with Paul's conscious, prophetic utterances in his letters (e.g., 1 Cor 2:1; 14:37; 2 Cor 13:3). The content of 1 Peter does indeed differ from 2 Peter, but that can, in large measure, be explained in light of a change of circumstances (both Peter's and his audience's).[1] Granted, the early church did not unanimously rally around Petrine authorship of this letter, but several prominent members within the early church ascribe authorship to Peter (e.g., Eusebius, *Hist. eccl.* 3.3.1).

DATE

Peter, probably writing from Rome once more, is aware that he is nearing the end of his life: "I will soon put it [his body] aside, as our Lord Jesus Christ has made clear to me" (1:14; cf. Jn 21:18-19). There is a strong tradition that Nero crucifies Peter upside down in AD 65 or 66 (Eusebius, *Hist. eccl.* 2.25.5; 3.1.2). So, we should date the epistle sometime before his death.

[1]D. A. Carson and Douglas J. Moo, *An Introduction to the New Testament*, 2nd ed. (Grand Rapids: Zondervan, 2005), 664.

OCCASION

It appears that the audience of 2 Peter is the same as 1 Peter (1:1). According to 2 Peter 1:1, the audience is quite general: "to those who through the righteousness of our God and Savior Jesus Christ have received a faith as precious as ours." But, 3:1 states, "this is now my second letter to you." If Peter is referring to the epistle known as 1 Peter here, then we can conclude that the audience of 2 Peter is the same as 1 Peter. Like many churches scattered throughout the Roman Empire at the time, false teachers have slipped into largely Gentile congregations in northwest Asia Minor. They must have arrived shortly after Peter wrote his first epistle. The false teachers are proclaiming a libertine and self-indulgent lifestyle (2:12-20) attributable to a failure to live in light of Christ's second coming (1:16; 3:3-4).

FIGURE 21.1. CRUCIFIXION OF ST. PETER

PURPOSE

The apostle Peter exhorts the churches in northwest Asia Minor to resist these false teachers and condemn them. As the true people of God, they are to live in accordance with the truth of the gospel and expect Christ's second coming as sovereign king.

RELATIONSHIP WITH JUDE

Borrowing material is not foreign to the New Testament authors. Matthew and Luke probably borrow from Mark. The issue crops up once again between 2 Peter and Jude. There are three main possibilities: (1) 2 Peter borrows from Jude; (2) Jude borrows from 2 Peter; (3) 2 Peter and Jude borrow from an independent source. Most commentators today generally prefer the first option as it allows Peter to modify and expand on Jude's letter.[2]

GENRE

Richard Bauckham argues that 2 Peter should be considered a letter and a "testament."[3] A testament is a genre found in Jewish literature that describes a prominent individual gathering his family together before death and offering them ethical instruction (e.g., T. Mos.; T. 12 Patr.). Part of the instruction tends to be strong apocalyptic and eschatological insights. By arguing that 2 Peter is a Jewish testament, Bauckham

[2]See Peter H. Davids, *The Letters of 2 Peter and Jude*, PNTC (Grand Rapids: Eerdmans, 2006), 136-42.
[3]Richard J. Bauckham, *Jude, 2 Peter*, WBC 50 (Grand Rapids: Zondervan, 1983), 131-35.

argues that the letter is written by a pseudepigrapher claiming to be Peter in the late first century. Second Peter does indeed share some similarity with the Jewish testaments, but it appears that the early church never considered 2 Peter as a testament. In addition, there is not one example in the early church of recognizing a clearly pseudepigraphical letter as canonical.[4]

OUTLINE

- I. Letter Opening (1:1-2)
- II. Confirmation of Identity as Participants of the New Creation (1:3-11)
- III. Reliability of the Apostolic Message (1:12-20)
  - A. Eyewitness Testimony of the Transfiguration (1:12-18)
  - B. The Testimony of Scripture (1:19-21)
- IV. Judgment Awaits the False Teachers (2:1-22)
  - A. Judgment on the False Teachers Within the Church of Asia Minor (2:1-3)
  - B. Judgment on the Deceivers and Wicked in the Old Testament (2:4-12)
  - C. Further Judgment on the False Teachers (2:10-22)
- V. The Day of the Lord and Letter Closing (3:1-18)
  - A. The Day of the Lord as Judgment on Wickedness (3:1-13)
  - B. Living in Light of the Day of the Lord and Letter Closing (3:14-18)

BIBLICAL-THEOLOGICAL THEMES

Undergirding Peter's second epistle is the Old Testament conception of the day of the Lord, an event that most likely originates in the divine warrior motif.[5] God fights on behalf of his people when they obey him but against them when they do not. Strictly speaking, the day of the Lord largely refers to God's judgment and defeat of his adversaries. If Israel disobeys the covenant, God promises to arrive in judgment on the day of the Lord. Joel 1:14-15, for example, says, "Summon the elders and all who live in the land to the house of the LORD your God, and cry out to the LORD. Alas for that day! For *the day of the LORD* is near; it will come like *destruction from the Almighty*" (cf. 2:1, 11, 31; Amos 5:18, 20; Zeph 1:7, 14; Mal 3:2, 5). But, together with judgment, the phrase sometimes also includes the deliverance of God's people (Obad 15-21; Zech 14). The day of the Lord can also include God's judgment poured out on pagan nations. Isaiah 13 prophesies the destruction of Babylon: "A prophecy against Babylon. . . . Wail, for the day of *the LORD is near*; it will come like *destruction from the Almighty*. . . . a cruel day, with wrath and fierce anger—to make the land desolate and destroy the sinners within it" (Is 13:1, 6, 9; cf. Ezek 30:3; Joel 3:14; Obad 15).

Much of the difficulty in understanding the day of the Lord lies in the nature of its fulfillment and the language employed. In some sense, the language is figurative, but in another sense it is literal.[6] Some passages in the Old Testament talk about the immediate,

[4]L. R. Donelson, *Pseudepigraphy and Ethical Argument in the Pastoral Epistles*, HUT 22 (Tübingen: Mohr-Siebeck, 1986), 10-11.
[5]Tremper Longman III and Daniel G. Reid, *God Is a Warrior* (Grand Rapids: Zondervan, 1995).
[6]G. B. Caird, *The Language and Imagery of the Bible* (Philadelphia: Westminster, 1980), 256.

historical fulfillment of the day of the Lord. When this happens the fulfillment is usually not complete, so that the fulfillment itself refers to an even greater, yet future culmination of the day of the Lord at the very end of history. Everson perceives that the Old Testament prophets use the day of the Lord "in interpreting various momentous events—past, future or imminent."[7] According to Isaiah 13, the day of the Lord is fulfilled when the Medo-Persian Empire conquered the Babylonians (Is 13:17). However, the eschatological future of the day of the Lord is in view in Isaiah 2:2-5 when the Lord restores Israel to her land.

When we move into the New Testament, we find a similar understanding of the day of the Lord. According to Acts 2, the day of the Lord in Joel 2 is initially fulfilled during Peter's sermon at Pentecost: "*This* is what was spoken by the prophet Joel: '*In the last days*, God says, I will pour out my Spirit on all people'" (Acts 2:16-17; cf. Is 2:2). Elsewhere in the New Testament, the day of the Lord refers to the final day of judgment in the future (1 Cor 5:5; 1 Thess 5:2; 2 Thess 2:2; 2 Pet 3:10). Second Peter builds on the Old Testament understanding of the day of the Lord as a future event when the Lord will return and "come like a thief" (2 Pet 3:10a). At the second coming of Christ, the old cosmos will come under God's judgment and a new order will emerge (3:10b): "the heavens will disappear with a roar; the elements will be destroyed by fire." Unbelievers and apostates bear God's wrath, but believers will enjoy a renewed physical existence and look forward to "a new heaven and a new earth" (3:13).

One interesting development is the shift in language in the New Testament. In the Old Testament, the phrase "day of the Lord" is quite common, whereas the New Testament unflinchingly identifies Christ with the day of the Lord. For example, 2 Corinthians 1:14 reads, "We will boast of you in *the day of the Lord Jesus*" (cf. 2 Thess 2:2). The word for "coming" in 2 Peter is the Greek term *parousia* that ordinarily means either "presence" or "coming" (2 Pet 1:16; 3:4, 12), and the former appears best in 2 Peter (cf. 1 Thess 3:13; 4:15; 5:23; 2 Thess 2:1, 8-9). Christ's coming does not indicate a physical motion from

FIGURE 21.2. JOHN'S VISION OF THE TWO HORSEMEN EXECUTING JUDGMENT

[7] J. A. Everson, "The Days of Yahweh," *JBL* 93 (1974): 335. Cf. Anthony A. Hoekema, *The Bible and the Future* (Grand Rapids: Eerdmans, 1979), 9-11.

heaven down to earth. Revelation 6:14, for example, refers to the end of the present cosmos in terms of a scroll that has been split and each of the two halves then rolled up. The present physical reality will in some way disappear and the formerly hidden heavenly dimension, where Christ and God dwell, will be revealed (Rev 11:19; 19:11; 21:1-3). The old-world reality will be ripped away, and the dimension of the new, eternal reality will appear along with Christ's presence. When Christ appears, he will not descend from the sky over London or New York or Hong Kong or any other localized area. When he appears, the present dimension will be ripped away, and Christ will be manifest to all eyes throughout the earth (see Mt 24:27).

LETTER OPENING (1:1-2)

The author identifies himself as "Simon Peter" and a "servant and apostle" of Christ (1:1a). Peter finds it necessary to underscore his apostolic authority given the occasion of the letter. His message is at odds with the false teachers, so the churches must embrace his role as a genuine apostle of Christ heralding the very words of God. Peter does not locate his audience in a specific geographic location like he does in 1 Peter 1:1 but only describes them as receiving "a faith as precious as ours" (1:1b).

CONFIRMATION OF IDENTITY AS PARTICIPANTS OF THE NEW CREATION (1:3-11)

Right out of the gate, Peter finds it necessary to furnish his readers with a strong understanding of their identity in Christ. The phrase "godly life" (1:3) is found with the phrase "precious promises" (1:4). The only other time this precise word for "promise" occurs in the New Testament is in 3:13, referring to the promise of the coming new creation: "In keeping with his *promise* we are looking forward to a new heaven and a new earth" (cf. Acts 13:32-34; 26:6-8; 1 Tim 4:8; 2 Tim 1:1; Titus 1:2; Jas 1:12; 1 Jn 2:25). According to 2 Peter 1:4, the future resurrection life

FIGURE 21.3. PETER STRIKING THE EAR OF MALCHUS

has broken into the present: "through them [the promises] you may participate in the divine nature, having escaped the corruption in the world caused by evil desires." The escape from the old, corrupted world occurs when believers begin to participate in the new creation. On the basis of believers' identity as participants in the new heavens and earth, Peter expects them to demonstrate and work out their identity through righteous living (1:5-9) and "confirm" their "calling and election" (1:10).

RELIABILITY OF THE APOSTOLIC MESSAGE (1:12-20)

After exhorting the churches to work out their identity as a new creation (1:3-11), Peter commands his audience to trust his and Scripture's testimony (1:12-21). Peter reminds the churches of these things because of the advent of the false teachers (1:12, 15). "These things" is probably a reference to Peter's initial exhortation of 1:3-11.[8] His response to the false teaching that Christ will not return a second time to judge is based on two realities: Peter's eyewitness testimony to the transfiguration (1:16-18) and Scripture's testimony (1:19-21).

Eyewitness testimony of the transfiguration (1:12-18). Peter explains to the church that "we did not follow cleverly devised stories when we told you about the *coming of our Lord Jesus Christ in power*, but we were *eyewitnesses of his majesty*" (1:16). The shift from "I" (1:12-15) to "we" (1:16-18) is notable and reinforces the general apostolic testimony of the transfiguration and not only Peter's. The apostle Peter recasts the transfiguration in a way remarkably similar to Matthew's account of the event (Mt 17:1-5). Peter also couches the transfiguration in language reminiscent of Christ's second coming. The New Testament often uses the word *coming* to describe the second advent or *parousia* of Christ immediately before the full restoration of the new heavens and earth (Mt 24:3; 1 Cor 15:23; 1 Thess 3:13; 4:15). Second Peter 1:17a explains Christ's coming on the mountain: "He received honor and glory from God" (cf. Dan 7:13-14). Peter then includes the quotation found in the Synoptics: "This is my Son, whom I love; with him I am well pleased" (1:17b). He alludes to texts such as 2 Samuel 7:14, Psalm 2:7, and Isaiah 42:1, highlighting the establishment of Israel's king, who will usher in the end-time kingdom. The transfiguration, therefore, demonstrates that Jesus is the long-awaited yet divine Messiah who obeys his Father perfectly, subdues his enemies, and spreads God's presence to the ends of the earth.

> ***The idea of Jesus being God's "Son" is reminiscent of Israel being God's "son," who is to obey God's law perfectly, subdue the earth of rebellion, and spread his glory to the ends of the earth (Ex 4:22).***

The general idea here in 1:16-18 is that Peter and the apostles experienced Christ as the long-awaited, sovereign king of Israel at the transfiguration. Therefore, the false teachers are wrong to say that Christ will not come a second time as cosmic king,

[8]Bauckham, *Jude, 2 Peter*, 197.

because "the Transfiguration was . . . a proleptic second coming."[9]

The testimony of Scripture (1:19-21). Not only does the transfiguration guarantee the second coming of Christ as sovereign Lord, so does the Old Testament (1:19-21). The "prophetic message" is also "completely reliable" (1:19) because as prophets "they were carried along by the Holy Spirit." The elusive phrase "prophetic message" refers to the Old Testament passages that anticipate the establishment of the end-time kingdom of God at the very end of history.[10] Another reason why the Old Testament expectation of the establishment of God's end-time kingdom is completely reliable lies in the initial fulfillment of those promises at the transfiguration and Jesus' ministry as a whole (e.g., Gen 49:9-10; Num 24:17-19; Dan 2:35, 44-45).[11]

JUDGMENT AWAITS THE FALSE TEACHERS (2:1-22)

The prophet Jeremiah alerted the Israelites that the Babylonian Empire would soon come and raze Jerusalem, hauling off the influential Israelites to exile. Jeremiah 6 warns Israel to "flee for safety, people of Benjamin! Flee from Jerusalem! . . . For disaster looms out of the north, even terrible destruction" (Jer 6:1). Later on in the chapter the prophet explains why God decrees utter destruction: "From the least to the greatest, all are greedy for gain; *prophets and priests* alike, *all practice deceit*. They dress the wound of my people as though it were not serious. 'Peace, peace,' they say, when there is no peace" (Jer 6:13-14; cf. 8:10-11). Israel's wicked leadership (Jer 6:15) attempt to convince the nation that God would not dare punish the Israelites. He made a covenant with them! But sin must be punished, and the nation of Israel and her leaders will indeed pay a steep price for their rebellion. The false teachers in Asia Minor are similar to these wicked Israelite leaders during Jeremiah's day. They, too, are trying to convince the churches that God will not punish wicked behavior (2 Pet 2:3, 13-14).

Judgment on the false teachers within the church of Asia Minor (2:1-3). In chapter 2 Peter launches an attack on the false teachers that prey on the local churches. The first section (2:1-3) addresses the false teachers within the church and their present judgment, while 2:4-12 looks back to the false teachers of the Old Testament and serves as the basis for such judgment. Peter sets up his discussion of the false teachers in 2:1: "There *were* also *false prophets* among the people, just as there *will be false teachers* among you." This statement connects the current events of the local church with the events of the Old Testament. The false teaching in the local church has been prophetically anticipated in the Old Testament. The church scattered throughout Asia Minor participates in the grand story of the Israel.

At the heart of the false teaching is a denial that Christ is "the sovereign Lord" (2:1; cf. Jude 4), a heresy that is proclaimed "with fabricated stories" (2 Pet 2:3a). Peter, without mincing words, outlines the result of the false teachers' behavior: "Their *condemnation* has long been hanging over them, and their *destruction* has not been sleeping"

[9]Davids, *2 Peter and Jude*, 201.
[10]Douglas J. Moo, *2 Peter, Jude*, NIVAC (Grand Rapids: Zondervan, 1996), 75.
[11]Moo, *2 Peter, Jude*, 76.

FIGURE 21.4. ANIMALS ASSEMBLING IN FRONT OF NOAH'S ARK

(2:3b). Judgment is at hand for these teachers, and God is, at the present, pouring out his end-time wrath on them for harming his congregations. God is at war with these heretics.

Judgment on the deceivers and wicked in the Old Testament (2:4-12). The next section, largely dependent on Jude 5-10, is the basis for the condemnation that has befallen the heretics. The general idea is that since the false teachers in the Old Testament did not escape judgment, neither will the false teachers in the present. Inaugurated eschatology forms much of the framework here as Peter draws a line from the Old Testament to the events taking place within these small churches in Asia Minor. These Old Testament examples of false teachers are a typological pattern of the false teachers that infiltrated the congregations. History will be repeated in the latter days, but the stakes are much higher.

In staccato-like fashion, Peter runs through the gamut of several Old Testament events that demonstrate God's commitment to punishing false teaching and deception. He begins with a particularly difficult reference to the angels who committed sin in Genesis 6: "For if God did not spare angels when they sinned, but sent them to hell, putting them in chains of darkness to be held for judgment" (2 Pet 2:4).[12] God's judgment of these evil beings began in the Old Testament, continues into the era of the New Testament, and will culminate in the climactic judgment at the very end of history. Verses 5 and 6 disclose two events—the flood and the destruction of

[12]Though it is quite possible that this refers to the fall of angels at the beginning of creation, even before the fall of Adam and Eve.

Sodom and Gomorrah—that are "an example of what is going to happen to the ungodly [teachers]." God's judgment on the false teachers in Asia Minor is assured because he has *already* judged the unbelieving wicked in Noah's day (Gen 7:18-24) and the immoral in Sodom and Gomorrah (Gen 19:24). Yet, in the midst of judgment, God promises to preserve the faithful who, like Lot, are "righteous" (2 Pet 2:7). The churches must take heart that God will preserve their souls if they continue to obey the truth of the gospel (cf. 1:10-11).

Further judgment on the false teachers (2:10-22). Peter shifts his focus in 2:10-22 to the present situation with the problem of false teachers. We can detect shades of political and spiritual subversion when Peter asserts that they "despise authority" (2:10). The wording of 2:10-12 follows Jude 8-10 but without the possible reference to the Testament of Moses. These false teachers wrongly assume full autonomy from the government and from the spiritual realm over which the risen Christ sovereignly rules. Their penalty for pursuing absolute independence from God is utter destruction (2:12b).

Verses 13-22 is a general modification of Jude 11-16 that outlines the selfish and immoral behavior of the teachers and their unfulfilled promises. They promise freedom to the churches "while they themselves are slaves of depravity" (2:19). Verse 21 is a stinging indictment of them: "It would have been better for them not to have known the way of righteousness, than to have known it and then turn their backs on the sacred command." These teachers are familiar with the gospel message about Christ, his identity, and what he accomplishes on the cross and in his resurrection. Yet, they turn their backs on this apostolic teaching and pursue their own version of the truth. The chapter ends with a quotation from Proverbs 26:11 and another from an unknown source. As D. A. Carson writes, "The true nature of these people never changed. A dog may leave its vomit for a while but will return to it; a sow might well be spruced up and look clean but will still find a mud pit enticing."[13]

THE DAY OF THE LORD AND LETTER CLOSING (3:1-18)

Adam and Eve's transgression affects not only all of humanity but also the entire cosmos. According to Genesis 3:17, God curses the ground because of their sin. Paul asserts in Romans 8:20-21 that "creation was subjected to frustration" and that it needs to be "liberated from its bondage to decay." The created order longs for its redemption: "The whole creation has been groaning" (Rom 8:22). Although Christ's death and resurrection wrought judgment on the created order, his work of redemption also began the process of renewal. Colossians 1:20, for example, says, that God "through him [Christ] reconcile[d] to himself all things, whether things on earth or things in heaven, by making peace through his blood." Christ's work puts the created order back together. Second Peter 3:10 is one of the most descriptive passages in the New Testament that speaks to God's full judgment on the cosmos: "The heavens will pass away with a roar and the elements will be destroyed with intense heat, and the earth and its works will be burned up" (NASB). A few verses later,

[13]D. A. Carson, "2 Peter," in *Commentary on the New Testament Use of the Old Testament*, ed. G. K. Beale and D. A. Carson (Grand Rapids: Baker Academic, 2007), 1058.

however, Peter provides comforting news to the righteous: "We are looking forward to a new heavens and a new earth, where righteousness dwells" (3:13; cf. Is 65:17; 66:22). What Christ inaugurated at the cross will arrive in its fullness when he returns at the second coming.

The day of the Lord as judgment on wickedness (3:1-13). Chapter 3 marks the culmination of the letter in which Peter confronts the false teaching about the day of the Lord. He begins with telling the churches that this is the second letter written to them "to stimulate you to wholesome thinking" (2:1). Peter then explains what wholesome thinking entails: "*Recall the words* spoken in the past by the *holy prophets* and the command given by our *Lord and Savior* through your *apostles*" (3:2). Although it is not crystal clear what words Peter has in mind, he is probably referencing the general apostolic proclamation of the gospel—Christ's life, death, and resurrection, particularly as these events pertain to his second coming. Christ's return is not detached from his ministry or peripheral; rather, it is the utter completion of his work of redemption. Jesus himself even spoke of his second coming (e.g., Mt 24:36–25:46). The church is to reject the slippery teaching of the heretics and hold fast to the sound teaching of the Old Testament and the message of Jesus as attested to by the apostles.

In this vein, Peter goes on to detail some of the specifics of false teaching in the following verses: "Above all, you must understand that *in the last days* scoffers will come. . . . They will say, 'Where is this "coming" he promised?'" (2 Pet 3:3-4). Second Peter and Jude remind readers that Christ and the apostles predicted the infiltration of the false teachers "in the last days" (3:3) and "in the last times" (Jude 18). Both letters contend that this expected latter-day tribulation of apostate teaching already has been expressed through the appearance of false teachers who pervert the truth in the midst of the Christian community.

> ***The Old Testament and Jesus prophesied that false teaching will creep into the covenant community, so Peter pleads with the community of faith not to be caught off guard and to expect its arrival.***

At the heart of the false teaching lies a failure to believe in God's creative power—"They [the false teachers] deliberately forget that long ago *by God's word* the heavens came into being and the earth was formed out of water and by water" (2 Pet 3:5). The same might that God used in creating the world will operate when he brings the new cosmos to its completed state: "*By the same word* the present heavens and earth are reserved for fire" (3:7). The teachers also fail to grasp that God judged wickedness through a deluge (3:6; Gen 7:21-24). God created the world, poured out judgment on it, and promises to do so again by fire.

Part of the issue at stake is God's relationship to time. The false teachers may have been casting doubt on Christ's second coming because there appeared to be a delay. Several decades have transpired since his ascension. But Peter reminds the church that "With the Lord a day is like a thousand years, and a thousand years are like a day" (3:8). The

FIGURE 21.5. THE ISAIAH SCROLL AT QUMRAN

wording here resembles Psalm 90:4: "A thousand years in your sight are like a day that has just gone by." God does not experience time the same way humans do.

Peter's portrayal of Christ's second coming is one of the most visually stimulating sections of the New Testament (3:10). At the time of judgment, "the earth and its works will be burned up" (3:10 NASB). The wording here is particularly straightforward: the cosmos will come under physical judgment. Peter envisions the transformation of the cosmos from an old, sin-infested world into a new cosmos where God dwells fully with humanity.

The language of "hastening[14] the coming of the day of God" (3:12 NASB) recalls Isaiah 60:22: "I, the Lord, *will hasten it in its time*" (NASB). In its immediate context, Isaiah prophesies of a time when the nations will come to Israel in obeisance (60:10-18). In 60:19, consummate restoration is at hand: "The sun will no more be your light by day, nor will the brightness of the moon shine on you." God will replace the old creation with a "new heaven and a new earth" (2 Pet 3:13). The wording here is reminiscent of Revelation 21:1: "Then I saw '*a new heaven and a new earth*,' for the first heaven and the first earth had passed away." Second Peter 3:13 and Revelation 21:1 allude to Isaiah 65:17 and 66:22: "See, I will create *new heavens and a new earth*"; "As the *new heavens and the new earth* that I make will endure before me." The allusion to these two key Old Testament texts is appropriate since Isaiah envisions the consummate restoration of all of creation. Peter (and John) employs these references from Isaiah to signal the future fulfillment of these prophecies at Christ's second coming.

Living in light of the day of the Lord and letter closing (3:14-18). The purpose of Peter mentioning the disintegration of the cosmos is pastoral and ethical: to encourage saints to be holy so that they might be found faithful when the day of judgment arrives (2 Pet 3:11-12, 14). In contrast to the ungodly, the righteous will find mercy on that dreadful day (cf. Jude 21). Even the timing of Christ's second coming is designed with the purpose that all individuals "come to repentance" (2 Pet 3:9).

Another remarkable insight comes from Peter's conviction that the writings of Paul are on par with Old Testament Scripture:

[14]Though the Greek word here can be translated "being zealous for."

"As our dear brother *Paul* also wrote you with the wisdom God gave him. . . . *His letters* contain some things that are hard to understand, which ignorant and unstable people distort, as they do *the other [Old Testament] Scriptures*" (3:15-16). The New Testament contains a number of references to the apostles' writings functioning as authoritative as the Old Testament itself (e.g., 1 Thess 2:13; 2 Thess 3:1; 1 Cor 14:37-38; 2 Cor 13:3; Eph 3:1-5; Rev 22:18-19). The authoritative testimony of the apostles is not only oral but also written.

Peter's final admonition nicely summarizes the thrust of his epistle: "Since you have been forewarned, *be on your guard* so that you may not be carried away by the error of the lawless and fall from your secure position" (2 Pet 3:17). The churches of Asia Minor have been warned on multiple fronts—the Old Testament, Jesus, and the apostles. They must come to grips with the reality of the inbreaking of the great tribulation and must resist false teaching at all costs. If they do not, they will fall from their secure position and begin to doubt the gospel itself. Peter sounds off on the antidote for the presence of heresy in the last verse of the letter: "But grow in the grace and knowledge of our Lord and Savior Jesus Christ" (3:18). All believers must abide in God's grace through faith in Christ's work on a daily basis and continue to cultivate a strong knowledge of apostolic doctrine.

JUDE

AUTHORSHIP

The author of the book bears the name Jude, but it is not immediately clear which Jude is in mind. Excluding Judas Iscariot, The New Testament mentions four men with the name Jude or Judas (all are spelled *Ioudas*): Judas, the half-brother of Jesus (Mk 6:3); the Christian prophet "Judas (called Barsabbas)" (Acts 15:22); one of the twelve disciples, "Judas son of James" (Lk 6:16); and "Judas the Galilean," a famous criminal (Acts 5:37). The book of Jude lends some help in determining which individual may have penned this short epistle: "Jude, a servant of Jesus Christ and a *brother of James*." The Gospels claim that a person bearing the name James is indeed the half-brother of Jesus (Mt 13:55; Mk 6:3). It is likely then that Jude, the half-brother of Jesus, writes this letter.

DATE

Pegging a date, even an approximate one, is tricky. Dating this epistle probably turns on its affinity with 2 Peter, as a textual relationship does indeed exist. If Jude has borrowed from 2 Peter, it may have been written shortly thereafter in the mid to late 60s. If, however, 2 Peter borrows from Jude, as many commentators agree, this book may have been written in the early 60s or even earlier.

OCCASION

Scarcely anything is known about the provenance of the letter or its intended audience. Certainly, Jude's concern is to address the ingress of false teachers into house churches. Much of the epistle is dedicated to the condemnation of these false teachers, and the churches' response to them. Evidently, false prophets have crept into the believing community, offering a self-indulgent lifestyle. It appears this group is analogous to those rebuked in 2 Peter 2. Unlike 2 Peter, however, this group in Jude does not share the same eschatological outlook that denies Christ's second coming (2 Pet 3:4).

PURPOSE

Jude writes to a gathering of largely Jewish Christians to resist the contamination of the gospel and adhere to sound doctrine.

OUTLINE

I. Letter Opening (vv. 1-2)
II. Purpose of the Letter (vv. 3-4)
III. Judgment on False Teachers (vv. 5-16)
  A. Condemnation of the False Teachers (vv. 5-10)
  B. Errant Ways of the False Teachers (vv. 11-13)
  C. Condemnation of the False Teachers Once More (vv. 14-16)
IV. Letter Closing and Doxology (vv. 17-15)

LETTER OPENING (VV. 1-2)

After identifying himself as a servant of Christ and the "brother of James," Jude reassures his readers of their spiritual position by labeling them "called," "loved in God," and "kept for Jesus Christ" (v. 1). Physical, emotional, and spiritual attack notwithstanding, their salvation remains safely in God's hands. Before launching into the body of the letter, Jude must first remind them of their identity in Christ. The combination of calling, mercy, and peace highlights their identity as the true Israel of God (cf. Gal 6:16). As such, they must hold fast to their calling and prepare to weed out the false teaching that flourishes in their midst.

PURPOSE OF THE LETTER (VV. 3-4)

Apparently, Jude originally intended on writing a letter pertaining to "the salvation we share" but changed his mind upon receiving news of the false teachers (v. 3a). Above all, this letter encourages the audience to "contend for

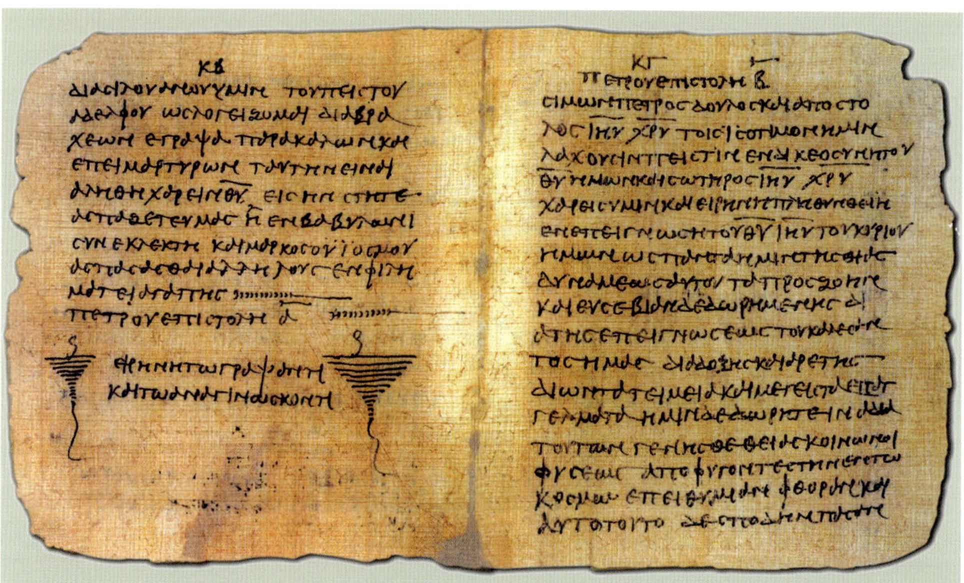

FIGURE 21.6. PAPYRUS 72 CONTAINING 1-2 PETER AND JUDE

the faith that was once for all entrusted to God's holy people" (v. 3b). The following verse then discloses the reason for Jude's earnestness ("certain individuals . . . have secretly slipped in among you"), and these false teachers are on the receiving end of God's wrath. At the core of their teaching is a perversion of "the grace of our God into a *license for immorality* and *a denial Jesus Christ our only Sovereign and Lord*" (v. 4). They abuse the gospel by commending the church to indulge in fleshly desires. For the false teaching to flourish, Christ's sovereign rule must be denied. The false teachers among the congregation advance a weakened gospel and an anemic view of Christ. In a word, one's view of Christ is related to one's ethics.

JUDGMENT ON FALSE TEACHERS (VV. 5-16)

At the heart of this epistle lies Jude's condemnation of the false teachers. The New Testament reserves its harshest words for false teachers, and Jude proves to be no exception. In a straightforward manner, he condemns this pernicious group and outlines their destructive ways. He not only resolutely condemns these teachers (vv. 5-10, 14-16) but also describes their sinful conduct in some detail (vv. 11-13). One of the most unique, even dizzying, aspects of the epistle is Jude's close reading of Old Testament narratives. In a span of just eleven verses, several Old Testament and two Jewish texts form the backbone of Jude's condemnation of the false teachers. What makes Jude's reading of the Old Testament instructive is his conviction that events, even large swaths of Old Testament narratives, prophetically anticipate the condemnation of these false teachers. Jude aligns false teachers in his congregation with the false teachers in the Old Testament that caused great harm to Israel. Just as there is one people of God running throughout both Testaments, it may not be a stretch to conclude that a spirit of evil corporately inspires a group of false teachers spanning the Old and New Testaments. This may be evident further from recalling that Israel was often typological of the New Testament church, just as Old Testament false teachers were sometimes typological of false teachers in New Testament communities.

Condemnation of the false teachers (vv. 5-10). In verses 5-7, Jude employs three Old Testament scenarios that foreshadow God's judgment on the wicked false teachers. Verse 5 describes God's punishment of rebellious Israel in Numbers 14, where the people of Israel disobey God by grumbling against Moses and God. In their eyes, Egyptian captivity is better than entering into the Promised Land and being destroyed by the Canaanites (Num 14:1-4). As a result of their lack of faith, God subsequently bans the first generation of Israelites from entering the Promised Land (Num 14:26-35).

Verse 6 is notoriously difficult to interpret, as Jude appears to be referring to God's punishment of the wicked angels of Genesis 6:2-4 and quite possibly to the narration of the judgment of evil angels in a popular Jewish work, the Book of Watchers (1 En. 1–36). Jude seems to be interpreting Genesis 6 as referring to angels intermingling with humans. Typically, three options are given in identifying the "sons of God" in Genesis 6: (1) angels (see 1 En. 6–19); (2) "divine" kings who desired great power and divine authority; (3) sons of Seth, which differs from the "daughters of human beings" (non-Sethian women) in that they are Seth's descendants.

A fourth view is possible, one that blends the first and second. In both Testaments, heavenly rulers, i.e., angels, influence earthly rulers (e.g., Deut 32:8; Ps 82; Judg 11:24; 1 Cor 2:8; Eph 3:10; 6:12). This is a notoriously difficult text to interpret and confidence about any four of the views is difficult to attain. Regardless of the precise identity of the "sons of God" in Genesis 6, Jude's main point is clear enough: since God's judgment upon the "sons of God" in Genesis 6 is sure, how much more sure will God's judgment be upon the false teachers.[15]

FIGURE 21.7. MICHAEL AND THE DRAGON

Verse 7 pertains to God's punishment of Sodom and Gomorrah. The men of Sodom, according to Genesis 19:1-9, desire sexual relations with other men (or possibly angels), so God punished them for their despicable actions. In the same way, God will punish these heretics who have led astray some within the congregation. Verse 9 is especially difficult in that it is not entirely clear what passage Jude is alluding to when he says, "Even the archangel Michael, when he was disputing with the devil about the body of Moses, did not himself dare to condemn him for slander." According to Clement of Alexandria, Jude "confirms the assumption of Moses," referring to a Jewish text also known as the *Testament of Moses* (Frag. 1.2). The problem is that this version of the Jewish text does not contain the story Jude is referring to. It is possible that our version of the *Testament of Moses* did indeed contain this event but the ending has been lost to us.[16] Nevertheless, the point of the Jewish reference is that "no one is a law to himself, an autonomous moral authority."[17] The angel Michael does not possess the authority to judge the devil; he only has the authority to deliver God's messages. God alone has the right to decide what is right and wrong. This probably explains why Jude goes on to quote Zechariah 3:2, in which the Lord condemns Satan for his slander. Therefore, these false teachers are committing slander and disrespect by claiming to be the chief arbiter of morality.

Errant ways of the false teachers (vv. 11-13). The next few verses state three additional failings of the teachers and their destruction. Instead of leading God's people in truth and sound doctrine, they corrupt and defile the community. Jude uses the Old Testament once more to describe the failings of the false teachers with regard to their leadership. Cain is regarded in Second Temple Judaism as the great corruptor of humanity, and Balaam is the great false prophet who leads Israel astray (Num 31:16). Korah also stirs a great rebellion against Moses (Num 16:1-3). Jude views Cain, Balaam, and Korah as prophetic anticipations of the false teachers in his congregation.

[15]Davids, *2 Peter and Jude*, 226.
[16]Bauckham, *Jude, 2 Peter*, 47.
[17]Bauckham, *Jude, 2 Peter*, 61.

FIGURE 21.8. GOD'S PUNISHMENT OF KORAH

Verses 12-13 employ six metaphors to describe the opponents: Like hidden reefs, these heretics instruct during intimate gatherings over meals and celebrations, thus shipwrecking the church. An allusion to Ezekiel 34:2 recalls the prophet's castigation against the shepherds who are concerned only with themselves and not the flock. Clouds are supposed to produce rain, but in this case it never materializes. Trees naturally bear fruit, yet these trees fail to live up to their expectations. In the same way, these teachers never live up to their claims. Instead of teaching God's Word, they proffer lies and destruction. Their teaching contaminates the church just like waves of the sea casts up its dirty foam. Like stars that have departed from their natural course, these teachers have strayed from the truth, resulting in their condemnation.

Condemnation of the false teachers once more (vv. 14-16). Repeating himself, Jude once again picks up the theme of God's judgment on the false teachers in verses 14-16. Here in verses 14-15 Jude quotes from 1 Enoch: "Behold, the Lord came with many thousands of his holy ones to execute judgment upon all, and to convict all the ungodly of all their ungodly deeds which they have done in an ungodly way, and of all the harsh things which ungodly sinners have spoken against him" (1 En. 1:9). Quoting from noncanonical sources is not entirely unique in the New Testament (though it is not common). The New Testament cites other extracanonical sources on several occasions: Epimenides (Acts 17:28; Titus 1:12), Aratus (Acts 17:28), and Menander (1 Cor 15:33). Jude agrees with 1 Enoch in that God and his angels will indeed come in the latter days to bring forth judgment on the wicked. Although Jude quotes an extracanonical book, he in no way attributes to it the title of Scripture.[18]

[18]See P. J. Gentry and A. M. Fountain, "Reassessing Jude's Use of Enochic Traditions (with Notes on Their Later Reception History)," *Tyndale Bulletin* 68 (2017): 261-86.

Letter closing and doxology (vv. 17-25). After condemning and describing the heretics, Jude tells the churches how they are to respond to these nefarious teachers. First, they should expect the arrival of false teachers: "Remember what the apostles of our Lord Jesus Christ foretold. They said to you, "In the last times there will be scoffers who will follow their own ungodly desires"' (vv. 17-18).

Second, the churches must cultivate a robust relationship with God through prayer and meditation: "By building yourselves up in your most holy faith and praying in the Holy Spirit, keep yourselves in God's love as you wait for the mercy of our Lord Jesus Christ to bring you to eternal life" (vv. 20-21). Although Jude does not unpack with great precision what he means by "building yourselves up in your most holy faith," he probably may have in mind learning more about the foundational truths of the Christian faith.

Third, Jude asks that his church be merciful and attempt to preserve those who struggle with false teaching: "Be merciful to those who doubt; save others by snatching them from the fire; to others show mercy, mixed with fear—hating even the clothing stained by corrupted flesh" (vv. 22-23). Although his words are somewhat enigmatic here, Jude exhorts the church to have mercy on and make an attempt to save those who have bought into aberrant teaching. Jude draws a clear distinction between the false teachers and those who have been deceived by false teaching. Jude reserves his harshest words of judgment for the purveyors of falsehood (vv. 5-10, 14-16) but asks his congregation to extend a hand of mercy toward those who have succumbed to it.

Jude ends his epistle with a wonderful doxology that praises God for his ability to preserve the saints. God ultimately is the one who possesses the power to keep the saints from stumbling (24a). The goal of such preservation is that believers may be presented to God without fault (24b). By God's grace, the believers in Jude's congregation must hold fast to sound doctrine so that they may be found blameless at the second coming of Christ.

22

JOHANNINE EPISTLES

AUTHORSHIP

The author of 1 John is not explicitly mentioned within the letter, but a few external considerations bring some clarity. Several prominent individuals within the early church believe the author of 1 John to be the apostle John, son of Zebedee, and the author of the Gospel of John (e.g., Irenaeus, *Adv. Haer.* 3.16.7-8). Whether the apostle John authors 2–3 John is a bit trickier since these two letters are less attested in the early church. According to Eusebius, Origen claims that John wrote "one Gospel . . . the Apocalypse . . . [and] left also an epistle of very few lines; perhaps also a second and third; but not all consider them genuine, and together they do not contain a hundred lines" (*Hist. eccl.* 6.25.9-10). One of the strongest arguments for considering the apostle John as the author of all three letters is the thematic and linguistic continuity between the epistles and the Gospel of John. The emphasis on light and darkness (Jn 1:5-9; 1 Jn 1:5-6), Jesus as the Word (Jn 1:1; 1 Jn 1:1), abiding in Christ (Jn 15:4-10; 1 Jn 2:27) and so on is striking.[1] Even the discussion of an antichrist figure in 1 John 2:18-23 and 2 John 7 binds these two epistles together. At the end of the day, it appears likely that the apostle John pens all three letters.

DATE

Dating the Johannine Epistles probably turns on their relationship with the Fourth Gospel. Many scholars are convinced that the three epistles were written *after* John's Gospel, and a few even argue that the epistles are partly a response to a misreading of the Gospel of John.[2] Whether these three letters are written confronting an aberrant view of John's Gospel is hard to say. If the three epistles presuppose the publication of John's Gospel, we probably should peg the

FIGURE 22.1. THE APOSTLE JOHN

[1]See Andreas J. Köstenberger, *A Theology of John's Gospel and Letters* (Grand Rapids: Zondervan, 2009), 86-89.
[2]D. A. Carson and Douglas J. Moo, *An Introduction to the New Testament,* 2nd ed. (Grand Rapids: Zondervan, 2005), 676.

date of their composition somewhere in the 90s. According to the early church, John spends his final years in the city of Ephesus at the end of the first century (Eusebius, *Hist. eccl.* 3.31.2; Irenaeus, *Adv. Haer*. 3.1.1).

OCCASION

The local churches in and around Ephesus find themselves in a difficult situation. A prominent group of individuals have left their communities. John claims that they departed from the church because "they did not really belong to us. For if they had belonged to us, they would have remained with us" (1 Jn 2:19). It is not clear, however, what provoked these individuals to leave. We can only guess that their departure stems from a repudiation of apostolic doctrine that focuses on the person of Christ (2:22-27) and perhaps a lack of sincere love for one another (3:10). Complicating matters is the lack of a clear portrayal of the false teaching, and 1 John contains only a handful of clues about certain aspects of their false teaching.

What prompts the apostle to write 2 John is also a bit unclear. Whereas 1 John opens without an explicit reference to the letter's author and its recipients, 2 John begins with the inclusion of both (v. 1). Importantly, 1 John and 2 John contain remarkable similarities in language and theology. It appears that false teaching still remains at the forefront of John's mind in the second letter. First John largely explains how the church should behave in light of the fallout of the secession of the false teachers from their congregations, while 2 John is preventive medicine for banning those same false teachers from infiltrating the local communities of faith (2 Jn 7-11). Although 3 John makes almost no mention of false teaching regarding Christ, such teaching may still be on the table. Second John is a stalwart defense against false teaching, whereas 3 John is going on the offense against

FIGURE 22.2. CHURCH OF MARY IN EPHESUS

the false teachers. The apostle John is pleased with Gaius's preservation of the truth in the midst of the constant threat of false teaching. Diotrephes, perhaps another elder of a house church, may have sided with the false teachers and rebuffed John's envoy.[3] In any case, John writes to Gaius to encourage him for his faithfulness to the truth (3 Jn 2-8) and warns the church about Diotrephes and his divisive behavior (3 Jn 9-10).

PURPOSE

John addresses a collection of churches probably within and around the city of Ephesus. He encourages believers to resist the false doctrine of those who departed from their churches and embrace a Christian lifestyle that is expressly marked by love, so that they may be confident in their inheritance of the new creation (1 Jn 2:25; 5:13). Second John encourages these congregations to prevent any infiltration of these false teachers into their community. Third John praises Gaius and exhorts him to remain steadfast.

OUTLINE

1 John

- I. Prologue (1:1-4)
- II. The God of Light and Life (1:5–3:10)
    - A. Fellowship with God (1:6–2:17)
    - B. The "Last Hour" and the Influx of False Teachers (2:18-27)
    - C. Remaining in Righteousness (2:28–3:10)
- III. The God of Love and Truth (3:11–4:21)
    - A. Love as an Expression of New Life (3:11-24)
    - B. Overcoming the False Teaching of Evil One (4:1-6)
    - C. The Love of God and New Birth (4:7-21)
- IV. Confidence in Eternal Life (5:1-21)

2 John

- I. Letter Opening (vv. 1-3)
- II. Love and Obedience as True Israel (vv. 4-11)
- III. Letter Closing (vv. 12-13)

3 John

- I. Letter Opening (vv. 1-4)
- II. Commendation of Gaius and Rebuke to Diotrephes (vv. 5-12)
- III. Letter Closing (vv. 13-14)

BIBLICAL-THEOLOGICAL THEMES

During Passion Week, Jewish leaders test Jesus' understanding of the Torah in order to accuse and convict him. According to Matthew 22:36-37, a Pharisee asks Jesus, "'Teacher, which is the greatest commandment in the Law?' Jesus replied: 'Love the Lord your God with all your heart and with all your soul and with all your mind.'" Jesus' response is directed toward one of the Pharisees, an expert in the law. Jesus here quotes Deuteronomy 6:5 and claims that the weightiest or greatest commandment of the Torah is to love God above all else. The previous verse is known as the Shema—an Israelite creed that confesses a firm belief in the exclusivity of Israel's God: "Hear, O Israel: The LORD our God, the LORD is one" (Deut 6:4). The hallmark of the Israelite faith, then, is a supreme love for God and a correct understanding of who he is. In the next verse of Matthew 22, Jesus states the second-greatest commandment by quoting Leviticus 19:18: "Love your neighbor as yourself" (Mt 22:39).

[3]C. Marvin Pate, *The Writings of John: A Survey of the Gospel, Epistles, and Apocalypse* (Grand Rapids: Zondervan, 2011), 328.

Leviticus 19 lists a series of admonitions directed toward the entire Israelite community (19:1). Nearly all of the Ten Commandments are alluded to in Leviticus 19 (19:3-4, 11-12, 18, 30) and summarized in the command to "Love your neighbor as yourself" (19:18).[4] Central to living holy lives in the midst of God's glorious presence is loving one another. Love toward one another is rooted in loving God. Those within the covenant community cannot love one another without first loving God.

In the Sermon on the Mount, Jesus says, "You have heard that it was said, 'Love your neighbor and hate your enemy.' But I tell to you, love your enemies and pray for those who persecute you" (Mt 5:43-44). His teaching on love here in verses 43-44 is an integral part of the Sermon on the Mount (Mt 5–7), but what is often overlooked is Jesus' relationship to the law in the immediate context. The Mosaic covenant, even the love commands, anticipate Jesus' person, his acts, and his teaching on kingdom ethics. The Old Testament expects that the coming Messiah will establish ethics or norms that are in keeping with the end-time kingdom. This explains Jesus' statement, "Do not think that I have come to abolish the Law or the Prophets; I have not come to abolish them *but to fulfill them*" (Mt 5:17).

FIGURE 22.3. SHEMA INSCRIPTION

With Jesus' establishment of the new age, his people are called and empowered to live as citizens of his kingdom (Mt 5:43-44). Kingdom ethics, particularly the command to love God and one another, are not antithetical to those commandments in the old covenant or Mosaic administration (Deut 6:5).They deeply internalize the love commands within the individual, reaching their intended state of fulfillment (Jer 31:31-34; Ezek 36:25-27). The Mosaic covenant certainly possesses an internal dimension (Ex 20:17), but it was largely external in nature. Saints living in the new age are equipped to love more deeply because of the presence of the end-time Spirit dwelling in their midst.

Since all believers equally participate in the kingdom, they are now bound to a set of latter-day kingdom ethics. All Christians belong to the new age and are required to live accordingly. As kingdom citizens, believers ought to pursue an ethic of love. First John 4:7-8 states the matter succinctly: "Let us love one another, for love comes from God. Everyone who loves has been born of God and knows God. Whoever does not love does not know God, because God is love." Above all, Christians' love of God and others must shine brightly in the new age. It is this deep love for God and others that propels a great deal of 1 John.

[4]L. Michael Morales, *Who Shall Ascend the Mountain of the Lord? A Biblical Theology of the Book of Leviticus,* NSBT 37 (Downers Grove, IL: InterVarsity Press, 2015), 208.

1 JOHN

PROLOGUE (1:1-4)

The letter opens in a somewhat unusual manner. Instead of identifying the sender and the recipients, John begins with reinforcing his eyewitness testimony. The first-person plural *we* dominates this section (cf. 4:14), a feature that Rickard Bauckham labels "we of authoritative testimony."[5] The point of the "we" section reinforces John's apostolic testimony to Jesus' life and ministry. John can testify that the historical Jesus indeed is the divine Son of God. In some sense, the apostolic testimony contained in the prologue of 1:1-4 reinforces John's eyewitness testimony contained in the Fourth Gospel. John 21:24 is relevant here: "This is the disciple who *testifies* to these things and who wrote them down. *We* know that his *testimony* is true."

Although we lack some of the nuances to the false teaching that John confronts in this epistle, we can be confident that the prologue strikes at the heart of it. Central to the prologue is the reference to Christ as the Word who is "from the beginning" (1 Jn 1:1). The wording reaches back to John 1:1 and, ultimately, to Genesis 1, underscoring Christ's eternality and his role as creator. Although distinct from the Father (1:3), Christ enjoys full authority and glory as God. Much of 1 John highlights what Christ accomplishes as an atoning sacrifice and what the Word who inaugurates the new creation by overcoming the devil (1:2; cf. 3:8). John also divulges why he bears witness to Christ—"that you also may have fellowship with us" (1:3). Grasping a true knowledge of Christ leads to a life marked by love and true fellowship within the people of God. The aim of the prologue is John's ultimate concern for these congregations and their participation in the covenant community.

THE GOD OF LIGHT AND LIFE (1:5–3:10)

Psalm 51 was penned in light of King David's illicit relationship with Bathsheba (2 Sam 11). David pleads with God, "*Cleanse me* with hyssop, and I will be clean; *wash me*, and I will be whiter than snow" (51:7). Although reparation for sin is offered through various sacrifices, David understands that sacrifices are still unable to remove the stain of sin completely. The prophets look forward to the day when God will forgive Israel's transgressions and deal with sin once and for all in the latter days. Jeremiah 33:8 asserts, "I will cleanse them from *all the sin* they have committed against me and will forgive *all their sins* of rebellion against me" (cf. Is 33:24; Jer 31:34; Mic 7:18). John claims that the time has arrived and absolute forgiveness of sin is available only in Christ, who purifies individuals "from all unrighteousness" (1 Jn 1:9). The Old Testament prophets foretold the day when God would offer complete and final forgiveness of sins, and John argues that such a time has indeed arrived.

Fellowship with God (1:6–2:17). Setting up the discussion for the first section, John asserts a key principle: "God is *light*; in him

[5]Richard Bauckham, *Jesus and the Eyewitnesses: The Gospels as Eyewitness Testimony* (Grand Rapids: Eerdmans, 2006), 370-83.

there is no *darkness* at all" (1:5). God's identity as light may partly have in mind the inbreaking of the long-awaited new creation. Isaiah 60:1-2, in speaking of the future restoration of Israel and creation, asserts, "Arise, shine, for your *light* has come and the glory of the LORD rises upon you. . . . Thick *darkness* is over the peoples, but the LORD rises upon you and his glory appears over you" (cf. Is 2:5; 58:10-11; Eph 5:8-9, 13-14). First John 2:8 even reads, "darkness is passing and the true light is already shining." God has begun the process of renewal, and believers must live in accordance with the arrival of the new creation to preserve the fellowship with one another and promote unity between God's people. Isaiah 60:3 goes on to say, "*Nations* will come to your *light*, and kings to the *brightness* of your dawn."

One of the hallmarks of the new creation is harmony between Israel and the nations.

The next section (1:7-2:2) underscores Christ's role as an atoning sacrifice and heavenly advocate. Not only is Christ described as existing before creation (1:1), he is also its "atoning sacrifice" (2:2; cf. 1:7). The Old Testament background of this important phrase is the centerpiece of the temple and its sacrificial system. A cognate of this term for "atoning sacrifice" pertains to the mercy seat in the holy of holies, where the high priest atones for Israel once a year (Lev 16:11-19). The high priest sprinkles blood on the mercy seat in order to make atonement for himself, his household, and all the Israelites. Sin defiles God's temple, so the sanctuary must be cleansed to resume its proper function as the dwelling place of God. Holiness and sin are always incompatible.

The New Testament affirms that God pours out his wrath on Christ, the true mercy seat (e.g., Rom 3:25). Likewise, the blood of the animal sacrifices that the high priest sprinkles on the mercy seat, typologically points to the greater sacrifice of Christ. God's glorious presence above the ark in the temple now blossoms in the person of Christ. The world that Christ formed (1 Jn 1:1) is the very world for which he died. Christ's work on the cross extends not only to Israel but also to Gentiles; he died for the "whole world" (2:2). Believers can be confident that when they sin, God will purify them of their sinful behavior (1:9; cf. Jer 31:34).

John addresses the churches as "dear children," "fathers," and "young men" in 2:12-14. The reference to "children" in 2:12, 14 probably refers to the entire congregation (2:1, 18, 28; 3:7; 4:4; 5:21), whereas "fathers" points to those who are older in age (2:13a) and "young men" to those who are indeed younger (2:13b).[6] Importantly, John addresses the young men because they have "overcome the evil one" (2:13b-14). Within the book of Revelation, the theme of overcoming is central to the book in that believers are called to overcome the world in a spiritual manner while being overcome by the world physically (e.g., Rev 2:7, 11, 17, 26-29; 3:12, 21). This behavior of overcoming is modeled after Christ, who overcomes the devil and the world at the

[6]Colin G. Kruse, *The Letters of John*, PNTC (Grand Rapids: Eerdmans, 2000), 89-90.

cross while being physically overcome (Rev 5:5-6; cf. Gen 3:15; Rom 16:20). The point is that the younger members and the congregation as a whole, if they persevere in their love for one another and embrace of the gospel, will continue to overcome the devil and the world.

The "last hour" and the influx of false teachers (2:18-27). The second half of chapter 2 is a response to the false teachers that have left the local congregation. This section develops Jesus' and Paul's predictions of an end-time opponent that are based on Daniel's earlier prediction that false teachers would infiltrate and deceive Israel in the latter days (Dan 7:25; 8:12, 23-25; 11:30-34; Mt 24:24-25; 2 Thess 2:3-10). John is attempting to persuade the local churches that the end-time prophecy concerning false teachers in Daniel 7–12, Matthew 24, and 2 Thessalonians 2 has initially been fulfilled as the false teachers spread lies about Christ and the gospel. John clues his audience in to this fulfillment when he mentions the "last hour" in 1 John 2:18: "Dear children, this is *the last hour*; and as you have heard that the *antichrist is coming*, even now many *antichrists have come*. This is how we know it is *the last hour*" (cf. Jn 5:25-29). The term *hour* recalls the Greek translation of Daniel 8, 11–12, where the end-time opponent attempts to deceive God's people at the final hour (8:17, 19; 11:35, 40; 12:1).

There is a sense in which the antichrist himself is active among the false teachers who are deceiving these churches in Ephesus: "Who is the liar? It is whoever denies that Jesus is the Christ. Such a person is *the antichrist*—denying the Father and the Son" (1 Jn 2:22). How can John say that the singular *antichrist* is already here? Although the antichrist has not yet come in his incarnate, physical form, his spirit has arrived on the scene, inspiring his false teachers (4:2-3; see 2 Thess 2:5-12).

According to 4:4, John tells the entire congregation that they can be assured of their identity as the true people of God because they have overcome the world, the devil, and the false teachers (4:3).

FIGURE 22.4. SERMON AND DEEDS OF THE ANTICHRIST

Determining some of the nuances of this false teaching is notoriously difficult. Perhaps those who seceded from the community held to a form of proto-Gnosticism. Gnosticism would later become one of the deadliest heresies that the church would face. But in the first century, it had not been developed into a full-blown system. Gnosticism is quite eclectic, borrowing from several strands of religions. Central to this heresy is the conviction that physical matter is inherently evil, so the goal is to free the body from any form of materialism and flesh. Using this as their rough framework, perhaps these false teachers proclaim that Jesus is not fully human; he only *appeared* to be human (docetism). The false teachers could not reconcile how the Son of God, a perfect, divine spirit, could enter a sinful, material body. Frank Thielman further explains the nature of the false teaching:

> As the divine revealer of the Father, Christ is free from this evil. Because of this, he only appears to take the form of Jesus and is not subject to the normal physical troubles of a human being, such as birth, suffering, and death. He came on Jesus in spiritual form at baptism and departed from Jesus prior to his crucifixion.[7]

Whatever the precise details of the false teaching may be, it is clear that they are denying a key tenet of the person of Christ, especially his identity as Israel's end-time king (1 Jn 2:22).[8]

Remaining in righteousness (2:28–3:10). John continues to connect eschatology to the lives of the churches in the following section. Uppermost in his mind is the second coming of Christ: "*Continue in him*, so that when he appears we may be confident and unashamed before him *at his coming*" (2:28). Christ's second coming motivates the church to hold fast to sound doctrine and repudiate sin. A few verses later, John argues, "We know that when Christ appears, we shall be like him, for we shall see him as he is" (3:2). When Christ returns at the very end of history and raises his people from the dead, believers will be fully transformed into his last Adam image (cf. 1 Cor 15:45-54). Between the two advents of Christ, believers are spiritually created in the image of the last Adam (2 Cor 3:18), but at Christ's final coming they will be physically created into his image. Once more, eschatology is wedded to the conduct of believers: "All who have this hope in him purify themselves" (1 Jn 3:3). The second coming of Christ fuels righteous living in the midst of a dark and hostile world.

Perhaps the false teachers also advocate a view of the Christian life that promotes a fleshly lifestyle. Throughout the epistle, John insists that believers must not continue to sin (3:6; 5:18) or "go on sinning" (3:9). Although Christians will inevitably sin (1:8, 10), their lives are not to be earmarked by sinful behavior. Instead, their lives are patterned after the risen Lord, who inaugurated the redemption of the cosmos. So, believers

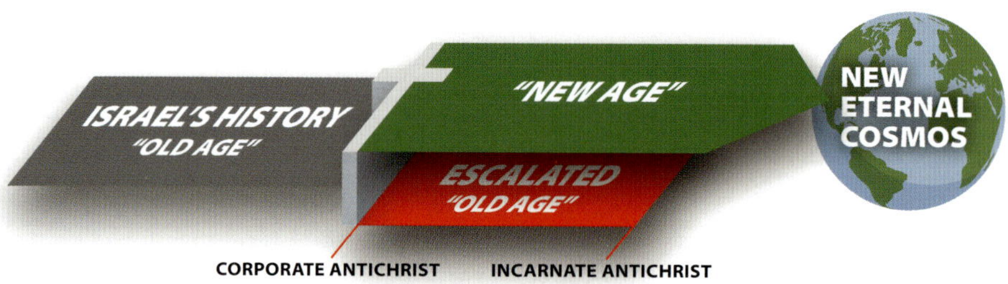

FIGURE 22.5. THE ANTICHRIST IN THE OVERLAP OF AGES

[7]Frank Thielman, *Theology of the New Testament: A Canonical and Synthetic Approach* (Grand Rapids: Zondervan, 2005), 541.
[8]Köstenberger, *Theology of John's Gospel*, 96.

are to live in light of the new eschatological order. Christ delivers a mortal blow to the evil ruler of the old age (3:8), and all those who identify with him participate in his victory over the devil (2:13-14). The resurrection life of the new eternal cosmos has begun in Jesus' resurrection and in the spiritual resurrection of his followers (1:2; 2:17, 25; 3:14; 4:9; 5:11-13, 20).

THE GOD OF LOVE AND TRUTH (3:11–4:21)

The Old Testament waits expectantly for the day when God will break the power of sin and raise his saints to life. David in Psalm 51:10 pleads that God would give him a pure heart. And Ezekiel 36 describes an end-time renewal using the language of a "new heart" and a "new spirit" (Ezek 36:26). Ezekiel 37 even relates this event to the end-time resurrection of Israel. God promises that he will "open your graves and bring you up from them" so that the Israelites will live in the Promised Land of the new creation (Ezek 37:12-14). The prophet Ezekiel envisions the Lord redeeming Israel from Babylonian captivity and transforming their bodies into an existence that is fit for God's unfettered presence in the new age. John recalls this theme of new life when he employs the language of being born of God (1 Jn 2:29; 3:9; 4:7; 5:1, 4, 18). Everyone who "believes that Jesus is the Christ is *born of God*" (5:1). In contrast to the local heresy that results in death, the message of Christ generates resurrection life.

Love as an expression of new life (3:11-24). Life in the new age is marked by supreme love toward one another and righteous living. If love marks the new creation, then hate and unrighteous behavior mark the old, sinful age. John commands the church to "not be like Cain, *who belonged to the evil one* and murdered his brother . . . Anyone who hates a brother or sister is a murderer" (3:12, 15). Cain's actions were consonant with the actions of the evil one. But the church has already "overcome the evil one" through Christ's work (2:13-14; 4:4). Where Cain is the epitome of selfish and unrighteous living, Christ is the epitome of righteous and selfless living. He "laid down his life for us" (3:16a; cf. Jn 10:17-18). Instead of imitating Cain, the

> *Christ's life and death irrevocably affected the cosmos, so that John can declare that the old, fallen world of darkness is passing away and "the true light" of the new creation "is already shining" (2:8, 17).*

church must imitate Christ (1 Jn 3:16b) because they belong to the light (1:6-7). True believers who partake of the new creation or have "passed from death to life" (3:14; cf. Jn 5:24) will inevitably relish their new identity through unabashed love toward one another. So much of John's letter to the church is encapsulated in 1 John 3:23: "This is his command: to *believe* in the name of his Son, Jesus Christ, and to *love* one another as he commanded us." Righteous living is always tethered to right doctrine.

Overcoming the false teaching of the evil one (4:1-6). Resuming his discussion of the false teachers, John once again touches on the end-time deception of the antichrist. The Old Testament prophesied the arrival of an end-time antagonist who would deceive many within the covenant community. Daniel 7:25, for example, says, "He [the antagonist] will speak against the Most High and oppress his holy people and *try to change the set times and the laws*" (cf. Dan 7:7-12; 8:9-12, 23-25; 9:26-27). John, as we have already seen in 1 John 2:18-23, refers to this figure as the antichrist. In direct fulfillment of Daniel's prophecy, this end-time figure arrives on the scene in the first century. But Daniel's prophecy is coming to fruition in an unexpected manner—the end-time antagonist has yet to emerge as a single, physical individual. Although the single antichrist figure still remains a future reality, he inspires false teachers to do his bidding. John claims that the spirit of the antichrist is mysteriously alive and well in the false teachers who have already infiltrated the local congregations (cf. 2 Thess 2:3-7). John's churches find themselves in the midst of the great tribulation, in which the devil and the corporate antichrist are accosting the church through false teaching. To combat this deception, believers must remain vigilant and vigorously hold fast to the "Word of life" (1 Jn 1:1; cf. 4:15).

FIGURE 22.6. CAIN SLAYING ABEL

The love of God and new birth (4:7-21). John returns to his discussion of love and once again couches it in the arrival of the new creation. The flow of thought in this section is generally clear: God is love (4:16), and only those who belong to him possess such love (4:7). God's incomparable love for humanity is discussed first, wherein he "sent his Son as an atoning sacrifice" (4:10; cf. 2:2). Christ's substitutionary death and resurrection is the means by which God gives individuals a spiritually resurrected existence.

Believers are "born" of God (4:7; cf. 2:29; 3:9; 5:1, 4, 18; Jn 3:3-8), a condition that designates the initial entry into the resurrection life of the eternal new cosmos. John's wording here echoes Ezekiel 36–37, which portrays the physical restoration of Israel from Babylonian captivity as a new birth through the power of the Spirit. One can also make the connection to Jesus' discussion with Nicodemus in John 3, a passage that also has Ezekiel 36–37 in mind. The point here in 1 John 4:7-21 is that true believers are emerging from spiritual captivity into the Promised Land of the new creation, a reality that Jesus inaugurates in his own body and spiritually in the hearts of believers. A tangible effect, therefore, of inheriting the new heavens and earth is a vigorous love for God and for one another (4:16-21).

CONFIDENCE IN ETERNAL LIFE (5:1-21)

So much of John's epistle rests on the idea that works, either good or bad, are indicative of

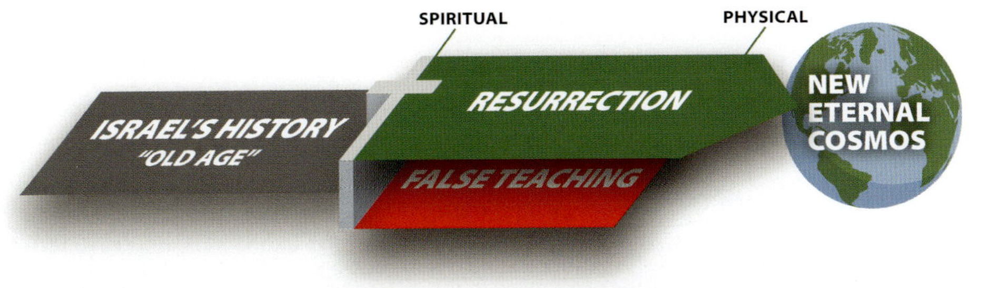

FIGURE 22.7. BELIEVERS' RESURRECTION IN THE OVERLAP OF THE AGES

one's relationship to Christ. True believers will inevitability display righteous behavior, whereas unbelievers manifest unrighteous works. First John 5:1 neatly summarizes the letter: "Everyone who believes that Jesus is the Christ is born of God, and everyone who loves the father loves his child as well." Genuine Christians believe that Jesus is truly the divine Son of God who died for sin and demonstrate selfless love for one another.

The last few verses of the letter give believers robust confidence in their salvation (5:18-20). God promises that those who place their faith in his Son and his work of redemption receive an inner, spiritual assurance that they have been rescued from the "evil one" (5:19). According to 5:9-15, eternal life springs from trusting in God's Son, and whoever believes in Christ "accepts this testimony" (5:9-12). This testimony is none other than the internal witness of the Spirit. John assures his audience that God's testimony is true that they have life in the Son. Otherwise God would be a liar (5:10). John elaborates on the saving message of Christ throughout 1 John. He writes so that those who "believe in the name of the Son of God . . . may know that [they] have eternal life" (5:13). Such genuine believers have confidence that God hears the prayers of those who request "according to his will," promising to grant "whatever we ask" (5:14-15). One implied request is that if they have asked for eternal life in the Son, then on the basis of God's promise to give such life, they are assured that he has given them this life of the new creation.

John finishes his letter in a remarkably abrupt manner: "Dear children, keep yourselves from idols" (5:21). While he may be referring to literal, physical idols, John is likely summarizing the entire argument of his epistle. He pens this letter as a warning against believing the false teaching concerning Christ. If his readers succumb to false teaching, they commit spiritual idolatry. False teaching is a blatant substitution for genuine truth; it promises life but delivers death. The church must guard itself from venerating false theology as a substitute for the true, unvarnished message of Christ that John and the apostles fight so hard to preserve (1:1-4).

> *Despite living in the midst of the great tribulation and being attacked by the "spirit of the antichrist" (4:3), John's churches can be confident in their eternal inheritance of the new heavens and earth.*

2 JOHN

LETTER OPENING (VV. 1-3)

Second John opens with the author self-identified as an elder. The word *elder* can refer to a person of authority within Judaism and early Christianity (e.g., Mt 16:21; Titus 1:6-9), but it may also have in mind a physically older person (e.g., T. Job 15:2; Lk 15:25). Both definitions of the word are appropriate for John since, on the one hand, he is an authoritative voice in Asia Minor at this time. On the other, John remains the *oldest* apostle. These two shades of meaning are found elsewhere in the early church (e.g., *1 Clem* 1:3). The larger issue, though, is why 2 and 3 John begin with the self-designation of elder, whereas 1 John immediately launches into the prologue. Although we will probably never know for certain, the answer may lie

FIGURE 22.8. WOMAN AND THE DRAGON IN REVELATION 12

in the general nature of 1 John. Perhaps 1 John is intended to circulate to all the local congregations in and around Ephesus (and beyond), while 2 John serves as a cover letter of sorts to 1 John directed toward specific churches.[9] It is possible that 1 and 2 John are dispatched together and that 2 John is read before 1 John. The point of 2 John is to ban from the church the false teachers that are condemned in 1 John.

The audience of 2 John is metaphorically portrayed as "the lady chosen by God" who has "children" (v. 1). Old Testament prophets sometimes portray Israel as an unfaithful woman (e.g., Is 1:8; Jer 6:2, 23; 14:17; 18:13). On other occasions they depict the nation of Israel as a faithful woman (cf. Jer 4:31). Several prominent passages within Isaiah figuratively anticipate the restoration of Israel in the end times using a marriage metaphor: "You will be a crown of splendor in the LORD's hand. . . . The LORD will take delight in you, and your land will be married. As a young man marries a young woman, so will your Builder marry you; as a bridegroom rejoices over his bride, so will your God rejoice over you" (Is 62:3-5; cf. 52:2; 54:1-6; 61:10; 66:7-13). The New Testament also picks up this theme when it describes the new covenant community as a bride or mother (e.g., Gal 4:26-27; Eph 5:25-33; 1 Pet 5:13). Indeed, one of the apostle John's favorite symbols for the church in Revelation is that of a woman and a bride (Rev 12; 21:2, 9; 22:17). Not coincidentally, Isaiah 40–66 refers several times to future restored Israel by the name of "elect" (*eklektos*). Isaiah 45:4 even states that God will "call" future restored and "elect" (*eklektos*) Israel an end-time "name." Along these lines Isaiah 62:2-5 portrays restored Israel as a

[9]Luke Timothy Johnson, *The Writings of the New Testament*, 3rd ed. (Minneapolis: Fortress Press, 2010), 497.

young woman whom God gives an eschatological "new name." By figuratively describing the local congregations as a chosen lady here in 2 John (see v. 13), could the covenant community be prominently identified as the restored Israel of God living in the latter days?[10] The believers in these local congregations must cling to their identity as God's people when they encounter false teaching and work out their identity in obedience to God's commands.[11]

FIGURE 22.9. MAN MOCKED BY WORSHIPING A CRUCIFIED DONKEY

LOVE AND OBEDIENCE AS TRUE ISRAEL (VV. 4-11)

Having laid a foundation that accentuates the church's identity as the true Israel of God (v. 1), John now turns to the heart of his message. He remains encouraged in the church's commitment to walk in the truth (v. 4) but pleads with them to love one another by walking in obedience (vv. 5-6). The twin themes of right doctrine and earnest love toward one another recall John's central exhortations in 1 John (3:23; 5:1; cf. Jn 13:34-35; 14:15-31). Love for God and one another is concretely expressed in pursuing pure, apostolic doctrine. When false teaching invades the local congregation, dissension and fracture inevitably result. Genuine love glues the community of faith together, whereas false doctrine creates fissures within the congregation. The early church often met in private houses, so any dissension would have drastic effects on the congregation.[12] For the church to survive, believers must preserve the two themes of love and sound doctrine at all costs.

John's exhortations are rooted in the advent of "many deceivers, who do not acknowledge Jesus Christ as coming in the flesh" (v. 7). We should identify these false teachers with those mentioned throughout 1 John (e.g., 2:18-27; 4:1-6). They err in their understanding of Christ in that they deny that Jesus is fully God and fully man who atones for sin and rules as the end-time Messiah. As in 1 John 2:18-27, John labels these false teachers as "the antichrist" (v. 7). Notice that John uses a singular title to describe a plurality of false teachers: "*those* who do not acknowledge Jesus Christ *as* coming in the flesh. *This* is the deceiver and

[10]Outside of Isaiah, the word *eklectos* refers to restored Israel only elsewhere in the Old Testament around six times (e.g., 1 Chron 16:13; Ps 88:3).

[11]See Raymond E. Brown, *The Epistles of John* (Anchor Bible: Garden City, NY: Doubleday, 1982), 651-55, who discusses five different identifications for the "elect lady," two of which refer to the church at large and to a local church. We think a local church is in mind, which is part of the larger church universal (likewise see R. W. Yarbrough, *1-3 John*, BECNT [Grand Rapids: Baker, 2008], 333-34).

[12]Eckhard J. Schnabel, *Early Christian Mission: Paul and the Early Church* (Downers Grove, IL: InterVarsity Press, 2004), 2:1585.

the antichrist" (NASB). Although the end-time antagonist of Israel has not arrived on the scene in his final, physical form, he inspires these false prophets to do his bidding (see 1 Jn 4:1-3; 2 Thess 2:3, 7-8). These local communities of faith find themselves in the throes of the great tribulation as the spirit of the antichrist is, quite literally, knocking on their doors.

The congregations, gathered in their house churches, are to refuse lodging to these false teachers. John commands the churches to "not take them [the false teachers] into your house or welcome them" (2 Jn 10). It is customary in the first century for individuals to take in those passing through the city. As Craig Keener points out, "Showing hospitality by taking in travelers was one of the most important virtues in Mediterranean antiquity, especially in Judaism."[13] In this context, to refuse lodging is countercultural. The false teachers are not given any opportunity to infect congregations with their heresy.

LETTER CLOSING (VV. 12-13)

John admits that while he has far more to say on the subject, it will have to wait for a personal visit. He hopes to visit with his congregations "face to face" (v. 12). The ultimate goal of his exhortation and visit is to make his and their joy complete. This is the same goal stated in 1 John 1:4. When we turn to the Fourth Gospel, we find the identical language once more: "I [Jesus] have told you this so that *my joy* may be in you and that *your joy may be complete*. My command is this: *Love each other* as I have *loved you*" (15:11-12). Possessing joy in its fullness is entwined with loving one another. The precise admonitions found in 1 and 2 John crop up once more here. Loving one another binds the true Israel of God together, thus producing supreme joy.

3 JOHN

LETTER OPENING (VV. 1-4)

As in 2 John 1, the author designates himself as "the elder" (v. 1a). We argued above that such a designation refers to John's authoritative role as an apostle over the church and that it may also include reference to his old age. The audience is mentioned, but this time a specific individual is in mind: "to my dear friend *Gaius*" (v. 1b). Gaius is found elsewhere in the New Testament and often associated with the apostle Paul. One Gaius is probably from Macedonia (Acts 19:29), another hails from Corinth (Rom 16:23; 1 Cor 1:14), and yet another from Macedonia (Acts 20:4). But it is unlikely that the Gaius mentioned here in 3 John should be identified with any of those. All that we can learn about this particular Gaius is probably contained in this short epistle.

It is unknown what precise role Gaius assumes in the local church, but he may in all likelihood be responsible for some sort of ecclesiastical oversight. The thrust of the first half of the epistle is an encouragement to Gaius for his hospitality toward John's envoy. It is probably safe to assume that Gaius owns the house in which the envoy lodged and is, to some degree, wealthy and influential in

[13]Craig S. Keener, *The IVP Bible Background Commentary: New Testament* (Downers Grove, IL: InterVarsity Press, 1993), 73.

the local community. We do not know for certain if the church met in Gaius's house, but it makes good sense.

The apostle John is delighted to hear that Gaius demonstrated "faithfulness to the truth" and is walking in it (v. 3). If we connect the thrust of 1 and 2 John to 3 John, we may be able to fill in a few historical gaps. Apparently, the apostle John dispatches an envoy with 1 and 2 John in hand. With 2 John serving as the cover letter to 1 John, letter couriers from the apostle visit Gaius and his church. These ambassadors most likely circulate among the local churches to determine their spiritual health in light of the threat of false teaching. John's envoy arrives at the house of Gaius and thankfully discovers that he heeded the apostle's instruction contained in 1 and 2 John. Gaius had rightly condemned the false teachers and barred them from infiltrating his congregation. The envoy then reports back to John with the good news. John now pens what we call 3 John to encourage Gaius in his model behavior in remaining confident in the apostolic message of Christ.

COMMENDATION OF GAIUS AND REBUKE TO DIOTREPHES (VV. 5-12)

The body of the letter breaks down into two halves—commendation of Gaius (vv. 5-8) and condemnation of Diotrephes (vv. 9-12). John remains encouraged with the conduct of Gaius, who is "showing faithfulness by whatever" he is doing "for the brothers, especially when they are strangers" (v. 5 HCSB). This is probably a reference to Gaius's hospitality toward John's envoy (the "strangers") that is sent to check in on the church and determine whether the false teachers infiltrated the house church. The envoy checks in on the congregations throughout Ephesus and the neighboring cities "for the sake of the Name" (v. 7). This is a somewhat unusual expression, yet there are some interesting parallels to other passages in the New Testament. Acts 5:41 reads, "The apostles left the Sanhedrin, rejoicing because they had been counted worthy of suffering disgrace *for the Name*" (cf. Jn 15:21; Acts 9:16, 21). The expression may be shorthand for "the name of our Lord Jesus Christ" (see Acts 15:26; 21:13), but what is noteworthy is that most of these references to name contain a tinge of suffering and rejection. This observation fits well with 3 John 7: "They went out, receiving no help from the pagans." John probably makes reference to the envoy not enjoying any hospitality as they travel from city to city, a clear sign of utter rejection.

The letter takes a turn for the worse in verses 9-10: "I wrote to the church, but Diotrephes, who loves to be first, *will not welcome us*. So when I come, I will call attention to what he is doing, *spreading malicious nonsense about us*. Not satisfied with that, *he even refuses to welcome other believers*. He also stops those who want to do so and *puts them out of the church*." Like Gaius, we do not know Diotrephes outside of 3 John. We are also unsure of his precise role in the local church, although it is probably safe to assume that he is an elder of a local congregation, perhaps even the owner of the house where the church meets. Whatever the case, John's words are firm. Diotrephes apparently rejected John's envoy as they circulated among the local congregations. Diotrephes may have rejected 1 and 2 John and allowed false teaching to spread within his congregation. He may have even sided with the false teachers. The apostle John plans on coming to Diotrephes's church to "call attention to what he is doing" (v. 10).

The last part of the letter encourages Gaius to avoid imitating Diotrephes, who "does what is evil" (v. 11). Themes discussed in 1 John begin to resurface as John argues that "anyone who does what is good is from God. Anyone who does what is evil has not seen God" (v. 11; see 1 Jn 3:6, 10). When viewed through the lens of 1 John, Gaius is a wonderful example of a saint who "has been born of God" in the new creation (1 Jn 4:7). Gaius is hospitable and demonstrates his love toward John's envoy. He also does not tolerate the false teachers and thus overcomes the antichrist and his teaching (1 Jn 2:14; 4:4). Diotrephes is, however, self-promoting and "loves to be first." He may be using the local church to build his own reputation. Finally, John commends Demetrius, probably the courier of the letter, to Gaius (3 John 12). Gaius must warmly welcome Demetrius and heed his message.

LETTER CLOSING (VV. 13-14)

John ends his letter with a brief closing like the one found at the end of 2 John. The apostle confesses that he has much more to say than what he outlines in this epistle and that he longs to see Gaius, his "dear friend" (vv. 2, 5, 11). John's colleagues at his home church send their greetings to Gaius. The stakes are high in this short letter, and John finds it necessary to maintain the bond of unity between the saints. Because these three letters exist within the New Testament canon, we can be confident that John's message to the church is successful and false teaching is kept at bay. The orthodox teaching of the apostle John won the day.

REVELATION

AUTHORSHIP

The author identifies himself as John, a servant of God who bears witness to Jesus Christ and who is exiled for his faith (1:1, 9).[1] He is either the apostle John, the one who penned the Gospel of John and three epistles, or another individual with the same name. He seems to be well known to all the churches of Asia, possessing authority to write a letter of this nature to the seven churches and expect his message to be heeded. Internally, many of the themes associated with John's Gospel and letters—Jesus as the Word, the Lamb and the Shepherd, manna, living water, life and light, conquering, keeping the word and the commands of God, and others—also appear in Revelation. Examining the evidence outside the book, we learn that some within the early church assume that John the apostle authored the book (Justin, *Dial.* 81; Irenaeus, *Haer.* 4.20.11). In the end, the apostle John, the son of Zebedee and brother of James, is likely the author of this book.

DATE

According to Revelation, Christians are suffering at the hands of local Jews and the Roman Empire (2:9, 13-14; 13:15). Early Christian writers, such as Irenaeus, believe that John receives his vision during the reign of Domitian (AD 81–96; Irenaeus, *Haer.* 5.30.1-3). At the end of the first century, emperor worship is prevalent throughout, especially in Asia Minor. Therefore, Revelation is most likely written in the 90s, when John is an old man.

OCCASION

The church is birthed in persecution and, by the end of the first century, the saints continue to face strong headwinds of adversity. More than ever, the culture is trying its best to force the church into conformity with its immoral values and idolatry. Dennis Johnson rightly avers, "Revelation is addressed to a church that is under attack. Its purpose, to reveal 'things which must soon take place,' is not to satisfy idle eschatological curiosity or feed a hunger for revenge but to fortify Jesus' followers in steadfast hope and holy living."[2] The church must understand that acquiescing to political and religious pressure in Asia Minor results in total abandonment of the gospel.

PURPOSE

John writes to the seven churches of Asia Minor to remind them of their position in

[1]This chapter is a distillation of G. K. Beale, *Revelation: A Shorter Commentary* (Grand Rapids: Eerdmans, 2015).
[2]Dennis Johnson, *Triumph of the Lamb: A Commentary on Revelation* (Phillipsburg, NJ: P&R, 2001), 16.

Christ. His victory is their victory. The faith of believers must not diminish in the face of adversity since the sovereign hand of God governs the course of history. God promises to punish the wicked, deliver the righteous, and receive all glory and honor.

STRUCTURE

Not many books of the Bible have been as controversial the book of Revelation. G. K. Chesterton famously quipped, "Though St. John the Evangelist saw many strange monsters in his vision, he saw no creatures so wild as one of his own commentators."[3] At the center of the debate lies the book's structure. How do the visions relate to one another? Does the book unfold in a strict chronological manner, or does it repeat the same general vision but from different perspectives? The futurist position generally argues that the material in 4:1–22:5 unfolds chronologically. The recapitulation position (the authors' view), however, argues that the series of judgments run parallel to one another and describe, more or less, the same events. Take, for example, the pattern of the judgments: at the end of each series, definitive final judgment gives way to salvation (6:12-17 and 7:9-17; 11:18a and 11:18b; 14:14-20 and 15:2-4; 16:17–18:24 and 19:1-10; 20:7-15 and 21:1–22:5).

FIGURE 23.1. ST. JOHN AND THE ANGEL

THE FOUR MAJOR MODELS FOR INTERPRETING REVELATION[4]

1. **Preterist**: The word *preterist* refers to the past. This view holds that Revelation is a prophecy of the fall of Jerusalem in AD 70 or the fall of the Roman Empire in the early fifth century AD and that everything in the book has *already* been fulfilled.
2. **Historicist**: The seals, trumpets, and bowls are the successive ages of the church. The symbolism of Revelation refers to a series of specific historical events leading up to the time of any particular historicist commentator, such as the collapse of the Roman Empire, the corruption of the papacy, the Reformation, and various events since.
3. **Futurist**: The futurist view holds generally that the entire book, apart from the letters to the churches in chapters 1–3, prophesies events surrounding the return of Christ at the end of history. Dispensational futurism interprets the visions in a straightforwardly more literal manner, attempting to relate them to physical, not spiritual, realities. Revelation is understood as a broad chronological outline of future events of history.
4. **Redemptive-Historical Idealist (Authors' View)**: The idealist view sees the entire book as a symbolic presentation

[3]G. K. Chesterton, *Orthodoxy* (New York: John Lane, 1908; repr. San Francisco: Ignatius, 1995), 21–22.
[4]The discussion of the four views is taken from Beale, *Revelation: A Shorter Commentary*, 7-9.

of the battle between good and evil. The seals, bowls, and trumpets speak repeatedly to actual events of human history in every age and give believers of all ages an exhortation to remain faithful in the face of suffering. But parts of Revelation indeed refer to future end-time events concerning the return of Christ, his final defeat of the enemy, and the establishment of his heavenly kingdom. Many of the events prophesied speak equally to the life of the church in all generations, excluding those particular events dealing with the very end of history and the return of Christ. And, of course, there are references to the first coming of Christ and events pertaining to the church in the first century (see especially chaps. 1–3).

GENRE

Revelation combines aspects of three different kinds of writing—apocalyptic, prophecy, and epistle. According to 1:3, the book is a prophecy: "Blessed is the one who reads aloud the words of this *prophecy*." The name of the book is the *apokalypsis*, often translated "Apocalypse" or "Revelation" (1:1). The word *apocalyptic* can refer to a literary category that includes latter-day events. According to Revelation, these end-time events have begun to be fulfilled but await a future, final fulfillment at the very end of history. Prophetic elements, such as visions of God's throne, descriptions of his glorious appearance, angels around the throne, descriptions of the heavenly temple in which the throne is located, etc., are critical elements of John's

The Sevenfold Pattern of Woes

	SEALS		TRUMPETS		BOWLS	
Four Catastrophes	6:1-2:	white horse, bow, crown, conquer	8:7	hall, fire, blood	16:2:	sores
	6:3-4:	red horse, sword takes peace from earth	8:8-9	fiery mountain in sea, 1/3 of sea became blood	16:3:	sea to blood
	6:5-6:	black horse, balance	8:10-11	star falls on 1/3 of rivers wormwood > water	16:4-7:	rivers to blood
	6:7-8:	pale horse, sword, famine, plague, wild animals	8:12:	1/3 sun, 1/3 moon, 1/3 stars	16:8-9	sun
The Woes Intensify: The End Approaches	6:9-11:	martyrs under altar, "how long," "little longer"	8:13:	"woe, woe, woe" demon locusts from dark pit	16:10	darkness
	6:12-17:	earthquake, sun and moon, stars fall, all fear	9:13-21:	200,000,000 demon cavalry form Euphrates	16:12-16	kings of east cross Euphrates to prepare for Armageddon
Interlude	7:1-8:	sealing 144,000/great multitude	10:1-11: 11:1-3:	eating scroll 2 witnesses	(pattern broken)	
The End	8:1:	silence	11:15:	end announced and celebrated but not described	16:17-21:	theophany "God remembered great Babylon"
					17-18:	then elaborate the 7th bowl Babylon as a continuation and elaboration of the fall of Babylon

FIGURE 23.2. SEVENFOLD PATTERN OF WOES

visions. The book of Revelation falls in line with Old Testament prophetic-apocalyptic works—Ezekiel, Daniel, and Zechariah. Standing on the shoulders of these prophets of Israel's past, the apostle John exhorts the church in the present and predicts what will befall God's people in the future. Revelation is also an epistle, a letter to the seven churches of Asia Minor. It begins and ends as a typical letter. Verse 1:4, for example, resembles other letters when it reads, "To the seven churches in the province of Asia" (cf. 1 Cor 1:2; Eph 1:1). In keeping with other New Testament letters, John addresses the needs and circumstances of his churches, especially in chapters 2 and 3.

OUTLINE

- I. Prologue (1:1-20)
  - A. Introduction and Salutation (1:1-8)
  - B. John's Commission (1:9-20)
- II. The Letters to the Seven Churches (2:1–3:22)
- III. God and Christ Glorified Through Christ's Resurrection (4:1–5:14)
  - A. God Glorified as Sovereign Judge and Redeemer (4:1-11)
  - B. God and the Lamb Are Glorified Through Christ's Death and Resurrection (5:1-14)
- IV. The Seven Seals (6:1–8:5)
  - A. Seals 1-6 (6:1-17)
  - B. The Interlude of 144,000 (7:1-17)
  - C. Seal 7 (8:1-5)
- V. The Seven Trumpets (8:6–11:19)
  - A. The Six Trumpets (8:6–9:21)
  - B. The Recommissioning of John's Prophetic Call (10:1-11)
  - C. The Prophetic Witness of the Church (11:1-13)
  - D. The Seventh Trumpet (11:15-19)
- VI. Seven Visions of Deeper Conflict (12:1–15:4)
  - A. Divine Protection from the Devil's Attack (12:1-17)
  - B. The Devil's Alliance with Political and Economic Powers (13:1-18)
  - C. The Vindication of the Righteous and the Punishment of the Unrighteous (14:1–15:4)
- VII. The Seven Bowl Judgments (15:5–16:21)
  - A. Introduction to the Seven Bowl Judgments (15:5-8)
  - B. The First Five Bowl Judgments (16:1-11)
  - C. The Sixth and Seventh Bowl Judgments (16:12-21)
- VIII. Final Judgment of Babylon and the Beast (17:1–19:21)
- IX. The Millennium (20:1-5)
  - A. The Inauguration of the Millennial Kingdom (20:1-6)
  - B. The Unsuccessful Assault on the Church (20:7-10)
  - C. Final Judgment (20:11-15)
- X. The New Heavens and Earth (21:1–22:5)
  - A. Dwelling in the Midst of God (21:1-8)
  - B. The Perfected Church in the New Creation (21:9–22:5)
- XI. Epilogue (22:6-21)

BIBLICAL-THEOLOGICAL THEMES

Daniel 7 and the Son of Man. Few passages in the Old Testament are as influential and enigmatic as Daniel 7. To both Judaism and early Christianity, Daniel 7 remains paradigmatic in its eschatological outlook on what events will transpire in the latter days. Jesus himself draws from Daniel 7 in his favorite title, *Son of Man*, and the New Testament writers mined this passage. Revelation drank deeply from the wells of Daniel 7.

This chapter in Daniel, with all of its complexity, is generally straightforward: the Ancient of Days (7:9) passes judgment on earthly pagan kingdoms and establishes his eternal kingdom through the "son of man" (7:13). Daniel 2 outlines four kingdoms (probably Babylon, Medo-Persia, Greece, and Rome) that will consecutively emerge, but the fourth and final kingdom will give way to God's eternal kingdom. This same end-time blueprint continues into chapters 7–12. These four beasts in Daniel 7 should be identified with the four parts of the statue in chapter 2.

The initial vision then reverts to the heavenly throne, where a divine, enigmatic figure "one like a son of man" travels on clouds up to the Ancient of Days (7:13). The son of man, an Adamic figure, then receives an inheritance: "He was given authority, glory and sovereign power; all nations and peoples of every language worshiped him. His dominion is an everlasting dominion that will not pass away, and his kingdom is one that will never be destroyed" (7:14). The kingdom that Adam fails to procure in the garden is the same kingdom the son of man establishes.

The second half of chapter 7 is devoted to the interpretation of the vision (7:15-27). The four beasts symbolize "four kings" or kingdoms (7:17). The final kingdom is discussed in some detail, particularly the little horn (7:8). The ten horns (which derive from the fourth kingdom) refer to ten kings (7:24). This final horn or king antagonizes other kings, persecutes and deceives the Israelites, and speaks against God (7:20-21, 24-25).

Perhaps the reason why the heavenly figure is described as a "son of man" stems from the close identification with true Israel. For example, the son of man receives "authority, glory and sovereign power," "an everlasting dominion," and a "kingdom" (7:14). According to the interpretation of the initial vision, the figure of the son of man is replaced by the remnant of Israel in 7:18, 22, and 27, where the righteous remnant will "receive the kingdom and will possess it forever" (7:18; see also 7:22, 27).

FIGURE 23.3. BELSHAZZAR'S FEAST IN DANIEL 5

Daniel 7 forms the background to the identity of Christ as the "Son of Man" in Revelation 1:7, 12-20 and the structure of chapters 4–5. The description of the two beasts in chapter 13 is also from Daniel 7. Thus, chapters 4–5 and 13 are patterned after the blueprint of Daniel 7. John is adamant that what was prophesied in Daniel 7 is initially fulfilled in Christ's work on the cross and the resurrection. God judges the antagonistic kingdoms of the earth and establishes the long-awaited kingdom through the Son of Man's death.

The ten plagues of Egypt. The ten plagues of Egypt are formative for John's depiction of God's judgment in the trumpet and bowl judgments. The plagues in Exodus 7–12 result in chaos and instability, whereas harmony and order mark creation in Genesis 1–2. The Egyptian plagues of judgment reverse God's original creative activity. The ten plagues harden Pharaoh so that he would *not* release Israel from captivity (Ex 4:21). The ten plagues demonstrate, above all, the Lord's incomparable omnipotence to the Egyptians (Ex 7:5, 17; 8:10, 22; 9:16, 29; 10:1-2). The God of the Israelites deserves all glory and honor.

The Egyptian plagues also reveal the seriousness of sin within the heart of Pharaoh and the Egyptians. As the narrative of Exodus advances, we learn just how intractable Pharaoh is. At every turn, he is unwilling to release the Israelites so that they may worship God at Sinai. The ten plagues, therefore, judge the Egyptians for their hardness of heart, idolatry, and oppression of God's people.

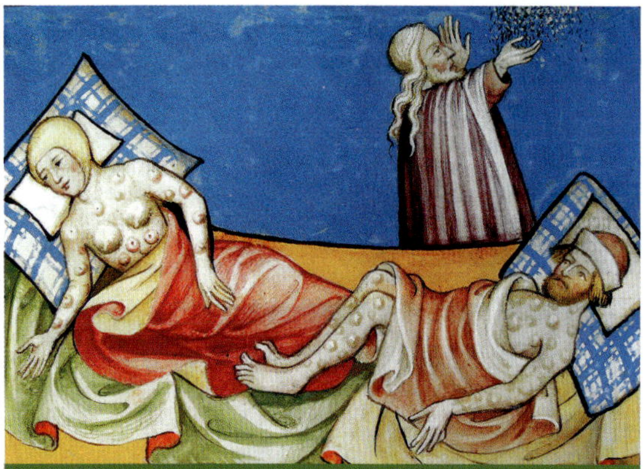

FIGURE 23.4. THE SIXTH PLAGUE OF EGYPT

The plagues of Egypt are a literary and a theological model for the trumpet (8:6–11:19) and bowl judgments (15:1–16:21). The blueprint or prototypical use of the Old Testament is probably in view here. The ten plagues are prophetic patterns or types of God's judgment on the world system. The trumpets and bowls follow the same general order: plagues strike the earth, the sea, rivers, the sun, the realm of the wicked with darkness, the Euphrates, and the world with God's final judgment. The bowls disclose that the trumpets are plagues of judgment directed against unbelieving humanity. The trumpets and the bowls symbolically illustrate God's unique identity and his righteous judgment (16:5-6), and serve to harden the hearts of intractably unrepentant people. Above all, God executes these judgments, like the ten plagues, for the fundamental purpose of bringing glory to himself (11:13, 15-16; 15:8; 16:9).

PROLOGUE (1:1-20)

Israel's history is filled with saints doubting the Lord's goodness, power, and presence. When the wicked Babylonians overthrow Israel, the prophet Habakkuk cries out in frustration, "How long, Lord, must I call for help, but you do not listen? . . . The wicked hem in the righteous so that justice is perverted" (Hab 1:2, 4). Habakkuk is not alone. Scores of Old Testament prophets echo Habakkuk's concern. Chapter 1 of Revelation addresses this issue and offers the church a concrete answer. As the "son of man" (Rev 1:13), Christ stands in complete authority over all of history, yet he does so walking amid his churches. In the Revelation, God the Father remains utterly transcendent, yet Christ draws near to the church to comfort and encourage the saints to overcome the world.

Introduction and salutation (1:1-8). The word *revelation* (or *apocalypse*) expresses the subject and nature of the book (1:1a). John begins by describing his vision as a revelation "which God gave him to show his servants what must *soon take place*" (1:1b). The wording recalls Daniel 2:28-30, 45-47, where Daniel predicts the establishment of the eternal kingdom in the latter days. What Daniel prophesied to happen at the very end of history John insists is coming to pass. The long-awaited kingdom is here, although not it its fullness.

The phrase "made it known" (1:1b) ought to be rendered *signified* or *symbolized* (see HCSB, KJV), and the word *signified* continues the allusion to Daniel 2. According to the LXX of Daniel 2:45, the word describes the symbolic vision that King Nebuchadnezzar saw: "the Great God *has symbolized* to the king what will come to pass in the latter days" (our trans). In Revelation 1:1, John deliberately employs the language from Daniel 2:45 to demonstrate that the general content of Revelation is likewise symbolic. As a rule of thumb, then, *the book of Revelation should be largely read and interpreted in a symbolic manner*. According to Dennis Johnson, "Revelation is a book to be seen, a book of symbols in motion. . . . Revelation is given in visions full of symbols that paradoxically picture the true identity of the church, its enemies, and its Champion."[5]

What is the purpose of John's visions in Revelation? John informs the churches of Asia Minor of God's perspective of the course of history—what has taken place in the past, what is taking place in the present, and what will transpire in the future. Looks can be deceiving. A proper view of reality instructs believers in God's true purposes for their lives and motivates them unto obedience. John identifies the church as a community fashioned "to be a *kingdom and priests* to serve his God and Father" (1:6). God's saints rule with Christ (1:5a) and partake of his priestly office (1:5b, "he freed us from our sins by his blood")[6] by virtue of their identification with his death and resurrection. What is true of Christ is true of his followers. John also alludes to Exodus 19:6: "You will be for me a *kingdom of priests* and a holy nation." God's purpose for Israel is never genuinely realized in the Old Testament but, on account of Christ's work, the churches of Asia Minor are now experiencing the realization of their original calling.

The description of the Son of man's hair as "white like wool" (1:14) is taken from the picture of the Ancient of Days in Daniel 7:9, indicating that Christ and God share the same divine attributes.

John's commission (1:9-20). After greeting the churches (Rev 1:1-8), John announces his commission from the risen Christ to write the book of Revelation (1:9-20). Placing himself on the same level with prominent Old Testament prophets, John uses language similar to Ezekiel's: "I was in the Spirit" (1:10; cf. Ezek 2:2; 3:12, 14, 24). The vision of Revelation 1:12-20 follows the typical pattern of Old Testament visions, whereby a vision is initially revealed and then later interpreted. In 1:12-16, John depicts Christ as a heavenly end-time priest, ruler, and judge. The interpretative section (1:17b-20) then discloses *how* he assumed these offices—his death and resurrection.

John sees "seven golden lampstands" (Rev 1:12), symbolizing two critical components

[5]Johnson, *Triumph of the Lamb*, 22.
[6]See also Rev 1:13 for Christ portrayed as a priest.

of the church in the book of Revelation: the saints' witness to the world and God's intimate presence dwelling among them (1:20; cf. Zech 4:2-6). John graphically envisions the son of man (Rev 1:13-16), arrayed with a "robe reaching down to his feet and with a golden sash around his chest" (1:13). In light of Daniel 7:13-14 and 10:5-6, Christ is the heavenly priest who tends the lampstands (the church) by spurring them on toward godly living. A few verses later, Christ describes himself as the "First and the Last" (1:17), using the same titles God attributes to himself in Isaiah 41:4, 44:6, and 48:12 and also in Revelation 1:8 (cf. 22:13). John's point is clear: Christ is the Lord of history, governing all events from beginning to end. No doubt Jesus presents himself as divine here. Christ's identity in the inaugural vision is the basis for his exhortation, mediated by John, to the seven churches in chapters 2–3 and all of Revelation. At the end of chapter 1, John stands at the beginning of the latter days whom the risen Christ commissions to record what is unfolding in the present and what will transpire at the very end of history (1:19).

THE LETTERS TO THE SEVEN CHURCHES (2:1–3:22)

It is no coincidence that John addresses *seven* churches in Asia Minor in chapters 2–3. Seven is a favorite number of Revelation. According to the Old Testament, it signifies completion or fullness, originally derived from the seven days of God's complete creative act. The number here in Revelation 2–3 signifies that these seven historical churches in Asia Minor embody all the churches scattered throughout the world. What is true of the seven churches of Asia Minor is true of the church at large.

Arranged as a literary chiasm, the seven churches fall into three groups. The first and last, Ephesus and Laodicea, have fallen into grave spiritual danger. They must

SEVEN CHURCHES IN ASIA MINOR

repent of their compromise to avoid judgment and inherit the new creation (2:1-7; 3:14-22). The three in the middle, Pergamum, Thyatira, and Sardis, are ambivalent in their commitment to Christ. Some within these churches remain faithful, whereas others are compromising with pagan culture. Among these three churches, Pergamum remains in the best condition (2:12-17), while Sardis is the worst (3:1-6). These three churches must not to cave in to the mounting pressure of idolatry. Succinctly, "what fellowship can light have with darkness" (2 Cor 6:14). Only the second and sixth churches, Smyrna and Philadelphia, have proven faithful in the face of persecution from Jews and pagans (2:8-11; 3:7-13). They may be physically poor and "have little strength" (2:9; 3:8), but they cannot give up.

The significance of this literary structure of the churches is that the Christian church, on the whole, is in poor spiritual condition. The churches in the worst condition form the literary boundaries of the letters, and the churches with serious problems form the very core of John's presentation. Above all, each letter climaxes with the promise of inheriting eternal life—the main point of each letter (2:7, 11, 17, 26-29; 3:5-6, 11-12, 21). Only those who overcome the allurements of the world and model their lives after *the* overcomer par excellence, the exalted Christ (5:5), will inherit the new creation. Christ overcomes the world spiritually by being overcome by it physically. Grant Osborne notes that "the overcoming theme in Revelation combines promise (God's blessing on those who persevere) and warning (God's judgment on those who fail to persevere)."[7]

GOD AND CHRIST GLORIFIED THROUGH CHRIST'S RESURRECTION (4:1–5:14)

According to 5:4, John "wept and wept" because "no one was found who was worthy to open" the book containing the end-time judgment of God. Christ, however, is the only qualified individual found worthy to open the book (5:5). Why is Christ alone deemed worthy? The answer lies in Genesis 1–3, where God promises Adam that, upon perfect obedience, he and his descendants would reign over the earth. Although Adam forfeits this promise because of his personal disobedience, Christ, the last Adam, inherits God's promise on account of obedience. Christ is also worthy to open the book because he suffers the final judgment as an innocent, sacrificial victim on behalf of his people, whom he represents and redeems (5:9).

The compact statement in 3:21b that Christ "was victorious and sat down with" the "Father on his throne" is unpacked in the vision of chapters 4–5, a section that is patterned after Daniel 7. Note the following points of comparison:[8]

1. Introductory vision phraseology (Dan 7:9; Rev 4:1)
2. The setting of a throne(s) in heaven (Dan 7:9a; Rev 4:2a)
3. God is sitting on a throne (Dan 7:9b; Rev 4:2b)
4. The description of God's appearance on the throne (Dan 7:9c; Rev 4:3a)
5. Fire before the throne (Dan 7:9d-10a; Rev 4:5)
6. Heavenly servants surround the throne (Dan 7:10b; Rev 4:4b, 6b-10; 5:8, 11, 14)

[7]Grant R. Osborne, *Revelation*, BECNT (Grand Rapids: Baker, 2002), 123.
[8]The parallels between Daniel and Revelation are drawn from Beale, *Revelation: A Shorter Commentary*, 97.

7. Book(s) before the throne (Dan 7:10c; Rev 5:1-10)
8. The opening of the book(s) (Dan 7:10d; Rev 5:2-5, 9)
9. A divine (messianic) figure approaches God's throne to receive authority to reign forever over a kingdom (Dan 7:13-14a; Rev 5:5b-7, 9a, 12-13)
10. This kingdom includes all peoples, nations, and tongues (Dan 7:14a; Rev 5:9b)
11. The seer's emotional distress on account of the vision (Dan 7:15; Rev 5:4)
12. The seer's reception of heavenly counsel concerning the vision from one among the heavenly throne servants (Dan 7:16; Rev 5:5a)
13. The saints are also given divine authority to reign over a kingdom (Dan 7:18, 22, 27a; Rev 5:10)
14. A concluding mention of God's eternal reign (Dan 7:27b; Rev 5:13-14)

Revelation's blueprint use of Daniel 7 indicates that Daniel's prophecy is beginning to be realized. Daniel 7 predicts the establishment of the end-time kingdom on account of the son of man's success over the fourth beast. As a result, the righteous saints benefit from the son of man's rule. Christ's victory over death and his resurrection inaugurate the long-awaited prophecy of Daniel 7. The church subsequently inherits what he accomplishes. Daniel 7 stands behind Revelation 4–5, and Revelation 4–5 stands behind Revelation 6–22. So the broad eschatological framework of Daniel 7 extends to nearly all of Revelation.

John is ushered into the timeless presence of God and his heavenly court. He is firmly in the company of Old Testament prophets, such as Isaiah, Ezekiel, and Daniel.

Chapters 4–5 take place in the throne room of God's heavenly temple,[9] demonstrating that God and Christ rule over the entire course of history in the heavenly temple. As the following visions unfold in Revelation, we discover that divine blessing and judgment emanate from the heavenly temple. The entire course of history, from beginning to end, is governed by the triune God from the throne. At the end of Revelation, the heavenly temple will descend and replace the old earth (21:2-3). At long last, God will consummately dwell with his people.

God glorified as sovereign judge and redeemer (4:1-11). The phrase "after these things" (NASB) in 4:1 does not refer to the events of the visions from chapter 4 to the end of the book as coming after the historical events narrated in chapters 1–3. Rather "after these things" indicates that John experiences a new vision after the previous vision (cf. 7:1, 9; 15:5; 18:1; 19:1). The order of John's visions does not represent the future historical order of history but only the visionary order of visions that come one after another. His visions are sequential, not historically chronological. As we journey

[9]Cf. P. Mauro, *The Patmos Visions* (Boston: Hamilton, 1925), 149-68; and Philip Carrington, *The Meaning of Revelation* (New York: Macmillan, 1931), 113, 381-90.

into the book of Revelation, we must never forget that the subsequent visions from 6:1 to 22:5 remain tethered to the central vision in chapters 4 and 5.

John mentions the divine throne seventeen times in chapters 4 and 5 (and a further twenty-one times in chaps. 6–22) to emphasize the sovereignty of God over all human history. The four living beings (4:7-8a) represent the entire created order, and the twenty-four elders or angels (4:4) represent the covenant community throughout the ages. The church on earth is represented in heaven by beings who attend the throne of God. The angelic elders operate in a priestly capacity by presenting the prayers of the saints to God and by interpreting heavenly visions to humanity. John carefully notes that everything is arranged *around* God's throne (4:4, 6, 8), demonstrating that "the throne is the very centre of the universe, not the physiographical but the spiritual centre."[10]

The hymns of 4:8b-11 interpret the preceding vision (4:2-8a). The vision of God on the throne surrounded by heavenly beings, fire, and a sea is interpreted to mean that he is holy (4:8b) and sovereign over creation (4:8b, 11b). He alone is worthy to be praised, worshiped, and glorified (4:9-11). The hymns bring to light the main point of the vision: God, as the Creator of all things, deserves all honor and glory because he is holy and sovereign.

God and the Lamb are glorified through Christ's death and resurrection (5:1-14). The heavenly scene of worship in chapter 4 continues unabated. The One seated on the throne holds a book "with writing on both sides and sealed with seven seals" (5:1). This book symbolizes the judgment of God, as the following chapters reveal. A book of judgment is not foreign to the Bible, as several Old Testament passages associate a book with judgment (Is 29:11; Ezek 2:9b-10; Dan 7:10; 12:4, 9). An angel addresses the cosmos, asking for someone who has the authority to step forward to open the book and break its seals (Rev 5:2).

FIGURE 23.5. LAMB AND THE TWENTY-FOUR ELDERS

But no one is found worthy to open the book or look into it, so John weeps (5:4). His despair is short-lived, as a declaration comes from one of the elders that the "Lion of the tribe of Judah" (Gen 49:8-12), "the Root of David" (Is 11:1-10), has overcome and can open the book. Both titles are messianic and describe a long-awaited king who will vanquish Israel's enemies. Christ, fulfilling the Old Testament, overcomes the devil through his death and resurrection, and now possesses the authority to carry out the divine plan of redemption. The book of righteous judgment can now be unsealed. The unsealing of a book symbolizes that Old Testament prophecy is now being fulfilled and the prophecies are now understood more fully (see Daniel 8:26-27; 12:4, 8-9).

[10]William Hendriksen, *More than Conquerors: An Interpretation of the Book of Revelation* (Grand Rapid: Baker, 2002), 84.

John sees a Lamb as slain, standing in the midst of the throne (5:6). "Slain" alludes to the Passover lamb and to Isaiah's prophecy of the lamb led to slaughter (Is 53:7). John depicts the conquering Lion as a slain Lamb because of the centrality of the cross. Overcoming evil begins at the cross, even before the resurrection. The concluding hymns in 4:11 and 5:9-13 function as interpretative summaries of each chapter: Christ continues God's work in creation by causing all things to return glory to their Creator. At the end of Chapter 5, all of creation worships Christ and God because they alone govern the cosmos.

THE SEVEN SEALS (6:1–8:5)

Much of Israel's career is marked by hostility and strife *within* the covenant community. Certainly, the nation of Israel suffers greatly at the hands of her neighbors, but the remnant within the nation was often under siege from wicked Israelite rulers and prophets. Israel's monarchy is earmarked by a slew of wicked kings who oppress the righteous and favor the unrighteous. Ahab and Jezebel, for example, promote idolatry and erect a temple for Baal (1 Kings 16:32) all the while persecuting righteous prophets (1 Kings 18:4). God designs the first four seals primarily to prune the ungodly within the covenant community and provoke hard-hearted Israelites and confessing believers to return to the Lord. In light of Revelation 4–5, Christ sits enthroned, controlling all the trials and persecutions that befall the church. Through his death and resurrection, Christ has made the forces of evil in the world his instruments to execute his purposes of sanctification and judgment for the furtherance of his kingdom.

Seals 1–6 (6:1-17). The first four seals (6:1-8) symbolize God's authority to purify the saints and punish unbelievers. It is a time of testing and refinement for the covenant community but a period of divine judgment for those who fail to overcome (2:7, 11, 17, 26; 3:5, 12, 21). These seal judgments begin at Christ's first coming and culminate at his second coming.

The most obvious Old Testament background to the first four seal judgments is Zechariah 6:1-8, where God commissions four groups of horses of different colors to patrol the earth and punish the nations that oppress his people (Zech 6:5-8). The use of Zechariah 6 in Revelation 6 is symbolic. The horses in Revelation 6:1-8 signify that Christ issues natural and political disasters throughout the world for two reasons: to judge unbelievers who persecute Christians, and to vindicate his righteous people. Another key Old Testament passages standing behind the first four seal judgments is Ezekiel 14:12-23. According to Ezekiel 14, all Israelites endure persecution because of rampant idolatry (cf. 14:3-11; Lev 26:18-28). The purpose of the trials in Ezekiel 14 is to punish the unbelieving majority in Israel while simultaneously purifying the righteous remnant within the nation. Suffering and purification mutually reinforce one another. Accordingly, Zechariah 6 and Ezekiel 14 are John's blueprint in his portrayal of the four horsemen in the symbolic vision of Revelation 6:1-8.

Whereas the first four seals depict the world's sufferings from the perspective of the heavenly decree of God, John envisions the fifth seal from the perspective of the slain and glorified saints (6:9-11). These individuals, who represent all true believers, have been persecuted for bearing witness to Christ. On the physical altar, located in front of the holy of holies, the high priest burns incense and pours out the blood of the sacrifice on the Day of Atonement (Lev 16:18-19). The heavenly altar, the counterpart to the earthly one, is where the sacrifice of Christ was made and where the saints also identify in their sufferings. The persecuted saints in heaven cry out "How long . . . until you judge the inhabitants of the earth and avenge our blood?" (Rev 6:10). Each believer then receives a "white robe" (6:11), symbolizing a tested, pure faith (cf. 3:4-5).

The events outlined in 6:12-17 are a response to the saints' question posed in 6:10. The calamitous scene of 6:12-17 assumes that the persecution of all Christians has finally run its course, and now all that remains is to execute final punishment on the persecutors, striking the very last note of world history. The cosmic language of 6:12-17 alludes to Old Testament passages that refer to the final day of the Lord: the shaking of the earth; the darkening and/or shaking of the moon, stars, sun, and heaven; and blood (e.g., Is 24:1-6; Ezek 32:6-8; Joel 3:15-16; Hab 3:6-11). Revelation contains several references to earthquakes representing the final judgment (Rev 6:12; 8:5; 11:13; 16:18), and all describe the identical events that take place at the very end of history (cf. Ex 19:16, 18-19).[11]

The interlude of 144,000 (7:1-17). Chapter 7 commences with a new vision, as indicated by the introductory phrase "after this I saw" (7:1). Although John experiences this vision subsequent to that of chapter 6, what it describes comes *before* what chapter 6 depicts chronologically. The section stands as a kind of parenthesis explaining how God preserves the saints throughout the seal judgments during the overlap of the ages (6:1-8).

Four godly angels restrain the evil forces of destruction from the earth, an event that has already occurred according to 6:1-8. The "four winds" (7:1) are probably to be identified with the four horsemen of 6:2-8, since the "four winds" of Zechariah 6:5 also refer to the four horse-drawn chariots. To survive the demonic wave of persecution, God's people are sealed with God's protective mark (7:3; cf. Ezek 9:4-6), which he bestows on them before they endure the tribulations inflicted by the four horsemen in Revelation 6:1-8.

The group of the 144,000 represents the entire church as true Israel in all ages.

FIGURE 23.6. VISION OF THE HORSES OF ZECHARIAH

[11]Richard Bauckham, "The Eschatological Earthquake in the Apocalypse of John," *Novum Testamentum* 19 (1977): 228.

Numbers in Revelation are symbolic, so this group, figuratively numbered as 144,000, symbolizes the redeemed church in its fullness (cf. 14:1-3; 20:2; 21:13-14). The number 144,000 is derived from 12 x 12 x 1,000. The multiples of 12 reflect back on and are rooted in the background of the 12 tribes of Israel, further identifying the church as true Israel. In addition, the numbering of 144,000 in Revelation 7:4-8 also suggests that God's people are an assembled army.[12] The book of Numbers contains a series of lists that organizes Israel into an army, ready to conquer the Canaanites (e.g., Num 1:21, 23; 2:32). According to Revelation 7, though, believers conquer their enemy not with a physical sword but in faithful devotion to Christ. Just as Jesus was victorious over sin and the devil by dying, so too God's people conquer evil by enduring persecution, which ironically is their great weapon.

John depicts the church in military terms to war against the world and the devil.

Revelation 7:1-8 pictures the church as a restored remnant of true Israel whose salvation the Son of Man guarantees, whereas the second half of chapter 7 describes the *same* group from the viewpoint of their future glorification in heaven (7:9-17). Having earned their reward through faithful perseverance in tribulation, they are now enjoying the presence of the Lord for all eternity in the new creation (7:1-9).

Seal** 7 **(8:1-5). At first blush, the seventh seal appears to have no content: "There was silence in heaven for about half an hour" (8:1). But silence in the Old Testament is associated with divine judgment (Hab 2:20–3:15; Zech 2:13–3:2). This final judgment of God is so awful that the whole world falls utterly silent before it. No words capture its horror. The seventh seal is a continuation of the sixth. Whereas the first five seals deal with the entire period of the interadvent age, the last two deal with the final judgment at the very end of history. Verses 3-5 connect the final judgment with the saints' petition in 6:9-10. By breaking the seventh seal, God vindicates the unjust death of the saints.

THE SEVEN TRUMPETS (8:6–11:19)

In Psalm 94, the psalmist cries out in frustration: "How long, LORD, will the wicked, how long will the wicked be jubilant? . . . They slay the widow and the foreigner; they murder the fatherless" (94:3, 6). The seal judgments of Revelation 6–8 answer this perennial dilemma. The time has come for God to judge Israel's oppressors and overturn the injustice of the world. Whereas the first four seal judgments refine the faith of God's people, the trumpet judgments punish the unbelievers who persecute the church. Both judgments, the seals and the trumpets, take place during the overlap of the ages, and the end of each series culminates in final judgment at the very end of time.

The six trumpets (8:6–9:21). By introducing the trumpet judgments in a parenthetical manner in 8:2, John suggests that these judgments, thought distinct from the seals, are

[12]Richard Bauckham, *The Climax of Prophecy: Studies in the Book of Revelation* (Edinburgh: T&T Clark, 1993), 217-29.

also a response to the requests of the saints in 6:9-10. The trumpets do not follow the seventh seal chronologically in history, but in the chronological order of the visions as John sees them. We have moved on to the next vision.

The Egyptian plagues typologically correspond to the first five trumpets in Revelation 8–9. The first trumpet (hail, fire, and blood [8:6-7]) corresponds to the plague of hail and fire (Ex 9:22-25), the second and third (poisoning of the sea and waters [8:8-11]) to the plague on the Nile (Ex 7:20-25), the fourth (darkness [8:12-13]) to the plague of darkness (Ex 10:21-23), and the fifth (locusts [9:1-12]) to the plague of locusts (Ex 10:12-15). The sixth trumpet (9:13-21) presents a picture of ferocious, demonic creatures who torment unbelievers through deception.

Like the Egyptian plagues, the plagues of Revelation punish hardness of heart, idolatry, and persecution of God's people. God does not intend for the Egyptians plagues to coerce Pharaoh into releasing Israel but to demonstrate his incomparable power to the Egyptians and the surrounding nations. The ultimate purpose of God pouring out the ten plagues is to bring glory to himself (Ex 7:5, 17; 8:10, 22; 9:16, 29; 10:1-2; cf. Rom 9:17). The same principle is at work here in Revelation 8–9: in the trumpet judgments, God judges unbelievers so that his sovereign power may reverberate throughout the whole world. The result of divine judgment maintains the pattern set forth in the exodus—God hardens recalcitrant unbelievers and receives all glory and honor.

The recommissioning of John's prophetic call (10:1-11). According to the next vision, John is recommissioned to exhort the seven churches to persevere in their evangelistic efforts and to inform the churches of the destiny of their persecutors. Chapters 10–11 are parenthetically inserted between the sixth and seventh trumpet judgment, a technique that connects the two halves of Revelation together. This literary device called interlocking introduces the second part of the book while also linking it to the first part. The parenthesis of chapters 10–11 offers further interpretation and theological reflection of the same period of the overlap of the ages covered by the first six trumpets.

FIGURE 23.7. ANGELS OF THE SEVEN TRUMPETS AND THE CENSER

John sees "another mighty angel coming down from heaven" (10:1), but this is no ordinary angel. He is clothed with a cloud (10:1), and in the Old Testament God alone comes in the clouds. The angelic figure also has a "rainbow above his head," resembling the appearance of God in Ezekiel 1:26-28 (cf. Rev 4:3). The angel's "face was like the sun," just like Christ in 1:16. The feet of the angelic figure are called "fiery pillars," evoking the presence of the Lord with Israel in the wilderness, where he appears as a pillar of cloud and a pillar of fire (Ex 13:20-22; 14:24; Num 14:14). The angel in chapter 10 is most likely, then, the divine Angel of the Lord, either God or Christ.

The divine angelic figure carries in his hand "a little book which was open" (10:2 NASB). The meaning of the little book is generally the same as the book of chapter 5. There the book symbolizes God's end-time plan of judgment and redemption. Chapter 5 also reveals that perseverance *through* suffering is the way in which Christ overcomes the devil and gained the authority to execute the book's contents. Following suit, the little book of chapter 10 continues the same ironic pattern—saints overcome evil through suffering (10:5-7). Believers experience on a small scale what Christ experienced on a grand cosmic scale.

The prophetic witness of the church (11:1-13). We learn in chapter 11 that God protects the church from the judgment that will befall those who reject the testimony of the saints. The events portrayed in 11:1-13 occur during the same time as the first six trumpets (8:6–9:21).

The command to "measure" the temple in 11:1-2 is derived from Ezekiel 40–48, where an angel measures the eschatological temple and all of its various features. In Revelation 11, the measuring connotes, in fulfillment of Ezekiel's prophecies, God's protective presence that dwells with the covenant community on earth. The temple and all the cultic parts outlined in 11:1-2 (the altar and the outer court) symbolize the church as the true, end-time temple of God. Believers are assured that God will protect them when the world does their worst.

For "forty-two months," or the entire period between the two comings of Christ, the church endures a period of tribulation that the prophet Daniel anticipates (Dan 7:25; 12:7, 11-12). Using language taken from the Old Testament narratives of Moses and Elijah, believers may undergo bodily, economic, political, or social harm, but their status as the covenant community will in no way be broken (Rev 10:3-6; Ex 7:17-25; 2 Kings 1:10-12).

FIGURE 23.8. THE BEAST OF REVELATION 11

When the prophetic witness of the church has run its course, at the very end of history, the beast will "attack" and "kill" the church (Rev 11:7). The beast here in Revelation 11 recalls the beast in Daniel 7 that symbolizes an evil king and his kingdom that wage war against the righteous saints. By all external appearances, the church seems to be defeated. But this is not how the story ends. Revelation 11:11-13 outlines the concluding events of world history. Just as Christ ascended into heaven and God vindicates him before the world (Acts 1:9-11), so God will summon the church into heaven and vindicate them. The seventh angel sounds off and a "severe earthquake" marks God's consummate judgment upon the world (Rev 11:13, 19; cf. 6:12; 8:5; 16:18).

The seventh trumpet (11:15-19). The literary and theological parenthesis of 10:1–11:13 has ended, so 11:14 begins where 9:21 leaves off. The section of 11:15-19 is probably the "third woe," an explanation of the consummation of history. The final fulfillment of the long-awaited messianic kingdom prophesied throughout the Old Testament has finally come to pass. Verse 15 recalls Daniel 7, in which the evil kingdoms of the world are defeated and handed over by the Ancient of Days to the authority of the Son of Man, who then reigns forever. Verses 18-19 take the reader back a step to the period immediately preceding the establishment of God's eternal kingdom in 11:15-18.

SEVEN VISIONS OF DEEPER CONFLICT (12:1–15:4)

The book of Revelation pulls back the curtains on the hostility between the church and the world, revealing the intersection of the spiritual and physical. The Old Testament is well aware of the spiritual dimension that is intertwined with the physical world. For example, Elisha prays that his distraught servant would perceive the angelic army that will deliver them from the Syrian threat. Immediately, the servant "saw the hills full of horses and chariots of fire" (2 Kings 6:17). This series of visions in Revelation opens readers' eyes to a great conflict between the covenant community and the world around them. By tracing the repeated introductory vision formulas such as "and I saw" or "and behold" throughout this section, we can discern seven discrete sections or signs (Rev 12:1-17; 13:1-10; 13:11-18; 14:1-5; 14:6-13; 14:14-20; 15:2-4). A new vision begins in chapter 12, yet it continues to develop the themes of the previous sections of the book. It delves deeper into the dimension of the spiritual conflict between the church and the world. Chapters 12–22 relate the same events as chapters 1–11 but explain in greater detail what the first chapters only introduce and imply.

> *The dragon attacks the saints and God (12:4; see Dan 8:10), but the crucifixion and resurrection snatch Jesus from the clutches of death and the serpent (Rev 12:5).*

Divine protection from the devil's attack (12:1-17). Chapter 12 portrays the destiny of believers between the first and second comings of Christ, particularly how the devil himself is the deeper source of evil. The chapter breaks down into three sections, each repeating the same period of time but from different perspectives (12:1-6, 7-12, 13-17).

The first section, 12:1-6, depicts the covenant community as a woman "clothed with the sun, with the moon under her feet and a crown of twelve stars on her head" (12:1). The sun, moon, and eleven stars metaphorically represent Jacob, his wife, and eleven of the tribes of Israel (Gen 37:9), who bow down to Joseph, representing the twelfth tribe (cf. Is 60:19-20). According to 12:1-6, the woman, representing God's covenant people, gives birth to Christ who inherits what is lost in the garden (Gen 3:14-16). The dragon symbolizes evil kingdoms who persecute God's people (Ps 74:13-14; 89:10; Is 30:7; 51:9; Ezek 29:3; 32:2-3; Hab 3:8-15), yet it is more than a mere metaphor for an evil kingdom. It also stands for the devil himself as the representative head of all evil kingdoms (Rev 12:9).

Verses 7-12 are a heavenly snapshot of the identical events depicted in 12:1-6, explaining how Michael and his angels defeated the devil and his angels in heavenly combat. Michael, representing God's covenant community and its messianic leader, wages war in heaven, even as Christ fights on earth (cf. Dan 10:5-21). The remainder of chapter 12 demonstrates that Christ's death and resurrection drastically curtail the devil's role of deception and slander (12:9-12). According to 12:7-12, the church is once again portrayed as true Israel, the woman, whom God spiritually protects by his presence in the wilderness.

FIGURE 23.9. JOSEPH'S DREAM

The devil's alliance with political and economic powers (13:1-18). Although defeated, the Devil still oppresses the saints. The section of 13:1-18 outlines the devil's agents through whom he inspires and executes his will. These agents are none other than the governing political and economic powers of the earth. In chapter 13, John largely draws from Daniel, especially chapter 7. The first agent of the devil is a "beast coming out of the sea" (Rev 13:1). The imagery of the sea monster is used throughout the Old Testament to represent evil kingdoms that persecute God's people. One of the heads of the beast appear to be slain (13:3), paralleling the Lamb who was slain (5:6). The comparison continues. In 13:14, the beast's miraculous recovery is even portrayed as a resurrection. The beast serves as a satanic counterfeit of Christ. Therefore, the identity of the beast should not be limited to a particular historical person or epoch, for his evil activities are manifested in the devil and his servants, spanning the entire overlap of the ages. The transhistorical nature of the beast is indicated in part by observing that the image of Daniel's four kingdoms, which spanned hundreds of years, is collapsed into the one figure of the beast (Rev 13:1-2).

Verses 11-17 concern the same situation as 13:1-8 but from the perspective of the state's ally, the second beast. Like the first beast, this second beast speaks with the full authority of the devil: he is speaking as a dragon. This beast is later called "the false prophet" (16:13; 19:20; 20:10), suggesting that its role is primarily religious. Whereas the first beast speaks loudly and defiantly against God, the second beast makes the first beast's claims appear plausible and persuasive. False teachers within the church promote compromise with the culture's idolatrous institutions. The oppressive state and the deceptive false teachers work hand in hand.

FIGURE 23.10. THE BEAST OF THE SEA

> *Instead of identifying with the idolatrous world, the redeemed identify with Christ: these are the ones who "follow the Lamb wherever he goes" (14:4). Like the sacrificial Lamb, they offer up their lives in sacrifice to God (cf. Rom 12:1).*

The vindication of the righteous and the punishment of the unrighteous (14:1–15:4). Chapter 14 marks the end of another cycle of visions. This cycle that began in chapter 12 with the anticipation of Christ's birth ends here with the final judgment. The juxtaposition of the Lamb in 14:1 with the beasts of chapter 13 contrasts Jesus, the true Lamb to whom allegiance is to be given, with the pseudo-lamb of 13:11 and the first beast. The 144,000 pictured with Christ here on Mount Zion are the same group as those sealed in 7:4—the saints of all ages. The name of Christ and of the Father are placed on the foreheads of the 144,000 in contrast to the "name of the beast" on the foreheads of unbelievers (13:16-17). Two people groups run throughout Revelation—those who identify with the triune God and those who identify with the beast.

The timeframe of Revelation 14:6-11 immediately precedes the very end of history, shifting from the redeemed (14:1-5) to the unredeemed. The angel here is a messenger not primarily of grace but of judgment. The section of 14:6-13 announces the final judgment by the son of man (see Dan 7:13) as a warning to professing Christians, whereas 14:14-20 depicts that same judgment as falling on unbelievers. Verses 6-8 are drawn from Daniel 4 where, despite Nebuchadnezzar's response to God, he never becomes a true monotheistic follower of God. Even as an unbeliever, Nebuchadnezzar had no choice but to acknowledge that God alone is sovereign. Probably functioning as an analogical use of Daniel 4, the same will happen at the end of time for the ungodly within the church.

The ungodly will worship God "who made the heavens, the earth, and the sea" (14:7), but, nevertheless, they will remain in unbelief.

The seventh vision (15:1-5) that began in 12:1 is interrupted by the introduction of the seven angels carrying bowls filled with God's wrath (15:1). Apparently, 15:2-4 concludes 12:1–14:20 and introduces the bowls of judgment in 15:5-16:21. The sight of "what looked like a sea of glass glowing with fire" (15:2) represents the heavenly counterpart to the Red Sea on the earth. John sees the mighty hand of God calming the chaotic powers of the sea. In a possible direct fulfillment of Daniel 7:2, the victory of the Lamb forges the way for the saints to overcome the beast of the sea. Just as the Israelites praised God by the sea after he had delivered them from Pharaoh (Ex 15; Deut 32), so the glorified church in heaven praises God for defeating the beast (Rev 15:3-4), the former being a typological foreshadowing of the latter.

FIGURE 23.11. POURING OUT OF THE FIRST THREE BOWLS

THE SEVEN BOWL JUDGMENTS (15:5–16:21)

Revelation 15–16 shifts back to the theme of God judging all the unrighteous who persecute his people. The four seal judgments generally refine the church, whereas the trumpets and bowls punish Israel's oppressors. The section of 15:5–16:21 rehearses the same series of judgments we saw before in the trumpet judgments, but this time the imagery is heightened and the effects of divine judgment are more pronounced. Although it is tempting to see the bowls in 15:5-16:21 as chronologically following the trumpets, the bowls go back in time and temporally overlap with the trumpets and explain in greater detail the woes throughout the age, culminating in the final judgment. The goal of all seven bowl judgments is not only to demonstrate God's incomparability and the just judgment of sinners but, ultimately, to give glory to God (15:8; 16:9; cf. 11:13, 15-16; 15:4; 19:1-7).

Introduction to the seven bowl judgments (15:5-8). John sees seven angels coming "out of the temple" (15:6). These angels possess the seven plagues that recall Leviticus 26:21: "If after this ye should walk perversely, and not be willing to obey me, I will further bring upon you *seven plagues* according to your sins" (LXX [Brenton]). According to Leviticus, God promises to send plagues on Israel if they commit idolatry. Five times it is repeated that God promises to judge them seven times if the Israelites become unfaithful to the covenant (Lev 15:1, 6, 8; 21:9; 26:21). Each sevenfold expression introduces a successively worse ordeal if Israel refuses to repent from the preceding woe. This is not the first time Revelation mentions a plague, for in 13:3 and 12 the beast receives a "fatal wound" or, literally, a "plague." Christ executes the plague of judgment through his death and resurrection, setting in motion the seven bowl judgments of 15:5-16:21.

In the Old Testament, priests use "golden bowls" in their service in the tabernacle or temple (1 Chron 28:17; 2 Chron 4:8, 22). Within Revelation 16, angelic priests minister with the bowls at the heavenly altar of the tabernacle of testimony. The image of bowls is also derived in part from Isaiah 51:17, 22. Isaiah spoke of the "cup of staggering; the bowl of my wrath" (ESV), first drunk by Jerusalem but soon to be poured out on Israel's tormentors, that is, Babylon (Is 51:22).

The first five bowl judgments (16:1-11). The first five bowls symbolize God's punishment of the ungodly between the two comings of Christ by depriving them of earthly security (Rev 16:2-11). Such punishment is just because they are hostile toward the church and blatantly idolatrous (16:5-7). The description of the first bowl's effect on unbelievers is based on the Egyptian plague of boils (16:2; cf. Ex 9:9-11). The punishment matches the crime: those who receive an idolatrous mark of the beast are physically marked by boils under God's judgment. The second bowl strikes the sea that transforms into "blood like that of a dead person; and every living thing in the sea died" (Rev 16:3). The wording recalls Exodus 7:17-21, where Moses turns the Nile into blood. The second bowl symbolizes a famine due to economic deprivation, and the third bowl is modeled after the same plague in Exodus and once again refers to the economic deprivation of the world system (Rev 16:4-7). The fourth bowl symbolizes God's judgment on those who blaspheme him (Rev 16:8-9; cf. Jer 7:20; Ezek 22:21-22). The fifth bowl, patterned after Exodus 10:21-29, refers to God's judgment on all who follow the beast (Rev 16:10-11). Although unbelievers experience great anguish and horror as they realize their spiritual bankruptcy, they still refuse to repent and give glory to God.

The sixth and seventh bowl judgments (16:12-21). The sixth bowl prepares the way for the execution of the seventh bowl—God assembles the ungodly forces in order to punish them at the very end of history (16:12-16). The figurative drying up of the Euphrates in Revelation 16 marks the prelude to the destruction of latter-day Babylon, the world system (cf. Is 11:15; 44:27). The three central opponents of God—the dragon, beast, and the false prophet (Rev 16:13)—deceive unbelievers into thinking they are assembling to exterminate the saints at Armageddon. The truth of the matter is that God is the one who ultimately gathers them to be judged by his Son (16:16; cf. 19:11-21). The seventh and final bowl, patterned after the theophany at Sinai in Exodus 19:16-18, symbolizes God's final judgment on the unbelieving world or "Babylon the Great" (16:19; see 4:5; 8:5; 11:19).

FINAL JUDGMENT OF BABYLON AND THE BEAST (17:1–19:21)

Revelation 17:1–19:10 is a snapshot of the sixth and seventh bowls that symbolically depict the final judgment on Babylon taking place at the end of history. The second section, 19:11-21, describes in greater detail the final, epic battle between Christ and the host of evil. A great deal of Revelation 17:1–19:4 concerns God's judgment of the harlot. We

FIGURE 23.12. WOMAN ON THE BEAST

learn here how the government and the false religious system interact with one another.

The main point of the vision is the "*punishment* of the great prostitute, who sits by many waters" (17:1). Symbolizing Babylon as a harlot reveals her alluring and seductive nature in drawing people away from Christ. Babylon is depicted as a prostitute with whom "the kings of the earth committed adultery" (17:2). She symbolizes the ungodly world as it works with the state socially, culturally, and economically to persecute Christians (17:6; 18:24; 19:2; cf. Dan 7:3-7, 20, 24). The woman rides the beast (17:3), informing the readers that the world system is deeply allied with the government. The kings of the earth gather together for war but, mysteriously, turn against Babylon (Rev 17:15-18). Her waters are dried up, and she is laid waste. The enemies of God, once united in their pursuit of oppressing the church, have self-destructed (17:5).

> ***The kings represent the political arm of the world system that turns against the economic-religious arm in a worldwide civil war.***

Chapter 18 opens with a new vision wherein Christ, portrayed as a magnificent angelic messenger, announces Babylon's destruction. Babylon is on the receiving end of God's judgment because it seduced the nations to trust in her economic resources (18:3). Instead of relying on the Lord and his provision, the nations trusted Babylon for well-being and security. Many gain considerable wealth on account of Babylon's alliance with the state, but their wealth is short lived. When Babylon falls, their wealth collapses (18:9-19). The prediction of Tyre's judgment in Ezekiel 26–28 forms the background of Babylon's downfall in 18:9-19. Chapter 18 ends with the ecstatic praise of the saints over Babylon's fall (18:20). The prayer in 6:10, "How long, Sovereign Lord, holy and true, until you judge the inhabitants of the earth," has finally been answered!

Revelation 19:1-10 constitutes a new vision, describing the result of Babylon's downfall—the effusive praise of the righteous. God has overcome the wickedness of the world with great finality, so the most appropriate response is "Hallelujah!" (19:1, 3, 4, 6). Although God's reign has always been, in some sense, timeless, in another sense his cosmic reign reaches its fullness in the final destruction of all the forces of evil (19:11-21).

THE MILLENNIUM (20:1-5)

There are three predominant views of the period known as the "millennium" (one thousand years), a term that is found in the Bible only here in Revelation 20. Some believe that the millennium will occur after the second coming of Christ. This view is traditionally known as premillennialism. Postmillennialism, by contrast, argues that the millennium occurs toward the end of the present church age and that Christ's climactic coming will occur at the close of the millennium. Others believe that the millennium inaugurates at Christ's resurrection and will be concluded directly before his final coming. This view has been called amillennialism or, better, inaugurated millennialism. We prefer the last view, as it resonates with the New Testament's conviction that the end-time kingdom of God began with Christ's ministry and continues throughout the overlap of ages. This view also fits well with the book of Revelation's penchant for rehearsing and recapitulating events from different angles in the successive visions, and it fits well with a close interpretation of Revelation 20:1-6. The kingdom, as described here in Revelation 20:1-6, is simply another depiction of the inauguration of the end-time kingdom that pervades the writings of the New Testament.

The inauguration of the millennial kingdom (20:1-6). John sees an angel with a key to "the Abyss" and a "great chain" in his hand (20:1). This key is identical to the "keys of death and Hades" (1:18) held in possession of Christ on account of his resurrection. Christ's success restrains Satan's operation during the overlap of the ages (cf. 3:7; 6:8; 9:1, 4). According to 20:2-3, the angel "bound" Satan for a "thousand years" in order to "keep him from deceiving the nations anymore until the thousand years were ended." A "thousand years" is symbolic of a long period of time (e.g., Deut 1:10-11; Ps 90:4; Is 7:23; 2 Pet 3:8). Satan's binding, expulsion, and fall from heaven portrayed in Revelation 12 and 20 must be interpreted in conjunction with other New Testament passages using similar terminology (e.g., Mt 12:29; Mk 3:27; Lk 10:18-19; Jn 12:31; Col 2:15; Heb 2:14). Satan's deceptive powers are not restricted absolutely in every way but only in two primary ways. During the overlap of the ages, he is unable to deceive the elect and powerless in restricting the establishment of God's church. Also, until God's appointed hour, Satan is not permitted to deceive the ungodly nations for a final assault on the church. When Satan is finally released at the very end of history, he will assemble the unbelieving nations to wage war against the church (Rev 20:7-9).

The focus on what transpires in the abyss in 20:1-3 shifts to what materializes at the same time in heaven as a result of the binding of Satan. The group in 20:4-6 should be identified with the saints in 6:9. During the overlap of the ages, these dead saints rule and reign with Christ in heaven, where they also serve as priests (cf. Ex 19:6; Is 61:6; Zech 6:13). While God's people on earth certainly reign with Christ, death brings to them an escalated state of ruling in heaven.

The unsuccessful assault on the church (20:7-10). With the release of Satan

FIGURE 23.13. ANGEL BINDING SATAN

from the abyss, the nations assemble at the very end of the age to exterminate the people of God (Rev 20:8). This section runs parallel to 19:17-21. Between the two comings of Christ, God restricts Satan in his ability to deceive the nations into joining forces to attack and completely annihilate the church, but this restraint is now removed. Satan will escort an army drawn from the "four quarters of the earth," an Old Testament expression for the whole earth (Is 11:12; Ezek 37:9; Dan 7:2). The assembling of these antagonistic forces against God's people fulfills the prophecy of Ezekiel 38–39, in which "Gog" and "Magog" and "many peoples" gather together for war against Israel in the end times (cf. Zech 12–14). The attack on the church, the continuation of true end-time Israel and the covenant community, is unsuccessful as the satanic trinity—the devil, beast, and false prophet—is cast into the lake of fire for all eternity (Rev 20:10).

Final judgment (20:11-15). The visions in chapters 4, 5, and 20 spring from Daniel 7, depicting God sitting on the throne and opening the books of judgment. Whereas much of the focus of the vision in chapters 4–5 is on the present reign and judgment of God and Christ, the scene in chapter 20 concerns the future culmination of that rule at the end of history. John envisions the destruction of the entire world system coming under absolute judgment. Unbelievers and believers are resurrected, and both groups stand "before the throne" (20:12). In fulfillment of Daniel 12:2, true believers who have held fast to Christ will inherit the eternal new heavens and earth, while unbelievers who have worshiped the devil and the world will be "thrown into the lake of fire" (20:14). Thus, the sequence of all the events portrayed in 20:1-15 is "Christ's first coming . . . followed by a long period during which Satan is bound; this, in turn, is followed by

FIGURE 23.14. THE NEW JERUSALEM

Satan's little season; and that is followed by Christ's second coming."[13]

THE NEW HEAVENS AND EARTH (21:1–22:5)

Revelation ends where Genesis begins—the creation of heaven and earth. John's vision is not simply a replacement of the created world in Genesis 1–2 but the realization of its ultimate goal. Although the created world was perfect before the fall, it remained in an incomplete state—it had the potential for corruption, and God's full, glorious presence remained in the invisible heavens. But in the new heavens and earth, as described here in Revelation 21–22, the created order is perfected and in a state of incorruptibility. Sin cannot enter into this new world, and, above all, heaven and earth are a single reality. God and humanity have a new home.

John does not see a physical temple in the new creation, because the "Lord God Almighty and the Lamb are its temple" (21:22). The entire created world is now the house of the Lord. Genesis 1–2 records God constructing a cosmic temple, and Revelation 21–22 narrates God moving into that temple once and for all. The resurrected saints will live in a physical environment, a world free from sin and persecution, and worship God for all eternity. William Dumbrell captures the heart of this passage when he states, "The history of salvation has ended, and the journey has been long. We have moved from creation to Adam to Israel and redemption, to Jesus as suffering Israel, to the creation of a new people of God through the cross and resurrection of Jesus. We have moved through the call of the Gentiles to come into the new people of God, through the difficulties of the overlap of the ages, into the reality of the new age itself."[14]

> ***In the new creation, God's presence will not be limited to a physical structure of a temple where his people are kept outside, but the people themselves will be the city and the temple, as well as priests dwelling in the midst of God's and Christ's presence.***

Dwelling in the midst of God (21:1-8). John sees a "new heaven and a new earth" (21:1a) in fulfillment of Isaiah 65:17 and 66:22. These prophecies, though fulfilled in an initial manner in Christ's death and resurrection, are now fulfilled in their fullness in the new heavens and earth. The phrase "no longer any sea" (21:1b) is rooted in the Old Testament conception of sin and rebellion, as it refers to the threat of evil and tribulation for God's people (e.g., Ps 74:12-15; Ezek 32:2; Dan 7:2). In the eternal state, then, there is no potentiality for evil and oppression. John then sees a "Holy City, the new Jerusalem . . . prepared as a bride" (21:2). The image of the city is symbolic, representing the fellowship of God with his people, both Jews and Gentiles, in the eternal new creation.

[13]Hendriksen, *More than Conquerors*, 185.
[14]William Dumbrell, *The Search for Order: Biblical Eschatology in Focus* (Eugene, OR: Wipf & Stock, 1994), 346.

The voice in 21:3 explains the city and marriage metaphors of 21:2: "God's dwelling place is now among the people, and he will dwell with them. They will be his people, and God himself will be with them and be their God" (see Lev 26:11-12; Ezek 37:27). In the new heavens and earth, God's people will no longer experience any of the forms of suffering characteristic of the old creation (21:4).

The perfected church in the new creation (21:9–22:5). The structure of the city in 21:9–22:5 is based on Ezekiel 40–48, a passage that predicts the pattern of the latter-day temple (chapters 40–44) and the arrangement of the city and its land (chapters 45–48). This section of 21:9-22:5 directly fulfills Ezekiel 40-48, by collapsing temple, city, garden of Eden, and new creation into one end-time picture portraying the one reality of God's communion with his people. Revelation 21:9–22:5 also recapitulates 21:1–8 by lending further insight into God's consummate communion with his people and their consummate safety in the new creation. The theme of God's glorious presence dwelling with his people in the new creation, briefly developed in 21:1-8, runs throughout 21:11–22:5.

EPILOGUE (22:6-21)

The introduction pronounces a blessing on all who obey the exhortation of Revelation (1:3), whereas the conclusion issues an emphatic curse on all who disobey it (22:18-19). The epilogue reveals that the purpose of the book is to promote godly living within the church so that the readers may receive their inheritance of the new creation (22:7, 9, 11-12, 14-15, 18-19). Verse 6 serves as a concluding statement for the vision of 21:1–22:5 and the book at large. John hears a voice declaring, "These words are trustworthy and true." The phrase, a verbal repetition of the phrase in 21:5, is based on Isaiah 65:16, asserting confidence in God's forthcoming act of new creation (cf. Dan 2:45).

The angel commands John, "Do not seal up the words of the prophecy of this book, for the time is near" (22:10 NASB). The prohibition against sealing is the opposite command given to Daniel, who was commanded to "seal the words of the scroll until the time of the end," indicating that the prophecy was not yet fulfilled and was not very understandable (Dan 12:4). Thus, the language of unsealing the book demonstrates the beginning fulfillment of Daniel's prophecies and the possession of greater insight into Daniel's (and other Old Testament) prophetic utterances.

The book ends with Jesus' affirmation that he is "coming soon" (22:20). Jesus assures the churches that the book of Revelation is true by guaranteeing that the second coming will fulfill what is promised throughout the book. Christ's death and resurrection set God's end-time promises in motion, and his second coming brings them to their consummation. The closing benediction in 22:21 is a typical conclusion to New Testament letters: "The grace of the Lord Jesus be with God's people." It is only by God's grace that John's readers can grasp and heed the contents of the letter, with the ultimate goal of bringing glory to God, the Lamb, and the Spirit.

BIBLIOGRAPHY

Abernethy, Andrew T. *The Book of Isaiah and God's Kingdom: A Thematic-Theological Approach*. NSBT 40. Downers Grove, IL: IVP Academic, 2016.

Alexander, T. Desmond. *From Eden to the New Jerusalem: An Introduction to Biblical Theology*. Grand Rapids: Kregel, 2008.

———. *From Paradise to the Promised Land: An Introduction to the Pentateuch*, 3rd ed. Grand Rapids: Baker, 2012.

Allison, Dale C. *The New Moses: A Matthean Typology*. Minneapolis: Fortress Press, 1993.

Arnold, Clinton E. *The Colossian Syncretism: The Interface Between Christianity and Folk Belief at Colossae*. WUNT 77. Tübingen: Mohr Siebeck, 1995. Reprint, Grand Rapids: Baker, 1996.

———. *Ephesians*. ZECNT. Grand Rapids: Zondervan, 2010.

Asher, Jeffrey R. *Polarity and Change in 1 Corinthians 15: A Study in Metaphysics, Rhetoric, and Resurrection*. HUT 42. Tübingen: Mohr-Siebeck, 2000.

Bauckham, Richard. *The Climax of Prophecy: Studies in the Book of Revelation*. Edinburgh: T&T Clark, 1993.

———. "The Eschatological Earthquake in the Apocalypse of John," *NovT* 19 (1977): 224-233.

———. "For Whom Were Gospels Written?" In *The Gospels for All Christians*. Edited by Richard Bauckham, pp. 9-48. Grand Rapids: Eerdmans, 1998.

———. *Gospel of Glory: Major Themes in Johannine Theology*. Grand Rapids: Baker, 2015.

———. "James and the Jerusalem Church." In *The Book of Acts in Its Palestinian Setting*. Edited by Richard Bauckham, pp. 415-480. Grand Rapids: Eerdmans, 1995.

———. *Jesus and the Eyewitnesses: The Gospels as Eyewitness Testimony*. Grand Rapids: Eerdmans, 2006.

———. *Jesus and the God of Israel: God Crucified and Other Studies on the New Testament's Christology of Divine Identity*. Grand Rapids: Eerdmans, 2008.

———. *The Jewish World Around the New Testament*. WUNT 233. Tübingen: Mohr Siebeck, 2008. Reprint, Grand Rapids: Baker, 2010.

———. *Jude, 2 Peter*. WBC 50. Grand Rapids: Zondervan, 1983.

Beale, G. K. "The Background of ἐκκλησία Revisited." *JSNT* 38 (2015): 1-18.

———. "Colossians." In *Commentary on the New Testament Use of the Old Testament*. Edited by G. K. Beale and D. A. Carson, pp. 841-871. Grand Rapids: Baker Academic, 2007.

———. *Colossians and Philemon*. BECNT. Grand Rapids: Baker, 2019.

———. "Eschatological Conception of New Testament Theology." In *Eschatology in Bible & Theology*. Edited by Kent E. Brower and Mark W. Elliott, pp. 11–52. Downers Grove, IL: InterVarsity Press, 1997.

———. *1–2 Thessalonians*. IVPNTC. Downers Grove, IL: InterVarsity Press, 2003.

———. *Handbook on the New Testament Use of the Old Testament: Exegesis and Interpretation*. Grand Rapids: Baker, 2012.

———. "The Old Testament Background of Reconciliation in 2 Corinthians 5–7 and Its Bearing on the Literary Problem of 2 Corinthians 4:14–7:1." *NTS* 35 (1989): 550-81.

———. "The Purpose of Symbolism in the Book of Revelation." *Calvin Theological Journal* 41 (2006): 57-58.

———. *Revelation: A Shorter Commentary*. Grand Rapids: Eerdmans, 2015.

———. *The Temple and the Church's Mission: A Biblical Theology of the Dwelling Place of God.* NSBT 17. Downers Grove, IL: InterVarsity Press, 2004.

———. *We Become What We Worship: A Biblical Theology of Idolatry*. Downers Grove, IL: IVP Academic, 2008.

Beale, G. K. and Mitchell Kim. *God Dwells Among Us: Expanding Eden to the Ends of the Earth.* Downers Grove, IL: InterVarsity Press, 2014.

Block, Daniel. *For the Glory of God: Recovering a Biblical Theology of Worship*. Grand Rapids: Baker, 2014.

Blomberg, Craig. "Matthew." In *Commentary on the New Testament Use of the Old Testament.* Edited by G. K. Beale and D. A. Carson, pp. 1-110. Grand Rapids: Baker Academic, 2007.

Bock, Darrell L. *Acts*. BECNT. Grand Rapids: Baker, 2007.

Bockmuehl, Markus. *Revelation and Mystery in Ancient Judaism and Pauline Christianity*. WUNT 36. Tübingen: J. C. B. Mohr (Paul Siebeck), 1990. Reprint, Grand Rapids: Eerdmans, 1997.

Bolt, Peter. *The Cross from a Distance: Atonement in Mark's Gospel.* NSBT 18. Downers Grove, IL: InterVarsity Press, 2004.

Boring, M. E., K. Berger, and C. Colpe. *Hellenistic Commentary to the New Testament.* Nashville: Abingdon, 1995.

Brendsel, Daniel J. *"Isaiah Saw His Glory": The Use of Isaiah 52–53 in John 12*. BZNW 208. Berlin: Walter de Gruyter, 2014.

Bruce, F. F. *The Book of Acts*. NICNT. Grand Rapids: Eerdmans, 1954.

———. *Philippians*. NIBC. Peabody, MA: Hendrickson, 1995.

Bryan, Steven M. "Consumed by Zeal: John's Use of Psalm 69:9 and the Action in the Temple." *BBR* 21 (2011): 479-494.

———. "The Eschatological Temple in John 14," *BBR* 15 (2005): 187-198.

Burridge, Richard A. *Four Gospels, One Jesus? A Symbolic Reading*. 2nd edition. Grand Rapids: Eerdmans, 2005.

———. "Gospel Genre and Audiences." In *The Gospels for All Christians: Rethinking the Gospel Audiences*. Edited by Richard Bauckham, pp. 113-146. Grand Rapids: Eerdmans, 1998.

———. *What Are the Gospels? A Comparison with Graeco-Roman Biography*. 2nd edition. Grand Rapids: Eerdmans, 2004.

Byrskog, Samuel. *Story as History—History as Story: The Gospel Tradition in the Context of Ancient Oral History*. Leiden: Brill, 2002.

Caird, G. B. *The Language and Imagery of the Bible*. Philadelphia: Westminster, 1980.

———. *New Testament Theology*. Edited by L. D. Hurst. Oxford: Oxford Press, 1995.

Carrington, Philip. *The Meaning of Revelation*. New York: Macmillan, 1931.

Carson, D. A. "1 Peter." In *Commentary on the New Testament Use of the Old Testament.* Edited by G. K. Beale and D. A. Carson, pp. 1015-1047. Grand Rapids: Baker Academic, 2007.

———. *The Gospel According to John*. PNTC. Grand Rapids: Eerdmans, 1991.

———. "Mirror-Reading with Paul and Against Paul: Galatians 2:11–14 as a Test Case." In *Studies in the Pauline Epistles: Essays in Honor of Douglas J. Moo*. Edited by Matthew S. Harmon and Jay E. Smith, pp. 99-112. Grand Rapids: Zondervan, 2014.

———. "Pseudonymity and Pseudepigraphy." In *The Dictionary of New Testament Background.* Edited by Craig A. Evans and Stanley E. Porter, pp. 857-864. Downers Grove, IL: InterVarsity Press, 2000.

———. "2 Peter." In *Commentary on the New Testament Use of the Old Testament*. Edited by G. K. Beale and D. A. Carson, pp. 1047-1063. Grand Rapids: Baker Academic, 2007.

———. "The Vindication of Imputation: On Fields of Discourse and Semantic Fields." In *Justification: What's at Stake in the Current Debates*. Edited by Mark Husbands and Daniel J. Treier, pp. 46-78. Downers Grove, IL: InterVarsity Press, 2004.

———. "What Is the Gospel?—Revisited." In *For the Fame of God's Name: Essays in Honor of John Piper*. Edited by Sam Storms and Justin Taylor, pp. 149-170. Wheaton, IL: Crossway, 2010.

Carson, D. A. and Douglas J. Moo. *An Introduction to the New Testament*. 2nd edition. Grand Rapids: Zondervan, 2005.

Chapman, David W. *Ancient Jewish and Christian Perceptions of Crucifixion*. WUNT 244. Tübingen: J. C. B. Mohr (Paul Siebeck), 2008.

Chesterton, G. K. *Orthodoxy*. New York: John Lane, 1908. Reprint, San Francisco: Ignatius, 1995.

Ciampa, Roy E., and Brian S. Rosner. "1 Corinthians." In *Commentary on the New Testament Use of the Old Testament*. Edited by G. K. Beale and D. A. Carson, pp. 695-753. Grand Rapids: Baker Academic, 2007.

Clowney, Edmund P. *The Unfolding Mystery: Discovering Christ in the Old Testament*. 2nd ed. Phillipsburg, NJ: P&R, 2013.

Crowe, Brandon D. *The Last Adam: A Theology of the Obedient Life of Jesus in the Gospels*. Grand Rapids: Baker, 2017.

Crump, David M. "Prayer." In *Dictionary of Jesus and the Gospels*. 2nd edition. The IVP Bible Dictionary Series. Edited by C. S. Green, Joel B. Green, Jeannine K. Brown, and Nicholas Perrin, pp. 684-693. Downers Grove, IL: IVP Academic, 2013.

Cullmann, Oscar. *Christ and Time*. Philadelphia: Westminster, 1950.

Davids, Peter H. *The Epistle of James*. NIGTC. Grand Rapids: Eerdmans, 2013.

———. *The Letters of 2 Peter and Jude*. PNTC. Grand Rapids: Eerdmans, 2006.

———. *A Theology of James, Peter, and Jude*. BTNT. Grand Rapids: Zondervan, 2014.

Dempster, Stephen G. *Dominion and Dynasty: A Theology of the Hebrew Bible*. NSBT 3. Downers Grove, IL: InterVarsity Press, 2003.

Dodd, C. H. *According to the Scriptures: The Sub-Structure of New Testament Theology*. London: Nisbet, 1952.

Donelson, L. R. *Pseudepigraphy and Ethical Argument in the Pastoral Epistles*. HUT 22. Tübingen: Mohr Siebeck, 1986.

Dumbrell, William J. "Genesis 2:1-17: A Foreshadowing of the New Creation." In *Biblical Theology: Retrospect & Prospect*. Edited by Scott J. Hafemann, pp. 53-65. Downers Grove, IL: InterVarsity Press, 2002.

———. *The Search for Order: Biblical Eschatology in Focus*. Eugene, OR: Wipf & Stock, 1994.

Ellingworth, Paul. *The Epistle to the Hebrews*. NIGTC. Grand Rapids: Eerdmans, 1993.

Everson, J. A. "The Days of Yahweh." *JBL* 93 (1974): 329-337.

Fee, Gordon. *The First and Second Letters to the Thessalonians*. NICNT. Grand Rapids: Eerdmans, 2009.

———. *The First Epistle to the Corinthians*. NICNT. Grand Rapids: Eerdmans, 1987.

France, R. T. *The Gospel of Mark*. NIGTC. Grand Rapids: Eerdmans, 2002.

———. *Jesus and the Old Testament: His Application of Old Testament Passages to Himself and His Mission*. London: Tyndale, 1971.

Fyall, Robert S. *Now My Eyes Have Seen You: Images of Creation and Evil in the Book of Job*. NSBT. Downers Grove, IL: InterVarsity Press, 2002.

Gaffin, Richard B., Jr. *By Faith, Not by Sight: Paul and the Order of Salvation*. London: Paternoster, 2006.

Gage, W. Austin. *The Gospel of Genesis*. Winona Lake, IN: Eisenbrauns, 1984.

Garland, David E. *Luke*. ZECNT. Grand Rapids: Zondervan, 2011.

———. *A Theology of Mark's Gospel: Biblical Theology of the New Testament*. Grand Rapids: Zondervan, 2015.

Gentry, P. J., and A. M. Fountain. "Reassessing Jude's Use of Enochic Traditions (with Notes on Their Later Reception History)." *TynB* 68 (2017): 261-86.

Gladd, Benjamin L. "Colossians." In *A Biblical-Theological Introduction to the New Testament: The Gospel Realized*. Edited by Michael J. Kruger, pp. 301-319. Wheaton, IL: Crossway, 2016.

———. "Mark." In *A Biblical-Theological Introduction to the New Testament: The Gospel Realized*. Edited by Michael J. Kruger, pp. 61-91. Wheaton, IL: Crossway, 2016.

———. "Philemon." In *A Biblical-Theological Introduction to the New Testament: The Gospel Realized*. Edited by Michael J. Kruger, pp. 401-410. Wheaton, IL: Crossway, 2016.

———. *Revealing the* Mysterion: *The Use of Mystery in Daniel and Second Temple Judaism with Its Bearing on First Corinthians*. BZNW 160. Berlin: Walter de Gruyter, 2008.

Gladd, Benjamin L., and Matthew S. Harmon. *Making All Things New: Inaugurated Eschatology for the Life of the Church*. Grand Rapids: Baker, 2016.

Green, Joel B. "Luke, Gospel of." In *Dictionary of Jesus & the Gospels*. 2nd edition. Edited by C. S. Green, Joel B. Green, Jeannine K. Brown, and Nicholas Perrin, pp. 540-553. Downers Grove, IL: IVP Academic, 2013.

Grizzard, Carol S. "The Scope of Theology in Wisdom Literature." In *An Introduction to Wisdom Literature and the Psalms: Festschrift for Marvin E. Tate*. Edited by H. W. Ballard Jr. and W. D. Tucker Jr., pp. 195-214. Macon, GA: Mercer University Press, 2000.

Guthrie, George H. "Hebrews." In *Commentary on the New Testament Use of the Old Testament*. Edited by G. K. Beale and D. A. Carson, pp. 919-997. Grand Rapids: Baker Academic, 2007.

Hafemann, Scott J. *2 Corinthians*. NIVAC. Grand Rapids: Zondervan, 2000.

Hamilton, Victor P. *Handbook on the Pentateuch*. 2nd. edition. Grand Rapids: Baker Academic, 2005.

Harmon, Matthew. *Philippians*. Fearn, Scotland: Mentor, 2015.

Harris, Murray J. *The Second Epistle to the Corinthians: A Commentary on the Greek Text*. NIGTC. Grand Rapids: Eerdmans, 2005.

———. *Slave of Christ: A New Testament Metaphor for Total Devotion to Christ*. NSBT 8. Downers Grove, IL: InterVarsity Press, 1999.

Hays, Richard. *Echoes of Scripture in the Letters of Paul*. New Haven, CT: Yale University Press, 1989.

———. *First Corinthians*. Interpretation. Louisville: Westminster John Knox, 1997.

———. "The Letter to the Galatians: Introduction, Commentary, and Reflections." In *The New Interpreter's Bible*. Edited by L. E. Keck, pp. 11:181-348. Nashville: Abingdon, 2000.

———. *The Moral Vision of the New Testament: Community, Cross, New Creation: A Contemporary Introduction to New Testament Ethics*. New York: HarperCollins, 1996.

———. *Reading Backwards: Figural Christology and the Fourfold Gospel Witness*. Waco: Baylor University Press, 2014.

Heil, John Paul. "The Narrative Strategy and Pragmatics of the Temple Theme in Mark." *CBQ* 59 (1997): 78.

Hendriksen, William. *More than Conquerors: An Interpretation of the Book of Revelation*. Grand Rapids: Baker, 2002.

Hengel, Martin. *The Four Gospels and the One Gospel of Jesus Christ: An Investigation of the Collection and Origin of the Canonical Gospels*. Translated by John Bowden. Harrisburg, PA: Trinity Press, 2000.

Hoehner, Harold W. *Ephesians: An Exegetical Commentary*. Grand Rapids: Baker, 2002.

Hoekema, Anthony A. *The Bible and the Future*. Grand Rapids: Eerdmans, 1979.

Hooker, Morna D. *From Adam to Christ*. Cambridge: Cambridge University Press, 1990.

———. "Philippians." In *The Cambridge Companion to St. Paul*. Edited by James D. G. Dunn, pp. 105-115. Cambridge: Cambridge Press, 2003.

Hühn, E. *Die alttestamentlichen Citate und Reminiscenzen im Neuen Testament*. Tübingen: Mohr Siebeck, 1900.

Jobes, Karen H. *1 Peter*. BECNT. Grand Rapids: Baker, 2005.

———. "The Function of Paronomasia in Hebrews 10:5-7." *TJ* 13 (2002): 181-191.

———. "The Greek Minor Prophets in James." In *'What Does the Scripture Say?': Studies in the Function of Scripture in Early Judaism and Christianity*. Edited by Craig A. Evans and H. Daniel Zacharias, pp. 2:147-158. New York: T&T Clark, 2012.

———. *Letters to the Church: A Survey of Hebrews and the General Epistles*. Grand Rapids: Zondervan, 2011.

Johnson, Dennis. *Triumph of the Lamb: A Commentary on Revelation*. Phillipsburg, NJ: P&R, 2001.

———. *Walking with Jesus Through His Word: Discovering Christ in All the Scriptures*. Phillipsburg, NJ: P&R, 2015.

Johnson, Luke Timothy. "Luke-Acts, Book of." *ABD* 4:402-419.

Johnston, Philip S. *Shades of Sheol: Death and Afterlife in the Old Testament*. Downers Grove, IL: InterVarsity Press, 2002.

Keener, Craig S. *The Gospel of Matthew: A Socio-Rhetorical Commentary*. Grand Rapids: Eerdmans, 2009.

———. *The IVP Bible Background Commentary: New Testament*. 2nd edition. Downers Grove, IL: InterVarsity Press, 2014.

———. "John, Gospel of," in *Dictionary of Jesus & the Gospels*. 2nd edition. Edited by C. S. Green, Joel B. Green, Jeannine K. Brown, and Nicholas Perrin, pp. 419-437. Downers Grove, IL: IVP Academic, 2013.

Kim, Mitchell. "The Blessing of the Curse: Fulfilling Genesis 1:28 in a Context of Suffering." PhD diss., Wheaton College, 2011.

Kim, Seyoon. *The Origin of Paul's Gospel*. WUNT 4. J. C. B. Mohr (Paul Siebeck), 1981. Reprint, Grand Rapids: Eerdmans, 1981.

———. *"The Son of Man" as the Son of God: A Selection*. WUNT 30. Tübingen: J. C. B. Mohr (Paul Siebeck), 1983. Reprint, Eugene, OR: Wipf & Stock, 2011.

Kline, Meredith G. *God, Heaven, and Har Magedon: A Covenantal Tale of Cosmos and Telos*. Eugene, OR: Wipf & Stock, 2006.

Klink, Edward W., III. *John*. ZECNT. Grand Rapids: Zondervan, 2016.

Köstenberger, Andreas J. *A Theology of John's Gospel and Letters*. Grand Rapids: Zondervan, 2009.

Köstenberger, Andreas J., L. Scott Kellum, and Charles L. Quarles. *The Cradle, the Cross, and the Crown: An Introduction to the New Testament*. Nashville: B&H: 2009.

Kruse, Colin G. *The Letters of John*. PNTC. Grand Rapids: Eerdmans, 2000.

Laansma, Jon. *I Will Give You Rest: The "Rest" Motif in the New Testament with Special Reference to Mt. 11 and Heb. 3-4*. WUNT 98. Tübingen: J. C. B. Mohr (Paul Siebeck), 1997.

Ladd, George Eldon. *A Theology of the New Testament*. Rev. ed. Grand Rapids: Eerdmans, 1993.

Lane, William L. *Hebrews 9–13*. WBC 47B. Grand Rapids: Zondervan, 1991.

Laniak, Timothy S. *Shepherds After My Own Heart: Pastoral Traditions and Leadership in the Bible*. NSBT 20. Downers Grove, IL: IVP Academic, 2006.

LaRondelle, Hans K. *The Israel of God in Prophecy: Principles of Prophetic Interpretation*. Berrien Springs, MI: Andrews Press, 1983.

Litfin, Duane. *St. Paul's Theology of Proclamation: 1 Corinthians 1–4 and Greco-Roman Rhetoric*. SNTSMS 79. New York: Cambridge University Press, 1994.

Longman, Tremper, III, and Daniel G. Reid. *God Is a Warrior*. Grand Rapids: Zondervan, 1995.

Machen, J. Gresham. *The New Testament: An Introduction to Its Literature and History*. Edited by W. John Cook. Edinburgh: Banner of Truth, 1976.

Marcus, Joel. "Son of Man as Son of Adam." *RB* 110 (2003): 38-61.

Marshall, I. Howard. "Acts." In *Commentary on the New Testament Use of the Old Testament*. Edited by G. K. Beale and D. A. Carson, pp. 513-606. Grand Rapids: Baker Academic, 2007.

———. "Philippians." In *New Dictionary of Biblical Theology: Exploring the Unity and Diversity of Scripture*. Edited by T. Desmond Alexander and Brian S. Rosner, pp. 319-322. Downers Grove, IL: InterVarsity Press, 2000.

Martin, Oren. *Bound for the Promised Land: The Land Promise in God's Redemptive Plan*. NSBT 34. Downers Grove, IL: IVP Academic, 2015.

Martin, Ralph P. *Philippians: An Introduction and Commentary*. TNTC 11. Downers Grove: InterVarsity Press, 1987.

Mathewson, Dave. "Reading Heb 6:4-6 in Light of the Old Testament." *WTJ* 61 (1999): 209-25.

Mathison, Keith A. *From Age to Age: The Unfolding of Biblical Eschatology*. Phillipsburg, NJ: P&R, 2009.

Mauro, P. *The Patmos Visions*. Boston: Hamilton, 1925.

McKnight, Scot. "Collection for the Saints." In *Dictionary of Paul and His Letters*. Edited by Scot McKnight, Gerald F. Hawthorne, Ralph P. Martin, and Daniel G. Reid, pp. 143-147. Downers Grove, IL: InterVarsity Press, 1993.

———. "The Warning Passages of Hebrews: A Formal Analysis and Theological Conclusions." *TJ* 13 (1992): 21-59.

Michaels, J. Ramsey. *1 Peter*. WBC 49. Waco, TX: Word Books, 1988.

Middleton, J. Richard. *The Liberating Image: The Imago Dei in Genesis 1*. Grand Rapids: Brazos, 2005.

Mihalios, Stefanos. *The Danielic Eschatological Hour in the Johannine Literature*. LNTS 436. New York: T&T Clark, 2011.

Moo, Douglas J. *The Epistle to the Romans*. NICNT. Grand Rapids: Eerdmans, 1996.

———. *Galatians*. BECNT. Grand Rapids: Baker, 2013.

———. *The Letter of James*. PNTC. Grand Rapids: Eerdmans, 2000.

———*The Letters to the Colossians and to Philemon*. PNTC. Grand Rapids: Eerdmans, 2008.

———. *2 Peter, Jude*. NIVAC. Grand Rapids: Zondervan, 1996.

Morales, L. Michael. *Who Shall Ascend the Mountain of the Lord? A Biblical Theology of the Book of Leviticus*. NSBT 37. Downers Grove, IL: InterVarsity Press, 2015.

Morris, Leon. *The Atonement: Its Meaning and Significance*. Downers Grove, IL: InterVarsity Press, 1983.

———. *The Gospel According to Matthew*. PNTC. Grand Rapids: Eerdmans, 1992.

Murphy-O'Connor, Jerome. *St. Paul's Corinth: Texts and Archaeology*. Collegeville, MN: Liturgical Press, 1983.

Nicole, R. "The New Testament Use of the Old Testament." In *The Right Doctrine from the Wrong Text? Essays on the Use of the Old Testament in the New Testament*. Edited by G. K. Beale, pp. 13-28. Grand Rapids: Baker, 1994.

Niehaus, Jeffrey J. *God at Sinai: Covenant and Theophany in the Bible and the Ancient Near East*. Grand Rapids: Zondervan, 1995.

Nolland, John. *Luke 9:21–18:34*. WBC 35B. Grand Rapids: Zondervan, 1993.

Osborne, Grant R. *Matthew*. ZECNT. Grand Rapids: Zondervan, 2010.

———. *Revelation*. BECNT. Grand Rapids: Baker, 2002.

Padgett, Alan. "Wealthy Women at Ephesus: 1 Tim 2:8-15 in Social Context," *Int* 41 (1987): 19-31.

Pao, David W. *Acts and the Isaianic New Exodus*. WUNT 130. Tübingen: J. C. B. Mohr (Paul Siebeck), 2000. Reprint, Grand Rapids: Baker, 2002.

———. *Colossians & Philemon*. ZECNT. Grand Rapids: Zondervan, 2012.

Pao, David W., and Eckhard J. Schnabel, "Luke." In *Commentary on the New Testament Use of the Old Testament*. Edited by G. K. Beale and D. A. Carson, pp. 251-415. Grand Rapids: Baker Academic, 2007.

Pate, C. Marvin. *The Writings of John: A Survey of the Gospel, Epistles, and Apocalypse*. Grand Rapids: Zondervan, 2011.

Pennington, Jonathan T. *Heaven and Earth in the Gospel of Matthew*. NovTSup 126. Leiden: Brill, 2007. Reprint, Grand Rapids: Baker Academic, 2009.

Perrin, Nicholas. *Jesus and the Temple*. Grand Rapids: Baker, 2010.

Peterson, David G. "Acts." In *New Dictionary of Biblical Theology*. Edited by David G. Peterson, D. G. Alexander, T. Desmond, and Brian S. Rosner, pp. 285-291. Downers Grove, IL: IVP Academic, 2000.

———. *The Acts of the Apostles*. PNTC. Grand Rapids: Eerdmans, 2009.

Poythress, Vern. *The Shadow of Christ in the Law of Moses*. Brentwood, TN: Wolgemuth & Hyatt, 1991.

Rapske, Brian. *The Book of Acts and Paul in Roman Custody*. Grand Rapids: Eerdmans, 1994.

Reumann, John. Introduction to the First Edition of *Corporate Personality in Ancient Israel*, by H. Wheeler Robinson. Philadelphia: Fortress, 1964.

Ribbens, B. J. "Typology of Types: Typology in Dialogue." *Journal of Theological Interpretation* 51 (2011): 81-96.

Ridderbos, Herman. *Paul: An Outline of His Theology*. Translated by John Richard De Witt. Grand Rapids: Eerdmans, 1975.

Rowe, C. Kavin. *Early Narrative Christology: The Lord in the Gospel of Luke*. Berlin: Walter de Gruyter, 2006. Reprint, Grand Rapids: Baker, 2009.

Schnabel, Eckhard J. Acts. *ZECNT*. Grand Rapids: Zondervan, 2012.

Schreiner, Thomas R. *Commentary on Hebrews*. Nashville: B&H, 2015.

———. *Galatians*. ZECNT. Grand Rapids: Zondervan, 2010.

———. *New Testament Theology: Magnifying God in Christ*. Grand Rapids: Baker, 2008.

Scott, James M. *2 Corinthians*. NIBC. Peabody, MA: Hendrickson, 1998.

Seifrid, Mark. *Christ, Our Righteousness: Paul's Theology of Justification*. NSBT 9. Downers Grove, IL: InterVarsity Press, 2001.

Silva, Moisés. "Galatians." In *Commentary on the New Testament Use of the Old Testament*. Edited by G. K. Beale and D. A. Carson, pp. 785-812. Grand Rapids: Baker Academic, 2007.

———. "Perfection and Eschatology in Hebrews." *WTJ* 39 (1976): 60-71.

———. "Philippians." In *Commentary on the New Testament Use of the Old Testament*. Edited by G. K. Beale and D. A. Carson, pp. 835-841. Grand Rapids: Baker Academic, 2007.

Smit, F. M. "'What Is Apollos? What Is Paul?' In Search for the Coherence of First Corinthians 1:10-4:21." *NovT* 44 (2002): 231-251.

Strauss, Mark L. *Four Portraits, One Jesus: A Survey of Jesus and the Gospels*. Grand Rapids: Zondervan, 2007.

Stuhlmacher, Peter. *Biblical Theology of the New Testament*. Translated by Daniel P. Bailey. Grand Rapids: Eerdmans, 2017.

Thielman, Frank. "Ephesians." In *Commentary on the New Testament Use of the Old Testament*. Edited by G. K. Beale and D. A. Carson, pp. 813-834. Grand Rapids: Baker Academic, 2007.

———. *Theology of the New Testament: A Canonical and Synthetic Approach*. Grand Rapids: Zondervan, 2005.

Thompson, Alan J. *The Acts of the Risen Lord Jesus: Luke's Account of God's Unfolding Plan*. NSBT 27. Downers Grove, IL: IVP Academic, 2011.

Thompson, Mark D. *A Clear and Present Word: The Clarity of Scripture*. NSBT 21. Downers Grove, IL: InterVarsity Press, 2006.

Tipton, Lane G. "Christology in Colossians 1:15-20 and Hebrews 1:1-4: An Exercise in Biblico-Systematic Theology." In *Resurrection and Eschatology: Essays in Honor of Richard B. Gaffin, Jr.* Edited by Lane G. Tipton and Jeffrey C. Waddington, pp. 177-202. Philipsburg, NJ: P&R, 2008.

Turner, David L. *Israel's Last Prophet: Jesus and the Jewish Leaders in Matthew 23*. Minneapolis: Fortress Press, 2015.

Twelftree, Graham H. *Jesus the Exorcist: A Contribution to the Study of the Historical Jesus*. WUNT 54. Tübingen: J. C. B. Mohr (Paul Siebeck), 1993.

Vance, A. B. "The Church as the New Temple in Matthew 16:17-19: A Biblical-Theological Consideration of Jesus' Response to Peter's Confession as Recorded by Matthew." ThM thesis, Gordon-Conwell Theological Seminary, 1992.

Vlachos, Chris. *The Law and the Knowledge of Good and Evil: The Edenic Background of the Catalytic Operation of the Law in Paul*. Eugene, OR: Wipf & Stock, 2009.

Vos, Geerhardus. *Biblical Theology: Old and New Testaments*. Grand Rapids: Eerdmans, 1948. Reprint, Carlisle, PA: Banner of Truth, 2000.

Wagner, J. Ross. *Heralds of the Good News: Isaiah and Paul in Concert in the Letter to the Romans*. Leiden: Brill, 2003.

Walton, John H. *Genesis*. NIVAC. Grand Rapids: Zondervan, 2001.

Waters, Guy Prentiss. "Galatians." In *A Biblical-Theological Introduction to the New Testament: The Gospel Realized*. Edited by Michael J. Kruger, pp. 249-265. Wheaton, IL: Crossway, 2016.

Watson, Francis. *Gospel Writing: A Canonical Perspective*. Grand Rapids: Eerdmans, 2013.

Watts, Rikki E. *Isaiah's New Exodus in Mark*. WUNT 2:88. Tübingen: Mohr Siebeck, 1997. Reprint, Grand Rapids: Baker, 2000.

———. "Mark." In *Commentary on the New Testament Use of the Old Testament*. Edited by G. K. Beale and D. A. Carson, pp. 111-251. Grand Rapids: Baker Academic, 2007.

Weima, Jeffrey A. D. "1-2 Thessalonians." In *Commentary on the New Testament Use of the Old Testament*. Edited by G. K. Beale and

D. A. Carson, pp. 871-891. Grand Rapids: Baker Academic, 2007.

Westerholm, Stephen. *Perspectives Old and New on Paul: The "Lutheran" Paul and His Critics*. Grand Rapids: Eerdmans, 2004.

Wheaton, Gerry. *The Role of Jewish Feasts in John's Gospel*. SNTSMS 162. Cambridge: Cambridge Press, 2015.

Winter, Bruce W. *Roman Wives, Roman Widows: The Appearance of New Women and the Pauline Communities*. Grand Rapids: Eerdmans, 2003.

Wright, N. T. *Colossians and Philemon*. TNTC 12. Downers Grove, IL: InterVarsity Press, 1986.

———. *Jesus and the Victory of God*. Minneapolis: Fortress Press, 1996.

———. *Surprised by Hope: Rethinking Heaven, the Resurrection, and the Mission of the Church*. New York: HarperOne, 2008.

IMAGE CREDITS

Figure 1.1. Thomas Cole, *The Garden of Eden,* Amor Carter Museum of American Art / Wikimedia Commons

Figure 1.3. Karnak Temple, Egypt: photo by Tizianok / Wikimedia Commons

Figure 1.4. Jan Brueghel the Elder, *The Garden of Eden,* Doria Pamphilj Gallery, Web Gallery of Art / Wikimedia Commons

Figure 1.5. Simon de Myle, *Noah's Ark on Mount Ararat* / Wikimedia Commons

Figure 1.6. Cosimo Rosselli, *Descent from Mount Sinai,* Sistine Chapel / Wikimedia Commons

Figure 1.7. Benjamin West, *Joshua Passing the River Jordan with the Ark of the Covenant,* Art Gallery of New South Wales: Google Art Project / Wikimedia Commons

Figure 1.8. Nicolas Poussin, *The Judgment of Solomon,* Louvre / Wikimedia Commons

Figure 1.9. *Ezra the Scribe,* folio 5r from the Codex Amiatinus (Florence, Biblioteca Medicea Laurenziana, MS Amiatinus 1) / Wikimedia Commons

Figure 1.12. John Thornton, Coventry glazier, York Minster, Great East Window, between 1405-1408 / Wikimedia Commons

Figure 2.1. Artist unknown, *Portrait du Scribe d'Eadwine,* Trinity College / Wikimedia Commons

Figure 2.3. Author unknown, *Great Isaiah Scroll,* The Israel Museum: photo by Ardon Bar Hama / Wikimedia Commons

Figure 2.5. Artist unknown, *The Three Hebrews in the Fiery Furnace,* the catacombs of Priscilla, Rome: Martha Hollander / Wikimedia Commons

Figure 2.6. Joseph-Marie Vien, *Joshuah Ordering the Sun to Stand Still,* Fabre Museum / Wikimedia Commons

Figure 2.7. Author unknown, *Greek Minor Prophets Scroll* / Wikimedia Commons

Figure 2.8. Lawrence Alma-Tadema, *Death of the Pharaoh's Firstborn Son,* Rijkmuseum / Wikimedia Commons

Figure 2.9. John Martin, *The Fall of Babylon*: Wellcome Images / Wikimedia Commons

Figure 3.1. Copied and illuminated by Abraham, the priest, in classical Armenian, *Portrait of St. Mark from the Four Gospels,* 1495: Asian Collection, Wellcome Library, London / Wikimedia Commons

Figure 3.2. Eadfrith of Lindisfarne (presumed), *Gospel of Matthew,* Lindisfame Gospels / Wikimedia Commons

Figure 3.3. Ende, *Beato de Gerona,* Girona Cathedral / Wikimedia Commons

Figure 3.4. Antioch Saint Pierre Church: photo by Volkan Hatem / Wikimedia Commons

Figure 3.5. Jacob Jordaens, *The Four Evangelists,* Louvre Museum / Wikimedia Commons

Figure 4.1. Michelangelo Merisi da Caravaggio, *The Inspiration of Saint Matthew,* Contarelli Chapel, Church of San Luigi dei Francesi / Wikimedia Commons

Figure 4.2. Pieter Aertsen, *Worship of the Statue of Nebuchadnezzar,* Museum Boijmans Van Beuningen / Wikimedia Commons

Figure 4.5. Isaac van Swanenburg, *Parable of the Weeds Among the Wheat,* Rijksmuseum / Wikimedia Commons

Figure 4.6. Possibly Rembrandt van Rijn or Gerrit Dou, *Parable of the Hidden Treasure,* Museum of Fine Arts, Budapest / Wikimedia Commons

Figure 4.7. Circle of Juan de la Corte, *The Israelites Crossing the Red Sea,* Fundación Banco Santander / Wikimedia Commons

Figure 4.8. Gerard van Honthorst, *King David Playing the Harp,* Centraal Museum: Google Art Project / Wikimedia Commons

Figure 4.9. Frescos (prophet Isaiah) in the interior of Oratorio dei Disciplini, Clusone / Wikimedia Commons

Figure 4.10. John Martin, *The Killing of the Egyptian Firstborn by God*: Wellcome Images / Wikimedia Commons

Figure 4.11. Krzysztof Lubieniecki, *Moses Strikes Water from the Stone,* National Museum in Warsaw / Wikimedia Commons

Figure 4.12. Unknown Serbian artist, *Saint Elijah,* Greek Orthodox Church and Museum, Miskolc / Wikimedia Commons

Figure 4.13. Source of Jordan River, northern Israel: photo by Shalom at Polish Wikipedia / Wikimedia Commons

Figure 4.14. Aerial view of the Judean Desert: photo by Andrew Shiva / Wikimedia Commons

Figure 4.15. View from Mount Sinai, Egypt: photo by Mark A. Wilson, Wilson44691 at English Wikipedia / Wikimedia Commons

Figure 4.16. Sea of Galilee: photo by Berthold Werner / Wikimedia Commons

Figure 4.17. St. Peter statue, Piazza San Pietro / Wikimedia Commons

Figure 4.18. Dome of the Rock, Jerusalem: photo by Berthold Werner / Wikimedia Commons

Figure 4.19. Arch of Titus in Rome, photo: Anthony M. from Rome, Italy / Wikimedia Commons

Figure 4.20. A model of Herod's Temple adjacent to the Shrine of the Book exhibit at the Israel Museum, Jerusalem: photo by Berthold Werner / Wikimedia Commons

Figure 4.21. Giotto di Bondone, *Scenes from the Life of Christ, Judas Receiving Payment for his Betrayal,* Scrovegni Chapel: Web Gallery of Art / Wikimedia Commons

Figure 4.22. Via Dolorosa, old city of Jerusalem: photo by magister at he.wikipedia / Wikimedia Commons

Figure 4.23. Garden tomb, Jerusalem: photo by Grant Barclay / Wikimedia Commons

Figure 4.24. Reverse side of Cyrus Cylinder: photo by Prioryman / Wikimedia Commons

Figure 5.1. Unknown artist, *Saint Peter,* Museum of the Warsaw Archdiocese / Wikimedia Commons

Figure 5.2. Vittore Carpaccio, *The Lion of St. Mark (detail),* Doge's Palace: Web Gallery of Art / Wikimedia Commons

Figure 5.3. Dura Europos, painting from Dura Europos synagogue / Wikimedia Commons

Figure 5.4. Cornelis de Vos, *The Anointing of Solomon,* Kunsthistorisches Museum / Wikimedia Commons

Figure 5.5. Hendrick van Balen, *Triumph of King David,* Musée Municipal d'Art et d'Histoire de Colombes / Wikimedia Commons

Figure 5.6. Paris Psaulter gr139 fol136, National Library of France / Wikimedia Commons

Figure 5.7. Bernard Meehan, *The Four Evangelist Symbols,* folio 27v in *The Book of Kells: An Illustrated Introduction to the Manuscript in Trinity College Dublin* (London: Thames and Hudson, 1994) / Wikimedia Commons

Figure 5.8. Duccio di Buoninsegna, *Maestà,* Altarretabel des Sieneser Doms, Museo dell'Opera del Duomo / Wikimedia Commons

Figure 5.9. Unknown artist, *Elijah the Prophet in the Desert,* Yaroslavl Art Museum, Yaroslavl, Russia / Wikimedia Commons

Figure 5.10. *Speculum Humanae Salvationis,* Westfalen oder Köln, um 1360, ULB Darmstadt, Hs 2505, fol. 41r, ULB Darmstadt / Wikimedia Commons

Figure 5.11. Guido Reni, *St. John the Baptist in the Wilderness,* Dulwich Picture Gallery: Google Art Project / Wikimedia Commons

Figure 5.12. Unknown, *The Synaxis of the Holy and the Most Praiseworthy Twelve Apostles,* Pushkin Museum / Wikimedia Commons

Figure 5.13. Marten van Valckenborch, *Parable of the Sower,* Kunsthistorisches Museum, Vienna / Wikimedia Commons

Figure 5.14. Antonio Balestra, *Prophet Isaiah,* Museo di Castelvecchio: De Agostini Picture Library / A. Dagli Orti / Wikimedia Commons

Figure 5.15. John Everett Millais, *Victory O Lord!,* Manchester Art Gallery / Wikimedia Commons

Figure 5.16. Caesarea Philippi: photo by Bill Rice from Flat Rock, MI, USA / Wikimedia Commons

Figure 5.17. Hubert van Eyck, Genter Altar, Altar des Mystischen Lammes, linker Außenflügel, äußere Lünettenszene: Der Prophet Zacharias / Wikimedia Commons

Figure 5.18. Unknown artist, *Parable of the Workers in the Vineyard,* Codex Aureus Epternacensis, fol. 76f / Wikimedia Commons

Figure 5.19. Josefa de Óbidos, *The Sacrificial Lamb,* Walters Art Museum / Wikimedia Commons

Figure 5.20. Annibale Carracci, *Holy Women at Christ's Tomb,* Hermitage Museum / Wikimedia Commons

Figure 6.1. Claude Vignon, *Saint Luke the Evangelist* / Wikimedia Commons

Figure 6.2. Stuttgarter Psalter, (9. Jh.) fol 23 / Wikimedia Commons

Figure 6.3. Kloster Wettingen, Ost 29 Detail, *Turmbau zu Babel* / Wikimedia Commons

Figure 6.4. Jacques Daret, *Visitation,* Staatliche Museen, Berlin / Wikimedia Commons

Figure 6.5. Cosimo Rosselli, *Crossing of the Red Sea,* Sistene Chapel / Wikimedia Commons

Figure 6.6. Flood at Kendem Stream, Judean Desert, Israel: photo by Yuvalr / Wikimedia Commons

Figure 6.7. Ruins of ancient Great Synagogue at Capernaum, shore of Lake Galilee, Israel: photo by Eddie Gerald / Wikimedia Commons

Figure 6.8. *The Great Isaiah Scroll* MS A (1QIsa), Israel Museum: Google Art Project / Wikimedia Commons

Figure 6.9. Hendrick ter Brugghen, *King David Playing the Harp,* National Museum in Warsaw / Wikimedia Commons

Figure 6.10. Galilee boat: photo by Konrad Summers / Wikimedia Commons

Figure 6.11. Ferdinand Bol, *Elijah Fed by an Angel,* Web Gallery of Art / Wikimedia Commons

Figure 6.12. Jacopo Bassano, *The Good Samaritan,* National Gallery in London: Google Art Project / Wikimedia Commons

Figure 6.13. Mustard seeds: photo by veganbaking.net / Wikimedia Commons

Figure 6.14. Second Temple in model Jerusalem, Israel Museum: photo by Daniel Case / Wikimedia Commons

Figure 6.15. David Roberts, *The Siege and Destruction of Jerusalem by the Romans Under the Command of Titus, A.D. 70* / Wikimedia Commons

Figure 6.16. Garden of Gethsemane, Mount of Olives: photo by brionv / Wikimedia Commons

Figure 6.17. Jean Colombe Limbourg brothers, *Très Riches Heures du Duc de Berry,* Folio 153v Psalm LXVIII, the Musée Condé, Chantilly / Wikimedia Commons

Figure 7.1. Andreas Ritzos, *St. John the Theologian Writing his Revelations on an Open Scroll,* Benaki Museum: Google Art Project / Wikimedia Commons

Figure 7.2. Edward Poynter, *Israel in Egypt,* Guidhall Art Gallery in London / Wikimedia Commons

Figure 7.3. *Speculum Humanae Salvationis,* Westfalen oder Köln, um 1360. ULB Darmstadt, Hs 2505, fol. 69r; untere Miniatur: Daniel, Belsazar und das "Menetekel", ULB Darmstadt / Wikimedia Commons

Figure 7.4. Model of the Tabernacle, Timna Park, Israel, photo: Ruk7 / Wikimedia Commons

Figure 7.5. *Moses Before Pharaoh,* Folio 8r of the Syriac Bible of Paris (Bibliothèque Nationale, MS syr. 341) / Wikimedia Commons

Figure 7.6. *Jacob's dream at Bethel,* Jacob's ladder in the Catacomb of the Via Latina / Wikimedia Commons

Figure 7.7. Tyrian shekels, photo: Hanay / Wikimedia Commons

Figure 7.9. Anthony van Dyck, *The Brazen Serpent,* Museo del Prado, Madrid / Wikimedia Commons

Figure 7.10. Four loaves and two fish, church in Tabgha, photo: Berthold Werner / Wikimedia Commons

Figure 7.11. Parrasio Micheli, *The Gathering of the Manna* / Wikimedia Commons

Figure 7.12. A very shoft sukkah, in "Neot Kedomim," Israel, photo: Ori229 / Wikimedia Commons

Figure 7.13. Juan de Flandes, *The Raising of Lazarus,* Prado Museum, Spain / Wikimedia Commons

Figure 7.14. Ruins of the ancient synagogue in Kibbutz Bar'am in Northern Israel, photo: MASQUERAID / Wikimedia Commons

Figure 7.15. Dedication inscription, Israel Museum, Jerusalem, photo: Carole Raddato / Wikimedia Commons

Figure 7.16. *David Playing the Harp,* from the Westminster Psalter, BL Royal MS 2 A xxii f. 14v, British Library / Wikimedia Commons

Figure 8.1. View of Acropolis, photo: Christophe Meneboeuf / Wikimedia Commons

Figure 8.2. Jean II Restout, *Pentecost,* Louvre Museum / Wikimedia Commons

Figure 8.3. Benjamin West, *The Expulsion of Adam and Eve from Paradise,* National Gallery of Art, Washington, DC / Wikimedia Commons

Figure 8.4. Pentecost icon / Wikimedia Commons

Figure 8.5. Lucas van Valckenborgh, *The Tower of Babel,* Louvre Museum / Wikimedia Commons

Figure 8.6. The Second Jerusalem Temple, Model in the Israel Museum, photo: Ariely / Wikimedia Commons

Figure 8.7. Giorgio Vasari, *Martyrdom of St. Stephen,* Vatican Museums / Wikimedia Commons

Figure 8.8. Andreas Brugger, Temple Plans / Wikimedia Commons

Figure 8.9. Unknown Russian icon painter, *The Baptism of the Eunuch of the Ethiopean Queen by Philip,* Icon Museum Recklinghausen / Wikimedia Commons

Figure 8.10. Caravaggio, *The Conversion on the Way to Damascus,* Cerasi Chapel, Rome / Wikimedia Commons

Figure 8.11. Caesarea maritima, photo: DerHexer / Wikimedia Commons

Figure 8.12. Jusepe de Ribera, *Saint Peter and Saint Paul,* Musées de la Ville de Strasbourg / Wikimedia Commons

Figure 8.13. Picture of Acropolis taken from the Areopagus in the afternoon, June 7, 2019, photo: Trajan 117 CE / Wikimedia Commons

Figure 8.14. Wolfgang Sauber, Rococo frescos, St. Peter and Paul parish church in Söll / Wikimedia Commons

Figure 9.1. Valentin de Boulogne (attributed to), *Saint Paul Writing His Epistles,* Museum of Fine Arts, Houston / Wikimedia Commons

Figure 9.2. Colosseum in Rome, photo: Diliff / Wikimedia Commons

Figure 9.3. Ford Madox Brown, *The Coat of Many Colors,* Walker Art Gallery / Wikimedia Commons

Figure 9.4. El Greco, *Mount Sinai,* Historical Museum of Crete / Wikimedia Commons

Figure 9.5. *The Commentary on Habakkuk Scroll* (1QpHab), Israel Museum / Wikimedia Commons

Figure 9.6. Peter Paul Rubens, *Cain Slaying Abel,* Courtauld Institute of Art / Wikimedia Commons

Figure 9.7. William de Brailes, *The Israelites Worship the Golden Calf,* Walters Art Museum / Wikimedia Commons

Figure 9.8. Ark of the Covenant, relief, Auch Cathedral, France, photo: Vassil / Wikimedia Commons

Figure 9.9. Rembrandt, *The Sacrifice of Isaac,* Alte Pinakothek, Germany / Wikimedia Commons

Figure 9.10. The Torah, photo: Lawrie Cate / Wikimedia Commons

Figure 9.11. Sebastiano Ricci, *The Fall of the Rebel Angels,* Dulwich Picture Gallery, London / Wikimedia Commons

Figure 9.12. John Martin, *The Seventh Plague,* Museum of Fine Arts, Boston / Wikimedia Commons

Figure 9.13. Jean-Honoré Fragonard, *Jeroboam Sacrificing to Idols,* National School of Fine Arts, Paris / Wikimedia Commons

Figure 9.14. Olive tree at Beit Hakerem Jerusalem, photo: Aviva zeevi / Wikimedia Commons

Figure 9.15. Karl Theoldo von Piloty, *Nero View the Burning of Rome* / Wikimedia Commons

Figure 9.16. Guido Reni, *Archangel Michael Tramples Satan,* Santa Maria della Concezione, Rome / Wikimedia Commons

Figure 10.1. Ancient Corinth, photo: Ploync / Wikimedia Commons

Figure 10.2. Stephan Kessler, *Daniel and King Cyrus in Bel's Temple,* Private collection, Salzburg / Wikimedia Commons

Figure 10.3. Daniele da Volterra, *Der Prophet Elias,* The Yorck Project / Wikimedia Commons

Figure 10.4. Unknown, *Sosthenes, Apollo, Cephas, Tychicus, Epaphroditus, Cæsar and Onesiphorus of 70 disciples* / Wikimedia Commons

Figure 10.5. Caravaggio, *David and Goliath,* The Prado Museum, Madrid / Wikimedia Commons

Figure 10.6. Socrates (perhaps a copy of a lost bronze statue by Lysippos), Louvre / Wikimedia Commons

Figure 10.7. Grape field, Barkan Winery, Israel, photo: Elgaard / Wikimedia Commons

Figure 10.8. William de Brailes, *The Stoning of Achan,* Walters Art Museum, Baltimore / Wikimedia Commons

Figure 10.9. Temple of Athena at Paestum, Italy, photo: Greenshed / Wikimedia Commons

Figure 10.10. Tefillin, Jerusalem, photo: Benjamín Núñez González / Wikimedia Commons

Figure 10.11. Votive plaque depicting elements of the Eleusinian Mysteries, National Archaeological Museum, Athens / Wikimedia Commons

Figure 10.12. Atrium of the House of the Young Bull, Pompeii, photo: Carole Raddato / Wikimedia Commons

Figure 10.13. Portion of the *Temple Scroll,* labeled 11Q19, Israel Museum / Wikimedia Commons

Figure 10.14. Adam Elsheimer, *The Three Marys at the Tomb of Christ,* Rheinisches Landesmuseum, Bonn / Wikimedia Commons

Figure 11.1. Fountain of Peirene, ancient Corinth, photo: Ploync / Wikimedia Commons

Figure 11.2. Magyar: San Paolo fuori le mura (Róma, Olaszország): *Szent Pál* / Wikimedia Commons

Figure 11.3. Unknown artist, *Vaux Passional,* National Library of Wales, Aberystwyth / Wikimedia Commons

Figure 11.5. Charles Le Brun, *Entry of Alexander into Babylon,* Louvre / Wikimedia Commons

Figure 11.6. Titian, *The Descent of the Holy Ghost,* Santa Maria della Salute / Wikimedia Commons

Figure 11.7. Arch of Titus relief, photo: Cassius Ahenobarbus / Wikimedia Commons

Figure 11.8. A print from the Phillip Medhurst Collection of Bible illustrations in the possession of Revd. Philip De Vere at St. George's Court, Kidderminster, England / Wikimedia Commons

Figure 11.9. Passing lion, brick panel from Procession Way in Babylon, Louvre, photo: Jastrow / Wikimedia Commons

Figure 11.10. Rembrandt, *St. Paul in Prison,* Staatsgalerie, Stuttgart, Germany / Wikimedia Commons

Figure 11.11. Shops in ancient Corinth, photo: Ploync / Wikimedia Commons

Figure 11.12. Kisan Gate, Chapel of St. Paul, Old City of Damascus, photo: Bassel Khabbaz / Wikimedia Commons

Figure 11.13. Apostles from Orcau, Museu Nacional d'Art de Catalunya / Wikimedia Commons

Figure 12.1. Unknown artist, *The Apostle Paul,* St. Sophia of Kyiv, Google Art Project / Wikimedia Commons

Figure 12.2. *Tikkunei Shabbat* (prayer book for the Sabbath), Israel Museum, Google Cultural Institute / Wikimedia Commons

Figure 12.4. Qumran archaeological site, Israel, photo: Dr. Avishai Teicher / Wikimedia Commons

Figure 12.5. Washington Allston, *Elijah in the Desert,* Museum of Fine Arts, Boston, Google Cultural Institute / Wikimedia Commons

Figure 12.6. Bekehrung des Heiligen Paulus Norditalien 16Jh / Wikimedia Commons

Figure 12.7. Fragment of the *Passover Haggadah,* a text that was stored in the Cairo Geniza, photo: Younes and Soraya Nazarian Library, University of Haifa & The Friedberg Genizah Project / Wikimedia Commons

Figure 12.8. Emperor Claudius marble, Louvre, photo: Jastrow / Wikimedia Commons

Figure 12.9. *Abraham Meets the Three Strangers* (the Old Testament Trinity), St. Sophia of Kyiv, Google Art Project / Wikimedia Commons

Figure 12.10. *Pedagogue and Boy,* Walters Art Museum / Wikimedia Commons

Figure 12.11. Joseph-Marie Vien, *Hagar to Abraham with Sarah,* Bare Museum / Wikimedia Commons

Figure 12.12. Michelangelo, *Moses,* San Petro in Vincoli (Rome), photo: Jörg Bittner Unna / Wikimedia Commons

Figure 12.13. Synagogue floor, Israel Museum, Google Cultural Art Institute / Wikimedia Commons

Figure 13.1. Celsus Library, Ephesus, photo: Benh LIEU SONG / Wikimedia Commons

Figure 13.2. Temple of Hadrian, Ephesus, photo: José Luiz Bernardes Ribeiro / Wikimedia Commons

Figure 13.3. Luxor Temple, photo: A.hariry / Wikimedia Commons

Figure 13.4. Aeriel photo of Al-Aqsa Mosque and the Dome of the Rock on the Temple Mount, in the Old City of Jerusalem; photo: Andrew Shiva / Wikimedia Commons

Figure 13.5. Albrecht Dürer, *Job and His Wife,* Jabach Altarpiece, Städel Museum / Wikimedia Commons

Figure 13.6. Jerusalem Temple warning, Istanbul Archaeology Museums, photo: onceawhile / Wikimedia Commons

Figure 13.7. Friedrich Stummel, inside dome of Sacred Heart Church, photo: Gottfried Grafe / Wikimedia Commons

Figure 13.8. Unknown artist, leaf from the Morgan Picture Bible, Getty Center, Google Cultural Institute / Wikimedia Commons

Figure 13.9. Marco d'Oggiono, *Altarpiece of the Three Archangels,* Pinacoteca di Brera, Milan / Wikimedia Commons

Figure 13.10. Artemis of Ephesus, photo: QuartierLatin 1968 / Wikimedia Commons

Figure 14.1. Fragment of Arc de Triomphe, Louvre, photo: Jérémy-Günther-Heinz Jähnick / Wikimedia Commons

Figure 14.2. Pieter Lastman, *Joseph Selling Corn in Egypt,* National Gallery of Ireland, Dublin / Wikimedia Commons

Figure 14.3. Nicolas Poussin, *The Jews Gathering the Manna in the Desert,* Louvre / Wikimedia Commons

Figure 14.4. William de Brailes, *Hannah Prays in the Temple,* Walters manuscript, Walters Art Museum, Oxford / Wikimedia Commons

Figure 14.5. Juan Correa de Vivar, *El Profeta Isaias*, Museo del Prado / Wikimedia Commons

Figure 14.6. Unknown, *The Martyrdom of Saint Timothy,* Walters Art Museum, Baltimore / Wikimedia Commons

Figure 14.7. Philippi, Roman Forum, photo: DocWoKav / Wikimedia Commons

Figure 14.8. Ancient Ostia, Via di Diana, photo: Massimop / Wikimedia Commons

Figure 14.9. Altar Tel Be'er Sheva, photo: Moshe David / Wikimedia Commons

Figure 15.1. *Codex Harleianus 5557* (minuscule 321 in the Gregory-Aland numbering), the first of the Epistles to the Colossians / Wikimedia Commons

Figure 15.2. Roman Temple, Evora, Portugal, photo: ho visto nina volare, ed. Alvesgaspar / Wikimedia Commons

Figure 15.3. Model of the Tabernacle, Timna Park, Israel, photo: Mboesch / Wikimedia Commons

Figure 15.4. Gustava Meukow, watercolor depiction of Adam and Eve stained glass, Hejde Church, Gotland, Sweden, Swedish National Heritage Board / Wikimedia Commons

Figure 15.5. *Daniel in the Lions' Den,* Chatzidakis, Byzantine art in Greece / Wikimedia Commons

Figure 15.6. Onyx intaglio: incantation in Greek letters, bequest of Mary Anna Palmer Draper, 1915, Metopolitan Museum of Art, New York / Wikimedia Commons

Figure 15.7. Synagogue mosaic, Jericho, photo: Avishair Teicher via PikiWiki / Wikimedia Commons

Figure 15.8. Mattia Preti, *Moses on Mount Sinai,* Montpellier, Musée Fabre / Wikimedia Commons

Figure 15.9. St. Mark and St. Luke; Right cover of *The Washington Manuscript of the Gospels,* Freer Gallery of Art / Wikimedia Commons

Figure 15.10. Laodicea on the Lycus, Phrygia, Turkey, photo: Carole Raddato / Wikimedia Commons

Figure 15.11. *Mosaic of the Cups*, Dougga, at the National Museum of Bardo, Tunisia, photo: Pascal Radigue / Wikimedia Commons

Figure 16.1. Roman agora, Thessaloniki, Greece, photo: Ian Kehoe / Wikimedia Commons

Figure 16.2. Salomon de Bray, *Joseph Receives His Father and Brothers in Egypt*, Web Gallery of Art / Wikimedia Commons

Figure 16.3. Rembrandt, *Jeremiah Lamenting the Destruction of Jerusalem*, Rijksmuseum / Wikimedia Commons

Figure 16.4. Francesco Hayez, *The Destruction of the Temple of Jerusalem*, Gallerie dell'Accademia, Venice, Italy / Wikimedia Commons

Figure 16.5. Francisco Collantes, *The Vision of Ezekiel*, Museo del Prado, Web Gallery of Art / Wikimedia Commons

Figure 16.6. Statue of a man in armor, from the Julian Basilica, Archaeological Museum of Ancient Corinth, Greece, photo: Carole Raddato / Wikimedia Commons

Figure 16.7. Rembrandt, *Balaam and his Ass*, Musée Cognacq-Jay, Paris / Wikimedia Commons

Figure 16.8. Paolo Veronese, *The Anointment of David*, Kunsthistorisches Museum / Wikimedia Commons

Figure 16.9. *Attack*, Alba Bible / Wikimedia Commons

Figure 16.10. *Jews Defending Jerusalem's Wall*, Alba Bible / Wikimedia Commons

Figure 17.1. Anastasis, symbolic representation of the resurrection of Christ, panel from a Roman lidless sarcophagus, Vatican Museums / Wikimedia Commons

Figure 17.2. Jan van Bronchorst, *Jethro Advising Moses*, Royal Palace of Amsterdam, Google Art Project / Wikimedia Commons

Figure 17.3. Gnostic gem with scarab, Walters Art Museum, Baltimore / Wikimedia Commons

Figure 17.4. Fra Angelico, *St. Peter Consecrates St. Lawrence as Deacon*, Niccoline Chapel, Web Gallery of Art / Wikimedia Commons

Figure 17.5. Mattia Preti, *The Martyrdom of Saint Paul*, Museum of Fine Arts, Houston, Google Cultural Institute / Wikimedia Commons

Figure 17.6. Master of the Dinteville Allegory, *Moses and Aaron Before Pharaoh*, Metropolitan Museum of Art, New York / Wikimedia Commons

Figure 17.7. *Uncial 0232* (Gregory-Aland), manuscript of the New Testament with the text of the Second Epistle of John 1-5 / Wikimedia Commons

Figure 17.8. Disc of Phaistos, Archaeological Museum of Heraklion, Crete, Greece, photo: Olaf Tausch / Wikimedia Commons

Figure 18.1. Giovanni Paolo Panini, Roman Capriccio: The Pantheon and Other Monuments, Indianapolis Museum of Art / Wikimedia Commons

Figure 18.2. Peter Paul Rubens, *The Sacrifice of the Old Covenant*, Museum of Fine Arts, Boston / Wikimedia Commons

Figure 18.3. Unknown artist, *The High Priest Aaron*, St. Sophia of Kyiv, Google Cultural Institute / Wikimedia Commons

Figure 18.4. Michelangelo, *The Prophet Zacharias*, Sistene Chapel, The Yorck Project / Wikimedia Commons

Figure 18.5. Peter Paul Rubens, *King David*, Städel Museum, Franfurt, Germany / Wikimedia Commons

Figure 18.6. Meister des Ashburneham-Pentateuch, *Moses Receiving the Law*, Folio 76 recto of the Ashburnham Pentateuch, Bibliothèque Nationale, France / Wikimedia Commons

Figure 18.7. Peter Paul Rubens, *The Israelites Gathering Manna in the Desert*, Los Angeles County Museum of Art / Wikimedia Commons

Figure 18.8. Peter Paul Rubens, *The Meeting of Abraham and Melchizedek*, National Gallery of Art, Washington, DC / Wikimedia Commons

Figure 18.9. John Singleton Copley, *Samuel Relating to Eli the Judgements of God upon Eli's House*, Wadsworth Atheneum Museum of Art / Wikimedia Commons

Figure 18.10. Domenico Fiasella, *Joseph's Brothers Bringing His Bloody Coat to Jacob,* El Paso Museum of Art / Wikimedia Commons

Figure 18.11. William De Brailes, *Eli's Sons Commit Sacrilege,* Walters manuscript W. 106, Waters Art Museum, Baltimore / Wikimedia Commons

Figure 19.1. Unknown, *James the Just, Lord´s brother,* Russian Orthodox icon, fragment from the icon "Selected saints," Russian Orthodox Church, Volga region / Wikimedia Commons

Figure 19.2. Frans Francken the Younger, *King Solomon Receiving the Queen of Sheba,* Walters Museum, Baltimore / Wikimedia Commons

Figure 19.3. *Job Rebuked by His Friends,* from the Butts set, The Morgan Library / Wikimedia Commons

Figure 19.4. Stephanus Garsia and other unnamed, *Vision of Daniel in the Apocalypse of Saint-Sever,* Bibliothèque Nationale, Paris / Wikimedia Commons

Figure 19.5. Rudolf von Ems, *Nabot's Stoning,* World Chronicle / Wikimedia Commons

Figure 19.6. James ossuary, photo: Paradiso / Wikimedia Commons

Figure 19.7. *Abraham's Sacrifice,* fresco, Old Church, Raduil, Bulgaria, photo: Edal Anton Lefterov / Wikimedia Commons

Figure 19.8. *A Teacher with Three Discipuli,* funerary relief, Rheinisches Landesmuseum, Trier, Germany, photo: Carole Raddato / Wikimedia Commons

Figure 19.9. *Crossing of the Red Sea by the Jews,* Byzantine illuminated manuscript, icon-art.info / Wikimedia Commons

Figure 19.10. Brick makers, *Tomb of Rekhmire,* Rogers Fund, 1930, Metropolitan Museum of Art, New York / Wikimedia Commons

Figure 19.11. Giovanni Lanfranco, *Elijah Receiving Bread from the Widow of Zarephath,* Getty Center, Google Cultural Institute / Wikimedia Commons

Figure 20.1. Claude Vignon, *Lament of Saint Peter,* Iris & B Gerald Cantor Center for Visual Arts, Standford University / Wikimedia Commons

Figure 20.2. *Adam and Eve,* north door of iconostasis / Wikimedia Commons

Figure 20.3. Ferdinand Bol, *Moses Descends from Mount Sinai with the Ten Commandments,* Royal Palace of Amsterdam, Google Cultural Institute / Wikimedia Commons

Figure 20.4. Attack mosaic from Villa Borghese / Wikimedia Commons

Figure 20.5. Judaean prisoners deported into exile, relief, The British Museum, London / Wikimedia Commons

Figure 20.6. Sarcophagus, Red Sea crossing, Arles Museum of Ancient Art, photo: Marsyas / Wikimedia Commons

Figure 20.7. Madam mosaic, National Museum of Carthage, Fabien Dany, www.fabiendany.com, www.datka.kg / Wikimedia Commons

Figure 20.8. *David flees Jerusalem,* Maciejowski Bible, Leaf 45 / Wikimedia Commons

Figure 20.9. Diego Velázquez, *Joseph's Tunic,* the Royal Seat of San Lorenzo de El Escorial /Wikimedia Commons

Figure 20.10. Zanobi Strozzi, *King David in Prayer* in an Initial B, Robert Lehman collection, 1975, Metropolitan Museum of Art / Wikimedia Commons

Figure 20.11. Byzantine mosaic artist from the 5th century, Great Palace, Istanbul, Turkey / Wikimedia Commons

Figure 20.12. *Nero and Agrippina,* Museum in Aphrodisias, Turkey, photo: Carlos Delgado / Wikimedia Commons

Figure 21.1. Caravaggio, *Crucifixion of Peter,* Santa Maria del Popolo, The Yorck Project / Wikimedia Commons

Figure 21.2. Philip James De Loutherbourg, *The Vision of the White Horse,* Tate Britain, London / Wikimedia Commons

Figure 21.3. Grégoire Guérard, *The Capture of Christ,* Musée des Beaux-Arts de Dijon, Bourgogne, France / Wikimedia Commons

Figure 21.4. Giovanni Benedetto Castiglione, *In Front of Noah's Ark,* Gemäldegalerie Alte Meister, Dresden, Germany, Web Gallery of Art / Wikimedia Commons

Figure 21.5. The Great Isaiah Scroll MS A (1QIsa), Israel Museum, Google Cultural Institute / Wikimedia Commons

Figure 21.6. Papyrus Bodmer VIII, Original: Biblioteca Apostolica Vaticana / Wikimedia Commons

Figure 21.7. Unknown Spanish painter, *Saint Michael and the Dragon,* Metropolitan Museum of Art, New York / Wikimedia Commons

Figure 21.8. Sandro Botticelli, *The Punishment of Korah and the Stoning of Moses and Aaron,* Sistene Chapel, Web Gallery of Art / Wikimedia Commons

Figure 22.1. Anonymous, *St. John the Evangelist,* Russian Orthodox icon / Wikimedia Commons

Figure 22.2. Church of Mary, Ephesus, Turkey, photo: Adam Jones / Wikimedia Commons

Figure 22.3. Shema inscription on the Knesset Menorah in Jerusalem, photo: SuperJew / Wikimedia Commons

Figure 22.4. Luca Signorelli, *Sermon and Deeds of the Antichrist,* Chapel of San Brizio, Web Gallery of Art / Wikimedia Commons

Figure 22.6. Lorenzo Ghiberti, *Gates of Paradise,* reliefs, photo: Sailko / Wikimedia Commons

Figure 22.8. *Woman and Dragon,* Frescos in abbey church of Saint-Savin-sur-Gartempe / Wikimedia Commons

Figure 22.9. *Man worshiping a crucified donkey,* graffito, museum on Palatine Hill, Rome / Wikimedia Commons

Figure 23.1. *John woken by angel,* Douce Apocalypse, Bodleian Ms180 / Wikimedia Commons

Figure 23.3. Rembrandt, *Belshazzar's Feast* / Wikimedia Commons

Figure 23.4. *The Black Death,* Toggenburg Bible, Kupferstichkabinett, Staatliche Museen / Wikimedia Commons

Figure 23.5. *The Lamb in the Midst of the Elders,* Burckhardt-Wildt Apocalypse, illuminated manuscript / Wikimedia Commons

Figure 23.6. Unknown, *The Vision of Zechariah,* Getty Center, Los Angeles, Google Cultural Institute / Wikimedia Commons

Figure 23.7. *The Seven Trumpets and the Angel with a Censer,* Bamberg Apocalypse, Folio 019v7 / Wikimedia Commons

Figure 23.8. *Folio 185,* Revelation 11:5-8, Augsburger Wunderzeichenbuch / Wikimedia Commons

Figure 23.9. Gaetano Gandolfi, *Joseph's Dream,* Web Gallery of Art / Wikimedia Commons

Figure 23.10. *The Beast of the Sea,* Tapestry of the Apocalypse / Wikimedia Commons

Figure 23.11. *The First Three Vials,* folio 39V of the Bamberg Apocalypse, Bamberg State Library / Wikimedia Commons

Figure 23.12. *The Woman on the Beast,* Lambeth Apocalypse / Wikimedia Commons

Figure 23.13. Philip James de Loutherbourg, *The Angel Binding Satan,* Yale Center for British Art, Google Cultural Institute / Wikimedia Commons

Figure 23.14. *The New Jerusalem,* Tapestry of the Apocalypse / Wikimedia Commons

SUBJECT INDEX

SCRIPTURE INDEX

Leviticus

Numbers

Jeremiah

Lamentations

Ezekiel

ANCIENT WRITINGS INDEX

Old Testament Apocrypha

Old Testament Pseudepigrapha

Dead Sea Scrolls

Other Jewish Texts

Apostolic Fathers

Early Christian and Classical Writings

Finding the Textbook You Need